Nelson's Navy

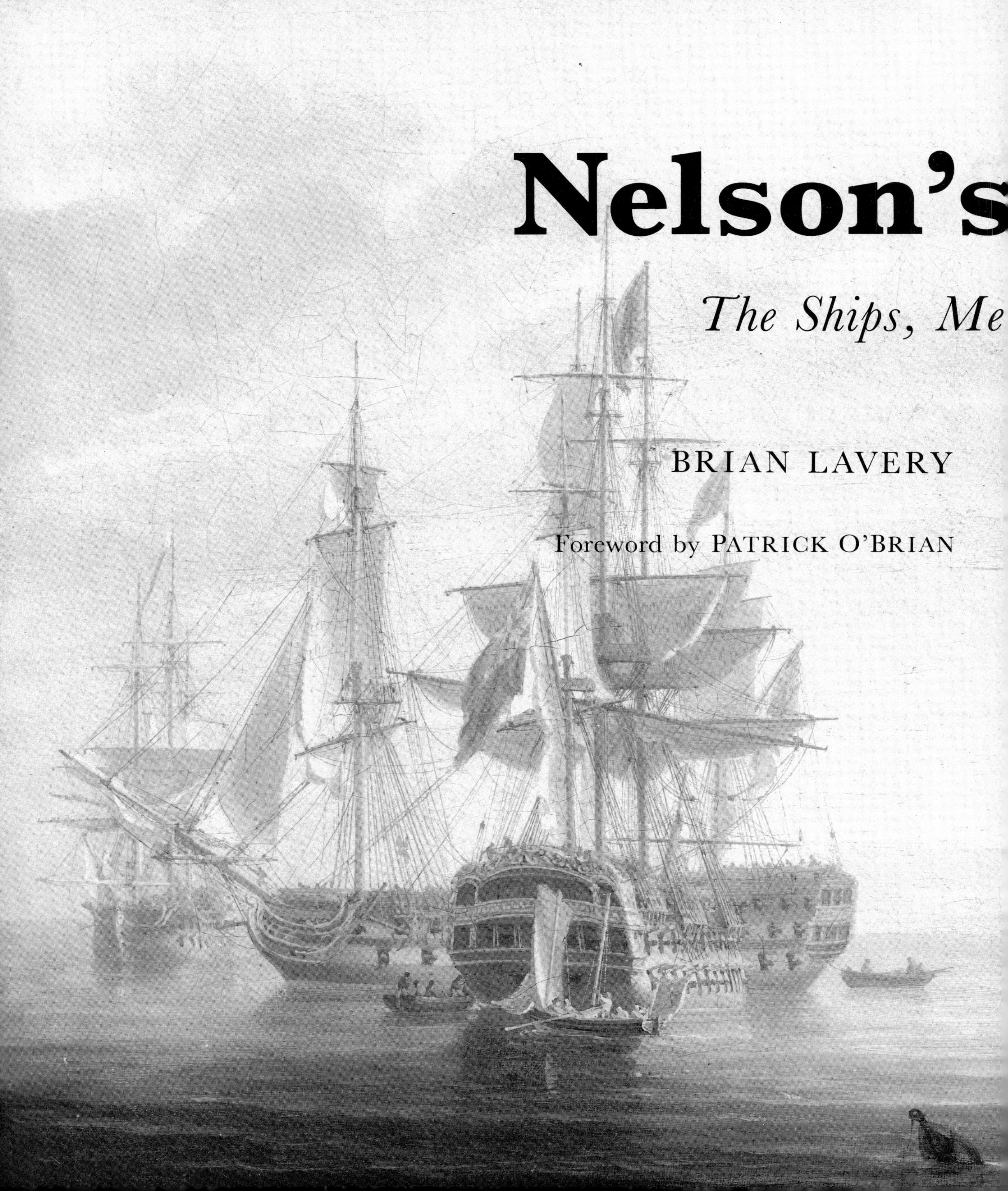

Nelson's

The Ships, Me

BRIAN LAVERY

Foreword by PATRICK O'BRIAN

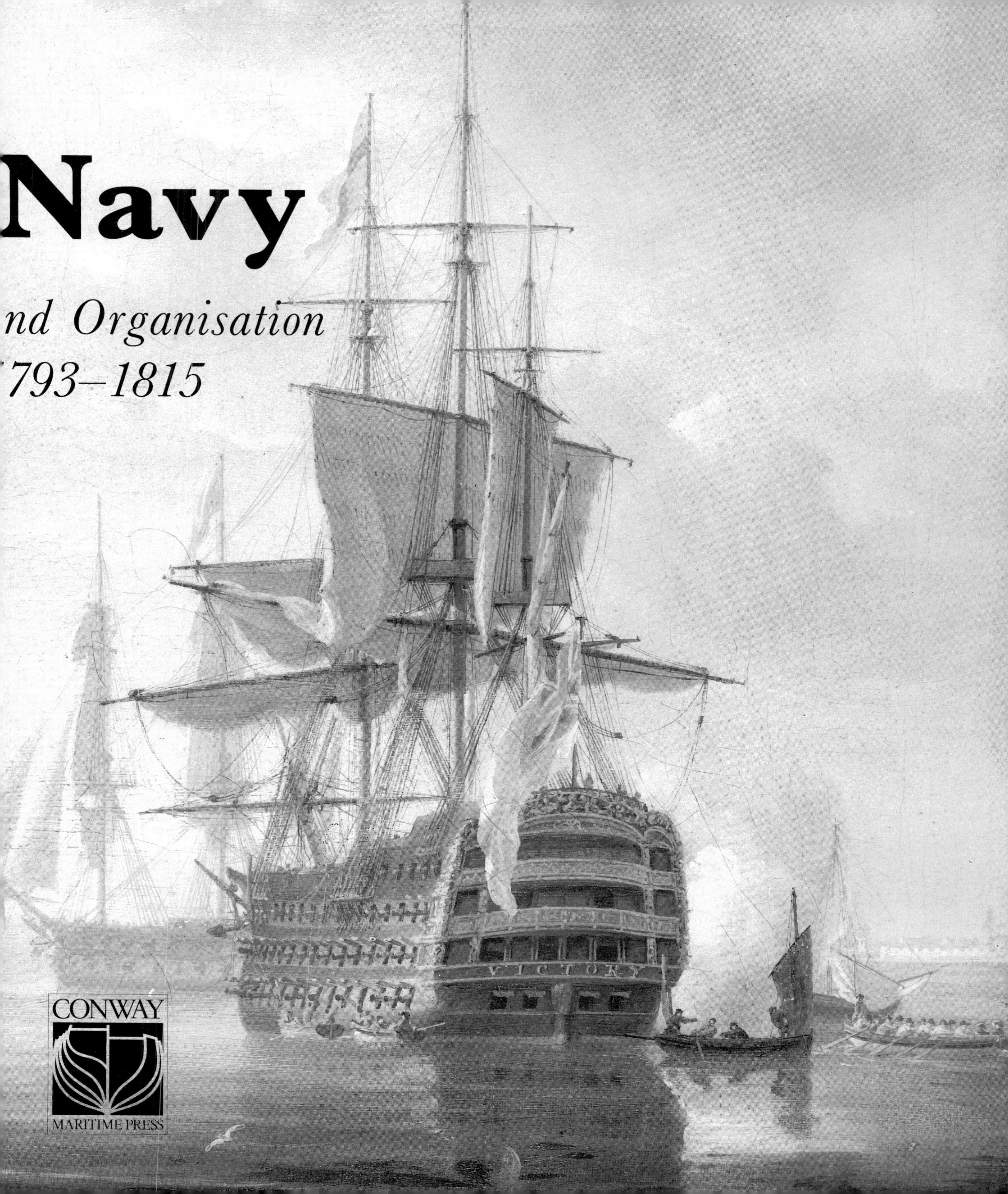
Navy
nd Organisation
793–1815
VICTORY
CONWAY
MARITIME PRESS

First published in Great Britain 1989 by
Conway Maritime Press Ltd
101 Fleet Street
London EC4
Revised edition 1990
Reprinted twice 1992
Reprinted 1993

British Library Cataloguing in Publication Data
Lavery Brian
Nelson's Navy
1. Napoleonic Wars. Naval operations by Great Britain. Royal Navy
I. Title
940.2′7
ISBN 0 85177 521 7

Designed by John Leath
Maps drawn by Denys Baker
Typeset by Lasertext, Stretford, Manchester
Printed and bound in Great Britain by The Bath Press

Frontispiece
A detail of Nicholas Pocock's Nelson's Ships, *an imaginary composition depicting five of the ships in which Nelson distinguished himself. Portsmouth lies in the distance.*
The National Maritime Museum

Contents

Foreword

From the earliest times until today people have loved to read about ships and the sea; the undying popularity of the Odyssey, of the Navigations of St Brendan, of Hakluyt, Purchas, Harris and Churchill, and the immense success of Sir Francis Chichester's and Thor Heyerdahl's more recent accounts prove the fact over and over again. And if even further proof were required one could bring forward the case of the Abbé Prévost: in his youth he led a less regular and perhaps somewhat less celibate life than is usual with monks, running away from his monastery to England and Holland and writing his incomparable *Manon Lescaut*; but later he settled down, became almoner to the Prince de Conti, and occupied his leisure with an enormous compilation, *l'Histoire générale des Voyages*, in no less than sixteen thick quarto volumes filled with engravings and maps, a modern publisher's nightmare, impossibly expensive to produce (the binding alone of my copy would cost well over £1000); yet it was so well received that after his death supplements were brought out in Amsterdam and Paris.

It is to be hoped that the dear man had a thorough understanding of the ships he wrote about, because one's pleasure in a sailor's account of his voyage is so very much enhanced if one can follow the more technical passages. This is even more true where the navy of Nelson's day is concerned, for by the time of Trafalgar the sailing man-of-war, line of battle ship or frigate, had reached its apogee, an immensely complex machine requiring extraordinary skill to handle it and, of course, a copious vocabulary to speak of its parts and their function.

Yet in spite of the continuing delight in ships and the sea, this thorough understanding is by no means usual. Only this year an eminent writer sent a 74-gun ship of the line to Australia in 1813 with no copper sheathing, no surgeon and no spare topmasts, though by way of compensation she did have plywood bulkheads and bilge-keels (bilge-keels with a draught of 22 ft!); while a well-known military historian, describing the battle of Trafalgar, could write '...with the wind behind, the best point of sailing for square-riggers'.

To be sure, there is no royal road to a knowledge of the navy of Nelson's time, no smooth and easy path to be followed without effort; but Brian Lavery's *Nelson's Navy* is the most nearly regal that I have come across in many years of reading on the subject. Before it was written, a man who wished to have a general view of the Royal Navy and to understand the finer points of, let us say, the battle of St Vincent or Sir Michael Seymour's splendid capture of the *Thetis*, or the ordinary life of a seaman on the Brest blockade would have needed more leisure than most possess and a well-furnished library at his command. For the general view he would have consulted Clowes' massive opus or one of the many later histories; for the day-to-day nature of life aboard he would, ideally, have been able to roam through the great number of contemporary autobiographies, the six volumes of James's *Naval History*, which deals with the Revolutionary and Napoleonic wars year by year in great detail, and the forty volumes of the *Naval Chronicle*, a monthly service magazine that ran from 1799 to 1818; while for the nautical terms Admiral Smyth's *Seaman's Word-Book* and Burney's edition of Falconer's *Marine Dictionary* would have been needed. For more specialised subjects such as social history, shipbuilding, ship handling, strategy, tactics, the influence of seapower, navigation, the Admiralty and naval administration, health, dockyards, signals, recruitment and particular battles he would, of course, have found a great many works, some, like Michael Lewis's *Social History of the Navy, 1793–1815* or Christopher Lloyd's *St Vincent and Camperdown*, both delightfully written and authoritative, others neither the one nor the other.

But in either case this hypothetical reader would have been confronted with bookshelves stretching away to the horizon — the London Library's catalogue contains hundreds and hundreds of titles — and it would have taken him a great while to find his way among them all. What is so particularly valuable about Brian Lavery's book is that it deals, and deals thoroughly, with all these matters as well as a great many more: you name it, *Nelson's Navy* has it. This is especially the case with the building and fitting-out of a ship, subjects upon which the author is an internationally recognised authority. I do not mean to imply that the other sections are less valuable; I make the point only because there are almost no other writers so well qualified to speak of these matters — fundamental, after all, to the existence of a ship — and very few who attempt more than a superficial treatment of them.

Of course, as the author says himself, *Nelson's Navy* does not exhaust the subject: there is still a very great deal of material in the Public Record Office and at Greenwich, in family archives, specialists' studies and out-of-the way printed books. But anyone who has read and digested the work will have a more than ordinarily sound knowledge of Nelson's navy; he will read the great man's letters and dispatches, and those of St Vincent, Collingwood, Keith and a great many more with a far keener relish, to say nothing of naval biographies, naval reminiscences, naval fiction, naval history, the publications of the Navy Record Society and the countless actions, great and small, recorded in James, which has recently been reprinted.

And should the reader have an inclination to join the ranks of historical novelists he may reflect that genius is an infinite capacity for taking pains, and since these pains have already been taken for him, all he needs to do is to find a plot and to lay in a store of paper and ink.

PATRICK O'BRIAN

Preface

Nelson's navy still fascinates many people, as is shown by the sales of naval fiction by C S Forester, Patrick O'Brian, Dudley Pope, Alexander Kent, Richard Woodman and others. It was a highly successful organisation which dominated the seas more completely than any human force before or since. It was often in the forefront of the latest technology, despite an unjustified reputation for backwardness. Yet it was rooted in antiquated and crude methods, such as the press gang.

This book is an attempt to present a rounded and balanced picture of Nelson's navy. Nelson himself does not figure very much, because he has already been given due prominence by historians, while the achievements and tribulations of others have been less recognised. It covers many aspects of the navy: social, historical and technical. The officer or seaman of the time would have understood all these aspects equally, and one of my aims is to show the service from his point of view. For the same reason, I have concentrated mainly on standard practices rather than innovations. I have attempted to represent the routine of day to day life as much as the few moments of high drama; the ordinary men as much as the great admirals; and the general run of ships, rather than the few which became well known, such as the *Victory*, *Bellerophon* or *Shannon*.

In a sense, such a work has to be superficial. It has sixty-one chapters, and the subject matter of many of them could make a book on its own — indeed several already have. Some aspects of the navy have been well covered in print; for others, there is little published material, but rich documentary sources. Therefore some chapters are more original than others, but I hope I have introduced some new material into all of them, except the first section, on background, which is intended for those who might be unfamiliar with the period.

I have referenced material in the text so that where there are several extracts from the same work, the reference number comes after the last item.

I would like to thank the staffs of all the libraries and institutions where I have researched this book — The National Maritime Museum, the London Library, the British Library, the Public Record Office at Kew, the Royal Naval Museum at Portsmouth, the Royal Marines Museum at Eastney, and the Science Museum in London. Some members of the staff of the National Maritime Museum have been particularly helpful over the years, raising interesting points for discussion — especially David Lyon, Roger Knight, Roger Morriss and Chris Ware. Thanks also go to N A M Rodger of the PRO, and Robert Gardiner of Conway Maritime Press.

Part I
BACKGROUND

1 The Wars with France

The Extent of the War

There were three wars with France during the years 1793 to 1815, plus war with the United States and various European countries. This period was dominated by war, with only thirteen months of peace. It also saw the Royal Navy at its greatest peak of strength and importance, with a dominant role in European waters and in almost every other part of the world's oceans. These wars were the culmination of a long series of conflicts with France, which had begun over a century before, in 1689, but they were far more extensive, intense, and 'total' than those which had gone before. They were fought for much deeper principles than the colonial wars of the middle part of the eighteenth century, and they involved a far greater mobilisation of national resources, in the form of manpower, shipping, industry and trade. (Both the Ordnance Survey and the national census began during these years, in order to assess these resources, and income tax was introduced to pay for the wars.) They were ideological as much as national wars, though they did much to create the idea of nationalism in itself. They were the last major wars to be fought by sailing navies, and, as such, they contained the climax of one kind of naval technology.

Until they began to be overshadowed by much more total and devastating conflicts nearly a century later, these wars were often called 'The Great War'. They could be called world wars, and have at least as much claim to that title as the first of the great twentieth-century conflicts. British troops fought in Europe, Africa, North and South America, the West Indies, Indonesia and India. Ships fought in the Baltic, North Sea, Mediterranean, Caribbean, Atlantic, Indian and Pacific Oceans, and in the English Channel. Every part of Europe was involved in the wars at one stage or another; and since a great part of the world was under European domination, the various colonies were also involved. Unlike the wars of the previous century and a half, victory eventually came through the invasion of the enemy's homeland and the imprisonment of the leader, rather than through negotiation. Since the war resulted in a victory for conservative principles, it did not lead to quite such a comprehensive re-drawing of the map of Europe as the First World War; but in many ways its social effects were just as profound.

The First Coalition

When the French Revolution first broke out in 1789, it was welcomed enthusiastically by radicals in Britain, and more cautiously by many sections of the ruling class, who thought it might lead away from absolute monarchy, towards the sort of constitutional monarchy which Britain enjoyed. But as government passed into more extreme hands, culminating in the 'Reign of Terror' and the execution of Louis XVI and Marie Antoinette in 1793, public opinion turned against the French. The British government began to suppress the radical movement at home, and to join with the ultra-conservative forces of Austria, Prussia, Spain, Naples and the French royalist emigrés in opposing the French republic.

Britain joined the war in February 1793, as part of an alliance later known as the First Coalition. At first, the government, under the leadership of William Pitt the Younger, treated the war as an old-fashioned colonial conflict. Subsidies were paid to the European allies, a small British force under the Duke of York was deployed in Flanders, and the navy was employed to blockade the French and to capture her overseas possessions, which it was intended would later be bargained away at the negotiating table. But this was not enough to defeat the French Revolutionary armies, which were much more heavily motivated than any army of the old regime. However, the navy had some successes. In 1793, the major French base at Toulon was delivered up by French royalists, and many French warships were destroyed there before it was abandoned by the British. In the following year, the first great fleet battle of the war was fought, on 'The Glorious First of June'. A British force of twenty-five ships-of-the-line defeated a French one of twenty-six ships, capturing six and destroying one; but the French grain convoy, vital to the economic survival of the country, was able to escape. The combined forces in the West Indies captured the French islands of Marie Galante, St Lucia, the Saintes, and Guadeloupe.

But meanwhile, the allied armies were being driven back in Flanders, and Holland had been overrun by 1794. During 1795 Prussia made peace with France, while Spain, worried about British gains in the Caribbean, declared war in 1796. The young General Bonaparte was making dramatic advances against the Austrian interests in Italy, and for a time the British fleet was obliged to abandon the Mediterranean. In 1797, Austria made peace with France, and Britain was alone against France, Spain and Holland.

William Pitt addressing the House of Commons in 1793, on the declaration of war with France. National Portrait Gallery

The Crisis of the Naval War

The year 1797 was a critical one at sea. The combined forces of France and her allies should have been enough to defeat the British, and several plans of invasion were made, largely concentrating on Ireland, where the disaffected population might be expected to give the French some support. But early in the year, Sir John Jervis, with the assistance of Horatio Nelson, defeated a superior Spanish force at the Battle of St Vincent, and removed the threat from that direction. In April, the Channel fleet at Spithead mutinied in protest about bad conditions, and gave the government its biggest problem yet. The seamen were granted virtually all they had asked for, including their first pay rise for nearly 150 years. In the following month, the North Sea fleet at the Nore also mutinied but they were much less successful; the mutiny eventually collapsed, and many of the leaders were hanged. In October of 1797, the same fleet, under Admiral Duncan, defeated a Dutch squadron at Camperdown, and the Royal Navy was back in command of the situation, though the Mediterranean remained firmly under French control.

French victory over Austria at Marengo in 1800. National Army Museum

In 1798, Napoleon captured Malta, and took a fleet and army towards Egypt, intending to open up the land route to India. Nelson was sent after him, and succeeding in annihilating his fleet at Aboukir Bay. Napoleon's army was now isolated, and its thrust towards Syria was defeated at Acre in 1799. Britain was again master of the seas, and the French hold on Europe was beginning to weaken.

The Second Coalition and Armed Neutrality

During 1798, Pitt began to gather allies for another assault against France. With the support of Russia, Portugal, Austria, and other powers, some moves were made towards an attack on France, but without any great success. Meanwhile the British captured Malta, which caused some dissension among the allies and the withdrawal of Russia from the coalition. Bonaparte, having returned from Egypt, was appointed first consul, and became effective head of the French government. He took command of the armies in Italy again, and defeated the Austrians heavily at Marengo in 1800. Another French army defeated them at Hohenlinden in the same year, and they sought peace, so the coalition was effectively destroyed.

The northern powers, Sweden, Denmark and Russia, proclaimed their Armed Neutrality during 1800. This, in effect, cut Britain off from the Baltic, and denied her many essential naval supplies. In response, Admiral Sir Hyde Parker was sent to Copenhagen, with Nelson as his second in command. Nelson led the fleet into the Battle of Copenhagen, ignoring Parker's signal in a famous gesture. He destroyed the Danish force of old ships anchored off the town.

In Britain, Pitt's government had fallen because of lack of parliamentary support. The new prime minister, Addington, concluded a treaty with France known as the Peace of Amiens, which took effect in March 1802. Britain was to give back all her colonial conquests except Ceylon and Trinidad, and was to evacuate Malta. The French were to abandon Egypt. The government believed that the conflict was ended, and the armed forces were largely demobilised.

The Outbreak of War

Despite the peaceful intentions of Addington's government, neither side trusted the other. Bonaparte continued to increase his power in France, and to take over parts of northern Italy. Britain, on the other hand, did not give up Malta. War broke out again in April 1803, and the British fleet was mobilised quickly and with some secrecy. The Addington government fell in 1804, and Pitt came back into office. Meanwhile Bonaparte crowned himself emperor, and began to prepare for an invasion of southern England, setting up camps in the north of France, and preparing a fleet of light gunboats. But, during 1805, Pitt began to build yet another coalition in Europe, gaining the support of Austria and Russia. On the other hand, Spain joined the French side after a squadron of British frigates captured her treasure fleet from America, and gave her an excuse for conflict.

The Trafalgar Campaign

At sea, the blockade of Brest had been resumed soon after the outbreak of war, and Nelson was sent to blockade Toulon. The French fleet there, commanded by Villeneuve, escaped and caused Nelson to search the Mediterranean and West Indies for it. Villeneuve made for the West Indies, then doubled back towards the English Channel. He was stopped by a British squadron under Admiral Calder, off Cape Finisterre. The resulting action was indecisive but it forced Villeneuve to retreat to Ferrol and then Cadiz, where he joined with the Spanish fleet and was blockaded by Nelson.

In October 1805, Villeneuve was goaded by Napoleon into leaving Cadiz and offering battle. Though he had thirty-three ships-of-the-

Napoleon as Emperor of France. From Bourrienne's *Memoires*, 1831 edition

line against Nelson's twenty-seven, the French and Spanish were so demoralised by recent British successes that they had no expectation of victory. Seventeen French and Spanish ships were captured, though most of these were lost in the storm which followed the battle. A few weeks later, four of the surviving French ships were also captured, making the British victory complete. But Nelson had been killed during the battle.

The Continental System

Meanwhile, the French were unstoppable on land. The Austrians and Russians were heavily defeated at Austerlitz in December 1805, and Austria left the war. Pitt died a few weeks later, and none of his successors as prime minister (Grenville, Portland, Perceval and Liverpool) had any of his great political skills. Britain had a land victory in Italy in 1806, at the Battle of Maida. Sir Home Popham captured the Cape of Good Hope from the Dutch, and attempted to take Buenos Aires, which was a disaster, for he was misinformed about the amount of support he could expect from the population, and forced to retreat. An attempt to force a passage through the Dardanelles and make war with Turkey also failed. Finally, in 1807, Russia made peace with Napoleon at the Treaty of Tilsit, leaving Britain isolated again.

Unable to invade Britain or defeat her at sea, Napoleon attempted to destroy her trade. As soon as his control of continental Europe was reasonably complete, he issued the Berlin Decrees, forbidding ships and ports under his domination to trade with Britain. Britain responded by blockading any port or country which implemented the decrees. Though the enemy fleets had been destroyed, there was more work than ever for the navy. Furthermore, there was always the danger than the French would build or acquire a new fleet, particularly with most of the shipbuilding resources of Europe at her disposal. In 1807, it seemed that the French were about to take over Denmark, with her powerful navy. Admiral Gambier took a fleet to Copenhagen, the army bombarded and severely damaged the town, and the ships of the Danish fleet were captured or destroyed.

The Peninsular War

In 1808, the Spanish began their revolt against French domination. A British army under the future Duke of Wellington was sent to Portugal to assist the rebels. The army landed and defeated the French at Vimiero, and marched on Lisbon. However, Wellington was superseded in command, and the French were allowed to evacuate Portugal. Sir John Moore took command, and marched into Spain. He was outmanoeuvred by the French, and forced to retreat to Corunna. Most of the army was evacuated, but Moore himself was killed.

Wellington landed in Portugal again in 1809, and resumed his war in co-operation with the Spanish guerrillas, as well as with Spanish and Portuguese regular soldiers. He continued his campaign over the next four years, defeating the French in several battles, but retreating when outnumbered. He depleted French resources, and developed the British army into a very effective force. His strategy depended very much on naval power; the navy blockaded the French-held areas, and often raided them in co-operation with the guerrillas. The climax of this war came in 1812, when Popham captured the town of Santander.

The British made other attempts to attack Napoleon's empire. In 1809 a major landing was made on the island of Walcheren, in the Netherlands, in an attempt to neutralise the naval base at Antwerp. It was a failure, and the force had to be evacuated with heavy losses. Colonial expeditions were more successful — Martinique, Senegal and Cayenne were taken in 1809; Guadeloupe, Amboyna and Mauritius in 1810, and Java in 1811. French trade was effectively stifled by the operation of the blockade, and the economy suffered.

1812

During 1812, both Russia and the United States joined the war, one in alliance with Britain, and one against her. Napoleon's dispute with Moscow was largely inspired by the Russian failure to close her ports to the British. A great French army was assembled and fought a bloody battle with the Russians at Borodino; Napoleon occupied Moscow in September. The city was burned, the French army was starved of supplies, and Napoleon left it to be harassed by Russian troops.

The war between Britain and America was provoked by the British claim to inspect American merchant ships, and impress British subjects from them. At sea, the Royal Navy was defeated in several single-ship actions with American frigates and sloops; for the Americans, with a small navy, had concentrated on quality rather than quantity, so that they had a natural advantage in this type of action. Eventually, the British began to prepare ships specially to deal with the big American frigates, and had some success. The war dragged on until 1815, with naval battles in the Great Lakes, and landings at Washington and New Orleans.

The Defeat of Napoleon

By 1813, the Russians were advancing westwards, and gaining allies as they went. In Spain, Wellington made a final offensive, and drove

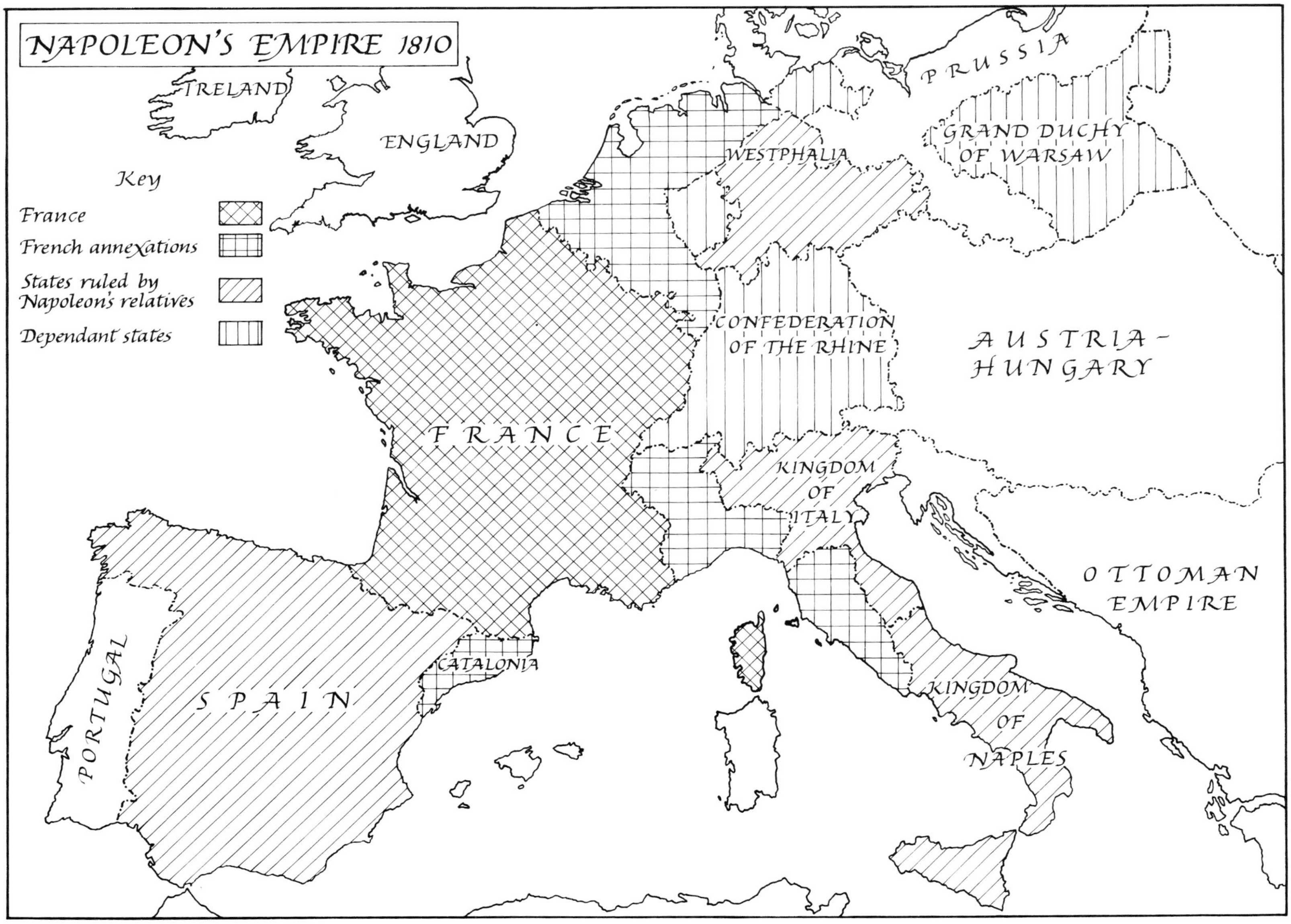

NAPOLEON'S EMPIRE 1810

Key
France
French annexations
States ruled by Napoleon's relatives
Dependant states

IRELAND
ENGLAND
PRUSSIA
GRAND DUCHY OF WARSAW
WESTPHALIA
CONFEDERATION OF THE RHINE
AUSTRIA-HUNGARY
FRANCE
KINGDOM OF ITALY
OTTOMAN EMPIRE
PORTUGAL
SPAIN
CATALONIA
KINGDOM OF NAPLES

Napoleon's empire at its greatest extent, c1810.

the French from the country. Another coalition was formed, and the French were defeated at the Battle of Leipzig, by combined Austrian, Russian, Prussian and other German forces. Napoleon had to retreat to France.

Early in 1814, Wellington crossed the Pyrenees, and defeated the French at Toulouse in March. The allied powers crossed the Rhine and marched on Paris. France surrendered, Napoleon was deposed and sent into exile on the island of Elba. The leaders of the victorious powers met at Vienna to arrange a re-settlement of Europe after twenty years of upheaval. The Bourbon line was restored in France in the person of Louis XVIII.

In March 1815, Napoleon escaped from Elba and was welcomed by the French armies. Louis fled, and Napoleon took power again. The Royal Navy was mobilised, while Britain, Prussia, Austria, Russia and the Netherlands sent armies against him. At Waterloo, Wellington and Blucher were victorious, and Napoleon fled, only to surrender to the Royal Navy some weeks later. He was exiled on St Helena, where he died. Europe was exhausted by war, and a long period of relative peace followed.

The Battle of Waterloo, and final defeat of Napoleon, 1815. National Army Museum

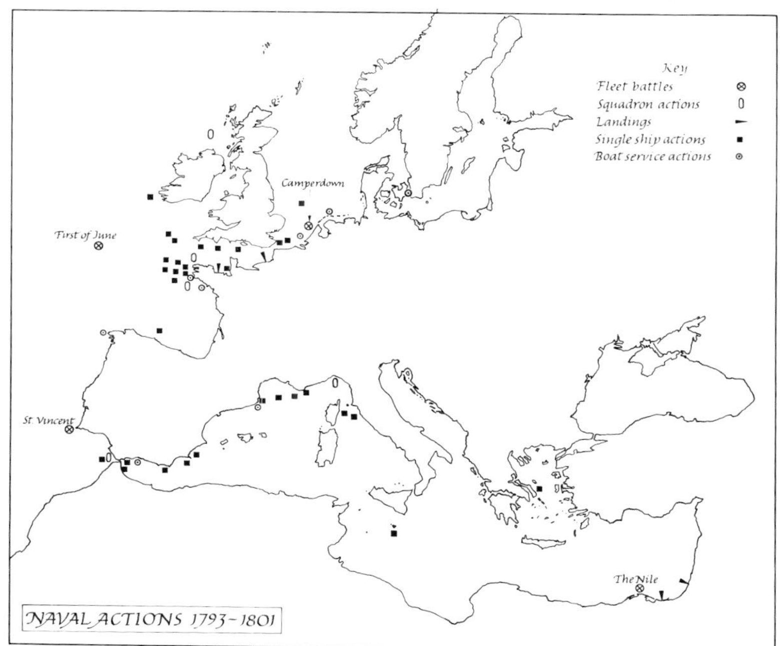

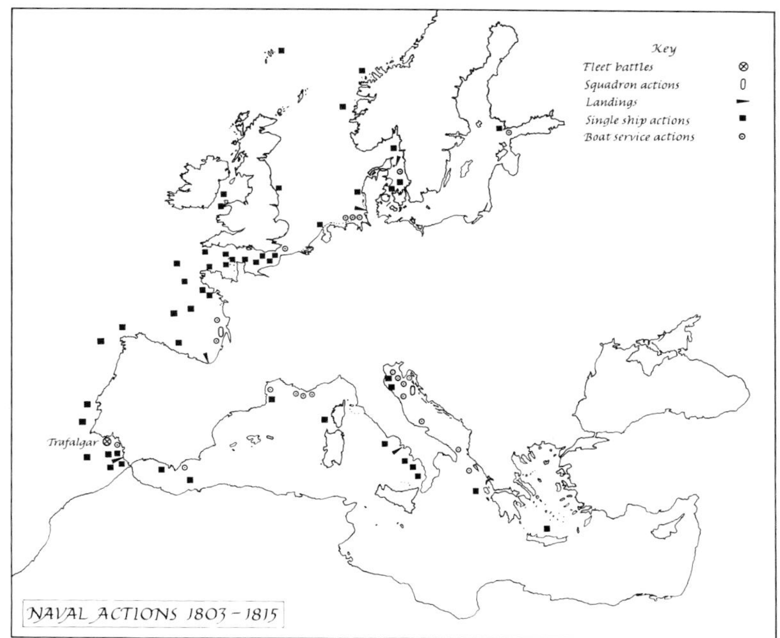

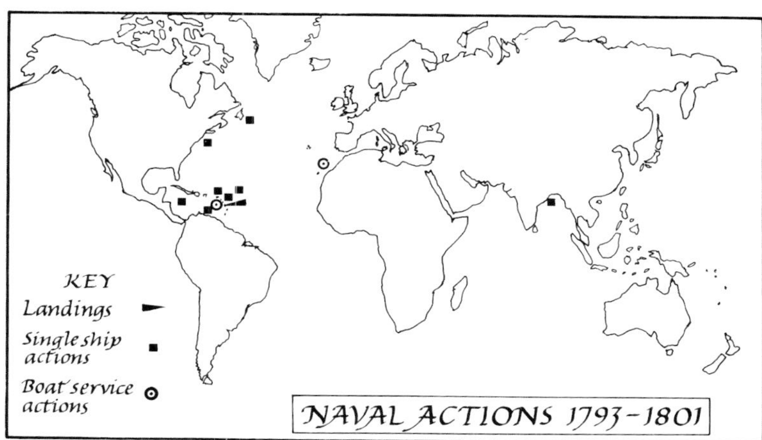

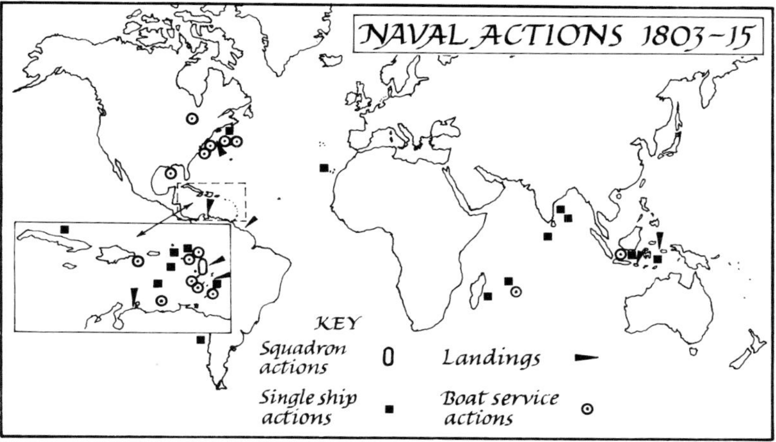

The extent of the naval war: naval actions, 1793-1815, for which the Naval General Service Medal was eventually awarded. Compiled from Douglas-Morriss, *The Naval General Service Medal*, 1982

2 Early Naval History

The Foundation of the Navy

King Alfred is usually credited with the foundation of the English navy, around 897. With the subsequent reduction of Viking invasions, there was no need for a navy and, after the Norman Conquest, the English Channel was no longer the national boundary. Only transport ships were really needed, and these were mostly provided by the Cinque Ports. When the French possessions were lost, King John was obliged to build another navy. Over the next few centuries, navies were created by kings with aggressive foreign policies — Edward III and Henry V, for example. They were invariably allowed to decline to almost nothing under their successors, so at that time the Royal Navy had no permanent existence. Before the days of gunnery, it was quite easy to convert a merchantman into warship; it was armed simply by providing it with soldiers and archers. Ships were generally small, though Henry V's *Grace Dieu* was around 1500 tons, and was one of a long line of royal prestige ships, but the ordinary ships could be built quickly in an emergency so there was no real need for a peacetime fleet.

Most of this was to change in the course of the sixteenth century. Guns were increasingly used aboard ship, and it became common to mount heavy ones firing through gunports cut in the sides, rather than small ones firing over the gunwales. Ships were now three- or four-masted, and much larger. The discovery of the Americas and the sea route to India raised the stakes, and provided new motives for naval power. After the Protestant Reformation of the 1530s, England was faced with the hostility of France and Spain, and needed a more permanent navy to protect herself. The continuous history of the English navy begins with Henry VIII, who built up a fleet which

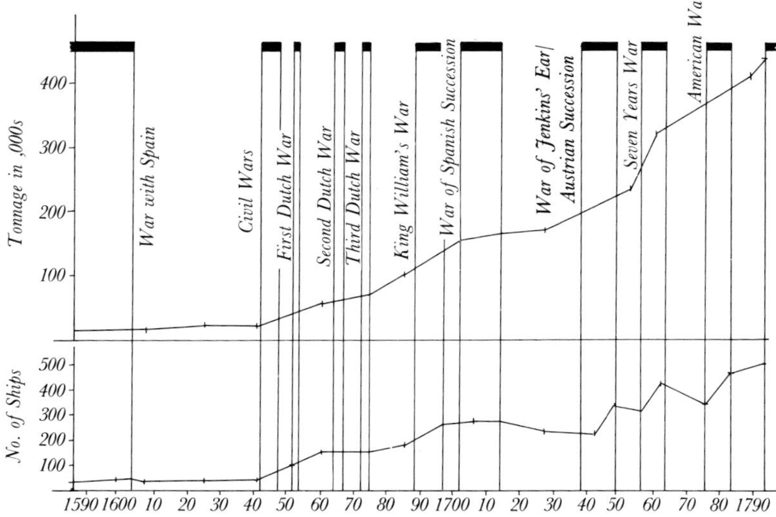

The growth of the navy, 1588-1790, showing numbers of ships, and tonnage.

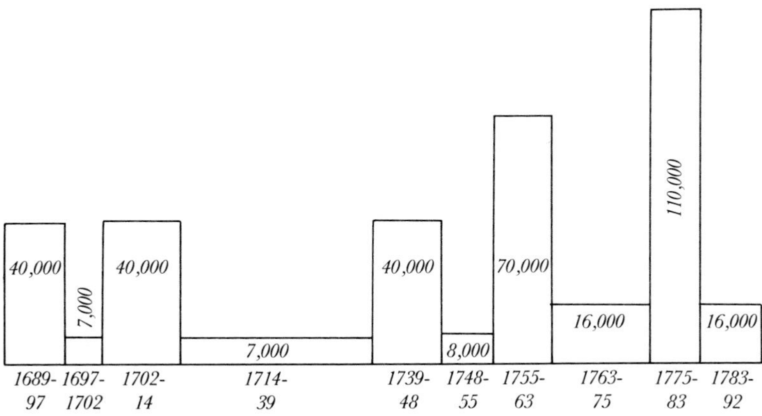

Numbers of men voted for the navy, 1689 to 1792, showing the largest numbers voted in each war, and the smallest numbers in peace.

reached a peak of fifty-eight ships and over 12,000 tons in 1546. These included the famous *Mary Rose* and the *Henry Grace A Dieu*, or *Great Harry*, of 1000 tons.

The War with Spain

The culmination of the Tudor navy came with the Armada campaign, under Henry's daughter Elizabeth. In the 1570s and '80s, Sir John Hawkins built up a new kind of navy, using fast 'race built' ships rather than the great floating fortresses of the past; and relying much more on the power of the big guns, rather than on boarding the enemy. The fight against the Spanish Armada, which took place along the length of the English Channel during a whole week of July 1588, is generally seen as the beginning of a new type of naval warfare. But although heavy guns were used far more than ever before, they had remarkably little effect, except in deterring the Armada's advance; only three Spanish ships were lost during this phase of the campaign, largely by accident. Later, much more serious damage was done, as the Armada headed home round the north of Britain. In effect, the enemy was destroyed by storms rather than the English fleet. The Armada campaign showed some of the potential for gun power, but it was only a beginning, and it was to be several decades before this was fully realised.

Elizabeth's fleet was not a 'royal' navy in the modern sense. There was no large corps of naval officers, merely privateer captains like Drake, and gentleman commanders like Howard of Effingham, who could be called on when necessary. Elizabeth's own fleet was still quite small, with only forty-two vessels at her death in 1603; however their tonnage, at 17,000 was substantially greater than her father's fleet. The royal fleet was not always fully mobilised during the fifteen years of war with Spain, and Elizabeth preferred to save money and conduct the war by private enterprise. However, the war did show some of the potential of gun power, and it convinced the English that they were destined to become a great sea power.

The Origins of the Line of Battle

It is often assumed that the first two Stuart Kings, James I and Charles I, had rather negative effects on the navy. True, James I

The defeat of the Spanish Armada in 1588. In the foreground is a Spanish galleass. The National Maritime Museum

made peace with Spain soon after his accession, and allowed Elizabeth's fleet to fall into some decay. However, this fleet began to revive after 1618, with the building of several 'great ships' to replace those which had been scrapped. James had already built his own prestige ship, the *Prince Royal* of 1610. This pointed the way towards the three-decker, and was the largest ship of her time. The process was completed by his son, who built the *Sovereign of the Seas*, of 1500 tons. Charles I continued to increase the fleet, to a strength of forty-two ships and 22,000 tons in 1641. He relied heavily on 'great ships' of 600 to 850 tons, clearly intended as heavy fighting ships rather than commerce raiders.

Early Stuart naval expeditions, to Cadiz, the Ile de Rhe, and La Rochelle, were uniformly disastrous. The commanders were inexperienced, the men were unwilling conscripts, and the supplies were totally inadequate. Thousands of men died through neglect, and the survivors had to wait months and years for their pay. However, the age did see a silent revolution in naval gunnery and tactics. In the previous century, guns had been loaded very slowly, and ships had to retreat from the immediate area of action to do this. As a result, they had tended to make full use of the guns already loaded, turning the ship to fire both broadsides, as well as bow and stern guns. During the first part of the seventeenth century, this began to change, and gun loading became more efficient. Large ships like the *Sovereign of the Seas* were too big to turn easily, and had to fight with one broadside, and more men were allocated to the guns, less to the sails and small arms, so that the ships could stand and fight. However, the tactical effects of this were not fully appreciated for some years.

◁ *Henry VIII's great ship, the* Great Harry *of 1514, from the Anthony Roll.* The Science Museum

Charles I funded the fleet by extending the unpopular Ship Money tax. This, and other attempts to extend the power of the king, eventually led to revolt and civil war in 1642. The fleet, tired of bad pay and victuals from the king, supported parliament against him. The old great ships were not of immediate tactical value in this conflict, for the main task at sea was to defeat Royalist gun runners and commerce raiders. To do this, small fast ships known as 'frigates' were copied from the Dunkirk privateers. These were long and narrow, and again they tended to shift the emphasis to the power of the broadside; they were difficult to turn, and had less room for bow and stern guns.

By 1649, Parliament was victorious, largely through its land victories under men such as Cromwell and Fairfax. The fleet had not expanded greatly, for only a few of the new frigates had been

The humiliation of the English fleet – the flagship, the Royal Charles, *is captured by the Dutch during the Medway raid in 1677.* The National Maritime Museum

Samuel Pepys, clerk of the acts, 1660-73, and secretary to the Admiralty, 1773-9 and 1684-9. The National Maritime Museum

built, bought or captured. But with the execution of the king in 1649, the leaders of the new republic had to prepare to face a new set of enemies.

The Dutch Wars

The execution of the King made the English republic unpopular throughout Europe. As well as fighting the exiled royalists, the state engaged in wars against Ireland, Scotland, France and Spain. However, the most important naval enemy was the United Netherlands, regarded as the leading naval power in the world after winning her independence from the Spanish, following many decades of war. By the time the First Anglo-Dutch War had broken out in 1652, the navy had been considerably increased; it had more than doubled in size, with 102 ships. The original frigate type had been expanded, and developed into a two-decker. The new type of ship relied much more on the broadside, and on a high rate of fire, than any which had gone before. However, the first battles of the Dutch War were fought on old tactical principles, with the fleet divided into several squadrons, each of which formed its own line. In 1653, when experienced army generals took command of the fleet, it was realised that the guns could be deployed much more effectively if the fleet formed a single line, the 'line of battle'. This was tried that year at the Battle of the Gabbard, and resulted in a crushing English victory. Peace was made in the following year.

After the death of Oliver Cromwell in 1658, the English republic failed to find a new system of government which offered stability, and the monarchy was restored in the person of Charles II in 1660. By this time, the navy had reached a total strength of 154 ships and 57,000 tons, and had more than trebled in eighteen years — the greatest expansion it ever experienced.

Two more wars were fought with the Dutch under Charles II, though neither was a great success. The Second Dutch War, 1664–7, had some English victories, and some defeats, largely because the Dutch had improved their ships and tactics since 1653. However, Charles's government, like those of his father and grandfather, was chronically short of money. In 1667, it was decided not to fit out a main fleet, and the Dutch were able to raid the Medway, doing considerable damage and capturing the English flagship, the *Royal Charles*. In the Third War, 1672–4, the English fought in support of the French, who were attempting to invade the Netherlands. This alliance was unpopular at home, where the people now regarded France as a much more dangerous enemy than Holland. The combined fleets failed to do any serious damage to the Dutch, and England made peace.

Charles II's government extended the shipbuilding policies of the republic. The ship-of-the-line, large enough to stand in the line of battle, was further developed. Several new 100-gun ships were built, including the *Royal Prince* and *Britannia*. The 90-gun three-decker was developed as a cheaper alternative to the 100-gun three-decker, while the 70-gun two-decker became the backbone of the line of battle. With the great shipbuilding programme of 1677, which caused thirty new ships-of-the-line to be added to the fleet, the idea of the ship-of-the-line reached a new peak of development.

One of the major influences behind the development of Charles's navy was Samuel Pepys, Clerk of the Acts and later Secretary to the Admiralty. Perhaps his greatest achievement was to begin to build a permanent corps of professional naval officers. He instituted a system of training and examination, and campaigned against the 'gentleman captains' who were said to have caused many of the defeats of the Second and Third Dutch Wars. Pepys became even more important after the death of Charles II in 1685, when his brother James II succeeded to the throne. However, James was overthrown four years later, and Pepys was too closely associated with him to stay in office. William III, Prince of Orange and Stadtholder of the Netherlands, became king and a new era began.

The Wars with Louis XIV

In the years between 1689 and 1714, Britain was to fight two European wars which in some ways paralleled those of 1793 to 1815. As in the later conflict, the enemy was often identified as a single person, Louis XIV. These wars also produced a large and effective British army, and a great general in the person of the Duke of Marlborough. They lasted for a period of about twenty-five years, with an ineffective truce in the middle. And they were started by a revolutionary event, the overthrow of King James II.

In many respects, the naval war was rather different. The war of 1689 to 1697 began rather badly at sea, for Louis had built up a great fleet which was able to defeat the combined British and Dutch forces at Beachy Head in 1690. However, the French failed to take the opportunity to invade England, and eventually the British had their revenge at Barfleur and La Hogue in 1692, when a large part of Louis's fleet was destroyed. Never again would the French fleet

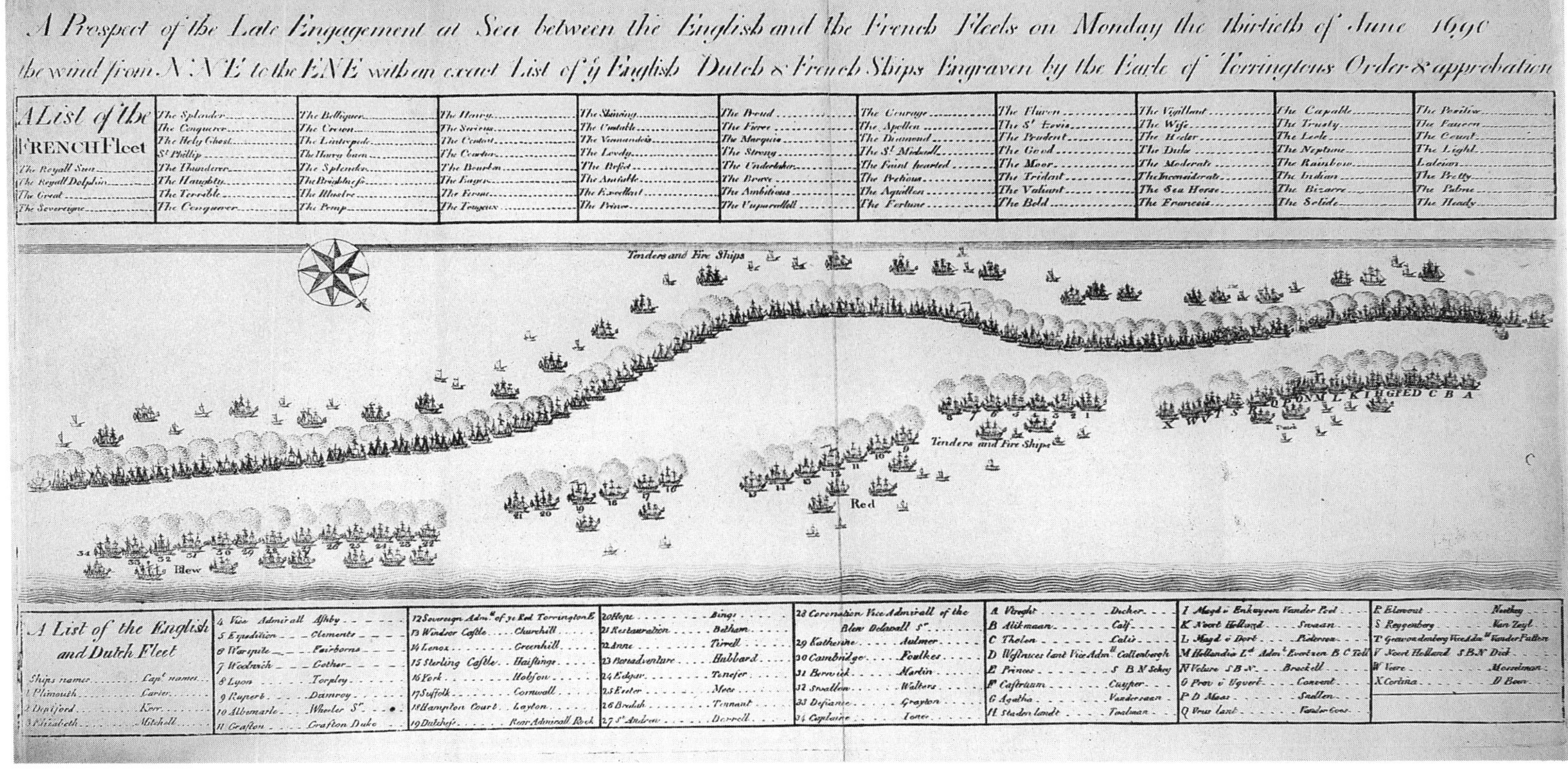

Battle of Beachy Head, 1690 – the last English defeat in a fleet battle. The Dutch squadron, to the right of the picture, is engaging the French, while the British squadrons hold back. From Charnock's *Biographia Navalis*

be numerically superior to the British. The French were a European power with a vulnerable northern land frontier, so they had to concentrate resources on their army. The French battlefleet would not be dangerous again for more than half a century.

But the French found new ways to harass their enemies. Since both Britain and Holland had large merchant fleets, the French fitted out small fast privateers to raid their commerce. It is doubtful if such tactics could really defeat a determined enemy, but they were enough to cause near panic among British merchants, and force the navy to move its resources away from the battlefleet and into commerce protection. After 1692, new shipbuilding was largely directed to smaller ships of 40 guns, 30 guns and 20 guns, which were expected to deal with the privateers, as well as ships of 50 guns which, it was hoped, could serve in the line of battle, or in commerce protection as required. None of these classes was particularly successful, and the British had not yet developed a suitable light warship. The development of the ship-of-the-line was not much more successful; a new shipbuilding programme, an imitation of that of 1677, was begun in 1691. The whole effort was misconceived, and the new ships, of 80 and 60 guns, were far inferior to the old 70, 90 and 100-gun ships.

The war ended in 1697, but was renewed in 1702, with Queen Anne as the English sovereign. The principal British aim was to put the Habsburg claimant on the throne of Spain, rather than the Bourbon one. In this, they were unsuccessful, though the British made many gains in other ways. Gibraltar and Minorca were captured, initially in the name of the Habsburg claimant. The Spanish lost their possessions in the Netherlands and Italy, and were forced to give Britain some trading concessions in their South American empire. Because the French did not fit out a full-scale battlefleet, there was only one fleet battle in the war, off Malaga in 1704. It resulted in no loss of ships on either side. For most of the war the British navy was occupied with the campaign against French privateers, which it pursued with a fair degree of success by means of patrols and convoys.

Colonial Wars

By 1714, the Royal Navy was a well established and permanent force. Though the active fleet was greatly reduced in time of peace, naval officers were now given half pay as a retainer until they were needed again. The fleet now consisted of 229 ships, and the great majority of these would be kept in the navy, in some kind of repair, though only a few would be at sea at any given moment. Against this, the navy was now ultra-conservative, and over the next thirty years it was to make few changes in its practices, or its ship design. Dimensions of ships were 'established' in order to enforce standardisation, but this ruled out any experimentation. Decayed ships were 'rebuilt'. Though hardly any timber of the old ship was re-used, the builders were committed to keeping most of her form. The unsuccessful types of ship, the 80-gun three-deckers for example, were thus kept in service over several decades. Though the permitted dimensions were slowly increased over the years, there was almost no progress in ship design. Admirals were totally committed to the official 'Fighting Instructions', a set of rules which allowed very little room for individual initiative or tactical aggression.

Meanwhile, the nature of naval warfare had changed. The British overseas empire had grown slowly throughout the seventeenth century, and by the middle of the eighteenth century it was a vital and expanding part of the economy. The colonies and interests in North America, the West Indies and India were highly profitable, and America absorbed some surplus population. However, they could be vulnerable in certain circumstances. With this in mind, the French built up a new fleet under Maurepas, the minister of the marine. They developed a 74-gun ship, which was to become the classic ship-of-the-line in the second half of the century. They also developed the frigate (rather different in conception from the frigate of the 1640s) as a fast, medium-sized warship suitable for reconnaissance, patrol and convoy escort.

Admiral Lord Anson, first lord of the Admiralty, 1751-62. The National Maritime Museum

The Battle of Quiberon Bay, 1759. During a November gale, the British fleet chases the French into the bay, and virtually destroys it. The National Maritime Museum

However, for a time, Britain's main enemy was Spain. There were brief wars in 1718 and 1727, and a much longer one, known as the War of Jenkin's Ear, began in 1739. Admiral Vernon captured the Spanish American base at Portobello, but got involved in a long and unsuccessful campaign against Cartagena. Commodore Anson was sent out with a force to raid Spanish possessions in the Pacific. He returned four years later after losing most of his ships and men, circumnavigating the world, and capturing a Spanish treasure galleon. For the first time, the main focus of the naval effort was outside European waters. But the Spanish fleet could come up with surprises, and it had some excellent ships, such as the *Princessa*, captured after a long struggle in 1741.

In 1744, there was an indecisive battle off Toulon, which led finally to war between France and Britain. The new French navy had many fine ships, and, for a time, there was a threat of invasion, until it was severely damaged by a storm. When Prince Charles led a Jacobite rebellion in 1745, he did so with very little support from the French fleet, and was eventually defeated.

In 1747, Anson defeated a French squadron at the First Battle of Finisterre, and, a few months later, Hawke defeated another in the same area. Though both victories were only achieved by weight of numbers, the French fleet was crushed and most of its best ships were in British hands. Peace was made in the following year. Anson rose to be First Lord of the Admiralty in 1751, and continued a programme of naval reform. In 1755 he began to build 74-gun ships in place of the older types, and the first 32-gun frigates were begun two years later. Admirals were led away from the old system of 'Fighting Instructions', and began to move slowly towards a more aggressive policy. Improvements were made in naval medicine, and this made it possible to carry out the close blockade of enemy ports, keeping ships at sea for long periods.

When the Seven Years' War broke out in 1755, the British fleet was not yet fully mobilised, and Minorca was taken by the French. Admiral Byng was made scapegoat and shot. However, the basic fleet was sound after Anson's reforms, and once the nation had found an effective war leadership, under William Pitt the Elder, it began to move towards victory. In 1758, it captured the French fortress of Louisbourg and opened the way to Canada. In 1759, it captured Quebec, and also defeated the French fleet in a major battle at Quiberon Bay, south Brittany. The Spanish entered the war in 1761, and a large part of their fleet was captured at Havana in the following year. When peace was made in 1763, the Royal Navy was triumphant as never before.

The American War

In the peace which followed, the Royal Navy began to build up its reputation for exploration, with Captain Cook's voyages in the Pacific. However, the main focus was in North America, where the colonists were beginning to revolt against British taxation. By 1775, open war had broken out. At first, only the smaller ships of the navy were involved, as the colonists had no battlefleet. But, in 1778, France joined the war against Britain, to be followed by Spain in 1779 and Holland in 1780. British diplomacy had failed to provide an ally on the Continent, so France could pursue the war undistracted, and for the first time in the century the British were outnumbered on the high seas.

There was one indecisive battle in the Channel, at Ushant in 1778. The allies failed to exploit their superiority, while the British developed some new devices to help them in the war — notably coppering of ships bottoms, which greatly increased their speed and reduced the need for maintenance, and the carronade, a short, large-bore gun which increased the short-range gun power of ships to a considerable degree. A massive shipbuilding programme was begun, though many of the ships were not launched until the war was over. In 1780, the emphasis of the naval war shifted to the West Indies, and several battles were fought there. Finally, in April 1782, Admiral Rodney defeated a large French fleet at The Saintes. Though the American colonies had to be given up, the rest of the British Empire, in Canada, the West Indies and India, was safe for the moment. Peace was made in 1783.

By 1793, the Royal Navy was a large, professional, well-equipped and vastly experienced force. It was never immune from incompetence, corruption and nepotism, but it was already recognised as the supreme human agency on all the seas of the world. Over the next twenty-two years, it would go on to win yet more victories, to increase its skills and daring and to reach the highest pinnacle that any sea power has yet achieved.

3 The Naval Administration

Government and Parliament

Britain was, and remains, a constitutional monarchy. In theory all executive power rested in the king, who had the right to appoint and dismiss all his ministers; in practice, this power was considerably reduced by the need for the government to command the support of parliament if it was to carry out its business. George III, ever since he had come to the throne in 1760, had shown considerable determination to exercise his powers. However, he was subject to long periods of insanity, which eventually became permanent in 1811. When the king was unable to perform his function, a regency was created, with his son, the Prince of Wales, as acting head of state. Since the prince was usually at odds with his father, both politically and personally, this caused a further complication in the political system.

The post of prime minister was recognised by no law, but since the 1720s, it had become the real centre of the administration. The prime minister was appointed by the king, but in most cases the choice was extremely limited, because of the need to command the support of parliament. The prime minister chose the members of the cabinet and other office holders, though in practice the king had a veto on his appointments. He 'managed' parliament, distributing favours, posts, and sinecures to try to maintain its support.

The cabinet, including the First Lord of the Admiralty, controlled the general business of government, though its power as a body depended largely on the personalities involved, especially that of the prime minister. It had a strong interest in naval affairs, and it, rather than the admiralty, was in control of naval strategy, deciding how many ships should be sent to different parts of the world, and what level of finance and manning should be asked from parliament.

The House of Lords was the 'upper house' of parliament, and in most respects it remained the most powerful of the two, being composed of a relatively small number of very rich landowners. The House of Commons was elected by a system which was very far from democratic, and by a franchise which varied from place to place. In general, it represented the smaller landowners and the merchants, though less wealthy classes sometimes found a voice. The two parties were the Whigs and Tories, but their organisation was embryonic, and most members showed more loyalty to friends and family than to party. The House of Commons voted the annual estimates which allocated money to the navy, and both houses maintained a general supervision over the conduct of the government, so that naval affairs were often debated.

The structure of naval administration, c1800.

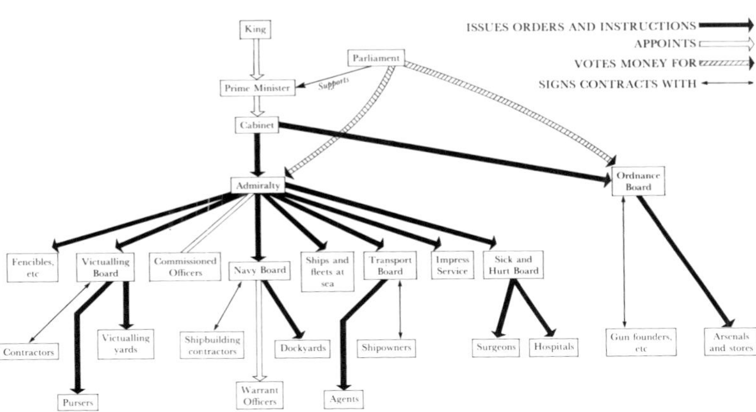

The Naval Estimates

Every year parliament voted a specific sum for the use of the navy. It came in three parts. The ordinary estimate was basically for maintenance of ships and dockyard facilities, and was a specific amount — £700,000 in 1787 and £653,573 in 1797 for example. One characteristic of the ordinary estimate was that it tended to be less in war than peace, because a large part of the maintenance of ships was then paid for under other heads. The second element was the extra estimate, which was usually intended to add to the strength of the navy by building new ships, or to catch up with a backlog of maintenance or debt. Something was paid under this head every year after 1753, and by 1805 it had risen as high as £1½ million. Finally, parliament voted each year for a specific number of seamen and marines, and this was the main determinant of the size of the naval force it expected to be fitted out that year. The highest number of men ever voted in the age of sail was 145,000, in each year from 1810 to 1813. This number was converted into actual money using a crude and antiquated formula, dating from the time of Oliver Cromwell: £4 per man was paid for each lunar month of the year, so that £52 was paid in total. The £4 was divided into three parts; 30s for wages, 27s for wear and tear of ships and equipment, 19s for victualling, and 4s for the Ordnance Board, to pay for guns and their equipment. In 1797, after the great mutinies raised wages, this was increased to £7 per man, with 37s for wages, £3 for wear and tear, 38s for victualling, and 5s for the ordnance.

The whole system was extremely unreliable. The number of seamen actually raised never quite corresponded to the numbers voted. No serious attempt was made to check whether the money was used as voted, and there was no real guarantee that the exact amount would really be paid. Most important of all, the money was never enough from year to year, so the navy was permanently in debt. However, this was accepted by the contractors, and payment was regular if slow, so the system worked. Seamen's pay was often years in arrears, and this was one of the causes of mutiny.

The Admiralty Board

The Admiralty Board was headed by the first lord of the Admiralty. Often he was a senior admiral, for at this time there was no bar on naval officers holding seats in parliament, and political office. The Earl of St Vincent and Lord Barham held the post during this period.

The naval estimates, 1792-1815. Based on figures in Clowes's History of the Royal Navy, *vol IV p 153, Vol V, p 9*

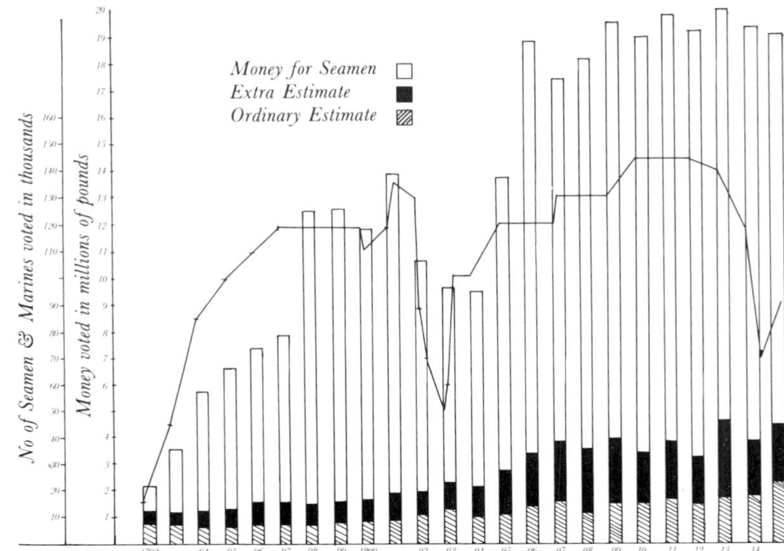

An Admiralty Board meeting, drawn by Rowlandson and Pugin, c1800. Around the walls can be seen the wind indicator, a globe, and pull-down maps of various parts of the world. The cords ring bells to summon clerks and messengers. The figures are too small, and exaggerate the size of the room. The National Maritime Museum

It was slightly more common for the first lord to be a politician. Civilian holders during the years 1793 to 1815 included Viscount Melville, the Earl of Spencer, and the Earl of Chatham; all of them were members of the House of Lords. Members of the Commons who held the post included Grey, Grenville and Yorke; but it is perhaps significant that two of these were the sons of peers.

Besides the first lord, the Admiralty Board had five or six junior members. Approximately half of these would be naval officers, and when the first lord was a civilian politician the senior naval officer would have considerable importance as an adviser, though the term 'First Sea Lord' was not yet common. The junior Lords did not tend to specialise, and some were quite lax in their duties, often leaving three or four members to carry on the work.

The Board considered promotions and appointments of commissioned officers, the movements of fleets and individual ships, and the allocation of resources. It exercised quite a close supervision over the Navy Board in its work with the *matériel* of the fleet. Despite the slowness of communication, the Admiralty Board considered thousands of detailed matters every month, and issued instructions on them.

The Admiralty Office

The Admiralty office in Whitehall, where the Board met daily, was the centre of naval administration. From 1796, when the first telegraphs were erected, the office was in constant communication with the main dockyards and anchorages (except when bad visibility prevented the use of the telegraph). The Board Room was fitted with a 'tell tale' linked to a weather vane on the roof, giving an instant reading of the wind direction. It walls were lined with globes and maps, reflecting the world-wide importance of the discussions taking place.

As well as the members of the Board, the building provided offices for a staff of officials who issued the orders of the Board. Because much of their work was delegated to other boards, the actual staff in Whitehall was quite small — a total of sixty-one in 1800.[1] This included the Marine Department, the Naval Works Department, and the Admiralty Court, as well as messengers, porters, and the 'necessary woman' (who was responsible for housekeeping). The actual clerical and administrative staff at the disposal of the Admiralty Board was only twenty-eight.

The two secretaries, first and second, were quite considerable figures. On relatively minor matters, they could issue instructions on their own authority, without reference to the Board. On more important issues, they were responsible for seeing that the Board's orders and instructions were sent out. The first secretary from 1795 to 1804 was Sir Evan Nepean, who had risen from a clerk, and later became Governor of Bombay. His successor from 1809 to 1830 was J W Croker, who had once held high office as chief secretary for Ireland; he was an important writer and journalist, and friend of many leading politicians. The second secretary from 1804 to 1845, with one brief gap, was John Barrow, who had been an explorer, and went on to write several important works on exploration and naval history.

The Admiralty also included the hydrographer, who was responsible for compiling some of the earliest official British government charts. The first hydrographer was Alexander Dalrymple, who was in office from 1795 to 1808. Previously, surveys had been carried out by men such as Greenville Collins, James Cook, and the Mackenzies, father and son. Dalrymple's was the first permanent appointment, and it signified the greater use of charts, in place of the practical experience of pilots.

Charles Middleton, Lord Barham, controller of the navy, 1778-90, lord of the Admiralty, 1794-5, and first lord, 1805-6. The National Maritime Museum

The Admiralty Office in Whitehall. This picture shows it shortly after the wars, when the shutter telegraph on the roof has been replaced by a semaphore telegraph. The National Maritime Museum

The Marine Offices

The headquarters of the Marines were situated in the Admiralty building. The head of the corps was the 'commandant in town', with the rank of lieutenant general. The Marine Department and the Marine Pay Department had small staffs of clerks, but the first and second secretaries of the former were also the first and second secretaries of the Admiralty. However, most of the administrative work connected with the Marines was done in the divisions, near the dockyards at Plymouth, Portsmouth, Chatham and later Woolwich.

The Navy Board

The Navy Board was responsible for the technical and financial aspects of naval administration. It was made up of a combination of naval officers, shipwright officers, and civilian administrators. They were more permanent than the members of the Admiralty Board, and rather more like civil servants than politians; but the distinction was not always clear in those days, and certainly some controllers of the navy indulged in politics.

The Navy Board was responsible for most of the warrant officers of the navy. Boatswains, carpenters, and cooks were examined by the Board and appointed to individual ships by them. Other warrant officers, such as masters, surgeons and pursers, were appointed by the board but not examined by them. The Board also oversaw the dockyards, and was responsible for the maintenance of ships and buildings. It supervised the subordinate boards of Victualling and Sick and Hurt. It was headed by the controller of the navy, who was an experienced naval captain. Next in importance were the surveyors of the navy, who were responsible for ship design, building and maintenance. Two of these were in office up to 1813, and three after that date. They were invariably shipwrights with long experience in the Royal Dockyards. Other members included the clerk of the acts, who acted as the secretary of the board; the controllers of the storekeepers, victualling and treasurers accounts, and several extra commissioners. The commissioners at the major dockyards were formally members of the Board, but they rarely if ever attended its meetings. The treasurer of the navy had once been a member of the Board, but now his office was regarded as a separate department.

One of the most important jobs of the Navy Board was to make agreements with civilian contractors, for building whole ships, at one end of the scale, and for every kind of object needed to run the ships and dockyards at the other. Contracts were put out to tender, with the lowest bidder usually being accepted, provided he could prove his reliability.

The Navy Board was often criticised for inefficiency and corruption, and, as a result, there were several long-running parliamentary enquiries into its affairs. The first one reported in 1788, and suggested a reorganisation of the way the Board carried out its business. Traditionally, it had met as a whole body, and according to one of its members, 'The Board's hours of business were spent in discussions of difficulties, till the pressing occasion forced them to leave things to take their course, and order them, not as they should, but as they could be done.'[2] The 1788 report recommended that the Board should be divided into three separate committees: correspondence, accounts, stores, with the controller as chairman of each, while the surveyors would form a separate specialised committee of their own. These suggestions were eventually adopted in 1796, and after this, the Board normally had ten members, excluding the dockyard commissioners — a controller, deputy controller, two surveyors and six commissioners. Despite the reforms, the Board remained an essentially conservative body, though it was responsible for implementing many new inventions in ship design and fitting.

Somerset House in the Strand, containing the offices of the Navy Board, Victualling Board, Transport Board, etc. From Lambert's *History of London*, 1806

The Ordnance Board

The Ordnance Board, unlike the others involved in naval administration, was neither directly nor indirectly under the control of the Admiralty. It was a separate government department, which controlled the supply of guns, ammunition and other stores to both the army and navy. It was headed by the master general, who was often a substantial figure in his own right — holders of the office included the Duke of Schomberg and the Duke of Marlborough. During 1793 to 1815, notable master generals included the Earl of Chatham (brother of William Pitt), Lord Mulgrave, and the Duke of Richmond. Its other officials, who took much more part in the actual running of the Board, included the lieutenant general, treasurer, surveyor general, and clerk of the ordnance. However, its most important official at this period was Thomas Blomefield, the inspector general of artillery; he designed a new type of cannon, which was in

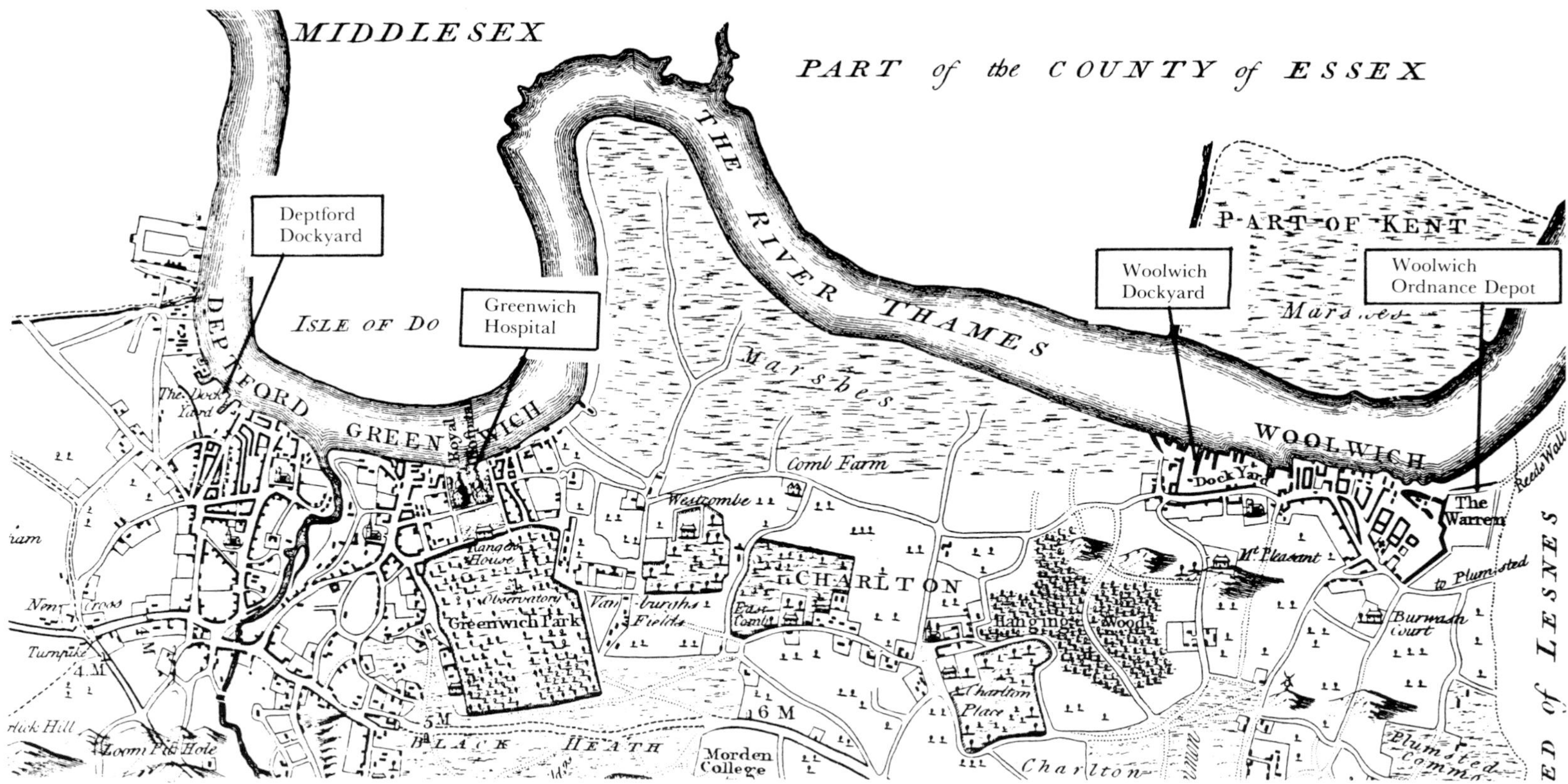

Naval and ordnance installations on the River Thames near London. Basic map from Hasted's *History of Kent*, 1787

Map of London from Lambert's History of London, *showing the main buildings used by government and the navy.*

1. *St James's Palace (King's main residence)*; 2. *Admiralty Building, Whitehall*; 3. *Downing Street (Prime Minister's residence)*; 4. *Houses of Parliament*; 5. *Somerset House (Victualling Board, Navy Board, Transport Board)*; 6. *Tower Hill (Rendezvouz for impress service)*; 7. *Tower of London (Ordnance depot)*

A. *Telegraph line to Portsmouth, Plymouth, Yarmouth, via Royal Hospital Chelsea*; B. *Telegraph line to Deal and Chatham*

general use by 1800, and he carried out many experiments in the making and firing of guns.

The Ordnance Board made contracts with private foundries (including Walker and Co of Rotherham and Carron Company of Falkirk) for the manufacture of guns. The Board controlled the great arsenal at Woolwich, where guns were received and tested. They were then issued to ships, by way of the ordnance depots near the main dockyards. The Board also supervised the gunpowder mills at Faversham and Waltham Abbey. It appointed gunners to ships, and supplied them with all the ammunition and stores necessary.

The Transport Board

The War of American Independence had created an enormous demand for hired merchant ships to carry troops and supplies across the Atlantic. In the past, this had been organised by the Navy Board, but in 1794 the Transport Board was set up to deal with it, and the Board survived throughout the French Revolutionary and Napoleonic Wars, because hundreds of supply ships were needed to handle naval and military commitments throughout the world. In 1794, the Board consisted of three senior naval officers; two of whom became rear admirals while on the Board. After 1795, it had three naval captains, and two administrators. It was disbanded in 1817, and merged with the Navy Office.

The Transport Office had a reputation for efficiency, unlike many other parts of the administration. As a result, the care of prisoners of war was transferred from the Sick and Hurt Board to the Transport Board in 1796. According to Sir Charles Middleton, 'The effect was a clear and constant transaction of the duty, without leaving any arrears of accounts.'[3] In 1804 another parliamentary commission recommended that the Sick and Hurt Board should also be merged with the Transport Department; this was done in 1806. The new board consisted of three naval officers, one as chairman; one civil administrator, and one physician as medical advisor.

The Victualling Board

The Victualling Board was an ancient institution, responsible for regulating and appointing the pursers of ships, and for supplying them with food and drink. It had seven commissioners, usually civilians. It had its headquarters at Somerset House in London, and its main depot at Deptford, and it ran the naval victualling yards at the main dockyards, and other depots around the world. It negotiated contracts for many thousands of pounds every year. It controlled several breweries, a large bakery at Portsmouth, and numerous warehouses. The Board had attracted much hatred in the past because of the generally poor quality of naval provisions, and because of allegations of corruption. Nevertheless, it pioneered some important improvements, including the introduction of canned food. It survived until 1832 when, with the Navy Board, it was merged with the Admiralty Board.

The Sick and Hurt Board

Originally the Sick and Hurt Board (or the Sick and Wounded Board) was responsible for ships' surgeons and their supplies, the running of naval hospitals, and prisoners of war. It consisted of five medical officers, though most of these were not men of distinction. Its neglect of prisoners of war led to these being transferred to the Transport Board in 1796. The members of the Sick and Hurt Board had no experience of administration or finance, and, though they oversaw some notable improvements in medicine, their affairs ran very heavily into debt — two and a half million pounds by 1792, and a million and a half more by 1804. The parliamentary enquiry recommended that it be merged with the Transport Board, and this was done in 1806.

4 Britain and the World

The United Kingdom

The Royal Navy of 1793 to 1815 reflected the society which created it. Life in the navy was hard, punishments were cruel, and death was never far away; all this was true, to a lesser extent, of British civil society. The navy also reflected the morals and values of British culture — the class system, the political ethos, and the ambiguous attitudes to liberty. It was an expression of the technology of the times — far more advanced than anything which had gone before, but primitive compared with the changes which would take place in the nineteenth century, not to mention the twentieth. It was supported by the British taxpayer, and hence by the British economy; its ships were a product of British industry, and its men were a product of British society. Often, the navy felt itself cut off from the rest of the British people, by geographical distance and by a different lifestyle; it was, none the less, part of the nation, and it cannot be considered in total isolation.

The United Kingdom was founded in 1707, when the Scottish parliament was persuaded to merge with the English parliament. The Crowns of the two countries had been merged a century before,

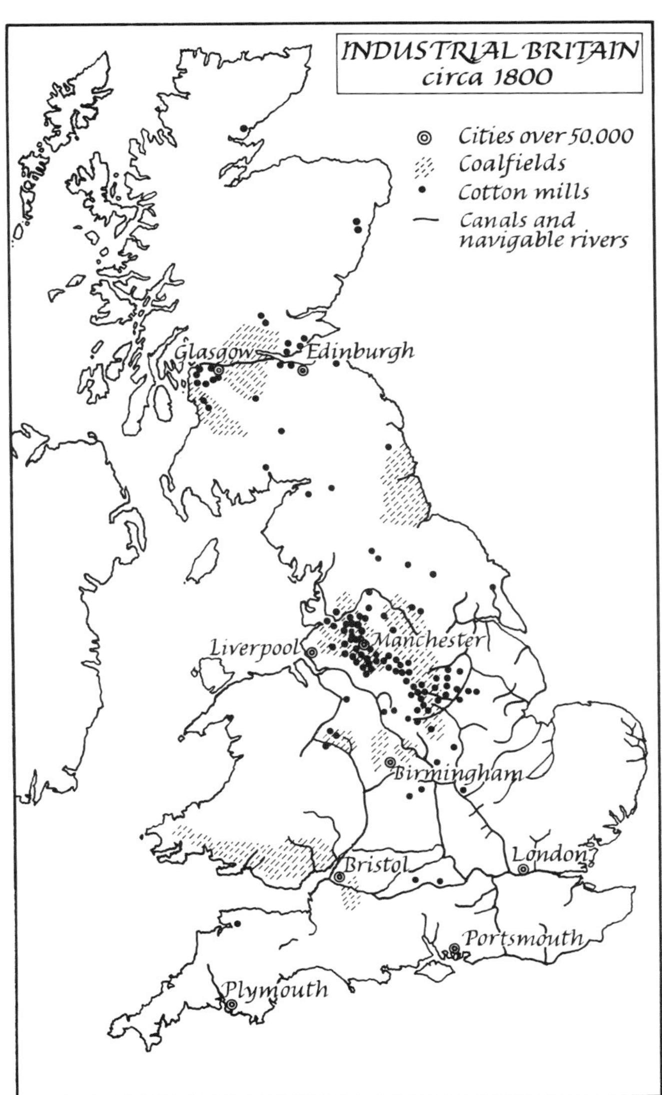

in the person of King James I and VI; Wales had been conquered by the English some centuries before. After 1707, the whole island became a political unity, though the Scots retained their own laws, Church and customs. The political consensus was based on the Glorious Revolution of 1688, when the Catholic James II had been overthrown, and parliamentary government guaranteed. Many people remained outside this consensus, especially the Jacobites of the Scottish highlands, who took part in several rebellions before they were crushed at Culloden in 1746, after which, the Jacobite cause ceased to be a serious issue. Mainland Britain was therefore quite united until the time of the French Revolution — following which, radicals began to campaign against the inequalities of the system of government. After 1793, they were put down quite effectively, by means of special laws passed against clubs, trade unions and other organisations. In Scotland, the government could be more ruthless, and several radicals were sentenced to long periods of transportation.

Ireland never became part of the general consensus. The people there remained Catholic, except for the landowning classes, those of the northeast and the government officials in Dublin. Until the end of the eighteenth century, the Irish had their own parliament, though the Catholics were not represented in it, and it was definitely subordinate to the London parliament. In 1800, the Act of Union was passed, and Great Britain and Ireland were governed by a single parliament in London. The Catholics had been promised emancipation, but this was withdrawn because of the king's refusal to countenance it. The Irish remained strongly disaffected with British rule, as expressed in the revolt of 1798 and in many other acts of defiance.

The Power of the State

Compared with most of its neighbours in Europe, Britain was quite liberal. Trial by jury was well established, and was conducted according to the rule of law. The political system was distinctly pluralist, compared with the autocracies on the Continent. The king, Cabinet, the two Houses of Parliament, the courts and the local officials such as the justices of the peace all had distinct and independent roles in the government of the country, and were jealous of their powers. The state had no arbitrary powers of imprisonment or dispossession. Though the political system was far from democratic, issues were debated more or less openly in parliament, and to a certain extent they were commented on by a free press. The upper and middle classes had a traditional fear of strong state power, and resisted any innovations which might increase it. However, this attitude was changing quite rapidly in the face of the war with France. On the less positive side, the state had some quite draconian powers, especially against the lower orders of society. The press gang was of course the most notorious, but the game laws imposed savage penalties on those who trespassed on the landowner's rights over his property. The powers of the state were increased in the aftermath of the French Revolution, and new laws were passed against trade unions and radical societies, while the freedom of the press was restricted.

Traditionally, the state had raised much of its money by means of taxes on land; either the national land tax, which supported most of the eighteenth-century wars, or the local rates. By the 1790s, wealth was as likely to be measured by money as by land, and it was necessary for the government to find new ways of tapping this. At first, it tried various new taxes on items which were difficult to conceal, such as windows, coaches and hair powder. In 1797, it was necessary to introduce income tax for the first time — an imposition which would have horrified the Tories of earlier years, and which was dropped again after the Peace of Amiens, but revived after the resumption of war.

A public hanging in 1803, by Rowlandson. Museum of London

Law and Order

Britain had no police force in the modern sense. In the countryside, law and order was the responsibility of the justices of the peace, who were mostly landowners, while in the towns it was supervised by the local magistrates. Aged constables were employed to patrol the streets, but they were inadequate and ineffective. Every citizen had a duty to help enforce the law, but this worked less and less well in the growing and chaotic cities. The crime rate was high, and the government's only answer was to impose severe penalties on the few who were caught. Over two hundred crimes were punishable by hanging — including the theft of quite small items; and public execution was a regular feature of town life. Other barbaric penalties still survived. The stocks and pillory were in use for minor offences, as was public flogging. For those convicted offenders who avoided hanging, the government had recently instituted the policy of transportation to Australia. Debtors could spend years in prison — prisons which were foul and ill run, such as Newgate in London. Those prisoners who could not afford to pay for more comfortable conditions might languish in extreme squalor, and possibly not be released until they had paid their gaol fees, despite being proved innocent. When considering the cruelties of the naval system of discipline, it is necessary to see it against the background of life ashore.

Population

In 1801, when the first national census was taken, the total population of Britain was just under eleven million. There are no accurate figures for the periods before that, but there is no doubt that it was rising rapidly, due to a reduction in infant mortality — enough to cause Malthus to predict disaster if it was allowed to rise any further. The

A well-off courting couple in 1805, by Rowlandson.

surplus population found little work in the countryside, and moved to the cities. London expanded to over a million people in 1811, while the new industrial centres, such as Birmingham, Manchester and Leeds, were growing rapidly. By 1811 the total population had expanded yet further, to twelve and a half million.

The Class System

The British class system was less rigid than that of many European countries, such as pre-revolutionary France; it was possible for a family to rise by several ranks in a single lifetime. The new merchants of the Industrial Revolution sometimes became as wealthy as members of the aristocracy, and there was nothing to prevent them from buying land to confirm their higher status. However, the class sytem was real enough, and quite rigid in its way. At the top was the aristocracy, made up of a few hundred very wealthy families, with vast estates and with the political power that came from a seat in the House of Lords, and perhaps the control of several parliamentary boroughs as well. Next, came the minor landowners, known as the 'squires'. Most had no title beyond that of Mr, and an income of only a few hundred a year; but collectively they controlled local government in the countryside, and had a great deal of influence over parliamentary elections. They provided most of the justices of the peace, and often the officers of the militia. In the older towns, the local government was controlled by the ancient guilds of tradesmen and artisans. The merchants could become very wealthy, especially through trade, including the slave trade. The artisans were trained by apprenticeship, so entry to the class was quite rigidly controlled. In a craft which benefited from the industrial revolution rather than being supplanted by it, men could rise quite high, becoming masters on their own account. Other trades were not controlled by apprenticeship, for example, the weavers. They suffered heavily when they were replaced by the power loom in the early years of the nineteenth century. In the countryside, the old class of yeoman — independent small farmers — was disappearing. The new type of farmer was a man with a good education and some capital for improvement, who rented his land from the larger landowners.

Rural prosperity, 1793, by Gillray. John Bull is represented as the traditional English yeoman, though this class was already declining.

The lower classes at Billingsgate fish market, by Cruikshank.

For the poor of the town and country, there were few privileges. Some became waged labourers in the new mines or factories (though there was a prejudice against men for factory work, where women and children were preferred); some lived by crime in the town or countryside; some remained in their old towns and villages, making a living from casual and seasonal labour; others enlisted in the navy in desperation. For those who could not make ends meet in any of these ways, the poor law existed to give them a minimum of help. Under the Speenhamland system of 1795, local magistrates supplemented the wages of the poorest-paid out of the local rates.

The Agricultural Revolution

The agricultural system of Britain had been in a state of change for some decades. The old medieval system, of fields divided into strips which were farmed in turn by different members of the village community, was rapidly dying. Landowners enlisted the support of parliament to divide their land into larger fields and farms, which were then let as single units. The old peasant farmers lost their

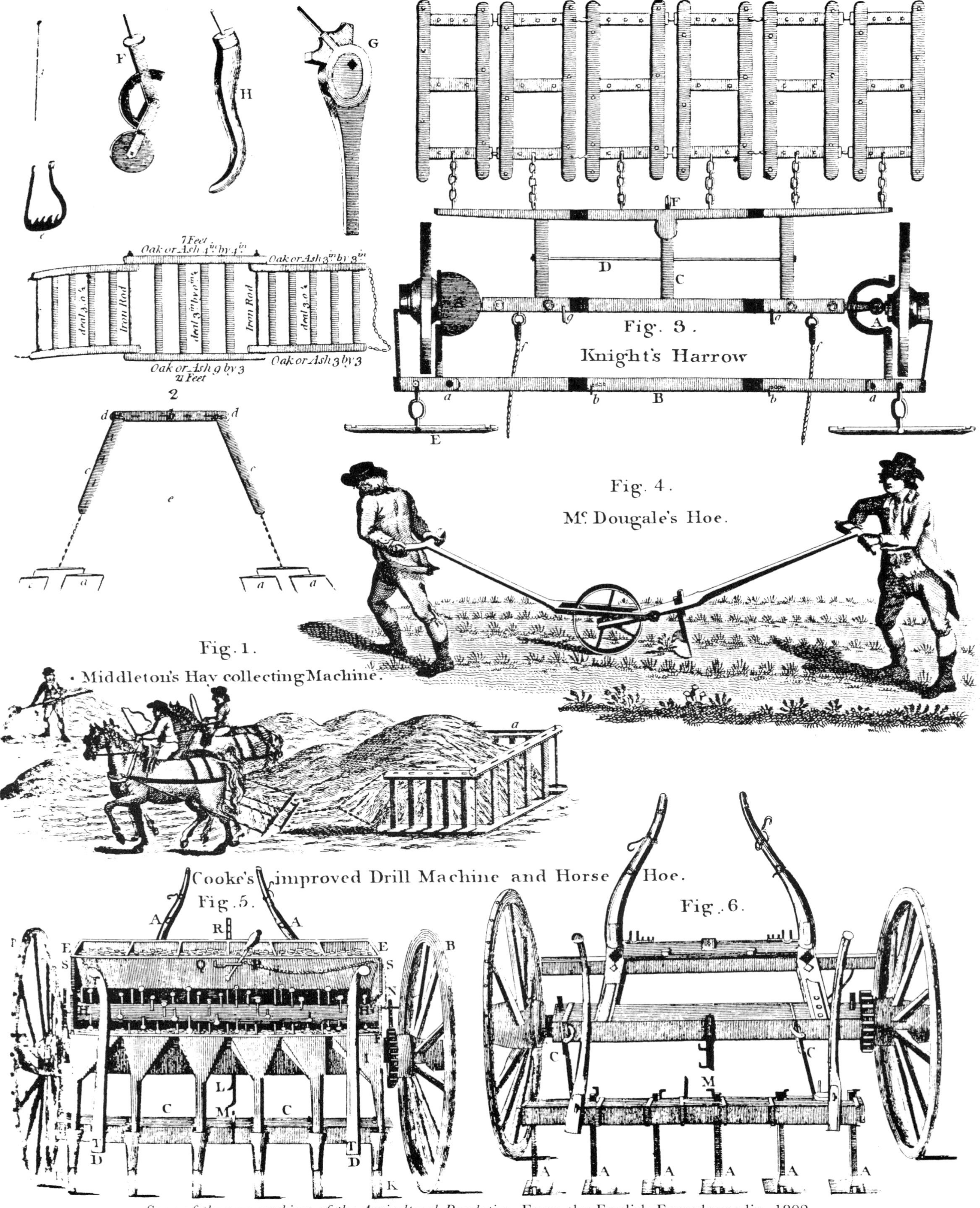

Some of the new machines of the Argicultural Revolution. From the English Encyclopaedia, 1802

customary rights, and joined the flow of labour to the towns and factories. New crops, such as turnips and potatoes, were introduced; many labour-saving devices were invented, and more efficient crop rotations were introduced. The process was well advanced by the 1790s, and agriculture was more efficient than ever before. However, the population was expanding, and the war sometimes reduced supplies of foreign food; as a result, the price of bread was very high, and the poor found it difficult to avoid starvation.

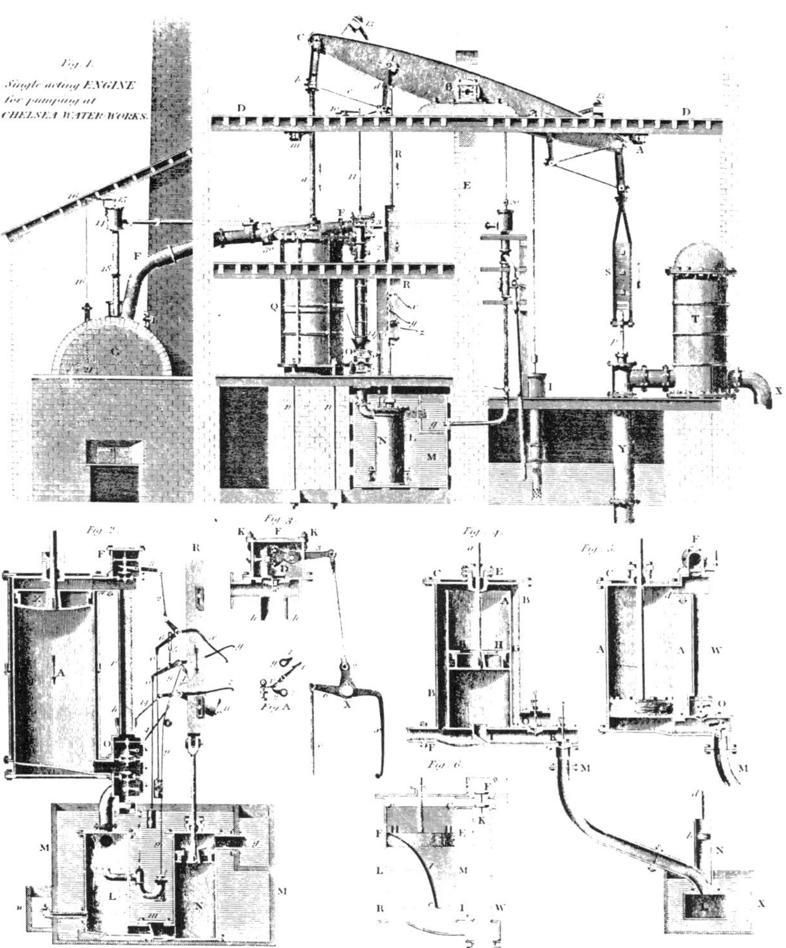
Watt's steam engine, from Rees's Cyclopaedia, *1819.*

The Industrial Revolution

The Industrial Revolution was under way by the 1790s. In certain industries, especially weaving, coal and iron, methods were revolutionised, production increased, and great advances brought about. Cotton and wool were made into yarn by Hargreaves' 'spinning jenny', by Crompton's 'mule' and Arkwright's 'water frame', which were often installed in factories, displacing the old-fashioned 'spinsters' working at home. The new factory workers were employed for long hours, and the work was hard and boring. After Cartwright's power loom of 1785, weaving was increasingly concentrated in the factories, and the old hand-loom weavers faced unemployment; this often drove them to join the navy.

The iron industry was growing rapidly, partly because of increased orders from the navy for guns, and also because iron was being used more and more to make tools and machinery. Iron was now smelted using coke instead of charcoal, and this created an increased demand for coal. Ironworks tended to be concentrated near the major coalfields, especially in Scotland and the north of England. The coal industry was developing its own technology, though its labour practices were primitive; young children were regularly used to haul coal underground, and, in Scotland, miners were technically serfs until the end of the eighteenth century.

As yet, industry was largely rural, because it had to be situated near its sources of raw materials and power. While water power remained predominant, textile factories were mostly built near suitable streams. But steam power was becoming increasingly important, and this allowed more concentration in major towns, while other towns, such as Birmingham and Leeds, were growing up round the industries. The Industrial Revolution affected only some industries; building, printing, and numerous other crafts survived almost unaffected. The Industrial Revolution was not yet total, in that only a small minority were involved in the factory system. It was only the beginning of a movement that was to change the world, for better or for worse.

The water frame, from Rees's Cyclopaedia, *1819.*

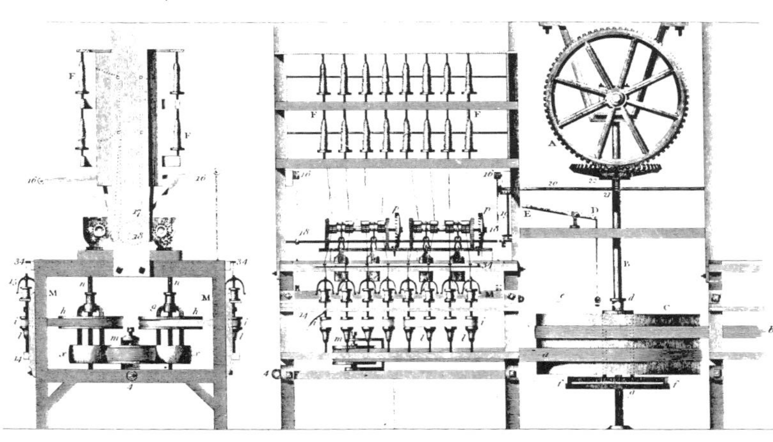

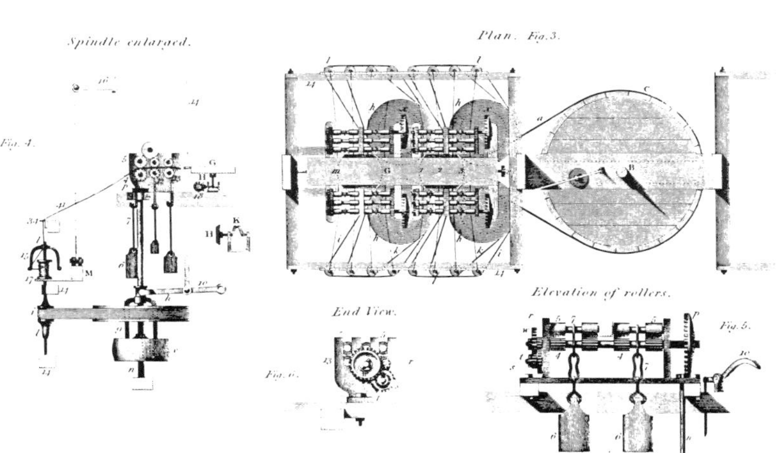

Transport

Obviously, industry and agriculture could only prosper if the products could be taken to market. As far as possible, the sea was used; when that was unsuitable, the growing canal network was exploited. Land transport came a poor third in terms of efficiency, but it was necessary to hold the country together — to bring the products from isolated places to market, or to the nearest seaport, and to allow the relatively fast passage of people and mails. Major roads were now turnpikes, so that users had to pay for their upkeep. As a result, it was possible to move about the country much faster than in the past; the country could be traversed in days rather than weeks.

Toll roads did much to improve transport in these years. A coach pays its toll. From Pynn's Microcosm, *1803-6.*

Culture

At its highest level, British culture was flourishing during the wars with France. Novelists like Sir Walter Scott and Jane Austen were at the peak of their powers. The Romantic movement was beginning to find its inspiration in the past, possibly to escape from the ugliness of contemporaneous factories and squalor. William Blake produced mystical and poignant verse and paintings, while Byron, Wordsworth, Shelley and Coleridge wrote some of the best-known poems in the English language. The landowners and merchants who had done well out of the agricultural and industrial revolutions were able to afford better houses, either as great country seats or in the elegant squares and terraces of cities such as London, Edinburgh and Bath. This produced architects such as Sir John Soane and James Wyatt. The Romantic Movement had its effect on architecture too, and there was a trend away from the Classicism of earlier years, and towards the Gothic Revival. In graphic arts, Turner was already well established in his career, while Constable was still seeking recognition by 1815. Though the rich and the better-off found expression so brilliantly, the culture of the poor was largely submerged. Traditional folk arts in the villages were barely surviving the onslaught of industrialisation; the new working class worked long hours and had little leisure time.

In general, it was not an age of strong religious feeling, though there were exceptions — Wesley had recently founded Methodism, which inspired large sections of the poorer classes. The wealthier and better educated were more likely to join the Evangelical movement. Atheism was unusual, and almost everyone expressed some kind of faith. In England, the Episcopalian religion, as expressed by Church of England, was still supreme in law, though a substantial minority of the population, especially in the north of the country, were 'dissenters' or 'nonconformists', following different Protestant faiths. In Scotland the Presbyterian Church of Scotland was the established church, and was supported by the majority of the population, though perhaps with less narrow-minded fervour than in the recent past. In Ireland, the great majority of the population was Roman Catholic, though that religion was repressed by law and custom. In the north east (the modern Northern Ireland), the people were largely Presbyterian, so the Episcopalian Church of Ireland was supported only by the upper and middle classes, the Anglo-Irish.

Opposition

In view of the contradictions and stresses of British society, it is not surprising that there were many movements opposed to the status quo. The government feared revolution on the French model, and was often quite ruthless in repressing any opposition. The Irish revolted in 1798, but were defeated; after that, the country was kept under control, though United Irishmen in the fleet caused many fears of a political mutiny. In England and Scotland, the middle classes, largely under-represented in the political system, had started off the period by supporting political reform, and forming Corresponding Societies to press for it. This movement faltered in the 1790s, partly because the middle classes were brought in to support the wars, but also because of government repression, culminating in the transporting of the 'Scottish Martyrs' in 1793. In later years, most of the opposition came from the lower classes. In 1797 the seamen aired their grievances with the Spithead and Nore mutinies. In the early nineteenth century, the artisans and labourers opposed the factory system, and formed gangs of 'Luddites', under their mythical leader 'Ned Ludd', to break into factories and destroy machinery. To all this, successive governments reacted with repression and staunch conservatism, and none of these issues had been resolved by the end of the wars in 1815. Parliamentary reform, the rights of the factory workers, and Irish nationalism were to dominate the political agenda for many years afterwards.

The British Empire

The old British empire had collapsed after the American victory in the War of Independence. The new one consisted of possessions in Canada, the Caribbean, Australia and India. Canada had French-

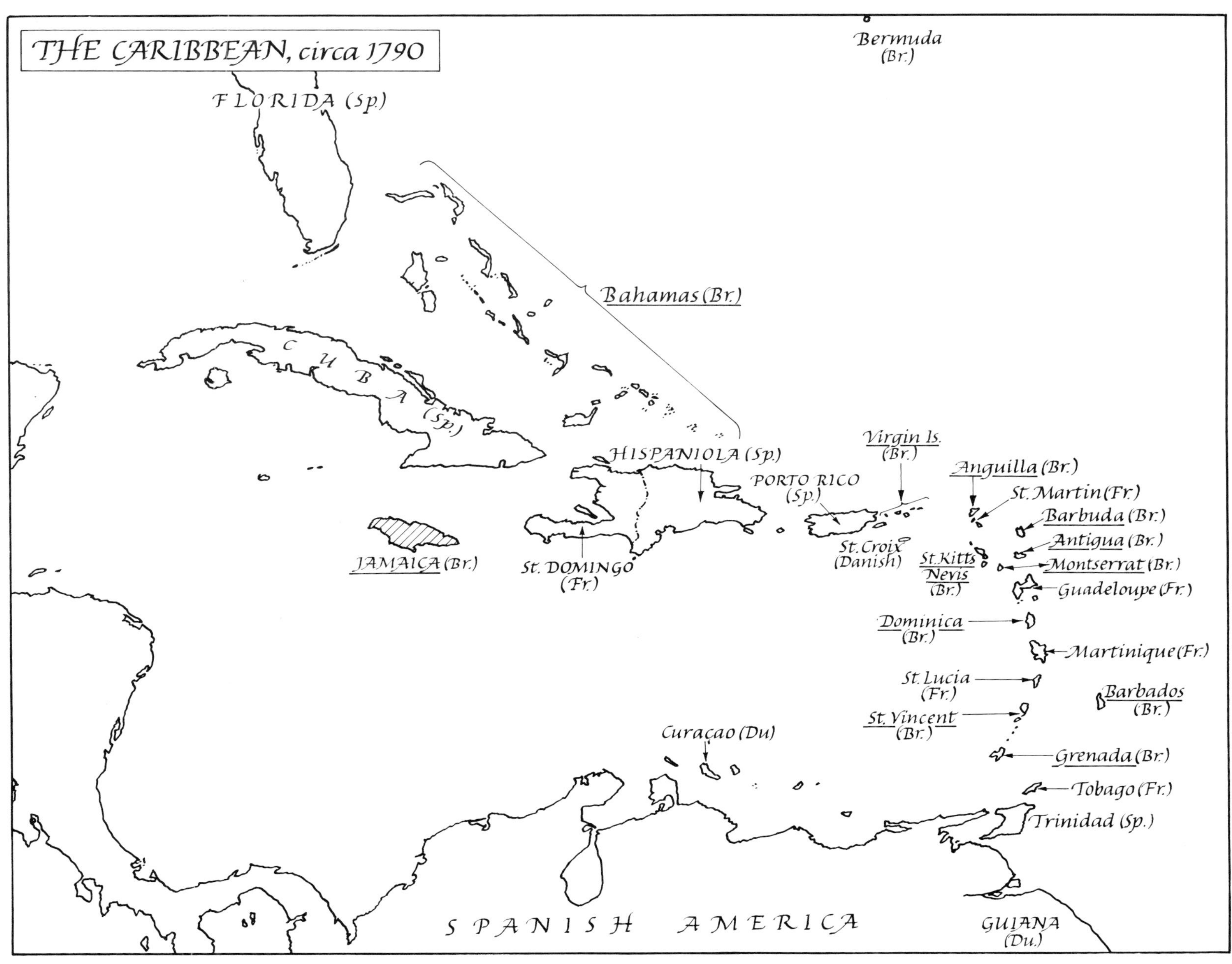

The Caribbean, c1790.

The African slave trade was abolished in 1808, but continued illegally for many years after that. This print of 1821 shows how the slaves were crammed into the ships.

speaking settlers in 'lower Canada' or Quebec, and English-speaking ones, mainly refugees from the American Revolution, in 'upper Canada', the modern Ontario. By an Act of 1792, Canada had some measure of representative government. Only the land around the Great Lakes had been colonised. There were separate colonies in Nova Scotia and Newfoundland.

In the Caribbean, the British held Jamaica, Barbados, Dominica, Grenada, the Bahamas, Antigua and a few smaller islands. The islands produced sugar for the home market or re-export, using slave labour originally brought over from Africa. The islands were very unhealthy for Europeans, and white settlers tended to stay long enough to make their fortunes, and then return home. As a result, there were few native whites. Naval power could prevent a serious threat of invasion, but slave revolt remained a constant fear, especially after the blacks of Haiti, inspired by the French Revolution, took power themselves. During the wars the British invaded many French, Dutch and Spanish islands, and some, such as St Lucia and Trinidad, became permanent possessions.

Australia was a very new colony in 1793. The First Fleet had arrived in 1788, with the first batch of convicts. It was to develop over the years, with new settlements, especially on Van Deimen's Land (Tasmania). It remained very backward, and was simply regarded by the home government as a dumping ground for the 'criminal classes' of Britain, with perhaps some hopes of future development as a naval base in the Pacific.

India was already regarded as the centre of the new British empire, though direct British rule only extended to Bengal, the Coromandel Coast, and Bombay, and was conducted by the East India Company rather than the British government. By 1805, under Sir Arthur Wellesley (later the Duke of Wellington), British rule had been extended to cover most of the south of the country, and parts of the north as far as Delhi. The native population was relatively little affected by British control. The East India Company made its profits by exporting luxury goods, such as silk, tea and spices from India, and importing manufactured goods, including cotton, from the homeland.

The British empire was to expand in other areas during the wars with France. Most notably, the Cape of Good Hope was to be taken from the Dutch, and remain a permanent part of the empire. Malta would also be acquired, along with several islands such as Tristan da Cunha, Ascension and the Seychelles, which could serve to protect the sea route to India.

The Condition of Europe

Before the Revolution of 1789, France was already regarded as the

Western Europe in 1789.

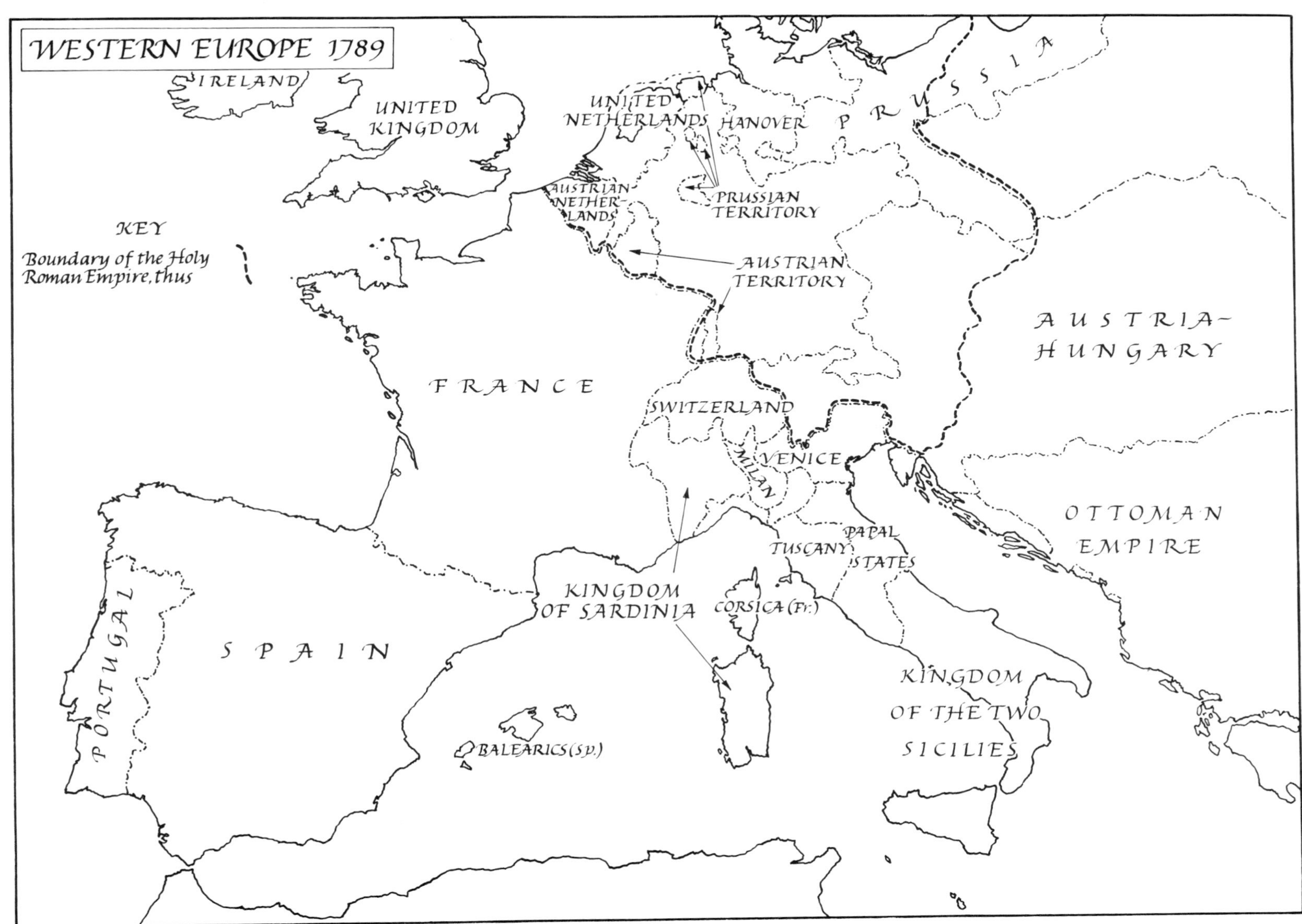

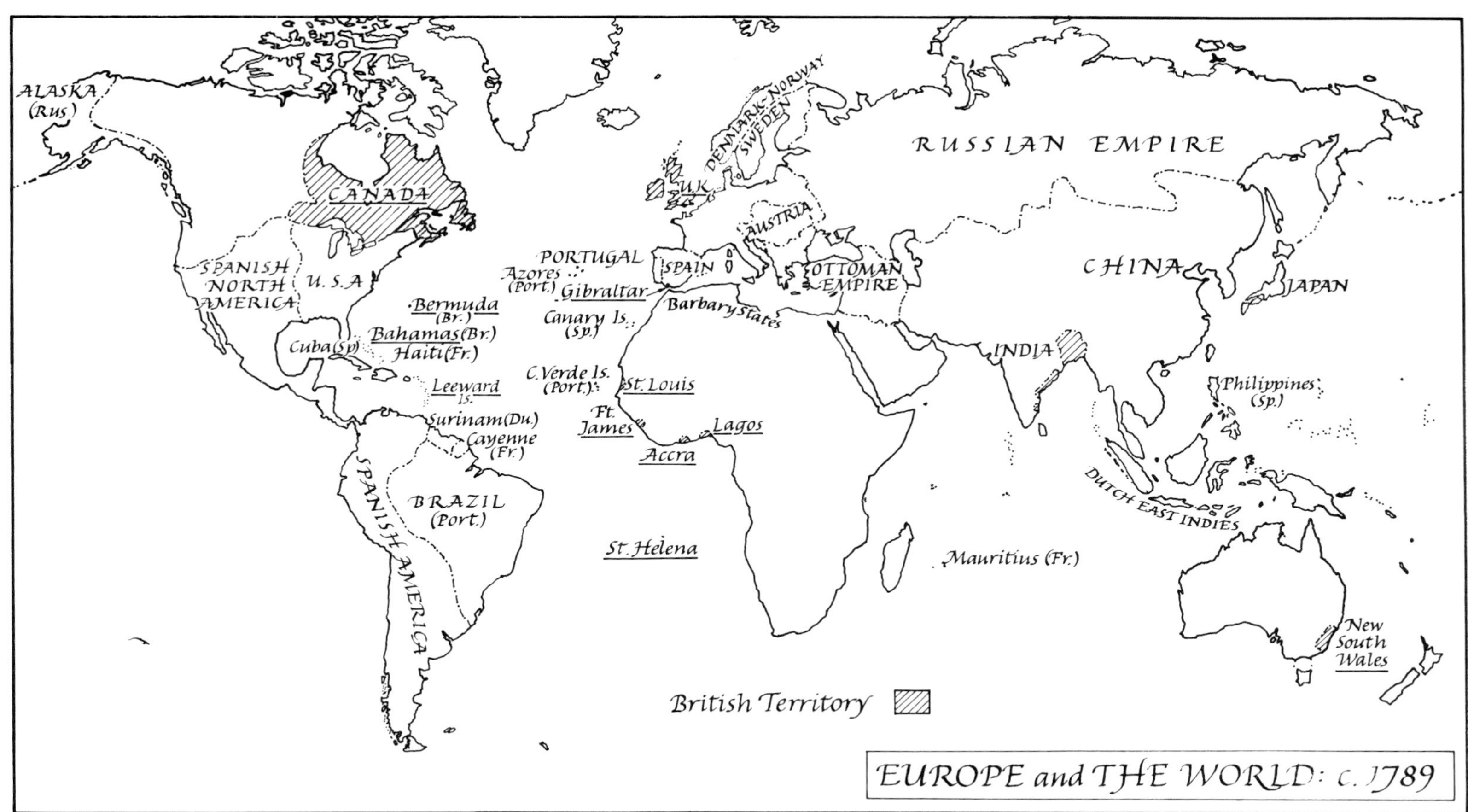

The world in 1789.

leading power of Europe, despite the increasing insolvency of the state and the backwardness of many of her institutions. Until 1789, she had an autocratic, Catholic monarchy, and was a strongly conservative part of the *Ancien Régime*. After the Revolution, she went through several forms of government, including the Directorate and the Committee of Public Safety, before settling down under the autocratic but more modern power of Napoleon Bonaparte. She had had a fairly large overseas empire, but most of that was conquered by the British during the wars.

The power of Spain had much declined by 1793, though she still had a vast overseas empire in Latin America and the Pacific. Like pre-revolutionary France, she was conservative and Catholic, was ruled by an absolute monarchy. Austria-Hungary was the main power of central Europe, and the joint monarchy ruled the modern areas of Belgium and Czechoslovakia, along with parts of Rumania, Poland, Italy and Yugoslavia. With such a diversity within Europe, the empire had no need for a policy of overseas expansion. Prussia, to the north, had expanded in the last decades from a small area around Berlin, and was now one of the great powers. The rest of Germany was theoretically part of the Holy Roman Empire along with Austria and Prussia. In practice, it was divided into dozens of states — some, like Bavaria, were moderately large, some were small, and some were tiny.

Russia was another expanding state, with developing interests in Siberia and to the south. It was ruled by the Tsar, who was even more absolute than other European rulers. The peasants were held in serfdom of almost medieval character, and individual life was cheap, even by the standards of the time. Yet weight of numbers, and a certain political cohesion, gave the Russian Empire some force in European affairs. Her main rivals in the Baltic were Sweden and Denmark-Norway.

Italy was divided into several states. The northern part was dominated by Austria, while the Pope ruled the central part around Rome. In the south was the Kingdom of Naples, including Sicily. The Ottoman Empire, based in Turkey, ruled the Balkans, including Greece. There were two republics in Europe: the Netherlands and Switzerland. Though very different in geography, both were distinguished from the rest of Europe by the difficulties of their terrain. Neither was in any sense democratic, as only the relatively wealthy had political power.

The Rest of the World

Europeans had already established some ascendancy over most of the world, though it was far from complete. Spain and Portugal controlled South and Central America. The United States of America had established her independence in the War of 1775–83, and was already beginning to look to expansion westwards, though the interior of the continent was largely unexplored, and the Indian tribes there lived undisturbed. North Africa was dominated by the corsair states of the Barbary coast, such as Algiers, Tunis and Morocco, while the Middle East, including Palestine, Syria and Arabia, was under the control of the Ottoman Empire. Sub-Saharan Africa was ruled by numerous native princes, though the slave trade had caused great disruption in their territories, especially in west Africa. European slave traders encouraged wars among them, so that they could take slaves and sell them. India was coming increasingly under British rule by this time, but the great empire of China remained undisturbed, and was little penetrated by Europeans. The Pacific islands were attracting attention from anthropologists who expected to find 'the noble savage' there, but formal colonisation was not far advanced. The east of Australia was coming under British rule, but throughout much of the continent, the aborigine continued in his ancient ways.

The Nelson, *a 120-gun ship of the Surveyors' class launched in 1814.* The National Maritime Museum

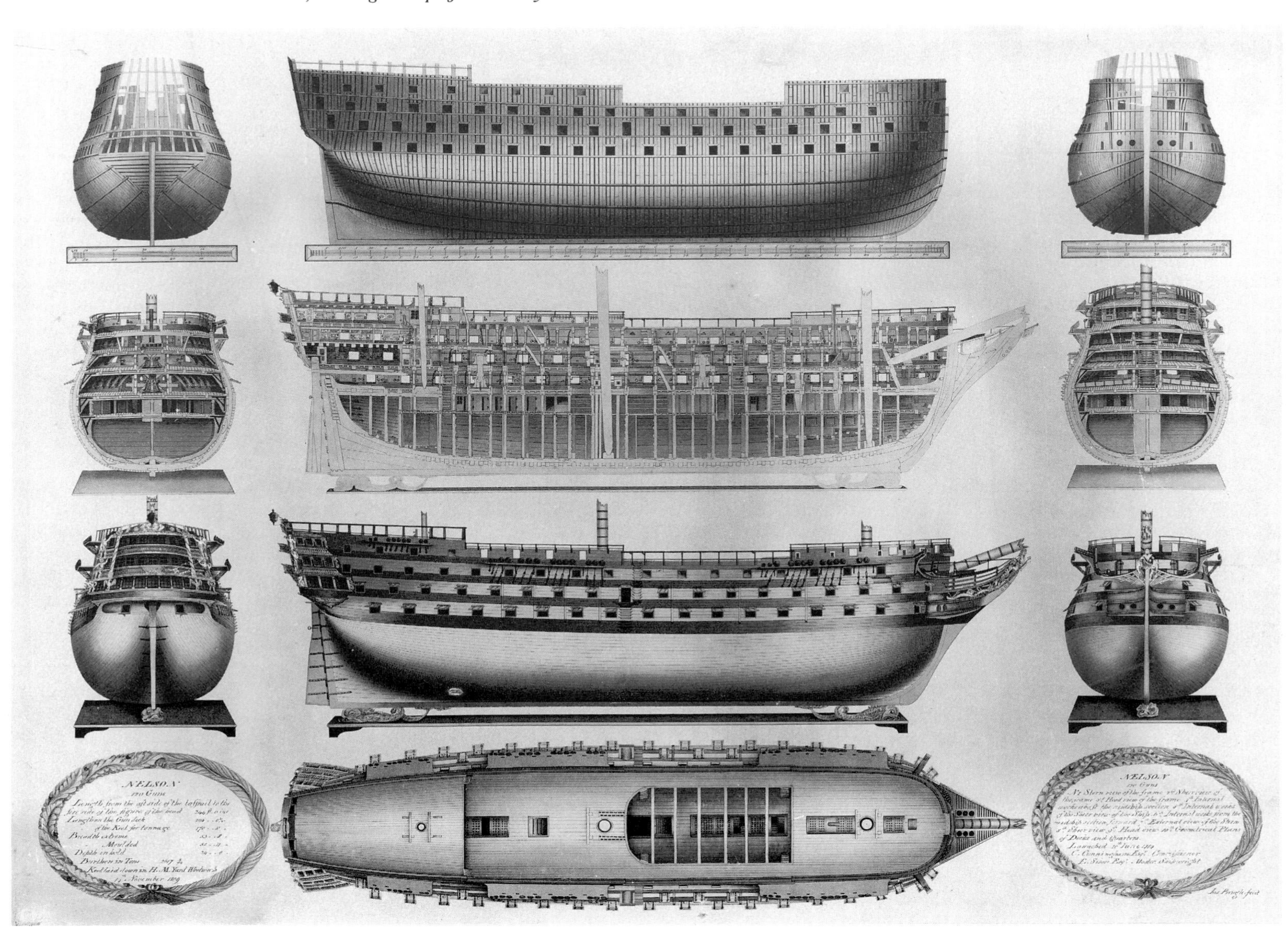

Part II
TYPES OF SHIP

1 The Principles of Ship Design

The Basic Questions

Ships were the basic ingredient of naval power. To build a large ship took several years, the wood from a small forest (which might have been growing for a century or more), and many thousands of hours of skilled labour. To replace the whole of the British fleet would have taken decades, as both timber and labour were in short supply. The ships represented centuries of tradition, experience, skill and growth of timber.

A warship was designed to carry a heavy armament, but at the same time it needed good sailing qualities, while it also had to accommodate its crew, and provide them with stores and provisions for a considerable period of time. Every ship design was a series of compromises; to increase armament might reduce sailing qualities, and vice versa. The sailing qualities themselves might vary in different conditions. Should ships be at their best in rough weather and strong winds, or in light breezes? Was speed more important than the ability to keep the seas in all weathers? Conditions of wind, tide, waves and currents were so variable that these questions had no single answer, and ships were designed after long experience of sailing and battle. Seaworthiness, speed in different conditions, armament, accommodation, maintenance, manoeuvrability, stability and many other factors had to be taken into account in the design of a ship.

The Broadside

The essential role of a warship was to carry a gun armament into action. The basic warship of the Napoleonic era carried the greatest part of its armament on its sides, firing outwards. In some ways, this was an inefficient use of gunpower; very little of it could be fired in the line of advance of a ship or fleet, so that naval tactics gave an inherent advantage to the defence. At best only half a ship's gunpower could be brought to bear on a given object, and a ship might fire dozens of rounds from the guns on one side, without firing the others at all.

The gun arrangements of ships were dictated by natural conditions. Ships are naturally long and narrow, and more guns can be mounted on the sides than at the bows and stern. Moreover, guns firing forward tend to be obstructed by the rigging and sails of the bowsprit. Guns of this period were still relatively small, because they were limited by the weight of ball a man could handle in action; 42-pounders were the largest guns employed on British warships, and these were largely obsolete by 1800, precisely because the ball was too heavy; 32-pounders were now the heaviest in common use, and these formed the basic armament of the line of battle. To give a ship a heavy armament it was necessary to use dozens of guns, and they could only be mounted on the broadside, firing through holes in the ships' sides.

In order to keep the centre of gravity as low as possible, it was necessary to keep the gundeck quite low. On the other hand, it had to be far enough above the waterline to keep out water when the ship was heeling, or when waves were high. Ship designers generally aimed to keep the lowest edges of the gunports of a ship-of-the-line or frigate about five feet out of the water, and in the 1800s this was raised to six feet for ships-of-the-line.

The heaviest guns were invariably mounted on the lowest gundeck, in any kind of ship. Ships of 74 guns or more had 32-pounders on their lower gundecks, with 18- or 24-pounders on the next deck. Three-deckers had yet lighter guns, 12-pounders, on the upper decks. A frigate had only one full deck of guns, 9-, 12-, 18- or 24-pounders, while brigs had only 6-pounders.

Deck Arrangement

Decks which were fitted with guns had to be strong enough to bear their weight. Main gundecks were invariably continuous throughout the length of the ship, except in the very smallest vessels. A gundeck was armed throughout its length, with a gun every few feet, firing through a port. A ship was identified by its number of complete gundecks — one, two or three. The distance between one gundeck and the deck above was one of the fixed factors of naval architecture. About five feet of clear headroom was needed to allow the men to operate the guns, and this did much to determine the height of a ship with a given number of decks. Decks which did not carry guns,

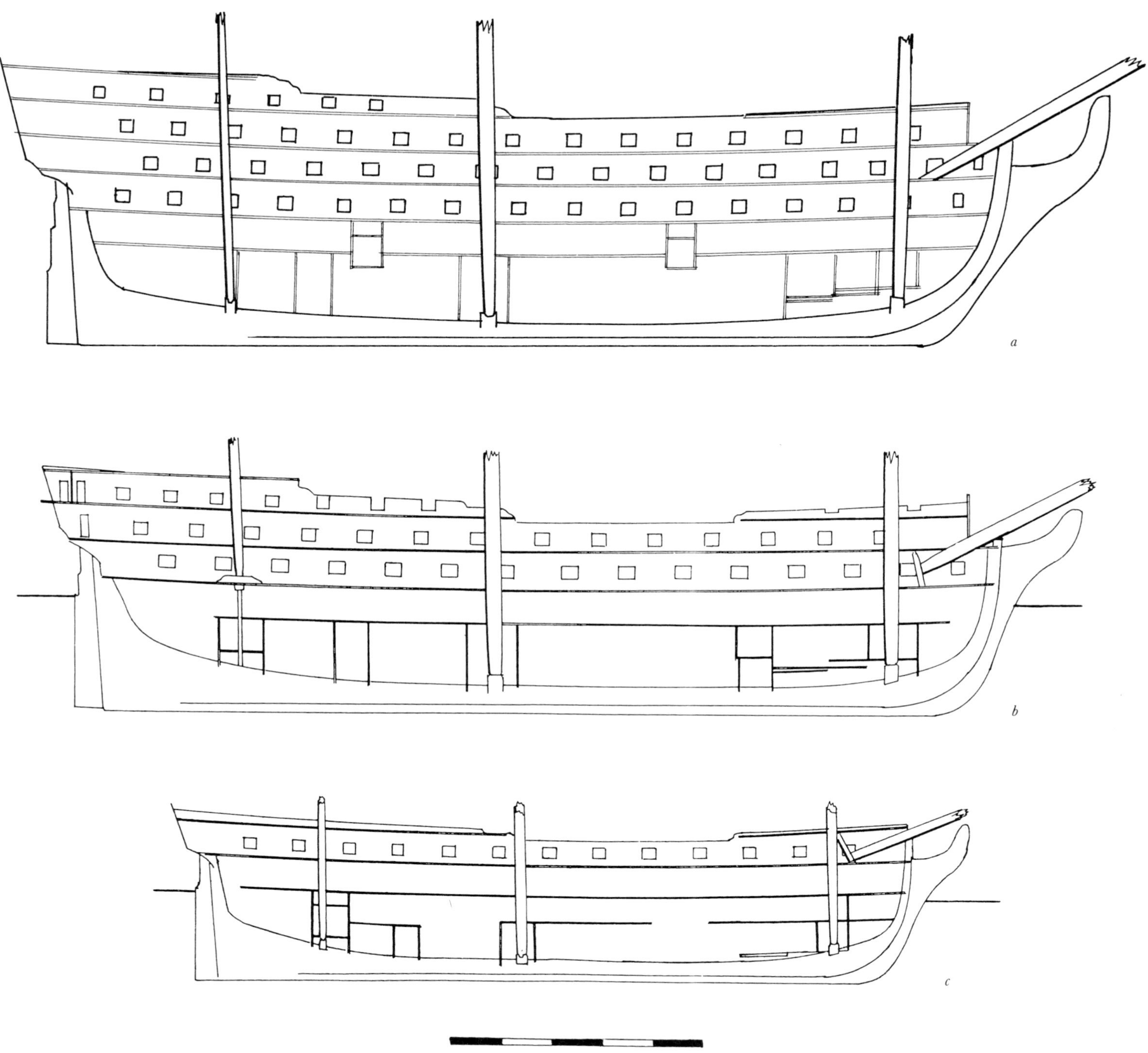

such as the orlop decks on ships-of-the-line, or the lower decks of frigates, needed less headroom, and were often closer to the one above.

In addition to the main gundecks, most ships also had armed quarterdecks and forecastles, and ships-of-the-line had a poop in addition. The quarterdeck ran for a little less than half the length of the ship, from the mainmast aft. The forecastle was rather smaller, and was level with the quarterdeck. The space between the two was known as the waist. It was gradually closed over the years, as the quarterdeck was gradually lengthened and the breadth of the waist was reduced by extending the gangways along its sides. Both the quarterdeck and forecastle carried broadside guns, from 6- to 12-pounders according to the size of the ship. By the 1790s these were gradually being replaced by carronades, of up to 32 or even 68 pounds. The forecastle also carried bow chasers, slightly heavier guns which were arranged to fire forwards.

The poop (or 'roundhouse') was only fitted to two- and three-deckers. It was about half the length of the quarterdeck, and originally it had served merely to cover the captain's cabin. By the 1790s it was becoming increasingly common to fit a few carronades to the poop.

Decks which did not carry guns were usually on or below the waterline. The standard frigate had an unarmed lower deck, also known as a berthing deck. It housed all the officers and crew of the ship, except the captain. Frigates had no continuous deck below that, but a large frigate had three platforms in the hold, forward, aft and

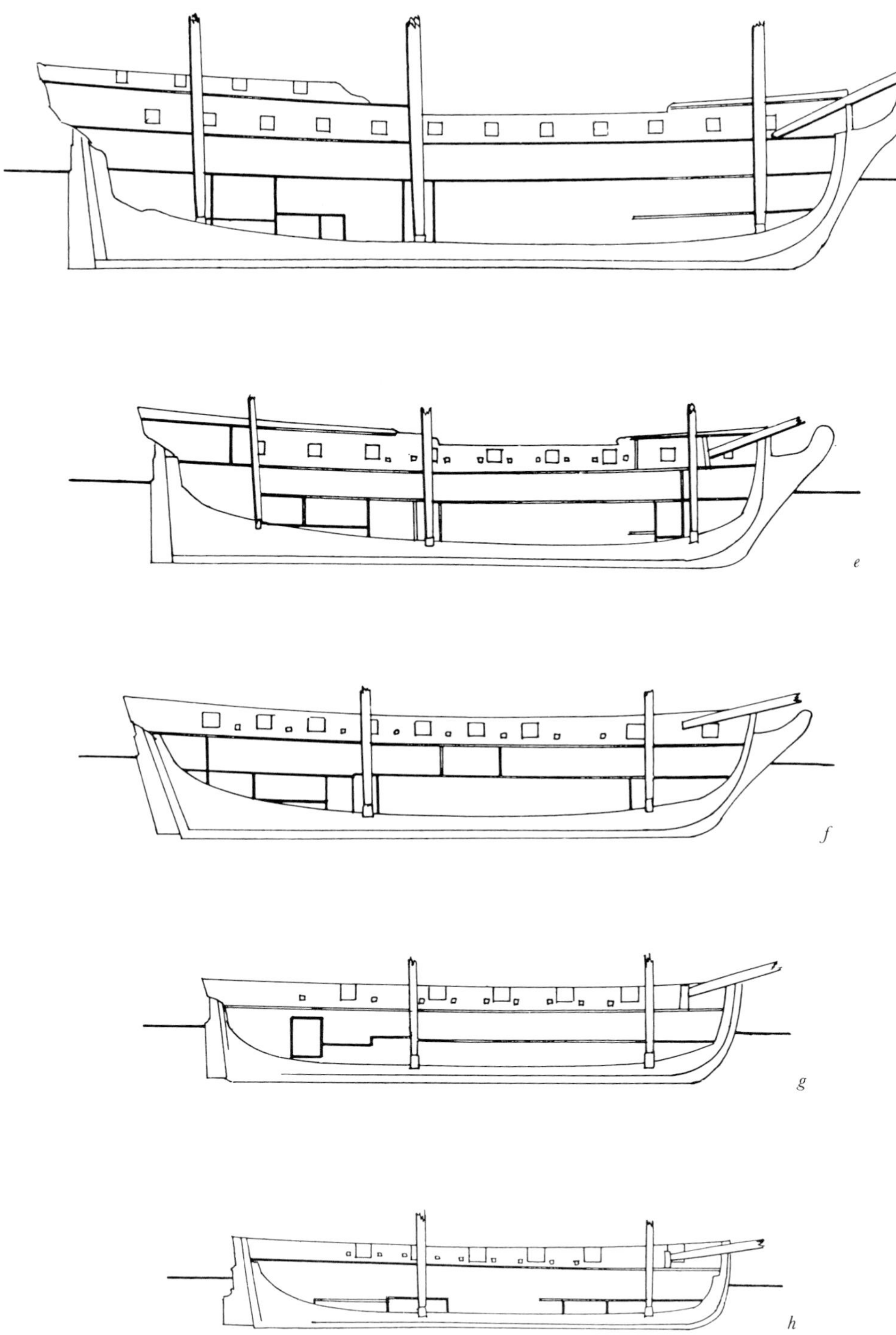

The deck arrangements of different types of ship.

a. The Victory *as rebuilt in 1803, a typical three-decker arrangement.*
b. A two-decker 74 of the 1790s.
c. A large frigate of the 1790s. Instead of a continuous orlop deck, it has three platforms in the hold, with the cable stowed on the middle one.
d. A late eighteenth-century sixth rate. Apart from being smaller, it differs from the frigate in having only two platforms in the hold, with the cables stowed on top of the casks in the hold.
e. A ship-rigged sloop.
f. A brig. It is generally similar to the ship-sloop below decks, but it has no quarterdeck or forecastle.
g. A gun-brig.
h. A small gunboat, with no continuous lower deck.

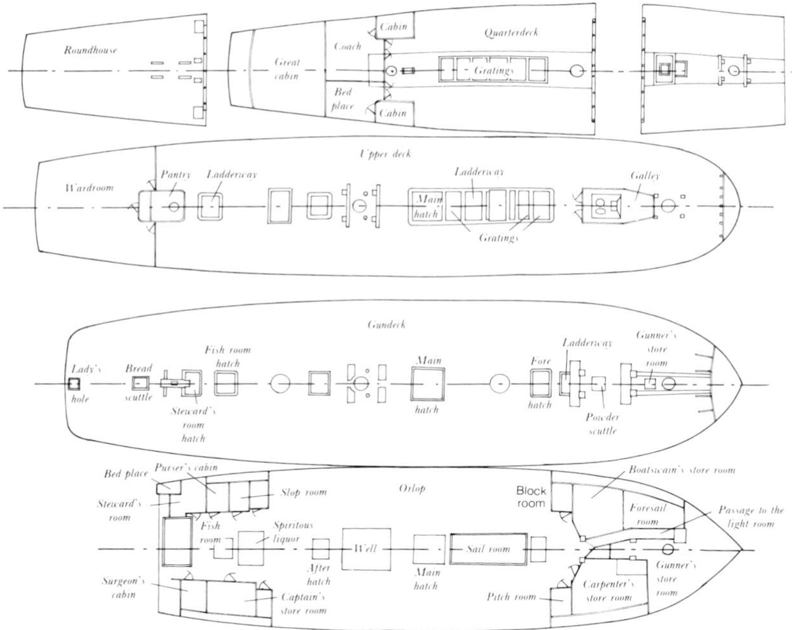

The deck plans of a typical 74-gun ship.

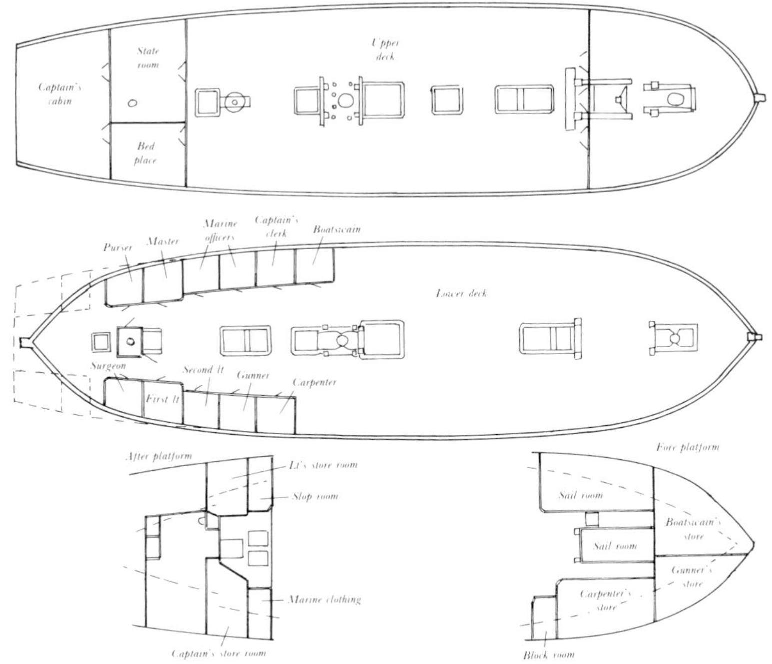

The deck plans of a sixth rate. A fifth-rate frigate would be similar, but with a central platform in the hold, and a few more officers' cabins on the lower deck, for extra lieutenants.

amidships. These were used for store rooms and to stow the cables. A sixth rate omitted the middle platform, while unrated ships generally omitted all three. A ship-of-the-line had an almost continuous orlop deck below the waterline, used for storage, accommodation, and for the cables.

Length

The principal measurement of a warship was the 'length on the gundeck'; the distance from the inside of the planking near the stem to that at the sternpost. This excluded the light framework of the head, the overhang of the stern galleries, as well as the length of the bowsprit, so that the total length of a fully rigged ship might be half as much again as the length on the gundeck. But the gundeck measurement was very useful, as it gave a real indication of the ship's ability to carry guns.

The optimum length for a ship depended largely on the number of decks she was to have. Three-deckers were longer than two-deckers, which were longer than single-decked frigates and sloops. At the smaller end of the range, ships which had a complete orlop or accommodation deck tended to be longer than those which had not. Longer ships needed the greater longitudinal strength which the extra decks gave. One of the great problems of ship design was 'hogging', or sagging at the ends. This was caused by 'the unequal distribution of the weight in different sections of the body, when compared with the quantity of water displaced in these places; and from the fore and aft parts being left unsupported by the water during the motions of pitching[1]. The bow and stern of a ship carried more guns, but were supported by less water than the midships, because of the narrowing of the hull in these areas. In practice, there was a safe limit for a ship of a given construction. If a two-decker was more than about 175ft long, it became increasingly liable to hogging — for example the *Kent*, a 74-gun ship of 182ft was found to have arched 17in at each end, despite being a 'ship of short standing'.[2] Apart from a few ships built in the 1790s, British two-deckers rarely exceeded 176ft, and further development of the 74-gun ship was not possible because of this, while the two-decker 80-gun was not often built in Britain until after 1815. According to one of the surveyors of the navy in 1806, there was a 'great similarity of forms' of ships, and 'little amendment is to be expected provided the principal dimensions are suitable to the required purpose of the ship, and the plane of flotation is such as to ensure stability'.[3]

The three-decker, on the other hand, had not yet reached its maximum. The 100-gun ship expanded to 110 guns, and then to 120 guns. Its length increased from 190ft to 205ft in the course of the wars. Likewise, frigates of large gun power became possible, and ships of 38 or 44 guns became increasingly common.

The Shape of the Hull

The first consideration in the shape of the hull was the breadth of the ship. A sailing ship could not be made too narrow or there would not be enough room to work her guns, and she would heel over too much in a wind. In most classes of ship the length/breadth ratio was between $3\frac{1}{2}$ and 4 to 1. The depth of the hull below the lower deck, known as the 'depth in hold', was another principal dimension, and was approximately half the breath. The midship section was drawn out from these two dimensions, using a system of tangent arcs. Merchant ships and transports were designed for carrying capacity, and were almost square in section, ships-of-the-line were approximately round, while sloops and small fast ships were closer to a triangular section; many French ships had a kind of 'six sided' section, with a sharp turn of the bilge.

The keel was of course considerably shorter than the length on the gundeck. The sternpost raked aft in a straight line, while the stempost formed a curve. The length of the keel was often used as one of the principal dimensions of a ship, but another, purely theoretical, keel length was used to determine tonnage. This was ascertained by the formula (keel x breadth x half breadth) divided by 94. This figure gave no real indication of the displacement of a ship, as it took no account of whether the ship had full bows and stern, or whether the midship section was square or triangular; nevertheless it was used to assess the size of a ship, and it was registered under this tonnage in the Navy List. It did give a reasonable indication of the amount of

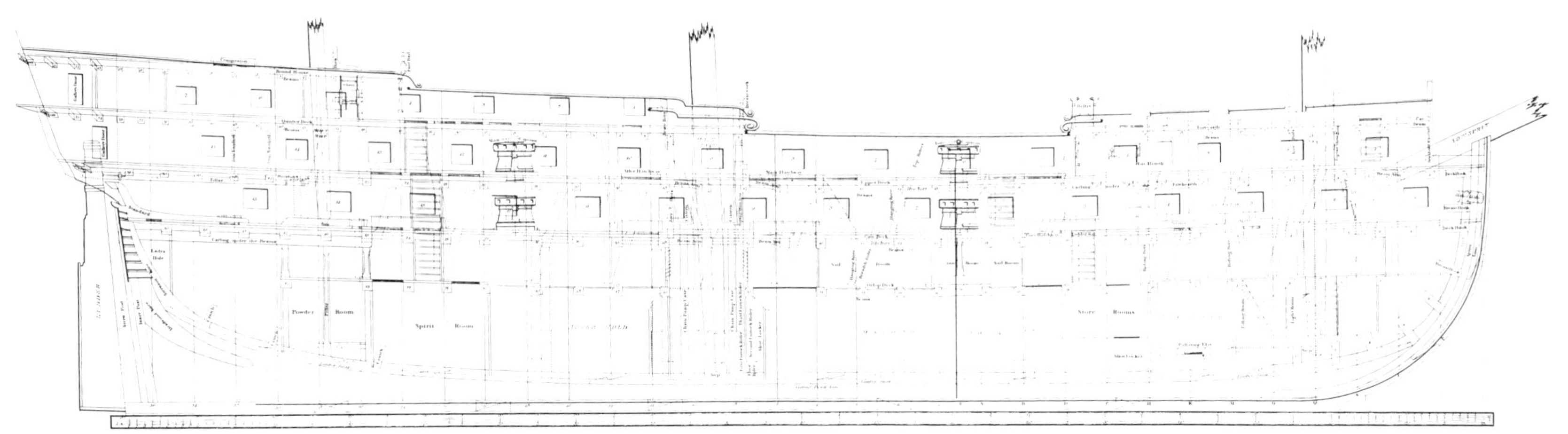

The longitudinal section of a 74-gun ship, c1795. From Rees's *Cyclopaedia*, 1819

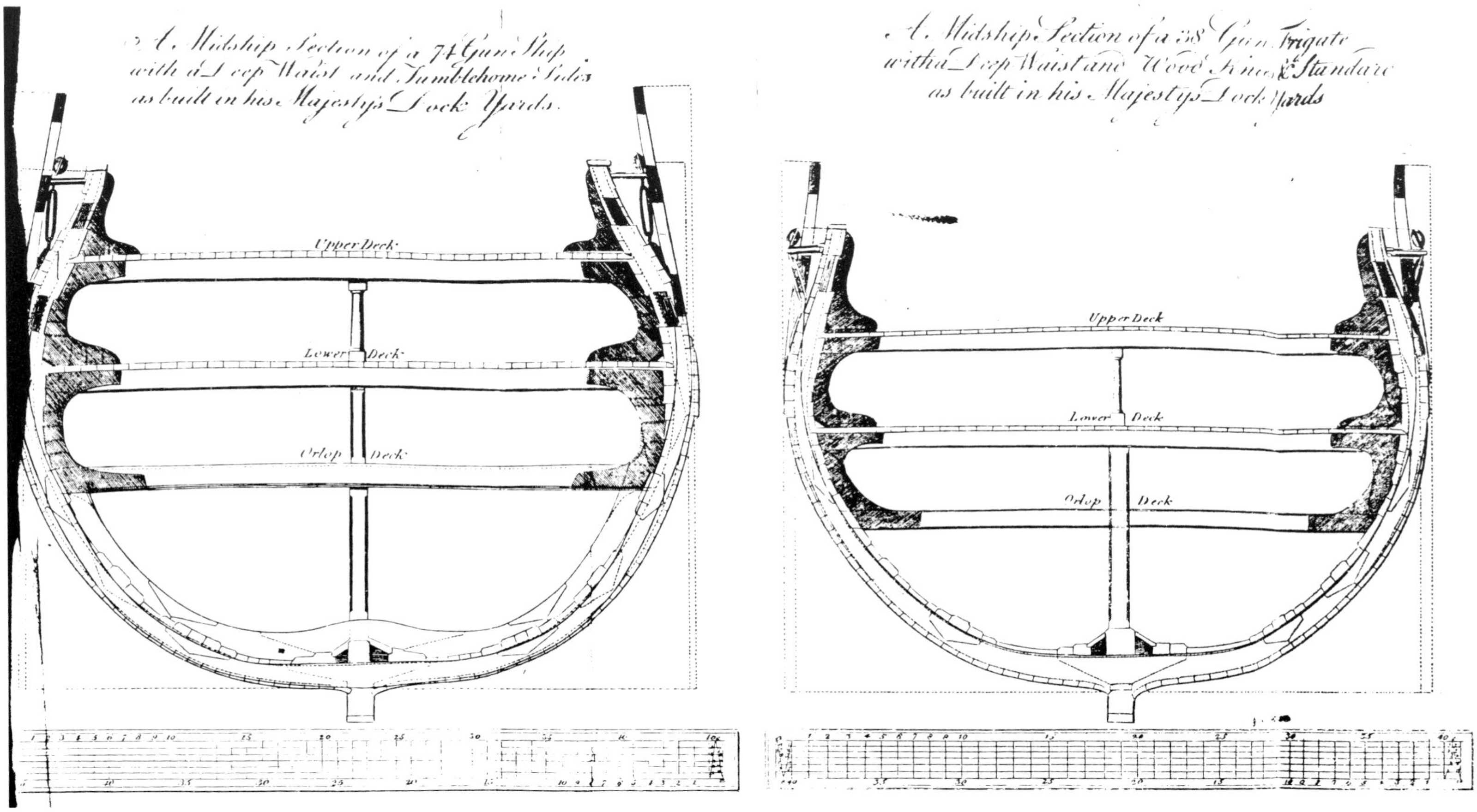

Midship sections of a 74-gun ship and a frigate. From the Naval Chronicle timber and labour needed for a vessel, and this was useful in drawing up contracts with private shipbuilders.

A print of 1804, reflecting the strength of the British fleet, and showing something of the rating system. The National Maritime Museum ▷

The Rating System

The Royal Navy had 498 ships and vessels at the beginning of the war in 1793, rising to 1017 at its peak in 1813. These were designed for a great multitude of tasks; to lead fleets, form part of the line of battle, patrol the seas, escort convoys, chase fast enemy ships, carry despatches, patrol the coasts, defend inshore waters against invasion, bombard enemy positions on shore, and to carry out more peaceful supporting roles. A few ships, such as bomb vessels, were designed for very specialised roles, but the majority could perform several different tasks, according to need.

Ships of 20 guns and more were rated, from first rate to sixth. Contrary to modern usage, the rating said nothing about the quality of a ship, but merely defined its size. All rated ships were commanded by officers with the rank of full (or 'post') captain, and were ship rigged, with three masts, all square rigged. The most important function of the rating system was to define the numbers of officers allocated to a ship, and their rates of pay; captains and heads of department had higher pay in larger ships, while the number of midshipmen, lieutenants, etc, depended on the rating of the ship. The rating also gave some indication of the role of a ship, and of its layout. All the ships of the first and second rates were three-deckers; those of the third and fourth were two-deckers, while virtually all those of the fifth and sixth rates were frigates, with a single complete deck of guns. However, there were some discrepancies at the boundaries of the rates. A third rate 80-gun ship had almost the same gun power as a three-decker 90. The fourth rate, made up of small two-deckers, was obsolescent by 1793. It had only twenty ships at the beginning of the war, and twenty-nine in 1813. Only three fourth rates were in commission in 1812, compared with ninety-four third rates and 119 fifth rates.[4]

First rates were three-deckers of 100 guns or more. The second rate comprised ships of 90 to 98 guns, though by this time virtually all of them had 98 guns. The third rate was made up entirely of two-deckers, but in other respects it was much more mixed, with ships of 80, 74, and 64 guns, and a few others with non-standard armaments. The fourth rate also included two-deckers, of 60 and 50 guns. The fifth rate was mostly made up of frigates, from 30 to 44 guns; but it also included a few old two-deckers of 44 guns. The sixth rate included small ships from 20 to 30 guns — frigates of 28 guns, and small 'post ships' of less.

Unrated ships were likely to be more specialised than rated ones. The biggest groups of unrated ships were the larger sloops, which were ship-rigged, with three masts. Apart from that, most unrated ships were defined by either their purpose or their rig — brigs, cutters, transports, bomb vessels and gunboats. They invariably carried less than 20 guns, and were generally less than about 500 tons, except for transports and static vessels.

Classes

The number of guns and the number of decks gave a rather better indication of the characteristics of a ship than its rate. The mere number '74', for example, gave a fairly clear definition of a ship type — two decks, 'fit for the line of battle', with a crew of 600 or more, with 32-pounders on the lower deck. Likewise, a 38 was a common type of frigate with 18-pounder guns and a crew of about 280. However, this classification was not always useful — there was an old type of 32-gun frigate, with 12-pounder guns, as well as a new one with 18-pounder guns. The two groups were very different in tactical value, and really need to be considered as separate entities.

The term 'class' was not often used in its modern sense, to denote a group of ships built to identical design. A class usually meant a number of ships of similar gun arrangement. Thus the 74s could be divided into three classes, some with 24-pounders on the upper deck, some with fifteen 18-pounders per side, and some with only fourteen. In this system of classification, the guns on the quarterdeck and forecastle were commonly ignored — the fitting of carronades created far too many discrepancies in these areas.

Ships built to identical designs were described as 'to the draught of' a particular ship. Other groups acquired nicknames in service, such as the 'Forty Thieves', a large group of 74s built between 1806 and 1810. It was becoming increasingly common to copy a successful ship many times, and, among the smaller vessels, large numbers were built to certain draughts — 58 gunboats to the draught of the *Archer* from 1801 to 1805, and more than 100 to the draught of the *Cruiser*, for example.

Foreign Influences

The Royal Navy shared a common technology with its most important competitors. In contrast to the days of the Spanish Armada or the Dutch Wars, the ships of all the major sea powers were similar in design and purpose, as is shown by the ease with which large numbers of foreign captures found places in the British fleet. It is a travesty of the truth to say that the Royal Navy relied on foreign captures for all its ideas — it developed copper sheathing, the Seppings system of construction and the round stern without any significant copying from abroad — but certainly foreign ships did much to inspire the development of ship design in Britain.

Information on foreign ships was available from several sources. Espionage was common enough, and provided some useful data. Like other navies, the British sometimes employed leading shipwrights from other lands, particularly after the French Revolution caused many Royalists to flee their native country. Marc Isambard Brunel, the father of the great Victorian engineer, carried out many improvements in the dockyards; and Jean-Louis Barrallier designed several ships for the British navy. However, the most important information on French, Dutch, Spanish, Danish and American ships came from their capture. During the French Revolutionary War, the Royal Navy captured thirty-seven ships-of-the-line alone, and dozens of frigates and sloops, as well as merchant vessels. Captured warships were carefully studied, and plans were often made of them in the dockyards. For fifty years the Royal Navy had paid particular attention to French prizes, and many improvements in hull design had come from them. Among 74s, the *Invincible*, captured in 1747, was still important, and was copied as late as 1798. The *Courageaux*, taken in 1761, was directly copied many times up to 1793. She also had considerable influence on the 'Surveyors Class', or 'Forty Thieves' of 1806. Among frigates, the *Hebe* of 1782 was particularly important — she was copied forty-seven times up to 1830. Danish ships were occasionally influential. The *Christian VII*, captured in 1807, inspired the design of the *Black Prince* class of 1810–15.

All this led many people to conclude that French ship design was far superior to British. But, in fact, the two nations designed their ships for slightly different purposes — the French for quick expeditions as part of a specific plan, the British for total control of the seas. Thus French ships were designed for speed, British ones for strength. Naturally, naval officers favoured the former, and delighted in the performance of captured ships; while the civil administrators, who were concerned with both maintenance and design, preferred strength.

A VIEW OF THE ROYAL NAVY
OF GREAT BRITAIN,
Dedicated by Permission to His Royal Highness The Duke of Clarence Admiral of the White
by His most humble, most obedient, and most dutiful Servant N. Heideloff
1804
1st RATE
10
2nd RATE
21
3rd RATE
158
4th RATE
27
5th RATE
164
6th RATE
192
572
154
Total 726
Admiral 3 Stars on each Epaulet & 3 Ships of Lace on the Cuffs
Vice Admiral 2 Stars & 2 Ships
Rear Admiral 1 Star & 1 Ships
Captain 2 Epaulets
Post Captain 1 Epaulet on the right side
Master & Commander 1 Epaulet on the left side
References to the figures
No. 1. Admiral
No. 2. Captain
No. 3. Lieutenant
No. 4. Midshipman
A Royal Standard &c.
B Admiral of the Fleet
C Admiral of the White
D Admiral of the Blue
E Vice Admiral of the Red
F Vice Adml. of the White
G Vice Adml. of the Blue
H Rear Adml. of the Red
I Rear Adml. of the White
K Rear Adml. of the Blue
L Commodore of the Red
M Commre. of the White
N Commre. of the Blue
O British Flag
Names of the Ships
Transports, Bomb Vessels, Cutters and other small Vessels

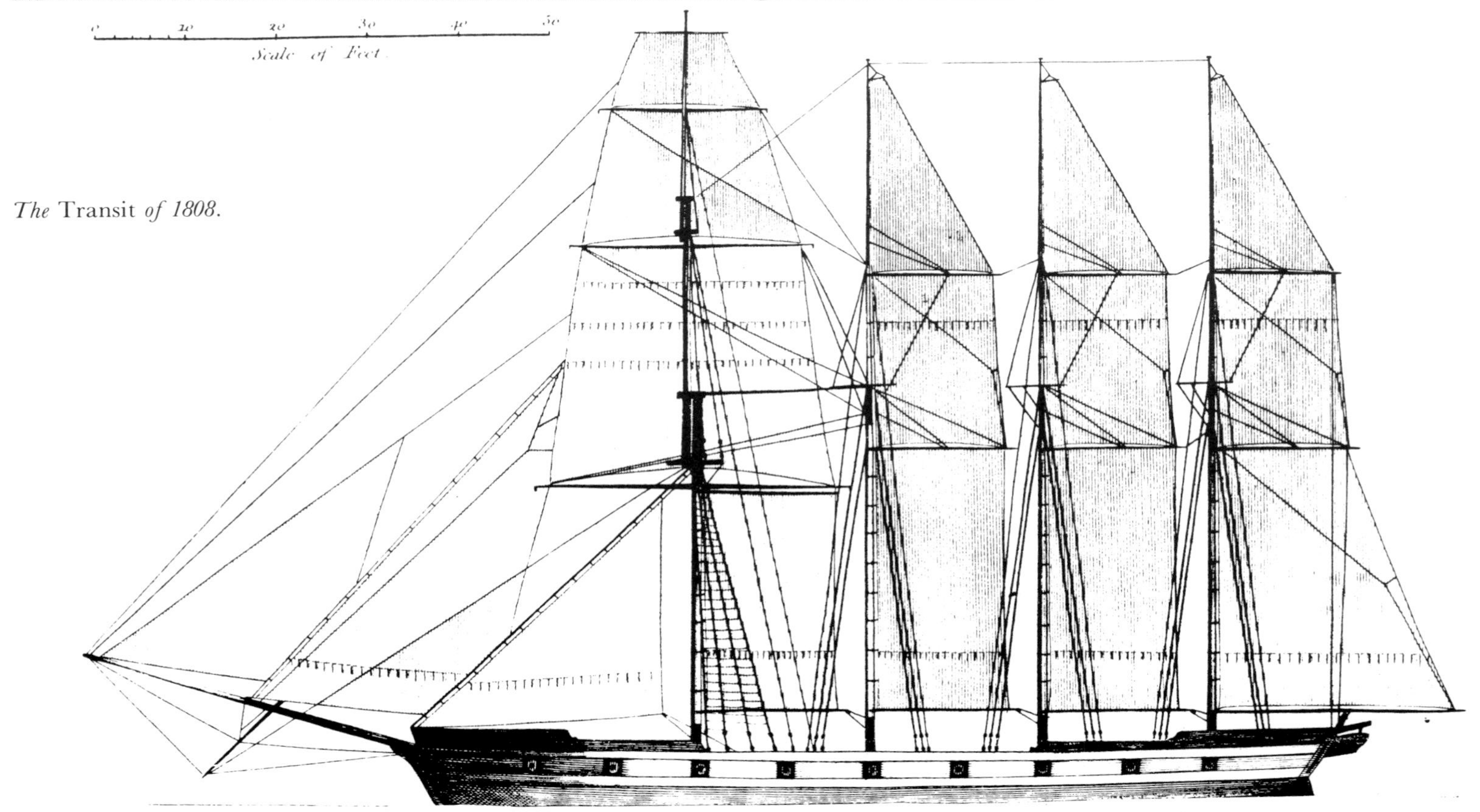

The Transit *of 1808.*

◁ *The French ships* Northumberland *and* Impeteux *at Portsmouth after being captured at the First of June Battle in 1794. Two British ships were built to the draught of the* Impeteux. The National Maritime Museum

Trends in Ship Design

It is not quite true to say that warship design from 1793 to 1815 was totally conservative. Captain Schank produced his sliding keel, similar to the centreboard of a modern dinghy. This was tried on various small warships and transports over the years, and had a certain amount of success. Sir Samuel Bentham designed two remarkable vessels called the *Arrow* and the *Dart*, with completely new hull shapes, and traverse bulkheads to give extra strength. A few small schooners were built to similar designs. The *Transit* of 1808 had a radical new rigging plan and hull shape, and was tested by the navy. Other experimental vessels included the *Spanker* floating battery, the *Inspector* sloop, and the *Mosquito* gunboat, designed by Sir Sidney Smith. However all of this was confined to the very smallest vessels, sloops and gunboats in particular, and affected only a tiny minority of them. The great majority of vessels, the hundreds of ships-of-the-line, frigates and sloops, remained unaffected, and followed rather different trends.

From about 1780, during the American War, there had been a general tendency to produce larger ships within a given rate. This was mainly due to the influence of the French, whose ships were at the peak of their reputation. First rates grew from 186 to 190ft, 74s from 168 to 172ft, while the 36- and 38-gun frigate began to replace the old 12-pounder 32. This movement reached its climax in the mid 1790s, when quite large ships were ordered in all classes. Many of these were to French designs, such as the *Hebe* frigate. During this period, the policy was to allow each of the two surveyors, Henslow and Rule, to design one ship each with every new order. Few successful designs were produced, apart from Rule's *Caledonia* class of 120-gun ships, and the *Cruiser* class of brigs.

The reaction set in during the following decade. The larger ships were expensive, and not completely successful, and design returned to older patterns, and some quite ancient draughts were revived and modified. The *Courageaux* of 1753 formed the basis for the Surveyors' class of 74s, and the *Amazon* of 1745 was adapted for several types of small vessel.

The Seppings system of construction, introduced in 1811, had the potential to change all that, by allowing much longer ships with a given number of decks. However, it was not to have its full effect until after the war; ship design remained essentially conservative and derviative during the first two decades of the nineteenth century.

2 Ships-of-the-Line

The Line of Battle

For nearly a century and a half, fleets had made the maximum use of their gun power by arranging their ships in line ahead. The 'line of battle' was made up of ships which were strong and well armed enough to make a contribution to the line, and to withstand the fire of the enemy. By 1793, the 64-gun ship was the smallest that was expected to stand in such a line, though there were many who believed that she was obsolete in such a role, and that the 74 was the smallest that should be employed (although a 50-gun ship, the *Leander*, found her way into Nelson's line at the Nile in 1798). However everyone agreed that a 'ship-of-the-line', or 'line-of-battle ship' had to be at least a two-decker. She might find many other roles, in convoy escort, patrol and reconnaissance, but her basic *raison d'être* was to stand in the line of battle with similar ships, and to oppose enemy ships-of-the-line. Such ships had to be big, and were therefore expensive; they required the largest pieces of timber, and cost much more per ton than frigates and sloops. In 1789 a 100-gun ship cost £24.10.0 per ton, a 74-gun ship cost £20.4.0, a 36 cost £14.7.0, and a sloop £12.3.0.[1] If necessary, a 74 could do the work of a frigate, but in a sense she was wasted in that role; a 74 cost £43,820 to build and fit, a 36 cost less than half that.

100-Gun Ships

Since the *Sovereign of the Seas* of 1637, the largest and most prestigious ships of the fleet had been 100-gun three-deckers. They had many disadvantages — they were large and clumsy, and were poor sailers compared with the two-deckers and frigates. They were expensive to build, and needed large crews. Their original role had been to represent the glories of the state, but this tended to decline over the years, as ships became more functional, and warfare more intense. Now their most important task was to provide a ship large enough to house an admiral and his staff. The extra deck allowed an extra set of cabins at the stern, where the admiral could live in comparative splendour. Poor sailing qualities were not a great disadvantage in this role, for a fleet was normally led by the slowest ship, so that all the others could keep station on her. At other times, a large three-decker could serve as a stationary headquarters for a port admiral at a major naval base. It could also be a floating embassy, representing British power over the seas, as when Admiral Collingwood ruled the Mediterranean in the 1800s.

Often 100-gun ships had longer lives than others, mainly because they were so expensive to build, and were therefore kept in good repair. The *Britannia* had been completed in 1762, to the 1745 Establishment of Dimensions; she was to fight at Trafalgar. Along with the ill-fated *Royal George* (lost at Spithead in 1782), she had been the largest ship in the fleet in her day, at 2116 tons. Her successor in that role was the *Victory* of 2142 tons, begun in 1759 and launched in 1765. She was a particularly well-designed ship, and her sailing qualities were excellent for a three-decker. The next to be built was the *Royal Sovereign* of 2175 tons, begun in 1774 and launched in 1786. There was a jump in size to the next 100-gun ship, the *Royal George* of 1788, of 2286 tons. Her sister ship, the *Queen Charlotte*, was launched in 1790, and blown up by accident ten years later. She was the last of the 100-gun ships; subsequently, this type of ship increased in size and was able to carry more guns. Apart from the 110-gun ships, which first emerged in 1788, three 104-gun ships were to be built. The new *Queen Charlotte* of 1810 was essentially the same as the *Royal George* of 1788, but with extra guns on the middle deck and quarterdeck. The total weight of guns was kept roughly constant by fitting 32-pounders instead of 42-pounders on the lower deck. Later, the *Princess Charlotte* and *Royal Adelaide* were built to the enlarged lines of the *Victory*, but neither of these ships was finished before 1815.

The armament of the 100-gun ship varied quite considerably. Until 1790, 42-pounders were standard for the lower decks, and it was not until 1807 that the last of these was replaced by 32-pounders. The older ships had 24-pounders on the middle deck and 12-pounders on the upper deck, but the *Royal Charlotte* introduced 18-pounders on the upper decks.

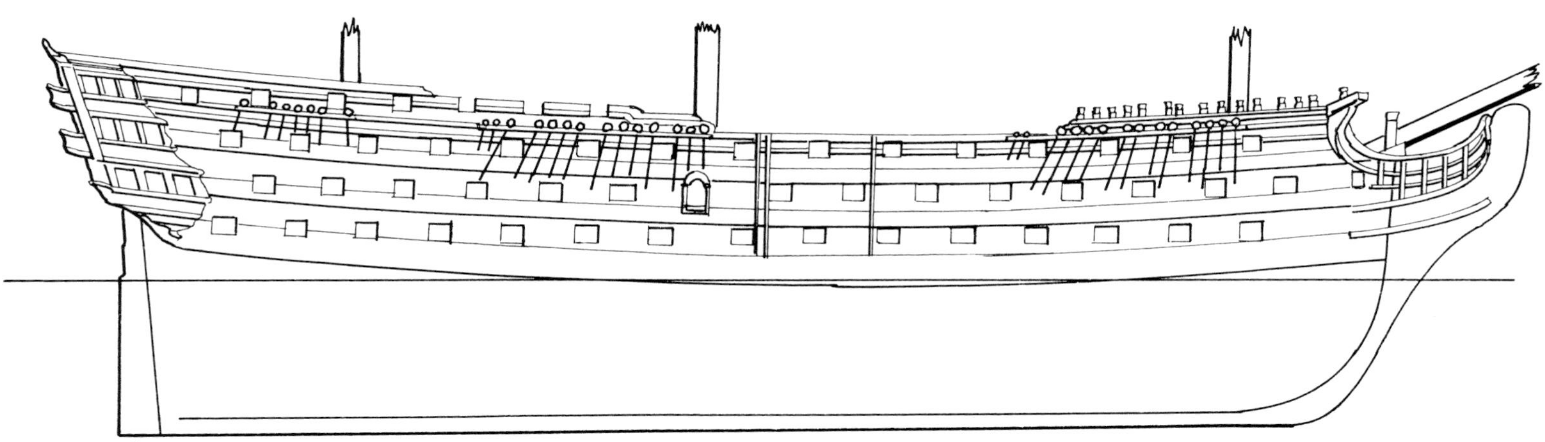

The Royal George *of 1788, one of the last 100-gun ships.*

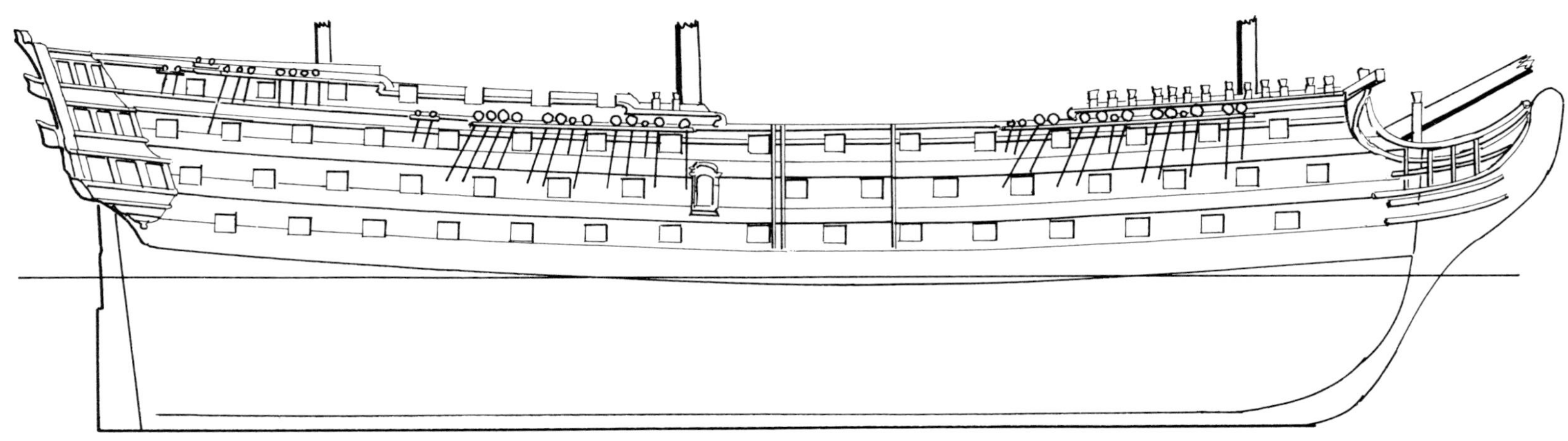

The Hibernia, *110 guns, of 1804.*

Ships of 110 and 120 Guns

With the design of the *Ville de Paris*, ordered in 1788 and completed in 1795, the first rate three-decker expanded to a length of 190ft, compared with 186ft of the *Victory*. This allowed ten extra guns — two on the middle deck, two on the upper deck, four on the quarterdeck and two on the forecastle. Another 110, the *Hibernia*, was built between 1790 and 1804, with length increased to 201ft, and tonnage to 2530. She carried a higher proportion of guns on her main decks, with only carronades on her quarterdeck and forecastle.

Long before the *Hibernia* was completed, the Admiralty ordered the first 120-gun ship, the *Caledonia*. She was ordered in 1797, but not begun until 1805. She was less than 100 tons bigger than the *Hibernia*, but carried 32 guns on the lower deck, with 34 each on the middle and upper decks. When she was finally launched in 1808 she proved to be a very successful ship, and it was said that 'This fine three-decker rides easy at her anchors, carries her lee ports well, rolls and pitches quite easy, generally carries her helm half a turn a-weather, steers, works, and stays remarkably well, is a weatherly ship, and lies-to very close.' She was 'allowed by all hands to be faultless'.[2] However, three more ships had been ordered before that, the *Nelson, St Vincent* and *Howe*. These were designed jointly by the two surveyors of the navy, and so were known as the 'Surveyors' Class'. Launched in 1814–15, they proved less successful than the *Caledonia*, and two more ships of the latter class were ordered by the end of 1815, though neither was completed by the end of the war. In later years the *Caledonia* was to become the standard design for British three-deckers.

Ships of 110 and 120 guns invariably carried 32-pounders on the lower deck, 24-pounders on the middle deck, and 18-pounders on the upper deck. Mostly they carried carronades on the quarterdeck and forecastle, with a few long guns.

Three-Decker Second Rates

The three-decker second rate had first been conceived in the 1670s, as a cheaper alternative to the first rate. In 1793, there were still several older ships, built before 1771, which carried 90 guns. These ships were about 177 ft long, and of 1900 tons; they had only two guns on the forecastle and none on the quarterdeck. The 98-gun ship was created merely by adding 8 guns to the quarterdeck. Second rates normally had 32-pounders on the lower deck, 18-pounders on the middle deck, and 12-pounders on the upper deck.

There were twenty-one second rates in the fleet in 1793. The class was generally in decline, because it had no real role, and was not a very efficient design. Such ships were short and high, which made them poor sailers — the *Prince* of 1788 'sailed worse than other ships', the *London* of 1766 'does not stand under her canvas particularly well', while the *Duke* of 1777 was 'neither weatherly nor fore-reaches with other men of war.'[3] According to a well-known work on naval architecture, it was 'the opinion of many competent judges that the classes between that of 100 guns and the 80-gun ships of two decks are very unnecessarily continued in the Royal Navy', because of 'instability, arising from that want of capacity which most first rates possess.'[4] The second rate could serve as a flagship, but not all admirals

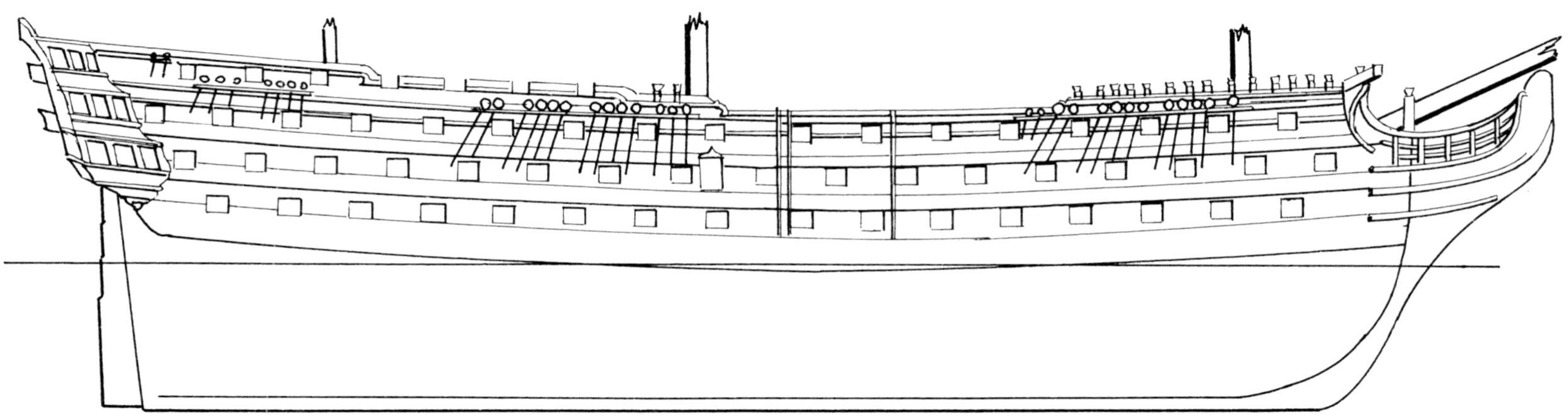

The Caledonia *of 1808, the first British 120-gun ship, and in many ways the most successful.*

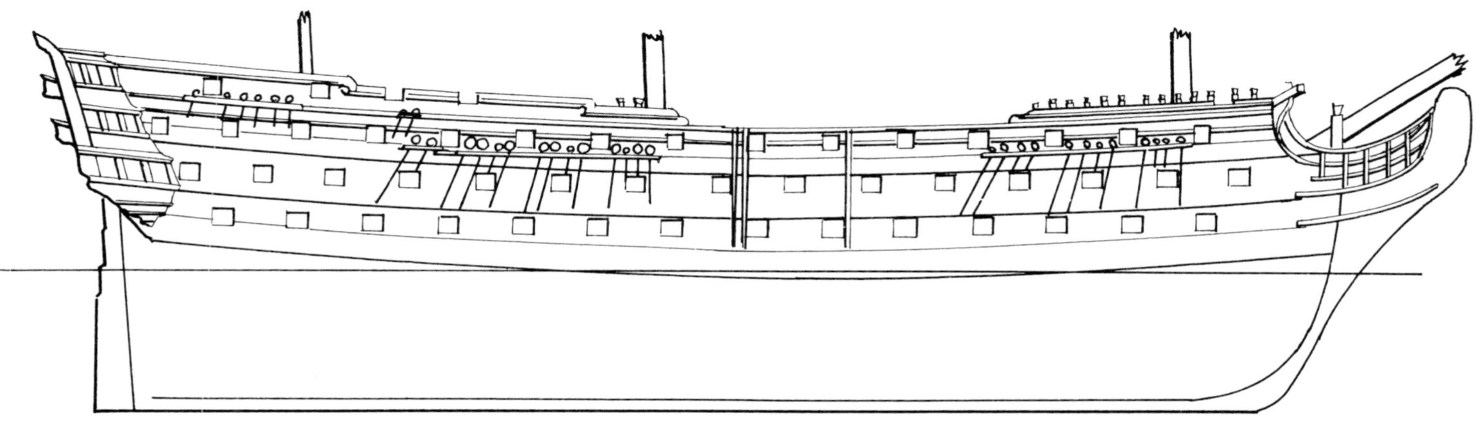

The Dreadnought, *98 gun, of 1801.*

A model of the Boyne, *a 98-gun ship launched in 1790.* The Science Museum

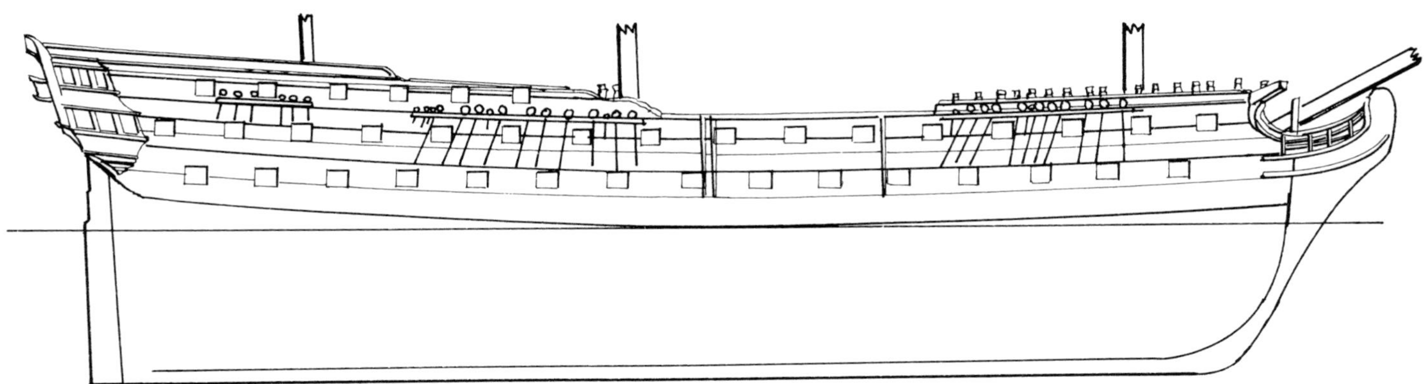

The Caesar *of 1788, the first British two decker 80-gun ship.*

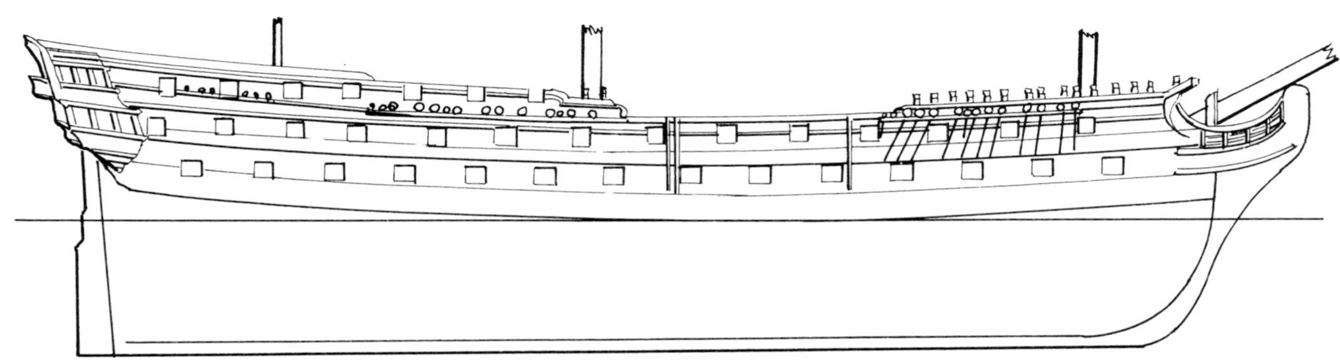

A 74-gun ship of the standard 168ft type, built between 1757 and 1780. The latest 74s were a few feet longer, but many of the old type remained in service.

used it — Lord Keith, when in command of the Mediterranean fleet, preferred to use a two-decker 80 despite the fact that there was a 98 serving as a private ship under his command. Nine 98-gun ships were ordered during the French Revolutionary War, including two, the *Boyne* and *Union*, to the lines of the *Victory*; they were all well over 2000 tons. Only one, the *Trafalgar*, was ordered after 1801, and she was not completed until 1820. By 1812, there were only seventeen left in the fleet.

Captured Three-Deckers

The most notable of the captured three-deckers was the *Commerce de Marseilles* of 120 guns, taken at Toulon in 1794. She was considered a very fine sailer for a three-decker, she had 'lines uncommonly fine, a good sea boat', and 'notwithstanding her immense size, she worked and sailed like a frigate'. However, her structure was found to be weak, and she was reduced to harbour service by 1800.[5] The Spanish *San Josef* of 110 guns, taken at St Vincent in 1797, was also highly regarded. She served for a time as the fleet flagship off Ushant, and later in the Mediterranean fleet. Other three-deckers were captured, but never served at sea with the British fleet.

Ships of 80 Guns

Until the 1750s, three-deckers of 80 guns had been built. They proved very unsuccessful, and were largely replaced by 74s, though the last of them, the *Cambridge*, was still in service as a hulk until 1808. The new type of 80-gun ship carried her guns on two decks, with 32-pounders on the lower deck and 24-pounders on the upper deck. This made her a very powerful ship, with a gun power almost equal to a three-decker 98. Since an 80 was considerably cheaper than a 98 (£53,120 compared with £57,120 in 1789), she had considerable advantages. However, the Admiralty remained satisfied with the 74 as a standard three-decker, and only four two-decker 80s were ordered before 1815. The *Caesar* of 1992 tons was begun in 1786 and completed in 1793, while the *Foudroyant* of 2062 tons was built between 1788 and 1798. The other two ships, the *Talavera* (later renamed *Waterloo*) and the *Cambridge* were not completed in time to serve in the wars.

The fleet had twelve ships of 80 to 84 guns in 1805, and fifteen in 1811. Most of these had been captured from the French, Spanish or Danes. Notable among these prizes were the French *Canopus* (ex *Franklin*), captured at the Nile in 1798, which served as the model for many ships built after 1815. The French ships *Tonnant*, *Spartiate* and *Malta* were used as models. The Danish *Christian VII* was copied for several 74-gun ships.

The 74-Gun Ship

The 74-gun ship had been evolved by the French in the 1740s, and prizes, especially the *Invincible* of 1744, had helped cause the British fleet to adopt it as standard in 1755. However, most 74s were not directly copied from the French, and the type was essentially an expansion of the traditional British 70-gun ship. By the 1760s it was the most common ship-of-the-line, and by the 1790s it made up about half of the line-of-battle ships in the navy list, and a considerably greater proportion of those in actual service. The 74 was a great success because it was the ideal compromise. It combined good sailing with strong gun power, being the smallest practicable ship to carry a full battery of 32-pounders on the lower deck. It had scantlings strong enough to withstand any likely attack, but, unlike the three-

A model of a Surveyors' class 74, possibly the Pitt *of 1816 or the* Vindictive *of 1813.* The National Maritime Museum

decker, it did not need the largest and most expensive pieces of timber. As a two-decker, it was well proportioned and weatherly. According to Falconer's *Marine Dictionary* of 1769, 'the ships of 74 cannon or thereabouts are generally esteemed the most useful in the line of battle, and indeed in almost every other purpose of war.'[6] According to Stalkaart's textbook *Naval Architecture*, published in 1781, the 74 united qualities which made her 'the principal object of maritime attention', and had given her 'so distinguished a pre-eminence in our line of battle'.[7]

Two types of 74 were officially recognised; the Large Class and the Common Class. The former had 24-pounders on the upper deck, and the latter had 18-pounders. In practice, the Common Class can be subdivided into those built in the British style, with fourteen ports per side on the upper deck, and those copied directly or indirectly from the French, with fifteen ports per side. The fourteen port Common Class was by far the most common up to the 1790s. It had largely been conceived by Sir Thomas Slade during his period as surveyor of the navy from 1755 to 1771, and his influence remained for at least ten years after his death. Other designers, such as Bately and Williams, also produced 74s, but none was as successful as Slade, whose plans were still being copied after his death. The standard 74 of this period was 168ft long on the gundeck, though a few shorter ships of the 1750s survived, and some slightly longer ones of 170ft were also built. 74s were often quite long-lived, and both the *Dublin*, the first real British-built 74, and the *Bellona*, the prototype of the 168ft version, saw considerable service in the wars of 1793 to 1815. During the 1770s the Large Class was represented only by captured ships, and by the *Triumph* and *Valiant*, copied from the French *Invincible*.

By 1780, there was a tendency to increase the size of 74s, largely because of the success of the newer French ships. The French *Courageaux*, captured in 1761, was copied for four ships of the *Leviathan* class, and the larger British designs of 170ft were revived. There was no single standard type in the 1780s and '90s, but expansion and the French influence continued. Eleven ships of the Large Class were built, and gundeck length reached 182ft with the *Ajax* and *Kent*, lengthened from the *Invincible* draught. A few ships were built with thirty 18-pounders on the upper deck, mostly copied from the French, while other ships of the common class averaged about 174ft on the gundeck. However, these ships were not generally successful; the *Plantagenet*, designed by Rule, had to have her poop removed to improve her sailing qualities, and the *Kent* suffered greatly from hogging. It became accepted that 176ft was a suitable maximum length for the gundeck of a 74.

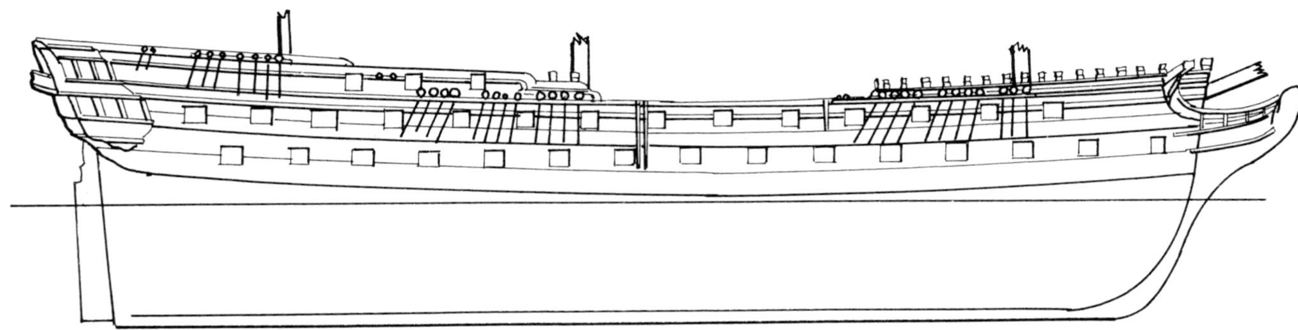

The Monmouth *64, one of the ships taken over from the East India Company in 1796. She was almost as long as an old 74, but with much less breadth and displacement.*

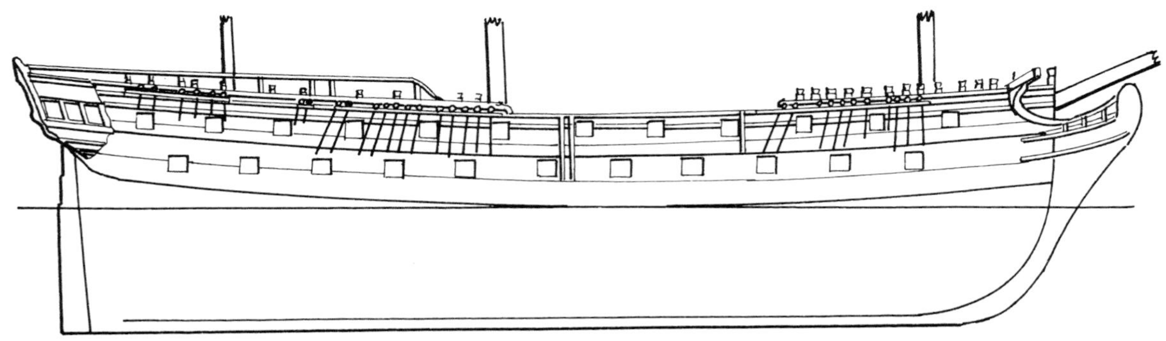

The Grampus, *an old 50 of 1780. She was broken up in 1794, but some of her class survived longer, often being converted to storeships.*

In the 1800s, design became increasingly conservative, as with other types of ship. The largest class of ships-of-the-line ever built for the British navy, known variously as the Surveyors of the Navy class, the *Vengeur* class, or the 'Forty Thieves', was begun in 1806, from the modified lines of the *Courageux*. Orders continued until 1812, and building until 1814. The class was not a total disaster, but it failed to meet the expectations of the sea officers, who mocked the designers. After that, the Danish *Christian VII* was copied for four ships, and some old designs were revived or modified. None of these was ready in time to take part in the war.

The 64

The 64-gun ship had had several false starts in the eighteenth century. Some had been built in the seventeenth century, and, in 1741, the type was revived as a reduced 70-gun ship. Then, and in 1755, there was an attempt to make the 64 carry 32-pounders on the lower deck, but this was never successful, and the 64 usually carried only 24-pounders. It developed from the old 60-gun ship, shortly after the 74 developed from the 70. It had a typical gundeck length of about 160ft, and a tonnage of about 1350. The 64 was essentially a cut-price 74; it had neither the gun power nor the sailing qualities of the latter, but more could be produced for the money, and this was important in the 1770s, when the Royal Navy had very extensive world-wide commitments. Building ceased after the American War, and the class was regarded as obsolete. In 1795 it was reported, 'There is no difference of opinion respecting 64-gun ships being struck out of the rates. It is a fact that our naval officers either pray or swear against being appointed to serve on board them.'[8] However, there remained thirty-nine on the list in 1793, making it the second biggest class of ships-of-the-line.

Numbers increased over the next few years. Some were captured, especially from the Dutch, who needed relatively small ships because of the shallowness of their harbours; but few of these saw active service. In 1796, as the naval war approached a crisis, five more were acquired by purchasing half-built merchant ships from the East India Company. These were much longer than naval 64s, with 173ft on the gundeck. They had the square midship section of merchantment, and a tonnage of about 1430. Despite everything, forty-one 64-gun ships remained on the list in 1812.

Fourth Rate Ships

Fourth rate ships were two-deckers, and carried from 50 to 60 guns. The 60 was still officially considered a ship-of-the-line, though this was purely theoretical by the 1790s. The 50 had been formally abolished from the line in the 1750s, though, as we have seen, one fought in the line at the Nile. Compilers of navy lists were unhappy about where to place it, and usually put it in a special category, neither frigates nor ships-of-the-line.

The 50 and the 60 had been very common in the first half of the eighteenth century, when it was considered desirable to build intermediate ships, in the hope that they would combine the qualities of the frigate and the ship-of-the-line. The 60-gun ship had virtually disappeared, and only one example, the *Panther*, survived into the 1790s. The 50-gun ship had been revived in the 1770s, largely as a patrol vessel and a flagship for small squadrons in peacetime. Nineteen of the class were on the list in 1793, and fourteen remained by 1812. They carried 24-pounders on the lower deck, 12-pounders on the upper deck, and 6-pounders on the quarterdeck and forecastle. The gundeck was about 145ft long, and the tonnage was about 1050. As short two-deckers, the 50s never had good sailing qualities. Several East India Company ships were converted to 54-gun ships, and a few more were captured from the Dutch.

3 Frigates

The Role of the Frigate

The frigate was the most glamorous type of ship in the navy. It was big enough to carry a significant gun power, but fast enough to evade larger enemies. It was likely to be given an independent role, while ships-of-the-line normally operated in fleets off the major enemy naval bases. It often fought single-ship actions against enemy frigates, and these were followed avidly by the press and public. Successful frigate captains like Cochrane and Broke achieved great fame, and some became extremely rich on prize money.

The frigate was designed with an unarmed lower deck, so that its guns were well above the waterline; this meant that it could be allowed to heel quite considerably, and carry sail in a strong wind and heavy sea. It also meant that it could use its guns in heavy weather, when a two-decker would be unable to open its lower ports. It was much cheaper than a ship-of-the-line (in 1789, a 38-gun frigate cost £20,830, and a 74, £43,820),[1] so more could be built for a given sum. The frigate was used for convoy escort, commerce raiding, and patrols. It also provided the main reconnaissance force for the battlefleet.

A frigate was expected to take on an enemy frigate, even one of superior gun power, such as the larger French and American frigates. It was not expected to take on a ship-of-the-line, because the difference in gun power was far too great — a 38 had half the broadside weight of a 64, and two fifths of that of a 74, and the hull scantlings were much weaker. By convention, ships-of-the-line in a fleet battle did not open fire on enemy frigates unless provoked. In other circumstances, a frigate would use its superior sailing to escape.

In ideal conditions there was not much difference between the speed of a 74 and that of a frigate; both types are recorded as doing 14 knots on occasion. However such speeds were very rare among ships-of-the-line. They could only be achieved by well-designed and well-trimmed ships, with daring captains, in ideal conditions of wind and sea. A frigate could maintain its speed in lighter winds, and make a slightly better course to windward; it could keep its gunports open longer than a two-decker, and it could operate with a smaller crew. For these reasons, the frigate was the best general purpose ship of war.

Trends in Frigate Design

Unlike the 74-gun ship, the frigate had not settled into a standard gun arrangement. The main reason for this was the increase in size of the guns carried on the main decks of frigates. The ship-of-the-line was now designed round the 32-pounder, but the optimum gun size for a frigate had not yet been found. At the beginning of the wars, most frigates carried 12-pounder guns, but these were outclassed by the latest enemy frigates. As a result, new construction concentrated almost entirely on 18-pounder frigates of 38, 36 and 32 guns. The American War of 1812 produced a dramatic series of defeats for British frigates, partly at the hands of large American ships with 24-pounder guns. The obvious answer was to build British frigates with 24-pounders, either by cutting down ships-of-the-line, or by building them from scratch. This began with a class of five ships built from pitch pine in 1813–14, carrying 24-pounder guns.

A model of a 38-gun frigate of the Diana class, c1794. The National Maritime Museum

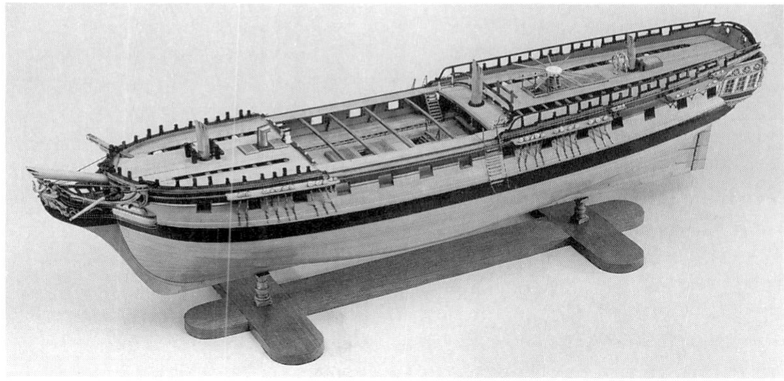

The 44-Gun Ship

The two-decker 44-gun ship was a relic of an earlier age, and represented a totally different concept of cruiser design. It carried twenty 18-pounder guns on the lower deck, twenty-two 12-pounders on the upper deck, and two 6-pounders on the forecastle. It was never intended to stand in the line of battle, but it was evolved as a cruiser before the development of the 'true frigate'. Nevertheless, it was occasionally referred to as a frigate, in particular by Admiral Kempenfeldt, who compared it unfavourably with the true frigate. The 44 had nevertheless been revived in the 1770s, largely as a patrol vessel in the years leading up to the outbreak of the American Revolution, and as a flagship for small peacetime squadrons. Twenty-one survived in 1793, but the last one was built in 1787. They saw service as troopships and transports rather than first-line fighting ships. The class had almost disappeared by the end of the wars in 1815.

The 44 appeared in another form, as a true frigate, during the last decade of the eighteenth century. A French ship, the *Pomone*, was captured in 1794, and another, the *Lavinia*, was built by the emigré French naval architect Barrallier in 1806, at Milford.

The 12-Pounder 32-Gun Frigate

The 32-gun frigate originated in 1757 with the *Southampton* class. It was the standard British frigate for thirty years after that, until it began to be out-gunned by larger French frigates, usually of 38 guns. After that, very few were built. The *Triton* of 1796 was built of fir, but remained an isolated example of new building within this class, until 1804. In that year, seven ships of the *Thames* class, modified from the old *Richmond* class of the 1750s, were begun. However there were always substantial numbers of 32-gun 12-pounder frigates in the fleet, because they had been built in large numbers in previous decades. In 1810, for example, there were 38 on the list, mostly dating from the American War. They invariably had twenty-six 12-pounders on the upper deck. In their classic form they had four 6-pounders on the quarterdeck, and two more on the forecastle; but by the 1790s most ships had carronades on the upper works, partly replacing the 6 pounders. The early 32s, up to the time of the American war, were about 680 tons. Like other classes, they tended to expand in size during the American War, to about 720 tons. The *Triton* of 1796 reached 848 tons, but the *Theseus* class was much smaller, at 657 tons.

The 18-Pounder 32

The 18-pounder 32 was an obvious response to the larger French frigates. It began with the *Pallas* of 1790, designed by Henslow. Six ships of the *Cerberus* class were ordered in 1793, and this was to be the largest single group. Ten more 32s were ordered to various draughts in the next few years, including some from the French ships *Topaze* and *Magicienne*.

The 18-pounder 32 was never a common type. In 1810, there were only twelve of them on the list, and they were easily outnumbered by 12-pounder 32s. The 18-pounder 32 had the same number of guns

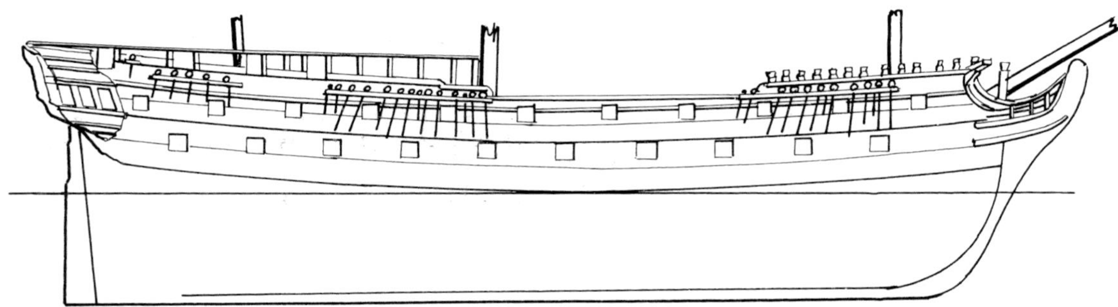

The Regulus, *an old 44-gun ship of 1785. She was reduced to a troopship in 1800.*

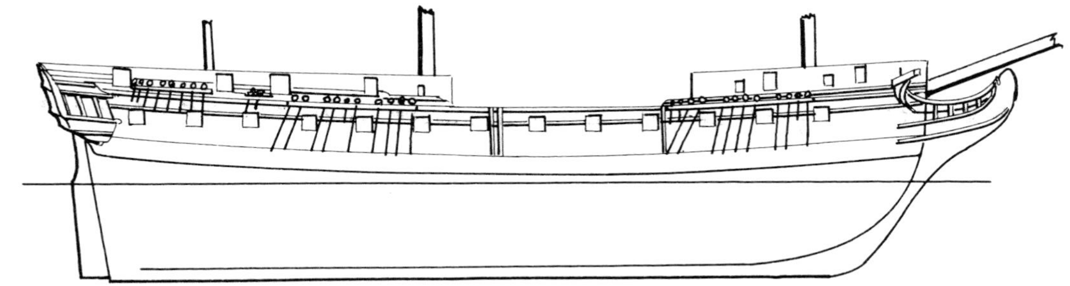

A 12-pounder 32-gun frigate of the later Richmond *class of 1805, based on a design of the 1750s.*

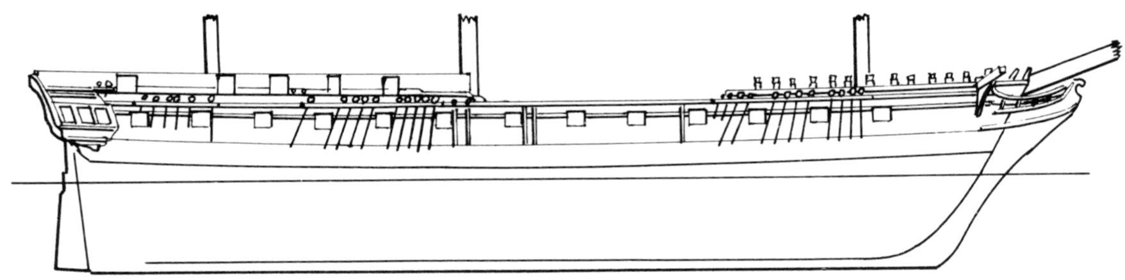

The Triton, *a fir-built 18-pounder 32 of 1796.*

on each deck as the 12-pounder 32, and also had 6-pounders on the upper works, except when replaced or supplemented by carronades. The earliest ships were of less than 800 tons, but the eight ships of the *Amphion* and *Narcissus* classes were of around 900 tons.

36-Gun Frigates

Three 36-gun frigates were built in the 1750s, at the same time as the 32 was introduced, but the type did not become common until much later. These ships carried only 12-pounder guns, like the old 32s, and one, the *Venus*, still survived with a reduced armament. In 1778 a new type of 36-gun frigate was originated, with the *Flora* class. These ships were the first British frigates to have 18-pounders instead of 12-pounders as their main armament. The 36 had become more common by the end of the American War, with seventeen on the list, including captures. Many more were built between 1794 and 1812, including 26 ships of the *Apollo/Euryalus* class, designed by Rule in 1798.

The 36 had the same guns on the upper deck as the 18-pounder 32, and differed from it in carrying eight guns on the quarterdeck instead of four. It had 9- and 12-pounders instead of 6-pounders on the upper works. In practice, ships were generally armed with carronades, and the main difference from the 32 was in the size of the ship. Most 36s were around 950 tons, though the three ships of the *Penelope* class of 1797 were of 1042 tons. Including captures, there were forty-three 36s on the list in 1805, and sixty-three in 1812.

The 38

There were already a few 38-gun ships at the beginning of the war in 1793, with seventeen on the list, mostly captured from the French. Of twenty-eight ships on sea service in 1801, twelve were of foreign origin.[2] By June 1813, there were more of this type of frigate than any other; there were eighty on the list, compared with seventy of 36 guns, and thirty-five of 32. In many ways, its design was more influenced by the French than any other class, and certainly the most successful ships were either captured or copied from the French.

The actual difference between the 38-gun frigate and the 36 was quite small — it had 28 instead of 26 guns on the upper deck. The first ships to be designed in Britain were the four ships of the *Minerva* class, launched in 1780–2. These were found to be too small, at 940 tons, to carry their armament. No more ships were ordered until the outbreak of war in 1793, when six ships of the *Artois* class, of nearly 1000 tons, were begun. Still the ships were not long enough, and the guns were too close together to be operated efficiently. In 1794 it was decided to copy the French *Hebe*, captured in 1782. She was 150ft long, compared with 146ft of the *Artois* class, and proved very successful. Forty-nine of these ships, known as the *Leda* class, had been ordered by 1815, and the design continued in use after the war. Meanwhile, attempts to develop a native British design continued; the *Naiad* and the *Amazon* of 1796, were not successful enough to be copied in later years. Nor were the *Hydra* and *Boadicea*, copied from

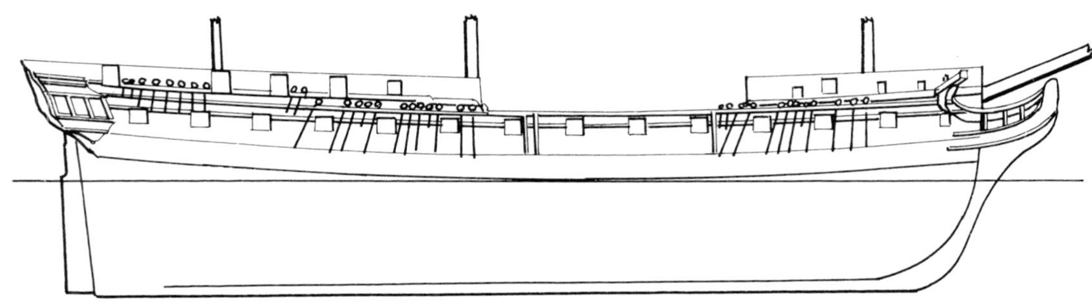

The Tribune, *a 36-gun frigate of 1803.*

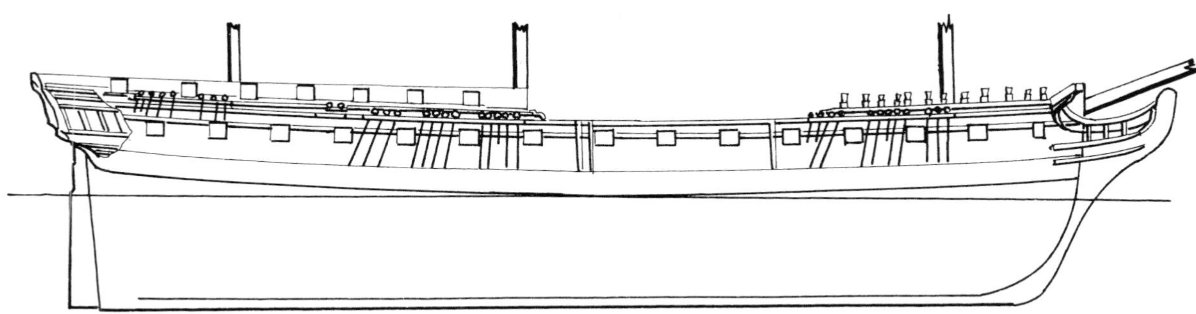

The Active, *a 38 of 1799.*

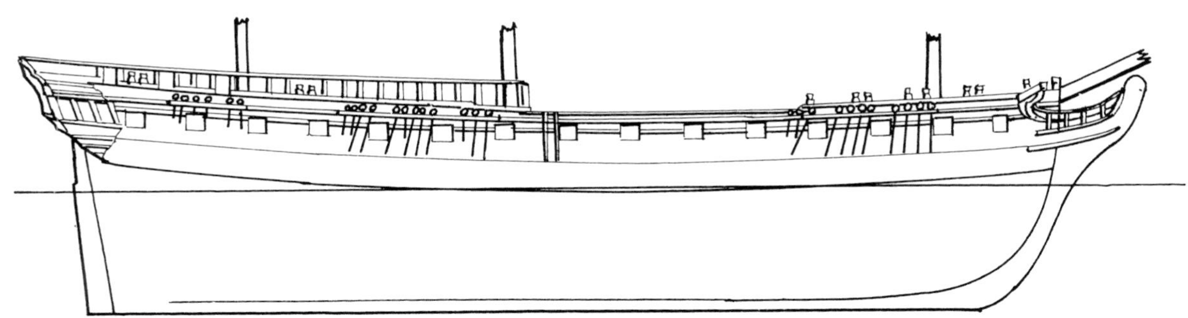

The Beaulieu, *a 40-gun frigate built on speculation by Adams of Bucklers Hard and purchased by the navy in 1790.*

the French *Melepone* and *Imperieuse*. The *Lively* class of 1799, designed by Rule, was more successful, and sixteen ships were built to this design between 1801 and 1812.

40-Gun Frigates

The class of 40-gun frigates was always quite small, with seven ships in 1801 and thirteen in 1813. Some of these were prizes and others were razees, but in 1797 the *Endymion* was based on the French 44-gun ship *Pomone*, while Henslow and Rule designed one each, the *Acasta* and *Cambria*. No more were built until 1813–14, when five ships were begun to the draught of the *Endymion*, largely in response to the large American frigates. They were made of pitch pine.

Captured Frigates

Foreign frigates, particularly French, made up quite a large proportion of the total number of frigates in the Royal Navy — in 1801, for example, exactly a third of the fifth rate frigates in sea service were foreign built.[3] During the French Revolutionary war alone, 206 frigates were destroyed or taken from enemy powers, including 143 from the French.[4] These comprised both privateers and national ships, but of course the latter group tended to include the largest classes, and the most advanced ships. Not all the captured ships were suitable for service, and it is notable that a high proportion of prizes were never used except for harbour service. In 1814, for example, twenty-five out of forty-five captured fifth rates were used only for harbour duties. On the other hand, some prize ships were very successful, particularly the French ones. Many French ships were copied, including the *Hebe, Pomone, Belle Poule, Magicienne* and *Imperieuse*. Spanish and Dutch frigates were often captured but never copied.

Razees

The practice of removing some of the decks of a ship, in order to reduce it to a lower rate and a smaller number of guns, had been established for many years. The *Royal William*, a 100-gun ship of 1719, had been reduced to a two-decker 84-gun ship in 1757, and was still in service until 1813. At the beginning of the French Revolutionary War three large frigates were produced by cutting down three 64-gun ships, the *Anson, Magnanime* and *Indefatigable*, to 38- and 40-gun ships. The *Indefatigable*, in particular, had some spectacular successes. During the American War of 1812 there was an urgent need for even larger frigates, especially with 24-pounder guns. An old 74, the *Saturn* of 1786, was cut down to a ship of 58

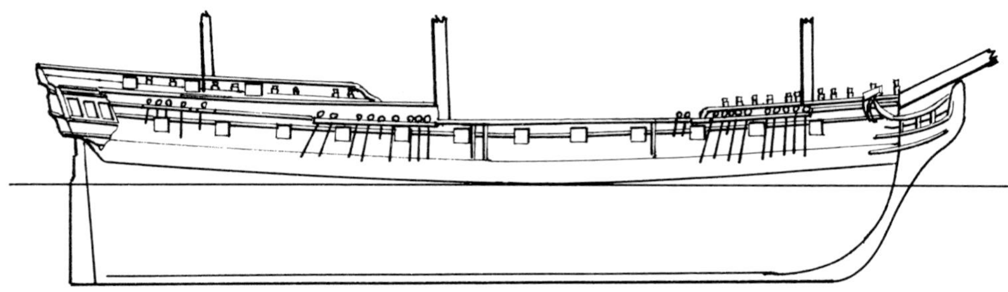

A 28-gun sixth rate of 1775. Some ships of this class survived into the 1800s, though no new ones were built.

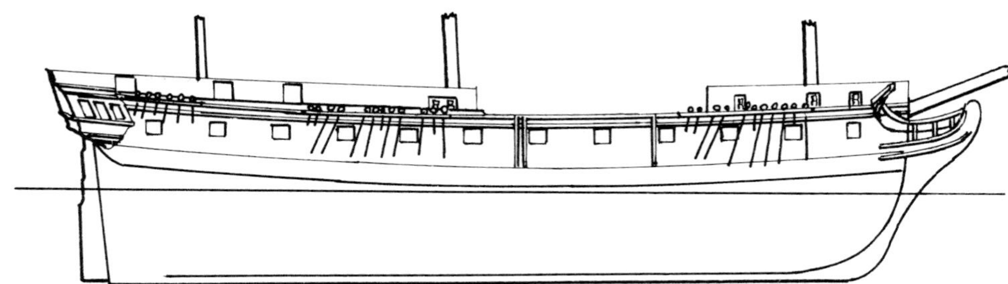

The Laurel *22 of 1806.*

guns, with two complete decks, but no quarterdeck or forecastle. However, all razee frigates had an inherent disadvantage, that they tended to carry their guns too close to the waterline; for frigates were designed to have a larger freeboard than ships-of-the-line.

The Sixth Rate

Apart from being smaller, the sixth rate differed from the fifth rate in that it had no platform in hold amidships, and the cables were stowed directly on the barrels in the hold. Like the small three-decker and the small two-decker, the small single-decker was largely discredited by 1793, and sixth rates were quite rare — only forty-one were on the list in 1793, and few more were added during the war.

The most common type of sixth rate was the 28-gun ship. This type has some claims to being the oldest kind of frigate in service, for it had been introduced as long ago as 1748.[5] It carried only 9-pounder guns, and was therefore very weak even compared with the old 32-gun frigate. No more of this class were added after 1793. The 24-gun ship also had 9-pounders on its upper deck. There were six ships of this type on the list in 1793, and only seven in 1808 — all old, or captured. The only kind of sixth rate which was developed at all was the so-called 22-gun ship. Two classes were ordered in 1805, one designed by Henslow, the other by Rule. The *Laurel* class was of 526 tons, and the *Banterer* class was of 537. Both carried twenty-two 9-pounder guns on the upper deck, along with eight 24-pounder carronades on the quarterdeck and forecastle, and two 6-pounder chase guns. Six ships of each class were built. In addition to these new ships, several prizes were added to the ranks of the sixth rates, so that there remained fifty-two on the list in 1813.

4 Unrated Ships and Vessels

Sloops

The term sloop, like many other nautical phrase, is deeply ambiguous. Originally, it meant a single-masted vessel, and in certain contexts it still does. The definition of a sloop of war was quite simply a vessel commanded by an officer with the rank of commander. It carried from ten to eighteen guns, but apart from that there was little unity within the group. The largest sloops were similar to sixth rates in deck layout, in that they had a quarterdeck and forecastle, an armed upper deck, unarmed lower deck, and two platforms in the hold. Flush-decked sloops, a relatively new class, had no forecastle or quarterdeck, and only rudimentary platforms in the hold; virtually all their accommodation and storage was on the lower deck. Sloops could be either ship rigged, with three masts, or brig rigged with two. There was considerable overlap between the ships and the brigs; sometimes the brigs were bigger than the ships, and sometimes both types were built with the same hull form, as in the case of the *Snake* and *Cruiser* classes.

The sloop carried out many of the functions of the frigate in commerce protection and patrol; however, it was rarely used for fleet reconnaissance, because in that role it was likely to have to deal with the enemy fleet's screen of heavy frigates. The number of sloops increased enormously in the latter part of the eighteenth century, from fifty-three in 1793 to over two hundred in 1801. This was partly because of the increased importance of commerce protection and patrol, inshore work against invasion, and the attack on enemy commerce; partly because sloops could be built quickly and cheaply in wartime; and also because the development of the carronade made it possible for a small ship to carry a respectable short-range armament.

Ship Sloops with Quarterdecks

The largest sloops were built like miniature sixth rates, with armed

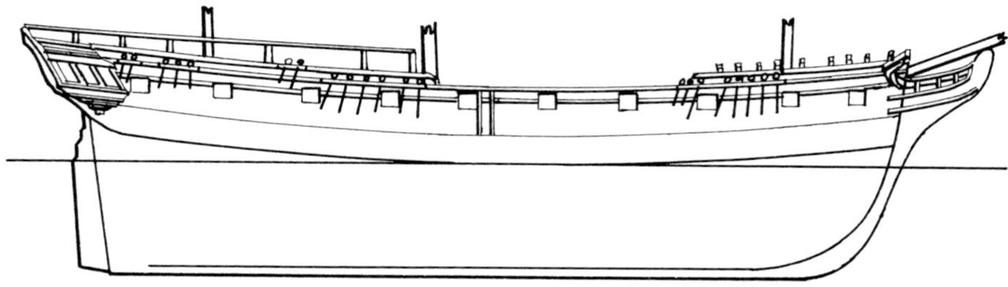

A large ship-sloop with a quarterdeck – the Buffalo, *purchased in 1797, and mainly used as a storeship.*

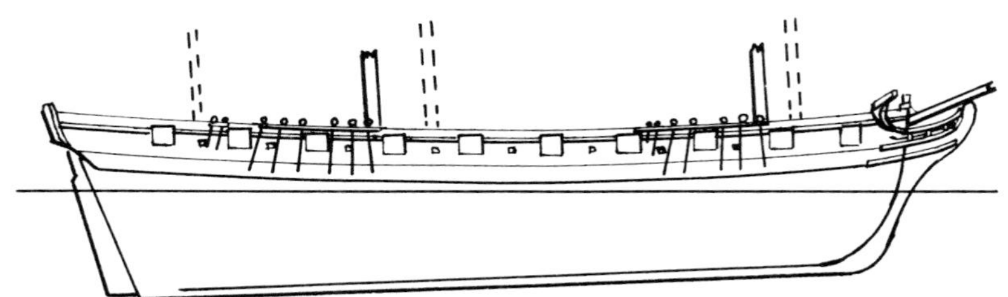

The common draught of the Snake *and* Cruiser *classes. It could carry three masts as a ship, or two as a brig.*

quarterdecks and forecastles. In 1793, there were thirty-one such ships, with fourteen or sixteen 6-pounder guns on the upper deck. The class expanded considerably with the *Cormorants* of 1793, based on the French *Amazon* of 1745. Twenty-three of these were built before 1806. After 1795, most new ships were designed for eighteen rather than sixteen guns on the main deck, and tonnage increased from 330 to 420. This began with the *Brazen/Termagant* class. Sixteen ships were built to the *Merlin* draught between 1795 and 1802, while experimental vessels included the *Cynthia* of 1795, with the Schank sliding keel, and the *Dart* and *Arrow*, built to Bentham's radical design.

On the quarterdeck and forecastle, early quarterdeck ship sloops carried swivel guns — usually twelve or fourteen. By 1795 it was becoming more common to fit carronades, usually 12-pounders. In the 1800s carronades were also fitted to the main deck on new ships. The ten ships of the *Conway* class of 1807 had eighteen 32-pounder carronades on the main deck, six 12-pounder carronades on the quarterdeck, and two 6-pounder long guns and two 12-pounder carronades on the forecastle. They had expanded slightly from the ships of the 1790s, with a tonnage of 444.

The quarterdeck sloop never became the largest group among sloops. There were thirty-two on the list in 1801, and in 1814 there were fifty-seven, none of which was foreign built.[1]

Flush-decked Ship Sloops

Most ship-rigged sloops were flush-decked, in that they had no quarterdeck or forecastle, or had only very small unarmed ones. Such ships tended to be better proportioned and more weatherly than the quarterdeck sloops, though they offered less accommodation for the officers. Flush-decked sloops were not necessarily smaller than the quarterdeck vessels, for many were of more than 400 tons; apart from the lack of guns on the quarterdeck and forecastle, they were not always more lightly armed, and most had sixteen or eighteen carronades.

The flush-decked ship sloop originated in 1796, with four ships of the *Snake* class, designed by Rule. The type was largely created by the carronade, and, from the begining, this gun formed the main armament — the *Snakes* carried sixteen 32-pounder carronades, and only two 6-pounder long guns as chasers. Small numbers were built in the next few years, but 24-pounder carronades were used on most. However, with the *Hermes* class of 1810, the 32-pounders were restored, and this practice continued with the *Cyrus* class of 1812. Sixteen ships were built to this draught, which was based on the lines of the *Myrmidon* sixth rate of 1781. There were forty-three flush-decked ship sloops in 1801, but by 1814 there were only twenty on the list.

Brig Sloops

The brig sloop was quite a well-established type, for it had originated in the adaption of a merchant ship design in the 1770s, begining with the *Childers* of 1779. Only eleven brig sloops were on the navy list in 1793. By this time, a brig sloop was not normally fitted with a quarterdeck, but in size and armament it overlapped quite considerably with the ship sloop; the *Snake* and *Cruiser* classes were identical, except that one had two masts and the other had three. But some of the brig sloop classes, such as the ten ships of the *Banterer* class of 1807, were quite small at 250 tons.

Wartime development of the brig sloop began with the eight ships built to the *Diligence* draught of 1795. Eight more were built to the draught of the *Albatross* of the same year, but the most successful design was the *Cruiser* of 1796. This was the first class to introduce carronades on the lower deck instead of 6-pounder long guns. Only the prototype was built in the eighteenth century, but, after 1803, new examples were ordered almost continuously until 1814. Eventually, more than a hundred were built, including postwar examples; the *Cruiser* class was the largest group of sailing warships ever built for any navy. Versions were built in fir and teak, as well as the conventional oak. As a result of this large-scale building, and of the capture of many ships from the enemy, there were 181 brig sloops in the fleet in 1814, including thirty-five prizes.[2]

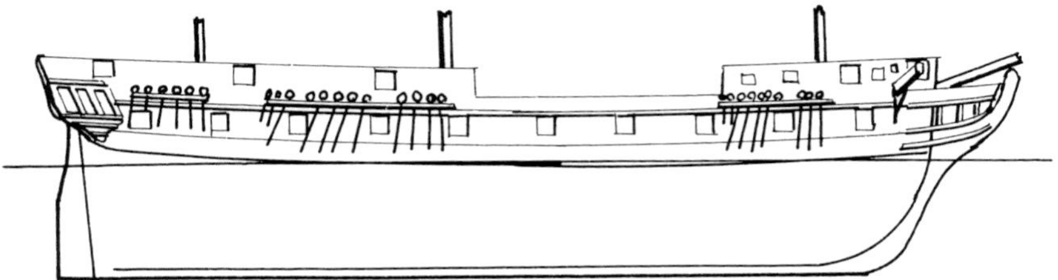

The Meteor *bomb vessel of 1812.*

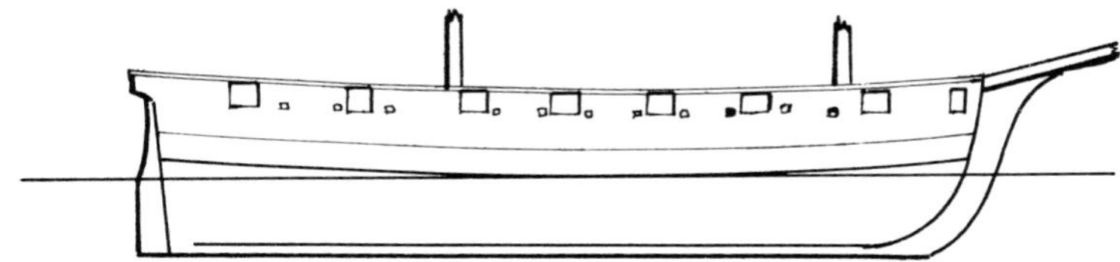

The Confounder *class of 12-gun brigs of 1805.*

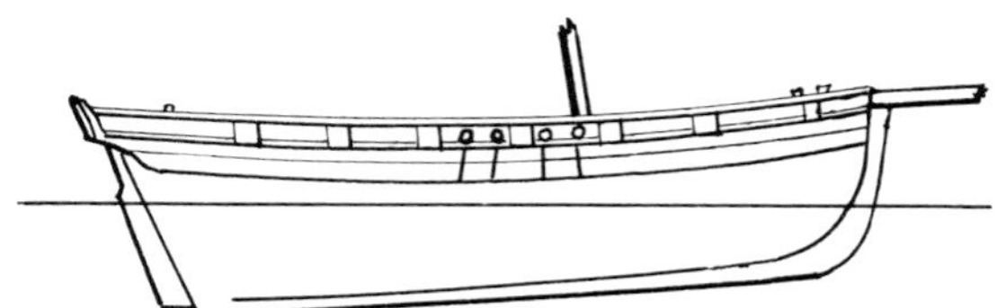

The Cheerful *and* Surly *cutters of 1806.*

Bomb Vessels

The bomb vessel was the most specialised fighting ship in the fleet. It was not intended to engage enemy ships except in self defence, but instead it was designed to bombard enemy towns and fortresses in the most effective way. For this, it was fitted with one or two mortars, angled to fire a high-trajectory shell for a considerable distance. It was the only kind of ship in the fleet to carry explosive shells. This had a considerable effect on the design, and special precautions had to be taken to protect them from accidental ignition. The bomb vessel had been developed in the 1680s, by the French for use against North African cities. It had been taken up by the British soon afterwards. Early examples were ketch rigged, as the lack of a foremast allowed the mortars to fire forward; but this led to an unbalanced rig and poor sailing qualities. By the 1790s, bomb vessels were ship-rigged, and the bomb-ketch, as such, was obsolete.

Most bomb vessels were purchased from merchant builders, and converted. They were from 300 to 400 tons, except for the *Perseus* of 1796, which was of 432 tons. Most had a complement of sixty-seven men, except for the *Perseus* which had ninety-six. Towards the end of the war, several ships were designed and built as bomb vessels — three ships of the *Vesuvius* class of 1812, and three more of the slightly large *Hecla* class of 1815. Unlike other types of ship, bomb vessels had a consistent naming policy: they were usually named after volcanoes, or in some way suggested hell and fire, such as *Belzebub*. There were only two bomb vessels in the navy at the beginning of 1793, but by 1799 there were fourteen. There were nineteen in 1805, and thirteen at the beginning of 1812.

Fireships

The concept of fireships was very old; they had been used with some success against the Spanish Armada in 1588. They had very little effect on eighteenth- and nineteenth-century battles, although fire was terrifying to a seaman in a highly inflammable wooden ship; a fireship was not too difficult to avoid, as its crew had to abandon it and set it on course to its target. No fireships were used (or 'expended') during the Great Wars with France, but some were always kept available — eight in 1795, thirteen in 1799, and five in 1805. Most fireships were converted merchant ships of around 300 to 400 tons, but six ships were built to the *Thais* draught of 1805, similar to the *Tisiphone* class of sixth rate of 1781. Like bomb vessels, fireships served as sloops when they were not needed for their primary role. At Basque Roads in 1809 they were used to launch rockets.

A fireship differed from other ships in that her gunports were hinged from the bottom instead of the top, so that they would fall open when the pot ropes burned through. Internally it was fitted with a fire-room, filled with combustible stores. A fireship was manned with a crew of forty-five or fifty-six, though only a small proportion of these were intended to remain with the ship on her final voyage.

Brigs

The brig was distinguished from the brig sloop by its smaller size, and the fact that it was commanded by a lieutenant rather than a commander. Apart from the gun brigs, upgraded from gunboats, most brigs had fourteen 24-pounder carronades. Their successors were the *Confounder* class, described as 'small brigs to carry fourteen 18-pounder carronades, of nearly the same tonnage of the last built gun brigs'. Twenty-one ships were built in this form, and the second batch, begun in 1811, had two 6-pounder long guns in addition. Eighteen more ships were built in this version.

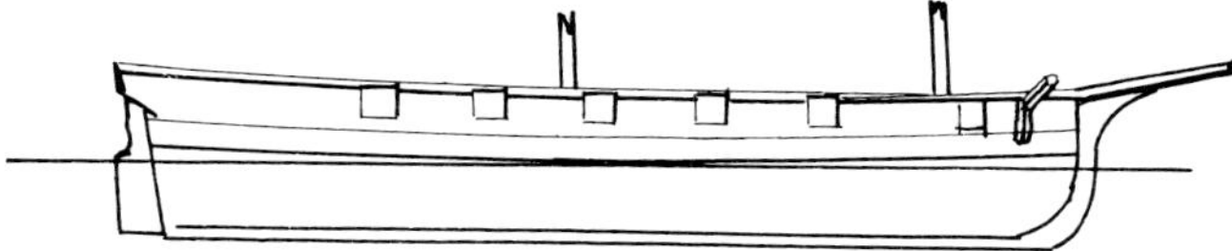

The Acute class of gunboat of 1797.

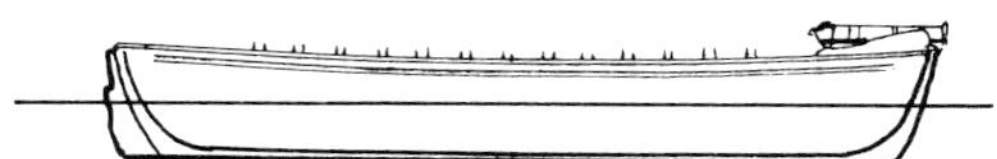

The type of small gunboat designed by Parkin and Smith in 1796. It was double ended, with a gun at each end.

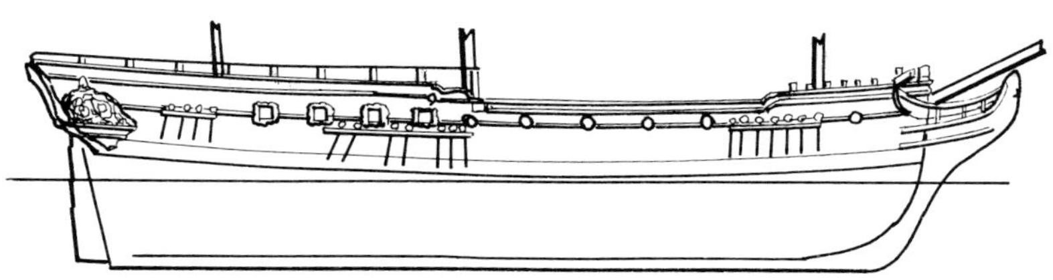

The Royal Sovereign, *a royal yacht of 1804.*

Schooners

The schooner had originated in North America; it was not a well established rig in Britain before 1800, and such ships remained quite rare in both naval and merchant service. Apart from the gunboats, there were only ten schooners in the navy in 1801, including those classed as 'galleots'. These included the two ships of the *Eling* class, smaller versions of the *Dart* and *Arrow*. The rig became much more common after 1803, with the inauguration of the *Ballahoo* class. These vessels were intended as despatch and advice boats, with a design 'similar to a Bermudian despatch boat'. Seventeen ships, all named after fish, were built in Bermuda, and twelve more, named after birds, were built in English yards. They carried four to six guns, with a crew of twenty men. About a third of the schooners which served in the navy had been captured from the French. The most famous schooner in the navy was the *Pickle*, which brought home the news of Trafalgar. She was built in a merchant yard in Bermuda, and purchased in 1800.

Cutters

Unlike the schooner, the cutter was a native British design, developed originally by the smugglers of Folkestone and surrounding areas. From the middle of the eighteenth century, it was adopted by the excise service, and by the navy itself. There were eighteen cutters in the fleet in 1793. A few more were built for the navy over the years, but the largest single group was the *Lady Howard* class, built to the lines of a Bermudan sloop of that name. They were 68ft long, 111 tons, and had forty men. Twelve were built, mostly armed with ten 18-pounder carronades; these were mostly rigged as schooners, although they were officially classified as cutters. Many other cutters were purchased from merchant builders in England, and there were forty-two in the fleet in 1813.

The cutter was designed for speed, and had a very large rig, which deployed both fore and aft and square sails on a single mast. It was suitable for patrols and despatch carrying, but not for close inshore work, as it had quite a deep draught.

Gunboats

The essential concept of a gunboat was a small vessel with at least one heavy gun, usually adapted to fire directly forward or aft and with little traverse, so that the vessel itself had to be steered to aim it. Within that definition there were several different types. The largest ones had a full broadside armament in addition to the fore and aft guns, and were not very different from ordinary brigs and schooners. The smallest had only one or two weapons, and were little bigger than ships boats.

Among the larger type, the first group were ordered to the draught of the *Conquest* of 1794. They were intended to row with eighteen oars, and were probably rigged as schooners or brigantines. They were of 146 tons, and carried two 24-pounder chase guns, and ten 18-pounder long guns. Other groups with similar armament were the *Acutes* of 1797, which were brig rigged, and were later fitted with Schank sliding keels; and the *Coursers* of the same year, which were similar in layout. Thirty-one ships were built of these classes. The ten ships of the *Bloodhound* class of 1801 had 18- or 32-pounder carronades as chasers. By far the most numerous group was the *Archer* class of 1801, of 177 tons. These ships had 32-pounder bow guns and ten 18-pounder carronades on the broadside. Fifty-eight were built between 1801 and 1805. All the larger gunboats were eventually reclassified as gun brigs or gun schooners, according to rig.

The smaller type of gunboat was developed through several experimental classes in the French Revolutionary War. They began with the double ended boat built by Parkin of Cawsand in 1796, and designed by Sir Sidney Smith. Ten flat bottom boats were built around 1801, with a single carronade or howitzer, and a displacement of 12 tons. Brenton's launches, built a few years later, were only 27ft long, and perhaps closer to ships' boats than independent ships. They were double ended, with a 12-pounder in the bows.

The classic form of small gunboat was designed by Commissioner Hamilton in 1805. The first group were clinker built, of 43 tons. Each carried two 18-pounders on slides near the bows, and an 18-pounder on a pivot aft. The first six were sent to Gibraltar for local

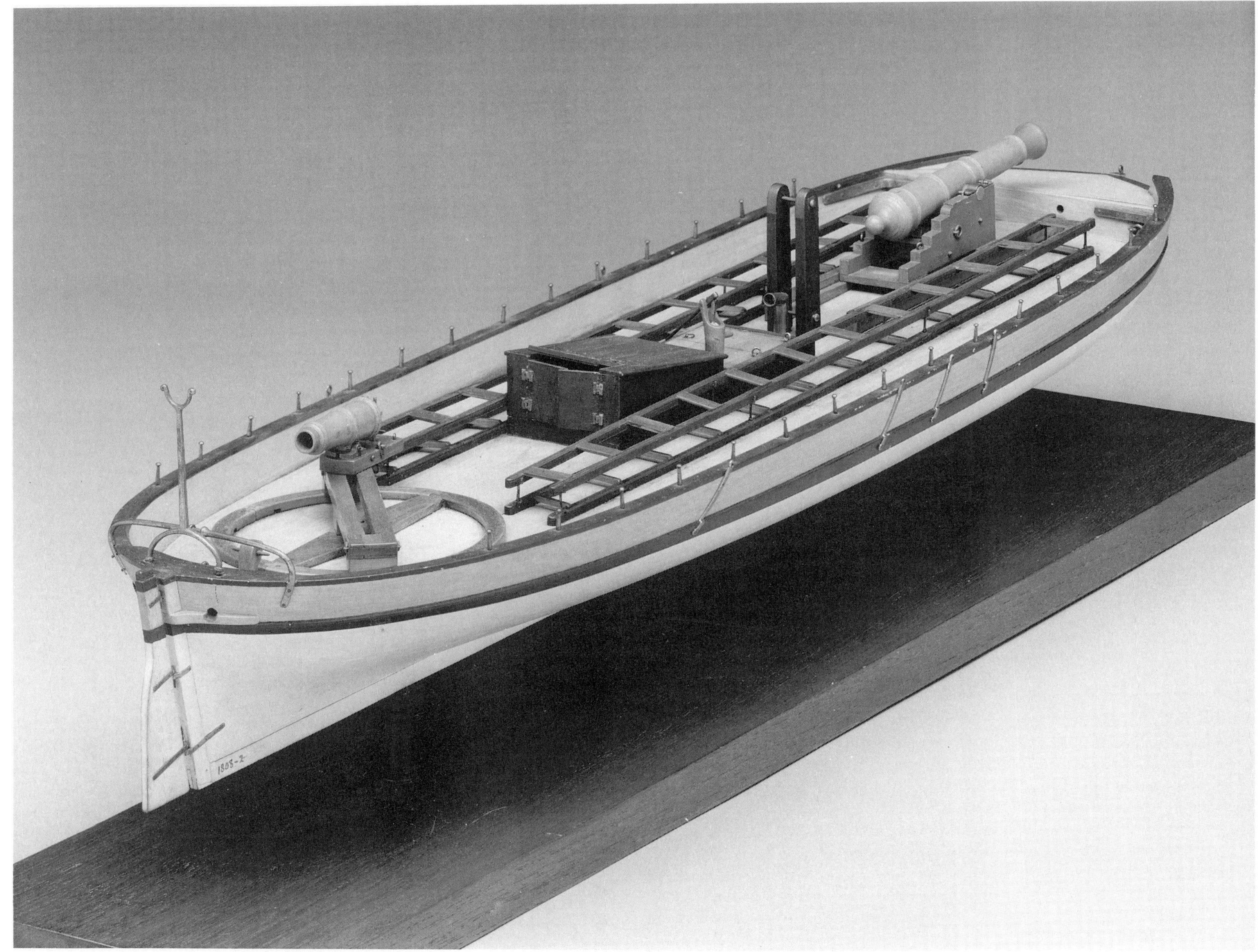

A model of Commissioner Hamilton's design for a class of gunboats, with a carronade and a long gun. The National Maritime Museum

defence. A further eighty-five were built from 1808 onwards, for coast defence and for operations in areas like the Danish Islands, where shallow draught was an advantage. They were built in several batches, of slightly different design; the last and largest group, of fifty vessels, were of 51 tons. The Hamilton gunboats were numbered, and were never given names.

Yachts

Yachts had first been introduced to the navy in 1660, when Charles II had been given one by the Dutch. The name reflected the origin, for it meant a swift craft, or hunter. Though none of the eighteenth-century kings shared the Stuart love for the sea, yachts had remained in the fleet ever since. The largest were essentially ship sloops, and were true 'royal' yachts, being often used to ferry the king on trips around his domain, and to his other kingdom of Hanover. These included the *Royal Sovereign* of 278 tons, built in 1804, and the *Royal Charlotte* of 231 tons, built in 1749. These ships were classed as second rates, although one historian commented 'It appears absurd to rank such toys among fighting vessels.'[3] Of course, this rating entitled their captains and officers to much higher pay.

Smaller yachts were used by various Admiralty officials. Each dockyard had a yacht for its principal officers, as did the Navy Board and the Admiralty itself. Appropriately, each yacht was usually named after the yard, or the board it was intended to serve. Most yachts were quite old, especially the *Bolton* of 1709, which was now used for training cadets at the Royal Naval College at Portsmouth. Newer yachts included the *Plymouth*, built in 1796, of 96 tons and 8 guns; and the *William and Mary*, built at Deptford in 1807, of 199 tons and 8 guns. There were eleven yachts on the list in 1793, and the same number in 1805.

Other Ships

Apart from standard rigs and classes, there were several small groups of ships. Some of these were experiments which had failed, or at least had not led to repetition — the *Spanker*, a floating battery designed by Mr Richard White, for example. The list of 1803 also included one lugger (the *Experiment* of 1792, the only one built for the Royal Navy), a 'lateen setee' of Mediterranean origin, and several types of support vessel. These latter have to be considered separately, though some of them were classed as warships and had naval crews.

Hired Vessels

The navy sometimes purchased vessels from merchant shipowners, including 64-gun ships bought from the East India Company. It also hired transports, but retained their original merchant crews. Between these two categories were the hired vessels which were used as warships, and carried naval crews. Naturally, there was not a great deal of uniformity about these vessels, but they were invariably small. At the end of the war in 1801, there were 130 on the navy list, all but twelve of them serving in home waters. Twelve were rigged as ships, and another twelve were brigs — all commanded by lieutenants. The great majority were cutters, commanded by lieutenants or masters. There were also schooners, luggers, and tenders for bomb vessels. Of those hired vessels outside home waters, seven were employed in the Mediterranean, three on the coast of Spain, and two, commanded by Matthew Flinders and James Grant, were on expeditions of discovery in the Pacific.[4]

A model of a typical naval cutter of around 1800. The National Maritime Museum

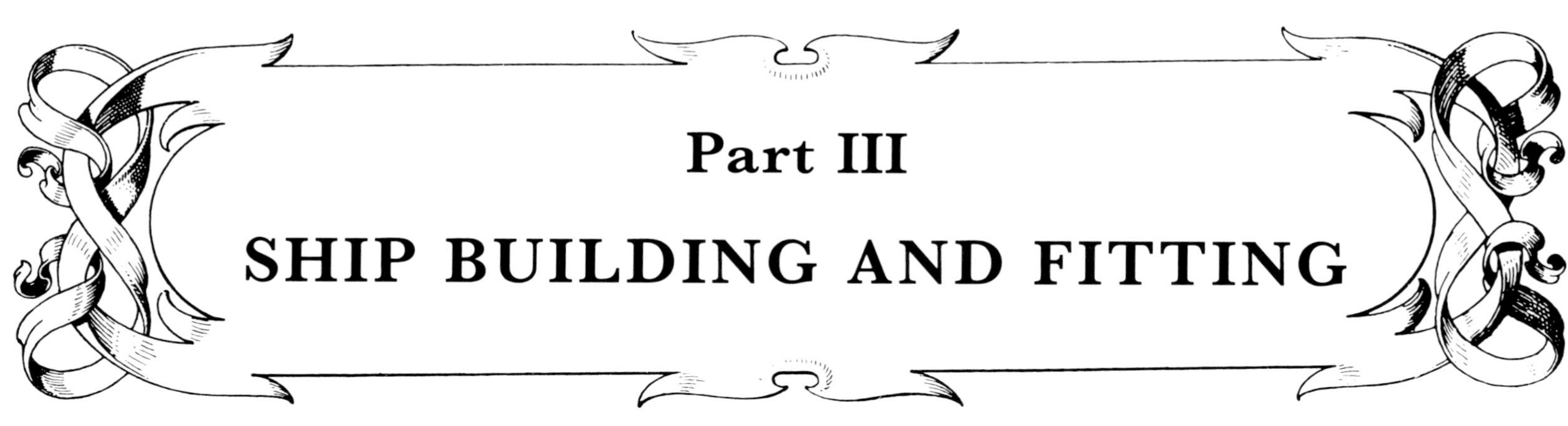

Part III
SHIP BUILDING AND FITTING

1 Ship Construction

Ship Designers

In the 1800s, naval architecture had not yet become a profession in its own right. In theory, all shipwrights were trained in ship design as well as construction, and could use a draughtsman's pen as well as an adze. In practice, there was an elite group among the shipwrights, consisting of men who would spend their lives in the drawing offices rather than cutting pieces of timber. To rise to the top of the profession, it was usually necessary to begin as an apprentice to a high official in the dockyards, rather than to an ordinary shipwright. After such a beginning, it was possible to climb through the ranks of the assistant master shipwrights at the dockyards, and then to master shipwright. After that, the successful careerist would move from one yard to another, ending at Deptford, the most senior; then to the Navy Office in London. As an alternative to the old system of apprenticeship, the School of Naval Architecture was opened at Portsmouth in 1811; but, of course, this had no effect on shipbuilding during the wars.

The design of the Royal Navy's ships was the responsibility of the surveyors of the navy, who were members of the Navy Board in London. Among past surveyors, the works of Sir Thomas Slade still had considerable effect on ship design; he had drawn the lines of the *Victory*, and designed many of the 74-gun ships and frigates still in service in the 1790s. According to one of his successors he was 'truly a great man in the line he trod'.[1] The surveyors in 1793 were John Henslow, who had entered the service in 1745 and been appointed surveyor in 1784, on the retirement of Sir John Williams; and William Rule, who had entered in 1758, and became surveyor in February 1793. In the 1790s the general policy was for each surveyor to produce a design for any new group of ships ordered. Rule's most successful design was the *Caledonia* of 120 guns, which became the standard design for first rates after 1814; but neither Henslow nor Rule was a great naval architect, and many French ships were copied because of lack of inspiration among native designers. Henslow retired in 1806, and was replaced by Henry Peake. At the same time, design policy changed, and it became common for the two surveyors to co-operate to produce a single design, known as the 'Surveyors of the Navy' class, for each major type of ship. Rule retired in 1813, and the number of surveyors was increased to three; Joseph Tucker and Robert Seppings were appointed to serve as junior surveyors. Of all the surveyors during the Great Wars, only Seppings was to have any major influence on shipbuilding, though that was in construction rather than design.

The great majority of ships, apart from those copied directly from the French, were designed under the direct supervision of at least one of the surveyors, and he signed the plan to guarantee its authenticity. It is not clear how much of the actual drawing was done by the surveyor himself; the Navy Board employed two assistant surveyors and three draughtsmen, who probably carried out the more repetitive tasks. On completion, the draught was sent to the Navy Board and the Admiralty for approval, though this was little more than a rubber stamp. It was copied as many times as necessary,

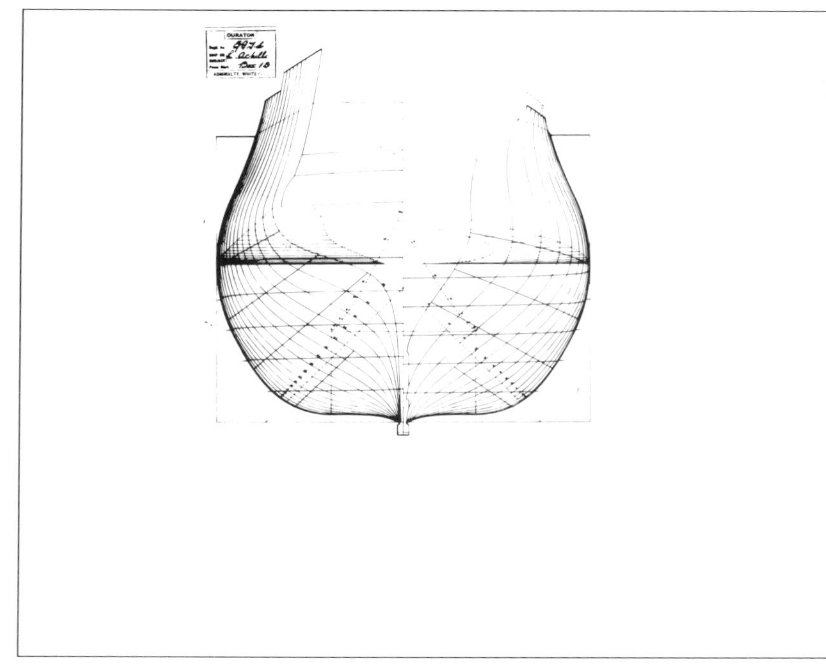

by pricking through the paper of the original. Then it was sent to the appropriate dockyards and shipyards for the ships to be constructed.

A few ships were built to other designs that were neither French copies nor done under the supervision of one of the surveyors. Barrallier, one of the assistant surveyors, was a French emigré and, perhaps because of the belief that the French were better at ship design, he was allowed to produce plans for several different types of ship, up to 74 guns; none was a great success. Other men, often amateurs at ship design, designed small experimental ships; Sir Sidney Smith, Captain Schanck, Gower of the East India Company, and Commissioner Hamilton, all produced plans, and some, like Hamilton's gunboats, were produced in quite large numbers.

The Sheer Plan

For a new ship, certain factors would have already been decided by the Admiralty and Navy Board before the ship designer started work. These included the length of the gundeck, maximum breadth, depth in hold and number and sizes of guns to be carried.

The main plan of a ship consisted of four views, all drawn on a single sheet of paper to a scale of 4ft to the inch. The side view, or sheer plan, was drawn first. The draughtsman would begin with the keel of the ship, which was straight. At the forward end he would draw the shape of the bow, formed by a combination of circles and

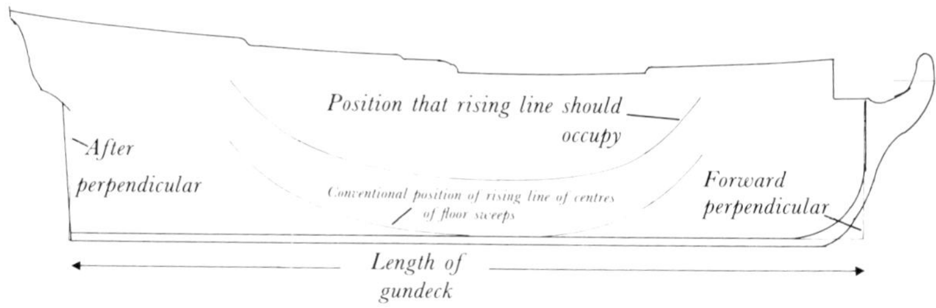

Sheer plan of a ship, showing the use of the rising line of centres of floor sweeps, and the length on the gundeck.

Sir Robert Seppings, master shipwright at Chatham from 1804 and joint surveyor of the navy from 1813; inventor of a new system of ship construction, the round bow and stern, and of many other shipbuilding techniques. The National Maritime Museum

The draught used for the 74-gun ships Achilles *and* Superb, *based on the captured French* Pompée. *It has all the usual features of ships' draughts, but it also shows the modifications to the bows and stern of 1796. The new closed stern replaces the old open one, and the new, simpler type of figurehead is shown.* The National Maritime Museum

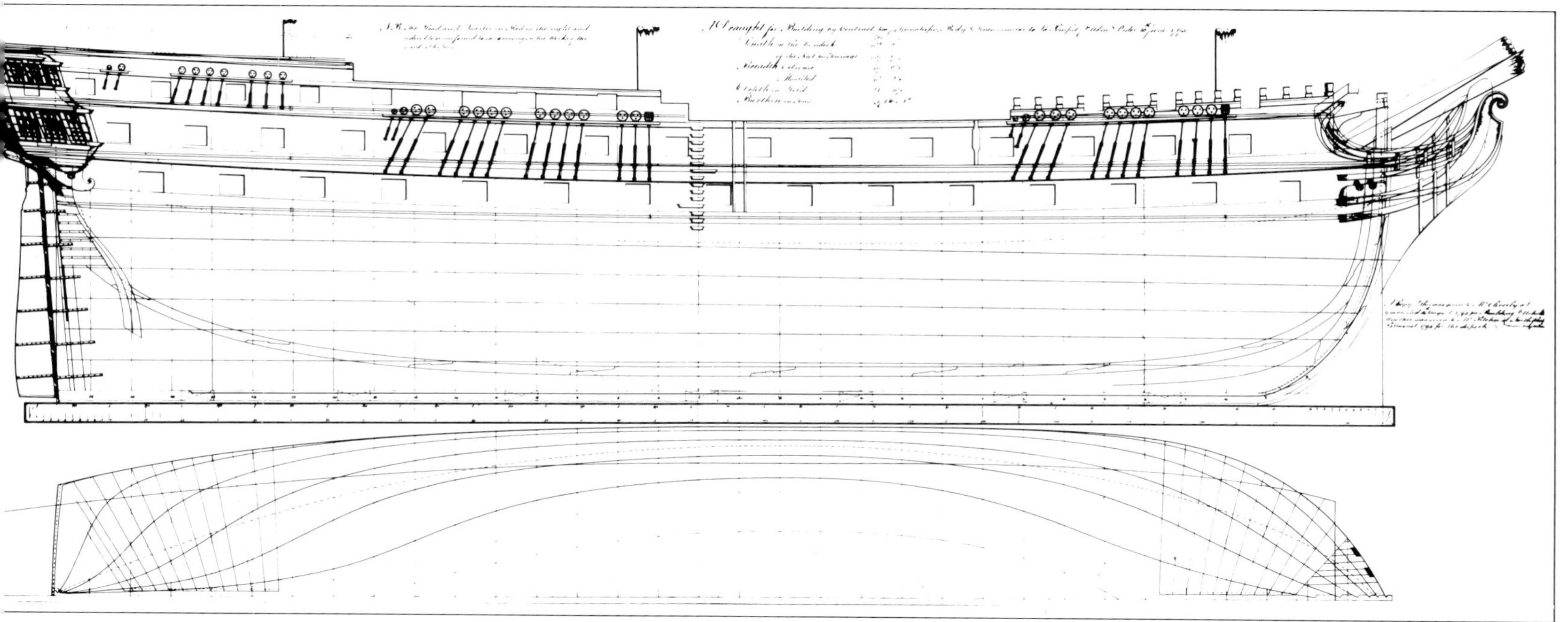

straight lines. The stempost, at the after end of the keel, was a straight line, rising from the keel at about 10 degrees to the vertical. The position of the lower deck was determined by the depth in hold, and by the need to keep the guns a certain height above the water. The sheer, or curve of the deck in this plane, would largely be decided by custom and experience. There was a tendency for sheer to reduce over the years, especially in the 1800s. The other gundecks would be placed at a certain distance above the lower deck, with enough space to allow the men to operate the guns. The orlop deck was placed below the lower deck, but here the 'height between decks' was less, because no guns were carried. All the decks were parallel, and had the same amount of sheer.

The gunports were evenly spaced along each deck, with a fixed height between the lower edge of the port and the deck itself. They were carefully staggered, so that the run of the timbers would not be interrupted by having one port directly above another. The beams which supported the deck were drawn next, arranged so that there was always a beam to support each gun. On the external hull, the wales were drawn under the rows of gunports, with rather more sheer than the decks. The channels which helped extend the rigging of the masts were drawn in, along with the chains and deadeyes associated with them. The tops of the sides were shown, with rails or timber heads. In the 1770s it had been common to produce 'as fitted' plans, showing the ship completed, with all its decoration. This practice had died out by the 1790s, and the builders draught was usually rather vague about the details of figurehead and carving. However, the shape of the stern, including the galleries, was shown. At the bows, the figurehead itself was represented by a block, but the shape of the head and its rails was drawn.

In earlier times, one sheer plan often served to give all the detail needed, with the external features drawn in black ink and the internal ones in red. By the 1790s, it was more common to draw separate plans. The longitudinal section gave full details of the decks and their beams, partitions in the hold and on deck, ladders and hatchways, the positions of the masts, and many other details. Sometimes a framing plan was also drawn, showing the hull before planking.

Hull Lines

The designer had a relatively free hand on the shape of the hull, though he was guided by his experience, and the need to produce a shape which was full enough to bear the weight of the guns, yet fine enough to allow good sailing qualities. The first step in designing the underwater hull was to draw the midship section, which was just forward of the middle of the hull, and represented the widest part of the ship. The position of the maximum breadth was found, just above the waterline; under that, the hull consisted of three curves, called the breadth sweep, the reconciling sweep, and the floor sweep. The section nearest the keel was usually represented by a straight line, which angled upwards from the horizontal to a greater or lesser degree. This was called the floor. Above the maximum breadth, there was normally a vertical straight line called the dead-flat. After that, the hull narrowed by means of a convex curve called the above breadth sweep, and then by a concave curve known as the toptimber sweep. This narrowing of the hull was known as tumble-home; its purpose was to increase stability, because it was believed that to keep the guns of the upper decks nearer the centreline would help reduce rolling. There was some truth in this, and furthermore tumble-home reduced the lengths of the deck beams, and also topweight, which also tended to increase stability. However, tumble-home had been far too great in the past, and was still being reduced during the French Wars.

The shape of the midship section was repeated for several frames, and then adapted for progressively smaller frames towards the bow

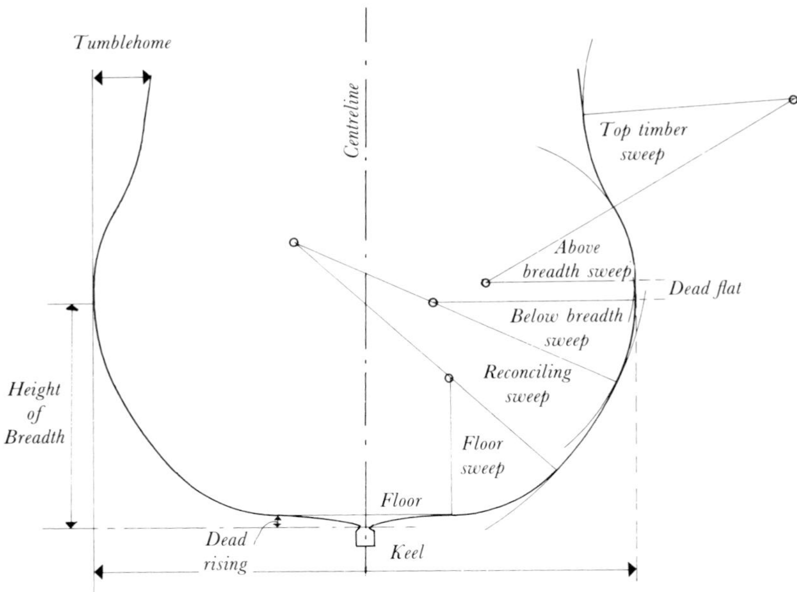

The various sweeps and other lines used in drawing out a midship section.

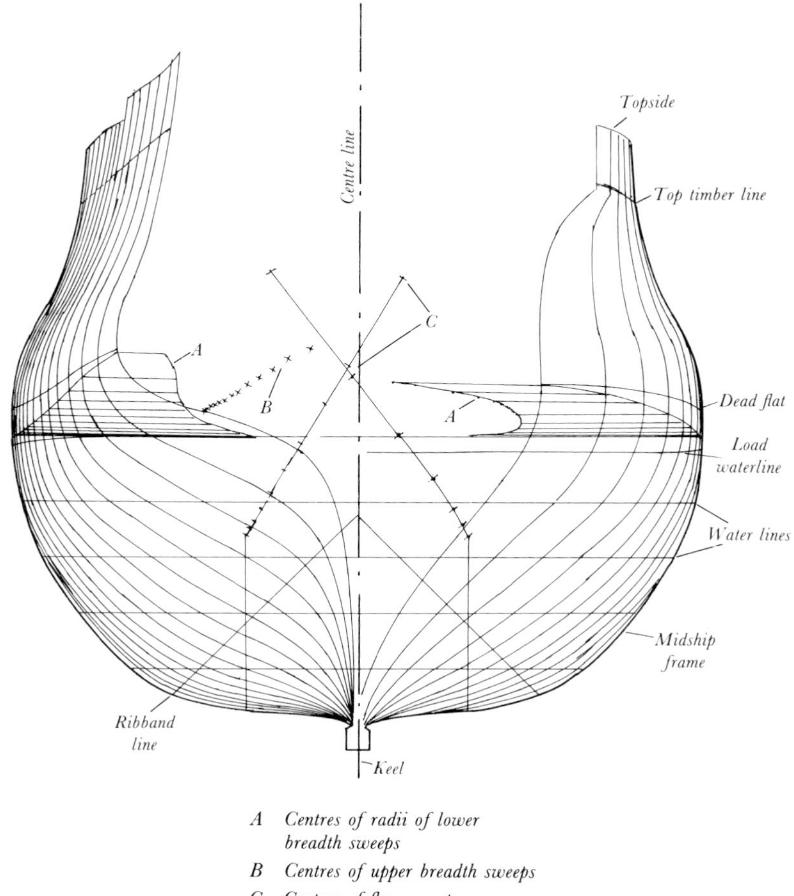

The body sections from a typical draught, showing the various construction lines.

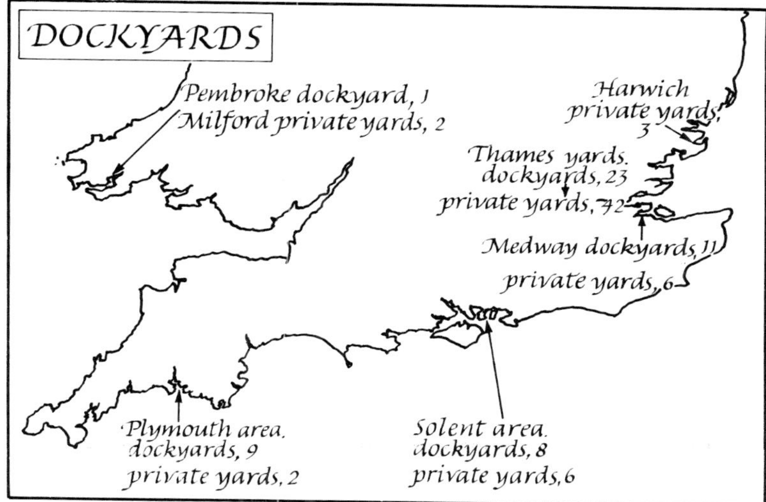

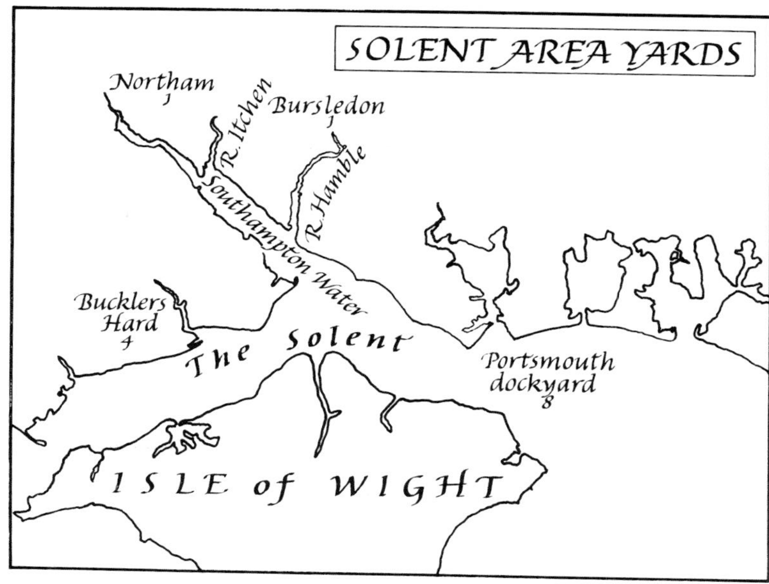

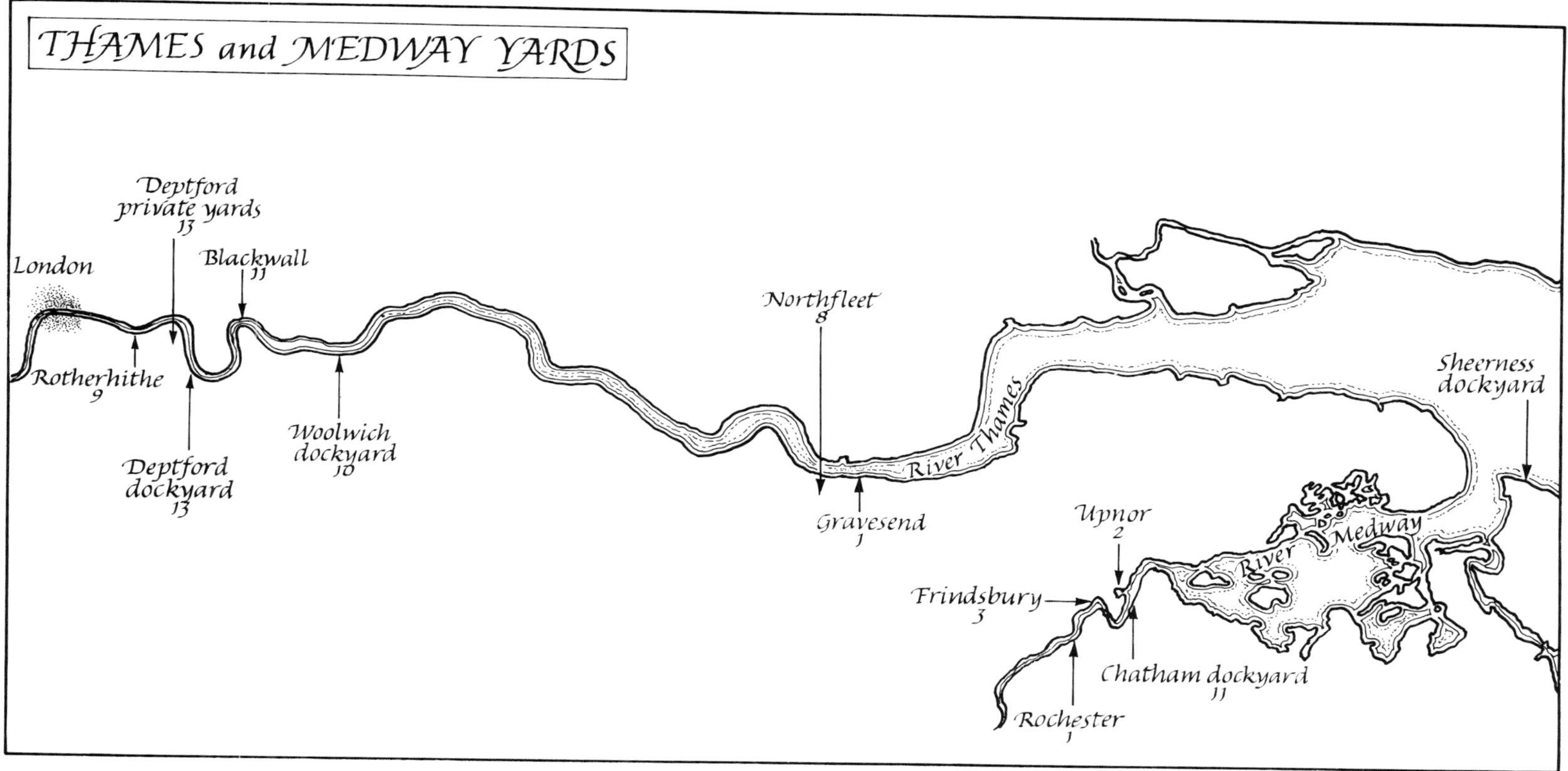

The major naval shipbuilding yards, giving the numbers of ships-of-the-line built in each, 1793-1815

and stern. This was largely controlled by the line of maximum breadth, which was drawn out in the horizontal plane. In the vertical plane, the height of the maximum breadth rose towards the bow and stern. The maximum breadth controlled the position of the breadth sweep. A similar line was drawn out for the toptimbers, in both vertical and horizontal plane.

The floor sweep for each individual frame was found by more complex geometrical means. By this time, the most common was the 'centre of floor sweeps' method. The guiding line was drawn on the sheer draught, though, by convention, it was placed tangential to the keel, not above the level of the maximum breadth where it ought to have been. A corresponding line was drawn in the horizontal plane, and, between them, these lines gave the positions of the centres of the floor sweeps for most of the length of the hull. The reconciling sweep had to be tangential to both the other sweeps. On most plans, the reconciling sweeps kept the same diameters along the length of the hull, but the breadth sweeps tended to reduce towards the bow and stern, while the floor sweep tended to increase. Towards the bow and stern the floor became purely theoretical; the sweeps were joined to the keel by means of reverse curves. This system gave little guidance on the shape of the bows and stern, and the draughtsman designed these according to his experience, and the intended role of the ship. In general, the bow was rounded and quite bluff, while the stern was much sharper, allowing the water a clear run to the rudder. The shipbuilder checked the fairness of his hull by drawing horizontal, vertical and diagonal lines in a fore and aft direction.

Deck plans were also produced, giving more detail of the deck beams, the position and sizes of the hatches and bulkheads, and such fittings as galley stoves and fixed cabins.

Shipbuilders

In peacetime, all ships were built in the Royal dockyards; most commentators believed that ships were much better when they were built under direct government control. In wartime, the dockyards continued to build the largest ships — the first and second rates. However, the space in the yards was largely needed for maintenance, and the great majority of ships of the third rate and below were built by private contractors. The administration was still fearful of building ships too far from where they could be supervised. A naval overseer, usually a dockyard foreman, was appointed to each ship under construction, but, away from dockyard control, there was a danger that he could be bribed to overlook bad workmanship or materials. Nearly all warships were built within a few hours' distance of major dockyards, in particular areas such as the Thames, the Medway, the Solent and Southampton Water, and Plymouth Sound. The largest private yard in the country was the Blackwall yard on the Thames, owned at this time by Perry, Wells and Green. It was capable of building several ships-of-the-line side by side.

The fixed capital required by a private shipbuilder was very small. His main requirement was a suitable site on the bank of a river which was wide and deep enough to allow the ship to be launched, and enough money to buy the timber and pay his workers while construction proceeded. The Navy Board allocated contracts for ships by competitive tender, and the lowest bidders were usually accepted; however, there was a screening process, and yards with a bad record would not be invited to tender. The builder was paid in instalments, beginning at the signing of the contract, continuing as various stages of construction were reached, and ending with the launch.

The actual work of building the ship was carried out by skilled shipwrights. The rules of apprenticeship were quite strict, and neither workers nor employers had any wish to introduce unqualified labour on the actual building of the ship, though labourers might be employed to carry timber and perform other menial tasks. The number of shipwrights needed on a ship was actually quite small — in 1804, Adams yard at Buckler's Hard employed only thirty-five, though there were two 74s being built there — but the demand for ships increased, while the supply of shipwrights was constant, so wages in the merchant yards tended to soar during the war years.

The Supply of Timber

The problem of timber supply was one that had dogged British naval administrators for more than a century. Traditionally, British ships had been built of oak, and shipbuilders were reluctant to move away from this. Many frigates and sloops were built of pine, but these were poorly received by naval officers, and did not last long. After 1801, it became increasingly common to build ships in India, using native supplies of teak. These ships were much more successful, and lasted for many years.

A timber wagon hauling a large piece to the nearest water transport. From Pyne's *Microcosm*

But oak remained the main material for shipbuilding. The most important pieces were the curved knees which supported the decks, and the curved futtocks which made up the frame timbers. The grain of the tree had to be suitable for this, and 'compass' timber, as it was called, could fetch very high prices. It might take a hundred years to grow timber suitable for an ordinary ship-of-the-line, and yet more for a first rate. This was the main reason why large ships were disproportionately expensive.

Shipbuilders preferred to use native oak if possible, and for more than a century landowners had been urged to plant trees. However, transport was always a problem, unless by water; timber more than about three miles from the sea or a navigable river declined rapidly in value. Native timber was never sufficient, and large supplies were procured abroad, particularly in northern Europe. This was one of the main reasons why the navy went to great lengths to keep the Baltic open in the 1800s.

The Frame

The first step in building a ship was to cut out the keel, and lay it in position on the building slip. On a ship of any size, the keel was made in several pieces fixed together by means of complex overlapping joins called scarphs. The keel was square in cross-section. Below it was the false keel, rather thinner and intended to protect the main keel from damage. Towards the bow and stern, the deadwood was placed above the keel. This served to hold the timbers at the sharper parts of the hull. The sternpost was a straight piece of timber, backed by the false sternpost and reinforced by an internal knee. The structure of the stempost at the bows was more complex, because of its curved shape. Ahead of the stempost was the knee of the head, which supported the decorations of the ship's head. This, like the stempost, was made up of several pieces scarphed together.

Meanwhile, the frame timbers were cut out. It was not possible to cut a whole frame from a single timber, so each was made up of several pieces. Usually two complete frames were placed side by side, and bolted together. The different sections were arranged so that the joins in one frame were not in the same place as those in the adjacent frame. The first pieces were the floor timbers, which fitted across the keel. The rest of the pair of frames were joined together and then fitted as one piece. They consisted of several curved pieces known as futtocks (up to four on each side according to the size of the ship) and the toptimbers. The first futtocks of each side would meet across the top of the keel; this frame also had the third futtocks and the toptimbers, while the adjacent one had the second and fourth futtocks. Towards the bow and stern, where the timbers rose much more steeply, the floor timbers were replaced by half timbers, which butted into the deadwood instead of going across the keel. After the timbers were in place, the kelson was placed over the floor timbers, directly above the keel, to help lock the system together. The frames which ran all the way from the keel to the top of the side, without interruption from gunports, were known as full frames and were fitted first. The port cills were pieces of horizontal timber fitted between them, to form the lower and upper edges of the ports. The remaining frames, known as filling frames, were placed in position above and below the cills. When completed the structure was quite solid, with about two thirds of the space under the planking being filled with frames.

Towards the foremost part of the ship, the ordinary frames, fitted at right angles to the keel, were replaced with cant timbers. These were fitted at increasing angles to the line of ordinary timbers, so that they followed the round shape of the bows. At the extreme foremost part were the hawse pieces, which were parallel to the line

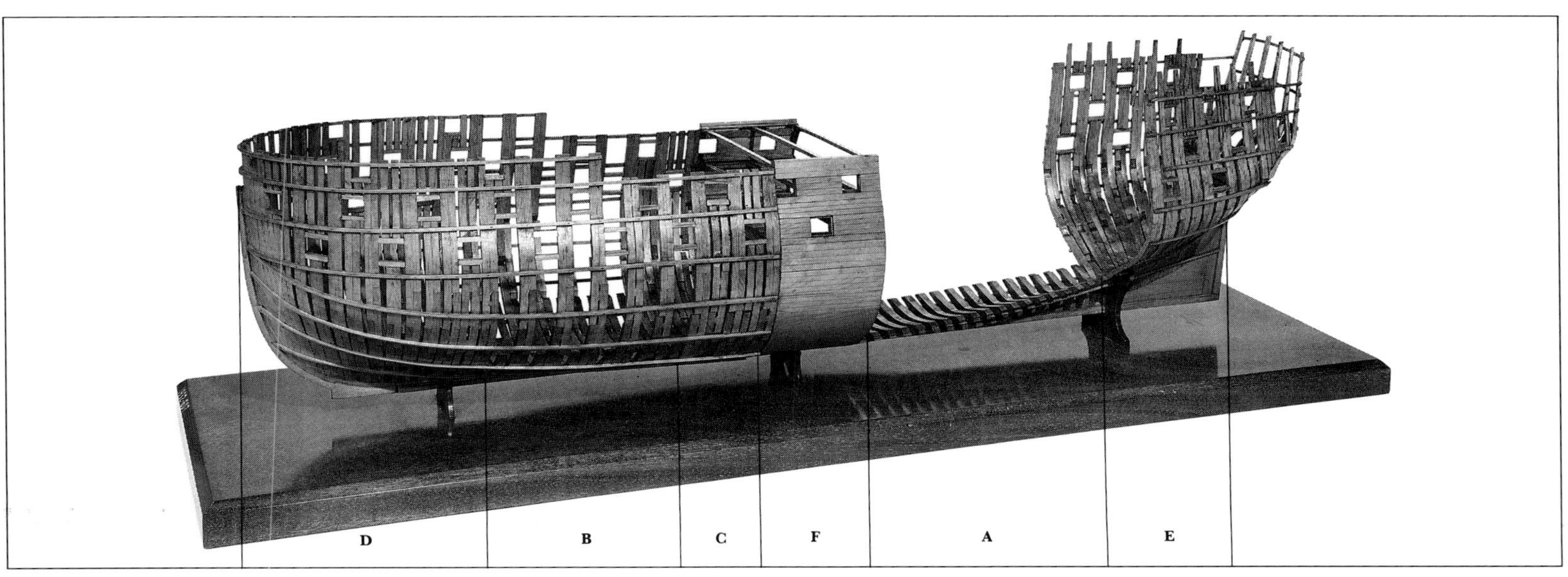

A model showing the stages of framing a 74-gun ship.
A. *The floor timbers crossed.*
B. *The full frames raised, and the port cills fitted.*
C. *The filling frames fitted.*
D. *The structure of the bow, showing cant frames and hawse pieces. This shows the round bow, as used after 1804. Before that, the structure of the foremost part would have ended one deck lower, and a beakhead bulkhead would have been fitted.*
E. *The stern, which also uses cant frames. The weakness of the after face of the stern can be seen; this was remedied by Seppings's round stern of 1817.* The Science Museum

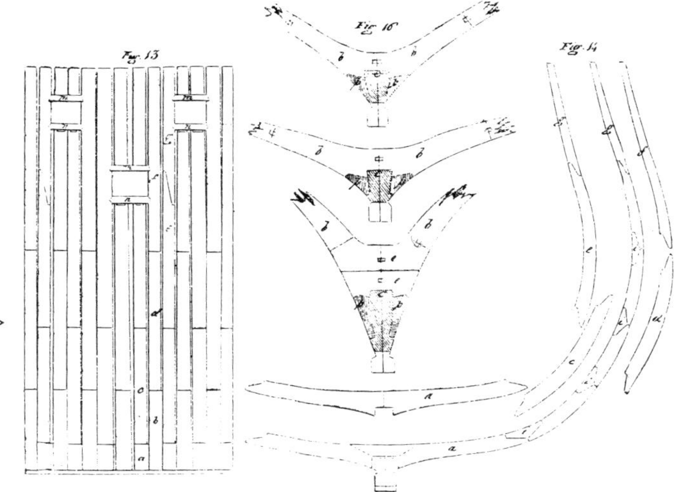

The structure of the frame. Fig 14 shows how the parts of a pair of frames fit together, and Fig 13 shows a profile of the completed assembly. Fig 16 shows various ways of fitting half timbers near the bow and stern. From Fincham's *Outline of Shipbuilding*, 1821 ▷

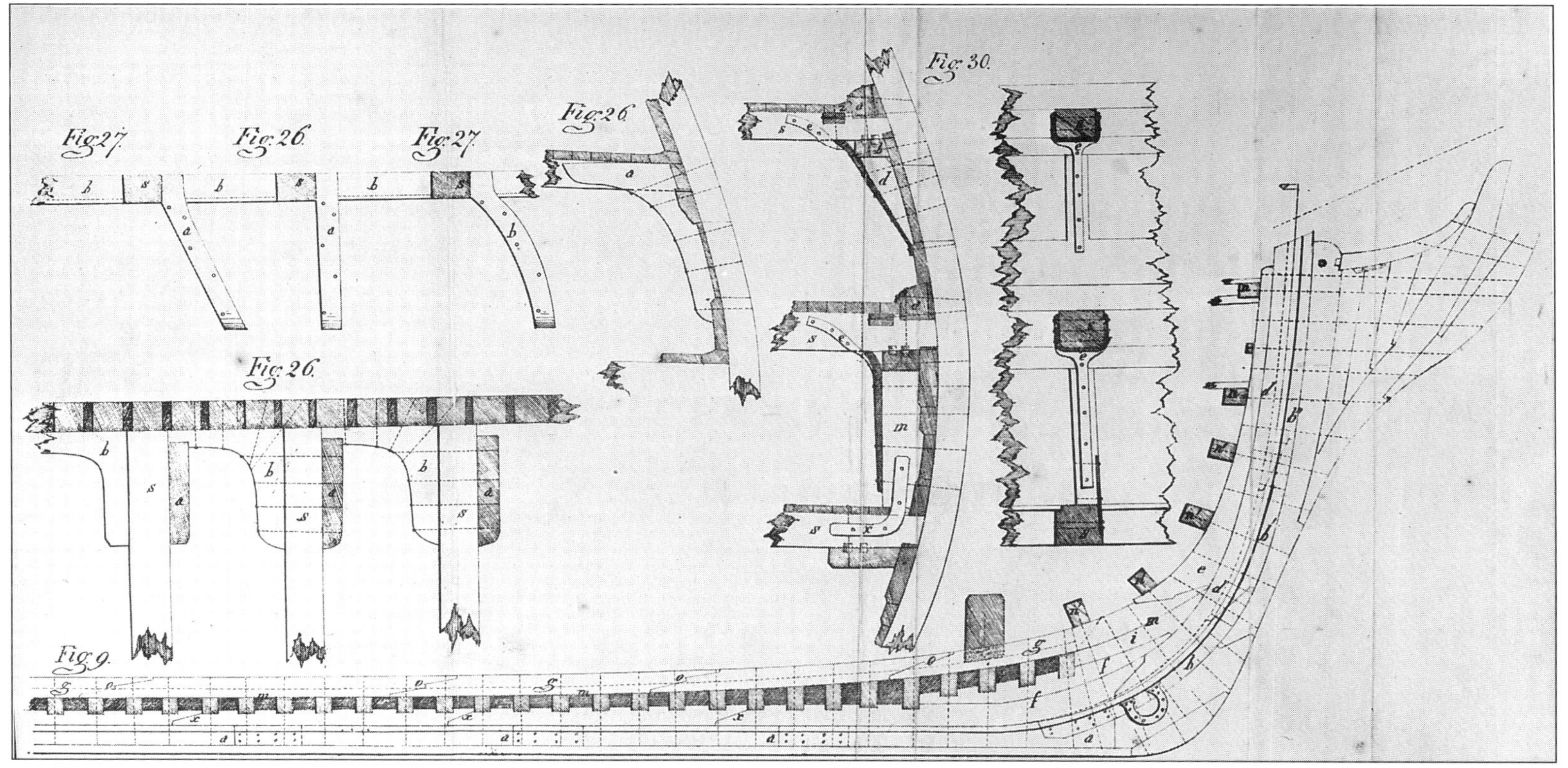

The structure of the keel and stem. From Fincham's *Outline of Shipbuilding*, 1821

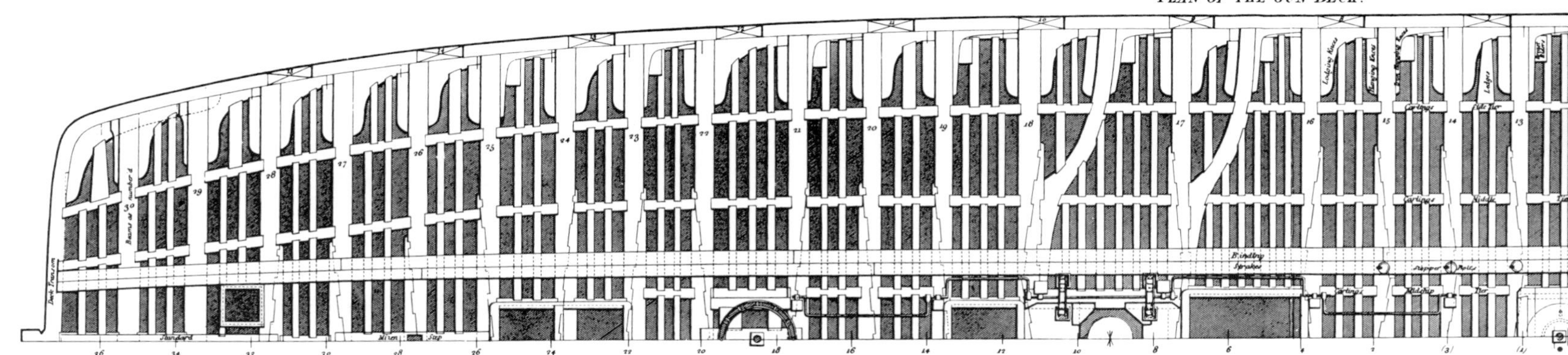

The deck plan of a 74-gun ship, showing the structure of beams, carlines, ledges and lodging knees. From Rees's *Naval Architecture*, 1819

of the keel, and fitted to the foremost cant timber. The hawse pieces were drilled with holes for the anchor cables. Cant frames were also fitted near the stern, and the last ones were called the fashion pieces. The aftermost part of the hull, above and below the level of the waterline, was made up of transoms — timbers fitted horizontally across the sternpost and shaped to give the form of the hull. Below the lowest transom, were small vertical timbers called filling pieces. Above the uppermost transom, known as the wing transom, was the structure of the stern, including counters and quarter galleries. This was much lighter than the rest of the hull, and was the weakest part of the ship.

The timbers of the hull were held together by metal bolts or wooden treenails. Underwater, iron could not be used because of interaction with the ship's copper plating, so a copper alloy was used. Above the waterline, iron bolts were employed. Treenails were used mostly for the planking rather than the frame.

Decks

The deck beams were stout pieces of timber, curved according to the camber of the deck and strong enough to support the guns. They were fitted quite early in the building of the ship, in order to keep the frames the correct distance apart. On larger ships, each deck beam was made up of two or three pieces scarphed together. The beams ran athwartships, while lighter pieces known as carlines ran fore and aft joining the beams together. Yet lighter pieces known as ledges ran between the carlines, parallel to the beams. At its ends, each beam was supported by vertical hanging knees, and lodging knees which were in the same plane as the deck. As well as strengthening the deck, these important timbers helped to brace the ship against all the stresses of its life. The deck was covered with 2in plank, usually in strakes 12in wide. The normal deck planking ran fore and aft in parallel strakes, but round the edges were the waterways. These followed the shape of the hull, and were slightly thicker than the rest of the deck planks, helping to keep deck water away from the sides of the hull. The edges of the hatches and gratings were trimmed with coamings, which prevented water on the deck from falling down.

Planking

Externally, thicker planking known as wales was placed under each row of gunports to give extra strength. Sometimes, the wales were constructed by a complex pattern known as 'anchor stock' or 'hook and butt' construction, but this was expensive, and ordinary straight planks were often used. The row, or strake, of planking just above and below each wale was slightly thicker than normal. The rest of the planking, including that of the bottom, was 2in to 4in thick according to the size of the ship. The shape of the underwater planking was the most complex, and some planks, known as stealers, did not run the full length of the ship but stopped short of the bows. At the stern, the ends of the bottom planks came to the counter, which ran almost horizontally under the stern galleries.

Ships were also planked internally. In the hold, thicker planking known as sleepers covered the joins in the futtocks, while the planking in the hold was known collectively as the ceiling. There was an even thicker strake of planking under each deck, called clamp; this did much to support the weight of the deck. The rest of the internal planking was known as spirketting. Inside the planking, riders and standards were placed across the keel and up the sides of the ship to give extra strength.

The planking of the ship was held in place by a combination of metal bolts and wooden treenails. The latter were wooden pegs, placed in holes drilled through the timber and the plank, and held in place by wedges inserted in their ends. Metal bolts were used at the ends of each plank, and treenails at each frame along the intermediate length.

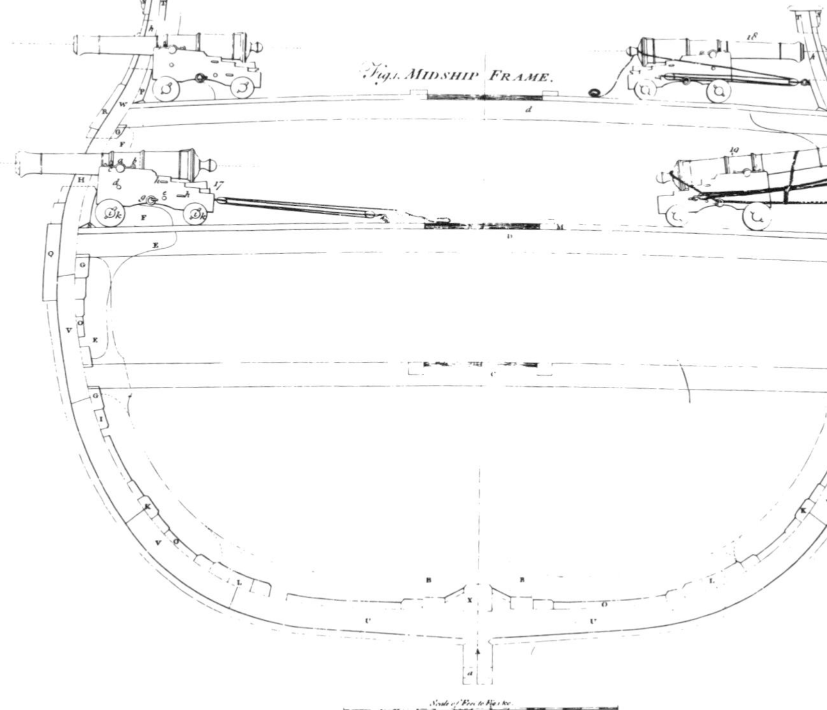

The midship section of a 74-gun ship. Though it comes from Falconer's Dictionary of 1769, little had changed in practice by the 1800s. E is a hanging knee of the lower deck, and F is a standard. Q is the main wale, with the planking of the bottom below. R is the channel wale. The print also shows the guns in various positions – no 18, run in for loading; with the train tackle in use.

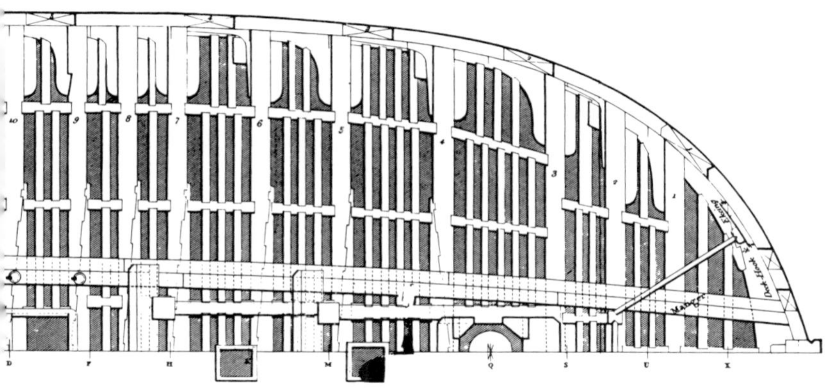

Figureheads, old and new style – for the Arrogant *of 1761 (still in service until 1801) and for the* Victorious *of 1808.* Based on drawings in The National Maritime Museum and the Public Record Office

Decoration

Carved decoration on ships had been progressively reduced since its heyday at the beginning of the century, but before the outbreak of the Revolutionary War it was still quite prolific, especially on the stern. All rated ships had stern galleries; either open, with external balconies, or closed, with a row of windows. In general each ship had the same number of galleries as decks — three on a three-decker, two on a two-decker, and one on a frigate. All the galleries after the first were open, which meant that a frigate had only a single closed gallery, while a three-decker had two open and one closed. In ships-of-the-line especially, the sides and taffrail of the stern were heavily decorated with carved figures and objects, and gilded or painted decoration. Frigates were less decorated, but still had some full and bas-relief carvings. At the bows, all ships of any size had a full-length figurehead, supported by a structure known as 'the head' which consisted of elaborate carved rails. Other features such as catheads were also decorated with carvings.

The stern decoration of the Boyne *of 1790, showing the old style of elaborate carving.* The Science Museum

Most of this came to an end in 1795, when the Admiralty decided to cut costs and 'explode carved works'. Open galleries were no longer fitted to new ships, or those under extensive repair (though a different type of gallery was allowed on two- and three-deckers after 1806). The fully-carved figures were replaced by simple bas-relief, and the figurehead became much shorter, showing only the head and shoulders of a man or woman, or perhaps a more abstract design known as a scroll head. Open galleries were restored in a slightly different form in the 1800s, but decoration remained much more moderate in the nineteenth century.

Painting

By the 1790s, it was normal to paint the sides of ships. The colour most used was the yellow ochre paint supplied by the dockyards, but the choice was left mainly to the captain, and red sides became quite fashionable — as with the *Zealous* and *Minotaur* at the Battle of the Nile.[2] The areas at the top and bottom of the hull were often painted black, following the run of the wales. Some two-deckers also had the upper wale painted black. This style was adapted by Nelson in time for the Battle of Trafalgar, with some changes — the black paint followed the lines of the decks rather than the wales, so that it was parallel to the lines of gunports; and the gunports themselves were also painted black, to give the classic 'Nelson chequer'. After the battle, the style marked out those ships which had taken part, known as 'Nelson's chequer players' among the fleet. The captain of the *Revenge* who tried to impose his own style on the ship, and substitute a single stripe, became very unpopular with his crew.[3] Nelson chequer became very common after 1805, and was the nearest thing to a standard system.

The names of the ships were painted on the counter of the stern. Figureheads seem to have been left white by the dockyard, but painted on the initiative of the captain. Around 1793, a list of twelve ships shows seven with white figureheads, four with coloured ones, and one, the *Edgar*, with a white one, the details of which were picked out in red and black.[4]

Launching

The time taken to build a ship varied according to its size; a sloop could be built in six months, a two-decker took two and a half years on average, while a first rate might spend ten years on the stocks. After the completion of the hull, the ship was launched into the water. The ship was built on a slip with its stern towards the water, and with its bows slightly higher than its stern. When the hull was completed, a pair of wooden rails were built under it, and the hull was supported by a launching cradle, which ran on the rails. The shipbuilder usually waited for a high spring tide for launching, and informed the Admiralty of his intention. Permission having been granted, notables were invited and a crowd gathered on the appointed day. At the right moment, the props supporting the stern were knocked away, and the ship slid into the water. Heavy ropes prevented it from moving too far, though accidents were not unknown. The shipbuilder informed the Admiralty of the success (or otherwise) of the operation, and claimed the final instalment of his payment. The ship was an empty shell, without guns, masts, fittings or stores; it now belonged to the navy, and arrangements were made to tow it to the nearest dockyard, where it could be fitted out.

The Seppings System

Even before his appointment as junior surveyor of the navy in 1813, Sir Robert Seppings had already carried out very important reforms in ship construction. The most radical of these was his system of diagonal bracing, first tried on the old 74-gun ship *Tremendous* in 1811. Seppings got rid of the internal planking and thwartships riders of conventional design. He filled in the spaces between the frames in the hold, to reduce movement, and fitted diagonal internal frames which crossed one another to provide much greater rigidity. The decks and spirketting were also planked diagonally, and the result was that the whole structure became much more rigid. Hogging, which had so far prevented the building of really large ships, was largely eliminated, and this opened the way for future developments. Seppings also used more and smaller futtocks for his frames, saving a considerable amount of timber. His new system had become standard by 1815, though only a few ships had actually been fitted with it by then.

Seppings also attempted to tackle the weak areas of the bow and stern. He extended the timbers of the fore part of the ship right up to the forecastle, getting rid of the weak beakhead bulkhead and creating the round bow (though such bows had been used on frigates for decades before they were introduced to ships-of-the-line). His radical new design for the aftermost part of the ship, the circular stern, did not come into use until after the war, but he altered the old structure of transoms under the counter, and replaced them with vertical timbers.

Seppings's reforms, though stimulated by the wars, did not have their full effect until after them. They allowed the building of much larger ships, so that 120- and 80-gun ships became standard, and the 90-gun two-decker was made possible.

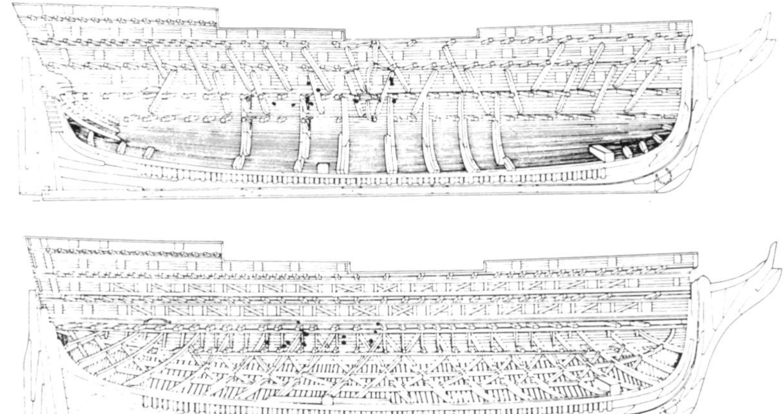

The old method of internal riders (above), compared with the Seppings method of diagonal riders.

A 40-gun frigate ready for launching. From Steel's *Shipwright's Vade Mecum* of 1805

2 Fitting of Ships

Steering

The ship's rudder of this period was fitted to the sternpost by means of hinges, consisting of gudgeons, attached to the sternpost, and pintles which were attached to the rudder. The rudder was quite long, and had the same breadth as the sternpost. In its fore and aft depth, it tapered towards its head, so that it was almost square in cross-section in its uppermost part. Two square holes were cut in the head, one for the main tiller, and another directly above that for a spare tiller. The head of the rudder passed through a hole in the counter, so that it was inside the hull, and protected from the sea and enemy action. The hole, known as the helm port transom, was often covered with leather to prevent leakage.

In frigates and ships-of-the-line, the tiller was fitted just under the level of the upper deck (or middle deck in three-deckers) but the head of the rudder protruded through the upper deck so that the spare one could be fitted at that level if necessary. On some classes of sloops and smaller vessels, the tiller was exposed on the upper deck. The tiller on most ships stopped just short of the mizzenmast, and its inboard end was supported by a sweep or quadrant, a curved piece of timber. The sweep was placed above the tiller, bolted to the beams of the upper deck; a small piece of timber known as a goose neck held it to the sweep.

The tiller rope ran round the sweep, guided by small wooden rollers. This allowed the ropes to be kept taut, as otherwise the geometry of the system would have demanded some slack. The ropes tended to stretch, and were tightened as needed by means of blocks and tackle running along the length of the tiller. The ropes ran up through holes in the decks and up to the wheel, which was situated on the quarterdeck. The mid part of the tiller rope was nailed to the barrel of the wheel, and several turns — traditionally seven — were taken round the barrel. The wheel was of the traditional ship's pattern, with spokes. In large ships it was double, with one wheel at each end of the barrel. On frigates and smaller ships there was no poop, so the wheel was placed in a very exposed position on the quarterdeck. The smallest ships, such as brigs and cutters, often had no wheel but steered with the tiller.

Some kind of helm indicator was usually fitted, to give the

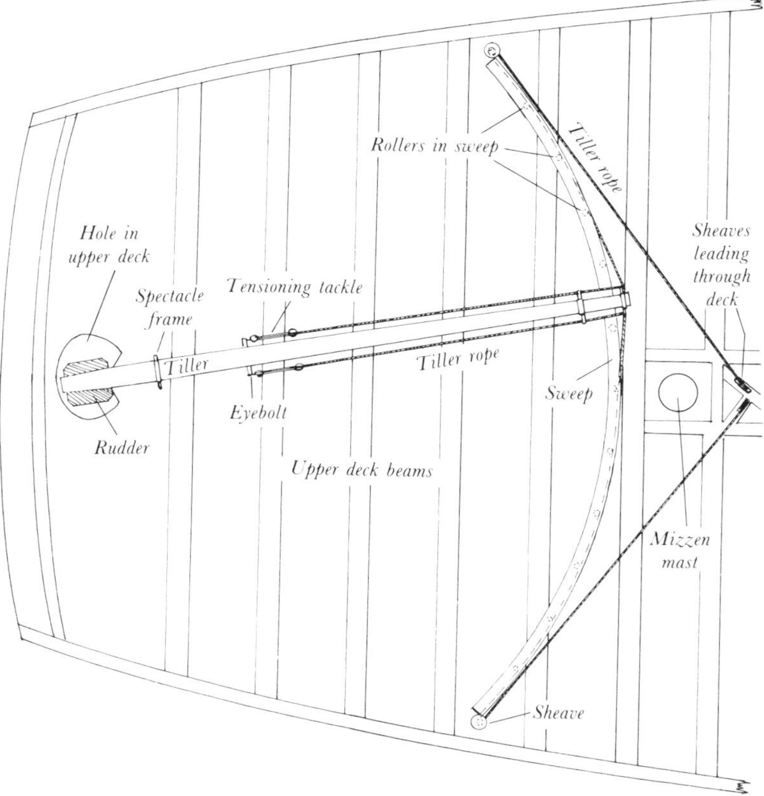

The fitting of the sweep, tiller ropes, etc, under the upper deck.

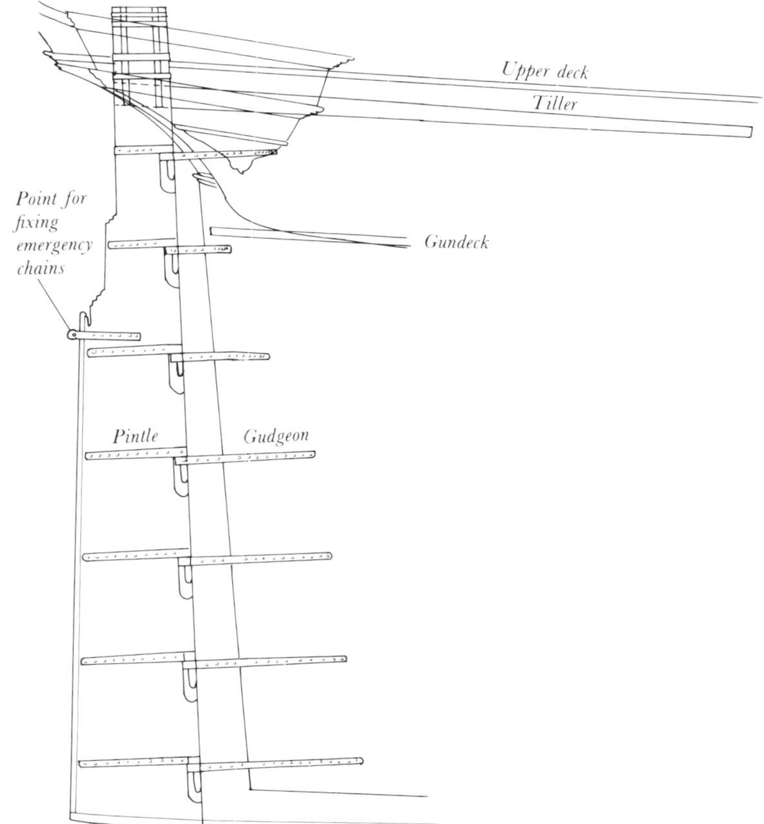

The fitting of a rudder to a ship-of-the-line. This shows the older type, where the fore and aft depth is reduced by means of a series of steps. In the later type, the shape was more rounded. Based on a drawing in the National Maritime Museum

The steering wheel and binnacle of HMS Victory. Author's photograph

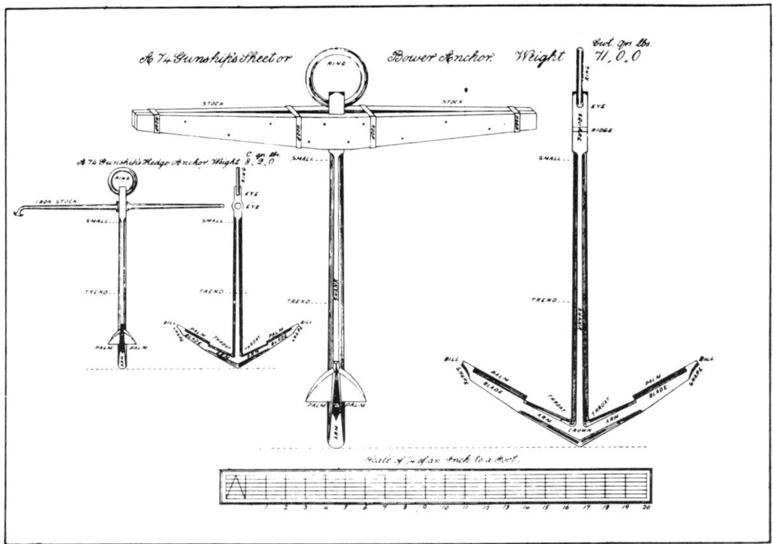

The anchors of a 74-gun ship. The National Maritime Museum

quartermaster or officer of the watch information about the direction in which the rudder was turned. On two-deckers this was placed along the foremost beam of the poop; in frigates, it took the form of a dial in front of the stanchion which supported the wheel. A wooden binnacle, containing two compasses and a light, was placed in front of the wheel.

Anchors

The anchor used by ships of 1800 was virtually identical to that in use for centuries. It had a wooden stock, attached to an iron piece consisting of shank, arms and flukes, one of which would bury itself in the sea bottom when the anchor was in use. In the standard British anchor, the two arms met at an angle, but the 'round crown' anchor was used by most foreign ships. The iron parts were made up of strips of metal welded together, either in the dockyards or by private contractors. At the end of the shank was an iron ring, which was covered with rope known as 'puddening' when in service.

Most ships of the sixth rate and above carried four large anchors, of similar size and weight. Two were kept permanently at the bows, and were known as the bower anchors. The other two were lashed against the channels of the foremast and known as the spare and the sheet anchors. The main anchors of a 74-gun ship weighed about 70cwt each in 1809; those of a 38, 44cwt, and of a 24, 29½cwt. Smaller ships had only three main anchors — those of a small sloop weighed 20cwt each.

Lighter anchors were also carried by all ships. Each ship had one stream anchor, about a quarter of the weight of the bowers, and used to hold the ship in certain conditions. A kedge anchor was about half the weight of the stream anchor. One was carried by each ship, and it was designed to be slung under a boat and rowed out ahead of the ship, to tow it in a calm or to get it out of difficulties in unfavourable winds. Three deckers had an extra kedge, half the weight of the ordinary kedge.

A typical ship had eight cables, made of very thick rope. A 74 had seven ordinary cables, 21in in circumference, and one stream cable, of 12½in. All cables were 120 fathoms long, and several could be joined together for use in very deep water. Towards the end of the war, chain cables were in use experimentally.

The capstan carried by the Neptune in 1796. The National Maritime Museum

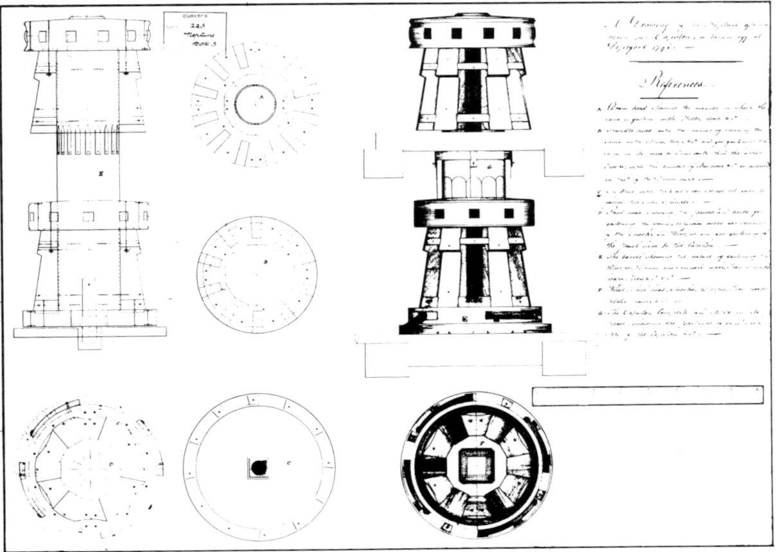

Capstans

All naval vessels except the very smallest used capstans to raise the anchors, and to carry out other heavy work, such as lifting guns and yards. Capstans could be either single or double; in the latter case, they operated over two decks, with barrels and bars at each level. Capstans normally held twelve bars, which could be removed when it was not in use. Round the barrel were placed whelps, intended to create friction with the cables, to increase the diameter of the system, and shaped to prevent the cable from riding up too far. Levers known as pauls were fitted to prevent the cables from surging back if there was a sudden pull on the ship.

Two- and three-deckers had two double capstans; the jeer capstan was in the waist, and the main capstan was under the quarterdeck. Both capstans were identical, so they could be interchanged if one was damaged. On three-deckers, the capstans were at the level of the lower and middle deck, so that they were covered by the upper deck; on two-deckers they were at the level of the lower and upper decks. A frigate had one double capstan, placed between the quarterdeck and the upper deck; smaller vessels often had only one single capstan, between the mizzenmast and the mainmast.

Pumps

Wooden ships always leaked, especially when racked by the sea or damaged in battle. The decks were cambered, and lead scuppers were placed to allow water on the decks to drain through the sides. The water in the hold, known as bilge water, was allowed to drain towards the area of the foot of the mainmast, the lowest part of the ship. There, the pumps were fitted, within a light rectangular structure known as the well. The principal pumps were chain pumps, based on a design of 1768 by Coles and Bentinck. The heads of these pumps were on the lower deck of a ship-of-the-line, or the upper deck of a frigate, as these were the lowest decks which were substantially above the waterline. The chain which gave the pump its name was fitted with saucers at suitable intervals; these were taken through tubes, one leading down into the well, and the other back up again. The chain was taken round a large wheel on the lower or upper deck, and a smaller one low down in the well. As the wheel turned, the water was drawn into the up-going tube, and carried to the deck, where it entered a cistern built round the pump. This drained through tubes known as dales, to the side of the ship. After that, the water was allowed to escape through the scuppers. The wheel was turned by means of handles, which could be extended for some distance so that quite a large number of men could operate the

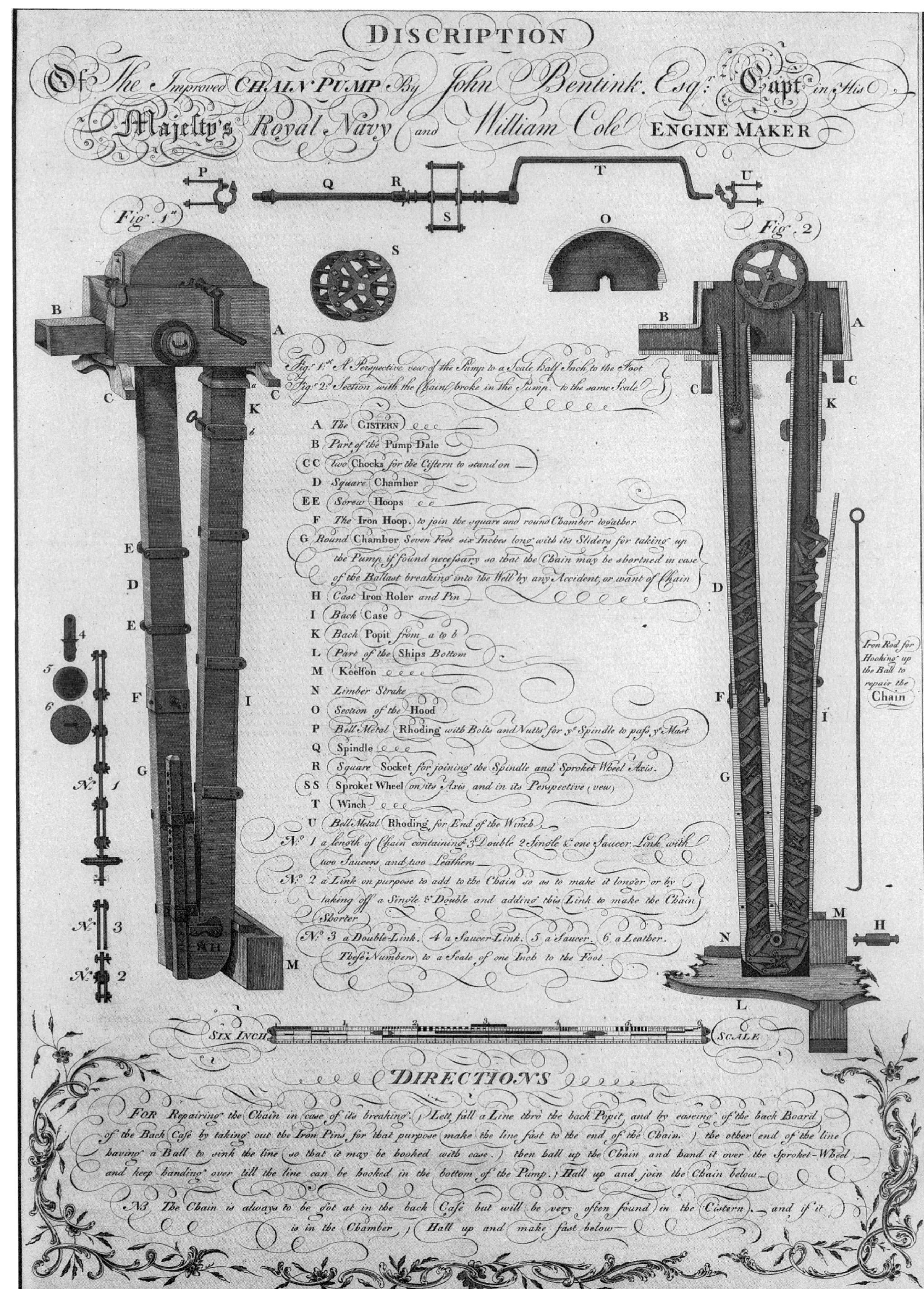

The construction of the Coles-Bentinck chain pump – the standard type since the 1760s. This print was supplied to the carpenters of ships to aid them with maintenance. The National Maritime Museum pumps at once — up to thirty on three-deckers. Ships-of-the-line had four pumps each, arranged round the mainmast. Frigates and sloops had two each, just forward of the mast.

The smallest vessels, such as schooners and gunboats, had no chain pumps, but used suction pumps instead. These were operated by a simple lever, known as a brake. Larger ships also used some suction pumps, to deliver water under pressure for fire fighting, and for washing the decks. On ships-of-the-line these sometimes operated above the level of the lower deck, so that water could be carried higher if necessary. Such ships also had small pipes just under the waterline, to allow the entry of water for such purposes.

Boats

In ships which relied almost entirely on the wind for propulsion, boats were needed for many reasons — for carrying men ashore, for moving the ship by means of anchors or cables, for communications between ships, and for bringing water and stores aboard. Several types were needed, and a ship-of-the-line had six boats. The longboat was virtually obsolete by this time, so the largest boat was the launch, less seaworthy than the longboat but better adapted for carrying heavy weights. A barge was narrower and often longer than launch; it was intended mainly for rowing, and especially for carrying captains and admirals. A pinnace was slightly smaller than a barge, and had fewer oars; it was used by the lieutenants and warrant officers. Cutters were good sea boats, clinker built, and with relatively fine lines; and the jolly boat was basically a small cutter, 18ft long.

A ship-of-the-line had a barge, 32ft long; a launch, from 30 to 34ft, according to the size of the ship; a 28ft pinnace; two 25ft cutters, and a jollyboat. A frigate had a barge, from 28 to 32ft; a launch, from 21 to 16ft; one or two cutters according to the size of the ship, and a jolly boat. Smaller ships had two or three boats; a longboat, pinnace and jollyboat in the case of a large sloop, and a cutter and jollyboat on a small brig. Captains often added other types of boat, according to personal preference or local availability. Gigs, wherries, galleys and other types were often used in service. Special landing craft, wide and shallow draughted, were provided for amphibious operations.

The larger boats were stowed in the waist, on booms fitted athwartships between the two gangways. To get a boat in the water from such a position required considerable time, and the use of a complicated tackle. Cutters were stowed under the quarter davits on each side of the stern, where they could be released quickly in an emergency. The jolly boat was often hung from the stern davits, which protruded directly aft of the ship, above the stern galleries.

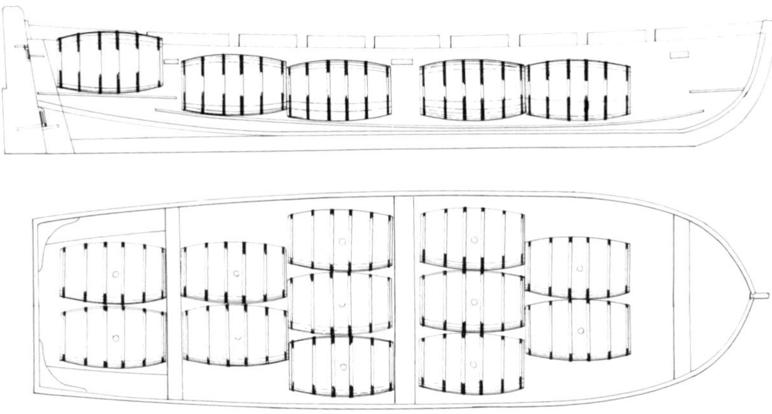

A third rate's launch of 1804, designed to carry twelve butts of water.

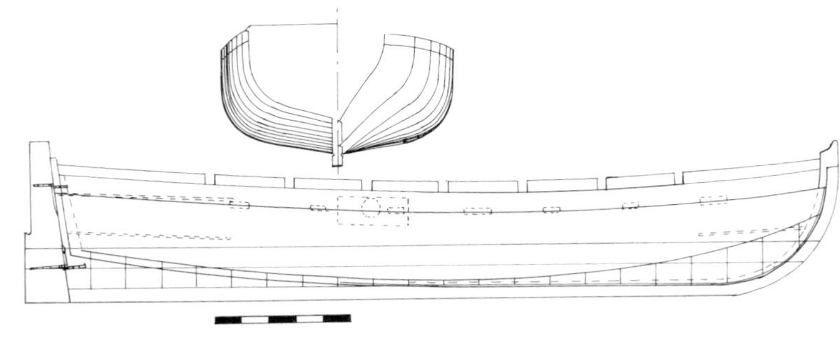

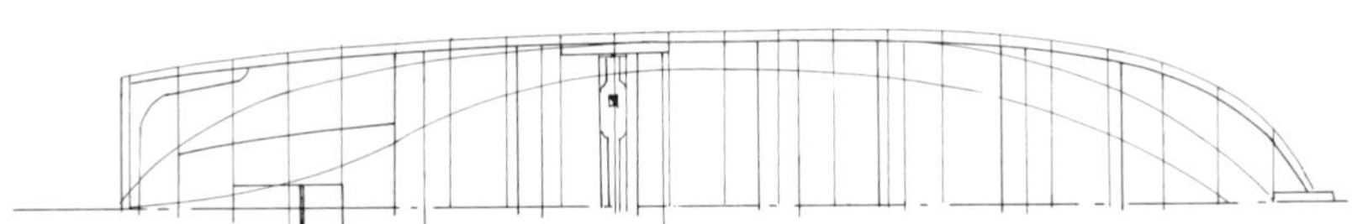

A 29ft launch, as used for 50-gun ships.

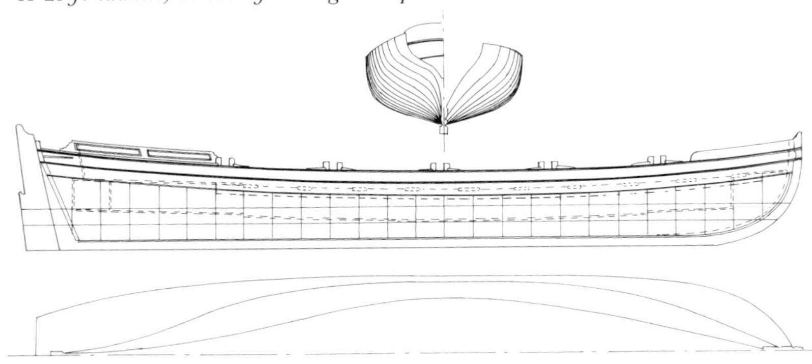

A pinnace of 1798, 32ft long, as used by all ships of 36 guns or more in 1805.

Coppering

Since the American War it had been normal policy to cover the bottoms of all naval ships with copper. This solved two perennial problems — it helped prevent weed growing on ships' bottoms, which slowed them down by creating extra friction; and it prevented ship-worm from getting among the timbers and eating its way through them. The thickness of the copper sheet varied according to the place in the ship; the thickest pieces were placed near the bows. The standard size of plate was 4ft by 14in, and the copper was laid in strakes, roughly following the line of the planking. The plates were held on by small nails, also made of copper alloy to prevent electrolysis. Copper was expensive, but it was very successful; among other advantages, it made it possible for ships to operate much longer away from dockyards and bases.

Hold Stowage

The hold of a ship was divided into several compartments, by means of bulkheads. In the stern was the bread room, raised above the level of the other storage areas to prevent bilge water reaching the bread. The fish room was partitioned off aft, to keep the smell away from other commodities. The spirit room was nearby, and it was separated for security reasons. Magazines were also partitioned off, because of the danger of fire and explosion. The pump well was right in the middle of the ship, kept apart from the rest of the hold to allow access to the pumps for maintenance. The remainder of the lower part of the ship was the main hold, used for general provisions such as beer, water, meat and cheese. The main hold took up about half the length of the ship, and a considerably greater proportion of the capacity, as the hull was fullest in that area.

The best sailing trim of the ship was achieved by distributing goods and ballast in the hold, and therefore the stowage of the hold was the responsibility of the master, though the goods themselves came

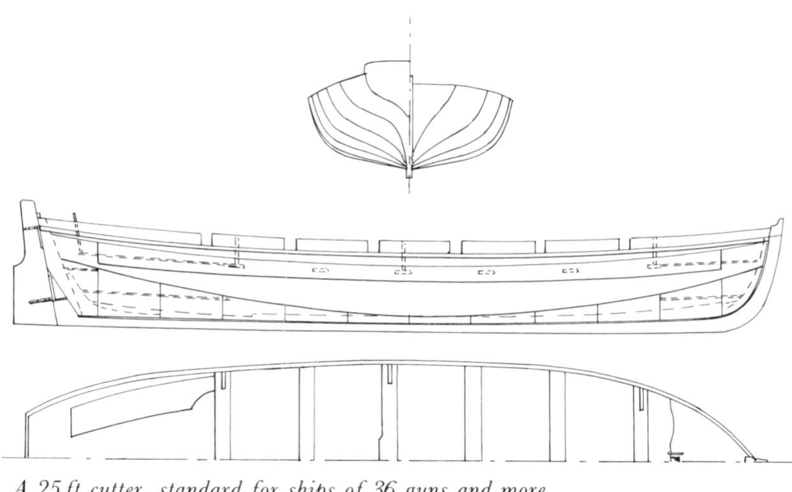

A 25 ft cutter, standard for ships of 36 guns and more.

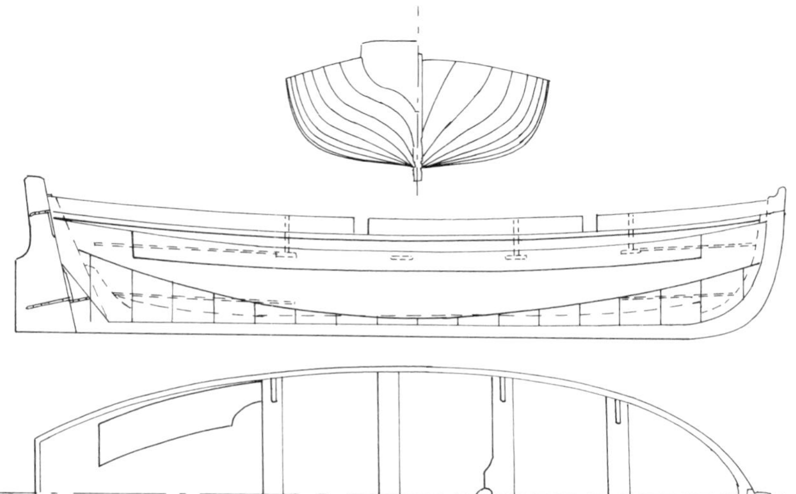

An 18 ft cutter or jollyboat, used by almost every kind of ship.

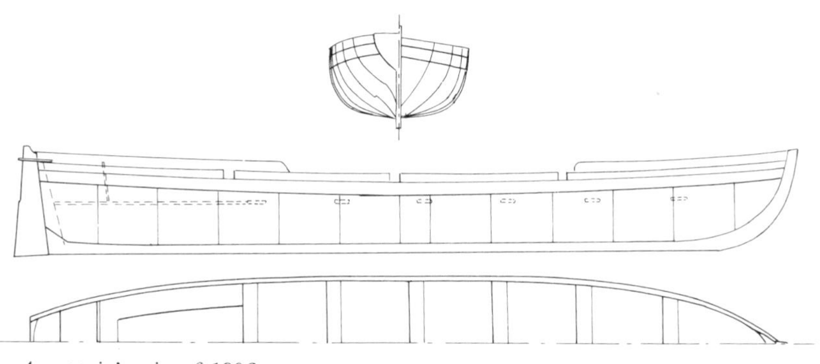

A captain's gig of 1806.
All from drawings in the National Maritime Museum

under the control of the purser. Most ships were trimmed by the stern, so that they were somewhat deeper in the water aft than forward. The total weight on the ship was important, as it could affect the height of the guns above the water; and the proportion of that weight in the lowest part of the ship could affect the position of her centre of gravity. All this had to be considered when stowing the hold.

At the very lowest level were iron pigs to serve as ballast. A 100-gun ship had 180 tons of this; a 38 had 70 tons. Above the iron was shingle ballast. This helped lower the centre of gravity, but it also formed a flat surface on which the provisions could rest. Most ship's supplies, with the exception of bread which was kept in bags, were contained in wooden casks. Water was the heaviest, and so it was placed on the lowest level, known as the 'ground tier'. Most ships had two more layers of casks, the second and third tiers. In large ships, the water was stored in large casks known as 'leaguers'; smaller casks — butts, hogsheads and barrels — made up the upper tiers. Yet smaller casks, such as half hogsheads, and rundletts, filled the awkward spaces near the sides. Wedges were driven between the casks as necessary, to prevent them from shifting.

The hold stowage of the frigate Artois *in 1794.* Public Record Office

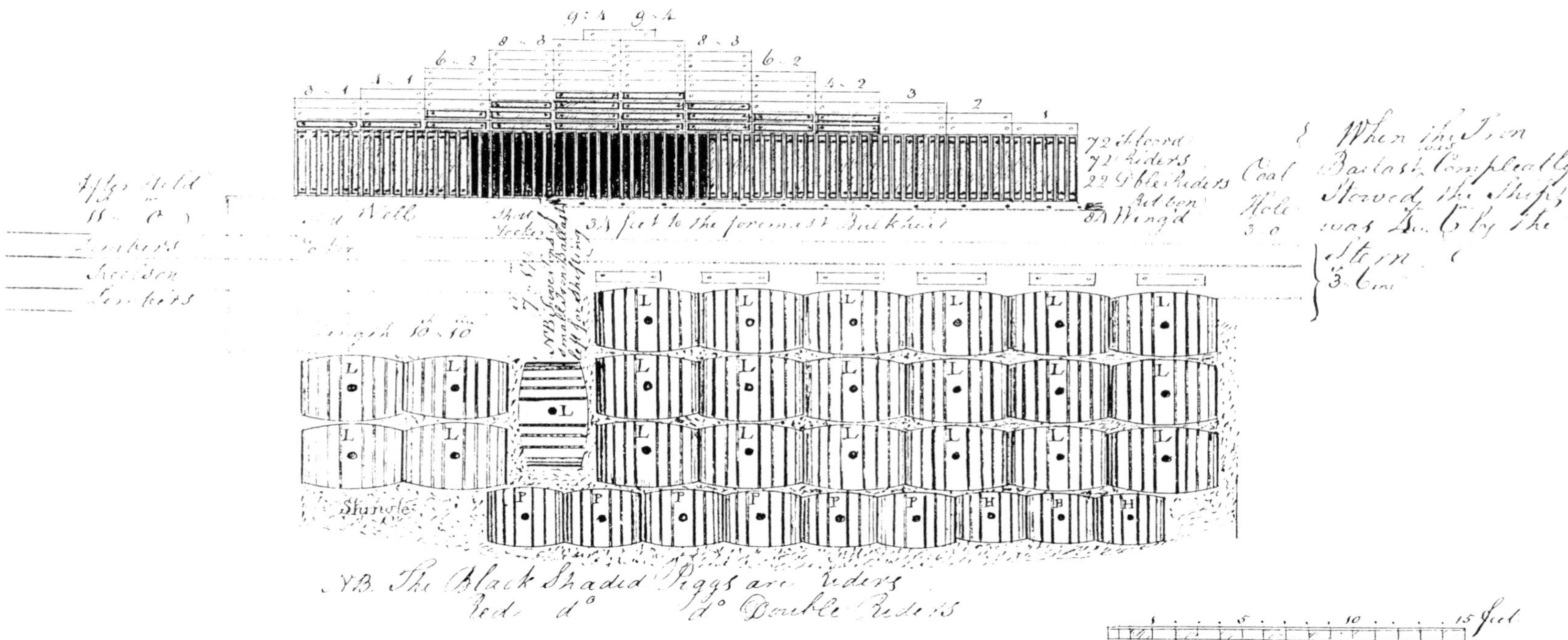

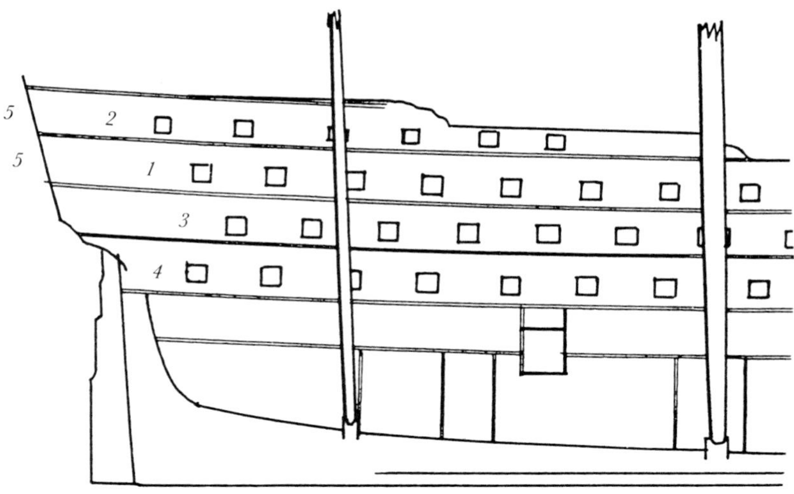

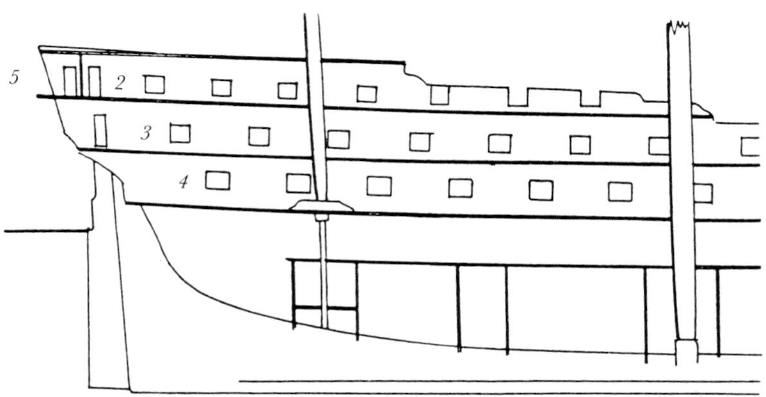

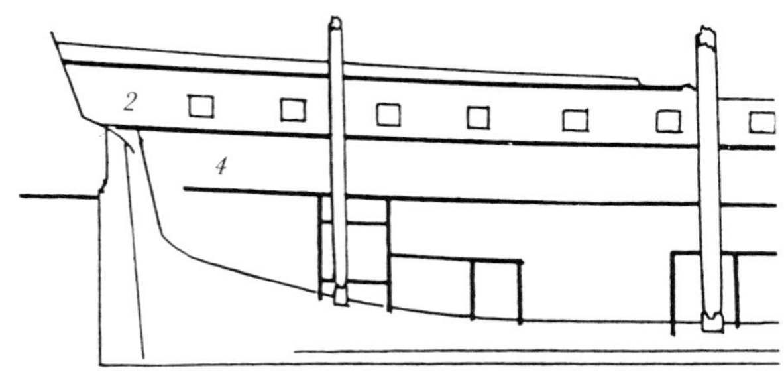

The stern cabins of a three-decker, two-decker and frigate.
1 Admiral's apartment
2 Captain's cabin
3 Wardroom
4 Gunroom
5 Decks with open galleries (pre 1796)

Fittings on the Orlop Deck

On a ship-of-the-line the orlop deck was continuous through the whole length. Aft was the upper part of the breadroom. Forward of that was the after cockpit, which contained clothing stores, the steward's room where the days provisions were issued, store rooms for the commissioned officers, and cabins for the surgeon and purser. Forward of the row of cabins was a midshipmen's berth on each side, where they ate; the area in the centre between the cabins served as a sleeping area for the midshipmen, and as an operating theatre in time of action. The centre part of the orlop deck was taken up with cable stowage, though some of the seamen and petty officers also slung their hammocks there. To allow the water from the cables to drain into the bilges, this part of the deck was not continuously planked, but had short pieces which could be taken up when necessary. The foremost part of the orlop was devoted to store rooms for the carpenter, boatswain and gunner. These areas were made quite secure. They were interrupted by a passage leading to the light room of the magazine.

On fifth rate frigates the orlop deck was divided into three parts, but the functions were similar, except that there were no cabins aft. On sixth rates the platform for the cables was not used. On the smaller sloops and gunboats, there was no separate orlop and the store rooms were merely divided off from the single 'tween decks space.

Cabins in the Stern

Warships invariably had cabins at the stern, with numbers and quality according to size of the ship and the status of her officers. All rated ships had a gunroom aft on the lower deck; this had no stern windows and was only lighted and ventilated by gratings in the deck and by gunports. On a frigate, the gunroom housed all the officers except the captain; rows of cabins were erected along each side, with midshipmen's berths at the forward end of each row. There was no wardroom as such, and the commissioned officers dined in the space in the centre of the deck, among the cabins. On a ship-of-the-line the gun room housed only lower status officers — the chaplain, junior marine officer, gunner and perhaps the pilot had small cabins at its corners, while the junior midshipmen or volunteers probably messed in the central area.

In a frigate, the captain lived aft on the upper deck under the quarterdeck, for there was no poop. In a two-decker, this space was allocated to the wardroom officers, twelve or so in a 74. About six canvas cabins were hung round the sides, and the space in the middle was occupied by a table, chairs and other furniture. The wardroom opened onto the stern windows, and to the quarter galleries on that deck, but it had no open gallery. On a three-decker the wardroom was on the middle deck. The captain lived on the quarterdeck on all ships-of-the-line, in a large cabin which was divided into three or four compartments. On a three-decker, there was an intermediate cabin on the upper deck, for the admiral. It was even larger than the captain's, and had similar conveniences — open galleries on the older ships, and access to the quarter galleries.

On two- and three-deckers, other cabins were placed forward on the upper deck, under the forecastle. These were for the boatswain, carpenter and cook. In 1801, the sick berth was fitted in this area, and the boatswain and carpenter were given cabins forward on the orlop deck, along with the gunner.

Galleys

The ship's galley was placed forward, usually on the upper deck under the forecastle — except on three-deckers, where it was on the middle deck. It was an iron structure, containing two cuboid copper kettles for boiling the food for the ship's company, and a furnace underneath. For more sophisticated cooking, chiefly by the officers' cooks, it was also fitted with an oven, a grill, and a turnspit operated by the smoke from the fire. It burned wood or coal, and a chimney carried the smoke up through the deck of the forecastle. The chimney had some form of cowl so that it could be turned away from the wind.

3 Masts, Sails and Rigging

The Use of Square Rig

Square rig, in which the sails in their neutral position were at right angles to the line of the ship, were by far the most common on ships of the navy. Even the small brigs, of less than 200 tons, were square rigged with two masts. Ship rig, with three square-rigged masts, was used for all major naval vessels, from about 400 tons upwards. The dividing line was set by the *Cruiser* class of 382 tons, which was brig rigged, and the *Snake* class of similar hull design was ship rigged. At the upper end of the scale, no ships carried more than three masts, and masts and sails were merely increased in size for larger ships.

Square rig had several disadvantages. It required large numbers of men to set and take in sail, and to trim and reef it to suit the winds; though this was not necessarily a problem, as ships needed large crews in any case, to man their guns. A square rigged ship could only sail to about six points, or $67\frac{1}{2}$ degrees, of the wind. A fore and aft rigged ship of the period could usually get within five points, or $56\frac{1}{4}$ degrees. Square rig had some advantages when the wind was behind the ship, or over the quarter. But the main disadvantage of fore and aft rig was that it was not easy to divide the sails up into manageable portions, and that the types of canvas and cordage available did not make the development of fore and aft rig very easy. As a result, all real fighting ships, big enough to carry a serious armament, were square rigged; fore and aft rig was confined to small vessels which were intended to sail rather than fight, and which would engage only merchant vessels or small privateers.

A full-rigged ship could carry four sails — course, topsail, topgallant and royal — on each of the main and fore masts, and three on the mizzen. It had about eight staysails, and four jibs, as well as studding sails; including spares, up to 40 sails would be carried. A ship would need about 1000 rigging blocks to lead the ropes and give mechanical advantage. The sails of the *Royal George* of 1788 weighed nearly 10 tons, and were said to cover an area of more than two acres.[1]

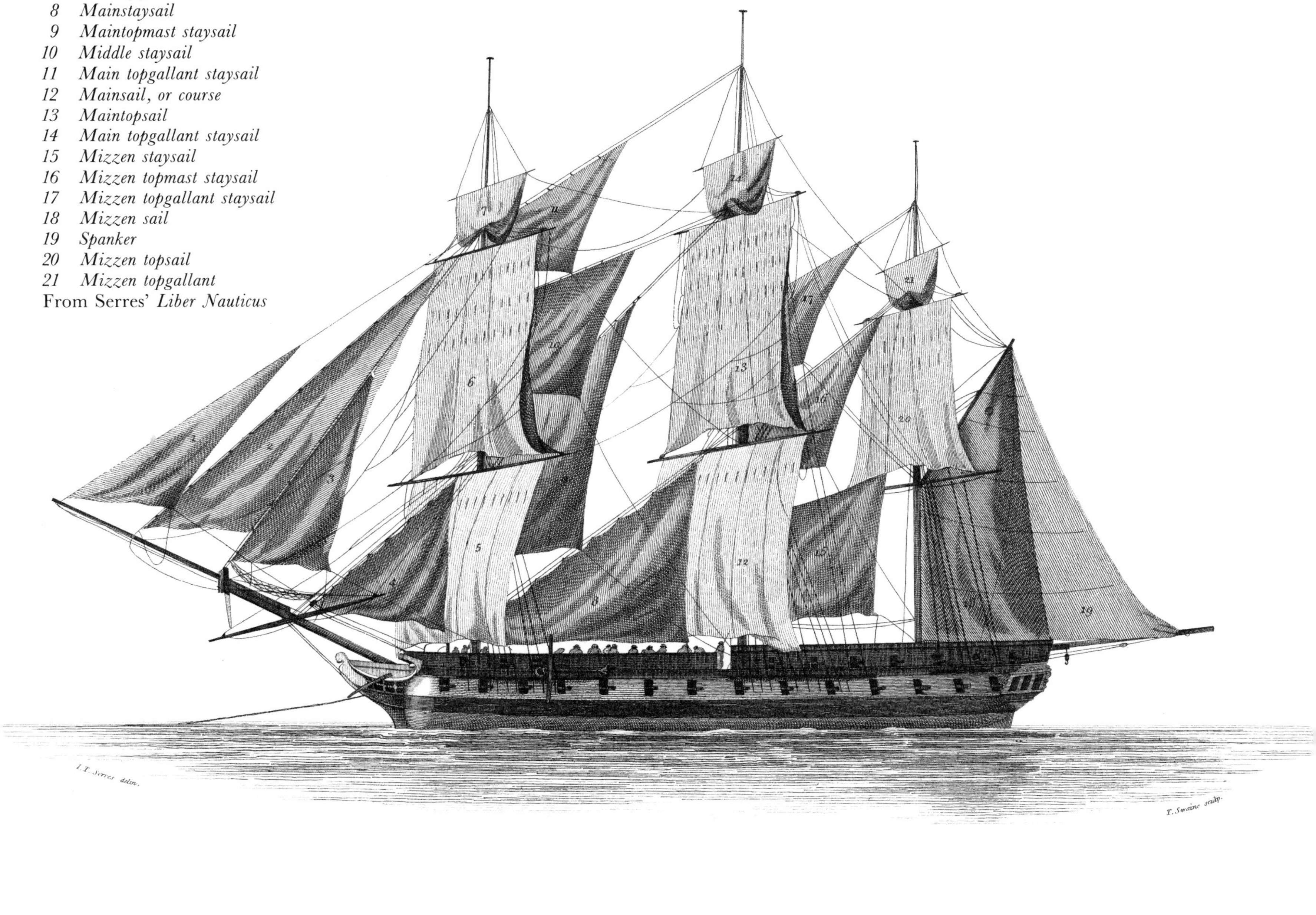

The sails of a square-rigged ship, hung out to dry in a calm.
1 *Flying jib*
2 *Jib*
3 *Fore topmast staysail*
4 *Fore staysail*
5 *Foresail, or course*
6 *Fore topsail*
7 *Fore topgallant*
8 *Mainstaysail*
9 *Maintopmast staysail*
10 *Middle staysail*
11 *Main topgallant staysail*
12 *Mainsail, or course*
13 *Maintopsail*
14 *Main topgallant staysail*
15 *Mizzen staysail*
16 *Mizzen topmast staysail*
17 *Mizzen topgallant staysail*
18 *Mizzen sail*
19 *Spanker*
20 *Mizzen topsail*
21 *Mizzen topgallant*
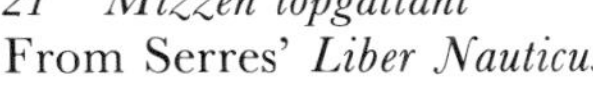
From Serres' *Liber Nauticus*

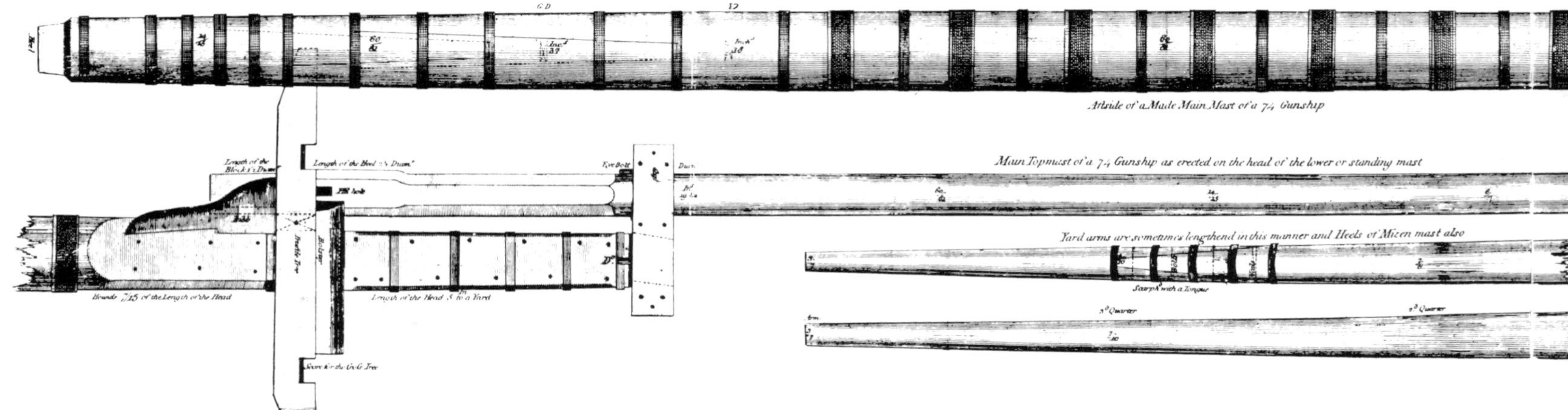

The spars of a 74-gun ship, showing the mainmast, the topmast and topgallant with the crosstrees and trestletrees joining them together, and the mainyard showing how the parts are scarphed together. From Steel's *Mastmaking, Sailmaking and Rigging*, 1794

Masts

A full-rigged ship had three masts, the fore, main and mizzen. The main was placed near the centre of the vessel, and was the largest. The foremast was placed at the forecastle, and the gap between it and the main was quite large. This was to prevent the main from masking the foresails in a following wind, and to help in tacking, when the yards of the fore and main would be braced in opposite directions for a time. The mizzen was considerably smaller than the other two, and was placed on the quarterdeck, quite close to the mainmast.

The term 'mast' was slightly ambiguous; it could refer to the whole structure right up to the highest point on the ship, or it could mean one of the two or three sections which were placed one above another. Thus the 'mainmast' consisted of the mainmast proper, or lower mast; the topmast, and the topgallant mast. Of course, the lower mast was the largest; it was often made up of several pieces of timber carefully joined together, and held in place with ropes until about 1800, and iron bands after that. The lower mast rested on the kelson of the ship, on a block of wood known as the step. It passed through holes in each deck, known as the partners, and was held rigid by means of wedges. It reached its maximum thickness where it passed through the upper deck, and began to taper after that. It was round in section for most of its length, and until it reached the hounds, where the top rested. After that, it was square. However, below the top, were projections from the mast — the cheeks running down the sides, and the front fish which went some considerable way down the front of the mast.

A top was a broad, flat, D-shaped structure, placed at the hounds of the mast. It served as a platform for the men working in the rigging, to spread the shrouds which supported the topmast, and to strengthen the join with the topmast. The latter was made in a single piece. It began just below the level of the top, and continued up to the level of the head of the lower mast, to which it was joined by means of a piece of timber known as the cap. It tapered after that, and became hexagonal in section under the hounds. Like the lower mast, it had a square head above the hounds. The topmast had no top as such, but only a structure known as the crosstrees, which had no large flat surface but otherwise served the same functions as the top. The topgallant mast came above that. It was similar to the topmast in shape, except that it ended in a button.

The bowsprit protruded from the bow at an angle of about 25 degrees to the horizontal. It was lengthened by means of the jib-boom. It served to support the rigging of the foremast, to lead the bowlines forward, and to take several sails, including the jibs and the spritsails.

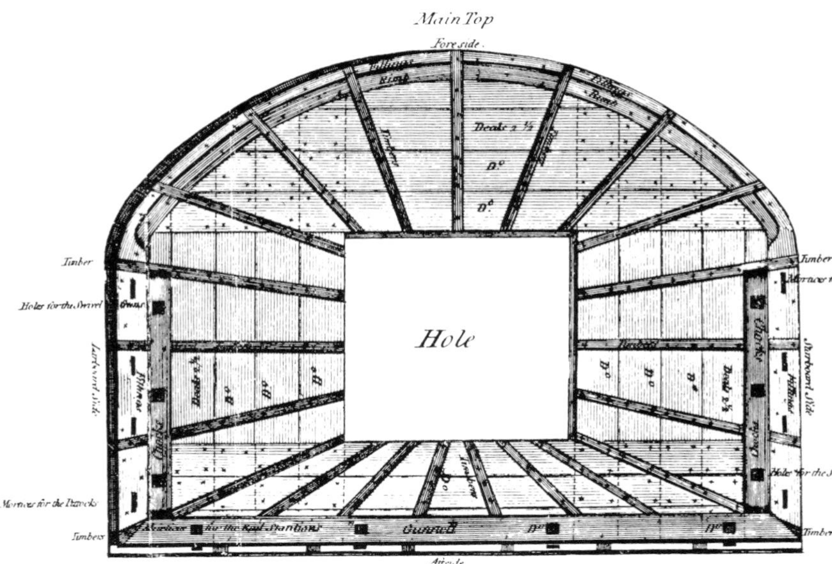

Plan view of the maintop of a 36-gun ship. From Steel's *Mastmaking, Sailmaking and Rigging*, 1794

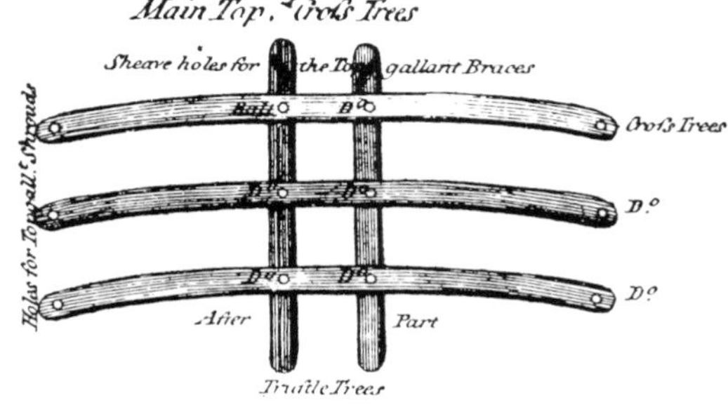

Plan view of the topmast crosstrees. From Steel's *Mastmaking, Sailmaking and Rigging*, 1794

The maintopmast cap. From Steel's *Mastmaking, Sailmaking and Rigging*, 1794

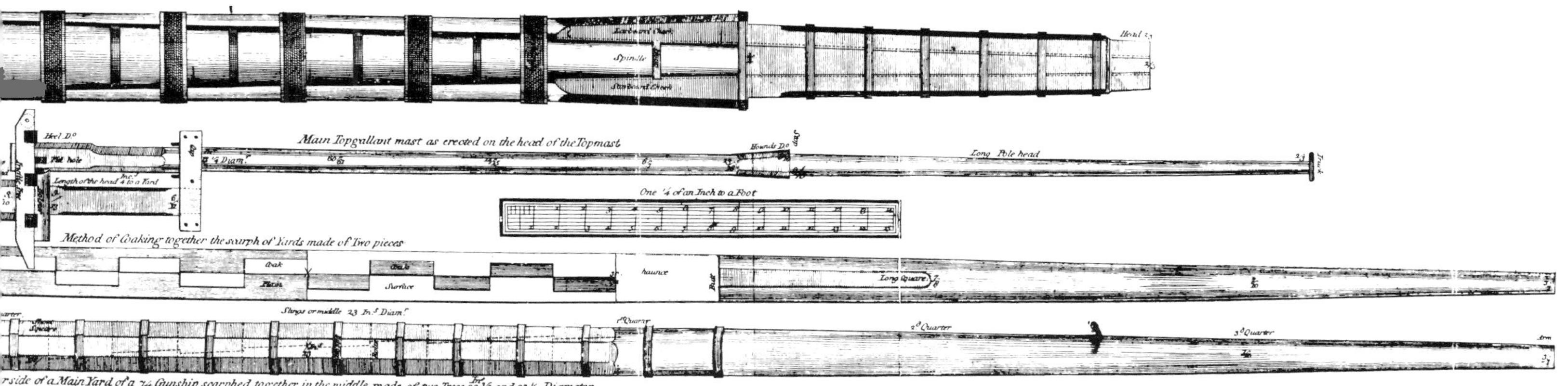

Standing Rigging

The masts were supported by the standing rigging. Unlike the running rigging this was relatively permanent, and so was prepared for long life. Much of it was 'wormed, parcelled and served', and all of it was tarred to give a black appearance. There were three main types of standing rigging: shrouds, backstays and stays.

The lower shrouds ran from the hounds of each lower mast to the channels which projected from the sides of the hull. They could be tightened to compensate for stretch, by means of a system of 'deadeyes' and 'lanyards'. The shrouds of the upper masts were similar, but ran to the top or crosstrees of the mast below. Under the top, the futtock shrouds led downwards to join on the shrouds of the lower mast. Catharpins were fitted between the shrouds on opposite sides, at the level where the futtock shrouds met the main shrouds; they were used to tighten the shrouds and allow more space to turn the yards into the wind. Both shrouds and futtock shrouds were fitted with ratlines — lighter ropes which were tied horizontally between the shrouds at regular intervals, giving a kind of ladder up which the men could climb to the tops.

Backstays were similar to shrouds in function, except that they ran from the hounds of a topmast or topgallant all the way to the deck. Some, the running backstays, were less permanent than the others.

A forestay ran forward from each mast, at an angle of about 45 degrees, to meet another mast, the deck, or the bowsprit. The backstays served to support the masts against any forces from forward, for example when the ship was tacking. They, too, were tightened by means of lanyards, though 'hearts' were used instead of deadeyes.

The bowsprit was held against upwards pressure by its 'gammoning', which lashed it to the knee of the head. The bobstays ran forward from the cutwater of the bow to near the end of the bowsprit, while the jib-boom was braced by means of the martingale stay, which passed through the dolphin striker, a piece of wood projecting downwards from the head of the bowsprit. This was relatively new, having been introduced in the 1790s.

Yards

Each square sail was hung from a yard. A yard was octagonal in cross-section near its centre part, the slings. It became circular after that, and it tapered towards the ends (the yardarms). It was fitted with several cleats to retain the rigging attached to it. On the very largest ships, the mizzensail, though a fore and aft sail, was also fitted to a yard, with one end projecting forward of the mast; though the foremost part was no longer used. After about 1800, every ship had its mizzensail attached to a gaff, which ended where it met the mast. The spritsail yards, attached to the bowsprit, were similar to those of the other yards. More specialised items included the studding sail booms and yards, which were used only in very light winds, to extend the normal sails.

Rigging to the Yards

A lower yard was hauled up by means of thick ropes known as jeers, passing through large blocks under the top. The upper yards were raised by halyards, which passed through a block set in the mast itself. The lower yards were held against the mast by a complicated arrangement of ropes and bead-like pieces of wood known as parrels. Trusses served a similar function for the upper yards. In both cases, the system had to allow the yard to rotate round the mast, and to be raised and lowered when necessary.

The yards were kept horizontal by means of lifts. Each lift led from the head of a mast, through a block at the yardarm, back through another block at the head of the mast, and then down to the deck. Footropes were slung under the yards, for the men to rest their feet while working on them. These were supported by stirrups hung from the yards themselves.

Braces were used to alter the angle between the yard and the fore and aft line of the ship, to suit the wind. The pendant of each brace led from the yardarm to a block. The pendant of the brace was taken through this block, with one end fixed near the deck, and the other at a cleat or kevel, so that it could be taken in or let out when necessary. The braces of fore and mainmast led forward; those of the topsails, topgallants and royals led through a block in the mast behind, and then down to the deck. The braces of the mizzen led forward, to the mainmast.

Sails

Sails were made from strips of canvas of different thicknesses, according to the intended use; thicker canvas, for heavy weather, was number 1, and weighed 44lb per 38yds; while light weather canvas was number 6, weighing 29lb. The strips of canvas were 2ft broad, and were sewn together with about $1\frac{1}{2}$in overlap. A kind of hem, known as tabling, was sewn round the whole sail, and round that was rope, known as bolt rope or head rope according to its position on the sail. Loops were formed in the corners of the sails, for attaching rigging lines. These were known as earrings at the upper corners and clews at the lower. Other loops, attached to the sides and bottom of the sails were known as cringles. Large sails, especially topsails, had lines of reefing points, light ropes which could be tied together to reduce sail in heavy weather. Some sails also had double thickness of canvas, known as lining, at crucial points.

There were four main types of sail. Square sails were hung under a yard. Only the lower sails, known as the courses, were approximately rectangular — the topsails invariably narrowed towards the head. The

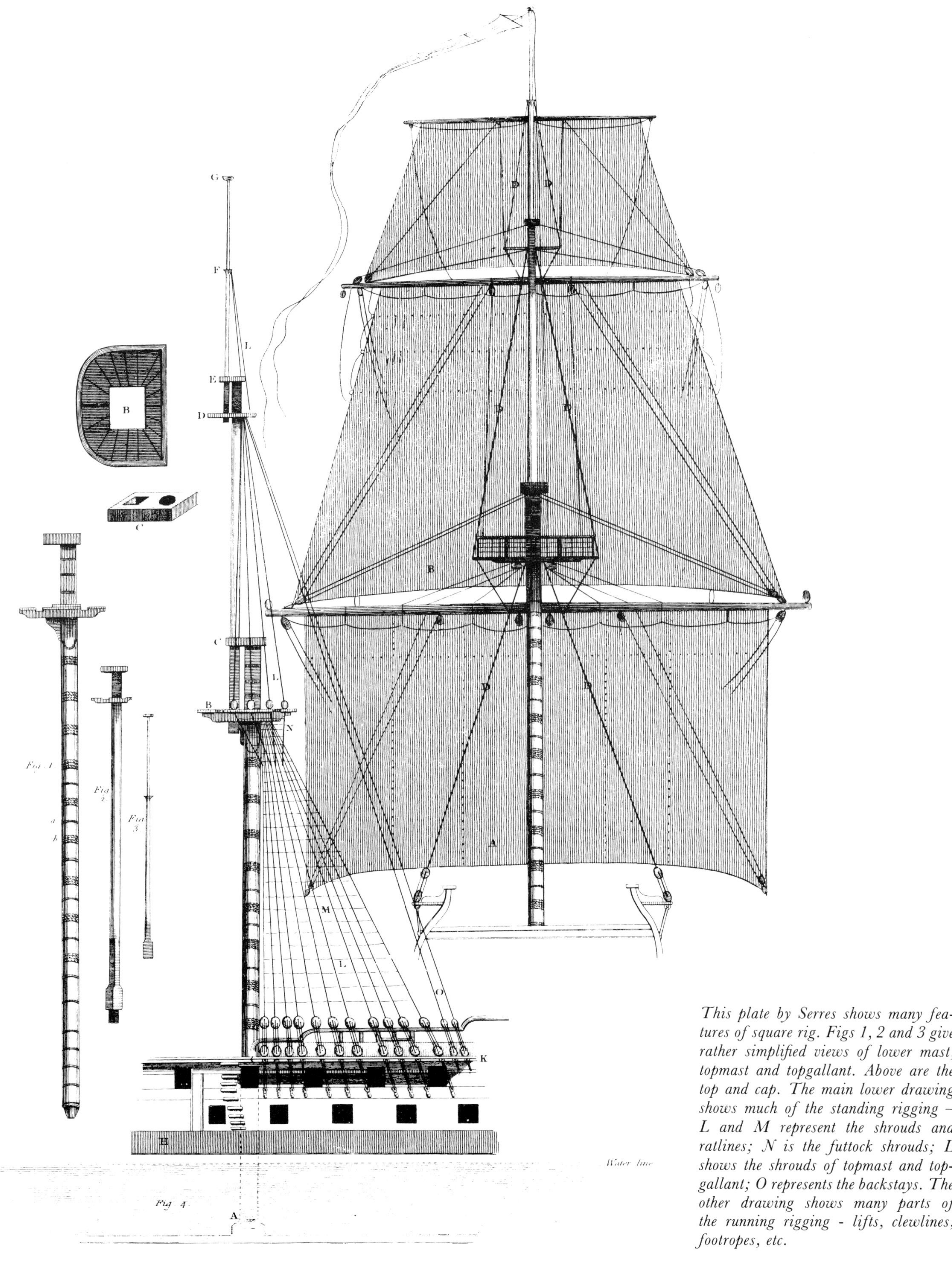

This plate by Serres shows many features of square rig. Figs 1, 2 and 3 give rather simplified views of lower mast, topmast and topgallant. Above are the top and cap. The main lower drawing shows much of the standing rigging – L and M represent the shrouds and ratlines; N is the futtock shrouds; L shows the shrouds of topmast and topgallant; O represents the backstays. The other drawing shows many parts of the running rigging - lifts, clewlines, footropes, etc.

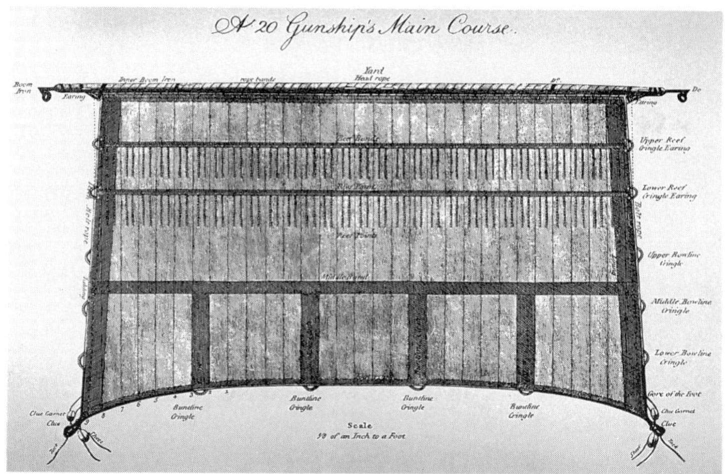

Course

Jib

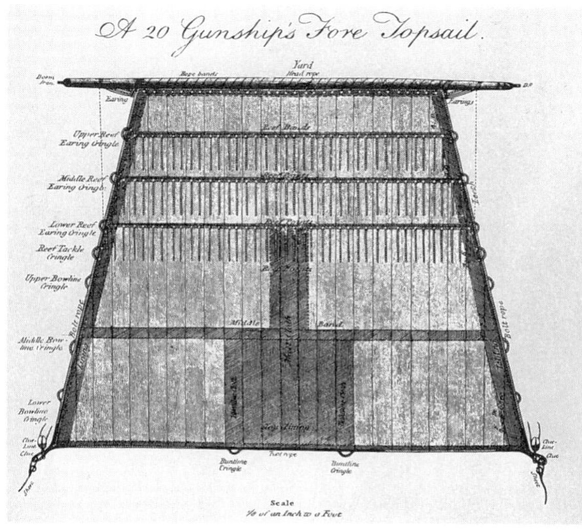

Topsail

Staysail

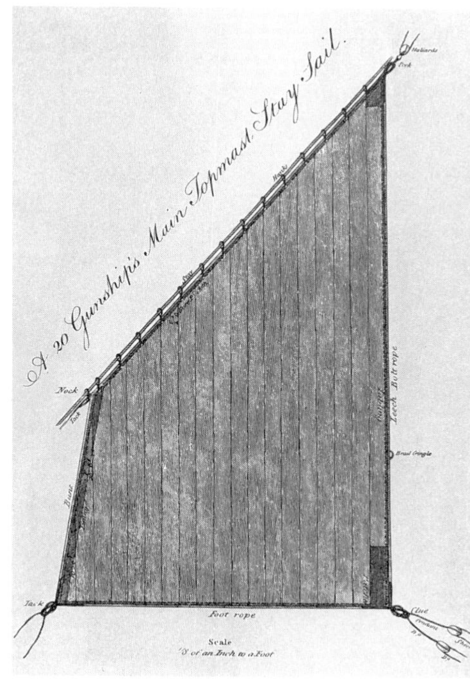

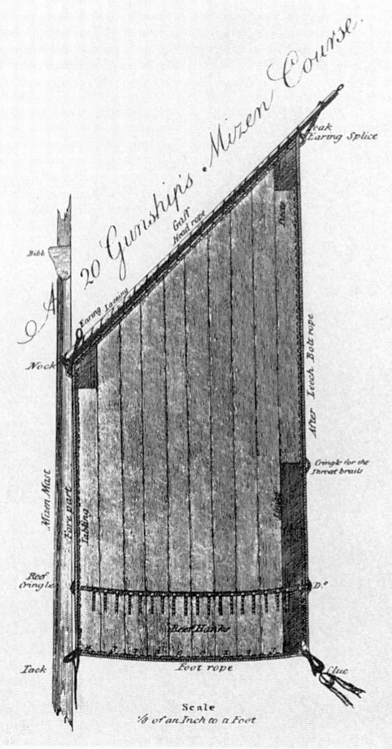

Mizzen course

Different types of sail, from Steel's Mastmaking, Sailmaking and Rigging., *showing the arrangements of lining, reef points, etc, and also the ropes attached to the corners.*

The fore and aft sails of a 74, from Rees's Naval Architecture.

Fig 1.

Fig 2.

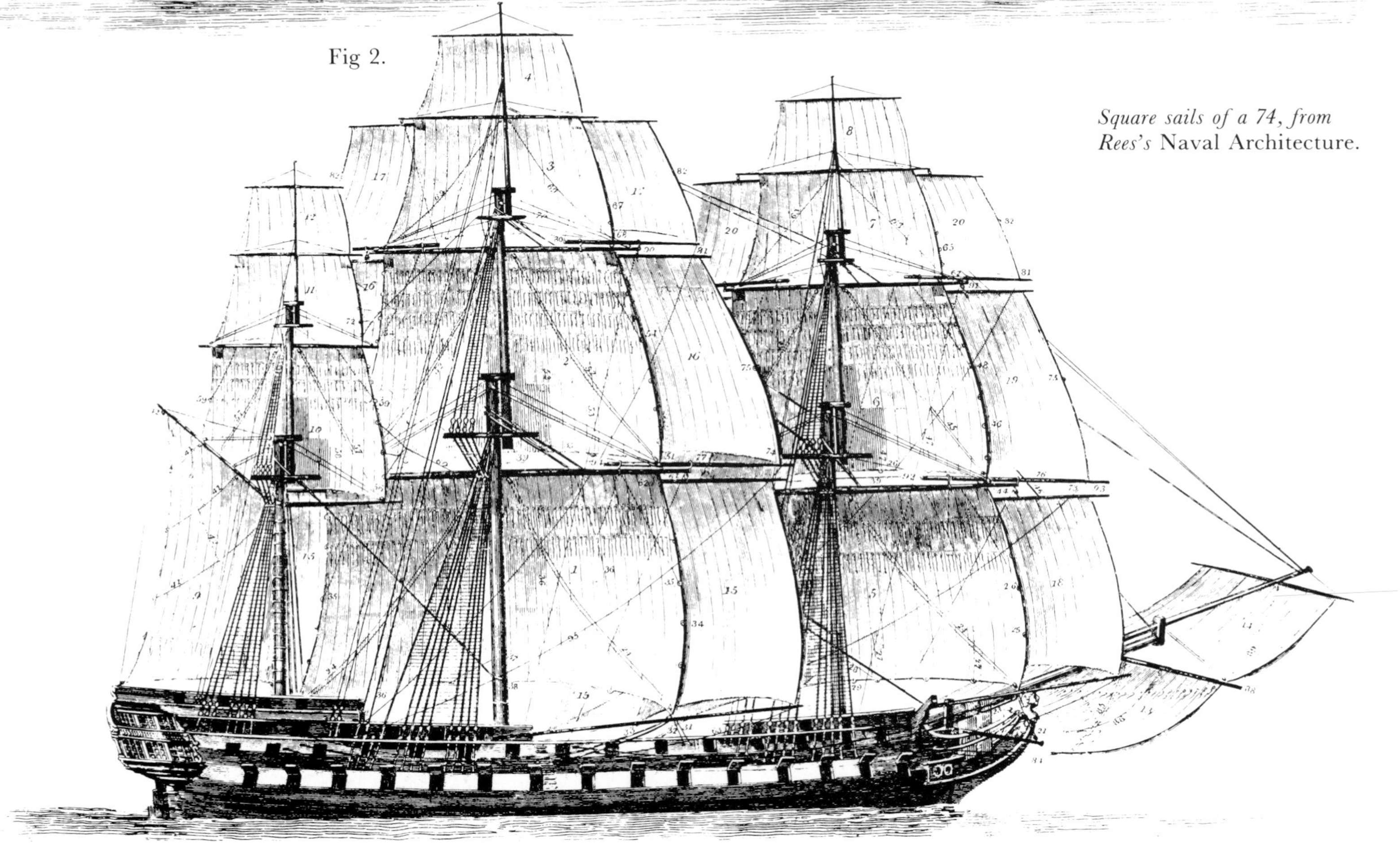

Square sails of a 74, from Rees's Naval Architecture.

mizzensail was essentiall a gaffsail, quadrilateral but not rectangular. Staysails were usually hung from under a stay, and were mostly quadrilateral, with parallel sides; while jibs, hung from the forestays, were triangular. In addition, studding sails had parallel head and foot, but angled sides.

Rigging Attached to the Sails

The sail was hung from the yard by means of robbands, passed through holes in the sail and tied over the rop of the yard. The outer ends were stretched along the yard by the earring, which was taken round the yardarm cleats.

The lower corners of square sails were controlled by means of sheets. In the case of the upper sails, these served mainly to stretch the sail out to the end of the yard below. The sheet was attached to the clew of the sail, and then led along the yard and down to the deck by means of blocks. On the fore and main courses, the sheets were crucial to the trim of the sails. They could be taken in on one side and let out on the other at the same time as the braces were moved, in order to alter the angle of the sails to the wind. Each of these braces had a pendant, with one end attached to the clew of the sail and the other to a block. The fall of the brace was attached to an eyebolt on the outside of the hull, and then went through the block on the pendant. It was led back through a sheave in the side of the hull, and it was this end which was used to trim the sail.

When necessary, the clews of the fore and main courses could be held forward by means of the tacks. This was especially necessary when the ship was sailing close to the wind. The fore tack led forward to the bowsprit, the main tack to a sheave in the hull. Bowlines served a similar purpose, in keeping the edges, rather than the corners, of the sails forward when sailing close to the wind. They were fitted to all square sails, by means of a system of bridles; they led forward to the mast ahead, or to the bowsprit, or, in the case of the fore course, to the boomkins — small spars projecting diagonally downwards and forward from the bows of the ship.

Sails were taken in and furled with the aid of clewlines and buntlines. Each clewline ran to the corner of a square sail, and was used to haul it up towards the centre of the yard. Buntlines ran aft of the sail, to cringles at the foot; they hauled the other parts of the sail vertically up to the yard. Slablines were similar, but ran forward of the sail. Reefing tackle led from the end of the yard to the reefing cringles, set in the edges of the sail on a level with the reefing lines. It was used to haul up the upper part of the sail when reefing.

Spritsails and spritsail topsails were square sails, hung from yards under the bowsprit. Their rigging was generally similar to that of other square sails, but they were nearly obsolete by this time, as their function had largely been taken over by the jibs. However, the rigging of their yards helped to brace the bowsprit against sideways pressure.

The Rigging of Fore and Aft Sails

The mizzen was the only gaff sail carried. It was hung from a yard or gaff, projecting from the mizzenmast at an angle of about 45 degrees. The outermost end of the gaff was held up by a peak halyard (sometimes known as a topping lift at this time), and the inner end by a throat halyard. The side to side movement of the peak of the gaff was controlled by vangs, leading to the rails on each side of the deck. The sail itself was laced to both the mast and the gaff. Its foot was loose, but it was controlled by means of a single sheet, leading from the clew of the sail to the taffrail at the stern of the ship. Its forward corner, the tack, was attached to an eyebolt in the deck. When not in use, the mizzen was hauled up to the mast and gaff by means of brails. In light winds, the mizzen course could be replaced by a larger sail known as a driver. Its foot was extended by means of a boom, as the normal sheeting arrangement would not work with such a large sail.

Stay sails were hung from the stays running between the mizzenmast and the foremast, and between the main and the foremast. The head of each was hung from the stay, and could be pulled back along it by means of a rope known as a downhaul, for furling. Conversely, it was hoisted by means of a halyard, which led up the stay to a block where it met the mast behind, and then down to the deck. A staysail needed two sheets, one for each side of the ship, to be used according to which tack the ship was on. Both were attached to the same clew, and led down to the appropriate side of the ship. Staysails were mostly quadrilateral, and therefore each needed a rope known as a tack, to control the other lower corner. This usually led to the mast just ahead of the sail.

Jibs were similar to staysails, except that they hung from the stays between the foremast and the bowsprit, and were triangular instead of quadrilateral. Their rigging was similar to that of a staysail, except of course that they needed no tacks. Their exposed position in the extremity of the ship caused some special difficulties; the foremost jib was attached to a special stay, which could be brought back some way aft by means of a traveller running along the bowsprit.

Other Ropes

Burton pendants were hung from the mastheads, rather like shortened shrouds. Each had an eye in one end, and this was used to attach the tackle which would be used for hoisting boats, guns, or other

Various types of fore and aft rig, from Steel's Mastmaking, Sailmaking and Rigging

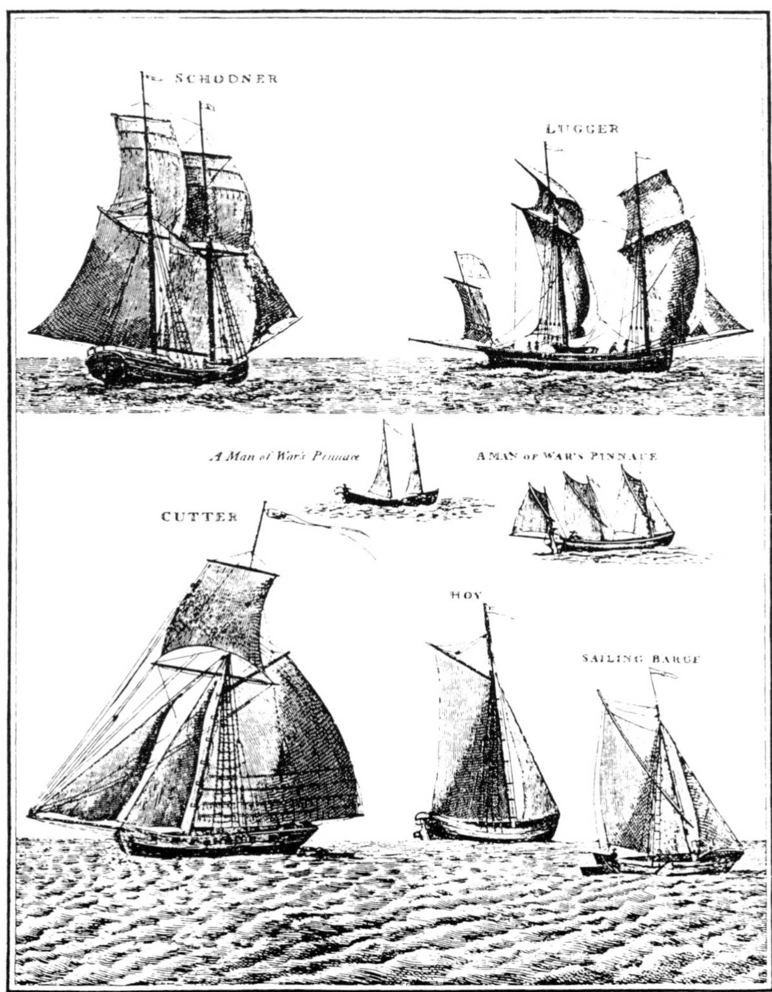

heavy weights. Numerous other ropes were used for towing boats, fitting awnings and boarding nettings, hauling casks up the side by a process known as 'parbuckling', for stern and side ladders, for mooring to a buoy or anchoring, and for dozens of other purposes.

Brigs, Cutters and Schooners

A brig was essentially similar to a ship rigged vessel, except of course that it had only two masts. The aftermost of these, the mainmast, was invariably larger. Apart from its size, the mainmast of a brig was similar to the mizzen of a larger ship; it had no square course, but a gaffsail instead; and naturally the braces of the yards ran forward rather than aft.

The cutter was essentially fore and aft rigged, though it could carry square yards when running before the wind. It had a single mast, very tall. Its mainsail was stretched by a boom, like the driver of a mizzensail on a larger ship. Her bowsprit was removable, and it was used to carry two jibs. Her topsail was square, with its head supported by a topsail yard, and its foot stretched by a lower yard, which could also take a square course when needed.

In this period, a schooner invariably had two masts, basically fore and aft rigged. According to one authority, 'The masts rake aft, but the bowsprit lies nearly horizontal'.[2] The courses were gaffsails, extended by booms as on cutters. It seems to have been normal to carry square topsails on both masts, and also a square course, used only when running before the wind.

4 Armament

The Supply of Guns

Guns, like all the other items which came under the heading of 'gunner's stores', were supplied by the Ordnance Board. By this time, ships' guns (except those of the Royal yachts, and a few cases where captains supplied their own light guns) were invariably made of iron. They were made in privately owned ironworks in England and Scotland, under contract to the Board of Ordnance. In the past, the iron industry had been based in the Weald of Kent and Sussex, and had used a production method based on charcoal; but because of the depletion of the southern woods, and the change to a method of iron founding based on coke, the ironworks were now situated in Scotland and the north of England, close to the major coalfields. The leading contractors included the Carron Iron Works in Stirlingshire. (It was famous for its invention of the carronade, and, after 1796, it was a major supplier of long guns as well.) Samuel Walker of Rotherham, who had played a large part in the development of the Blomefield pattern gun; and many others such as Wiggin and Graham, Gordon and Harley, Sturges, and Dawson.

The basic dimensions of each gun were set by the Ordnance Board, and by the 1790s standards were increasingly rigidly enforced. The gunfounder made a full scale model of the gun, mostly from clay. This was used to form a mould for the main part of the gun, with a separate mould for the breech and cascable at the rear. The bore was formed by a cylinder, which was placed inside the mould. Molten iron was poured in, and after cooling the mould was split apart. By this time, it was normal to cast the guns solid, and then bore them out with a drilling machine.

Completed guns were sent to Woolwich by sea, to be tested by the Board of Ordnance. Standards of proof varied over the years, but the basic method was to pack the gun with explosive, well beyond its normal service charge. It was fired, and, assuming it survived intact, it was carefully inspected for any signs of holes or cracks. If it passed, it was eventually sent to one of the naval ordnance depots— the Ordnance Wharf at Chatham, Priddy's Hard near Portsmouth, or the gunwharf at Plymouth.

The Shape of Guns

Stated simply, a muzzle-loading gun was merely a tube closed at one end. As the closed end, the breech, had to take most of the force of the explosion of the powder, it was made somewhat thicker than the other end, the muzzle. The very thickest part of the gun was the base ring; behind that was the cascabel, where it tapered rapidly, usually by way of curves and reverse curves. A large ball known as the button was fitted at the extremity of the gun. Forward of the base ring, the gun was divided into several areas known as 'reinforces' — named after the 'reinforce rings' which were moulded round the gun at intervals. Forward of the reinforces was the chase, where the gun reached its narrowest part, at the 'neck of the muzzle'. After that, it widened to form the 'swell of the muzzle', and then tapered again to the face.

Internally, the gun had a round bore with parallel sides. The aftermost part of the bore was the chamber, where the powder was placed for firing. In long guns, it was the same as the rest of the bore, while on a carronade it had a smaller diameter. The touch hole was drilled from the top of the breech down to the chamber; it was used to ignite the powder.

Externally, a long gun had trunnions on each side. These projected some way aft of the centre of gravity of the gun. They were cylindrical in shape, and allowed the gun to rotate for elevation and depression after it had been fitted to its carriage. Like all the rest of the gun proper, they were cast as part of the weapon during its original moulding.

Types of Guns

All guns were classified mainly by their weight of ball, and also by their length. The largest guns were 42-pounders, used only on the lower decks of the older first rates, and largely obsolete; 32-pounders were much more common, being the standard lower gun of nearly all ships-of-the-line, except 64s. They were 9ft 6in long, and weighed around 55cwt. The 24-pounder was used on the upper and middle decks of large ships-of-the-line, and as the main armament of small two-deckers, and a few large frigates. It was 9ft or 9ft 6in long, and weighed 47 or 50cwt. The 18-pounder was the upper deck gun of most 74s, and the main weapon of modern frigates. As fitted on ships-of-the-line, it was 9ft long and weighed 42cwt; on frigates, it was 8ft long and weighed 37cwt. The 12-pounder was used on the upper decks of many three deckers, and as the main armament of the older frigates. It came in four different versions, from 9ft and 34cwt to 7ft and 21cwt, with the shorter guns being used on frigates. The 9-

Various methods of boring cannon, from Rees's Cyclopaedia.

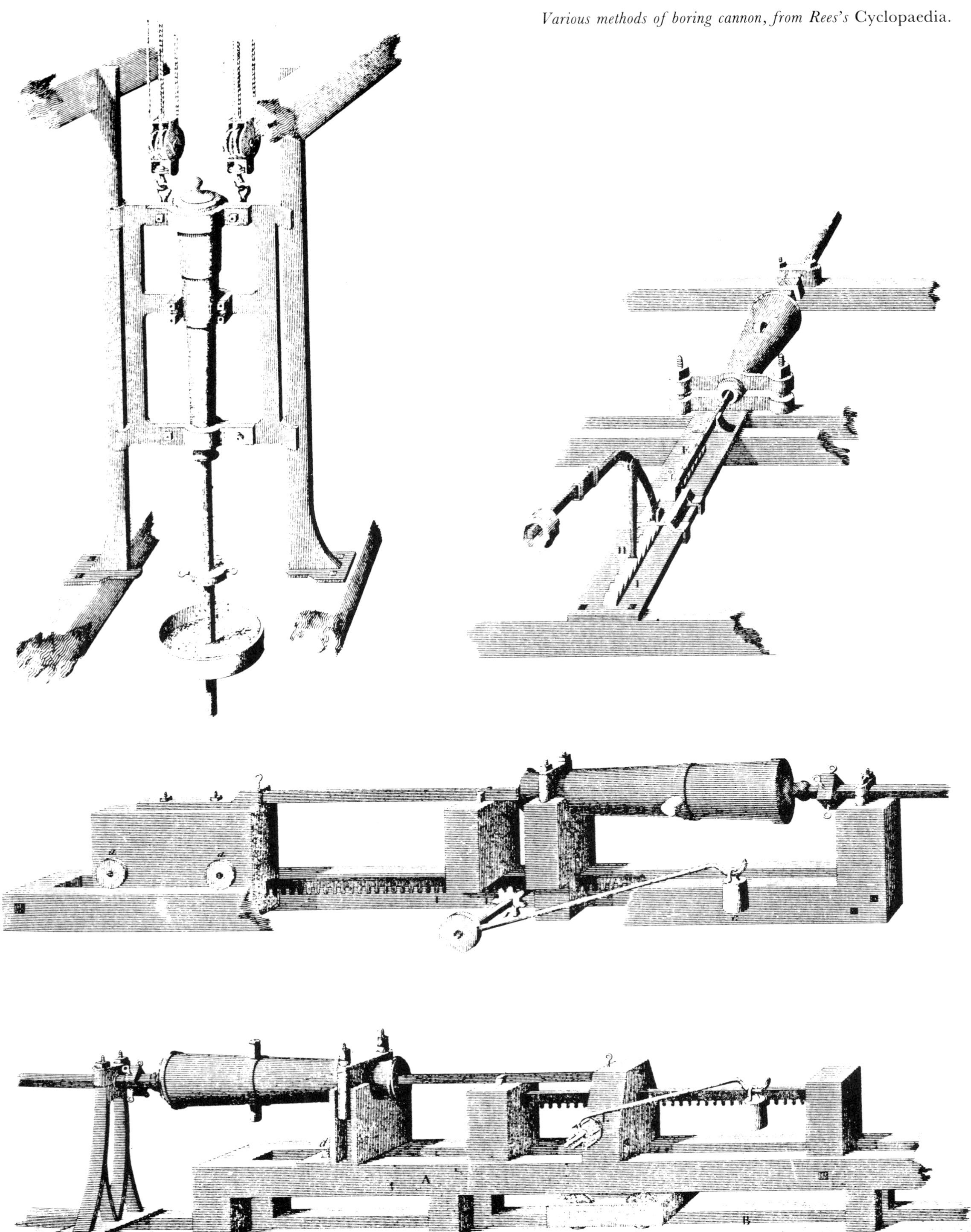

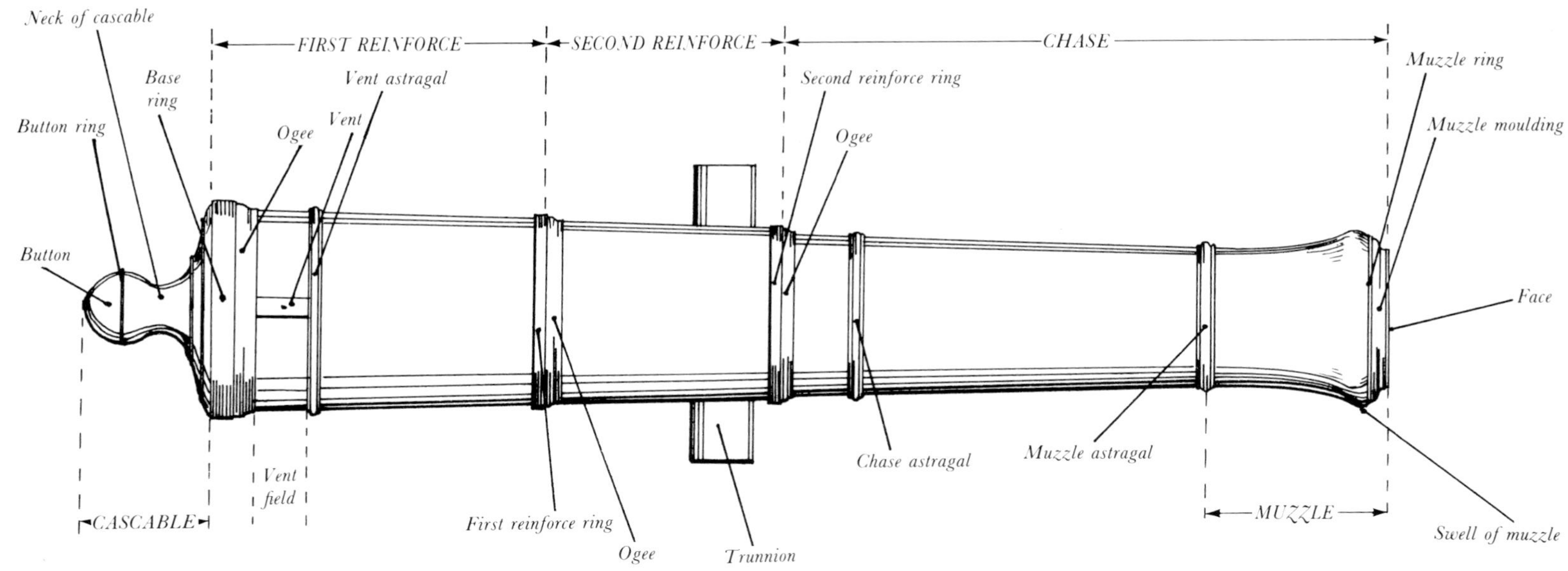

The main parts of a gun. This shows the old Armstrong pattern gun, without the loop on the beach.

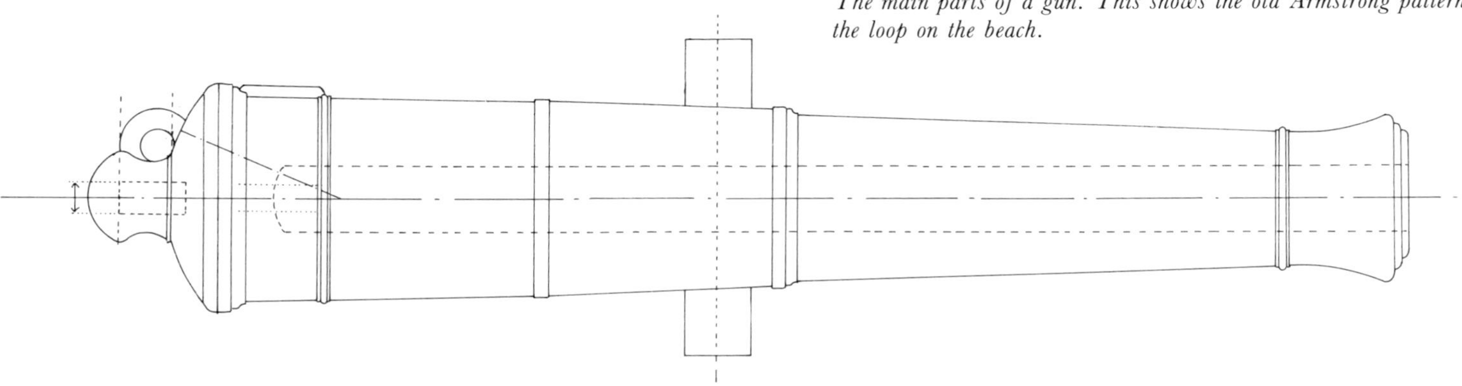

The Blomefield pattern gun – a 32-pounder is shown here. The drawing demonstrates how the centre of the circle forming the cascable is situated in the centre of the chamber. From a drawing in the Carron papers, Scottish Record Office, Edinburgh

pounder was the forecastle and quarterdeck gun of most two-deckers and many of the larger frigates, but it was largely superseded by the carronade. It also armed many sixth rates. It too came in four versions, with length varying from 9ft to 7ft, and weight from 31 to 25cwt. The 6-pounder was used as the subsidiary armament of smaller frigates, and as the main armament of sloops, though again it tended to be superseded by the carronade. It came in six versions, from 8ft 6in to 6ft long, and weighing 22 to 17cwt. Even smaller guns, of 4 and 3 lb, were also available, but were rarely used on fighting ships.

Armstrong and Blomefield Patterns

Standard patterns for gun design had been imposed on the founders since the early years of the eighteenth century. Despite attempts at improvement, the Armstrong pattern, first designed in the 1720s, remained standard until after the American War. It had a traditional form, with curves and ogees on its cascable, and a simple button without any loop. From 1786, Thomas Blomefield, the inspector of artillery, began to develop a new pattern of gun, in co-operation with Samuel Walker and Co. He attempted to lighten the gun by taking weight away from the chase, but the invention of cylinder powder defeated this, because the more powerful charge demanded a stronger gun. As a result, Blomefield guns were no lighter than their predecessors. He did succeed in simplifying and strengthening the cascabel, by designing it as a single curve, centred in the middle of the chamber. He also added a loop to the top of the button, to give the gun its most distinctive characteristic. This served to hold the breech rope. On older guns the breech rope was fixed to the button, but this caused difficulties when the gun was fired at an angle, creating differing pressures on each side of the rope. On the Blomefield gun the rope passed through the loop, so that the pull was equalised on each side.

The Blomefield pattern gun was standard by 1794, when it was ordered that no more of the old type were to be received at Woolwich. Of course, it took years to replace the old guns, and as late as 1808 some ships were still carrying the Armstrong pattern. However, the Blomefield gun was certainly the most common by the time of Trafalgar.

The Introduction of Carronades

The carronade was first invented in the late 1770s, by Melville, Gascoigne and Miller, as a short gun with a relative large bore. It was developed by the Carron Company, and was first adopted by the navy in 1779. It was fitted to the quarterdecks, forecastles and poops of various ships — but only if the captain applied for them. By 1782, 167 ships had been fitted but only forty of these remained by 1793. In 1794, a new establishment of carronades was drawn up, making the gun compulsory on most types of ship, though, in the first instance, only for ships to be fitted out in the future. The most common were 32-pounders and 24-pounders, even on quite small

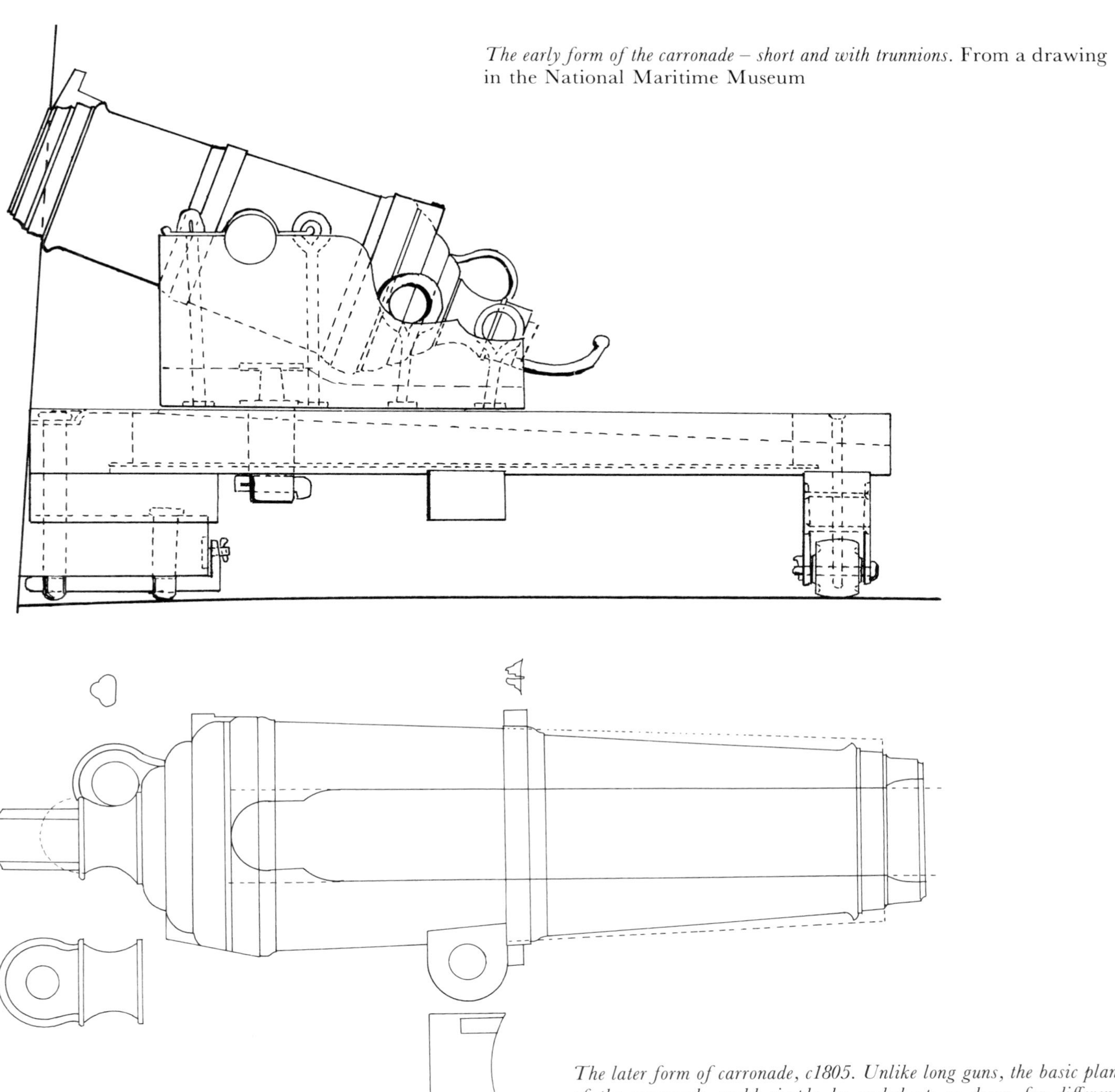

The early form of the carronade – short and with trunnions. From a drawing in the National Maritime Museum

The later form of carronade, c1805. Unlike long guns, the basic plan of the carronade could simply be scaled up or down for different calibres. From a drawing in the Carron papers

ships. In the following year, the first brig sloops to be designed round a main armament of carronades were begun, and, in 1797, carronades began to replace long guns, rather than supplement them, on the quarterdecks and forecastles of ships-of-the-line and frigates. As a general rule, the smaller the ship the greater proportion of carronades among her armament. Brig sloops were often armed almost entirely with carronades, while a first rate like the *Victory* carried only two, albeit 68-pounders. By the 1800s, most ships carried carronades in one form or another, though 'so unequally on board ships of the same class, that it is not possible to give general statement of the ordnance now in use.'[1]

The carronade also inspired several types of gun intended as a compromise between it and the standard long gun. This began with a 32-pounder invented by Sadler in 1796. It weighed 24cwt, and was tested aboard the *Dart* experimental sloop, but it was never adopted generally. In 1805 a 24-pounder of 33cwt was designed by Captain Gover. It was first used aboard the frigate *Narcissus*, and, in 1806, it was fitted to several old ships-of-the-line, as part of total 24-pounder armament — long guns on the lower deck, Gover guns on the upper deck, and carronades on the upper works. In 1812 Blomefield developed another short 24-pounder, while Congreve, the inventor of the naval rocket, designed another. They were tested aboard two frigates in 1813, and 300 of the Congreve pattern, rather like an elongated carronade in shape, were ordered before the end of the war.

The Design of Carronades

Early carronades, of American War vintage, were short, fat and had trunnions. The weapon seems to have been redesigned during the peace of 1783–93, and emerged somewhat longer, with a loop underneath instead of trunnions, and with a nozzle at the muzzle in place of a conventional swell. Instead of a button, a carronade had a ring at the breech, bored with a hole to take the elevating screw. The pattern did not change much after 1793. All carronades, of whatever calibre, were designed to a standard set of proportions. They had a chamber which was narrower than the bore. Typically, a carronade was about a quarter of the weight of a long gun of the same calibre. The largest gun was the 68-pounder, which weighed 36cwt. It gained fame aboard the *Victory* at Trafalgar, but it was never standard, and it was little used except as the subsidiary armament of bomb vessels. The 42-pounder, which weighed 22cwt, was more common, but it was not standard either. The 32-pounder weighed 17cwt, and was used on a wide variety of ships, from sixth to first rate. The 24-pounder weighed 13cwt, and was often used as the main armament of sloops and brigs. The 18-pounder, of 10cwt, had been common in the American War but tended to decline after that. The 12-pounder, of around 6cwt, similarly, was largely being replaced by heavier weapons.

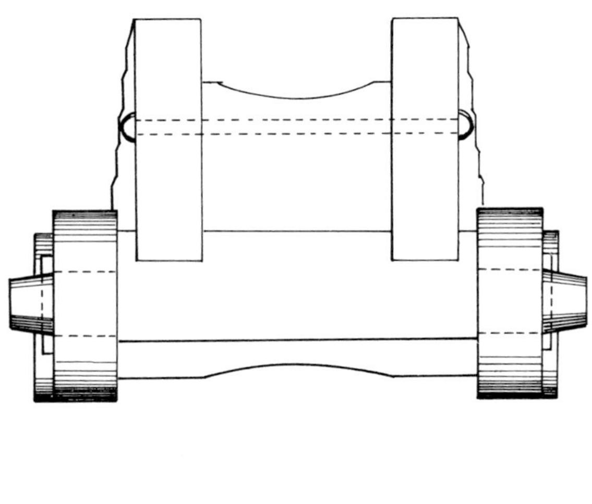

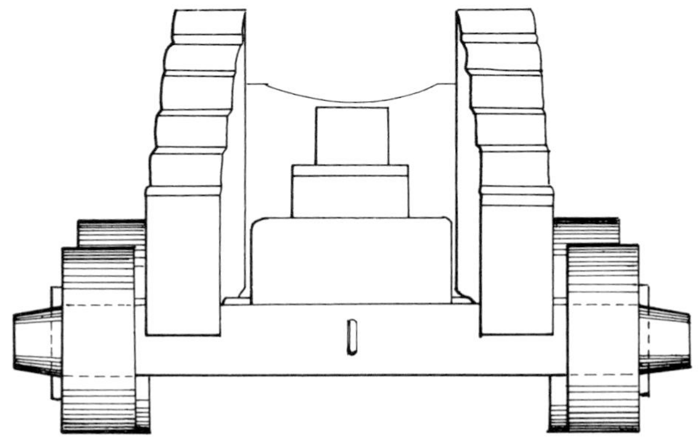

Gun Carriages

The standard ship's gun carriage was known as the 'truck' carriage — named after the four small wheels on which it was mounted. The two sides of the carriage, known as brackets, were each made from two pieces of timber. The rearmost part of each bracket had a system of steps, which provided surfaces against which the breech could be levered up. The forward part was mainly straight, except for a semi-circular hole for the trunnion of the gun. The brackets were held apart by the forward and rear axle, and also by a large piece of timber known as a transom, fitted above the forward axle. Iron work included: the linch pins which held the tricks in place on the axle, the capsquares which hinged over the trunnions and were locked in position by means of the forelock key, the ringbolts and eyebolts for the gun tackle, and the long bolts which held the structure together. At the rear of the assembled carriage was the stool bed. This supported the quoins, or wedges, which were moved in and out to elevate and depress the gun.

Gun carriages were made in different sizes, according to the type of gun they were designed for, and the height of the gunports of the ship. They were made and issued by the Ordnance Board, and stored at the armament depots.

Carronade carriages, in contrast, were made by the Carron Company and came with the guns. A few carronades had conventional truck carriages, but most had the specially designed carriage. This had two main parts — the bed, which was basically a solid piece of wood with an iron fitting to receive the bolt for the loop of the gun; and the slide, along which the bed slid up and down for recoil or loading. The carronade carriage was always easier to traverse than that of an ordinary gun, though methods of rotating the slide varied somewhat over the years. In the 1780s the pivot had been fitted outside the hull of the ship, but, after about 1790, it was placed inside. The rear part of the carriage was fitted with small wheels, set across the gun, aiding the traversing movement. After 1804, it became quite common to fit carronades on the 'non-recoil' principle (though it is not always clear what this meant). After 1808, some guns had normal trucks in addition to the small wheels, so that they could be taken away from their gunports at the sides of the quarterdeck and used over the stern if necessary. The carronade was elevated by means of a screw passing through the cascable.

Gun Tackle

A gun was allowed to recoil during firing, to bring it into the loading position. The rope which limited this recoil was the breech rope. This was quite thick — 7in in circumference for a 32-pounder. Its ends were fixed to eyebolts on the side of the ship, beside the gun ports, and with the Blomefield pattern it passed through the loop at the end of the gun, and the ringbolts on the brackets. The gun tackle proper was used to haul out the gun for firing. It had a double and a single block, with a rope passed through them to form a block-and-tackle arrangement. One block hooked into an eyebolt in the bracket of the carriage, and the other to another eyebolt on the side of the ship. Each gun needed two tackles, one on each side. The train tackle was similar to the gun tackle, but it operated at the rear of the gun, from an eyebolt at the rear of the carriage, to another fixed to the deck near the centreline of the ship. It served to keep the gun from rolling back out during reloading. When not in service, the gun and breeching tackles were lashed together, or frapped, and the muzzle was lashed to another pair of eyebolts fixed above the gun port.

A gunport lid was approximately square, and often fitted with a scuttle, or a 'bull's eye' of glass, to allow some light to enter when the port was closed. The port lid had two hinges, and it was opened by means of the port tackle, which was attached to the ringbolts at the lower ends of the hinges. It passed through the side of the ship, and was hauled in by means of an arrangement of blocks, fitted to the beams of the deck above. Guns in the waist, quarterdeck and forecastle had no deck above, and their ports were not fitted with lids.

Gun Implements and Gunners' Stores

One of the most important tools for loading and firing the guns was the flexible rammer, made of thick rope, with a wooden rammer head at one end, and a sponge at the other. Ladles were provided for powder, but these were mainly used in making up cartridges, not

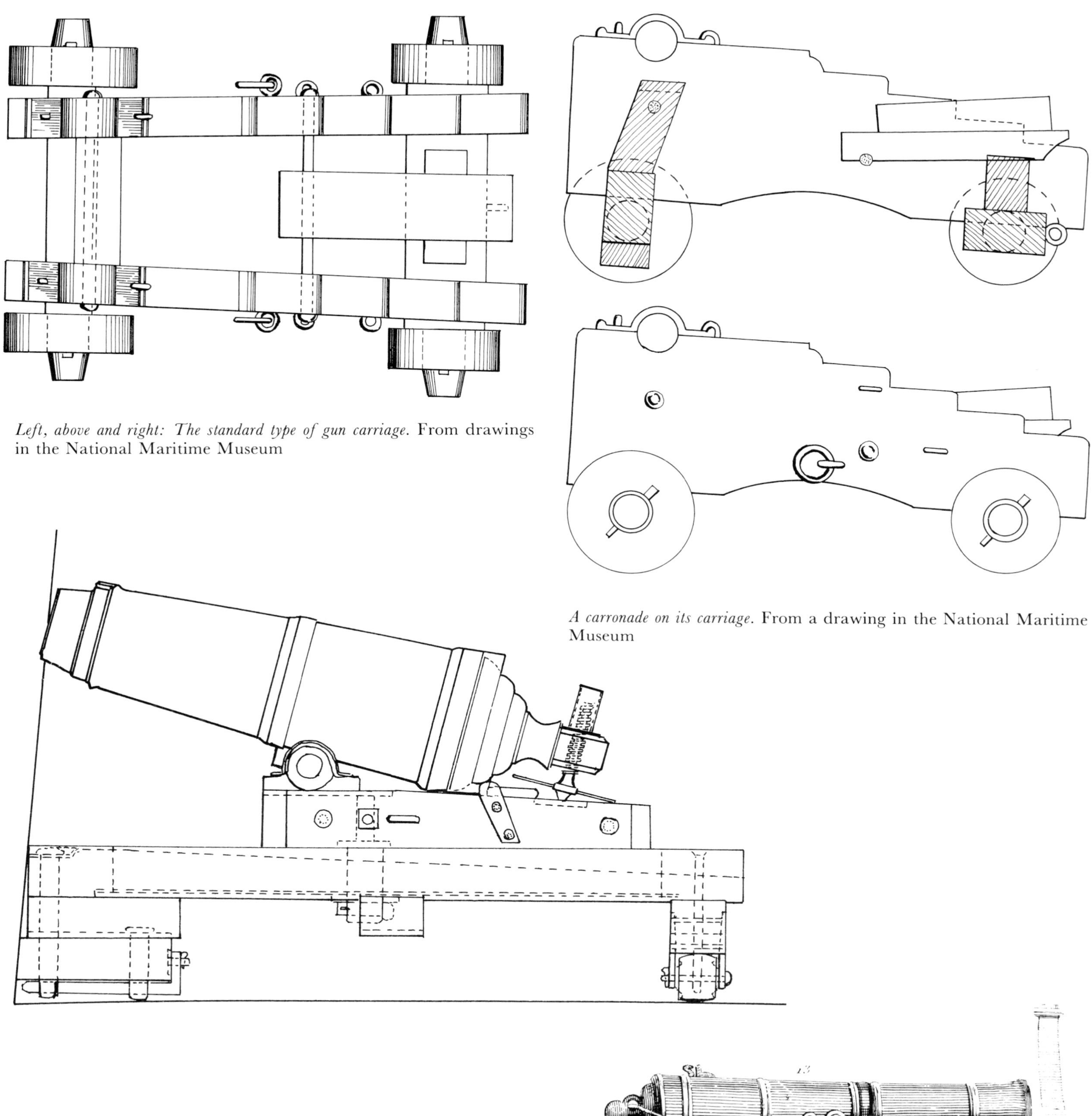

Left, above and right: The standard type of gun carriage. From drawings in the National Maritime Museum

A carronade on its carriage. From a drawing in the National Maritime Museum

A Blomefield gun, showing the gun tackle with its blocks, and the breech tackle, with one end loose. From Serres's *Liber Nauticus*

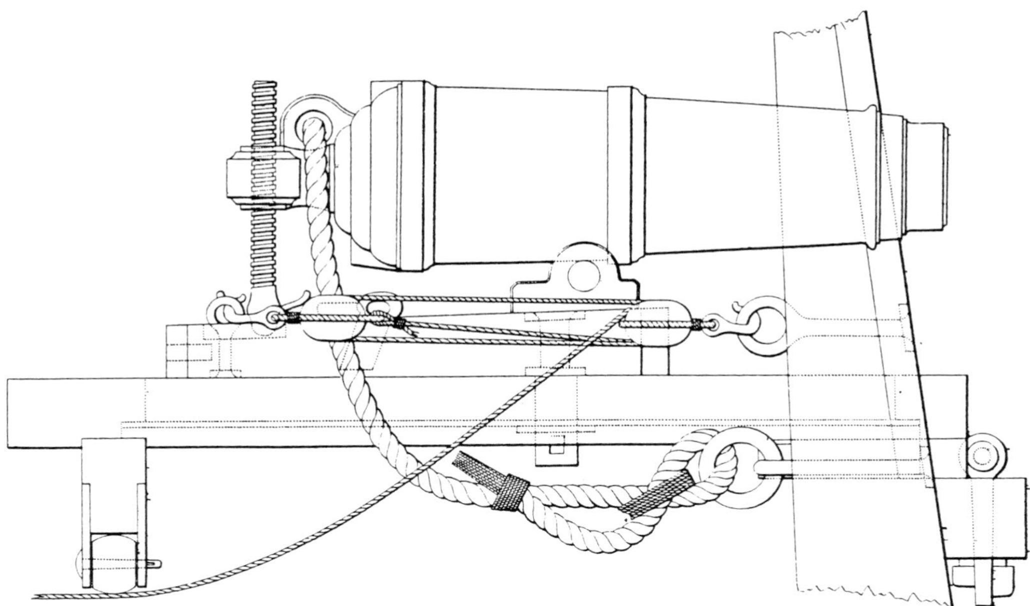

A carronade and its tackle. From Charles Dupin's *Voyages dans la Grande Bretagne*, 1821

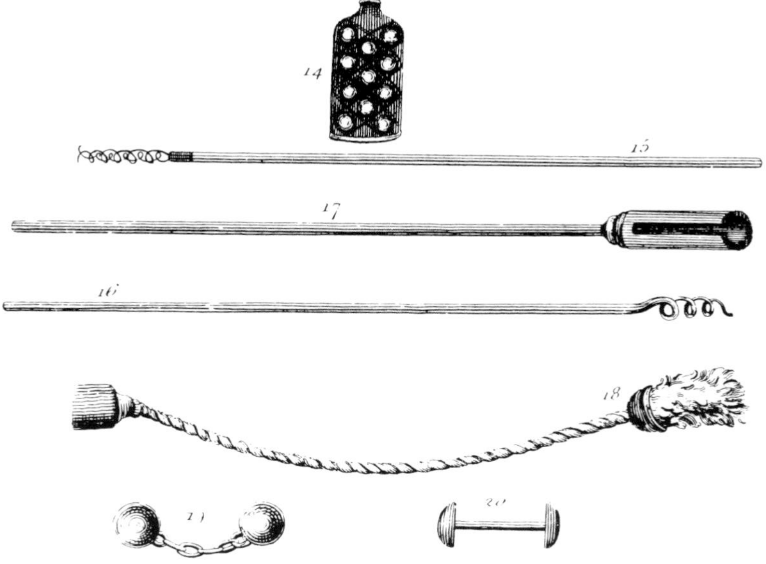

Gun implements, from Serres's Liber Nauticus. *15, a worm for removing charges. 16, another type of worm. 17, a ladle, used to measure out powder to fill cartridges. 18, the rope rammer, with a sponge at one end and the rammer at the other. Also shown are: (14) case or canister shot, (19) chain shot, and (20) bar shot.*

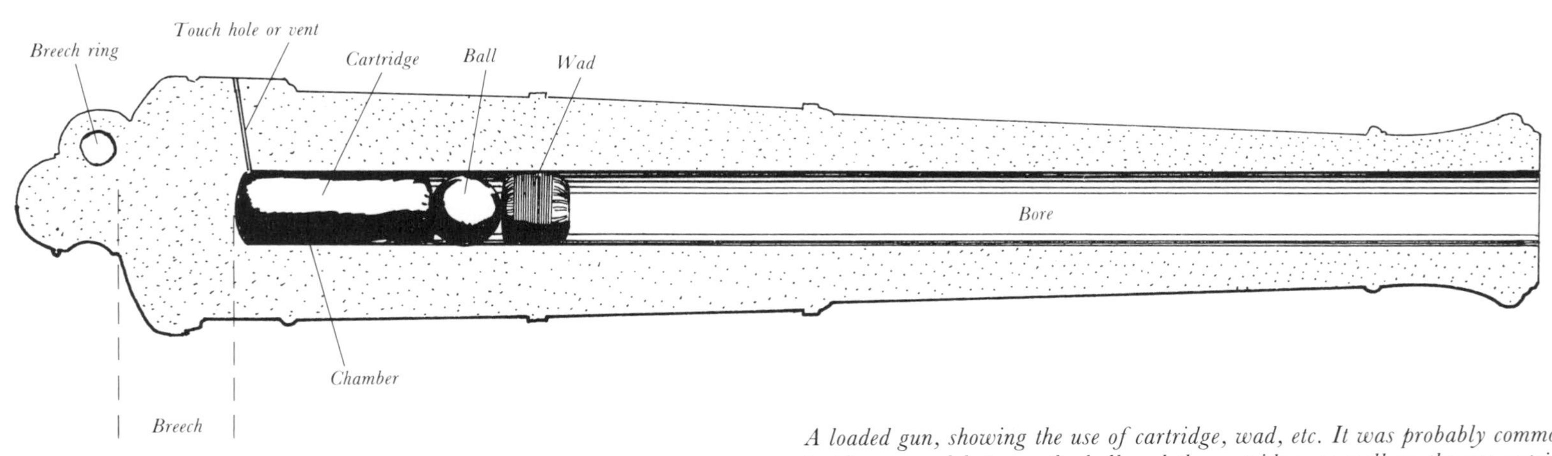

A loaded gun, showing the use of cartridge, wad, etc. It was probably common to place a wad between the ball and the cartridge, as well as the one outside the ball. From a drawing in the Public Record Office

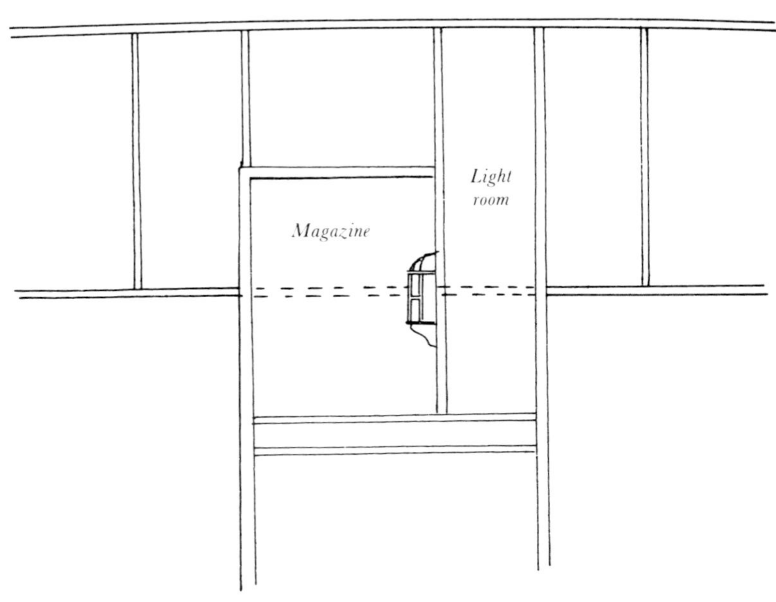

The type of magazine fitted to small frigates, of 32 and 28 guns. Larger ships had more elaborate versions. From a drawing in the Public Record Office

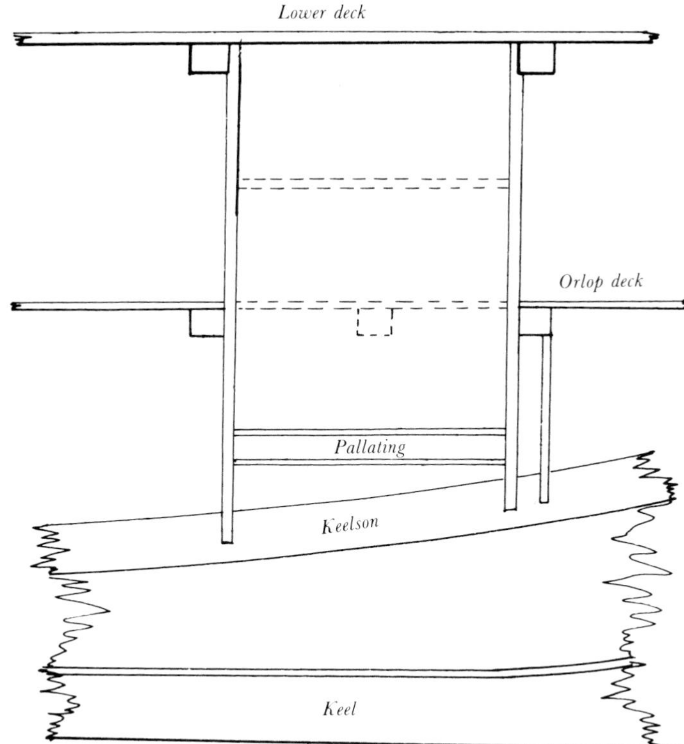

in action. A wadhook, rather like a giant corkscrew, was used for removing the charge from a gun. By this time it was common to fit locks to guns, so that matches were not normally needed. Powder horns were provided, for placing small amounts of powder down the touch hole for priming. 'Crows of iron', and wooden 'hand crow levers' were used to traverse the gun, by lifting under the rear axle and levering it round. Tampions were used to plug the mouth of the gun when not in use; they were very simply made on a lathe, and had none of the decoration of the modern equivalent. When the gun was kept loaded, an 'apron' of lead was placed over the touch hole and tied round the gun. If locks were fitted, a specially shaped apron fitted over the lock as well.

The gunners' stores included hundreds of other items — spare parts for the guns, carriages, and tackle; old rope ('junk') to make wads; paper, and flannel to make cartridges; and a complete set of armourers' tools, including a portable forge which could be set up on shore when necessary.

Powder and Shot

Gunpowder was made in mills at Faversham and Dartford in Kent, and at Waltham Abbey in Essex. It was a mixture of charcoal, saltpetre and sulphur; for the great guns, it was 'corned' — it was wetted and formed into grains to increase its consistency, and aid the circulation of air. In 1783, it was discovered that charcoal made in cylinders was much more efficient than the old type, and the new 'cylinder' powder was introduced to the navy around 1800. It had to be kept separate from other powder, because of the danger of overloading guns. It was stored in containers with red lettering, instead of blue or white. Powder was issued in wooden casks with copper or wooden hoops. Aboard ship, it was made up into cartridges of flannel or paper.

Powder was potentially the most dangerous of the commodities aboard ship. Besides its combustibility, it also had to be protected from damp, and magazines were especially constructed to keep out these dangers. No fire or iron were allowed into the magazine, and it was lit by means of a light room — a completely separate compartment with lanterns, lighting the magazine through panes of glass. The magazine was constructed to keep the powder away from the sides of the ship, and the deck was specially constructed, with small panels filled with charcoal to absorb any damp. On a ship of any size, the main magazine was invariably situated in the forward part of the hold. Forward of the magazine proper was the filling room, used for making up cartridges and storing them on racks. Two-deckers usually had a small powder room aft, and three-deckers had an additional one in midships.

Shot was easier to store, though it had to be kept dry to prevent rust. The shot lockers were amidships, forward and aft of the pump well. Around 1800, it became common to fit another shot locker, just aft of the main magazine. Solid iron round shot was the most common type — a 74-gun ship carried sixty rounds of this per gun in the 1790s. Grape shot, intended for use against personnel was carried at the rate of five rounds per gun, and double-headed hammered shot, in the shape of a barbell and used against rigging, at three rounds per gun. Only bomb vessels carried explosive shells.

Small Arms and Other Weapons

The ship's muskets, including those of the marines, were under the care of the gunner, and were repaired by his assistant, the armourer. Around 1790, a 74-gun ship carried 184 with bright metalwork, and 46 blackened ones, in addition to those for the marines. In 1797, this was reduced to 130, all black. She also had 70 pairs of pistols, 200 hand grenades, and various edged weapons for use in boarding — 60 poleaxes, 230 swords and 100 pikes. Later, it became common to carry tomahawks as well.

Part IV
OFFICERS

1 Officers' Entry and Training

The Need for Training

Commissioned officers, or 'sea officers' as they were often known in the eighteenth century, were the only group of men who had most of their training within the Royal Navy. Seamen were largely recruited from the merchant service, and surgeons, pursers and carpenters learned their professions ashore before going to sea. Masters, boatswains and gunners were usually promoted from among the seamen, as were the petty officers. However, the regulations demanded that a man must serve for at least three years as a midshipman or master's mate in the Royal Navy before qualifying for lieutenant, and have served a total of six years at sea.

The training of potential officers was not very systematic. There was a Naval College at Portsmouth, but only a small minority of entrants passed through it. Otherwise, the training of midshipmen and others was left almost entirely to the captain of each ship, with or without the assistance of the schoolmaster. Most 'young gentlemen' served on several ships before qualifying as lieutenant, and their training must have been erratic. However, a lieutenant had great responsibilities, whether in charge of a watch, as commander of a small vessel, in charge of a prize or landing party, or as a divisional officer. There were plenty of abuses in the system, and some incompetent lieutenants; but the majority were capable and well qualified, with a sound knowledge of seamanship and navigation.

Servants and Volunteers

The regulations demanded that no-one 'be rated as master's mate or midshipman who shall not have been three years at sea, and . . . [is] in all respects qualified for such an appointment'.[1] There were several ways of getting in this three years. Someone with good connections in the service (as most midshipmen had) could have his name borne on the books of a ship for several years, though the young man himself was still at school, or even in the nursery. Lord Cochrane was perhaps the most famous example; he had been entered at the age of five, and carried on one ship or another commanded by his uncle until he reached the age of eighteen. In 1801, a lieutenant was convicted of drawing the pay for his son, aged one, registered as an able seaman.[2] Naturally, it is impossible to collect statistics on such practices, but they were certainly quite common.

But many young men did serve the appropriate time at sea, though not, of course, as common seamen. Until the French Revolutionary War, the most usual practice was to enter as a 'captain's servant'. Each captain was allowed four such men for every hundred men in the complement of his ship. Clearly the captain of a 74 did not need twenty-four servants, but perhaps twenty of them were young men who intended to become officers. This period would usually be followed by another when they were rated as 'able seamen' on the ship's books.

In 1794, an Order in Council abolished this system and created a new class of 'Volunteers Class I' — 'to consist of young gentlemen intended for the sea service (whether the sons of sea officers or not) provided they are not under the age of eleven years; to be styled Volunteers, and allowed wages at the rate of six pounds per annum.'[3] Later, the regulations were changed so that only sons of officers could enter at eleven; the rest had to wait until thirteen. Basil Hall reckoned that thirteen was the latest age at which a young man should go to sea, although 'the early age of thirteen, at which they must of necessity go on board ship, renders it almost impossible to acquire any great stock of what is usually called knowledge'.[4] The regulations do not specify how the 'youngsters' were to be taken on, but clearly personal or family acquaintance of the captain of a ship was the major factor.

Traditionally these 'youngsters' were placed in the care of the gunner, and lived in the gunroom on a ship-of-the-line. 'In the *Irrisistible* I again messed with the gunner, Mr Gallant, who took great care of me.'[5] In 1805 the gunner was moved out of the gunroom, but it seems that the 'young gentlemen' stayed there. On frigates, they probably berthed among the older midshipmen.

The Royal Naval College

The third method of beginning the path to a commission was through the Royal Naval College, Portsmouth. This had been founded in 1729, for forty students aged between thirteen and sixteen, who would each take up to three years to complete a 'plan of learning', in the form of an illustrated book. Those with some previous sea experience were encouraged, and preference was given to the sons of officers. The school never became popular, possibly because there was an

A young man packs his chest before going to sea, while the family and servants look on. The National Maritime Museum

The Royal Naval College, Portsmouth. From the Naval Chronicle

aversion to book-learning in the navy, or because it tended to infringe on the captains' privileges in the matter of taking on volunteers and 'servants'. In 1806 its establishment was increased to seventy students, of whom forty were sons of naval officers on scholarships. Its staff included James Inman, the author of a famous set of nautical tables. Students were taught seamanship, navigation, mathematics, physics, astronomy, gunnery, fortification and other subjects. But only a small proportion of naval officers were trained in this way.[6] At Gosport, there was a similar institution, supported by private enterprise, and known as the Naval Academy. It had eighty students per year, and they attended at the ages of eleven and twelve before going to sea.[7]

Social Background

Midshipmen came from a wide social background. The highest of all was Prince William, the future King William IV, who served as a midshipman in several ships between 1780–5, before being commissioned. Several came from the highest ranks of the aristocracy, though mostly younger sons rather than the principal heirs to the estates — Howe was the grandson of a viscount, and Cornwallis the son of an earl. Naturally, the total numbers of these people were small, but their promotion prospects were good, and they had considerable influence on the navy. The landed gentry provided a much higher proportion of midshipmen, and it has been estimated that about 27 per cent of naval officers came from their ranks.[8] The largest group was the sons of professional men, who made up 50 per cent of the officer corps. Nelson was the son of a Norfolk parson, though his family also had strong naval connections. The professional group, of course, included the sons of naval officers themselves, and they made up about a quarter of the total number of officers. There were many well-established naval families, such as Samaurez, Hood, and Parker. A captain or an admiral in the family was an obvious advantage to any young man's career, because of the power of promotion that these officers held, and this power was sometimes abused. Admiral Rodney promoted his son to captain at the age of fifteen in 1780; the young man was later court-martialled for negligence, and debarred from any further promotion, so that he served longer as a captain than anyone else in naval history. Edward Pellew also had his son promoted at an early age; but he in fact proved a very capable officer. Other officers had fathers in medicine, the law, the army and the civil service. Far less common, were men from commercial or working-class backgrounds. Together, these made up only about ten per cent of officers. Perhaps, there were more sons of merchants among the midshipmen, but they failed to reach commissioned rank, because of lack of 'influence'. There were probably fewer sons of labourers and artisans in the midshipmens' berth, and the few who reached commissioned rank did so by other means.

The Midshipman

According to the regulations, a first rate was allowed twenty-four midshipmen, a 74-gun ship was allowed twenty, a small or medium-sized frigate six, and a sloop two. In addition, Volunteers First Class were carried, though the exact number was not specified.

Not all midshipmen were young. Some continually failed in their examination for lieutenant, or were passed over for an actual commission, but nevertheless served on one ship after another. Billy Culmer was a noted character in the navy, proud to be called 'the oldest midshipman in the fleet'. He had first entered in 1755, and was not promoted to lieutenant until 1790, at the age of fifty-seven.[9] Basil Hall mentions one midshipman 'who was more than twice as old as most of us, say about thirty'.[10] However, the typical age of midshipmen was between fifteen and twenty-two.

Some youthful midshipmen let power go to their heads, and became tyrants over the lower deck. According to Jack Nastyface,

> We had a midshipman on board of a wickedly mischevious disposition, whose sole delight was to insult the feelings of seamen and furnish pretexts to get them punished... He was a youth of not more than twelve or thirteen years of age; I have often seen him get on to the carriage of a gun, call a man to him, and kick him about the thighs and body, and with his feet would beat him about the head; and these, though prime seamen, at the same time dared not murmur.[11]

In the midshipmen's berth the atmosphere was more light-hearted, though many of the pranks were cruel and dangerous. Apart from such harmless pursuits as sending newcomers to 'go and hear the dogfish bark', there was much bullying of younger or unpopular members of the mess. 'Mr Cullen, as usual with all novitiates, had tricks and annoyances played upon him by the young mids; in particular one was very annoying, more than the others.'[12] Offenders against the code of the mess could be 'cobbed' or beaten by the others.

Midshipmen's Training and Duties

Midshipmen took a full part in the watch system of the ship. According to Basil Hall, 'These young gentlemen are divided into three watches, and the individuals of each part are stationed on different parts of the deck. The mate of the watch, who is the principal person amongst them, with two or three youngsters, walks on the quarterdeck... Another midshipman, generally the second in seniority, has the honour of being posted on the forecastle; while a third, stationed abaft, walks on the poop.'[13] As a seaman, Robert Wilson saw midshipmen differently. 'Their duty in watches is to call the officer of the next watch, to heave the log and mark the log board, and many other things as required.'[14] During tacking ship, 'The midshipmen are treading on each other's toes in the quarterdeck, except one or two who are on the forecastle.' Another was in charge of signals.[15] However, at other times the midshipman's life was more exciting. He often had command of one of the ship's boats, and might even be allowed to take command of a prize, and navigate into port. In action, he might act as aide-de-camp to the captain, or deputy to one of the lieutenants in command of a division of guns.

Some captains laid down regular training schemes for midshipmen. Aboard the *Amazon* in 1802, they were 'to be assembled every afternoon on the quarterdeck'. On Mondays they were to train at casting the lead, or practise on the mizzen topsail yard, on Tuesdays, to exercise at the small arms under the sergeant of marines, on Wednesdays, to learn knots and splices under the boatswain, on Thursdays, to exercise on the mizzen topsail again; on Fridays to exercise at the great guns; and on Saturdays, to 'attend with the boatswain'.[16] Midshipmen were expected to keep detailed navigational logs on all ships, and on the *Hyperion* in 1811, Captain Cumby ordered that they send them into the captain each day, 'as soon as may be after noon, their *own* account of the ship's way and position to be ascertained by log, chronometer and lunar observation'.[17]

Midshipmen were often punished, largely because their high spirits needed to be kept in check. One well-known form of punishment was 'mastheading' — sending the alleged offender to sit at the crosstrees of the main for several hours. Another was 'kissing the gunner's daughter'; though midshipmen were not publicly flogged like seamen, they — and more especially the youngsters — could be put over the barrel of a gun and flogged, usually by the gunner or one of his mates.

Midshipmen's Living Conditions

Towards the end of the eighteenth century, two midshipmen's berths

The after cockpit of a ship-of-the-line. Like most drawings, it greatly exaggerates the height between decks, but it gives an impression of the subdivision of space, and shows something of the attempts to decorate it by painting. The National Maritime Museum

A slightly more realistic view of the midshipmen's berth, with the new arrival being shocked at conditions on board. The National Maritime Museum

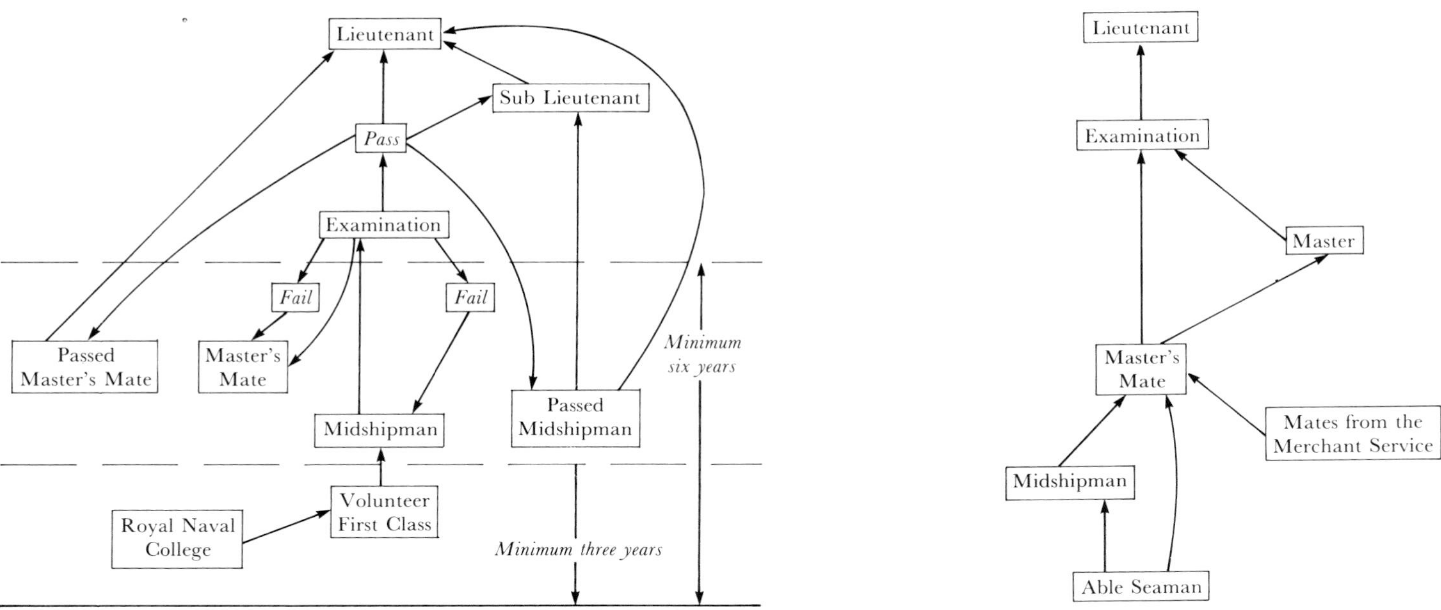

Possible routes to a commission.
a. Normal entry, as volunteer and then midshipman
b. Lower deck routes

A newly promoted lieutenant (post 1812) shows off his epaulette. The National Maritime Museum were fitted on the orlop deck of each ship-of-the-line, being added to the forward end of the row of cabins on each side of the after cockpit. On a frigate, the two berths were on the lower deck, forward of the rows of officers' cabins. Aboard the frigate *Squirrel* in 1789, 'There were eight midshipmen and two mates belonging to the ship, divided into two berths, the starboard or right hand side of the ship and larboard or left hand. Mr Cullen [the new surgeon's mate] by recommendation by Mr Fisher was admitted into the starboard, as it was then, and continued to be the best.'[18] Hall describes his mess aboard a small two-decker in the early 1800s, 'it is a place about twenty feet long, with a table in the middle of it, and wooden seats upon which we sit... There are fourteen of us in the mess at the same time.'[19] According to William Dillon, 'as soon as the appearance of more mids enabled us to form a mess, I joined the larboard berth. We had a number of fine gentlemanly young men, but only four that could be called youngsters.'[20] The midshipmen dined on the same food as the men, unless they had enough money to buy their own, or were favoured by the other officers. 'Captain Harvey always sent the remains of his pudding to us midshipmen, and we regularly looked for them.'[21] The meals were served by two or three servants.

The berth was used for eating, study and recreation. At night the midshipmen slung their hammocks in the open space in the middle of the cockpit, and had to take them up in the daytime in the same way as the seamen; Richard Parker, future leader of the Nore mutiny, was court-martialled in 1793 for refusing to take up his hammock as ordered, and reduced to seaman.

The midshipman was expected to supply all his equipment, including uniform, bedding, books and navigational equipment. This could be quite expensive, and some financial backing from parents or guardians was usually needed. James Gardner was devastated by the loss of his chest in 1794. 'I found that the ship had gone into dock, and that my chest, and that of another gentleman's who had lately joined, had not been removed to the hulk, but left in the ship, where it was broke open, and everything I possessed, with the exception of my quadrant, stolen.'[22] Midshipmen and volunteers first class had the social privileges of officers, in that they were allowed to take their recreation on the quarterdeck.

Masters' Mates

Originally, a master's mate was an experienced seaman, assistant to the master, but not in line for promotion to lieutenant. By the mid-eighteenth century, he was far more likely to be a superior midshipman, still waiting to pass his examination or to receive his commission, but taking rather more responsibility aboard ship. Six master's mates were allowed on a first rate, three on a third rate, and two on most frigates. Normally, they worked on a three-watch system, with the lieutenants, so that one served as the deputy to the lieutenant on each watch. The senior master's mate was the head of the midshipmen's berth.

Promotion from the Lower Deck

Some men reached commissioned rank after entry as a common seaman — perhaps 3 per cent of the whole officer corps. Some of these were rated midshipmen for a time, but had never served as 'captain's servant' or volunteer first class; presumably they were older than the other midshipmen. Others had served in the merchant service, usually as mates. Some became masters' mates immediately after entry. 'We pressed him and several mates of merchantmen out of a cartel from Marseilles to Gibraltar, and put them on the quarterdeck.'[23] One notable case of a man from the merchant service was James Bowen, who served as master of the flagship *Queen Charlotte* at the First of June battle in 1794. He was one of the few masters to be commissioned, as a reward for services during the battle; he eventually became a rear admiral, though he was not a lieutenant until the age of forty-three. Similarly, Phillip Lovell had entered the navy as an ordinary seaman in 1778, served to 1782, mostly as a captain's clerk, then re-entered in 1801. He became midshipman at the age of thirty-six, and was passed for lieutenant at the age of forty-one. William Millet had a similar career, passing at the age of thirty-eight.

Passing for Lieutenant

The examination for lieutenant, after at least six years' sea service, was one of the great ordeals in an officer's career. He had to be at least nineteen years old, and to produce journals and certificates for his service. Originally, a candidate had to go to London for his exam, but later one was held on the first Wednesday of every month, in each of the main home ports. The candidate was summoned before the board of three captains and questioned about seamanship and navigation. Basil Hall thought that this was not enough: 'There is a third branch, at least of equal importance to the well being of every ship that swims, and of the Royal Navy in particular, which is hardly ever alluded to, and never, as far as I know, made to form any part of these examinations; I mean the science of discipline.'[25]

The actual severity of the exam varied quite considerably. Boteler records that he was examined by a captain who knew him already, and he persuaded the others to pass him on the basis of what he had done aboard ship. '"And now as to seamanship?" "Well, so good that I once gave him charge of a watch and he acquitted himself entirely to my satisfaction." Such was my passing,' wrote Boteler, 'and I venture to say it stands alone in the service.'[26] However, James Anthony Gardner's examination does not sound very different. 'One of the Commissioners was an intimate friend of my father, and Sir Marshall Samuel... was a particular friend of... my mother's uncle... Commissioner Harwood, after a few questions had been put to me, said, "I think we need not ask you any more".' One of the examiners insisted on one more question, but, after that, the three agreed to pass him, giving certificates 'which ought to get me a commission without interest.'[27] Basil Hall also had an easy ride. 'In fact the examination, instead of turning out, as I had anticipated, an over-strict one, proved so ridiculously easy.'[28]

Charles Middleton, later Lord Barham, was a much more conscientious officer. Around 1790, he made a list of about thirty questions he intended to ask, including the following:

> You are sent to a ship ordered to be fitted out, the captain not having appeared; the lower masts and bowsprits are in, but not rigged; what part of the rigging goes first over the mast heads?
>
> Your ship being now under courses, you are supposed to be in such a situation as to oblige you to wear; give the proper orders, and wear your ship.
>
> An enemy is observed; give orders for clearing your ship, and make all the necessary preparations for engaging.[29]

Many candidates could be defeated by such questions; Boteler records some of the reactions of those who had been questioned before him. He describes 'The entry of a mid. who had missed stays, saying, "if it were not for going to the devil he would jump overboard." Then came another with "Hurrah, steward, some grog, by return of packet there will be my promotion. A bottle of champagne for luck. I have passed," in great glee.'[30] The passed midshipman was able to convince the board of 'his diligence and sobriety'. He could 'splice, reef a sail, work a ship in sailing, shift his tides, keep a reckoning of the ship's way by plane sailing and Mercator; observe by sun or star, and find the variation of the compass, and is qualified to do the duty of able seaman and midshipman'. In a later form he was also 'well qualified to take charge of a watch on board any of His Majesty's ships'.[31]

Sub Lieutenants and Passed Midshipmen

Even passing the examination did not guarantee promotion to lieutenant, for a commission was to an individual ship, and did not come until there was a suitable vacancy. It was said that, in 1813, there were nearly 2000 men who had passed but were waiting for an appointment.[32] Here again, 'interest' played a part. Midshipmen serving on the flagship had a natural advantage, as admirals on foreign stations had power to promote them. Those with good family or political connections could attract the notice of the Admiralty, and get an immediate appointment. Possibly those who did very well in the examination were given preference, as Gardner hints. The rest often had to wait some years for an appointment; those still waiting at the end of the war were mostly promoted on the half-pay list, though they never served as commissioned officers aboard ship.

While waiting for a commission, it was possible for an officer to serve as a sub lieutenant. This was a purely temporary rank, held during a particular appointment. Gun brigs and similar small ships were commanded by lieutenants, who needed qualified seconds in command. They were to be 'taken from the list of young men who have passed an examination and are qualified to serve as lieutenants in Your Majesty's Navy but that they should not be placed on the general list of the lieutenants in your Majesty's fleet'.[33] The rank was initiated in 1804, and seems to have lapsed at the end of the war. A sublieutenant counted as a commissioned officer while he held the rank.

2 Commissioned Officers

The Sea Officers

The commissioned sea officers, from lieutenant to admiral of the fleet, were distinguished from other naval personnel in several ways, apart from their training. Besides marine officers, they were the only officers who held commissions from the Admiralty — other officers, such as surgeons and masters, held only warrants from the Navy Board. They had a much more clearly defined rank structure than other officers, for they could rise to command fleets and squadrons, whereas other officers had few opportunities above the individual ship. The commissioned sea officers were the 'fighting' officers, who gained most of the prestige from successful naval actions. Marine officers were equal to them in social prestige, but they had a purely subordinate role in the ship hierarchy.

All commissioned officers were sea officers, trained in navigation, seamanship, and gunnery to a roughly equal extent. There was no attempt at specialisation among them, for navigation was the province of the master, ship maintenance of the carpenter, supply of the purser, and so on. A competent sea officer could be expected to oversee any of these departments, but he would not devote undue attention to it. An officer might specialise in signals for a short time, perhaps as flag lieutenant to an admiral; but this was not a recognised branch of the service, and had no established career pattern.

The sea officers could trace their pedigree back to the middle ages, or perhaps earlier. In those days it had been common to take merchant ships into the naval service for a short campaign, with their own crews led by the master. A company of soldiers would be put on board, headed by a captain and lieutenant. With the development of naval gunnery in the sixteenth century, the role of the soldier declined, but the captain and lieutenant grew somewhat in importance. It became increasingly necessary for a captain to have

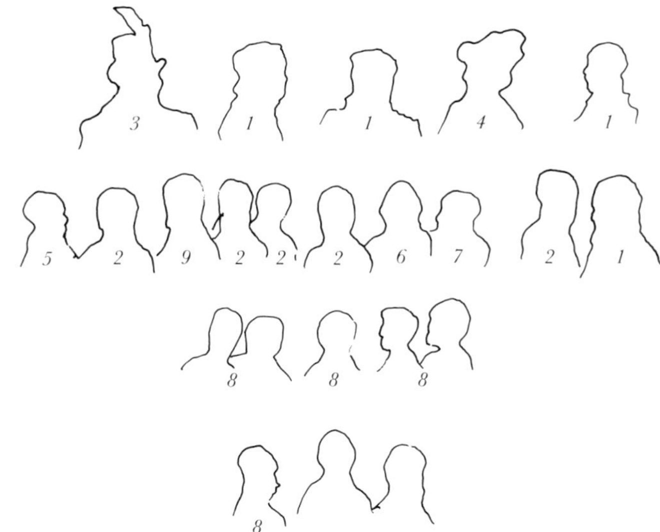

Above and right: Officers involved in the Diamond Rock affair, 1804
1 Captains
2 Lieutenants
3 Captain of marines
4 Lieutenant of marines
5 Master
6 Purser
7 Surgeon
8 Mishipmen
9 Admiral's secretary
The National Maritime Museum

Admiral of the Fleet (1)
Admiral of the Red (21)
Admiral of the White (20)
Admiral of the Blue (20)
Vice Admiral of the Red (22)
Vice Admiral of the White (19)
Vice Admiral of the Blue (24)
Rear Admiral of the Red (19)
Rear Admiral of the White (17)
Rear Admiral of the Blue (24) [Superannuated Rear Admirals (31
Captains and commodores (777) [Superannuated and retired Captains (29)]
Commanders (586) [Lieutenants superannuated with the rank of Commander (54)]
Lieutenant (3104) [Lieutenants unfit for sea service (213)]

Numbers of officers in the different ranks, 1812. Numbers from Burney's Dictionary

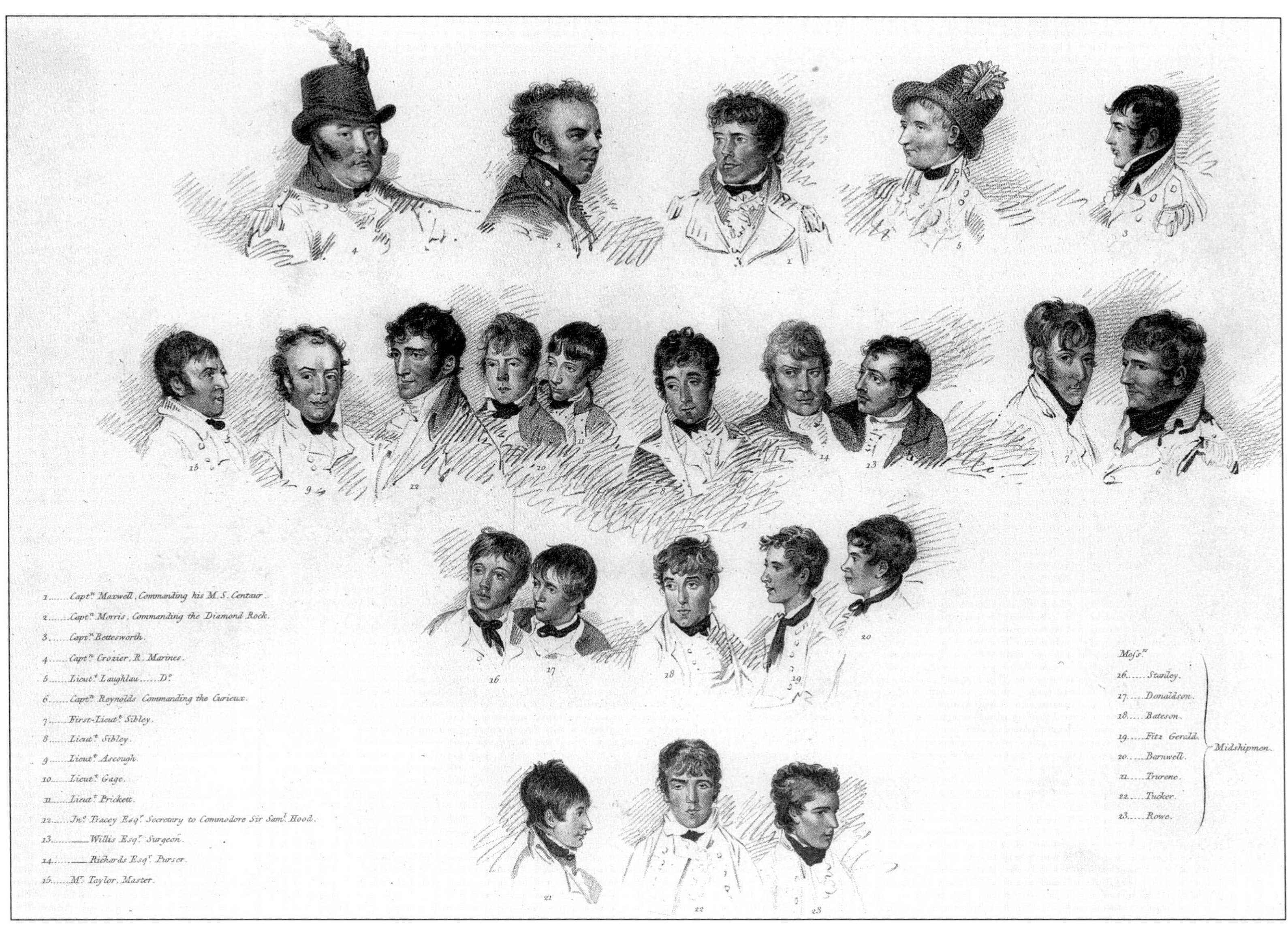

knowledge of seamanship as well as soldiering, though it was the late seventeenth century before any steps were taken to ensure that captains and lieutenants had any form of training and examination. After that, and in particular with the development of half-pay by 1714, the naval profession began to develop as a full career.

The commissioned sea officers were still occasionally referred to as the 'military' branch of the service (as distinct from the masters and other warrant officers). This was a relic of the older system, but in general the sea officers were prouder of their seamanship than their fighting skills. As Captain Mahan had observed, 'the naval officer came to feel more proud of his dexterity in managing the motive power of his ship than of his skill in developing her military efficiency'.[1] Despite many changes over the years, a naval officer's career was still a series of individual commissions linked by short or long periods on half-pay. A commission was issued to a particular post in an individual ship, eg, as captain or third lieutenant. Thus an officer might be issued with many different commissions from the Board of Admiralty, even though he was never promoted above lieutenant. An officer had a certain security, in that he was allowed half-pay, calculated at the rate of his last commission, when peacetime demobilisation, short term gluts in particular ranks, or his own incompetence or old age kept him away from active service at sea. But, as with many other aspects of naval affairs, the traditional fiction of short-term service was maintained, and it was implied that an officer served his king in an unconnected series of individual appointments.

The commissioned officers of the navy were always concerned with their status, especially in relation to the army. They felt that they were more skilled than army officers, and more successful in battle. Nevertheless, the army officers tended to have higher pay for an equivalent rank (though these things are always difficult to assess because of costs and fringe benefits). According to the facetious *Advice to Sea Lieutenants*, 'In regard to your pay, as you have the rank *in service* of a captain in the army, you should have incomes accordingly, particularly as an idea has been lately started that you do not *in private* enjoy the same rank, seeing that His Majesty, God bless him, neither you esquires, nor enables you to support their consequence.'[2] Army officers had grander uniforms, with epaulettes for junior ranks; the terms of an army officer's commission seemed to make him an intimate of the king, referring to him as 'trusty and well-beloved', while that of a naval officer warned him 'Hereof nor you nor any of you may fail as you will answer the contrary at your peril.' Naval officers were touchy about any hint that they were not gentlemen, and in 1803, when Captain Brisac was sentenced to stand in the pillory, many officers signed a petition asking the Admiralty 'to intercede with His Most Gracious Majesty for a remission of that disgraceful part of the sentence, so wounding to the feelings of the whole corps.'[3]

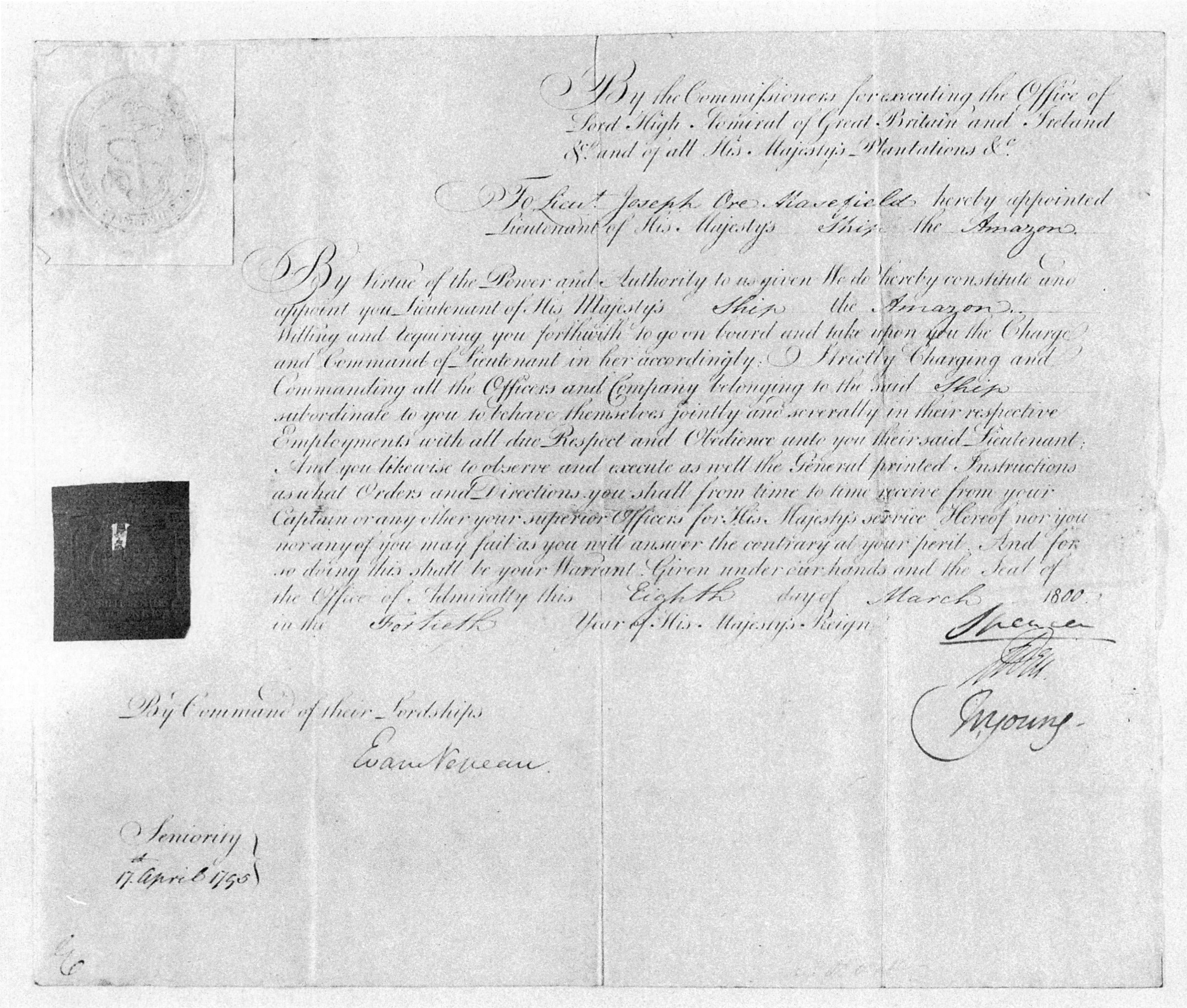

By the Commissioners for executing the Office of Lord High Admiral of Great Britain and Ireland &c. and of all His Majesty's Plantations &c.

To Lieut. Joseph Ore Masefield hereby appointed Lieutenant of His Majesty's Ship the Amazon

By Virtue of the Power and Authority to us given We do hereby constitute and appoint you Lieutenant of His Majesty's Ship the Amazon Willing and requiring you forthwith to go on board and take upon you the Charge and Command of Lieutenant in her accordingly. Strictly Charging and Commanding all the Officers and Company belonging to the said Ship subordinate to you to behave themselves jointly and severally in their respective Employments with all due Respect and Obedience unto you their said Lieutenant; And you likewise to observe and execute as well the General printed Instructions as what Orders and Directions you shall from time to time receive from your Captain or any other your superior Officers for His Majesty's service Hereof nor you nor any of you may fail as you will answer the contrary at your peril. And for so doing this shall be your Warrant Given under our hands and the Seal of the Office of Admiralty this Eighth day of March 1800 in the Fortieth Year of His Majesty's Reign

Spencer

J Young

By Command of their Lordships

Evan Nepean

Seniority
17 April 1795

A lieutenant's commission, 1800. Public Record Office

Lieutenants

In theory, a lieutenant should have been at least nineteen years of age, though a few were rather younger. The passing certificate kept an open mind on this issue by stating that the applicant 'appears to be' a certain age, and in the days before birth certificates it was difficult to prove otherwise. There was no upper age limit for a lieutenant, and some quite aged men remained in service. In 1812 there were 3327 lieutenants in the navy, including 223 who were unfit for sea service.

A lieutenant's pay remained constant in all rates of ship — it was £8.8.0 per month in 1808, exactly half that of the captain of a sixth rate. The number of lieutenants varied according to the size of the ship; eight on a first rate, five on a common class 74, three on a fifth rate frigate, and one on a sloop. A lieutenant could also be put in command of a ship smaller than a sloop, such as a schooner or gun-brig. However the great majority of lieutenants served as subordinate officers on sloops and rated ships.

According to the Admiralty Regulations, a lieutenant 'when appointed to one of His Majesty's ships, is to be constantly attentive to his duty, and is diligently and punctually to execute all orders for His Majesty's service which he may receive from the captain, or from any senior lieutenant of the ship'.[4] The first lieutenant was responsible for the administration of the crew, and did not normally keep watches. On a fifth rate and above, the other lieutenants kept watch in turn, and this was regarded as their main duty. According to the Admiralty Regulations, the lieutenant of the watch was to be constantly on deck during his watch, 'to see that the men are alert and attentive to their duty; that every precaution is taken to prevent accidents from squalls, or sudden gusts of winds; and that the ship is as perfectly prepared for battle as circumstances will admit'. The lieutenant had full responsibility for the ship after the watch was set, but he would be expected to call the captain in certain circumstances, for example if there was a change in the weather or land was sighted. The exact latitude allowed to the lieutenant varied according to the captain's inclination. Most lieutenants also had subsidiary duties. Each was in charge of a division of the crew, giving him some responsibility for the welfare of the men. Traditionally the junior lieutenant was to instruct the crew in the use of the small arms, but this duty had largely been taken over by the master at arms and the marine officers and NCOs. One lieutenant would probably take charge of the running of the wardroom mess, while another might be responsible for signals. In action, the first lieutenant stood by the captain, ready to advise or take over if his commander was wounded. Each of the subordinate lieutenants took charge of a section of the ship's guns, usually half a deck each.

Lt Elleston King. He was commissioned as a lieutenant in 1797, but despite long service and participation in several important actions, he was never promoted. From the Naval Chronicle

In smaller ships, with only one or two lieutenants, there was no question of each watch being commanded by a lieutenant, and the master's mates took over some of their duties. When large ships were short handed, due to casualties or illness, it was sometimes necessary for the lieutenants to stand extra watches, or for the captain to take a watch himself. Otherwise, midshipmen or masters' mates could be promoted to acting lieutenant, until such time as they were superseded or had an opportunity to pass the examination; however, acting lieutenants were sometimes quite young, and had not yet had enough service to qualify. In 1810, for example, Acting Lieutenant William Weiss of the *La Nereide* was 'a very young man who had not yet served his full time as a midshipman'.[5]

Promotion from Lieutenant

Patronage and 'interest' counted at every stage in an officer's career, but never more so than in his promotion from lieutenant. Below lieutenant, his progress largely depended on passing the examination, and on the support of his captain. As a captain, his future promotion was entirely by seniority. But as a lieutenant, his only way to rise above his thousands of companions was to attract the attention of higher authority. His captain could not help him; captains and commanders could only be made by commanders-in-chief on foreign stations, or by the Admiralty itself. There was no system by which captains reported on the abilities of their subordinates, and no formal method of assessing who was fit for promotion. A commander-in-chief might well have hundreds of lieutenants under his command, and the Admiralty had thousands. Essentially, there were three ways in which a lieutenant could attract enough notice to ensure his promotion.

The first was to have political influence where it counted most, at the Admiralty. Sons of the peerage had automatic influence, as their father's support in the House of Lords was worth favours from the government. Commoners whose families had influence in the election of Members of Parliament for counties and boroughs could often gain an advantage. Byam Martin wrote that he 'had the happiness to learn . . . from my father . . . that an arrangement was under consideration for promoting me to the rank of commander, not on account of the capture of the *Enterprise*, or any other account than the good name, interest and services of my father.'[6] This was common enough in the electoral politics of the eighteenth and early nineteenth centuries. A strong first lord would resist such pressures, and try to appoint and promote officers on merit. Lords of the Admiralty were bombarded with requests, and Lord Barham complained 'With regard to patronage the service has become too extensive to make it any longer an object; and I declare to you that since my coming to this Board [the Admiralty], I have made but one Master and Commander; and when I read the claims before me — from admirals and captains for their children, from the King's ministers, members of parliament, peers, eminent [illegible] I do not see when I am to make another.'[7]

Secondly, a lieutenant could attract the attention of his commander-in-chief. According to the Admiralty Regulations, a C-in-C 'is not to appoint by commission or warrant, any officer to any ship under his command, without being authorised to do so by . . . the Lords Commissioners of the Admiralty; but if vacancies should occur in any ships, he is to appoint officers to act in them, until the pleasure of the Admiralty shall be known'. However, he was 'never to exercise that power within the Channel surroundings, or in the North Sea, or on any of the coasts of the United Kingdom'.[8] In practice, the acting appointments made by a commander-in-chief abroad were usually confirmed by the Admiralty, so he had a considerable power of promotion. Furthermore, if a vacancy was created by death or court-martial, the commander-in-chief had absolute power of promotion.[9] Naturally, the lieutenants most under his eye were those of his own flagship, so appointments to the flagship were eagerly sought. Once he had obtained such an appointment, a lieutenant's promotion was practically guaranteed. Aboard the flagship *Ville de Paris* in 1797, seven lieutenants were removed because of promotion.[10] In 1805, Admiral Cornwallis complained that he had little opportunity for such promotions. 'It hath been usual, I believe, for two sets of lieutenants to have been promoted from the commander-in-chief's ship during the period I have been serving here.'[11]

Thirdly, a lieutenant could distinguish himself in some way, usually in action. After each of the major battles, such as the First of June and Trafalgar, the first lieutenant of every ship was immediately promoted to commander. The same thing happened after notable single-ship actions. However, the action had to be dramatic enough to attract attention, and some officers only gained promotion to commander after several minor actions. John Richards, for example, became a lieutenant in 1790. He was highly commended by his captain after an action in the West Indies in 1796. However, he remained a lieutenant, though he also served as acting captain of his ship, the 74-gun *Alfred*. In 1798 he led a boarding party on a French corvette, and captured it in a distinguished action. In 1799 he was transferred to the *Queen Charlotte*, flagship of his patron, Admiral Thompson. From this he was soon promoted commander, though he had to take part in several more notable actions before becoming a post-captain.

Ideally, an officer needed to combine several advantages for early promotion. Nelson showed himself as an officer of very great ability even in his youth, and showed great promise as a lieutenant, at the age of eighteen. Furthermore, his uncle was controller of the navy, and his promotion to commander came in 1778, at the age of nineteen. He became a captain by the age of twenty, and this flying start later allowed him to become a rear-admiral at the age of thirty-eight.

Commanders

The rank of 'master and commander' had originally been created in the late seventeenth century, for the captains of sixth rates. Such vessels had been considered too small to carry a master as well as a captain, so the duties were combined in one man. Later, sixth rates came to be commanded by post-captains, but the master and commander was retained, to take charge of the growing class of sloops. The rank had become established by 1747, when it was equated with a major in the army. For some time, it remained a 'seaman's' rank, reflecting its origins in a superior class of master; but by the 1750s it had become recognised as the natural step between lieutenant and captain. Promotions directly from lieutenant to captain are rare, and nearly everyone had to go through the rank of master and commander. In 1794, the traces of its humble origin were obliterated when the 'master and' was dropped, and the rank became simply 'commander'.

Lord Cochrane as a captain. He had problems with his promotion from commander because of differences with St Vincent, but eventually became a post captain in 1801. From James's *Naval History*

A commander was captain of a sloop, usually between ten and eighteen guns. His duties were virtually identical to those of a captain in relation to his own ship, though, unlike a captain, he had no automatic rights to promotion to the flag list. There were 586 commanders on the navy list in 1812, and this was one of the main problems with the rank — for there were only 168 sloops and brigs suitable for them to command.[12] Many lieutenants had been promoted after they or their ships had distinguished themselves in action, creating something of a promotion block. Often, advancement to commander could be a false step in a man's career, for after his first commission he might find himself on half-pay for the rest of his life, without any real prospect of command of a post-ship. This difficulty was not really solved until 1827, when it became common to use commanders as the seconds-in-command of large ships.

Captains

A full captain, the commanding officer of a ship of the sixth rate or above, was known as a 'post-captain'. The origins of the term are obscure, but it was generally taken to mean an officer who held the actual rank and title of captain, as distinct from a commander or a lieutenant-in-command, who merely held the courtesy title of captain. The ranks of the post captains were divided up in two different ways — by seniority and by the type of ship they commanded. Captains, like junior officers, always took rank from the date of their first appointment to their present rank, and this was particularly important to captains, who would eventually reach the flag list in the same order. Furthermore, after he had achieved three years seniority, a captain gained certain extra privileges. He was now equivalent to a full colonel in the army, instead of a lieutenant-colonel; and between 1795 and 1812 he was entitled to two epaulettes on his uniform instead of one.

On the other hand, his pay rate was controlled by the size of ship he commanded. Pay was graded according to rate — in 1808, the captain of a first rate had £32.4.0 per month, of a third rate £23.2.0, and of a sixth rate £16.16.0. The post-captain was the only type of commissioned officer whose pay varied in this way. There was a certain correlation between the captain's seniority and the size of his ship, as it was normal for a captain to begin with the command of a fifth or sixth rate, and progress to larger ships. One exception to this rule was the flag captain, who was often quite junior in seniority. Thus Captain Worth commanded the *Bulwark* and the *Venerable* 74 in 1812 to 1814, bearing the flag of Rear Admiral Durham, though he had only been promoted captain in 1810.

Commodores

The promotion structure above captain was by seniority only, and this created a great deal of rigidity. The only flexibility was given by the rank of commodore, which was a temporary rank given to a captain in command of a particular squadron. This allowed the Admiralty to advance particular captains, even though they had not enough seniority to become admirals. He was appointed by the Admiralty on a temporary basis, and ranked with a brigadier-general in the army.

Admirals

Though there were only three permanent commissioned ranks below admiral, there were nine different grades of admiral, and ten after

Sir William Hoste as a captain, wearing the full-dress jacket closed. From James's *Naval History*

1805. There were three separate ranks: admiral, vice admiral and rear admiral. Each of these ranks was divided into three squadrons, titled, in order of seniority, red, white and blue. Vice and rear admiral were divided into these three squadrons. Full admirals were slightly different, in that until 1805 there was no rank of admiral of the red; admiral of the fleet took its place. The system of rank had originated in the mid-seventeenth century, when the fleet was divided into three divisions, each carrying a different colour of ensign; each division was divided, in turn, into three squadrons. The navy no longer fought as a single unit, and the system had long become

Earl Howe as an admiral. From James's *Naval History*

obsolete, but, like so many other aspects of naval rank, the titles remained even when the substance was greatly changed. In the past, only one man had been appointed to each rank, so that there were only nine admirals in the fleet. This system had been abandoned in the 1740s, and any number could be appointed, except that there was only one admiral of the fleet. Thus in 1814 the Duke of Clarence was admiral of the fleet, as he had been since 1811; there were twenty-one admirals of the red, twenty admirals of the white, twenty admirals of the blue, twenty-two vice admirals of the red, nineteen vice admirals of the white, twenty-four vice admirals of the blue, nineteen rear admirals of the red, seventeen rear admirals of the white, and twenty-four rear admirals of the blue.[13]

Any post-captain could expect to reach flag rank eventually, but the system allowed the Admiralty to leave aside incompetent or aged admirals. In the first instance, captains who reached the top of the list but were not considered capable of commanding a squadron or fleet were appointed 'to an unspecified squadron', popularly known as the 'yellow' squadron. Such officers were entitled to the half pay of rear admirals, but had no further prospects of either employment or promotion. An officer who had avoided this, and been promoted to the general list of admirals, would continue to be promoted until he died, but there was no guarantee that the Admiralty would employ him. In 1814, there were only forty-three admirals in employment at sea, out of 168 non-superannuated admirals.

Conversely, if the Admiralty wanted to promote a distinguished captain, it had to 'reach down' the captain's list, and promote a few less successful captains above him, either to full or to 'yellow' flag rank. This was quite common when distinguished officers, such as Nelson, were to be advanced.

Shore Duties

If a commissioned officer tired of the sea, or became infirm, there were several ways in which he could use his experience in a shore job, still as part of the navy. One of these was in the impress service, which employed an average of about thirty regulating captains, and about seventy lieutenants. Each of the coastal signal stations was commanded by a lieutenant, while the Sea Fencibles employed many experienced officers. Certain dockyard appointments were reserved for experienced sea officers, and Agents of Transports were usually naval lieutenants. More senior posts in the civil service were to be found among the commissioners of the navy. Some of those at the Navy Office in London, and virtually all of those in charge of the yards, were post-captains. Officers who held this type of civilian appointment were debarred from promotion to flag-rank, but could resume their naval career on leaving office. Finally, captains and admirals, especially those who combined a parliamentary career with a naval one, could sometimes be appointed to the Board of Admiralty, which always included at least three experienced naval officers.

Half-pay

All commissioned officers were entitled to half-pay when not actively employed, provided they held themselves in readiness for an appointment. Until 1814, it was paid every six months, and after that every three months. Within each rank the actual amount varied with seniority. According to the 1814 regulations, the 300 most senior lieutenants had 7s per day, the next 700 had 6s, and the rest had 5s. Likewise, captains were divided into three groups, with the most senior receiving 14s 9d per day, while the admiral of the fleet had £3.3.0 per day. An officer on half-pay was not subject to naval discipline, and could not be ordered to take up an appointment with the fleet. However, if he declined a post, he could have his half-pay stopped. Officers who took up civil appointments, or duties in other branches, normally had their half-pay stopped while the appointments lasted, except in certain cases, such as officers in signal stations, where arrangements were made to take it into account.

Retirement

There was no general concept of retirement in 1800, and no all-embracing system for naval officers. Those who were too old for active service could simply remain indefinitely on half pay, but since this was intended as a retainer for future service rather than a reward for the past, it was an abuse of the system. Another possibility was promotion in lieu of superannuation. This of course had begun with the appointment of 'yellow' admirals in the 1740s, but over the years it was extended to other ranks. By 1814, there were thirty-seven 'superannuated and retired captains' on the navy list, and the oldest had seniority dating back to 1762. There were also fifty 'lieutenants superannuated with the rank of commander', and this group was considerably extended at the end of the wars, beginning in January of that year, when thirty more officers were appointed to it. After the end of the wars, many of the 'passed midshipmen' were promoted to lieutenant; between April 1814 and the end of 1815, 1372 new lieutenants were created.[14]

Wounded or invalid officers had other options. Greenwich hospital had places for four captains and four lieutenants. The 'Naval Knights of Windsor' included seven retired lieutenants of reduced means. The charity had been founded by one Samuel Travers in 1795, and had a 'college' near Windsor Castle, 'consisting of seven houses adjoining each other, with a general dining hall'. Income was raised from estates, mainly in Essex.[15]

Other officers were compensated by individual pensions, settled by the Admiralty. Each ship carried one 'widow's man' per 100 of her complement. These men were purely fictitious, but their pay went to a fund for the relief of widows and dependents of officers killed in service. In 1814, pensions were paid at the rate of £120 per annum for the widow of a flag officer, £90 for a senior captain, and £50 for a lieutenant.

3 Warrant Officers

Types of Warrant Officer

The simple definition of a warrant officer was that he was appointed by warrant from the Navy Board, rather than the commission of the Board of Admiralty. Warrant officers, therefore, included all specialised officers, including men like surgeons who would certainly be commissioned in a modern fleet. It also included men of much lower status, such as sailmakers and caulkers, who were equivalent to petty officers in most respects. In fact, there were four levels of warrant officer — those entitled to walk the quarterdeck and live in the wardroom, and therefore almost equal to commissioned officers in status; gunroom warrant officers, including masters' and surgeons' mates, who could expect to reach the wardroom in time; the 'standing officers', largely responsible for maintenance, who were so called because they stayed with the ship when she was out of commission; and the lower grade officers, such as the master at arms, the cook and the sailmaker, who were explicitly equated with petty officers

A boatswain's warrant of 1790, issued in this case by the admiral commanding at Jamaica. Normally, such warrants were issued by the Navy Board. They were on paper, whereas officers' commissions were on parchment. Public Record Office

By Philip Affleck Esq. Rear Admiral of the Blue Commander in Chief of his Majesty's Ships & Vessels employed & to be employed at & about Jamaica

BY Virtue of the Power and Authority to me given, I do hereby appoint you Boatswain of His Majeſty's ~~Ship~~ Sloop the Cygnet in the Room of Jonas Boulton appointed Gunner of ye Bourke requiring and directing you forthwith to Repair on Board the ſaid ~~Ship~~ Sloop, and take upon you the Employment of Boatswain in her accordingly, and to be obedient to ſuch Commands as you ſhall from Time to Time receive from the Captain of the ſaid ~~Ship~~ Sloop, or any other your Superior Officers, to hold the ſame Employment till further Order, together with ſuch an Allowance of Wages and Victuals, for yourſelf and Servant as is uſual for the Boatswain of the ſaid ~~Ship~~ Sloop, and for ſo doing this ſhall be your Warrant. Dated on Board His Majeſty's Ship the Centurion, Port Royal Harbour Jamaica the 15th of September 1790.

P. Affleck

To Mr [illegible] Bell hereby appointed Boatswain of His Majeſty's ~~Ship~~ Sloop the Cygnet

By Command of the Commander in Chief
James Culforth

355

The master of HMS Gloucester, *from Mangin's journal of 1812.* The National Maritime Museum

by the Admiralty Regulations, and therefore needed to be treated separately.

The wardroom warrant officers included the master, who was the senior warrant officer, and in many respects in a class of his own; the three 'civilian officers', so called because their jobs were essentially similar to those they pursued ashore, the surgeon, purser and chaplain. The standing officers were the gunner, boatswain and carpenter; they were the most like warrant officers in the modern armed forces, in that they had invariably risen from the ranks, and the boatswain, in particular, had some of the characteristics of a sergeant-major.

Literacy was one thing that all warrant officers had in common, and this distinguished them from the common seamen. According to the Admiralty Regulations, 'No person shall be appointed to any station in which he is to have charge of stores, unless he can read and write, and is sufficiently skilled in arithmetic to keep an account of them correctly.'[1] Since all warrant officers had responsibility for considerable quantities of stores, this was enough to debar the illiterate.

Masters

The master was the senior warrant officer, entitled to mess in the wardroom on a two-decker, and usually given one of the best cabins there. In rank, he was 'with but after' the lieutenants. His pay, like that of all the senior warrant officers, varied according to the rate of the ship, from £12.12.0 on a first rate in 1808, to £7.7.0 in a sixth rate. In a fifth rate, his pay was equal to that of a lieutenant, and, in larger ships, it was greater. His status could cause confusion; when captured he was often not treated as an officer, and in the wardroom the lieutenants sometimes resented him. 'As the master, though only a warrant officer, from his being sometimes allowed to take watch, and put the ship about, is apt to give himself airs of consequence, and frequently has the astonishing impudence to think himself your equal.'[2]

The master was responsible for the navigation of the ship, in the broadest sense of the term. As well as setting courses and finding the ship's position, he was to supervise the pilotage, and 'represent to the captain every possible danger in or near to the ship's course, and the way to avoid it'. He was to supervise the midshipmen and mates in taking noon sights of the sun, and look after the maintenance of the ship's compasses. Like all craftsmen of the age, he was partly responsible for supplying his own tools, and was 'to provide himself with such charts, nautical books and instruments as are necessary for astronomical observations and all other purposes of navigation.'[3] He was in charge of the stowing of the hold, for that had a considerable effect on the ship's trim, and therefore her sailing qualities. He was responsible for the security and issue of the beers and spirits on board, and also for the sails and rigging. He was to take responsibility for the ship's anchors, and, when the ship was at single anchor, he was 'to be very attentive in keeping the cable clear'.[4] He kept the official ship's log book, for the books kept by the captain and other officers were merely personal journals. He was a considerable figure on board ship, usually the best-paid officer apart from the captain, and the best accommodated apart from the captain and the first lieutenant.

There was no single promotion path to becoming a master. Some may have started on the lower deck, and perhaps picked up the art of navigation as quartermasters or masters' mates. Others had been volunteers and midshipmen, and despairing of getting commissions as lieutenants, had settled for the better pay, but poorer promotion prospects, of the master. Many had entered from the merchant service. To qualify for the rank, a prospective master would be examined by 'one of the senior captains and three of the best qualified masters'.[5] He might then serve for a time as a second master. Such officers were appointed to ships of the third rate and above, with the pay of £5.5.0 monthly in 1808. Second masters were apparently accommodated in the midshipmen's berth. They were given priority for promotion to full master when vacancies occurred.

Surgeons

A surgeon usually learned his trade before coming on board ship. It was not yet necessary for a surgeon to have a medical degree, and he was usually trained by apprenticeship. Many entrants to the profession were young Scotsmen, and these included some of the greatest naval surgeons of the age, such as Lind, Trotter, Robertson and Baird. The system of training on shore was less than effective, and an applicant for a naval post had to pass an oral examination at Surgeon's Hall in London, before receiving his warrant from the Navy Board. Overseas, he could be examined by 'the physician of the fleet, the physician and senior surgeon of the hospital, where there is one, and three surgeons of the squadron'.[6] After that, he had to serve for a period as a surgeon's mate before qualifying for the rank of surgeon.

There were over 550 surgeons in the fleet in 1793, 720 in 1806, and 850 in 1814. This does not include assistant surgeons, or shore-based officers such a 'dispensers'.[7] It was said that 'A naval surgeon of abilities and circumspection is generally the most independent officer in the ship, as his line of duty is unconnected with the others. He has the entire charge and management of the sick and hurt seamen on board his ship; is to perform surgical operations on the wounded as he may deem necessary to the safety of their lives; and to see that the medicines and necessaries with which he is supplied from the said board, or their agents, are in good in kind, and administered faithfully to the sick patients under his care.'[8] He also had to keep a journal of his treatments and send it in to his superiors, to send sick men to the hospital ship, or shore hospital, to supervise the general health of the ship's company, as well as those who were actually sick, and to act as adviser to the captain on matters affecting health.

At the beginning of the French Revolutionary Wars the status of the surgeon was still rather low, and it was generally felt that naval surgeons were drunken and incompetent men who had failed to make a living ashore. It is said that the surgeon of the *Defence* at the First of June Battle, though an 'amiable man', 'could not perform the operation of amputating a limb'.[9] Conditions for surgeons were improved soon afterwards; the most senior ones were allowed half-pay, while full-pay was raised, and some drugs were provided by the government rather than by the individual surgeon. However, there were still forty vacancies for surgeon's mates in the following year. Surgeons missed out on a general pay rise of 1802, but in 1805 they had a substantial rise, to 11s per day, and all of them were now entitled to half-pay. The surgeon's mate was renamed 'assistant surgeon'.

Pursers

To become a purser, a man had to have served at least one year as a captain's clerk, or eighteen months 'in the office of the secretary to a flag officer'.[10] Unlike other officers, he was not paid a straightforward salary. He was paid at the same rate as the boatswain and gunner, and therefore less than his colleagues in the wardroom; he was expected to make up the difference by saving provisions, for which he was paid at standard rates. In view of the value of the stores under his care, he had to put up a bond as security: £1200 in first rates to £400 in sixth rates and below. In the circumstances, it is not surprising that pursers were suspected of embezzling the crew's food, and enriching themselves at their expense. The trade certainly had its risks, and some pursers were bankrupted by their service; but there was never any shortage of applicants for the post, and it must have been reasonably profitable.

Chaplains

The status of the chaplain was quite low throughout the eighteenth century. Only disreputable parsons were likely to apply, but unlike the surgeon, the chaplain was not seen as essential aboard ship. His status as a wardroom officer was in doubt, and in 1758 a satirical petition was printed, asking that the chaplain be allowed to use the quarter gallery instead of having to 'ease himself' in full view of the common seamen. His pay was that of an ordinary seaman, though he also had a 'groat', or fourpence, for every member of the crew. By the 1790s he was well-established as a member of the wardroom mess, and, in 1812, there was a considerable revision of his pay and conditions. He was entitled to half-pay after eight years' service, and a basic pay of £150 per annum. He was guaranteed 'to have a cabin allotted to him in the wardroom or gunroom where he is to mess with the lieutenants and be rated for victuals'.[11] Although every ship of the fifth rate and above was now allowed a chaplain, few served in ships below the third rate, and, by 1814, recruitment had not improved greatly. In February of that year there were only seventy-nine chaplains in the navy, and fifty-one of these were serving aboard ship. The religious head of the navy was Archdeacon John Owen, chaplain-general to the fleet, appointed in 1812. Of course, all

A purser, c1800, by Rowlandson. The National Maritime Museum

chaplains were Anglicans; English dissenters, Irish Catholics and Scottish Presbyterians served in the fleet in large numbers, but their faiths were not officially recognised.

Boatswains

The boatswain had usually risen from the ranks of seamen, and regulations specified that he serve at least one year as petty officer in the navy. He had to be literate like all warrant officers, but, apart from that, he needed no special qualifications. He was generally responsible for the sails and rigging of the ship. He supervised the cutting of rigging lines when the ship first fitted out, and after that he was to inspect the rigging every day, 'to discover as soon as possible any part which may be chafed, or likely to give way, that it may be repaired without loss of time'. He was also responsible for ensuring that boats, anchors and booms were properly secured. The sailmaker and ropemaker of the ship were under his command. He was to be 'very frequently upon deck in the day, and at all times both day and night, when any duty shall require all hands being employed. He is, with his mates, to see that the men go quickly on deck when called, and that, when there, they perform their duty with alacrity and without noise and confusion'.[12] This is a rather euphemistic way of describing the cries, calls and beatings which the boatswain and his mates mustered and 'encouraged' the crew.

The chaplain of the Vanguard *preaches to Nelson and the crew of the ship after the Battle of the Nile in 1798.* The National Maritime Museum

Boatswains tended to be colourful characters, and this sometimes led them into trouble. Fifty-five boatswains were found guilty by court-martial between 1807–14, mostly of drunkenness or stealing stores. This compares with thirty-seven carpenters, twenty-four gunners, fourteen pursers and one surgeon.[13] In 1808, a boatswain was paid from £4.16.0 to £3.1.0 per month, the same rate as a gunner.

Carpenters

Unlike the other standing officers, the carpenter had to learn his trade ashore. 'No person shall be appointed carpenter of one of His Majesty's ships, unless he shall have served an apprenticeship to a shipwright, and has been six calendar months a carpenter's mate of one or more of His Majesty's ships, and shall produce certificates of his good conduct.'[14] Some carpenters had worked in the royal dockyards, and spent time at sea to gain experience. Others had been carpenters' mates of merchant ships, and were impressed. The press gang often took up shore-based shipwrights, because they were useful aboard ship; any proof that they had ever served at sea would make them liable to impressment.

The carpenter had a large crew, of up to ten men on a large ship. He had equal pay with the boatswain and gunner in ships of the fourth rate and below, but in large ships he had £1 per month more in 1808, giving him a maximum rate of £5.16.6. He was responsible for keeping the ship afloat, for routine repair and inspection, and for repairing battle damage. He and his crew were hard worked when a ship fitted out, for they had to make all the tables and benches for the officers and crew. They were to examine all wooden parts regularly, including masts and yards. The carpenters, like the other standing officers, had a store room forward on the orlop deck, with a supply of timber and nails.

Gunners

The science of gunnery was little developed in the eighteenth-century navy, and the ship's gunner had little opportunity to learn it in any case. He had to pass an examination, though the regulations did not specify who was to conduct it. He also had to serve at least one year as a petty officer. However, William Richardson found himself appointed acting gunner of the frigate *Prompte* without meeting any of the formal conditions. 'Captain Leveson-Gower... ordered me to take charge of the gunner's stores, and said he would soon get me a gunner's warrant; but I begged him to excuse me, as I knew little of gunnery, and indeed have never been so much as in a gunners crew.' He was sent for the examination before 'the passing gunners and a mathematical master', but he found that 'they could not pass anyone who had not been four years in HM service.' Richardson returned to his ship as acting gunner, and 'with leisure began to study the art of gunnery from books my brother James brought for me'. Eventually he was able to pass the examination.[15]

The gunner was mainly responsible for the maintenance of the guns and their equipment, rather than their actual firing, which was supervised by the lieutenants in action. The gunner's crew was quite large, with one or two mates, an armourer, and a quarter gunner for every four guns. They had to make the breechings and tackles for the guns when the ship fitted out, and to keep up a supply of cartridges and wads for the guns. They had to keep the powder dry in the magazine, but also well aired so that it did not decay, and safe from fire. The gunner was 'frequently to examine the state of the guns, their locks and carriages that they may be immediately repaired or exchanged if they be defective'.[16] He was also responsible for the small arms, and for gunnery implements such as powder horns and rammers. Traditionally, the gunner was in charge of the gunroom, and of the boys who lodged there, but this duty was largely taken away from him in the early nineteenth century.

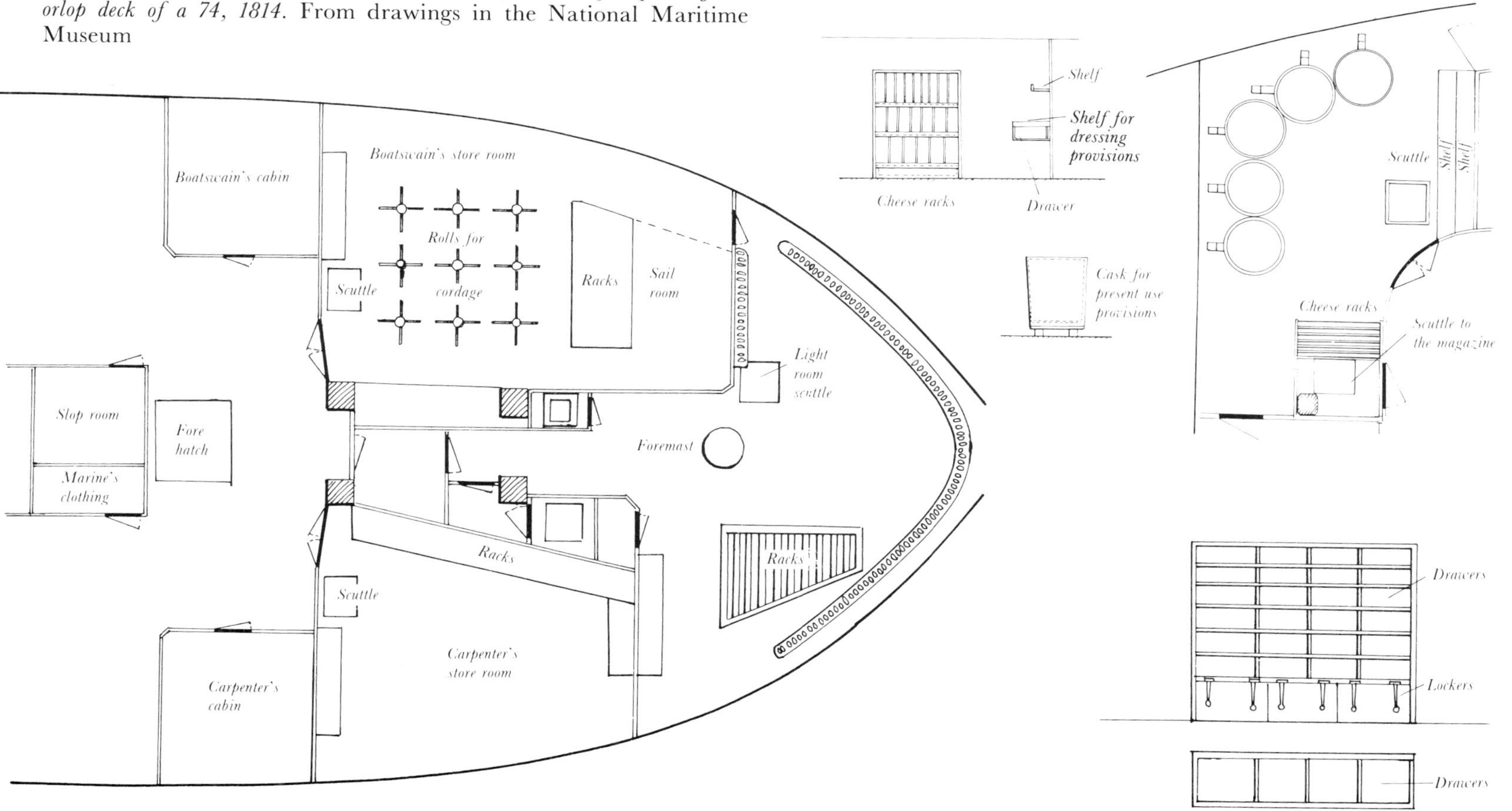

Details of the warrant officers' store rooms in the fore and after parts of the orlop deck of a 74, 1814. From drawings in the National Maritime Museum

Like all the standing officers, the gunner had no clear promotion path. There was no 'gunner of the fleet', or 'carpenter of the fleet', so the only promotion was to a higher rate of ship. Richardson complained of this. After an action, the senior lieutenants were promoted to commander, while 'I, who had sole charge of fitting them up, the most trouble, and my clothes spoiled by the stuff, did not get so much as a higher rate, which I applied for, and which from my services I thought myself entitled to; such is the encouragement that warrant officers meet in the navy.'[17]

Schoolmasters

The exact status of the schoolmaster was not clear, and in some senses he was more of a petty officer than a true warrant officer. He had no place in the wardroom, and no right to a cabin of his own. He had to be examined by 'the master, warden and assistants of the Trinity House of Deptford Strond; and obtain from them a certificate of his being well skilled in the theory and practice of navigation, and in all such branches of the mathematics as may be necessary to qualify him to instruct young men'.[18] As well as instructing the midshipmen, he often taught the ships' boys to read and write. His pay was the same as that of a midshipman, so it was difficult to attract suitable candidates. According to Boteler, 'We youngsters had a schoolmaster, a clever seedy-looking creature, whose besetting sin was love of grog; with very little trouble it floored him and then, I don't like to record it, we used to grease his head and flour it.'[19]

4 Officers' Living Conditions

Uniform for Commissioned Officers

Naval uniform had first been introduced in 1748, for commissioned officers and midshipmen only. The use of the navy blue coat, with white breeches, trimming and waistcoat, and gold braid for the more senior ranks, was immediately established. Though it had been introduced at the request of the officers themselves, they tended to adapt it to their own purposes, and individual officers often varied the details to suit themselves. The uniform regulations of 1787 were still in force at the beginning of the French Revolutionary War. There were two types of uniform — full dress, which was worn only on formal occasions, and 'undress' (or 'frock') uniform, for everyday use.

An admiral wore an open full-dress coat, with a horizontal strip of gold lace from each buttonhole. It had a stand-up collar, also trimmed with wide gold lace. There was yet more lace round the cuffs and the pocket. The coat was usually worn with a white waistcoat and breeches, and with a black cocked hat, with gold trim. A captain had a full-dress coat with wide white lapels, reaching down to the waist. It could be worn either open or closed, and also had gold lace round the edges of the lapels. A captain of three years' seniority had two rows of gold lace round his cuffs, while a more junior one had only one row. A master's and commander's coats were similar, but the lapels were blue rather than white. A lieutenant's uniform had virtually no gold lace, but had the white lapels of the captain. Cocked hats were normally worn with these uniforms; regulations said little about them, but ranks above lieutenant normally wore gold lace round them.

The undress uniform of an admiral included a double-breasted coat which could be worn open or closed. It had strips of horizontal lace on the lapels, which were exposed when the coat was open. A captain had a fall-down collar rather than a stand-up one; the strips of gold lace on the buttonholes tended to be shorter than those of an admiral. For a junior captain, the buttons were arranged in pairs, while a master and commander had them arranged in threes. The lieutenant's undress coat had no gold lace, but a narrow white trim.

Epaulettes formed no part of a naval officer's uniform at this time, a fact which caused some resentment when compared with the splendour of the army and the marines. Sometimes, officers wore them unofficially when ashore, but Nelson regarded such officers as 'coxcombs', who were 'a little cheap for putting on part of a Frenchman's uniform'.[1] However, the new uniform regulations of 1795 did allow epaulettes for ranks above lieutenant — one on the left shoulder for a commander, one on the right for a captain of less than three years seniority, and one on each shoulder for senior captains and admirals. The different ranks of admirals were distinguished by the badges on the epaulettes — an admiral had three stars on each epaulette, a vice admiral had two, and a rear admiral one. The epaulettes themselves had gold bullion fringes.

Other changes were introduced in 1795. The admiral's full-dress coat was now double breasted, with lace bars and trim. The captain's dress coat lost the white of its lapels and became similar to that of the commander, except for the epaulettes. On dress uniform, a captain or commander had a 'slash' cuff, with an irregular pattern of lace trim. The admirals' full-dress cuffs had a number of rings of gold lace — one broad ring and three narrow ones for a full admiral, one broad and two narrow for a vice admiral, and one broad and one narrow for a rear admiral. Such cuffs also had vertical stripes of gold lace.

The undress uniforms of all ranks were now virtually without gold lace, except on the cuffs of admirals; these had three rings for a full admiral, two for a vice admiral, and one for a rear admiral. All undress uniforms had blue lapels, with buttons down the side. The uniforms of lieutenants were unchanged by the new regulations.

Yet more changes were introduced in 1813. Captains and admirals now had white lapels and cuffs on their full-dress uniforms, and the use of epaulettes was extended, by popular request, to lieutenants. Three-year captains had a silver crown and a silver anchor on each epaulette; junior captains had an anchor only, while commanders had plain epaulettes on each shoulder, and lieutenants had one on the right shoulder only. Time was allowed for the changeover to the new uniforms, and this caused confusion. 'The signalman would report a post captain coming and the guard turn out to receive him, when it proved to be only a lieutenant.'[2]

Other Officers' Uniforms

Since 1787, warrant officers had worn a plain blue coat, rather civilian in cut, with a fall-down collar, and only buttons to indicate the naval status of the wearer. That worn by masters' mates was slightly different, with white edging. Masters, regarding themselves as the equal of lieutenants, regularly petitioned the Admiralty for a more military uniform, with epaulettes; when taken prisoner, they had difficulty in persuading their captors that they were entitled to officers' privileges. However, this had little effect, except that in 1807 masters and pursers were allowed a full-dress uniform, with a stand-up collar. Surgeons were given a uniform of their own in 1805, with a stand-up collar. This had one embroidered buttonhole on each side for a ship's surgeon, and two buttonholes for hospital surgeons. The collars of physicians were edged with gold lace.

Officers' uniforms, 1795-1812, from a print of 1804.
1 Admiral
2 Captain with three years' seniority
3 Lieutenant
4 Midshipman
The National Maritime Museum

Officers' rank distinctions, 1795-1812.

		Full Dress			*Undress*		
	Epaulettes	*Lapels*	*Cuffs*	*Collars*	*Lapels*	*Cuffs*	*Collars*
Admiral							
Vice Admiral							
Rear Admiral							
Captain (over three years)							
Captain (under three years)							
Commander							
Lieutenant							
Midshipman	*No full dress*						

Above: Nelson's Trafalgar uniform, with the undress cuffs of a vice admiral. Author's photograph, courtesy of the National Maritime Museum

Right: The full-dress cuffs of a captain. Author's photograph, courtesy of the National Maritime Museum

◁ *Top: The cuffs of an admiral's full-dress uniform.* Author's photograph, courtesy of the National Maritime Museum

Bottom: The full-dress cuffs and lapels of a vice admiral. Author's photograph, courtesy of the National Maritime Museum

Details of a presentation sword issued by the City of London. The National Maritime Museum

Midshipmen had worn uniform since it had been introduced in 1748. Since then, and until the present day, the distinguishing feature of the midshipman's uniform has been the white collar patch. He wore a long single breasted coat, which was unchanged by the regulations of 1795 and 1812. However, there were slow unofficial changes, and by 1812 his coat tended to be cut shorter in front, becoming more like a jacket than a coat. The uniform regulations allowed plenty of scope to the individual, both in the cut of his coat and in the accessories. According to Boteler, 'We were considered a crack ship, and the midshipmen dressed in cocked hats, tight white pantaloons, and Hessian boots, with a gilt twist edging and a bullion tassel!'[3]

Decorations

Medals for individual gallantry were not generally recognised at this time, and the concept of the campaign medal was barely established. Gold medals were issued to captains and admirals after battles such as the First of June and St Vincent. Private enterprise provided medals for every man involved in the battles of the Nile and Trafalgar, but it was 1848 before the government issued the Naval General Service Medal, with bars for more than 200 actions in the years 1793 to 1815. Officers sometimes wore the Nile and Trafalgar medals on ribbons round their necks. The Nile medal was issued in gold for admirals and captains, silver for lieutenants and warrant officers, bronze-gilt for petty officers, and bronze for seamen and marines. The Trafalgar medal was issued in gold for admirals, silver for captains and lieutenants, and pewter for men of lower rank.

Apart from that, senior officers were sometimes awarded orders of chivalry. By far the most common was the Order of the Bath, which entitled the holder to a red sash, worn over the right shoulder, and a badge in the form of an elaborate star. The order was conferred on all the most distinguished admirals of the wars, including Nelson and St Vincent. Some officers were also awarded foreign decorations. Nelson, in particular, wore stars of the Turkish Order of the Crescent, the Sicilian order of St Ferdinand, and the order of St Joachim of Leiningen. In his full-dress hat, he wore an amazing emblem called the 'chilingk', presented by the Sultan of Turkey, which included a part that rotated by clockwork. Like other officers, he wore embroidered versions of the stars of his orders on his dress uniform; he was wearing these when he was killed at Trafalgar.

Swords

A sword had always been regarded as part of the dress of an officer and a gentleman, though until 1805 there were no specific regulations about naval swords. Before that, both fighting swords and dress swords were in use; the fighting sword often had a curved blade, while the dress sword was usually straight. As a fighting weapon, some officers adopted the dirk; it was not yet associated with midshipmen, but was worn by officers of all ranks.

Design of the sword was often copied from standard army patterns — the so-called infantry pattern of 1786, and the light cavalry pattern of 1796. A sword usually had a knuckle guard, and the 'five ball' pattern, with five balls moulded as part of the guard, was common. The shape of the grip varied considerably, and sometimes it was decorated with naval patterns. The pattern of 1805 was similar to the light cavalry pattern, but had a lion's head on the outside of the grip. Senior officers, with the rank of commander and above, had ivory grips, usually bound in gold wire. Lieutenants and junior officers had black grips.

Presentation swords were given to officers by various organisations; the City of London, the Egyptian Club (for the Battle of the Nile) and the Patriotic Fund at Lloyds. The latter organisation presented swords of different value according to the merit involved — eighteen of the £30 pattern, ninety of the £50 pattern and thirty-nine of the £100 pattern were issued, along with twenty-nine of the Trafalgar pattern. It is unlikely that such swords were worn in action, or even at sea.

There was no regulation way of wearing a sword, but it was usually carried inside a scabbard, often made of black leather and decorated in the same style as the sword. It was worn at the left hip, and often supported by a shoulder belt. The shoulder belt tended to be replaced in the early nineteenth century by a waist belt. Dirks and small swords were nearly always carried from the waistbelt.

The Captain's Cabin

The captain's cabin was invariably in the upper stern of the ship — on the quarterdeck on a two- or three-decker, where it gave immediate access to the steering position; on the upper deck of a frigate, which had no poop; and on the only deck of a smaller ship. It had a row of stern windows on a frigate, and an open stern gallery on the older ships-of-the-line. It was the full width of the ship, and extended over two or three pairs of guns. It was separated from the rest of the ship by a removable wooden partition, with doors guarded by a marine sentry. Internally, it was divided into several compartments — usually a 'day cabin', which was right aft, with one side made up of the stern windows, a 'sleeping cabin' or 'state room' with a swinging cot on one side of the ship, and the 'steerage', or dining cabin, on the other. The captain had access to two quarter galleries; he used one as a toilet, and the other merely for observing the set of the sails.

Captains furnished their own cabins according to personal taste. They could live in solitary splendour, or they could surround themselves with their own servants and followers, or they could dine frequently with their officers; the latter was probably the most common.

The Wardroom and the Gunroom

On a ship-of-the-line, the senior officers, apart from the captain and admiral, lived in the wardroom aft on the upper deck. The wardroom had first begun to emerge at the end of the seventeenth century, and it was recognised in Admiralty orders by 1745. By the 1790s, its membership was quite well established — all the lieutenants, the master, surgeon (but not his mates), purser, chaplain, and the marine officers. On a 74-gun ship this meant twelve officers, if there was a chaplain. The wardroom itself was placed between the rows of officers' cabins on each side of the ship. According to Mangin, 'It is usually in a line-of-battle ship, about 35 feet in length, and 16 or 18 feet wide. Within the walls, which are of painted canvas, are the cabins of six officers; the centre of the room is occupied by the mess-table; and the extremity, under the stern windows, by a projection called the rudder head. The opposite end is arranged to do the office of a side-board; with the door or entrance on one side of it; and a space to sling a quarter cask of wine, on the other.'[4] The cabins were arranged so that a corridor led between them to one of the quarter galleries; the other opened from the first lieutenant's cabin, and was reserved for his use alone. The wardroom of a ship-of-the-line was well lit by several stern windows.

A frigate had a gunroom instead, aft on the lower deck. It had no natural light except what might come in through an open gunport, or the gratings of the deck above. Again, it was placed between two rows of cabins, but it tapered towards the stern, because of the shape of the hull in these parts. It opened out again at the extreme stern, where there were no cabins. All the officers had cabins in the area, including the standing officers and the midshipmen; but probably only those who would have qualified for the wardroom on a ship-of-the-line would have been allowed to eat at the gunroom table.

Food and Drink

The officers of the wardroom or gunroom were entitled to the same food as the seamen, but they usually provided themselves with something much better at their own expense. The normal way was for one of the members of the mess to act as caterer and treasurer of the mess, and to collect a subscription from the others. William Dillon held such a post aboard the *Aimiable* in 1797. 'We remained a few days longer at anchor than usual, and I, as caterer, was enabled to lay in plenty of stock for the mess. The prize money admitted of our

The wardroom of the Gloucester, *from Mangin's journal.* The National Maritime Museum

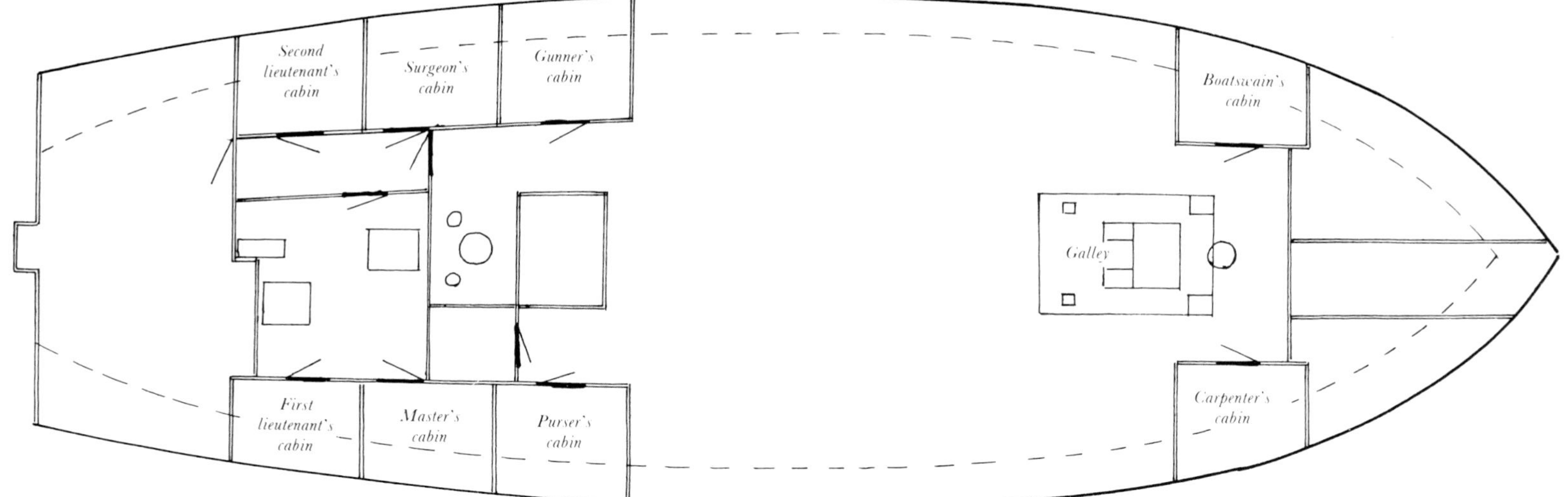

The cabins of an early nineteenth-century sixth rate. Based on drawings in the Public Record Office

adding some wine, and I took care to lay in a plentiful stock of claret.'[5] The members of the mess were not always happy with the amount of money spent. According to Edward Mangin, 'The expenses of the twelve members of the wardroom mess, for dinner, wine, tea, sugar, etc, were calculated by Captain Inches [of the marines], our caterer, at something above sixty pounds per annum; but, in my opinion, this sum would not have answered; especially when I found it was resolved, after various debates on the subject, that we could not decently drink less than half a pint of wine each day of the week, and that we ought to drink as much as we pleased on Sundays.'[6] Wardrooms often entertained the captain to dinner, and invited guests from the shore. This too caused disputes among the members, and Dillon reports, 'Therefore the surgeon and self made a proposal to our messmates to give an entertainment on board to a certain number of ladies and gentlemen. It was approved by only two; the other two would not join in anything leading to expense. Consequently there were four of us to issue the invitations and find the cash.'[7]

The various groups of officers, the captain, the wardroom or gunroom officers, the midshipmen, and the standing officers, usually had some kind of financial stake in the live animals kept on board; hens in coops on the quarterdeck, cows and pigs under the forecastle, or in the waist. The standing officers probably messed separately, in their own cabins, especially if their wives were with them. Richardson mentions 'cooking utensils' among the items a standing officer had to transfer from ship to ship.[8]

Officers' Cabins

Officers' cabins were usually about 8ft square, with variations according to the location in the ship. The best cabin in the wardroom was given to the first lieutenant. It was slightly larger than the others, with its own stern window, and direct access to one of the quarter galleries. The master's cabin was opposite, with a stern window, but no direct access to the quarter gallery on that side. Usually, there were three more cabins on each side of the wardroom, for the junior lieutenants and the captain of marines. Each of these included one of the ship's guns, and the occupant often had to sling his cot above it. Officially, all the cabins in the wardroom consisted only of canvas curtains, which could be rolled up in the daytime; however, there are signs that slightly more substantial partitions, of canvas stretched on frames, were now being made by ships' carpenters. But these partitions, like those of the captain's cabin, were taken down when the ship cleared for action.

Other officers, such as the chaplain and the junior marine officers, had canvas cabins in the gunroom of a ship-of-the-line. Room was rather restricted there because of the movement of the tiller. Mangin describes his cabin. 'This apartment was formed into what appeared to be a room of about 8 feet broad and long; and nearly 6 feet in height; one end and one side being composed of the ship's timbers; the other end, and the external side, of canvas strained on wooden framework; with a door of the same materials, and a small window in each.'[9]

On the orlop deck, or the lower deck of a frigate, there were no guns and the cabins could be more permanent. They were usually made of wood, with slats on the doors to allow ventilation. On a ship-of-the-line, there was a row of cabins on each side of the after cockpit, though only two of these were used as sleeping accommodation, by the surgeon and purser. The others served as store rooms for the various officers. On a frigate, all the officers' cabins, from first lieutenant to captain's clerk, were arranged on either side of the gunroom, and the midshipmen's berths were placed at the forward ends of the rows.

Recreation

Mangin describes some of the recreations of the off-duty officers in the wardroom.

> Several still linger behind, for the various purposes of writing letters, playing backgammon, fencing, singing (with a laudable energy of voice and a thorough contempt for music) practising on a violin, or a German flute . . . while perhaps, a subaltern of marines, very much devoted to the pursuits of literature, may indulge himself by trying to spell his way through a newspaper of three weeks date, or turn over a Steel's list, or a volume of Naval Instructions.[10]

Dinner was the high point of wardroom life, especially if guests were invited. However, the wardroom was a closed society, and unlike the seamen, the officers did not have the right to change mess if they did not get on with their companions. Trivial differences tended to become magnified in such circumstances. Aboard one ship, a wardroom discussion between the captain and one of his officers about whether women from the West End of London were superior to those from the East End eventually led to a court-martial. Captain Griffiths warned 'It is a notorious and melancholy fact, that in several instances of mutiny, it has been traced, if not to have positively originated in the conversations of the wardroom mess.'[11] Mangin wrote, 'I have as yet designedly omitted to mention our second lieutenant of the ship; we disliked each other, I believe mutually; at least I greatly disliked him, and those feelings are generally reciprocated.'[12] James Anthony Gardner served with dozens of

Mangin's cabin aboard the Gloucester. The National Maritime Museum

This picture is of a civilian passenger climbing into a cot, but it shows the standard type of cot used by naval officers. The National Maritime Museum

different officers during his career, including some who were 'crabbed as the devil', 'waspish, snappish and disagreeable', or 'a snappish cur'. He served with one purser who insisted on taking his meals by himself in the cockpit, and showed fear when anyone approached him.[13] But many more officers were described as 'a droll fellow', 'a good natured fellow', or 'half mad, but good natured'.

Personal Belongings and Cabin Furniture

Officers provided their own beds, cabin furniture, and all the necessities of life. In 1787, Surgeon Gillespie's belongings consisted of 'a large medicine chest, black trunk containing linen and books, a hair trunk with instruments, writing box, books etc, two cases of books, a cot with feather bed and two pillows.'[14] Most of these, of course, were necessary for the practice of his profession. As a chaplain, Edward Mangin needed less equipment; he provided himself with 'an assortment of shirts, neckcloths, stockings, black silk handkerchiefs, bed and bedding, two silver spoons and a silver fork for the mess, four table-cloths, a black silk gown, half a dozen bands, Bibles and prayer book, etc.'[15] As a gunner, William Richardson complained, 'No officer in shifting from ship to ship has more bother than a warrant officer; he has not only his chests and bedding to lug about but also his cabin furniture, cooking utensils, and if he has his wife with him so much the worse.'[16]

The standard officer's bed was the 'cot'. 'This is a machine of about 6ft in length, and usually about 3ft 3in wide; made of coarse canvas, and strained on an oaken frame; provided with such bedding as the owner may choose; and when slung, suspended by cords from each extremity, to hooks in the beams above. It is commonly slung athwartship; but I found it more convenient to hang mine fore and aft, in the direction of the ship itself. And it must be observed that were it not for the concomitant circumstances, a more luxurious bed could not be conceived than a cot thus suspended.'[17]

5 Ship Administration

The Need for Administration

A large ship of war was a cross-section of society, except that few, if any, women and young children were on board when at sea. A captain could call on the resources of many different experts — the seamen, petty officers, master and lieutenants who made the ship mobile; the medical team under the surgeon; skilled craftsmen such as the carpenter and his crew, the caulkers, coopers, armourers, tailors, and sailmakers; intellectuals like the chaplain and schoolmaster; a unit of disciplined soldiers under the officers of marines; clerical and administrative staff such as the purser and captain's clerk; and experienced artillerymen under the gunner and his mates. A ship could be free of the shore for up to three months at a time, and independent of the naval supply organisation for longer than that, if the captain was able to find water and food on his own initiative. Its men had to be fed and paid, reports had to be made to the Admiralty and to the commander of the fleet, and logs and journals written up. The administration of the ship began on the day she was commissioned, and ended when she was laid up after her service.

Fitting Out

Once completed, a new ship might remain laid up for years, if there was no immediate need for her; but in wartime, she would probably be fitted out as soon as possible. The work of fitting out largely devolved on her captain and crew. She would first be put in dock to have her bottom cleaned, and coppered if necessary. Once she was afloat, her rigging, fitting and armament would be carried out under the direction of the ship's officers, with some help from the dockyard. She would probably be moored at a buoy in a large naval harbour, and all stores would be brought out to her by hoys and other small craft. Her lower masts would be put in by a sheer hulk, and then the shrouds and stays would be rigged, and the topmasts hoisted into place. The boatswain would direct a large party of seamen, along with dockyard riggers, in the setting up of many miles of rope. After the lower yards were fitted, it was possible to hoist in the guns, using the yardarms to rig tackle to lift them. Hundreds of barrels would be stowed in the hold under the direction of the master, who would have to take account of the trim of the ship. The carpenter and his assistants would be busy setting up cabins for the officers and making tables for the crew. The purser would have to supervise the receipt of stores issued by the government, and at the same time acquire other items, such as coal and candles, out of the necessary money supplied by the Navy Board. The lieutenants would be mustering the crew and recruiting more men by means of inducements and impressment. If men and materials were available in sufficient quantities, a ship could be fitted out in about three weeks of back-breaking toil. But the stores and fittings would have to be removed,

A ship fitting out at Chatham. The National Maritime Museum

and the same procedure repeated, every time the ship went into dock.

The frigate *Galatea*, for example, began fitting out on 24 May 1794, when the first lieutenant appeared on board and commissioned the ship; the captain did not arrive till a few days later. The ship spent the next three months alongside the *Mercury* hulk, taking in stores and setting up rigging. By 7 June she had only thirty-seven officers and men on board, but some artificers were sent from the dockyard to help with the work, as the crew slowly increased. By the 10th, the iron ballast had been laid in the hold, and shingle ballast was being lifted on board from dockyard hoys. On the 21st the ground tier of casks had been completed, and work began on the lower rigging. The main yard and the fore crosstrees were brought on board on the 24th, and the tops were fitted the next day. By the end of the month, the crew had risen to 118, and work proceeded with the rigging. The seamen worked aloft, while landmen were set to work scraping and painting the outside and inside of the hull. On 5 July the topmasts were swayed up, and two days later the topgallants. Yards were swayed up and crossed during the next few days, and on 14 July the seamen began tarring the standing rigging. Some of the provisions had been consumed during this period, and the ground tier was again completed on the 20th. The fore and after holds were stowed on the 28th and 29th, and on the 30th the sails were bent to the yards. The landsmen were still painting the inside of the ship, and on 4 August the painters of the dockyard arrived on board to help them. The powder was brought on board on the 6th, and finally on 11 August a hoy came alongside with the ship's guns. They were hoisted on board, set on their carriages, and the ship was ready for sea.[1] Ships could be fitted out more quickly if men were available, but there were often delays.

Raising a Crew

The captain was also responsible for finding the crew for a newly commissioned ship — according to the Admiralty regulations he was 'to use his utmost endeavours to get her manned'[2] — though he was given the help of the port admiral and the impress service. The captain himself could also send out press gangs; on the night of 24 June, for example, the captain of the *Galatea* 'sent an officer and a gang of hands on shore on the impress service'. They left at 10 pm and returned at 2 in the morning with an unspecified number of men; five of these were retained in service. Ships often got large drafts of volunteers or newly pressed men from the receiving ships, and after the war had been going some time they might get men 'turned over' from ships taken out of commission. The manning of the *Galatea* was slow. She had a total complement of 260, but one month after commissioning, less than half that number were on board. After seven weeks the number had risen to 163, and the situation was eased in the following week, when the first party of 24 marines arrived on board. By the time she sailed she was nearly up to full strength, but many ships of that period sailed about ten per cent short of complement.[3]

If a ship had serious difficulty in finding men but was nevertheless needed urgently, men might be lent from other ships, or from receiving ships. Robert Hay was lent in such a way in 1803. 'A Lieutenant Archibald, commander of the *Eling* schooner, was on board, and was to be furnished with the loan of six boys during a cruise on which he was shortly to sail. The favour was granted of choosing these six boys, and I to my great satisfaction happened to be one of the chosen number.'[4] Men lent in this way were listed in the muster book as 'supernumeraries for wages'. 'Supernumeraries for victuals' were fed, but not paid as part of the ship. They were essentially passengers, such as seamen or soldiers being carried to a foreign station, or wives of soldiers. Women were usually given two thirds of the full victualling allowance.

Logs and Reports

Once commissioned, a ship required a considerable amount of paperwork to keep her in good order. The recognised office staff consisted only of the captain's clerk, the purser and his steward, and the writer to the first lieutenant — the rest of the writing had to be done by the officers themselves. Captains, lieutenants, mates and midshipmen all had to keep individual logs, and to present them to the Admiralty before they could be paid. In practice, logs mostly gave a bare record of navigational matters, with note on punishments given, provisions received, and a few other matters which the admiralty was known to be interested in. Often the wording of several different logs is identical, suggesting that in practice the officers colluded with one another. The log kept by the master was the official ship's log, and it gave rather more detail of navigational matters, with hourly accounts of winds, and courses steered. It gave even less information on other matters than the logs of the other officers. Any officers who wanted to give more detail of the life of the ship usually confided it to unofficial private diaries.

The other warrant officers were not expected to account for their time in quite the same way, though the surgeon was ordered to 'keep a journal of his practice'. The standing officers had to 'keep an account of... the receipt, expenditure, condemnation by survey, or supplying of stores'.[5] All these had to be sent to the Navy Board or appropriate authority before the officer could be paid.

The Captain's Office

In order to have his accounts passed at the Admiralty, a captain had to present at least twenty-five different completed books and forms.[6] Some of these were quite simple: a 'Certificate of no backstays shifted or top-masts lost', and a copy of his commission. Others largely depended on the nature of the cruise, and the enthusiasm of the individual: 'Remarks on coasts, roads, & co, or a certificate none were made.' Some were completed by others, such as the warrant officer's accounts. Some were very elaborate, such as the two copies of the log book, and the muster books which had to be sent in periodically. The main job of the captain's clerk was to prepare such documents, and to copy out the general correspondence of the captain — instructions to officers and crew, letters to the Admiralty and Navy Board, to the Admiral commanding, or to junior officers on other ships. There was no means of duplicating, except to copy out the whole document by hand, so letter books also had to be written out, containing office-copies of letters sent and received. Numerous other forms had to be made out in certain circumstances — a 'list for prisoners landed', 'receipt for clothing for the party of marines', and a list of all merchant ships spoken to during the cruise. The captain's clerk worked in a small office on the quarterdeck just forward of the captain's cabin, and lived in another in the gunroom. He had to work in close co-operation with the purser, especially in the making up of muster books, which were also used for victualling the crew.

Purserage

The purser was the ship's supply officer, responsible for the items most necessary to support life — food, clothing, heat, light and bedding. His exact financial position was rather complex, somewhere between a supply officer proper and a sub-contractor. Despite his name, he did not normally handle the government's money, and had little to do with the payment of the crew. However, his whole scheme of payment was based on cash and accounting.

The largest part of his responsibility was to do with the supplies of food and drink. These were provided by the government, but the purser was financially responsible for all of them. They were charged

An Account of Clothes and other Effects belonging to the following Persons, deceased, sold at the Mast on board His Majesty's Ship the , Capt. , Commander, between the and the to be transmitted to the Navy Office.

When sold	No. on the Ship's Books	To whom sold	Belonging to George Matthews.	Amount.
18				L. s. d.
10th May	9	James Fray	A waistcoat, a pair of breeches, and a pair of stockings	0 10 0
	10	James Owen	Two shirts and a pair of shoes	0 7 6
	11	John Griffiths	A jacket, two books, and a bed	0 15 0
	109	Charles Rowe	Two pair of trowsers and a Dutch cap	0 7 0
	127	John Price	A pair of silver buckles	0 16 0

A. B. Commander.
C. D. Master.
E. F. Boatswain.
G. H. Purser.

Pork.

Time Received	Place where	From whom	On the Casks: Marks	On the Casks: No.	Contents in Pcs. of 4 lbs ea.	When: Opened	When: Out	Whom present when opened	Proved pieces: Contents charged: Over	Proved pieces: Contents charged: Short	Remarks, &c.
18 Jan. 3.	Jamaica	F. G. Esq. Contractor Per K. L. his Agent.	F.G.P. Cork	620	80	4Mar.18	12 Mar.	Mr. S.T.	1		
				673	80						
				631	80	2Feb.18	3 Mar	Mr. S.T.		1	
				646	80						
			F.G.B. Dublin	37	80						
				21	80						
				75	80						
		Per Receipts given 5 Jan.			560						

to his account at fixed prices — $4\frac{1}{2}$d per pound of beef, 9s per bushel of peas, and 6d per pound of cheese, for example. He had to account very carefully for their use, by keeping an accurate muster book, showing exactly how many men were victualled each day. This task was complicated by several factors. Officers often contracted out of the ship's victualling and took payment in lieu; when provisions were short, the whole crew might be on short rations and be given money in compensation; men were entitled to change their messes as often as they wished; there were complicated rules for the substitution of one form of provision for another; men were often transferred in or out of the ship, or deserted and died; and supernumeraries were often borne at different rates of victualling. Detailed accounts of all this had to be produced before the purser could be paid.

The purser had certain ways of making profits on these victuals.

Form of a Short Allowance List.

A List of all the Officers and men belonging to His Majesty's Ship the as well such as are sick on shore, discharged, or dead, as such as are actually on board, beginning short allowance the and ending the of , of the nature and kinds undermentioned, viz.

No. of days.	Rate per diem.	Sum

No. on Ships Books	Men's Names	Quality	Entry for the time of this List	D. D. D. or R.	Discharge for the time of this List	To deduct for any that may within the time, be absent, either by Sickness, on shore, or otherwise. When absent from the Ship.	When Returned	Sum due to each Man for short Allowance	Solving Column	To whom paid.

Foms of Vouchers for payment of Savings of Provisions.

An Account of the Quantities of Provisions saved by the Company of His Majesty's Ship out of their daily allowance, between the and the ; with the value thereof, at the prices settled for the payment of Savings; the name of the person appointed to receive for each mess; and to whom the amount was paid: viz.

No. of the Mess.	No. of Persons in the Mess	Name of the Psrson appointed to receive for the Mess	No. on the Ship's Books of the Persons receiving.	Quantities of Provisions saved by each Mess. Bread lbs.	Wine Gallons.	Spirits Gallons.	Beef Pieces, including Flour, &c.	Pork Pieces.	Butter lbs.	Cheese lbs.	Value of the Provisions due to each Mess. L.	s.	d.	When Paid.	Signatures of the Persons to whom paid.	Signatures the Witnesses to the Payment.

A selection of the forms used by the purser. From Admiralty *Regulations and Instructions*, 1808

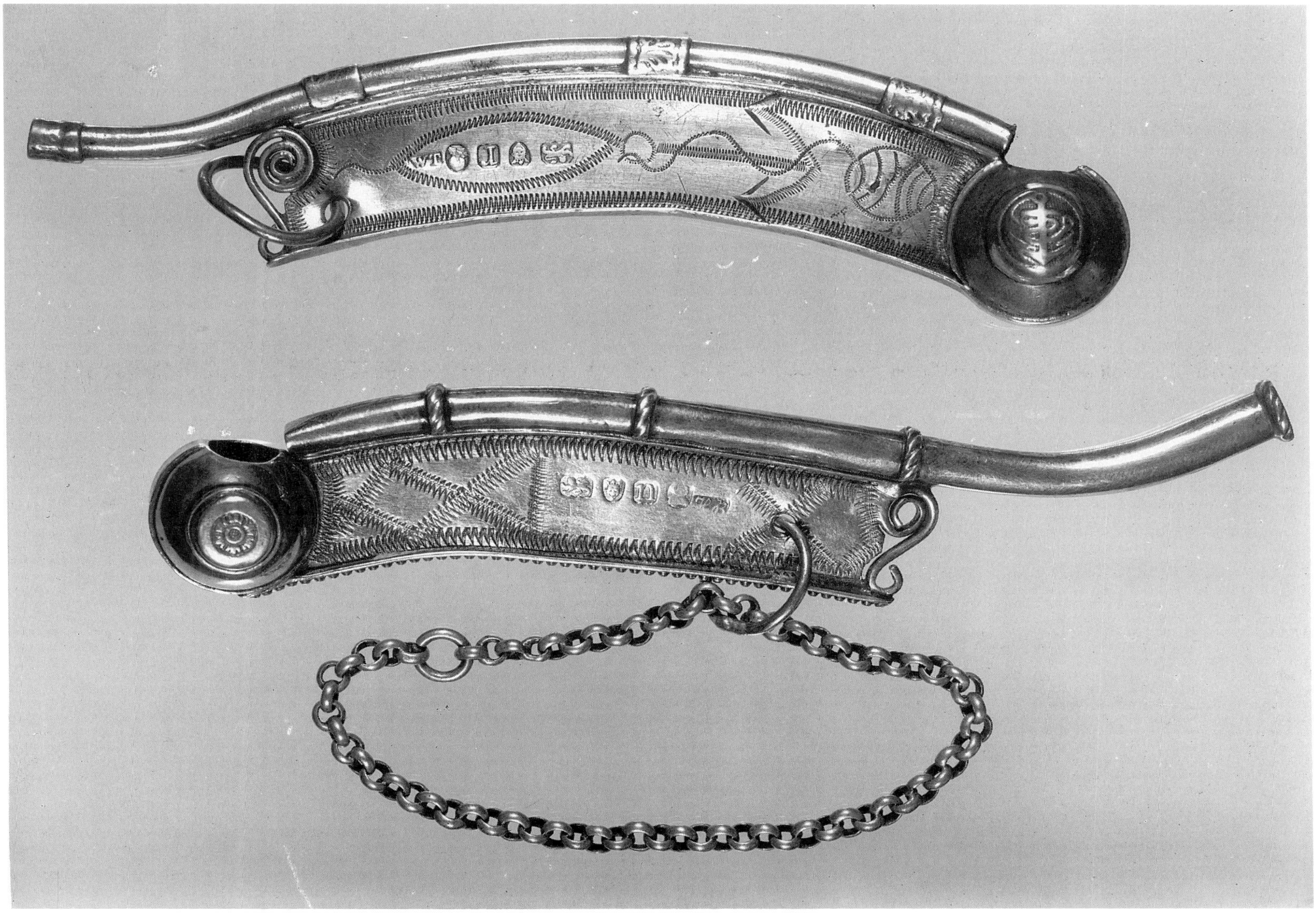

Two boatswain's calls. The National Maritime Museum

A speaking trumpet. Author's photograph, courtesy of the National Maritime Museum

He was allowed one eighth for wastage on all items except meat. If wastage was less than this, the profit went to the purser. Unconsumed provisions could be sold back to the government, though at much lower prices than the purser's account was charged: only 1¾d per pound of bread, 4s per bushel of peas, and 3d per pound of cheese. He was paid the full price on bad provisions condemned by survey.

While in harbour, or at anchor near one of the major naval ports, a ship was on 'petty warrant' (or 'Peter Warren') victuals. This meant that fresh food (unsalted meat, green vegetables and soft bread) was sent from the shore, and this had to be accounted for separately. In a port where there was some kind of British naval or consular presence, no money passed through the purser's hands, and he was strictly debarred from buying provisions except through the government agents. In other ports, he was allowed, in cases of necessity, to trade for provisions on the local market, and to send his bill to the Victualling Board.

The purser also had to supply the ship with 'necessaries', for example, 'coals, wood, turnery-ware, candles, lanthornes and other necessaries'. He had to pay for these out of his own pocket in the first instance, though he was eventually reimbursed at a rate which varied according to the number of men on the ship; a halfpenny per man day on a ship of more than 343 men, and 2s 6d per man per lunar month on a ship with a complement of less than sixty-seven, in 1807.[7] Pursers sometimes neglected to supply enough of these items, and the captain of the *Audacious* issued a standing order to the effect that 'Should the ship be obliged to return for want of such necessaries and her water and provisions would have kept her longer upon the services she was employed on, he will be answerable for the consequences.'[8]

Pursers were also responsible for the bedding and slops issued to the men. These were supplied by the Navy Board, and sold to the crew by means of deductions from their wages. This perhaps allowed a little scope for illicit profit; pursers were often accused of selling slops to men who had died or deserted. The purser was invariably suspected of starving the men, or feeding them rotten meat, in order to line his own pocket. In fact, his trade carried many risks, and he was often unpopular aboard ship.

Internal Communications

Orders aboard ship were conveyed in various ways. The boatswain's mates roused the crew for watches, and when action or danger threatened. The boatswain's call allowed a limited number of signals to be transmitted to the crew: 'as hoisting, heaving, lowering, veering away, belaying, letting go a tackle, & co, and the piping of it is as attentively observed by sailors, as the beat of the drum to march, retreat, rally, charge & co is obeyed by soldiers'.[9] Other signals were transmitted by the marine drummers — a continuous roll or 'Hearts of Oak' was used to 'beat to quarters', or call the crew to action stations. Variations on this, perhaps with one or two extra beats after the roll, told the crew that this was an exercise of one kind or another. To communicate with the crew on deck or in the rigging, the officer of the watch used a speaking trumpet to direct and magnify his voice; or possibly he ordered one of the boatswain's mates, usually chosen for his loud voice, to convey his orders. The speaking trumpet was part of the equipment of every sea officer. If the captain needed to call an individual officer or man to his cabin, he would 'pass the word'. The name would be called by the sentry at the cabin door, repeated by others who shouted it down the various hatchways, and then sent along the decks until the man was found. In action, a captain had several midshipmen as aides-de-camp, and he sent them to the lower decks to transmit orders to the officers on the gundecks. Some ships were also fitted with voice pipes to the different decks. These may have been used to transmit orders in action, but their main purpose was to communicate with the gunroom — if the steering wheel was put out of action, orders could be sent immediately to the men on the tackles on the tiller.

Prize Money

Prize money was one of the great inducements in the naval service, especially to officers. Admirals could make many thousands of pounds, and even lieutenants and warrant officers could become quite wealthy, given luck. Since the early years of the eighteenth century, it had been customary to issue a proclamation at the beginning of each war, allowing the whole value of ships captured from the enemy to be divided up among the officers and crews of the ships which took part in her capture. To be eligible for prize money, certain conditions had to be met. On capture, the hatches of the ship had to be nailed up, to prevent embezzlement of the stores (though the rules were much less strict about goods found above the deck). It had to be proved that the ship did in fact belong to an enemy country; many ships sailed under false colours, or with false papers, so it was quite easy for a captain to make a mistake. This issue was adjudicated by the Admiralty Court. Apart from the High Court of Admiralty in London, Vice Admiralty Courts existed round the coast of Britain and in various foreign possessions, such as Gibraltar, Barbados, Madras and Calcutta. The corruption of some courts was notorious; Cochrane found at Malta that the Proctor and Marshall were the same person, allowing vast scope for deceit. In another case, a prize was sold for £291, and the expenses of the court came to £221.[10] It often took some time for judgement to be reached, by which time the ship had often sailed. Advertisements were placed for money which was ready to be paid, and most naval officers had agents to claim the money for them — taking a commission of course.

The money was distributed according to a fixed scale. Before 1808, three eighths of the value went to the captain; if he was under the orders of an admiral, one of these eighths went to the flag officer; if he was sailing under orders direct from the Admiralty, he was allowed to keep it. Another eighth went to 'captains of marines, land forces, sea lieutenants and masters', to be divided equally among them. An eighth went to 'lieutenants and quartermasters of marines, lieutenants, ensigns and quartermasters of land forces, boatswain, gunner, purser, carpenter, masters' mates, surgeons and chaplains'. Yet another eighth went to the midshipmen, surgeons' mates, sergeants of marines and various petty officers, while the remaining quarter went to the crew and marines.[11] The new system of 1808 gave only a quarter to the captain, with a third of that going to the flag officer if applicable; the commissioned and warrant officers remained at one eighth for each group, while the petty officers and crew had a half between them. There were special rules for captures by small ships, or those with reduced crews. Prize money was shared out between all the ships in sight at the moment when the enemy surrendered; even a ship which took no part in the action could help in 'adding to the encouragement of the captors, and the terror of the enemy.'[12]

Undoubtedly, prize money was an unfair system. An admiral in command during an active phase in the West Indies could amass hundreds of thousands of pounds without leaving his headquarters; frigate captains could make large sums from enemy merchant shipping, while ships-of-the-line had much less opportunity. Ships were thereby encouraged to prey on merchant shipping, with its rich cargoes, rather than attack warships, which fought back and had much less value after their capture. The government took certain steps to reduce the obvious disadvantages of the system. Honours and promotions were given for the capture of warships only; 'head money' was paid, at the rate of £5 for each of the crew of the enemy ship, for privateers and warships. Parliament often voted sums of money after great victories, to be distributed among the fleet in the same way as prize money. All this did little to reduce the lust for prize money among many officers.

Part V
NAVAL RECRUITMENT

1 The Problem of Naval Recruitment

The Role of Impressment

The notion of the press gang, grabbing innocent victims from the streets and forcing them into unpleasant and extremely hazardous service in the fleet, is deeply ingrained in British consciousness. It has influenced the language in several ways. 'Prest' was originally a small sum of money given to the seaman on recruitment, but it became intertangled with the verb 'to press', and acquired very unpleasant associations. A 'gang' was originally a group of seamen allotted to a particular task, but through the press gang it began to take on overtones of violence and criminality, which survive to this day.

Undoubtedly impressment was a very cruel and inefficient system of conscription, but it must be remembered that by law it applied only to professional seamen. There were many cases where non-seamen were taken up by gangs during a 'hot press', but the vast majority of them were soon released on proving their identity. Captains of ships of war needed skilled men to run their ships, and had no real wish to take up landmen. Perhaps some were unable to prove their identity, and lacked the means to pursue their case through law; but there can be no doubt that the great majority of pressed men were seamen.

Seamen's Attitudes to the Navy

The navy never had any great problem in attracting officers. The aristocracy, gentry and the rising middle class competed to have their sons entered as midshipmen, for, despite all its hazards, a naval career offered the chance of fame, riches, and an entry into the highest places in the land. Professional men were taken on as surgeons and pursers, sometimes bribing their way into an appointment. Those of lower social origin became carpenters, gunners or boatswains, and were happy with the security that these careers offered. While the seamen were hiding from the press gang in every nook and cranny, the waiting room of the Admiralty was filled with officers soliciting appointments.

Obviously it was not the hazards of naval service which created this difference, for they were borne equally by officers and men. Bad victuals and draconian discipline may have played a part, but the conditions in the merchant service were often no better. William Spavens believed that 'His Majesty's service is, in many respects, preferable to any other', because, among other reasons, 'the provisions are better in kind, and generally more plentiful'.[1] Low pay was a factor, but it must be remembered that merchant service pay was also low in peacetime. According to Adam Smith, 'In time of war, when forty or fifty thousand sailors are forced from the merchant service into that of the king, the demand for sailors to merchant ships necessarily rises with their scarcity, and their wages commonly rise from a guinea and 27s to 40s and £3 per month.'[2] Recruitment to the navy prevented the seaman from sharing in this bonanza, but pay was not the only problem. The rise after the mutinies of 1797 seems to have done little to solve the problem of recruitment.

The biggest deterrent to naval service was its indefinite nature, the fear that it might last for years without end. On being impressed in 1794, John Nicol considered himself 'in a situation I could not leave, a bondage which had been imposed on me against my will, and no hope of relief until the end of the war'.[3] To Samuel Bechervaise, 'the dread of a ship of war was next to a French prison'.[4] The problem was that seamen were not released at the end of a voyage, like merchant seamen, but transferred from one ship to another until the end of the war brought release — unless they deserted, died, or became unfit for service. In earlier years, warships had been fitted out for the summer only, and seamen paid off during the winter; this practice had ceased by the beginning of the eighteenth century, but many relics of the old days remained. The seamen had all the disadvantages of long-term service, but none of the advantages of belonging permanently to an organisation. They often lost rank on transfer from one ship to another, and their back-pay sometimes took years to catch up with them. Shore leave was solely at the discretion of the captain, and was not guaranteed to any seaman. Even while awaiting transfer from one ship to another, or while their ship was in dry dock, the seamen were not allowed ashore, but accommodated in hulks.

The navy had been caught in a vicious circle for two centuries or more. Since the later stages of Queen Elizabeth's reign, money had been short, conditions bad, and the seamen had usually suffered from the taxpayer's reluctance to contribute. Trust between the government and the seamen had rarely been high, and it had declined steadily since the 1690s. The officers would not let the seamen ashore in case they deserted, and the seamen would not enter the navy because they could see no prospect of release.

By the Commissioners for Executing the Office of Lord High Admiral of the United Kingdom of *Great Britain* and *Ireland*, &c. and of all His Majesty's Plantations, &c.

IN Pursuance of His Majesty's Order in Council, dated the Sixteenth Day of *November*, 1808, We do hereby Impower and Direct you to impress, or cause to be impressed, so many Seamen, Seafaring Men and Persons whose Occupations and Callings are to work in Vessels and Boats upon Rivers, as shall be necessary either to Man His Majesty's Ship under your Command or any other of His Majesty's Ships, giving unto each Man so impressed One Shilling for Prest Money. And, in the execution hereof, you are to take care, that neither yourself nor any Officer authorised by you do demand or receive any Money, Gratuity, Reward, or other Consideration whatsoever, for the sparing, Exchanging, or Discharging, any Person or Persons impressed or to be impressed, as you will answer it at your Peril. You are not to intrust any Person with the execution of this Warrant, but a Commission Officer, and to insert his Name and Office in the Deputation on the other side hereof, and set your Hand and Seal thereto.---This Warrant to continue in Force till the Thirty-first Day of December 1809, and in the due execution thereof, all Mayors, Sheriffs, Justices of the Peace, Bailiffs, Constables, Headboroughs, and all other His Majesty's Officers and Subjects whom it may concern, are hereby required to be aiding and assisting unto you, and those employed by you, as they tender His Majesty's Service, and will answer the contrary at their Perils.

Given under our Hands, and the Seal of the Office of Admiralty, the [illegible] 1809.

Captain [illegible]
Commander of His Majesty's [illegible]
the [illegible]

By Command of their Lordships,

A press warrant issued to a captain in 1809. This would be countersigned by the captain on the other side, and issued to one of his lieutenants as his authority to press men. The National Maritime Museum

Supply and Demand

The second problem was simply one of supply and demand, as Adam Smith hinted. It took several years to train a good seaman, and in time of war both the navy and the merchant shipowners competed for his services. John Nicol was hounded by press gangs in the 1800s, and suffered great financial hardship because of this. Yet he took a perverse pleasure in his value as a seaman, and said to his friends who teased him about it, 'Could the government make perfect seamen as easily as they could soldiers, there would be no such thing as the pressing of seamen, and I was happy to be of more value than all of them put together, for they would not impress any of them, they were of so little value compared with me.'[5] The seaman was seen as being from a different race, almost a different species, from the rest of mankind, with his own dress, vocabulary and manners. The expression 'bred to the sea' recurs throughout the age of sail, and it highlights some of the difference. It was generally felt that adults could not easily be made into seamen. 'Boys soon become good seamen; landsmen rarely do, for they are confirmed in other habits', wrote one captain in 1838.[6]

One estimate suggests that there were just over 118,000 merchant seamen in 1792, on the eve of the French Revolutionary War. Within five years, Parliament was voting for a navy of 120,000 men.[7] Of course, not all the men borne on ships of war were professional seamen. Deducting officers, artisans, servants, landsmen and marines, it seems likely that only about half the complement of any given ship was experienced, and Captain Marryat suggests that no ship he served on in wartime was as well manned as that.[8] In five years both the navy and the merchant service would have a chance to train up new men, and the latter was allowed to recruit foreigners in wartime, so the navy would not really have to take up half the men of the merchant service. Nevertheless, the demand for seamen was intense, and the supply could only be expanded slowly.

The navy was a consumer rather than producer of seamen. Occasionally, training schemes were devised so that boys, landmen or marines could qualify to become seamen, but these were unofficial or half hearted, and largely ineffective. In general, the navy expected its seamen to have been trained in the merchant marine, and it persisted in the fiction that they were serving temporarily in the navy before returning to the merchant service. This fiction became increasingly unreal in an age when major wars could last for eight or eleven years without interruption. Bounties could sometimes lure seamen into the navy, but the only way to raise a fleet quickly was by impressment.

The Origins of Impressment

In a feudal society, where all men were obliged to help in the defence of the realm when needed, impressment was perfectly normal, and was applied equally to raise soldiers and sailors. In the revolutions of the seventeenth century the concepts of personal liberty and the limited power of the state developed side by side, and impressment of landmen was abolished. Parliament had debated the abolition of the impressment of seamen in 1641, on the eve of the Civil War, but it had concluded that it needed the navy too urgently to give up this prerogative.[9] At successive changes of regime, in 1649, in 1660 and in 1688, the new government was always too insecure, too dependent on a strong navy for its survival, to tamper with impressment in any way. As Britain developed into a European and world power, the navy became too important to be weakened, and no-one could devise an alternative means of raising a fleet quickly in an emergency. With the great growth of the navy, the burden of defending the state fell increasingly heavily on the seamen, and they suffered simply because they were more useful to the government than other groups of men. Thus impressment survived into an age when it was totally at variance with ordinary conceptions of liberty, and, if anything, it became more oppressive over the years, as seamen became more mutinous and resentful.

Impressment and the Law

There was no specific law which allowed impressment, but on the other hand, there was none which banned it. The issue had come before the courts in 1743, and the judge had commented,

> The question touching the legality of pressing mariners for the public service is a point of very great national importance. On one hand a very useful body of men seem to be put under hardship inconsistent with the

temper and genius of a free government. On the other, the necessity of the case seems to entitle the public to the service of this body of men, whenever the safety of the whole calls for it... I think His Majesty, as head of the community, concerned to see the good and welfare of the whole... has a right to demand the service of these people whenever the public safety calls for it. The same right that he has to require the personal service of every man able to bear arms, in case of sudden invasion or a formidable insurrection. His right in both cases is, I take it, founded upon one and the same principle, the necessity of the care and welfare of the state.[10]

Landmen were, however, rarely called upon to sacrifice their liberty in this way, because the navy was so successful in preventing 'sudden invasion', or 'formidable insurrection'.

In 1776, there was a similar judgement, when it was concluded that 'the power of pressing is founded on immemorial usage, allowed for ages... And the practice is deduced from that trite maxim of the constitutional law of England, that private mischief had better be submitted to, than that public detriment and inconvenience should ensue.'[11]

To be legal, it was assumed that a press gang had to be headed by an officer holding the king's commission, and also bearing a warrant to impress men, signed by the Lords of the Admiralty. Even so, it was not difficult for an officer to find himself on the wrong side of the law, for local magistrates often took a dim view of gangs which used excessive force, or impressed men who were not subject to it. In most cases, the Admiralty tried to protect its officers from the worst effects of this. In 1794, for example, a press gang from the frigate *Aurora* boarded the merchant ship *Sarah and Elizabeth* of Hull. In the scuffle which followed a carpenter's mate was killed, and a local coroner's jury decided that he had been murdered by the captain and part of the crew of the *Aurora*. The captain was rapidly transferred to another ship and sent to the West Indies for a period of years.[12]

The law did prescribe a long list of types of seamen who were exempt from the press. These included apprentices, who were already bound to another master. Men who had spent less than two years at sea were exempted, to encourage new men to enter the trade. Captains and mates of merchant ships were also exempt, along with all the men in certain trades, such as the Greenland fishery. Foreigners were not supposed to be impressed, but it was difficult for Americans to prove their nationality to the satisfaction of the Admiralty. A pilot was exempt, unless he ran the ship aground. Men employed in the service of the government, under the Transport Board, Navy Board, Ordnance Board etc, were also protected, as were some classes of fishermen. All these men carried protections issued by the Admiralty, though there were many others who carried forged protections.

Opposition to impressment

Though it was recognised that impressment was necessary for the defence of the country, almost everyone was opposed to it in practice. Seamen, of course, resisted it as far as possible. Ordinary citizens resented the disturbance and chaos it caused. Merchants and shipowners, who often formed the local government in a seaport town, did not like to lose the prime hands who might be employed on their own ships.

Opposition took many forms, both legal and illegal. One of the headings in the Admiralty index of letters was to 'Rescuing seamen and riots on the impress service'. In 1803, a regulating captain wrote to the Admiralty, 'Lieutenant Bounton has this instant come away from Sunderland to inform me that he durst not attempt to impress at that place last night, as mobs of hundreds of seamen, soldiers, and women, got round the rendezvous and threatened the lives of himself and his people, whether they acted or not.' A few days later the gang returned, 'the seamen all fled, but we were attacked by large mobs, principally women, who by throwing things hurt several officers and rescued several men.'[13] Such incidents were common in the life of an officer on impressment duty, for there was no effective police force, and the press gang did not have public support. One wrote 'On one occasion I was assaulted by a shower of brickbats: on another, a volley of either musket or pistol balls was fired into my room one evening as I was reading at my table.'[14]

A man - probably a tailor, with his scissors and tape hanging out of his pocket - is seized by a press gang. At least one of the gang seems to be enjoying his work, but the officer, to the right, looks rather apprehensive as the local people attack the gang with brooms and other weapons. The National Maritime Museum

On a milder level, those who saw a press gang at work were often inspired to abuse. 'The vagabond press gang seized me and dragged me along through rag fair to their rendezvous at Rosemary Lane, and being market day, the old Jewesses abused the gang in high style, making me think they were going to show fight and attempt rescue, but they let abusive language serve'.[15] William Dillon reports that while in the impress service in Hull, he was regularly supplied with attractive dancing partners, as the merchants attempted to distract him from his duties. In a similar vein, one young midshipman

The gang attempts to drag a seaman away from his wife and family. This was a common image of the press gang, and it was often shown grabbing a man on his wedding day. From *The Log Book*, or *Nautical Miscellany*, 1830

A London waterman is taken by a ruffianly press gang, while his upper-class passengers look on in horror. The National Maritime Museum

was sent down to Chatham to pick up a party of pressed men. 'In a public House, the Kings Arms, near the Marine Barracks, Brompton, I found half a dozen men with their women, who began to pet me, trying to make me drink, till I nearly cried with vexation; when one of the men said, "Oh come along; we shall get the young gentleman into a scrape", and so they all came down to the boat, and I brought them on board.'[16]

Dozens of pamphlets were written against impressment in these years; attempts were made to find seamen other ways, by means of quotas, bounties and so on; but despite all the hostility and ingenuity directed against it on many levels, impressment survived throughout the Napoleonic Wars, because no other means of recruitment could be found to replace it.

2 The Press Gang

Mobilisation for War

On the threat of war, the government usually took immediate action to mobilise the navy. Press warrants were issued from the Admiralty to the relevant officers. Marines and the crews of guardships were sent into the ports to form the nucleus of the press gangs. A bounty was proclaimed for all seamen who would enlist voluntarily, and an embargo was placed on trade, preventing British ships from leaving port for the immediate future, until the press gangs had time to do their work. Such embargoes were lifted progressively, one trade at a time, according to economic need. In 1795, there was the 'great embargo', in which shipping was kept in port until the numbers demanded by the Quota Acts had been raised.

Such mobilisations were quite common in the eighteenth century, but were not always followed by war. In the period before the French Revolutionary War, the 'Spanish Armament' of 1790 and the 'Russian Armament' of 1791 led to full mobilisation, but the differences were settled before hostilities broke out. Of all the mobilisations using the press gang, that of 1803 was probably the most effective, because the press warrants were issued in great secrecy, and executed ruthlessly.

Press Gangs from Ships

Essentially, there were two types of press gang — those regularly employed as part of the impress service, and used for no other duties; and those taken from a ship's crew, to gather men for that particular ship. Both types could be employed afloat or ashore, but the men of the impress service were mostly shore-based, while those from ships could land for a quick foray ashore, or take men from passing merchant ships.

Of the two, the press gang from the ship was the oldest. Captains were issued with press warrants as a matter of course when a ship was commissioned in wartime. These forms, signed by the Lords of the Admiralty, authorised the captain to appoint lieutenants to 'impress seamen, seafaring men, and persons whose occupations and callings are to work in vessels and boats upon rivers'. The press warrant itself gave details of the powers of the press gang, and listed types of men exempted. It gave the lieutenant power to press both ashore and afloat. If he boarded a merchant ship, he was to assemble the crew and inform them that if they volunteered for the navy they would be eligible for bounties: if not, they might be pressed anyway. The head of a press gang was rewarded with £1 for every seaman taken.

The shore-going press gangs from ships were perhaps the most notorious. Unlike the gangs afloat, they were likely to take landsmen by mistake or out of malice. Unlike the permanent gangs of the impress service, they did not wait around to see the effects of their actions. According to Samuel Leech, such gangs often took American citizens. 'To prevent the recovery of these men by their consul, the press gang usually went ashore on the night previous to our going to sea; so that before they were missed they were beyond his protection. Sometimes they were claimed on our return to port.'[1] One problem for the captain was to find suitable men who could be trusted ashore — according to Leech a gang 'was made up of our most loyal men, armed to the teeth'. It was surprisingly easy to find gangs from among newly pressed men; during the hot press of 1803, a midshipman observed, 'One fact deserves notice; I frequently captured men who, though inclined to be violent at first, soon resigned themselves to their fate, and became valuable members of the press gang, to which they became very valuable auxiliaries'.[2]

The Impress Service

In the seventeenth century the mass of press gangs competing with one another in the great ports, especially London, had caused chaos. Regulating captains were appointed to control the work of the ship-based gangs, and to inspect recruits. After 1755, they were also responsible for the impress service, which consisted of permanent shore-based gangs. By 1795, the impress service included 85 gangs, with 84 lieutenants, 162 petty officers, and 754 men in Great Britain and Ireland. There were thirty-two regulating captains, each with a district under his control. He set up his headquarters in the main port of his district, and inspected recruits with the aid of a surgeon. He directed the efforts of the gangs in the area, and with the help of his clerk he sent regular returns to the Admiralty.

Each regulating captain had a number of gangs under his control — two in the smallest districts, and up to seven in London. As with the gangs from ships, each was headed by a lieutenant, who was assisted by two petty officers or midshipmen. The lieutenants were usually fairly old, and William Dillon, on being appointed to the impress service, was 'completely taken aback', because 'none, generally speaking, but worn out lieutenants were appointed to that service.'[3] According to another account, 'Some officers, from being so many years at a rendezvous, lose sight of the service in every other point of view.'[4]

The lieutenant found a local inn or tavern for his headquarters.

The Impress Service in 1795. Based on information in Steel's Navy List

It was known rather optimistically as the 'rendezvous', implying that it was used mainly for voluntary recruiting. The inn had to be large enough to accommodate most of the gang, and needed a secure room known as the press room, where men could be locked up while awaiting transfer to a ship.

In contrast to the lieutenants, the midshipmen and petty officers of the gang were often quite young, and had no experience of the sea. For his gang, the lieutenant was encouraged to recruit experienced seamen, who could lure young men with tales of the sea; but such men were rare, and there was always the temptation to send them off to the fleet as recruits. Probably the majority of gang members were landmen. Normally a shore-based gang had ten men, but pay returns suggest that many were under strength.

The Work of the Gang

The first task of the press gang ashore was to find seamen; this was usually done by searching the streets and the seamen's favourite taverns, and sometimes their homes. Local knowledge was useful here, and often the gang tried to recruit at least one member who was familiar with the area. However, there was a certain risk in this, and such men were often in severe danger. In 1811, one Jackey White of Hull was attacked by a crowd at his lodgings, and had to be rescued by soldiers and taken to the pressing tender.[5] (See page 122.)

Having found men, the gang had to attempt to identify them as seamen. If they had recently left their ships they would be dressed in seamen's clothes, and the gang would have no problem. But if the seamen had warning, they would change into the 'long clothes' of landmen. The gang would approach likely looking men, and sometimes take them to the rendezvous for questioning. Violence was a part of their way of life, and they were not gentle in their approach.

> I was when crossing Tower Hill accosted by a person in seamen's dress who tapped me on the shoulder enquiring in a familiar and technical strain, 'What ship?' I assumed an air of gravity and surprise and told them I presumed he was under some mistake, as I was not connected with shipping. The fellow, however, was too well acquainted with his business to be thus easily put off. He gave a whistle and in a moment I was in the hands of six or eight ruffians who I immediately dreaded and soon found to be a press gang. They dragged me hurriedly along through several streets amid bitter execrations bestowed on them, expressions of sympathy directed towards me and landed me in one of their houses of rendezvous.'[6]

The gang often inspected men's hands for traces of tar, a sure sign of a seaman.

Local Government and Chartered Corporations

Though local magistrates and mayors often obstructed the press gang, they had long been given the responsibility of finding men for the navy by themselves. The oldest duty was that of the Cinque Ports in southeast England, who on mobilisation of the navy were ordered 'to impress as many seamen and seafaring men for His Majesty's service, as can be procured within the jurisdiction or limits of the said ports, towns, and members respectively, and cause them to be sent from time to time on board . . . His Majesty's ships and vessels'.[7] Like all pressing bodies, they were to be allowed £1 for every man so recruited. It is not likely that they pursued their task with any enthusiasm, and the numbers obtained by such means were usually quite small.

Another body charged with raising men was Watermens Hall, which licensed the boatmen who rowed passengers about the River Thames in London. They were generally expected to find a fixed number of men out of their members, and send them to the fleet. Again, the numbers obtained were not great in a fleet of up to 135,000 men, and there were often complaints about the quality. In addition, even inland local authorities were charged with apprehending deserters, and finding 'straggling' seamen who had fled inshore to escape the press gang. But in general the navy had learned to rely on its own resources, and to trust no-one else in the matter of impressment.

The press gang on Tower Hill, London. The National Maritime Museum

Pressing Tenders

Having found men ashore, the navy preferred to get them afloat as quickly as possible, so that they should be relatively immune from rescue attempts, or legal action to cause their release. Small hired vessels known as pressing tenders were moored near the main areas of activity, and a party of men was taken aboard from the press room daily, if possible. For many seamen, time spent in the pressing tender was the worst experience of their naval service. Even volunteers might spend weeks aboard awaiting assignment.

> Upon getting on board this vessel, we were ordered down in the hold, and the grating put over us; as well as a guard of marines placed round the hatchway, with their muskets loaded and fixed bayonets, as though we had been culprits of the first degree, or capital convicts. In this place we spent the day and the following night huddled together, for there was not room to sit or stand separate.[8]

And another recruit:

> A lanthorn was soon brought and hung up; we then discovered that we were in a dungeon! 'Gracious God, what a place!' It was somewhere in the bowels of the ship. There was a kind of platform where several persons were sitting, reflecting seriously on their state, and some swearing furiously, as if they had been brought on board by force.[9]

After the tender had been filled, it was sent to one of the major bases, where the recruits were put on board a receiving ship, usually an old man-of-war. It was considerably bigger than the tender, but no more comfortable. After that, the men would be assigned to any ships which had vacancies.

The Hot Press

Occasionally, the international situation was so serious, and the need for mobilisation so desperate, that the government waived the normal rule governing the press gang. Permission was given for a 'press from protections' — the certificates which would normally have protected a man from impressment were suspended. One such occasion was in the spring of 1803, when the fleet was mobilised for the next stage of the war. At Harwich, according to John Wetherell,

> They commenced their man plunder as I term it. The market house was to be their prison, where a lieutenant was stationed with a guard of marines and before daylight next morning their prison was full of all denominations, from the parish priest to the farmer in his frock and wooden shoes. Even the poor blacksmith, cobbler, tailor, barber, fisherman and doctor were all dragged from their homes that night.[10]

A pseudo-gentleman is held by the press gang outside a rendezvous, as denoted by the flag. To the right, a more seamanlike recruit has his hands tied behind his back. The National Maritime Museum

Of course most of them would soon have to be released, on establishing that they were not seamen. At Brixham, only ten men out of those taken could be kept; those released included shipwrights, a sailmaker, fishmonger, coal factor, grocer, cooper, watchmaker, ostler, waggoner, labourer, shoemaker, constable, basket maker, and a man who was apparently dumb.[11]

At Margate, numerous inhabitants were taken on board the *Texel*, moored in the Downs, and the local mayor had to obtain their release. Admiral Lord Keith apologised for the incident, and pointed out, 'that on such occasion as a general impress, it is morally impossible to carry the orders of the government into execution without incurring some risk of seizing upon individuals who are not liable to be impressed; but I hope that there is no room to believe that on the present occasion it has been wantonly done.'[12] It is said that at Plymouth the whole gallery of a local theatre was cleared, while in the Portsmouth area, 'A general press took place . . . Every merchant ship in the harbour and at Spithead was stripped of its hands, and all the watermen deemed for for His Majesty's service were carried off. Upwards of six hundred seamen were collected in consequence of the promptitude of the measures adopted.'[13] Many American seamen were taken on the Thames, which led to a protest by the ambassador; this issue was to become more serious in later years.

Impressment Afloat

Some tenders were employed solely for pressing men afloat, stationed in places like the Downs, where thousands of merchant ships passed every year. In other cases, ships of war sent out boats to impress men from passing ships. In theory they could only take men from ships homeward bound, and they were expected to provide replacement men for those pressed. The 'ticket men' were to return to their ships after they had done the job. Captains were sometimes accused of getting rid of their useless men in this way, and exchanging them for prime seamen; but, in 1795, the Admiralty employed a force of 528 seamen at Dover, specially for such duties. If the ship was outward bound or far from home, a captain might content himself with two or three men from a merchant ship.

The experience of being pressed afloat, often close to home, was one of the most traumatic of all for seamen.

> The lieutenant said, 'Come here my lad, who are you? . . . Jump in the boat, we just want such fellows as you.' I thought my very heart would burst, but I knew there was no chance, but by putting a good face on the matter, so I went in the boat. The officer having examined all hands, found them too old for him, except two apprentices; these he ordered into the boat, shoved off, and I found myself on my way to a ship of war.[14]

Evading Impressment

When avoiding the press gang, the sailor did not lack ingenuity. At Newcastle in 1813, a sailor named Bell was held in the press room. His sister gained access to him, they exchanged clothes, and the sailor 'walked off unmolested in female attire'. Of course the gang still had the woman, but they could not press her, and she was soon released by order of the magistrates.[1]

In Cork, the natives had less success.

> I was here told off to attend a press gang; we had intimation of a lot of seamen hid in a small public house, and after a scrimmage secured very prime hands, such a scene; a wake was got up, women howling over a coffin, where a corpse was said to be, but our lieutenant would not believe them, and sure enough out popped a seamen, who laughed himself, when all was over.[16]

A seaman pressed aboard a merchant ship. From Marryat's *Poor Jack*, 1875 edition

Another method of rescuing men from the press room was by 'fictitious arrest', this was common enough to earn a page in the Admiralty index. Friends of the pressed man would get up an action for debt or some minor matter, and have him transferred to the local gaol. It would soon be found that there was no evidence against him, and he would be released, to escape impressment unless the gang was very vigilant.

Sometimes, simple evasion could lead to riot.

> One evening in January 1815, a sailor passing over North Bridge was seized by the press gang, and whilst they were dragging him along, he slipped his arms out of his jacket, and leaving it in their hands, ran away down Bridge Street, hotly pursued by the gang . . . A number of workmen joined the mob and liberated the sailor. A regular chase, or running fight, was kept up through Low-gate. The gang applied in vain for assistance at the Mansion House, and dispersed to their several homes; but the mob, now exasperated, proceeded in a riotous manner through the market place and Humber Street to the press gang's rendezvous. Here the Riot Act was read, to no avail, for the mob (many of whom were sailors) completely wrecked the house.[17]

Forged protections were also common enough to earn a place in the index. Bechervaise found one easy to obtain. 'Aware that I should very soon become victim to the impress, I applied to the agent on shore, who kindly gave me a shipping paper as a fisherman, which in all cases was a sure protection for the whole time it was in date.'[18]

3 Other Methods of Recruiting

Volunteers

Although the press gang was at the centre of naval recruiting, and was certainly its most important element, it was not the only means of raising men. Estimates vary, accurate statistics are hard to come by, and even those available are distorted by the circumstances; but reasonable estimates suggest that about half the navy's men were impressed, and the rest were raised by other means.

Despite everything, there were probably several thousand men in the navy who were genuine seaman volunteers — not escaping from disgrace or imprisonment, not lured by enormous wartime bounties, not starry-eyed young landsmen with a dream of adventure, but regular Royal Navy seamen who liked the life for one reason or another. This group probably included most of the peacetime seamen, who manned the guardships and the small number of vessels in sea service. Such men formed the press gangs at the outbreak of war, and then went on to become the nuclei of the crews of the newly commissioned vessels. Volunteers were probably men who followed a particular captain or admiral from one ship to another, as part of his personal retinue. The regulations specifically allowed this, and permitted a captain to take a particular number of men with him out of each rate of ship. A popular captain such as Collingwood was

VOLUNTEERS.

G. R. III.

God Save the King.

LET us, who are Englifhmen, protect and defend our good KING and COUNTRY againft the Attempts of all *Republicans* and *Levellers*, and againft the Defigns of our NATURAL ENEMIES, who intend in this Year to invade OLD ENGLAND, *our happy Country*, to murder our gracious KING as they have done *their own*; to make WHORES of our *Wives* and *Daughters*; to rob us of our Property, and teach us nothing but the *damn'd Art of murdering one another*.

ROYAL TARS

Of OLD ENGLAND,

If you love your COUNTRY, and your LIBERTY, now is the Time to fhew your Love.

R E P A I R,

All who have good Hearts, who love their KING, their COUNTRY, and RELIGION, who hate the FRENCH, and damn the POPE,

T O

Lieut. W. J. Stephens,

At his Rendezvous, SHOREHAM,

Where they will be allowed to Enter for any SHIP of WAR,

AND THE FOLLOWING

BOUNTIES will be given by his MAJESTY, in Addition to Two Months Advance.

To Able Seamen, - - - *Five Pounds.*
To Ordinary Seamen, - - - *Two Pounds Ten Shillings.*
To Landmen, - - - *Thirty Shillings.*

Conduct-Money paid to go by Land, and their Chefts and Bedding fent Carriage free.
Thofe Men who have ferved as PETTY-OFFICERS, and thofe who are otherwife qualified, will be recommended accordingly.

LEWES: PRINTED BY W. AND A. LEE.

A recruiting poster issued at Shoreham in 1803. The National Maritime Museum able to recruit men in a way that was almost feudal: 'being particularly connected with Newcastle, I engaged my friends there to use their influence with the seamen, which they did so effectively that near fifty men entered.'[1]

Probably, a proportion of petty officers were also regular navy men, at least at the beginning of the war. They had prospects of promotion to secure berths as gunners or boatswains. Unfortunately, we know little about such men. They were so used to naval life that it seemed unremarkable to them, and in general they were not highly literate, so they were not often inspired to put their thoughts on paper. Other men joined quite casually, without any motives other than friendship. George Watson was already an experienced seaman when he joined at the age of sixteen. He had gone to visit a friend aboard the *Fame*, and after a time, 'I felt reluctant to part with my friend, and instead of doing so, I volunteered to serve His Majesty.'[2]

The next type of volunteer was the boy or landman who wanted adventure. One such man was John Nicol, who volunteered at the age of twenty-one. 'I had read Robinson Crusoe many times over and longed for the sea . . . Every moment I could spare was spent in boats or about the shore.' Robert Hay was aged fourteen when he joined, and was probably more motivated by lack of work as a weaver. 'After rambling about the greater part of the day, we towards evening repaired to the naval rendezvous. Here we found a naval lieutenant, to whom we offered our services and as hostilities with France had lately commenced, they were readily accepted of.'[3]

None of these men suggests that simple patriotism was a motive. Perhaps such matters had not reached the consciousness of the ordinary seaman; perhaps they were too reticent to boast about it; but certainly the officers of the impressment service made full use of it in their posters. 'Let us, who are Englishmen, protect and defend our good King and country against the attempts of all republicans and levellers, and against the designs of our natural enemies, who intend in this year to invade old England, our happy country, to murder our gracious King as they have done their own; to make whores of our wives and daughters; to rob us of our property, and teach us nothing but the damned art of murdering one another.' Another famous poster appealed to more pecuniary motives. 'The rest of the galleons with the treasure from La Plata are waiting half loaded at Cartagena . . . Such a chance perhaps will never occur again.' The lure of prize money, especially the enormous sums to be gained from Spanish treasure galleons, certainly had some effect and a few frigate captains, such as Lord Cochrane who had a reputation for taking valuable prizes, could sometimes man their ships entirely with volunteer seamen.

Bounties

If the navy had relied entirely on adventure, patriotism, prize money and loyalty, it is doubtful if it would have manned a tenth of its ships in wartime, when merchant wages were so high. The next method of attracting volunteers was by offering bounties on enlistment; these were quite small to begin with — £5 at the beginning of the war — but they are said to have risen to as much as £70 per man at the time of the Quota Acts (see page 128).

Obviously, many seamen who took the bounty did so because of the immediate threat of impressment; this was specifically allowed in the case of crews of merchant ships. When the pressing lieutenant went on board, he was to offer the bounty to those who volunteered, 'but that, otherwise, if they refuse to go voluntarily, they will be excluded from those advantages.' Probably there were many other men who were pressed on shore, who agreed to volunteer after the press gang had already caught up with them, in order to get the bounty — this procedure makes it difficult to assess who was a true volunteer, and who was a pressed man in disguise. At another remove, there may have been substantial numbers of seamen who offered themselves at the rendezvous because they were tired of being hunted by the gang, and preferred to earn the bounty before it was too late. Such men could be called volunteers, but really they were only there because of the press gang.

The Recruitment of Landmen

The rating of 'landman' was held by an adult who was new to the sea, and had been attracted by the bounty, or caught up in the quota system. Since it was reckoned to take about two years to train a seaman, and since most men were aboard for much longer than that in wartime, it seemed sensible to encourage this type of recruitment. However, the navy had no regular system for making landmen into seamen, and their presence was resented by both officers and seamen. Many were sceptical about the possibilities of training — in order to undergo 'the fatigues and perils of sea life' it was necessary to be 'inured to it from an early age'.[4]

Nevertheless, landmen were recruited in large numbers. They were offered bounties at all periods of the war, usually to about half the value of those offered to able seamen, and the Quota Acts encouraged them — 2742 were raised in London alone by the act of 1795. By the end of the wars, Captain Marryat reckoned that a total of 47 landmen to 120 petty officers and able seamen aboard a frigate was quite satisfactory. Aboard the *San Domingo* of 74 guns, the proportion was rather similar, with 107 landmen to 273 able seamen.[5]

One organisation which aided the recruitment of landmen was the Marine Society, found by Jonas Hanway in 1756. This was a charitable body, dedicated to recruiting poor boys from the streets and giving them clothes and a minimum amount of training for sea service, and also to giving sea clothes to newly recruited landmen. Throughout the twenty-two years of war, it provided 22,973 landmen with sea clothes, and it was instrumental in recruiting some of these, though most came by means of the Quota Acts or by normal recruiting. Obviously the total numbers of landmen recruited over the years were quite high, but it is not quite clear what became of them — how many deserted at the first opportunity, and how many went on to become skilled seamen.

Boys

Though it took a good deal of interest in landmen, the main concern of the Marine Society was to recruit boys to the navy. Its aims were to encourage 'the industrious poor to send their children to sea'. The principal design of the society with regard to boys, 'is to contribute towards maintaining a nursery of seamen for the public service, and to lay the foundations of the good fortune of those who are willing to serve their country'. The society found poor and destitute boys in the streets of London and other cities, equipped them with clothes and bedding and perhaps a rudimentary education, and sent them on board ship. In the mid-1790s it was sending five or six hundred boys a year to the fleet, and the final total must have been quite high.

Prisoners

Edward Thomson's remark that the crew of his ship was made up of 'the pressed refuse of gaols and the scum of the streets' has created the impression that the navy systematically emptied the prisons of murderers and thieves in order to man its ships. Though it is true to say that many men were recruited from one prison or another, very few of these were criminals in any accepted sense of the term. In 1805, when the Admiralty was asked to take on a man convicted of grand larceny, it replied that it 'did not consider persons of this description fit for the service'.[6]

The first category of prison recruit was prisoners of war. The navy

An allegory of the work of the Marine Society, showing ragged boys being brought in from poor families on the right, and fitted out with seaman's clothes on the left. The National Maritime Museum

sent officers round the prison hulks to find foreign seamen who were willing to serve, and it had a certain amount of success. A few French royalists were recruited, but not many. Far more came from the nations fighting reluctantly under the French flag, or in alliance with Napoleon.

Those recruited from ordinary prisons fell into several categories. Seamen who had been convicted of minor offences often asked to serve in the navy, and sometimes this was allowed. Debtors could possibly gain release from prison by using their bounty to pay off their debts. Other men were victims of the prison system itself. In 1797, for example, the regulating captain at Gravesend was allowed to pay the gaol fees of five seamen who had completed their sentences, but could not be released until they had paid for their upkeep. Smugglers were obviously desirable recruits. Their crimes were not regarded as anti-social in the sense of robbery or murder, and they were invariably good seamen. In 1805, for example, the regulating captain at Whitehaven asked the revenue service to send him any men found smuggling, in lieu of prosecution. It was proposed to regularise this by a bill before parliament.

The Fleet debtor's prison in 1808 (the name referred to the river which once ran through the area, and gave its name to Fleet Street). The Museum of London

Another type of minor offender was the 'Lord Mayor's man', defined as 'those who enter to relieve themselves of public disgrace, and are sent on board by any of the city magistrates for a street frolic or night charge'. The term was much abused, and seamen applied it to any young landman who found himself in the navy; whereas, since the system was only used in London, the numbers must have been relatively small.

The unemployed had long been regarded as fair game for the press gangs, and this was regularised by a statue of 1795 (35 Geo III c34) which allowed the local authorities to 'raise and levy under certain conditions such able bodied and idle persons as shall be found within the said counties to serve in His Majesty's Navy'. Among those liable were idle persons, rogues, vagabonds, smugglers and embezzlers of naval stores. This clearly gave local authorities an opportunity to get rid of undesirables and sometimes the numbers sent were quite large; forty-two from Dublin in November 1795, thirty from Newgate in April, and fourteen from the Savoy prison. Such men were blamed for the mutinies of 1797, and in later years the Admiralty became far more careful about who it recruited from prison. In May 1811, it informed one local authority, 'Their lordships have too much regard for His Majesty's service to introduce convicted rogues and vagabonds into it, and they have no intention either to send for or receive the men in question.' Two months later, it was stated that 'their lordships have given the most pointed directions not to receive into the navy any rogues or vagabonds the magistrates may be disposed to get rid of'.[7]

A young drunk arrested by a watchman. Such incidents could sometimes lead to men being sent to the navy as 'Lord Mayor's Men'. The Museum of London

Foreigners

One way or another large numbers of foreigners found their way into the navy. In theory they were exempt from impressment, but those serving in British merchant ships would often be picked up, and at sea there was no effective right of appeal. A list made aboard the *Warspite* in 1812 includes twenty-nine foreigners who were said to have been impressed.[8] Yet more were recruited from the prison ships — thirty-two aboard the *Warspite* — while others volunteered, presumably motivated by money or adventure, as were other recruits.

The proportion of foreigners was quite high in all ships for which figures are available. On the *Victory* at Trafalgar, they made up 8 per cent of the complement, and came from twelve different nationalities. On the *Implacable* in 1812 there were eighty, or 14 per cent — though half a dozen of these came from British colonies in the Indies.[9]

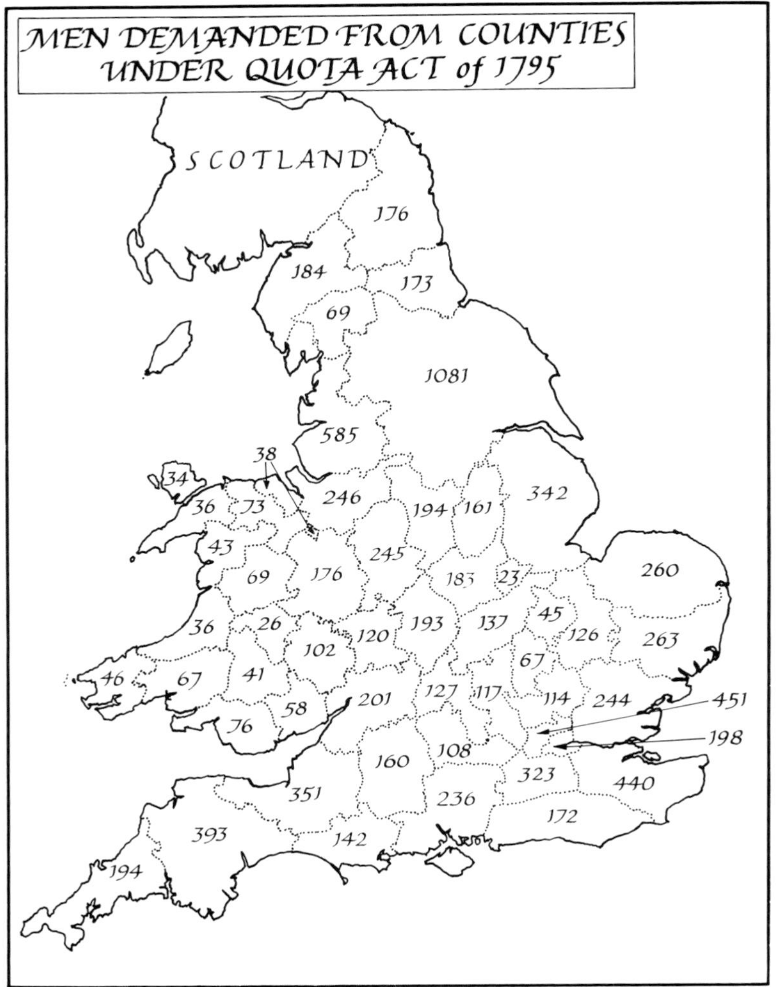

The Quota Acts of 1795.
a. The numbers of men demanded from each county in England and Wales, including inland ones.

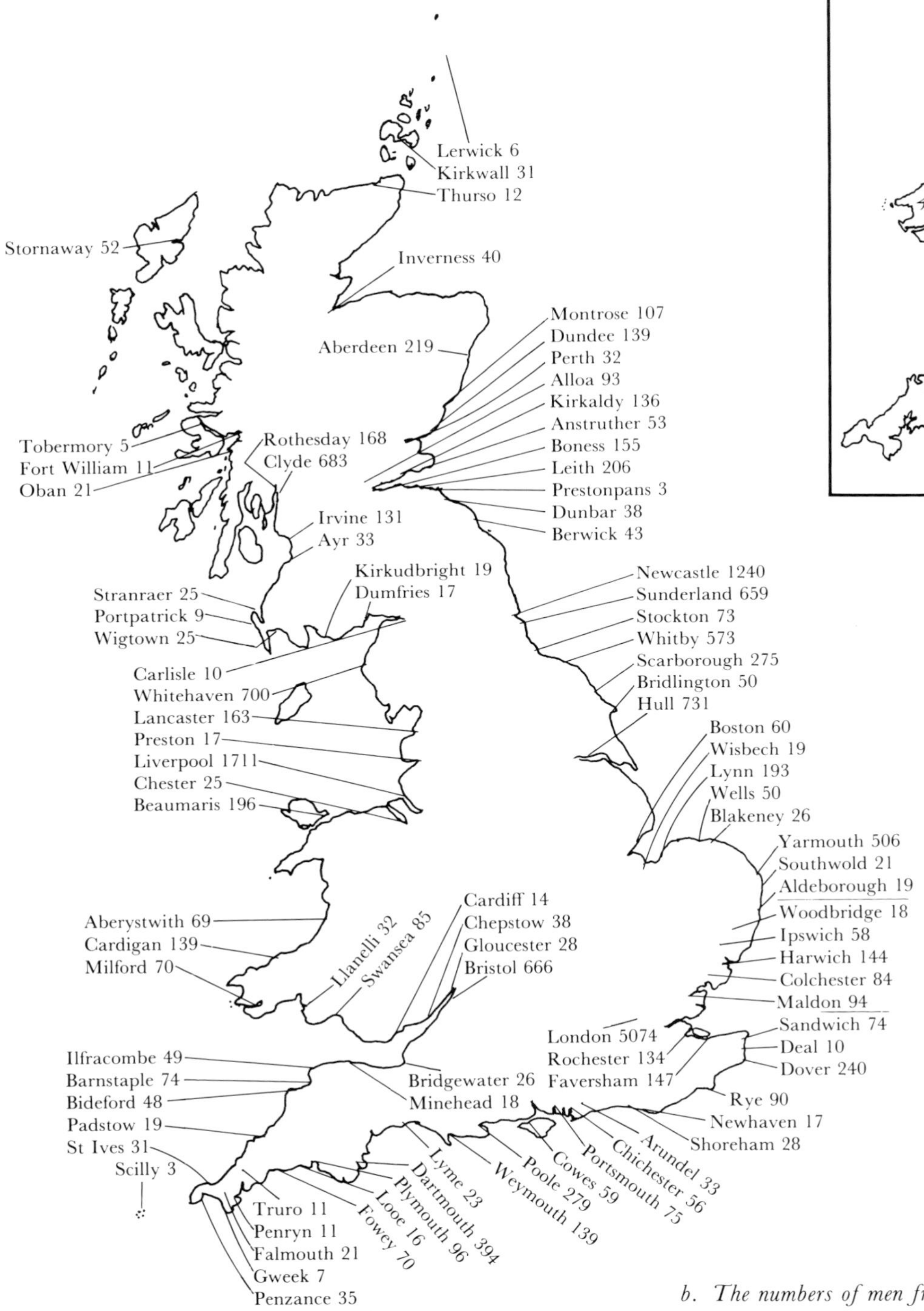

b. The numbers of men from the seaports.

A protection issued to a foreign seaman. It is signed by the first lord, two or more lords of the Admiralty, and the secretary. Public Record Office.

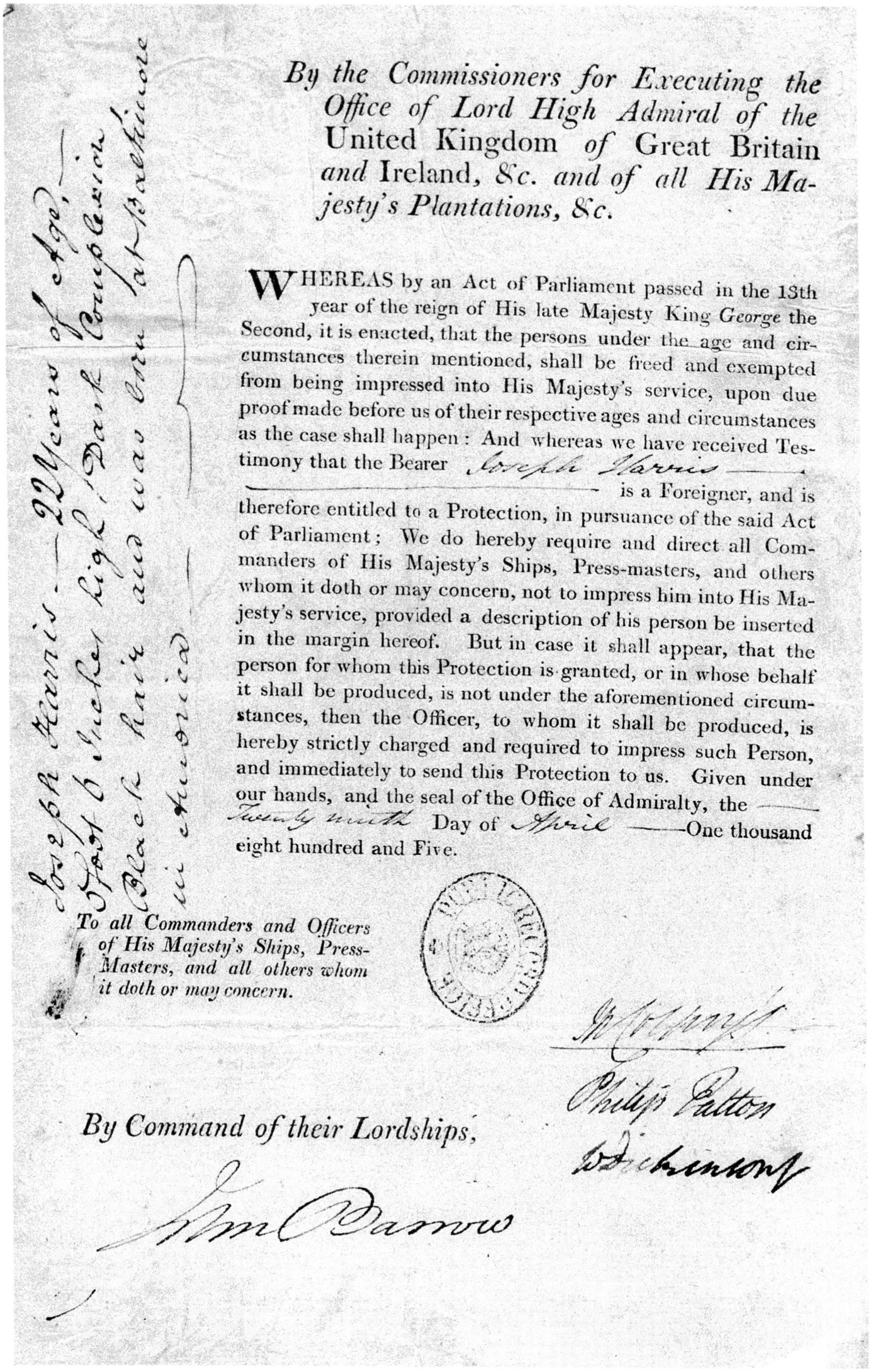

By the Commissioners for Executing the Office of Lord High Admiral of the United Kingdom *of* Great Britain *and* Ireland, *&c. and of all His Majesty's Plantations, &c.*

WHEREAS by an Act of Parliament passed in the 13th year of the reign of His late Majesty King *George* the Second, it is enacted, that the persons under the age and circumstances therein mentioned, shall be freed and exempted from being impressed into His Majesty's service, upon due proof made before us of their respective ages and circumstances as the case shall happen: And whereas we have received Testimony that the Bearer *Joseph Harris* is a Foreigner, and is therefore entitled to a Protection, in pursuance of the said Act of Parliament; We do hereby require and direct all Commanders of His Majesty's Ships, Press-masters, and others whom it doth or may concern, not to impress him into His Majesty's service, provided a description of his person be inserted in the margin hereof. But in case it shall appear, that the person for whom this Protection is granted, or in whose behalf it shall be produced, is not under the aforementioned circumstances, then the Officer, to whom it shall be produced, is hereby strictly charged and required to impress such Person, and immediately to send this Protection to us. Given under our hands, and the seal of the Office of Admiralty, the *Twenty ninth* Day of *April* One thousand eight hundred and Five.

Joseph Harris — 22 Years of Age, — 5 Feet 6 Inches high, Dark Complexion, Black hair and was born at Baltimore in America

To all Commanders and Officers of His Majesty's Ships, Press-Masters, and all others whom it doth or may concern.

By Command of their Lordships,

Wm Barrow

Philip Patton

W Dickinson

The *Warspite* had no less than 96, out of a complement of about 600;[10] while the *San Domingo* had 61 out of 439 among the seamen. By the later stages of the Napoleonic Wars, it seems that about 15 per cent of the fleet was of non-British origin.

A few of the foreigners seem to have become regular naval seamen. Eleven of those aboard the *Warspite* had served for ten years or more, and twenty-one of the others had served for more than five years. Americans made up the biggest single nation among the foreigners; but Dutch, Scandinavians and Italians were quite well represented.

The Quota Acts

It was not just humanity which inspired the government to seek alternatives to impressment for manning the navy. Over the past century, governments and naval administrators had become hardened to impressment, and had ceased to think in terms of replacing it. However, by the 1790s impressment was clearly not enough. As parliament began to vote for estimates of more than 100,000 men, new means had to be sought.

The answer was found in the two Quota Acts, passed through parliament in 1795. The first of these (35 Geo III c5) demanded that each county provide a certain number of 'able bodied men to serve His Majesty in the navy of Great Britain'. Bedford was to provide 57, Berkshire 108, Buckinghamshire 117, and so on. The men were to be raised by the justices of the peace, from the separate parishes and other divisions of the county. Each area was expected to find the men from among the poor of the district, or to raise the bounty to encourage volunteers, and could be fined for failing to do so. The inhabitants of every parish were to be called together, 'to consider the most effectual means of raising men; and, with their consent to agree with volunteers to serve in the navy'. Having been raised, the men were to be brought before naval officers at a rendezvous, and accepted or rejected; though a provision of the act gave the justices some power to overrule the naval officers. The second act (35 Geo III c9) applied to the ports of the country. Aberystwyth was to raise 69 men, Aldborough 19, Arundel 33, while London was to find 5704. An able seaman was considered equal to two landmen, and was to count as such. To ensure that the enlistment was carried out, and that seamen were not able to escape by sailing off, an embargo was to be placed on all British vessels in each port, beginning on 18 February 1795, and lasting until the quota of men had been raised.

In a sense, this was a return to an older system of recruiting, where the local authorities had been responsible for finding men, and the unemployed and the petty criminal had been taken into the service. The division of the country according to parliament's estimate of local strength, and the placing of responsibility on the local authorities, were measures entirely typical of the eighteenth century, though rarely carried so far. There are no overall figures on the success of the act, though it is known that London raised most of its quota, producing 1371 able and ordinary seamen (equal to 2742 landmen) and 2522 landmen, making a total of 5264. At Stockton the local authority issued a poster offering 'the largest bounties ever given' (£31.5.0 for an able seaman) and calling for volunteers.[11] The embargo on shipping continued until December 1795, when it can be assumed that all the areas had raised their quotas. As a result, several thousand men were added to the navy, increasing the strength from 87,331 in 1794, to 114,365 in 1796. The prime minister, William Pitt, was able to tell the House of Commons that the acts had been a success, without being challenged by the opposition.

The effects on the navy were not entirely beneficial, however. According to Collingwood, who was in command of a ship-of-the-line at the time, the acts contributed to the mutinies of 1797, by bringing in men who were not professional seamen:

> What they call Billy Pitt's men, the county volunteers, your ruined politicians, who having drank ale enough to drown a nation, talked nonsense enough to mad it; your Constitution and Corresponding Society men, finding politics and faction too rare a diet to fat on, took the county bounty and embarked with their budget of politics and the education of a Sunday's school into the ships, where they disseminated their nonsense and their mischief.'[12]

Protections

A 'protection' was a certificate issued by the Admiralty to a man who, for one reason or another, used the sea but was not liable for naval service. Most of the rules allocating protections were established by law, and they had three main aims: first, to allow the merchants necessary to the war effort to carry on their business undisturbed; second, to let the merchant navy continue to provide a 'nursery for seamen' for the Royal Navy; and third, to allow a certain minimum of trade to be carried on in wartime.

Ships and vessels belonging to and hired by the Ordnance Board, the Transport Board and the Navy Board were protected for the first reason. In effect this included all government transports and troopships. In the second category, apprentices, boys under eighteen, and landmen who had served for less than two years at sea were exempt from impressment, so that they could learn the trade. Certain classes of fishermen were protected too, partly because they were part of the 'nursery for seamen', but also because the nation's food supply would be serious affected if they were pressed without restraint. To allow trade to continue in wartime, the crews of outward-bound merchant ships were exempt from impressment, and masters and chief mates of ships of more than fifty tons were protected in all circumstances. However, the protection given to a vessel allowed her a specific number of hands; any more were regarded as supernumeraries, and liable to be pressed.

A protection was addressed 'To all commanders and officers of His Majesty's ships, prestmasters, and all others whom it doth or may concern'. It contained a description of the person protected, and instructions not to impress him while he remained in the circumstances which had caused it to be granted. There was a flourishing trade in forged protections, and lieutenants of press gangs had instructions to check very carefully for false ones. But, in general, officers seem to have respected protections when they were shown to them, except during a 'press from protections', as in 1803, when they were temporarily invalid.

The Effects of the System

Clearly the system of impressment, and naval recruiting in general, was very far from satisfactory. It brought discontent in the navy, and in the country at large. Even as a means of mobilising the navy quickly, there are doubts about its effectiveness. In most wars of the eighteenth century, it took three or four years to get the navy to its full strength, and the Royal Navy was often at a disadvantage because of the slowness of its mobilisation. But perhaps this was caused by the fact that British seamen were spread over the world at the beginning of a war, rather than any inherent defects in the system.

In any case, the methods of naval recruitment had a brutalising effect on the whole fleet. Though the navy professed to want a 'nursery for seamen' to provide its future strength, the fear of impressment was probably the greatest single deterrent to a seafaring career. The sight of grown men being dragged through the streets must have caused many a young man to think twice about going to sea. The system worked, in the sense that it provided the men to win the wars, and the professionalism of the British seamen was enough to overcome his resentment; but no-one was happy with it, and those most involved hated it most.

Part VI
SEAMEN AND LANDMEN

1 Seamen's Conditions of Service

The Relics of Short-term Service

The Admiralty paid little attention to the career of the individual seaman. His name was listed in the muster books of all the ships he served in, but, unless he applied to become a warrant officer or to enter Greenwich Hospital, no summary of his career was prepared. In the past, seamen and landmen had not 'joined the navy' as such; they merely joined particular ships, at the responsibility of the captain. This fiction was maintained until well into the nineteenth century, though it became increasingly difficult to sustain. Men were more likely to be recruited by the impress service than at the rendezvous run by individual ships, and once in the service they were often transferred from one ship to another by administrative order. The old system had originated in the seventeenth century, when ships had been commissioned for summer service only, and paid off at the end of the fighting season. It was long out of date in a navy with world-wide commitments; far from being paid off at the end of their ship's commission, the men were nearly always transferred to another ship, often against their will. To a certain extent, the system allowed the Admiralty to avoid much of the responsibility for the seamen, and delegate it to the captains. The seamen had all the disadvantages of long-term service, but often missed out on the security it ought to have given.

Entry

The seaman or landman, whether volunteer or pressed man, usually arrived on board ship by way of the press tender and receiving ship. His naval service did not properly begin until he was entered on the pay book on board a man-of-war in commission, for there was no provision for keeping sailors on shore bases, and the men were paid only as part of the complement of particular ships. There was no great formality about his entry — no swearing in or signing on. Perhaps it would have been too easy for pressed men to subvert the system by refusing to swear or sign; or perhaps seamen were regarded as too irreligious to take oaths, and too illiterate to sign on. Perhaps it was a relic of an earlier age; in 1592 it was considered that putting seamen on oath was 'lost labour and offence to God'.[1]

Instead, the new men were brought before the first lieutenant. 'On your first appearance on board, you are summoned before the first lieutenant, who interrogates you concerning your profession, your abilities as a seaman, place of nativity and dwelling; name and age, length of time you have been at sea, whether in ships-of-war or merchantmen, etc, to which questions you are looked to for prompt answers.'[2] These facts were needed for the ship's muster book, which contained columns headed 'Bounty paid', 'Number' (of the man in the muster book), 'Date and year of entry', 'Time of appearance on board', 'Whence and whether prest or not', 'Place and county where born', 'Age at the time of entry in this ship', 'Number and letter of tickets' (in the case of men transferred from other ships), 'Men's names' and 'Qualities', followed by other columns on the time and circumstances of discharge, slop clothes issued, and wages paid.

The men were examined by the ship's surgeon, who had orders to report any unfit men and send particulars of them to the senior officer on the station. The full description of each man was written down by the captain's clerk, along with 'your parent's, relation's or friend's dwelling; in short, of all your connections, in case of your desertion.'[3]

Rating

Another duty of the first lieutenant was to decide the rating of each man. Several different options were available to him. Youths under fifteen years of age were rated Boys Third Class, while those under eighteen became Boys Second Class. (Boys First Class were training to become officers.) Adults with no sea experience were rated landmen; and an ordinary seaman was 'One who can make himself useful on board, but is not an expert or skilful sailor.'[4] An able seaman was 'one who is not only able to work, but is also well acquainted with his duty as a seaman'.[5] If a man seemed very well qualified, he might be rated petty officer right away. Obviously a first lieutenant would be reluctant to do this without knowing the man personally, or having a reference from another officer; but in the bustle of a quick mobilisation, when a ship had to be manned and fitted out in a few weeks, risks had to be taken. According to Wilson, the first lieutenant rated men 'without prejudice or favour being shown to anyone. Should it so happen that you are found not competent to the rating you had at first, you are disrated'.[6]

The lower ratings, up to able seaman, depended on the man's ability and experience, so one would not expect a man to be reduced unless he had misrepresented his abilities on entering the ship. However, such disratings were quite common. For example, James Elton rose from landman to ordinary seaman between 1804 and 1805, and was then reduced to landman again on the same ship. He became an ordinary seaman again on another ship in 1805, and then went back to landman in 1810. He finally made able seaman in 1815, but was reduced again to ordinary seaman after the peace.[7] James Sparks entered as a landman in 1803, and had risen to able seaman by 1809; he was reduced to landman aboard the same ship, presumably as a punishment, in the following year, and then promoted to ordinary seaman, a rank he retained until discharge in 1814.[8] William Smith, on the other hand, had a fairly steady rise. He joined the *Niobe* as a second class boy in 1807 at the age of seventeen. He rose to landman in the same year, and to ordinary seaman in 1810. He became an able seaman in 1814, and a quartermaster's mate later in the year.[9] Physical fitness was a factor in the able seaman's rating, and it was quite common for men to be reduced to ordinary seaman shortly before being invalided out of the service.

A seaman at Trafalgar, praying that the enemy's shot be distributed in the same proportion as the prize money, with the greater part going to the officers. The National Maritime Museum

Similarly, petty officers had no kind of security of tenure. They were of course disrated quite casually for incompetence, especially when they had been equally casually rated by the first lieutenant while the ship was fitting. They were often disrated as punishment for minor offences such as drunkeness and quarrelling. Much worse, they frequently lost rank merely because they were transferred from one ship to another. This was a constant complaint, and did much to demoralise seamen. William Smith's steady rise was interrupted in 1814 when he was transferred to another ship, and reduced to able seaman for a time. Likewise, Robert Stewart became a cook's mate aboard the *Castor* in 1793. He was transferred to the *Colossus* and went back to able seaman for several months, before becoming cook's mate again.[10]

The actual proportions of the different rates within one ship could vary considerably. She might be well equipped if her crew was recruited at the beginning of a war, or had been a long time at sea, giving her men time to gain experience. The regulations merely gave the total complement of each vessel, and the number of officers, petty officers, servants, artisans and marines. Deducting them, left the mass of the crew, whose numbers within the individual rates were unspecified — there was no theoretical reason why they should not all be rated as able seamen, if the captain could find enough well-qualified men. Examples are difficult to come by, but in 1793, the *Prince* was well manned with 47 per cent petty officers and able seamen, 22 per cent ordinary seamen, and 31 per cent landmen. In the same year the *Bellerophon* had 35 per cent petty officers and able seamen, 27 per cent ordinary seamen, and 38 per cent landmen.[11]

Prospects

Starry-eyed boys might have joined the navy from a sense of adventure, and a few landmen were recruited with the promise of advancement; but the majority of experienced seamen had no great hopes of a naval career. Nevertheless, it offered as many prospects for advancement as any career at the time, except perhaps the merchant service. It was possible to rise from the lower deck to become a commissioned officer, and reach the rank of captain, as James Cook did; or even admiral, as Benbow did early in the eighteenth century. There was no-one from the late eighteenth century to compare with these two, but the road was not closed. At least 120 men reached the quarterdeck by way of the lower deck between 1793 and 1815, and at least eighteen of these were originally pressed. However, the chances of an individual seaman reaching commissioned rank were not good — it has been estimated that he stood one chance in 2500 of becoming a lieutenant, and one in 100,000 of becoming an admiral.[12]

The warrant officer ranks were more open to the common seaman. Boatswains and gunners were invariably recruited from their ranks, as were such lower grade warrant officers as cooks, and most masters at arms. Others could become petty officers such as boatswain's mates or quarter gunners, while landmen might eventually learn the trade and become able seamen. Some men made good after an unpromising beginning; William Savery was recruited as a landman in 1804, but immediately deserted. He was entered again in 1808, rated briefly as able seaman, and then reduced to landman. He eventually became an able seaman in 1814, and captain of the foretop soon afterwards.[13] Given luck, a seaman might see large parts of the world in days when most people had hardly gone beyond their own towns and villages; he might witness the great events of history, such as the Battle of Trafalgar; and, if he avoided all dangers, eventually come home with prize money and a great fund of stories to tell.

Pay

Until 1797, the common seaman had not had a pay rise since 1653. Able seamen had 24s per lunar (28 day) month; ordinary seamen had 19s. Deductions were made for Greenwich Hospital (6d per month) the Chatham Chest (a fund for distressed seamen, at 1s per month), 4d for the chaplain and 2d for the surgeon. The actual rate of pay of an able seaman was £14.12.6 per annum, while an ordinary seaman had £11.7.6, and a landman £10.11.6.[14] Other wages, including those of soldiers, had risen in the last few decades, and the mutineers of 1797 were well aware of this, especially since many soldiers were serving in the fleet. This comparison was a regular theme of seaman's petititons. As a result, pay was increased by 5s 6d per month for petty officers and able seamen, and 4s 6d for lower rates. There was a further increase in 1806, so that able seamen had 33s 6d per month before deductions, ordinary seamen 25s 6d, and landmen 22s 6d.

Wages were paid irregularly. They were invariably kept in six months arrears, to deter the seamen from desertion, except when the ship was finally paid off. The crew was normally paid before leaving on a foreign voyage, for crews had been known to refuse to sail without such payment. In theory, a ship should have been paid once a year in home waters, after one year in commission; but the exigiencies of naval service often prevented this. On foreign service, a ship might go for years without being paid. For example, the 74-gun *Audacious* was paid at Plymouth in March 1797. She went to the Mediterranean for four years and returned in 1801. The ship was then paid off, and seamen received up to £79 in back pay.[16] However, seaman had the right to have part of their wages deducted at source, and sent to their dependents shore. If seamen were turned over to another ship, or sent to hospital before their own ship was paid, they were issued with tickets instead. These were only cashed after considerable delay by the navy, or at considerable discount by private enterprise.

Payment was made by the clerk of the cheque in one of the home dockyards, after the ship's muster books had been sent to the Admiralty for checking. It was quite an event.

> In the early part of the day, the commissioners came on board bringing the money which is paid the ship's crew, with the exception of six months pay, which is the rule of the government to hold back from each man. The mode of paying is, as the names are, by rotation on the books. Every man is called, is asked for his hat, which is returned to him with his wages in it and the amount chalked on the rim. There is not perhaps one in twenty who actually knows what he is going to receive, nor does the particular amount seem to be a matter of much concern.[17]

Debts to the women on board were paid, and shore boats clustered round to sell their wares to the seamen.

Prize Money

In the distribution of prize money, petty officers, seamen and marines had only a small amount compared with the officers. The petty officers, 'Midshipmen, captain's clerks, master sailmakers, carpenter's mates, boatswain's mates, gunner's mates, masters at arms, corporals, yeomen of the sheets, coxswains, quartermasters, quartermaster's mates, chirurgeon's mates, yeoman of the powder-room, sergeants of marines and land forces on board' were to have one eighth, up to 1808. The lower ranks, 'trumpeters, quarter gunners, carpenter's crew, steward's cook, armourers, steward's mate, cook's mates, gunsmiths, coopers, swabbers, ordinary trumpeters, barbers, able seamen, ordinary seamen, and marines, and other soldiers, and all other persons doing duty and assisting on board' were to have a similar proportion. After 1808, the system was more complex. The whole group, petty officers and seamen and their equivalents, were allowed a quarter share of the whole. This was divided up into a number of shares, so that $4\frac{1}{2}$ shares went to each of the midshipmen and senior petty officers; 3 shares to each of the junior petty officers, including newly recognised categories such as the captains of the tops, etc; $1\frac{1}{2}$ shares each to the able and ordinary seamen, one share to each of the landmen and servants, and a half share to each of the boys.[18]

Occasionally, seamen and petty officers could make quite substantial sums from prize money. The record-breaking case had been the capture of the Spanish frigate *Hermione* in 1762, which had yielded £485 for each seaman. In 1799, the capture of more Spanish treasure ships gave £182 each for the seamen, and £791 for the petty officers. More modest examples included the capture of Colombo in 1796, when captains got £7000 each, petty officers got £76 each, and seamen £9. After the taking of Amboyna and Banda, the commander-in-chief got £28,300, the petty officers got £242, and the seamen £45 each.[19] Seamen on frigates perhaps earned enough on a typical cruise to double their wages; those on ships-of-the-line had less opportunity. But often seamen simply drank their money. Samuel Stokes wrote, 'I think I was not sober one hour when I was awake, while the money lasted.'[20]

Undoubtedly prize money was some kind of inducement, and it helped recruitment, and to keep men from desertion or mutiny. It was fully used by the recruiting posters, which often promised enormous sums. It probably gave the seaman some residual hope, like winning a lottery, but it is quite difficult to assess its full effect, in view of the uneven distribution.

Turnovers

One of the greatest of the seamen's grievances was the custom of 'turning over' men from one ship to another. Many years before, a secretary of the admiralty had commented, 'This custom is very disagreeable to the seamen, and has begot that aversion we have seen in them to the service. It takes from them the freedom of serving where they like, and many times the small [ie, petty] officers are turned before the mast. It abridges them from the pleasure of seeing their families.'[21] Men might have signed on for one ship because they liked the captain or had friends aboard; but there was nothing to stop them from being transferred to another against their will. It was

Discharged seamen demanding their prize money from a disreputable agent, by Rowlandson. The National Maritime Museum

Greenwich pensioners, with Greenwich Hospital in the background. The National Maritime Museum

quite normal for a petty officer to lose rank on transfer, if the new ship had all the appropriate posts filled. If the men missed pay day aboard their old ship they were issued with tickets instead, and it might be years before these were paid. Established groups of men were broken up, and little regard was paid to the men's feelings.

Even worse, ships first back from long foreign voyages often had their men turned over to another ship, without setting foot on land. William Richardson complained that 'without having a moment's liberty on shore, thirty-seven of us were drafted on board the *Royal William* at Spithead, and the same day drafted again into the *Prompte*, a frigate of 28 guns (Captain Taylor) ready for sea. Here was encouragement for seamen to fight for their King and country! A coolie in India was better off!'[22] The administration was aware of the problem, but pressure on its resources prevented any solution.

> To meet the wants of the public service in every quarter of the globe, the calls upon the navy were *incessant*... a means was, therefore, resorted to for keeping up the requisite number of men which became vexatious by growing into a practice, instead of being used only occasionally, as an emergency of the moment might require. I mean the plan of turning the men over to newly commissioned ships, on their return from foreign service, and perhaps again sending them abroad or what was worse, keeping them at home without the opportunity of leave of absence.'[23]

The rate at which a man was turned over varied considerably. James Everitt spent his whole career, from 1794 to 1802, aboard the *Polyphemus*; while William Eastburgh served on eight different ships in sixteen years, James Elton on ten ships from 1804 to 1816, and John Satchell on fourteen from 1793 to 1820.[24]

Discharge

On entry to the navy, the seaman had no idea when his service might finish. Obviously, he could not predict the end of the war, and release before then was only by death, desertion, illness and incapacity, or very special circumstances. According to the Admiralty Regulations, a captain was 'not to discharge any men but for one of the following reasons, viz, Death or preferment, into some other of His Majesty's ships; unfitness for service, to be determined by survey; not returning from being sick; or the order of the Admiralty, or of his superior officer.'[25] Death and desertion were common enough, but those who avoided both might find themselves serving for the whole of the war. James Elton, for example, served from 1804 to 1816, and Edmund Sheeham from 1804 to 1815. The Admiralty order necessary to pay them off only came after the end of the wars with France.

Retirement

On leaving the navy, the seaman did have a few privileges. In particular, he was entitled to a place in Greenwich Hospital if he was unable to support himself any longer; or he might be given a pension by the same institution, and remain at home.

Greenwich Hospital had been set up in the 1690s, by King William III and Queen Mary. It occupied a very distinguished building designed by Sir Christopher Wren, and was headed by senior officers, including a master and governor, a lieutenant governor, four captains, eight lieutenants, and various other officials. Nurses were recruited from the widows of seamen, provided they were under forty-five years of age. It was funded by the contributions deducted from the seamen's wages.

By 1805, it had an establishment of 2410 in-pensioners, provided with bed and victuals; and 3243 out-pensioners. For entry, a seaman had to apply to the board of the hospital, and examinations were held at the Admiralty four times a year. His service was carefully checked against the muster books of ships he claimed to have served in, and the surgeon examined him to see if old age or injuries prevented him from following his profession.

Sons of naval seamen were entitled to receive their education at Greenwich School. This had places for 200 boys, who were intended to enter either the naval or the merchant service. There was also an infirmary attached to the Royal Hospital, for the care of former seamen.

2 Seamen and Petty Officers

Seamen's Skills

The object of all the impressment effort, the basis of all British naval power, was the common seaman. What made him so valuable? He was not a member of a guild or a professional body, so he was not, in contemporary terms, normally regarded as an artisan. Sometimes he joined the trade by means of an apprenticeship, but this was more likely to train future masters and mates, with some knowledge of navigation, rather than common seamen. In other cases, apprenticeship was used as a means of avoiding the press, for those bound by indenture were protected. In any case, it is clear that very many seamen did not enter the trade by means of apprenticeship.

Despite this, the skills of a seaman were considerable, and could not be acquired without years of experience. He had a vocabulary of several hundred words unrecognisable to the landman. A sailing ship of the age had many miles of rope rigging, and a good seaman was expected to know it intimately, to find the right line in the dark, in a storm, or in the rain. He could tie twenty or thirty different knots without hesitation, and perform various kinds of splices. He could prepare ropes by worming, parcelling and serving. He knew about seizings, mouses, points, gaskets, mats, turk's heads and a dozen other ways of preparing rope. He could run 100ft up the ratlines on the orders of his officer, and then out to the end of a yardarm, with only an inch of footrope between him and death. He could spend half his waking life up there, as the ship tossed about with the motion of the sea. He could grapple with a wind-filled sail, helping to furl or reef it as a storm threatened. On coming down from the rigging, he could swab decks, push at the capstan bars, row the ship's boats, rig all kinds of tackle for hoisting weights or for raising and lowering the anchor. He had to be able to tolerate hardship, while the ship spent days in a storm and the pumps had to be worked continually; he had to be able to manage when the

A seaman at the lead, by Atkinson. The National Maritime Museum

The public image of seamen – carousing in a tavern ashore, and wasting most of their hard-earned money. By Cruikshank

victuals ran short on a long voyage. In action, he helped serve the guns, loading them and running them out — and by muscle power alone.

That was enough to make an ordinary seaman, but an able seaman needed more. He had to be able to take over as main helmsman and keep the ship on course with her sails filled; to stand in the main chains and heave the lead so that the navigator could know the depth of water; and to carry out these tasks with the utmost reliability, for the safety of the ship could depend on him alone. Aboard the *Blake*, such men were assessed on their ability to 'steer', 'take the lead' and 'sew a seam'.[1] According to Captain Basil Hall,

> The letters A.B., which mean Able Seaman, are placed against the names of only those who are thorough-bred sailors, or who, in the sea phrase, can not only 'hand reef and steer', but are likewise capable of heaving the lead in the darkest night, as well as in the daytime; who can use the palm and needle of a sailmaker; and who are versed in every part of a ship's rigging, in the stowage of the hold, and in the exercise of the great guns... In these, and twenty other things which might be pointed out, he ought to be examined by the Boatswain and other officers before his rating of A. B. is fully established on the books.[2]

The Character of Seamen

To an outsider, such as a ship's surgeon, the seaman seemed quite exotic in his habits.

> It is only men of such description that could undergo the fatigues and perils of sea life; there seems a necessity for being inured to it from an early age. The mind, by custom and example, is thus trained to brave the fury of the elements in their different forms, with a degree of contempt at danger and death that is to be met with nowhere else, and which has become proverbial. Excluded by the employment which they have chosen from all society but people of similar dispositions, the deficiencies of education are not felt, and information on general affairs is seldom courted. Their pride consists in being reputed a thorough bred seaman; and they look upon all landmen, as beings of inferior order. This is marked, in a singular manner, by applying the language of seamanship to every transaction of life, and sometimes with pedantic ostentation. Having little intercourse with the world, they are easily defrauded, and dupes to the deceitful, wherever they go; their money is lavished with the most thoughtless profusion; fine clothes for his girl, a silver watch, and silver buckles for himself, are often the sole return for years of labour and hardship. When his officer happens to refuse him leave to go on shore, his purse is sometimes with the coldest indifference consigned to the deep, that it may no longer remind him of pleasures he cannot command.[3]

Chaplain Edward Mangin noticed the seaman's unconcern for danger, and questioned 'whether bravery in men of the lower classes of society should not rather be termed insensibility; or is it that they have the sensibility of the enlightened, but want expression?'[4]

As a consequence of his separation from shore life, and the specialised vocabulary and skills of his calling, the seaman had distinctive manners, dress and speech, which marked him out from his contemporaries. A thousand pamphlets, broadsheets and cartoons parodied his style of conversation. 'He ran foul of me on my larboard side as I was steering through Wapping — so a hove him a gentle topper and knocked him down', says a sailor in a cartoon, accused of assault.[5] 'Tell him he may go on deck if he likes,' says another, temporarily rich from prize money, hiring a whole stage-coach for himself in the 1780s, 'and I hope he'll look after you, and see that you are steady at the helm, and dont sarve us the same as one of your land-lubbers did about three years ago, when he run foul of one of the landmarks, and pitched us all overboard.'[6] His dress was equally distinctive, for his trousers and short jacket, which made it easier for him to work on deck and in the rigging, contrasted with the long coat, breeches and stockings of the landman.

Seamen's Careers

Many men were probably quite content with the rank of able seaman, and aspired no higher. One veteran was Isaac Copland, who first entered as an able seaman in 1759. He served through four different wars in that rank, giving his age as forty in 1778, and again in 1803. He finally reached the rank of quarter gunner in 1804, but was invalided out soon afterwards, with twenty-four years' service.[7] Another confirmed able seaman was William Eastburgh, of Stockholm. He spent sixteen years in the rank, with only a few months as a quartermaster.[8] Others entered as ordinary seamen, presumably from the merchant service, and remained in that rank for some time such as Robert Elliot, who entered at the age of twenty-six in 1803, and left in 1809 with the same rating. Some men became petty officers very quickly, such as Robert Satchell. He entered as an able seaman in 1793 at the age of twenty-three, and was quickly promoted to boatswain's mate. He obviously had considerable qualities, as well as defects. He had risen to boatswain in 1801, but was broken by a court-martial for drunkeness and fighting. He was a boatswain again by 1807, but was reduced again, for selling his stores. In between these appointments, he had been a quartermaster's mate, a boatswain's mate (three times), a yeoman of the sheets (twice), a sailmaker's mate, a gunner's mate, and a quartermaster (twice).[9]

Petty Officers with Warrants

Some men, though appointed by Navy Board Warrant, were specifically excluded from most of the privileges of officers. According to Admiralty Regulations, such men, 'though appointed by warrants, are to be considered as petty officers, any of whom he [the captain] may disrate if their misconduct be such as shall absolutely require it'. Some of these, such as caulkers and armourers, were artisans rather than seamen, but others had usually spent their early careers as seamen. The master at arms, however, was in an ambiguous position. According to Captain Marryat, 'The master at arms's berth can never be filled up by a seaman, a soldier would answer the purpose much better.'[10] This is perhaps reflected in the career of Benjamin Chapman, who served in the marines from 1776–83, reaching the rank of sergeant. He served as an able seaman and gunner's mate from 1788–91, and received his warrant as master at arms in 1794. However, it seems likely that the majority of masters at arms had served as seamen.

Every rated ship had a master at arms. His duty, according to Robert Wilson, was 'narrowly to inspect into the conduct of the ship's company at large, and to report any impropriety he may witness, derogatory to the discipline of the ship. He has to see all lights and fires out at the proper time. In short, he has great power and is what is called a great man among the little ones.'[11] Traditionally, his duty had included teaching the men the use of small arms and muskets, hence his title; this was not entirely obsolete, but had largely been taken over by others. In ships of the fifth rate and above, he had two assistants known as ships corporals. In sixth rates, he had one corporal, while in unrated ships, the corporal worked alone, with no master at arms over him.

There was no doubt that the ship's cook was a seaman, though his work no longer took him aloft, or called on him to handle the guns. According to Wilson, 'The cooks in most ships are men that have lost a precious limb, or otherwise maimed in the defence of their king and country; so as a compensation they receive a warrant as cooks… They are for the most part elderly men who have seen much of the seafaring life.'[12] His pay was little more than that of an able seaman, but he often received a pension for his disabilities in addition, and had certain perquisites as well. He was assisted by his mates. They were paid as able seamen, but their number was not fixed by regulation. The 74-gun *San Domingo* had three.[13]

Boatswain's Mates

The boatswain's mates were the most vocal, and the most feared, of the petty officers. They had to wake the crew in the morning, with 'a voice designedly of most alarming loudness'.[14] They wielded the cat at floggings, and used their 'starters' on other occasions. Their 'calls' were an essential part of the signalling system of the ship. The regulations allowed four in first and second rates, two in third and fourths, and one in sixth rates. Perhaps some captains appointed more unofficially, for Wilson records that aboard the frigate *Unite* 'There are four of them. The first or chief one keeps no regular watch but is up all day and inspects with the boatswain into the tasks allotted to the crew, etc; the others are in three watches.'[15] Presumably

A boatswain's mate of the Gloucester, *from Mangin's journal. He carries a 'ropes end' to beat seamen, and has had the name of his ship painted on his hat – the origin of the present day custom.* The National Maritime Museum

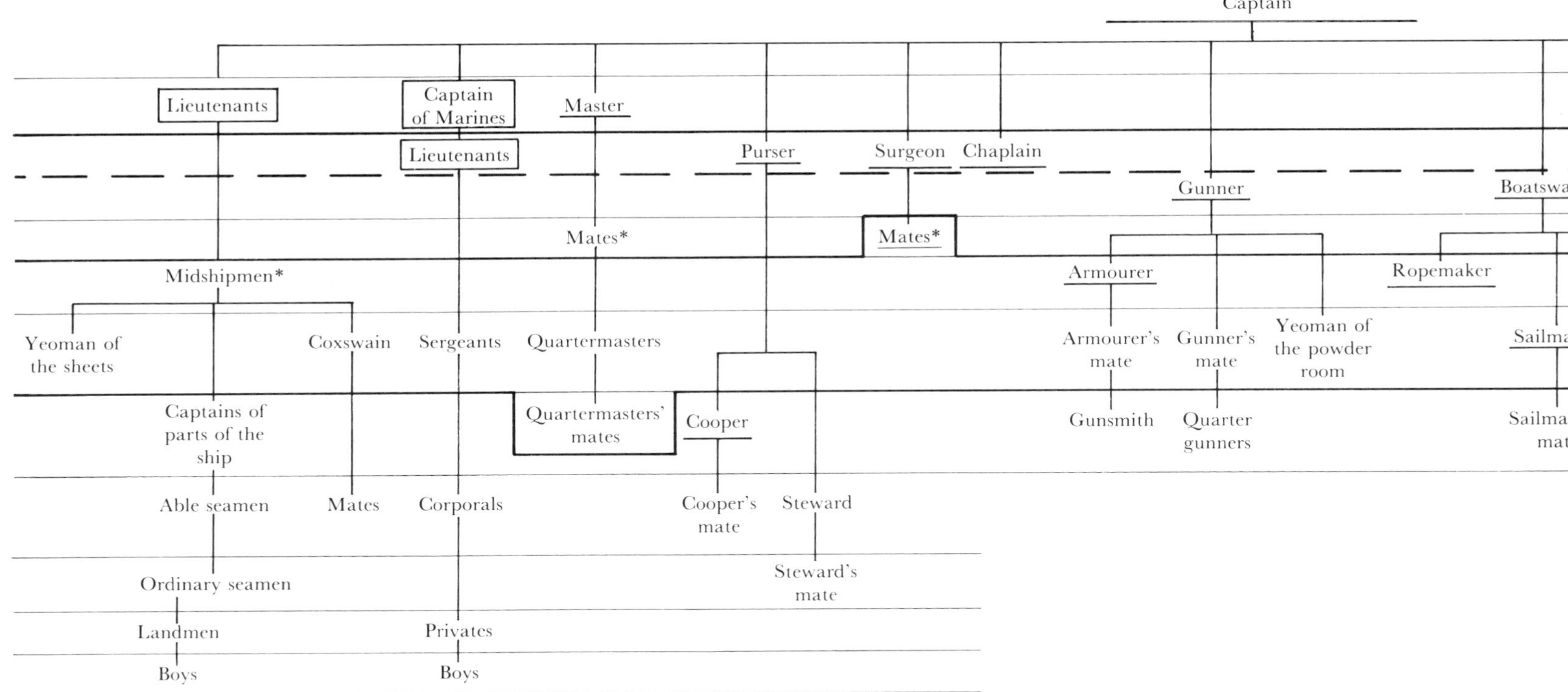

Relative ranks in the navy, c1810. These have been compiled using pay rates, division of prize money, responsibilities, privileges, etc. There are some major anomalies: for example, the surgeon's mates are very well paid, but placed in a lower category for prize money, and the first lieutenant has greater responsibilities, but he has no formal status in pay, privileges, etc. Commissioned officers are enclosed in boxes. Warrant officers are underlined. The thick solid lines mark the divisions for prize money. Those above the thick dotted line are the wardroom officers. Cockpit officers are marked with an asterisk.

the extra men were not paid as such, but a regular boatswain's mate was paid from £2.5.6 to £1.16.6 per month in 1806, according to the size of the ship.[16]

Quartermasters and Mates

The quartermasters were more skilled, and less abrasive than the boatswain's mates. They were 'fine old seamen, who conn, or direct the steerage of the ship'. Their other duties included 'stowing the ballast and provisions in the hold, coiling the cables on their platforms, overlooking the steerage of the ship, keeping the time by the watch glasses, and, in turn, over-looking the purser's steward in the delivery of his provisions'.[17] There were eight quartermasters on a three-decker, seven on an 80-gun ship, six on a smaller third rate, four on a fourth rate, three on a fifth rate, two on a sixth rate or sloop, and one on the very smallest vessels. They were paid at the same rates as boatswain's mates.

The quartermasters also had mates, six on the largest ships and one on the smallest. In 1806, the mates were paid £2.0.6 on first and second rates, and £1.15.6 on sixth rates.

Gunner's Mates and Quartergunners

The gunner's crew made up the largest single group of petty officers. The gunner had four mates on ships of 80 guns or more, two on other third rates, and one on smaller ships and vessels, paid at the same rates as boatswain's mates and quartermasters. Below them, were the quartergunners, one for every four guns on the ship, so that a 74 had eighteen, and a 38 had nine. In 1806, they were paid at a rate of £1.16.6 on large ships, and £1.15.6 on fourth rates and below, 1 or 2s more than an able seaman. Their duties were 'to assist the gunner in every branch of his duty; as keeping the guns and their carriages in proper order, and duly furnished with whatever is necessary; filling the powder into cartridges; scaling the guns, and always keeping them in a condition for service.'[18] This was not usually enough to keep them fully employed, and the quartergunners were also employed as an elite division of seamen. Aboard the *San Domingo*, they kept watches, and had duties during various evolutions — when tacking ship, for example, half of them were to 'attend on both gangways to see the fore and main tacks and sheets clear', and the others were to operate the 'main top bowline'. On the *Unite*, 'The gunner's crew are composed of the best seamen in the ship. Their duty is to attend to the mainyard and rigging, to the guns and whatever relates to them, so far as they may receive orders from the gunner of the ship. They are allowed 1s per month more than any other able seamen; what with the making of cartridges and wads, etc, they earn it.'[19]

Captains of the Tops, etc

For many years, it had been common to put one seaman in charge of each part of the ship, in each watch. Thus there were four captains of the tops, two each for the main and main masts; two captains of the waist, two of the afterguard, and two of the forecastle. These ranks were unpaid, and William Richardson wrote, 'As soon as I joined the *Prompte* I was made a captain, but it was a captain of the maintop — a great rise certainly, but with only the same pay as I had before.'[20] In 1806, these ranks were established, with the same pay rates as quartermaster's mates.

Yeoman of the Store Rooms

The three standing officers—boatswain, carpenter and gunner—had

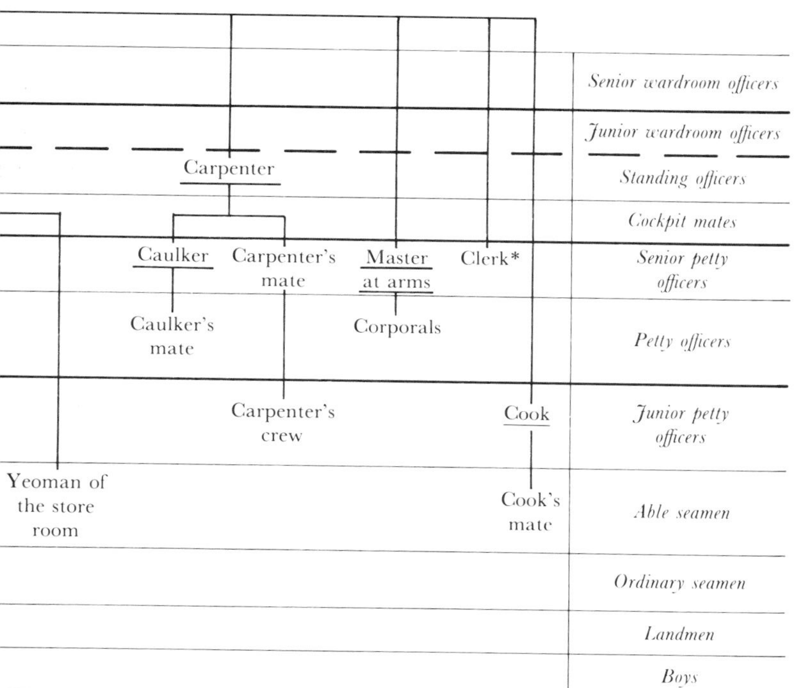

large quantities of stores and spare parts under their care. These were kept in three separate store rooms forward on the orlop, locked when not in use. Each of these rooms was in the care of a yeoman. In addition to these, the yeoman of the powder room was paid at the same rate as a gunner's mate, because of his great responsibility; the others were paid as able seamen. Ships of the third rate and above had two yeomen of the powder room. Their duty was 'to attend the fore and after magazines, and to receive and deliver the powder when wanted for action, or otherwise.'[21]

Other Petty Officers

Ships of the third rate and above had four yeoman of the sheets; fourth and fifth rates had two, sixth rates one, and unrated ships none. They were paid from £2.2.6 to £1.16.6 per month, according to the size of the ship. Their duty was 'to see that the fore and main sheets are properly belayed on working the ship, and that they are kept clear for running'.

Each ship had one coxswain paid at the same rate as the yeomen of the sheets. He was presumably in charge of either the ship's launch or the captain's own boat. Coxswains were also appointed to the other boats, though not paid as petty officers. A coxswain was 'The officer who steers a boat, and has the command of the boat's crew, and all things belonging to it. He has a whistle to call and encourage his men, and must be ready with his crew to man the boat on all occasions; he sits at the stern of the boat, and steers.'[22]

The Status of the Petty Officer

The position of the petty officer was often quite difficult, especially when the officers tried to use them as spies against the men. This apparently happened aboard the *Prosperine* in 1797, when the crew complained of four petty officers 'continually going fore and aft the deck to listen what is said, which is repeated by them to the commander'.[23] Conversely, petty officers often identified with the crew in times of mass mutiny. Out of thirty-three delegates in charge of the mutiny at Spithead, sixteen were petty officers and four were midshipmen.[24]

3 Landmen, Artificers and Servants

Landmen's Occupations

Landmen came to the navy from many different backgrounds. A large ship had representatives of forty or more different trades, mostly irrelevant to their naval duties. By the early nineteenth century, the Agricultural Revolution was causing many farm workers to seek other employment, which was often aboard ship. There were thirty-five 'labourers' on the *San Domingo*, nineteen 'husbandmen' on the *Caledonia* in 1811, and even the tiny *Dromedary*, with a total complement of 121, had eight 'farmers' labourers'. Weavers too were well represented, for their trade was losing ground to the power loom — seven on the *San Domingo*, twenty-two on the *Caledonia*, and five on the *Dromedary*. One weaver, Robert Hay left his home in Paisley in 1803 because 'trade was exceedingly depressed', and joined the navy because no other prospect offered itself. There were hairdressers, tinmen, shoemakers (eighteen on the *Caledonia*), stocking weavers, blacksmiths, saddlers, millwrights and dozens of other trades.[1]

Landmen's Duties

Some landmen could find employment aboard ship which was in keeping with their old trades. The *San Domingo* had butchers, bakers, tailors and servants among its idlers. The Admiralty Regulations allowed for barbers and tailors to be paid at the same rate as ordinary seamen. However, the weavers, farm labourers or tin miners would find no use for their old skills. They could either carry out menial duties above or below deck, or learn to become skilled seamen. There was no Admiralty training system for landmen (or for anyone else except future sea officers), but a captain might initiate one of his own. Thus, Marryat suggested that aboard a 36-gun frigate, one landman per watch should be allocated to each group of topmen, for training. Seven more would be 'idlers', serving as gun room steward, gun room cook, poulterer, midshipmen's servant, cook's mate, captain of the head (responsible for cleaning the toilet accommodation), and 'Jack in the dust' (a 'stout man' to 'keep order' in the gun room). This left twenty-two landmen for the afterguard, and ten for the waist, where they would clean decks, haul on ropes, and have little chance to qualify as fully-fledged seamen.[2]

Prospects for Landmen

Landmen were almost invariably depressed by their first few weeks aboard ship. One wrote to his wife 'If I had known how bad it was I would not have entered. I would give all I had if it was a hundred guineas if I could get on shore.'[3] But, undoubtedly, many landmen eventually became skilled seamen. Aboard the *Blake*, men's names were ticked off in the ship's description book according to their ability to 'steer', 'take the lead', and 'sew a seam'. Among those qualified at all three were a former husbandman, a servant (who was eventually rated as quartermaster), a shipwright, a calico printer, and an armourer.[4] On the other hand, William Isaac joined the navy as a landman in 1810 at the age of thirty-one, and had still not been promoted six years later; Peter Elliot was a landman for six years after his entry at the age of twenty-seven; Joseph Selade was thirty-eight on entry, and took eight years to reach ordinary seaman. Younger men tended to be more successful. Thomas Justice joined at twenty-one, became ordinary seaman after two years and an able seaman after three more; John Imbert entered at twenty-five, becoming an ordinary seaman after two years' service and able seaman after four.[5] Because of these differences, captains were sceptical about the possibilities of training adults for sea service. 'Such boys [aged fourteen to sixteen] soon became good seamen; landsmen very rarely do, for they are confirmed in other habits.'[6]

Boys

The Admiralty Regulations specified the number of boys (also known as 'volunteers') to be borne on ships of each class — thirteen of the second class and nineteen of the third class on first rates, ten and fourteen on the 74, and six and ten on large frigates. Third-class boys were normally used as servants to the officers. Robert Hay had spent some time aboard a schooner, and learned some seamanship, before being drafted to the *Culloden* in 1803. He resented being reduced to a servant. 'This arrangement is not at all agreeable to me, especially at the first. With all my skill, or at least fancied skill, in seamanship, to be degraded into a shoe boy!'[7] Occasionally, however, boys were put straight on to seamen's duties. On the *Swiftsure* of 74 guns in the 1800s, 'We received a number of boys to complete the complement of the ship; they were not allowed to be employed as servants, as is customary, but were stationed in the tops, where they soon became expert seamen.' Collingwood supported this plan, and commented, 'One hundred Irish boys came out two years since, and are now the topmen in the fleet.'[8] Second-class boys, between the ages of fifteen and seventeen, were to be 'divided into watches with the seamen, in order to bring them forward as such.'[9]

However, it seems likely that many captains preferred to keep them as servants. Most took some time to reach ordinary seaman status, via the rating of landman. Hay was promoted landman in 1808, and became an ordinary seaman two years later.[10] Others had similar careers. George Jones started as a gunner's servant at the age of thirteen in 1793. His ship was soon paid off, but he rejoined as a boy second class in 1795, and became a landman in 1797. He was rated ordinary seaman in 1800, and able seaman a year later.[11] David Everitt was a boy in the merchant service before joining the navy as a landman in 1803. He was invalided out three years later, still a landman.[12] Clearly, boy service did not necessarily give a flying start to a naval career.

A sailmaker at work. Aboard ship he would have to adapt to the available space, but the techniques would be similar. From Steel's *Mastmaking, Sailmaking and Rigging*

The Status of Artificers

Many artisans aboard ship had the status of warrant officer, as did the master at arms and the cook. Possibly, this was intended to lure them into the service and protect their privileges. Skilled men like sailmakers, ropemakers and armourers were not seamen, and could not be pressed into the navy. Warrants from the Navy Board gave them a certain guarantee of status, and kept them from the more menial duties of the seamen. Such men could only be disrated 'if their misconduct shall be such as their conduct shall absolutely require it'.[13] However, there were others on board who had no such protection. The carpenter's crew was quite large, but only the carpenter himself had a warrant. Some, at least, of the crew must have been skilled men, but it was possible to find ships' carpenters aboard merchant ships, and not all of them were exempt from impressment.

Carpenter's Crew

The carpenter had two mates on 80-gun ships and above, and one on smaller ships, including unrated vessels. They were paid £2.10.6 on first rates and £2.0.6 on sixth rates. In addition, the carpenter had a large 'crew' of skilled or semi-skilled men — twelve on a first rate, eight on most third rates, and two on sloops. They were paid at the same rate as quartergunners. In addition, one caulker was appointed by warrant to each rated ship, under the orders of the carpenter. He was responsible for the tightness of the hull, and the maintenance of the oakum driven between the planks of the ship. He was 'to be very attentive in examining frequently the caulking of the ship's sides and decks', and was to 'report to the carpenter any part of the caulking which he finds defective', and to repair it with oakum that was 'dry and in good condition'.[14] He had the same wages as a carpenter's mate in a first rate, but this pay remained the same in all ships, so in fact he had higher status.

Many members of carpenters' crews had trained as shipwrights in yards ashore, or had served as carpenters or mates of merchant ships. Others apparently learned the skills while in the navy. Robert Stewart joined as an able seaman in 1793 at the age of twenty-three, but later served as carpenter's crew or carpenter's mate on several ships.[15] Robert Hay was trained aboard the *Culloden*. 'After we had been a year or two in India our admiral found a considerable want of shipwrights and caulkers and to remedy this inconvenience he appointed several boys to learn these branches.' He was rated as ordinary seaman while learning the trade.[16]

Sailmakers and Ropemakers

One sailmaker was appointed by warrant to each ship, with the same rate of pay as boatswain's mates in large ships, and a higher rate in smaller ones. He had a mate in each rated ship, chosen from among the crew and paid £1.18.6 in all rates. In addition, he had two crew in fourth rates and above, and one in smaller ships and sloops. The ability to 'sew a seam' was part of the qualification of an able seaman, so such men could become part of the sailmaker's crew. In addition to this, other seamen could be drafted in to help the sailmaker if needed.

The sailmaker came under the command of the boatswain. He and his crew were to inspect the ship's sails as they came on board during fitting out. They stored them in sail rooms, with wooden tallies to identify them. They inspected them, repaired them when necessary, and had them aired to dry and prevent mildew.

The ropemaker was also appointed by warrant, and was under the boatswain. One was appointed to each rated ship, paid at the same rate as the caulkers. The ropemaker was to make rope with the help of any of the ship's company 'directed to assist him', and deliver it to the boatswain.[17] He had no regular mates, but on the *San Domingo* one man was appointed to assist him.[18]

Armourers

The armourer was yet another artificer appointed by Navy Board Warrant to all rated ships, and under the command of the gunner. He was the leading metal-worker of the ship, and often worked with the iron of the hull and rigging, as well as the armament. He was particularly concerned with the maintenance of the muskets of the crew and the marines. He was supplied with an elaborate set of tools, including a portable forge which could be set up on shore when the opportunity arose. He was paid at the same rate as the master at arms. He had two mates on third rates and above, and one on smaller vessels, including sloops which had no armourer as such.

Coopers

A cooper had rather lower status than the other artificers, being paid only as an able seaman. There was no regular establishment before 1806 but 'Captain in the Royal Navy' recommended two in first and second rates, and one in smaller ships. The *San Domingo* had two.[18] According to Robert Wilson, 'the cooper and his mates are employed in their line, but seldom having much to do, the cooper generally acts as assistant to the ship's steward and his mate graces the afterguard'.[20]

Stewards

The ship's steward was the purser's chief assistant, responsible for the actual issuing of provisions to the various messes. According to Burney, he was 'appointed by the purser to distribute daily the different species of provisions, to the officers and crew, for which purpose he is assisted by a mate, who is rated steward's mate, and commonly called Jack of the bread room, and sometimes by the cooper of the ship.' The steward was paid from £1.15.6 to £1.9.6 per month in 1806, though he also had 'beside his wages, an annual allowance from the purser, as a remuneration for his service under him.'[21] A steward's mate was authorised only in ships of the fourth rate and above, and was paid £1.5.2 per month. However, two mates were appointed on the *San Domingo*, and 'Captain in the Royal Navy' advised two mates in a third rate and above, two on a fourth or fifth, and one on a smaller vessel.[22]

Cooks' Mates

The cooks' mates were paid at the rate of able seamen. Their number was not specified by the regulations, but 'Captain in the Royal Navy' recommended two for third rates and above, and one on fourth and fifths.[23] The *San Domingo* had three, and Marryat recommended one, a landman, for a 36-gun frigate.[24] According to Wilson, 'The cook's mate does all the drudgery work, the cook inspects him.'[25] This is not surprising, in view of the age and disablement of most cooks.

Clerks

The captain's clerk was 'a person employed by the captain, to keep all the books necessary for passing his accounts.'[26] The Regulations demanded that a purser serve some time as a captain's clerk, so the latter was often a young man working his way up. He had quite high status, with an office on the quarterdeck or upper deck on most ships. He was paid at the same rate as a midshipman, and probably lived among them on the orlop — though on the *Gloucester* he had a cabin in the gunroom.

The captain's clerk was the only clerical worker recognised by the regulations, but on most ships the first lieutenant was allowed a

Coopers at work. From Pyne's *Microcosm*

'writer' to help him draw up the watch and station bills. He was presumably chosen from among the more literate landmen. On most ships, there were no other clerks, but on the *Gloucester*, Mangin mentions the clerk's assistants working in the gunroom. Apart from that, the rest of the clerical work of the ship was done by the warrant officers and their assistants — the purser and his steward, the yeomen of the store rooms and so on.

Trumpeters

Traditionally, trumpeters had been appointed to ships to make signals to the crew. The regulations still allowed one trumpeter for each rated ship, to be paid at slightly lower rates than the captains of parts of the ship; but no other source makes any mention of them, except possibly as part of the ship's band; presumably the custom had lapsed.

Captain's Servants

In the past, a captain of a ship-of-war had a considerable following. He was entitled to four servants for every hundred men of the ship's complement, which meant that a captain of a 74 was entitled to twenty-four. Most of these were in fact 'young gentlemen', serving the time needed to become midshipmen. The system was changed in 1794, so that potential officers began their careers in other ways, and captains' servants were now true domestic staff. The regulations merely allowed an unspecified number of captains' cooks, at the pay of able seamen. A captain also had a steward, 'a person nominated by the captain, having an optional rating on the ship's books, to take charge of his sea stock & co.'[27] 'Captain in the Royal Navy', suggests a total of four captain's servants on a ship of the fourth rate and above, and three or two on smaller ships; but many captains would have had more. The idlers list of the *San Domingo* is less specific, giving two officers' cooks and three officers' cooks' mates, but not saying which were allocated to the captain, and which to the wardroom. Only two servants are mentioned, apart from those specifically allocated to the wardroom or the midshipmen. Presumably these men, both marines, were the captain's servants. Marryat's 36-gun frigate had only a captain's cook and a captain's steward, rated as able seamen.[28] According to Robert Wilson, 'The captain's steward and servants are the highest in the line of domestics. They give themselves great airs, and are pampered and... little to do. The gunroom steward looks upon himself as an equal with the captain's, which the latter cannot brook; so that they too are in rivalship eternally, for the dignity of their to-be-envied situation is at stake. They try hard to vie with each other in dress, etc.'[29]

Wardroom Servants

Wardroom servants (or gunroom servants, who were their equivalents on frigates or sloops) fall naturally into two categories; those working for the wardroom as a whole, and those serving individual officers. Those in the first category included the wardroom cooks — two on third rates and above, and one on smaller ships, according to 'Captain in the Royal Navy'; and the wardroom servants — three, two or one according to the size of the ship. The *San Domingo* had three of the latter, and Marryat's thirty-six had a gunroom steward and a gunroom cook, all rated as landmen. The duties of the wardroom servants are hinted at by Mangin, 'Soon after day-break, several seamen are here employed to wash and scrub the flooring; they have scarcely finished, when the wardroom steward makes preparation for breakfast.' Later in the day, there were visits of 'the wardroom steward and his assistant, to inspect and regulate the state of the glasses and decanters.'[30] According to Wilson, 'The servants of the commissioned officers and those that mess with them in the gunroom are a steward or two and two or three other men or boys, who wait at table.'[31] The officers' cooks were 'most haughty in their exalted stations. They have not the least connection with the ship's cook.'[32] The officers' cooks used the forward part of the ship's galley stove, with such sophisticated fittings as an oven, a grill and a spit, whereas the food of the crew was merely boiled.

A woman, with a child, helping a wounded seaman during a battle. From *The Log Book*, or *Nautical Miscellany*, 1830

Each wardroom officer had a personal servant, usually a boy or a marine. Edward Mangin had 'a marine as servant (one Thomas Clarke, a Cheshire lad, very civil and attentive)'.[33] Robert Hay served as one, to Lt Abel Hawkins. 'It was now my object to see that no officer surpassed my master in a well brushed coat, in the brilliancy of his boots and shoes, and in the neatness and order of his cabin; to appear, which his kindness enabled me to do, clean and tidy the back of his chair at dinner, and to take care that if he missed his share of the good things at the wardroom table, it would be no fault of mine.'[32]

Other Servants

The standing officers — boatswain, gunner and carpenter — were entitled to one servant each. In two- and three-deckers, where the gunroom was used for various purposes including the lodging of the 'volunteers first class', an old seaman known as the 'lady of the gunroom' or 'Jack of the dust' cleaned the area and served the food. The midshipmen had a few servants — three on the *San Domingo*. According to Robert Wilson, 'The servants of the midshipmen, which are reckoned the lowest, are two, one man and a boy — or two boys — who cook and do everything for them in an epicurean way. They find it pretty difficult to please their masters.'[35]

Women at Sea

Despite the regulations, women were often carried to sea. Many of these were the wives of officers or petty officers, and had a definite role aboard ship, often looking after the sick and wounded. In the 1840s, when two women applied for the Naval General Service Medal, on the grounds that they had been present at the Battles of the Nile and Trafalgar, it was refused because it would create a precedent which would be followed by 'innumerable applications' from many others. At the battle of the First of June, a chaplain observed, 'The women of the ship were almost all quartered in the cockpit to assist the surgeon.'[36] Though marines had no right to take their wives to sea, soldiers were covered by different rules even when at sea; married women were allowed to follow their men, at the rate of five per company. Thus when soldiers were drafted aboard ships in the 1790s, women were taken with them, and appeared on the ship's muster books — three on the *Captain*, five on the *Egmont*, and eleven on the *Britannia*, for example.[37]

4 Mutiny and Desertion

The Offence of Mutiny

With intolerable living conditions and no means of release, sailors found two outlets — mutiny and desertion. Mutiny was endemic in the navy from 1793 to 1815. There are no figures on the actual numbers, but there were twelve courts-martial in 1805 alone, and fifteen in 1813;[1] and these were probably among the quieter years, after the peak of 1797. These figures take no account of offences that were dealt with by captains on their own, or where the men got their way and no court-martial followed. Probably, the total number of mutinies from 1793 to 1815 was more than a thousand.

In fact, the term 'mutiny' was used rather liberally by the law officers of the navy. It was applied to individual acts of disobedience, and the majority of trials were of one man alone. It also applied to acts of mass resistance, such as the Great Mutinies at Spithead and the Nore, and many mutines aboard single ships. In a much more extreme form, it was used to describe violent and revolutionary insurrections, where the officers of a ship were either killed or put off the ship, and a new set of leaders took over. Such cases were rarer, but the category included the mutiny on the *Bounty* in 1789, the *Hermione* mutiny of 1797.

The law made no distinction between these categories, but it did recognise four types of mutiny. 'Mutinous assembly' and 'mutinous language' were both charged under article 19. 'Concealment of mutinous designs' was under article 20, and mutiny itself was under article 34. In addition, striking or attempting to strike a superior officer was generally regarded as tantamount to mutiny, though the actual word was not used in Article of War 22. All these offences could be punished by death, or lesser punishments.

Individual Disobedience

Courts-martial for individual disobedience were naturally the most common. In 1798, in the aftermath of the Great Mutinies, the authorities were highly sensitive about any connection with the radical or Irish Nationalist movements ashore. A man who mentioned the 'tree of liberty', the symbol of the radical movement, or made any reference to republican sympathies, was likely to suffer extra penalties. As late as 1805, a captain's clerk was given 150 lashes and two year's imprisonment for expressing republican views — an unusual sentence for a man in such a position. Other acts of mutiny were rather less explicitly political; Benjamin Thompson of the *Ganges* said, 'If you mean to teach me better manners, you must hang me first. I have pen, ink, and paper, and can make use of them as any of you, and will be heard.' This was enough to earn him a court-martial. When women were refused on board the *Mars* in 1798, Thomas Perkins said, 'Come you men, what do you say? Let's all go on shore after the women. I will be the first that will make a break.' In the same year Robert Nelson of the *Belliqueux* apparently went mad and cut the breechings of the guns of his ship, in an attempt to sink it.[2] All these offences were treated as mutiny.

Mass Disobedience Before 1797

The navy had a long tradition of mass disobedience, going back for many decades. In the middle of the century, there had been several cases of crews refusing to sail with particular officers, and sometimes they were successful in their demands — in 1746 Captain Brett of the *Sunderland* was replaced because of this. There were yet more cases where crews became disgruntled because they felt they were being mistreated over pay; when one crew was paid before another, or when the ship was not paid before a foreign voyage. Such mutinies involved little or no threat against the officers of the ship, and did not lead to court-martial or punishment of the crew.[3]

By the later stages of the American War, violence was becoming more common on both sides. In 1783, the crew of the *Janus* revolted because of a rumour that they were not to be paid off at the end of the war. Officers were locked in their cabins, and the guns were run out in defence of the ship. The affair was settled through the negotiation of Admiral Lord Howe. In 1793, the crew of the *Culloden* battened themselves below decks and refused to come up, demanding a ship in better condition. Captain Pakenham persuaded them to come up, but then ten of the alleged ringleaders were taken and court-martialled; five were eventually hanged. Such incidents did nothing to improve trust between officers and the lower deck. In the following year, there was a mutiny in the *Defiance* 74, in Leith Roads. The *Edgar* was ordered to go alongside her, 'to engage her, if necessary, to restore order'. One of the *Edgar's* crew described his feelings on this occasion: 'When bearing down upon her, my heart felt so sad and heavy, not that I feared death or wounds, but to fight my brother, as it were. I do not believe the *Edgar's* crew would have manned the guns. They thought the *Defiance* men were in the right.'[4] Later in that year the crew of the *Windsor Castle*, in the Mediterranean, demanded that some of their officers be replaced, and were largely successful.[5]

The leaders of the Nore mutiny in council. According to this cartoon, the French and the parliamentary opposition are the instigators of the mutiny, and the ignorant seamen are dupes. The National Maritime Museum

Spithead and the Nore

Mutiny broke out among the ships of the Channel fleet, moored at Spithead under the command of Lord Bridport, in April 1797. It had been preceded by several petitions to the Admiralty about pay and conditions, but nothing had been done about these. On 15 April, the men of the flagship, the *Queen Charlotte*, refused to weigh anchor, and cheered. This was a pre-arranged signal, which informed the other ships that the mutiny had begun. They too refused to weigh, so a fleet of sixteen ships-of-the-line, the main defence of the country, was immobilised. The men sent a list of grievances to the Admiralty, demanding an increase in wages, better quantity and quality of provisions, and better treatment for the sick and wounded. Most of their demands were granted within a week, including the first pay rise since 1653, and a pardon was given to all the mutineers. However, the demand that flour should not be issued in port was not granted, and this led to an extension of the mutiny, aboard the *London* at St Helens, early in May; the marines opened fire, and five seamen were killed. The seamen, eventually, took control, disarmed the marines and imprisoned the officers. The mutiny spread to other ships, and Lord Howe, who had some credit among the seamen for the *Janus* affair, was sent to negotiate. The men's demands were conceded, and the fleet put to sea on 16 May, one month after the start of the mutiny.

The Nore mutiny began immediately afterwards. Some commentators, at the time and later, have seen it as a much more political affair than Spithead, more influenced by the radicals and revolutionaries ashore. There is no real evidence for this, and probably the seamen at the Nore merely saw it as an extension of the gains made at Spithead. It began on 20 May, when delegates from each ship took some demands to the vice admiral commanding at the Nore. They wanted more shore leave, more regular payment of wages, a fairer distribution of prize money, the removal of some unpopular officers, and the mitigation of certain parts of the Articles of War. The delegates took control of the ships, and sent some of the officers ashore. By the end of the month all the ships except the *Venerable*, flagship of Admiral Duncan, and one other, had joined the mutiny. Duncan kept his station off the Dutch coast with these two, making signals to imaginary ships to make the enemy think he had a full fleet. The mutineers attempted to blockade London by stopping trade in the Thames, but meanwhile the authorities were preparing against them. Special Acts of Parliament were passed to prevent communication with the mutineers. Shore batteries were set up to cover the fleet, and other ships were brought against the mutineers. The seamen sensed that they would not have an easy victory, and by 10 June several ships had begun to give up. On the 14th, the

Sandwich, the leading ship in the mutiny, surrendered, along with the best-known leader, Richard Parker. Many men were hanged, including Parker. Others were flogged or imprisoned, and no concessions were gained from the Admiralty.

Later Disobedience

The Nore affair did not mark the end of naval mutiny. There were at least fifteen other single-ship mutinies in the same year, and a particularly difficult situation in the Mediterranean fleet, where St Vincent, with characteristic ruthlessness, forced the crew of the *Marlborough* to hang one of their own number. Mutiny became gradually less common after that. In 1798 there was a serious affair aboard the *Defence* in the Mediterranean, with nineteen men sentenced to death. In 1801, there was another protest aboard the *Temeraire*, and eighteen men were sentenced to hang. As late as 1805, eleven men were sentenced to death for mutinous conduct aboard one ship[6] but large-scale mutiny was much less common by this time.

The men tried for mutiny aboard the Témeraire *in 1802.* From a contemporary pamphlet

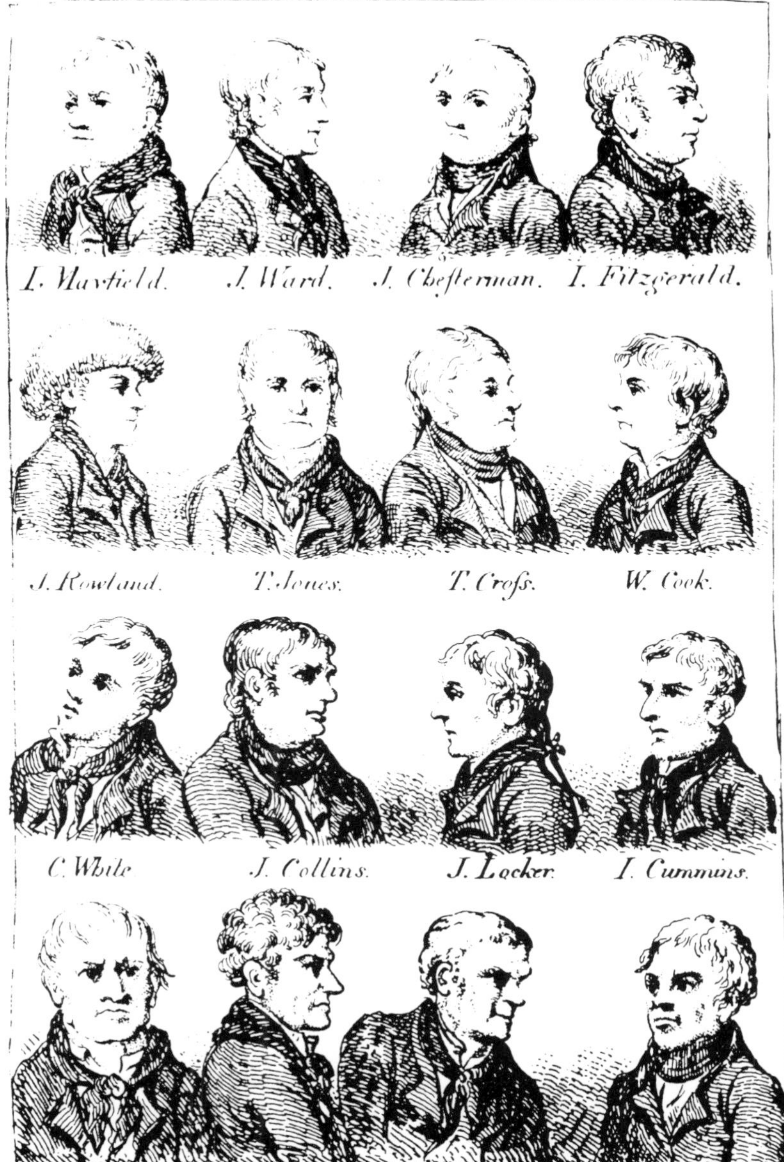

Violent Insurrection

Most mutinies involved a minimum of violence, necessary to restrain the officers and put the ship under the effective control of the crew. They were usually made for specific demands, subject to negotiation, and rarely took place while the ship was at sea, or in the presence of the enemy. However, there were some cases which broke these rules, and usually resulted in the ship being turned over to the enemy. The most notorious was of course the *Hermione* mutiny of 1797. That frigate was in chase of a privateer off Puerto Rico on 22 September, when Captain Pigot ordered sail to be shortened. Dissatisfied with the work of the topmen, he threatened to flog the last two men off the yards. As a result, there was a panic to get down, and two men fell to their deaths. Pigot callously ordered their bodies to be thrown overboard. That night, the crew began by rolling shot about the decks (a well-known sign of impending mutiny), and then rose, killing the captain and eight other officers. The ship was taken into La Guayra and handed over to the Spanish. She was later recaptured by a daring cutting-out expedition launched by the frigate *Surprise*, and many of the mutineers were eventually captured and hanged.

There were other insurections of this kind, though on a smaller scale. In 1795, the crew of the tiny *Shark*, 4 guns, took her into the French port of La Hogue. In 1800, the *Albanaise*, bomb vessel, was taken into Malaga by her crew. It seems that this type of mutiny was characteristic of small ships.

The Scale of Desertion

According to Dr Thomas Trotter, the average seaman often harboured some thoughts of desertion in his mind. After being impressed, he came on board with 'a sulkiness of disposition, which is gradually overcome, when he recollects that he only resigns his liberty for a season, to become a champion for that of his country. It, however, often preserves a determination to watch every opportunity for effecting his escape... A well regulated ship soon reconciles all disaffection. This war [up to 1804] has been singular for few desertions.'[7] Discussing the same period, Admiral Phillip Patton calculated that 5662 seamen, 3909 ordinary seamen and 2737 landsmen deserted in just over two years from 1803 to 1805 — a total of over 12,000 men, in a fleet with a total strength of 109,000 in 1805.[8] Nelson guessed that 42,000 men had deserted from 1793 to 1802, though this may well be an underestimate. He also claimed that 'whenever a large convoy is assembled at Portsmouth and our fleet in port, not less than 1000 men desert from the navy.'[9] Aboard an unhappy ship, men would seize every possible opportunity, and the captain was hard put to find men to send ashore for essential purposes. For example, the *Alfred* of 74 guns, lost twelve men from a watering party in the West Indies in January 1810, fifteen men two days later, and nine more on the next day — six per cent of the crew in four days.

Methods of Desertion

Ships of war rarely came alongside a quay or jetty, partly because of difficulty in manoeuvring, but also because of the fear of desertion. Men who wished to desert, therefore, had to get ashore in some way. Sometimes this was by failing to return from shore leave. Because of this, captains were often extremely reluctant to grant any leave at all. If they did grant it, they sometimes allowed only ten men ashore at a time, out of a crew of several hundred, and they held the rest of the crew as hostage for the behaviour of the others. Nevertheless,

The Hermione *is cut out after her surrender to the Spanish, following the mutiny of 1797.* The National Maritime Museum

they often assumed that they would lose a proportion of men from any liberty party.

Without any shore leave, men would mostly use the ship's boats to escape. Watering parties were commanded by an officer and sometimes guarded by marines, but this did not prevent men taking to their heels, as the example of the *Alfred* shows. Inhospitable territory was not always a deterrent to desertion. Robert Wilson records that four men from a boat's crew deserted in Turkey, although 'the men must have had a great aversion to any ship to desert in such a place as they did, in a country, to whose manners, language, destination from one place to another, they were perfect strangers to . . . I would not wish to treat any more of this place, but that they certainly had their reasons for deserting.'[10]

Failing to be sent ashore, men sometimes stole one of the ship's boats as it lay astern during the night, and made their way ashore. Many men were brought to court-martial for stealing boats in this way, but presumably far more got away with it. Not all seamen could swim in those days, but they used their ingenuity to the full. In 1811, Robert Hay and his companion on the *Ceres*, guardship in the Nore, used seven bladders strapped to their backs to carry them ashore.

Prevention of Desertion

One way to help prevent desertion was to make sure that the boats were not easy to steal. Captain's orders often demanded that the boats be hoisted in at night, or at least dropped well astern with a reliable boatkeeper in each. In harbour it was quite common to 'row guard' round the ship — a boat under the command of an officer or midshipman spent the night on patrol round the ship, to prevent men stealing boats or swimming ashore. Marine sentries were posted at the gangways of the ship, and the officers on deck were instructed to keep a sharp look-out; but men still managed to get away.

Punishments for Desertion

The great majority of deserters probably escaped. Some entered on foreign ships, especially American ones, and this was to contribute to the causes of the war of 1812. Many re-entered the merchant service, and some of these were pressed again, under a false name. Only a few suffered any punishment.

As soon as it became clear that a man had deserted, an 'R' (for 'run') was put against his name on the ship's muster books. All his wages and prize money were forfeit, unless he could subsequently clear his name. If a man was caught in the act of deserting, or soon afterwards, he was likely to be brought back to his own ship, and probably punished by the captain with twelve or more lashes. If he was caught long afterwards, or his captain felt like making an example of him, he would go before a court-martial.

During 1805, thirty-seven men were convicted of desertion by court-martial. Only one was an officer, a carpenter, who was dismissed from the service — a rather pointless punishment in the circumstances. One seaman was hanged, because he had escaped several times. Several more, who had been given good characters by their officers or had surrendered voluntarily, were given about fifty lashes. For the rest, the standard punishment was flogging round the fleet, usually with 300 lashes. One, who was suspected of serving the enemy, was given 700, as was another man who had served aboard a privateer. Such sentences were indeed harsh, but as a deterrent they failed. Probably six or seven thousand had deserted in that year, and the chances of severe punishment were quite small.

Part VII
MARINES

1 Role and Organisation

History

The Royal Marines celebrate 28 October 1664 as their foundation day, for it was then, in the early stages of the Second Dutch War, that The Admiral's Regiment, or The Duke of York and Albany's Maritime Regiment of Foot, was ordered to be raised. But, in some respects, the date is not quite appropriate. In the first place, troops had been used aboard ship since naval warfare began, and, until the great gun achieved pre-eminence, they provided the main armament of the ship. Secondly, the corps had no continuous existence after 1664; it was disbanded at the end of each war, and re-formed, often with a different composition, at the beginning of the next. Perhaps a more appropriate date would be 1755. In that year, a new corps of marines was formed, on the eve of the Seven Years' War. It was to be administered by the Admiralty rather than the War Office, and the marines have a continuous history from that year, for at the end of each war they were kept on as dockyard guards, and to provide a nucleus for rapid mobilisation.

The vast majority of marines served aboard ship, in small detachments forming part of the crew. Since every warship with more than about ten guns had some kind of marine detachment, it is not surprising to find that they served in every naval engagement of the Seven Years' War and the American War of Independence. With the growing importance of colonial warfare, they took part in many amphibious operations, and occasionally got involved in slightly more protracted land operations, such as the capture of Belleisle in 1761. They were present at the attack on Bunker's Hill which opened the war against the American colonists, and they formed a major part of the First Fleet which founded the British colony of Australia, guarding the convicts who were sent there in 1787. When the war began in 1793, they had a strength of about 4500 officers and men.

The Traditional Role of the Marines

The most ancient role of the marines was to fight as sea-going infantry, using virtually the same weapons and tactics as on land. At the time of the Spanish Armada, soldiers had made up about a third of a ship's complement, and in battle they fired their muskets and led boarding parties. Since then, their role had been steadily declining. After the invention of the line of battle in the 1650s, the musket and sword were very definitely secondary weapons. By the 1790s, a ship of 74 guns, with about 120 marines, used only about a dozen of them as small-arms men in action. The highly aggressive tactics introduced by Nelson in the 1790s increased the importance of boarding, but there is no real reason to believe that marines were particularly effective at this. The seaman would be more skilled at clambering from one ship to another, and his cutlass or pistol would often be more effective on the crowded decks of a ship than the marine's musket. In action, most marines worked the great guns alongside the seamen, but, as yet, they had no special training for this role.

When the marines were re-formed in 1740 to serve in the War of Jenkin's Ear, a totally different role was envisaged for them. It was felt in parliament that they could serve as a 'nursery for seamen', and that eventually some of them would become skilled mariners. Some vestiges of this view were still to be found in the 1800s.[1] Captains' orders often suggested that marines should be allowed to work aloft if they wanted, for training. However, the Naval Regulations stated that they were 'not to be obliged to go aloft, or to be beat or punished for not showing an inclination to do so'. The Naval Regulations of 1806 stated that 'No marine serving on board any of His Majesty's ships is to be discharged as such, and entered as a seaman, without particular order from the Board of Admiralty'.[2] Presumably, such cases were rare, and that role of the marines was obsolete. Moreover, by this time the navy used the rating of landmen for adults under training as seamen, and did not need to draw them from the marines.

Prevention of Mutiny

Marines are often associated with the suppression of mutiny, and this role was vastly expanded during the Napoleonic Wars. They had always carried out guard duties aboard ship, and had enforced regulations about conduct below deck. In the past, it had been normal to keep the marines socially separate from the seamen, giving them their own area for berths and messes; under St Vincent during 1797 — the year of the great mutinies — these rules were greatly reinforced. In command of the squadron off Cadiz, St Vincent called

A marine forming part of a gun crew at the Battle of Camperdown. He is wearing the standard uniform jacket, with a light cap. The National Maritime Museum

the marine captains from the various ships on board his flagship, 'under pretext of informing them about uniformity of dress, in exercise and economy: but really to give them some sense about keeping a watchful eye, not only upon their own men, but upon the seamen'.[3] Marines were to stand guard whenever punishment was inflicted; they were deliberately separated from the seamen, and in harbour, when mutiny was most likely, they were to be kept 'constantly at drill or parade, under the directions of the commanding officers of marines, and not to be diverted therefrom by the ordinary duties of the ship'.[4] When St Vincent took command of the Channel fleet two years later, exactly the same rules were applied. As a result, there were no major mutinies on the ships under St Vincent's command. In 1802, St Vincent was instrumental in having the title 'Royal' granted to the marines. As he said shortly before his death, 'In obtaining for them the distinction of Royal, I but inefficiently did my duty. I never knew an appeal to them for honour, courage or loyalty that they did not realise more than my highest expectations. If ever the hour of real danger should come to England, they will be found the country's sheet anchor.'[5]

The marines were not always effective in suppressing mutiny. At Spithead and the Nore, they often took a full part alongside the seamen. Some marines were commended for their loyalty, but others were hanged or flogged for supporting the mutiny. Admiral Phillip Patton believed that the Admiralty's reliance on the marines was misplaced, as they 'feel a very great inferiority to the seamen when at sea'.[6]

Landing Parties

There was no dispute about the marines' importance in amphibious warfare. Co-operation between the army and the navy often led to disputes about authority and precedence, and to tactical impotence. The marines were indisputably under naval discipline, and more effective. They were accustomed to the sea, and could often specialise in amphibious tactics. When marine companies were grouped together and used under an enterprising commander, as in the Peninsular War under Popham and others, they proved to be very effective. The role of amphibious warfare was increasing continually, and the marines found an important role here. Of course not all ships' marine detachments were used regularly in amphibious operations; but the opportunity to disembark men often occurred unexpectedly, and it was essential to have some marines available.

Marines' duties on shore were not restricted to amphibious warfare. They could be landed as guards in a friendly port, to keep the seamen from desertion, as at Brixham when boats' crews were sent ashore to collect water. Their smart uniformed appearance, in contrast to the informal manner and dress of the seamen, was used to impress enemies and allies. They were all, in theory, volunteers, so they were less likely to desert if sent on shore. Occasionally, they were used for impressment duties, either as part of press gangs, or as guards to prevent seamen escaping.

Continuity of Service

One further advantage that the marines had over seamen was that they could be employed much more easily in shore bases, even in peacetime. There was no real provision for employing seamen ashore on a long or medium-term basis, but marines were recruited and trained there, and lived in barracks when not needed at sea. In peacetime, many of them were kept on as guards for the dockyards. At the beginning of a war, that duty was relinquished to militia regiments, but the marines provided a nucleus of the crews for the ships being fitted out. They provided a large amount of semi-skilled labour in fitting out the ships, until the press gangs could bring a suitable number of seamen. In a sense, this was part of their amphibious nature, which was their greatest strength.

Recruitment

Since marines were essentially landmen, they could not be impressed like seamen. The recruiting organisation of the marines resembled that of the army. The country was divided into four districts, each under a field officer; another station was opened in Edinburgh in

The numbers of marines voted, 1793-1815.

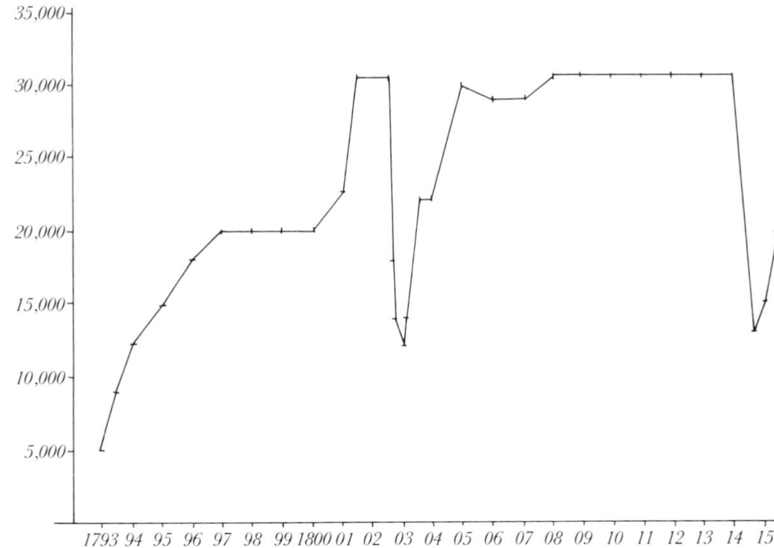

GREAT ENCOURAGEMENT.

AMERICAN WAR.

What a Brilliant Prospect does this Event hold out to every Lad of Spirit, who is inclined to try his Fortune in that highly renowned Corps,

The Royal Marines,

When every Thing that swims the Seas must be a

PRIZE!

Thousands are at this moment endeavouring to get on Board Privateers, where they serve without Pay or Reward of any kind whatsoever; so certain does their Chance appear of enriching themselves by PRIZE MONEY! What an enviable Station then must the *ROYAL MARINE* hold,---who with far superior Advantages to theſe, has the additional benefit of liberal Pay, and plenty of the best Provisions, with a good and well appointed Ship under him, the Pride and Glory of Old England; ſurely every Man of Spirit muſt bluſh to remain at Home in Inactivity and Indolence, when his Country and the beſt of Kings needs his Assistance.

Where then can he have ſuch a fair opportunity of reaping Glory and Riches, as in the Royal Marines, a Corps daily acquiring new Honours, and there, when once embarked in BRITISH FLEET, he finds himself in the midſt of Honour and Glory, ſurrounded by a ſet of fine Fellows, Strangers to Fear, and who ſtrike Terror through the Hearts of their Enemies wherever they go!

He has likewise the inſpiring Idea to know, that while he ſcours the Ocean to protect the Liberty of OLD ENGLAND, that the Hearts and good Wiſhes of the whole BRITISH NATION, attend him; pray for his Succeſs, and participate in his Glory!! Loſe no Time then, my Fine Fellows, in embracing the glorious Opportunity that awaits you; YOU WILL RECEIVE

Sixteen Guineas Bounty,

And on your Arrival at *Head Quarters*, be comfortably and genteely CLOTHED.—And ſpirited Young BOYS of a promiſing Appearance, who are Five Feet high, WILL RECEIVE TWELVE POUNDS ONE SHILLING AND SIXPENCE BOUNTY, and equal Advantages of *PROVISIONS* and *CLOATHING* with the Men. And thoſe who wish only to enlist for a limited Service, ſhall receive a Bounty of ELEVEN GUINEAS, and Boys EIGHT. In Fact, the Advantages which the *ROYAL MARINE* poſſeſses, are too numerous to mention here, but among the many, it may not be amiſs to state,—*That if he has a WIFE, or aged PARENT, he can make them an Allotment of half his PAY; which will be regularly paid without any Trouble to them, or to whomsoever he may direct: that being well Clothed and Fed on Board Ship, the Remainder of his PAY and PRIZE MONEY will be clear in Reserve for the Relief of his Family or his own private Purposes. The Single Young Man on his Return to Port, finds himself enabled to cut a Dash on Shore with his GIRL and his GLASS, that might be envied by a Nobleman.---Take Courage then, seize the Fortune that awaits you, repair to the ROYAL MARINE RENDEZVOUS, where in a FLOWING BOWL of PUNCH, in Three Times Three, you shall drink*

Long live the King, and Success to his Royal Marines.

The Daily Allowance of a Marine when embarked, is---One Pound of BEEF or PORK.---One Pound of BREAD.---Flour, Raisins, Butter, Cheese, Oatmeal, Molasses, Tea, Sugar, &c. &c. And a Pint of the beſt WINE, or Half a Pint of the best RUM or BRANDY; together with a Pint of LEMONADE. They have likewise in warm Countries, a plentiful Allowance of the choicest FRUIT. And what can be more handsome than the Royal Marine's Proportion of PRIZE MONEY, when a Serjeant shares equal with the First Class of Petty Officers, such as Midshipmen, Assistant Surgeons, &c. which is Five Shares each; a Corporal with the Second Class, which is Three Shares each; and the Private with the Able Seamen, One Share and a Half each.

☞ *For further Particulars, and a more full Account of the many Advantages of this invaluable Corps, apply to SERJEANT FULCHER, at the EIGHT BELLS, where the Bringer of a Recruit will receive* THREE GUINEAS.

S. AND J. RIDGE, PRINTERS, MARKET-PLACE, NEWARK.

A recruiting poster issued during the war of 1812. Royal Marines Museum

1798, under Colonel Duncan. Officers and sergeants were sent out from the divisional companies to 'the most proper places to raise recruits' — usually the market towns up and down the country. Posters were printed and stuck up in market places, and recruiting sergeants roamed the area, trying to impress likely young men with tales of action and adventure. Mere persuasion was not enough, and, in wartime, a substantial bounty had to be offered. In 1794, it was raised to 8 guineas per man, and then to 15. By 1801, it had apparently reached £26 per man, and in 1808 up to £30 was offered. All this brought in a steady flow of recruits, probably driven by unemployment or poor prospects in their own trades; around 1805, the marines of the *San Domingo* included fifty former labourers, presumably agricultural, among 121 NCOs and men. There were also twenty weavers (for that trade was beginning to be supplanted by the power loom) and representatives of twenty-seven other trades.[7]

But ordinary recruiting was never enough in wartime, and other methods had to be adopted. In 1795, the rapid expansion of the navy caused a crisis, as the recruitment of marines was not keeping up with the impressment of seamen. In the short term, an old expedient was tried — using soldiers from the army. Men from at least twelve regiments — the 1st, 11th, 25th, 30th, 50th, 51st, 69th, 86th, 90th, 91st, 97th and 118th Foot — served afloat during that year. This arrangement caused many difficulties. A certain proportion of soldiers was allowed to take wives with them, and some of these women were present during naval engagements. More important, it was disputed whether the authority of a naval court-martial could be extended to soldiers serving afloat. Naval officers resisted any attempt to reduce their power in this way, and pointed out that 'Marines, on the old approved establishment are much desired as assisting the preservation of discipline and order on board'.[9] To get round this, soldiers were offered bounties of 5 guineas to transfer to the marines. This seems to have been quite successful, and it was reported that nearly every man eligible in the 91st wanted to transfer.[9] Ten years later, a similar recruiting method was attempted, and one in every ten men joining the army was allowed to volunteer for the marines.

The marine corps continued to expand throughout the wars; the numbers voted by parliament were 15,000 in 1795, 20,000 in 1797, 30,000 in 1805, and 31,400 after 1806. Various new expedients were tried to find men. By an act of 1805, the militia regiments raised by the counties were each required to find a certain number of men to serve in the marines. The militia regiments were themselves raised by a form of limited conscription, men being selected by lot, for home service only. The offer of a bounty, and the promise of adventure overseas, was enough to inspire many to volunteer. By March 1805, 358 men had been raised in this way at the Portsmouth depot alone, from Somerset, Essex, Cardigan, Merioneth and Lancashire. Eventually, about 2000 men were recruited from this source.

In 1804, the regulations were altered to allow the recruitment of boys, who were to be paid as men on reaching the age of fifteen. Standards for men were reduced, so tht those of more than 5ft 2in tall were to be accepted. In 1805, the *San Domingo* had eighteen youths under twenty years of age among its marines, but probably the majority of boys were kept in barracks until they were old enough to serve effectively.

Many foreigners were recruited as marines during these years. In the 1790s, recruiting officers were sent round the hulks and prisons holding prisoners of war, and found a certain number of men, especially among those, such as the Dutch, who had been unwillingly taken under French rule. This exercise was repeated in the Napoleonic Wars, with seventy-three men being recruited from prison ships into the Portsmouth division between April and November 1804. Orders were sent to recruit any Swiss who had been conscripted into the French service, and this had some effect. In 1805 a recruiting station was opened on Malta, and had sent eight-two men to Portsmouth alone by the middle of the year. When the *Hercules* attacked Fort Piscadero in 1803, thirty out of her sixty-seven marines were Poles, recruited from prisoners taken in the West Indies. More foreigners were recruited when a station was opened in the West Indies, and some free negroes were enlisted. Recruiting of foreigners was stopped in 1810, but the number in the Royal Marines seems to have become quite substantial by this time.

Terms of Service

Traditionally, marines, like other soldiers, had been recruited for an unlimited period of service, for life or until the government had no further use for them. During the 1790s, there was some attempt to recruit them for the duration of the war, though there was some misunderstanding about this, and often men were unclear about their terms of engagement. The act of 1807 quite clearly allowed service for the duration, and this was probably the most common means of recruitment. In other cases, men agreed to serve for fixed terms of five or seven years. Those recruited overseas were offered a free passage home on completion of service. A recruit to the marines had to attest before a magistrate. In one oath he swore: 'I have no rupture, nor was ever troubled with fits, and am in no ways disabled by lameness or otherwise, but have perfect use of my limbs, that I am not an apprentice, and that I do not belong to the militia, or to any other regiment or corps, or to His Majesty's navy.'[10]

At the end of a war, the government invariably reduced the marines to a much smaller force, and tried to get rid of the least useful or deserving of its men. In 1802, the men 'were to be paraded

The marine barracks at Portsmouth, showing officers on duty and recruits drilling. Royal Marines Museum

by the commandant and all men who appear unfit or over forty years of age' were to be discharged, preference being given for retention to, 'those who have longest service at sea or are most in debt to the crown. Drummers to be persuaded if possible to remain and serve in the ranks'.[11] In 1814, those discharged first included foreigners and men under 5ft 3½in, as well as older and unfit men.[12]

The Marine Divisions

Marine shore organisation was centred on the three divisions, with barracks near the dockyards at Chatham, Portsmouth and Plymouth. These divisions were roughly equal in strength, with about forty companies to each in 1793. The Chatham division was known as the First Division, and its companies numbered 1, 4, 7, etc; Portsmouth was the Second Division, with companies numbered 2, 5, 8, etc; and at Plymouth they were numbered 3, 6, 9, etc. A Fourth Division was formed at Woolwich in 1805, with companies numbered consecutively from 144 to 183. By 1813, there were forty-eight companies at Chatham, forty-nine each at Portsmouth and Plymouth, and forty-one at Woolwich. After 1804 each division had an artillery company in addition. Originally, the divisions had resembled army regiments, in that each had two elite companies, called the grenadier company and the light company. These could have served little purpose in practice, and were abolished in 1804.

Each division was commanded by a commandant, with the rank of colonel or major general. The companies carried out the administration and training of the corps, and sent men on board ship. There was no relationship between the shorebased company and the detachment at sea, for men were sent on shipboard in ones and twos from each company. In wartime the companies were reduced to skeletons, with a few officers and NCOs to carry out the training and administration, and an average of about fifteen privates on hand. In 1803, the commandant at Portsmouth complained that his forces had not been included in a roster of men available for home defence in the event of an invasion, but he was forced to admit

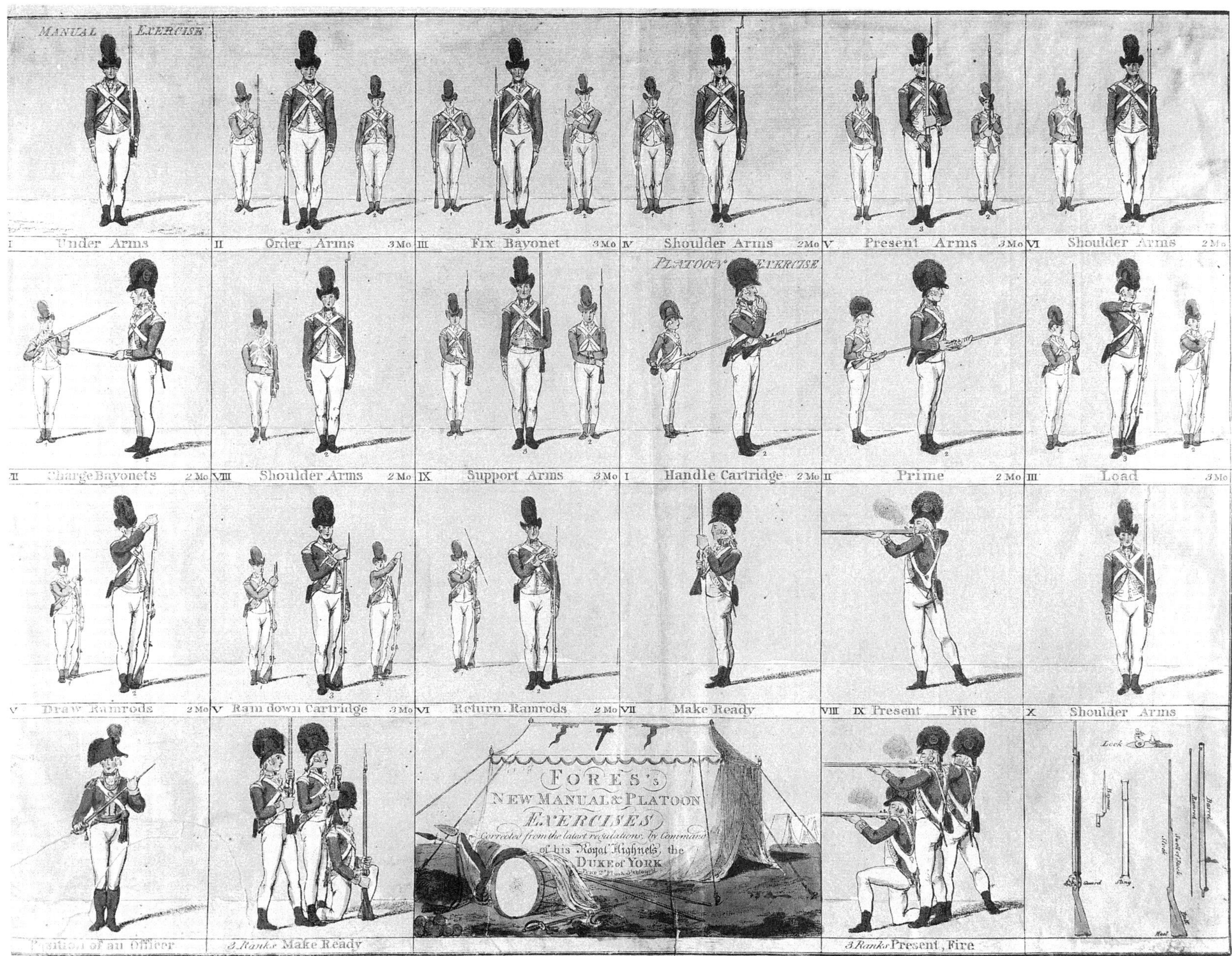

Infantry drill. Although designed for the army, this probably shows similar techniques and uniforms to those used by the marines at that time. National Army Museum

that he had few soldiers available. 'A reference to our weekly returns will show that though there be few men at quarters (the great body being actively employed on the element where they have gained their proved and invaluable distinction) yet there is a list, a long list, of officers who might in a variety of ways be made useful.'[13]

Nor did the company have much relation to the units in which the men drilled under training. According to a well-informed officer, 'Every marine recruit should intimate to his wife or kindred . . . the number of the *divisional company* to which he has been attached. Young men too frequently name only their *parade companies*, which is no use after they are embarked on board.' Use of the divisional company number would 'correct mistakes when two or more, of similar name, shall happen to belong to the same ship or division',[14] for the number of his company was marked opposite the man's name in the ship's muster book.

Each division had its own barracks. Those at Portsmouth were probably the worst, being situated at Southsea. They were too small, and men often had to be quartered in inns, or sent to Hilsea barracks some distance away. At Plymouth the marines used the Stonehouse barracks, completed in 1783 and still used by them today. They were often overcrowded in wartime, and other quarters sometimes had to be used. At Chatham, the new barracks had been completed in 1779, and were quite well equipped. 'The barracks . . . are capable of containing 825 men, with a due proportion of officers. To each room containing 12 men is a superintending sergeant and his wife, by the latter of whom they are kept in clean and good order.'[15] At Woolwich the men of the new division had to be accommodated in the dockyard until an old brewery was converted into a barracks in 1808.

The nominal size of a company increased over the years, from 120 officers and men in 1795, to 178 in 1810. The officers attached to each division in 1805 included a colonel (who was in fact a naval officer in an honorary position), a commandant and a second commandant, three lieutenant colonels, three majors, two adjutants, a quartermaster, deputy paymaster, barrackmaster, surgeon, and a surgeon's mate. Two sergeants in each division were designated 'squad sergeants', and were responsible for accounting and administration, under the quartermaster.

Training

There does not appear to have been a fixed training period for marines, and everything depended on how quickly men were needed at sea. Training on shore was entirely in the skills of an infantryman. In 1809, Thomas Rees was sent on board ship after nearly a year in barracks, 'so ignorant of everything belonging to a ship when I first went on board, I scarcely knew the head from the stern'.[16] On shore, a marine would be trained in loading and firing his musket, and in elementary infantry drill (for marines did not need to move in large formations like ordinary infantry). In 1809, each man was allowed twenty rounds of ball cartridge, forty rounds of blanks, and two flints for training. It appears that bayonet exercise was not regularised until 1811. A new system was devised by Lt Faden at Woolwich, and selected NCOs were to be taught it 'for the purpose thereafter of instructing men in the same, so that officers can proceed with the exercise as part of their drill as soon as the men are expert in their arms and otherwise for duty'.[17] In 1813, the men were paraded for an Admiralty inspection, and it was reported, 'The effective men at quarters being drawn out in the barrack square, saluted by presenting arms, went through the manual exercises with great precision, and marched past in ordinary and quick time, after which they were ordered to their divisions.'[18]

Pay

Marines were paid by two different systems, with a lower rate when they were afloat than when ashore. In 1797, the pay of a private was raised to 1s per day, or £1.8.0 per lunar month, in parity with the army. But when they were afloat, this was reduced to 19s 3d per month. The reason was that, while ashore, the marine was charged for the cost of his victualling and accommodation. At sea, he also had deductions, in the form of contributions to the Chatham Chest, the surgeon and chaplain; but his food was supplied free of charge. The marine afloat also had to pay for his bedding (but not his hammock), and also for the 'slops' which he used for working clothes when not on guard duty.

Within a particular rank, pay often increased with length of service. A private with more than seven years' service was paid 2s 4d extra when on shore, and 1s 9d when afloat. After fourteen years, these allowances were doubled. A sergeant had £2.11.4 ashore and £2.0.3 afloat. Artillerymen were paid more; a gunner had a minimum of £1.15.7 ashore, and a sergeant had £3.18.2.[18]

2 Marines in Service

Marine Officers

Marine officers above the rank of lieutenant colonel rarely served afloat, and were generally confined to administrative and staff duties at the barracks, or at the corps headquarters in London. Even lieutenant colonels were quite rare at sea, but in 1797 Lt Col Flight was appointed inspector of marines in St Vincent's fleet. However, the great majority of officers in sea service were captains and lieutenants. Field officers had no special rate of sea pay, because they were 'not liable to serve afloat'.[1] When majors and lieutenant colonels were found in command of shipboard marines, they usually held only brevet rank, given for special service but not carrying any increase in pay.

Captains commanded the marine detachments of all ships of fifty guns or more. They were equal to naval lieutenants in rank, and in the distribution of prize money. First lieutenants were usually put in command of the detachments in frigates, though occasionally one might act as second in command of the marines on a very large ship, such as a first rate. Second lieutenants were not allocated the command of any detachments, according to the established rules; if a ship was too small to have a first lieutenant, its marines were commanded by a sergeant.

In some ways, the position of marine lieutenants was anomalous aboard ship. They were clearly junior to naval lieutenants, and therefore to masters, who were only warrant officers, while the marine lieutenants were commissioned officers. The Admiralty Regulations recognised this dilemma: 'though lieutenants of marines share in prizes only with warrant officers of ships, upon consideration of their different sea duty, yet it is not intended to degrade their rank; and they are, while they do their duty, to be considered and treated in all respects as a commissioned officer should be.'[2] Though their economic status was no greater than that of a warrant officer, they were to be allowed all the privileges of commissioned status, with their own cabins and access to the wardroom and quarterdeck. Admiralty Regulations demanded that the marine detachment be divided into divisions, with a subaltern in charge of each.[3] Marine officers were appointed by the Admiralty, largely through influence. They did not purchase their commissions like army oficers; promotion was strictly by seniority and tended to be rather slow.

NCOs and Men

Until nearly the end of the Napoleonic Wars, there were only two non-commissioned officer ranks in the marines. Sergeants and corporals were usually appointed in approximately equal numbers, though if there was to be an odd number of NCOs, it was common to have fewer corporals than sergeants. Proportions varied according to the size of the ship; large ones had one NCO to about twenty men, while small ones had one to ten men. NCOs took charge of the guard at sea, and often led small parties ashore to prevent desertion. In action, they gave orders to the marines firing their small arms, and they were responsible for drilling the men in exercises. They probably messed apart from the privates. There is no sign that marines were divided into regular platoons and sections for service, but they were probably put into small groups for administrative and inspection purposes, as part of the divisional system of the ship.

Sergeants were distinguished from other non-commissioned personnel in that they carried halberds or pikes instead of muskets, and did not fall in with the ranks on parade. Corporals carried muskets like privates. The rank of lance corporal does not seem to have been formally recognised, though it certainly existed in the form of a private doing acting duty as a corporal. It is not clear whether the lance corporal was allotted a single stripe, as in the army, when chevrons were introduced in 1807.

The rank of colour sergeant was not officially recognised until 1814, though it had been used by the army for several years. In August of that year, each division was allowed to promote a number of sergeants to the new rank, with extra pay of 6d per day. However, there are signs that the rank was used informally aboard ship before that, and certainly the senior sergeant of a detachment had special responsibilities. There are frequent references to sergeant majors as the senior NCOs of detachments. According to the marine orders of the *Blenheim* in 1796, 'The sergeant who is appointed sergeant major of the detachment . . . is to be answerable for the proper military appearance of all guards.'[4] Sergeant majors were also needed when marines began to be formed into battalions for service on shore, and, even then, the rank was not officially sanctioned. In 1811, each division was asked to make up the extra pay of 1s 6d per day for

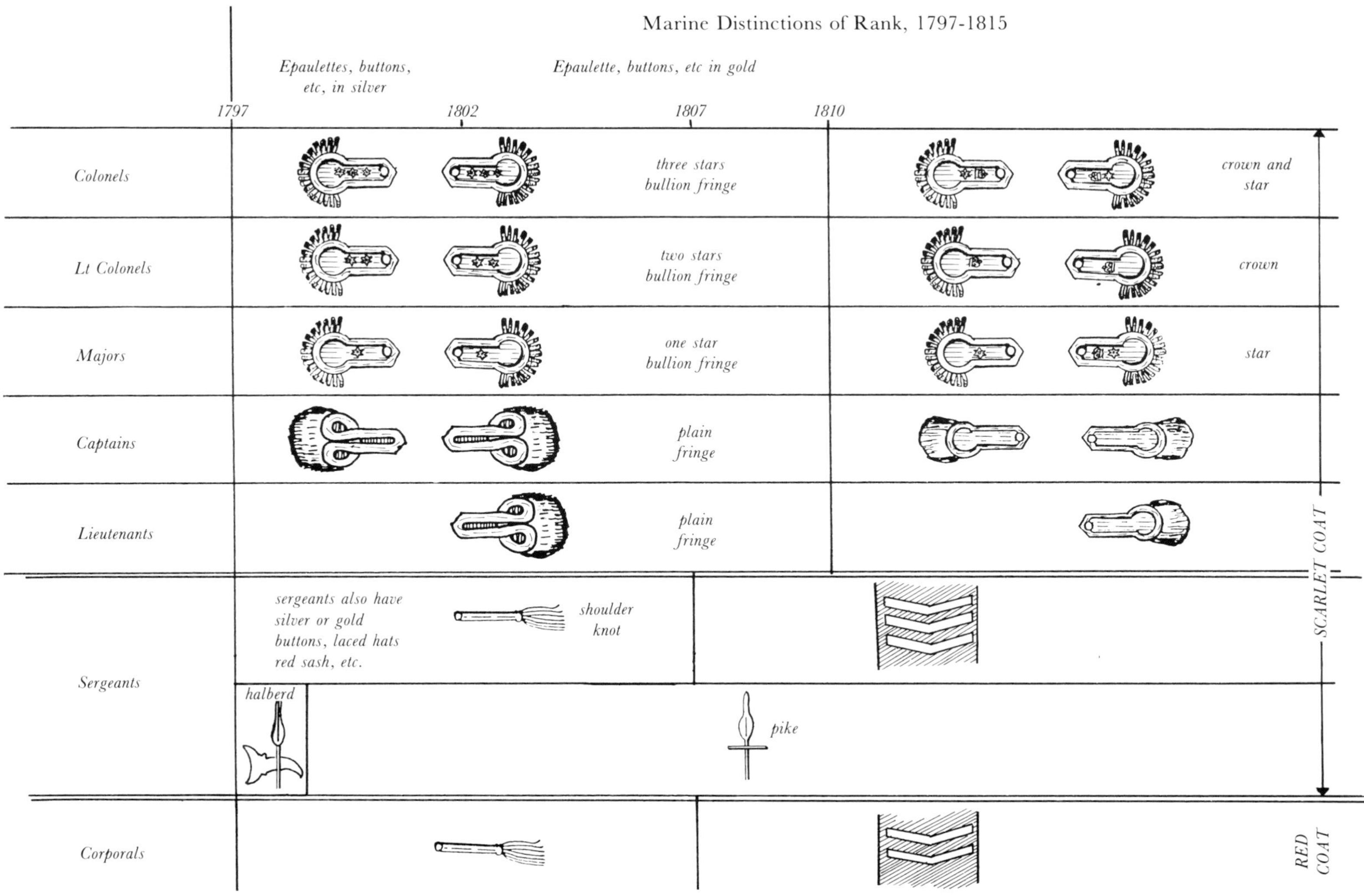

Marine distinctions of rank, 1797-1815. The exact shape of the epaulettes is far from certain, and the details of rank distinctions are often rather obscure. The position is even more vague before 1797.

Sergeant Hewit, sergeant major to the first battalion. Promotion to commissioned officer was rare, though not unknown. In 1798, Sergeant Mooney was promoted to second lieutenant for 'long service and exemplary conduct', and Sergeant O'Neale was given the same rank for revealing a conspiracy among United Irishmen aboard his ship, the *Caesar*.[5]

Drummers were senior to privates, being paid at the maximum rate for a private of fourteen years' service in 1808. Unlike the army, the marines do not seem to have used boys in this role.

Shipboard Detachments

When a ship was ordered to be commissioned, the captain was to apply to the nearest barracks for marines, according to an established number laid down by the Admiralty. The local commandant would select them from the companies in barracks, and send them on board. The captain had a certain discretion in refusing any of those sent whom he considered to be unfit: 'If he refuses to receive any of them, or any others that may at any time be sent to him, he is strictly required to send back the men he shall so refuse, to the commanding marine officer at quarters, his reasons in writing under his hand.'[6]

The size of a shipboard detachment varied according to the size of the ship, and according to the period. By the orders of 1801, on larger ships about one sixth of the complement was marines. In smaller ships, it was about one in seven. In 1808, the proportion of marines was increased, perhaps because of fear of mutiny, or because it was difficult to find any more seamen. Large ships now had about one fifth marines, smaller ones about one sixth.

Once on board, a certain proportion of the marines was employed on guard duty. The captain was obliged to post a sentry permanently at the hatchway to the magazine, and he would normally have sentries on other posts — at the door to his own cabin, at the spirit room hatch, and at the entrances to various store rooms. On a 74-gun ship about thirty men would normally be kept in full uniform, to provide a 'rotation of sentries'. According to the orders for the marines of the *Centaur* in 1803, sentries were 'to walk brisk on their posts, backwards and forwards, never to sit down, read or sing, whistle, smoke, eat or drink, but be continually alert and attentive to the execution of their orders, nor ever to quit their arms on any pretence whatsoever.'[7]

Relations with Seamen

According to one captain who had served in the Napoleonic Wars, the difference between seamen and marines was absolute.

> No two races of men, I had well nigh said two animals, differ from one another more completely than the 'Jollies' and the 'Johnnies'. The marines as I have said before are enlisted for life, or for long periods as in the regular army, and, when not employed afloat, are kept in barracks, in such constant training, under the direction of their officers, that they are never released for one moment of their lives from the influence of strict discipline and habitual obedience. The sailors, on the contrary, when their ship is paid off, are turned adrift, and so completed scattered abroad, that they generally lose . . . all they have learned of good order during the

Marines firing small arms at Trafalgar. The NCO's chevrons are presumably anachronistic, since they were not officially introduced until 1807. The National Maritime Museum

> previous three of four years. Even when both parties are placed on board ship, and the general discipline maintained in its fullest operation, the influence of regular order and exact subordination is at least twice as great over the marines as it can ever be over the sailors.[8]

Captain Glascock also illuminated the difference, pointing out that

> The sailor of our wars with France had so much *esprit de corps* for his own branch of the national service that he genuinely and heartily — not to say unreasonably — despised all that pertained to soldiering and pipeclay. But in most of the affairs we are able to relate, marines and seamen were able to work most perfectly together; the former, efficient soldiers as they were, holding the enemy's troops and covering the no less efficient cutting out and demolition work of the seamen.[9]

Relations between the two groups were of course uneasy on many occasions, particularly when there was any question of mutiny. Seamen had no great inclination to mix with marines, and this was deliberately encouraged by authority, which demanded that they eat and sleep separately. There was also a certain amount of resentment between the officers of the two services. Mixed parties were nearly always put under the command of naval officers, and the sinecure 'colonel of marines' was reserved for naval officers of distinguished service. On the other hand, the marines had a more impressive uniform, and a marine lieutenant had the same epaulettes as a junior naval captain, equivalent to a lieutenant colonel in the army or marines. The marine officer's commission was written in much more generous terms — like those of army officers — while that of the naval officers ended with the ominous phrase 'you may fail as you will answer at your peril'. Such differences caused some jealousy in the wardroom.

Landing Parties

Landing parties varied according to the task in hand. If it was intended to guard the press room, or escort a deserter back to his ship, a corporal's guard of four or six men might suffice. Quite often a ship's whole marine detachment might take part in a raid or shore operation — perhaps with a part of the seamen as well. For more important operations, the marines might be drawn from several ships on the station. In 1808, a party of 300 marines was gathered from several ships on the Portugal station, and landed at Figueras in support of a local rising. A few days later a large fleet arrived with the Duke of Wellington's army, and landed 16,000 soldiers; this was the first major British intervention in the Peninsular War.

Battalions

It had long been common to employ large bodies of marines ashore for quite extended periods, and this practice was developed during the wars. In December 1795, parties were landed on the French islands of St Marcou, off the coast of Normandy, to watch the movement of enemy vessels. They were to remain there until 1801. The original party came from the *Diamond*, but were soon replaced by 'invalid marines', sent from Portsmouth. By 1799, the garrison had been increased, to nearly 300 officers and men. These were borne on the books of two tiny gunboats, the *Badger* and *Sandfly*, and the fiction was maintained that they were on sea service.

In 1810, steps were taken to form larger bodies of marines on a more permanent basis, for service at Lisbon. The different divisions were each ordered to provide men to form a battalion at Chatham. By November, a force of two majors, five captains, twelve lieutenants, thirty sergeants and 473 rank and file had been formed. The marine battalion formed part of the garrison of Lisbon, but was also in readiness to serve aboard the fleet when necessary. In 1812, the battalion returned to Britain and was re-equipped, and made up to an effective strength of 500 rank and file. It was then sent to join Sir Home Popham's force on the north coast of Spain, where it took part in many landings, including the taking of Santander.

Meanwhile, a second battalion was formed at Portsmouth, again by forming companies at the different divisions and then assembling them together. It was sent to Santander in August. In 1813, the battalions returned home, being sent to Plymouth and to Berry Head, Torbay. They were increased to a total of 753 officers and men each, plus eighty-one artillerymen, and were sent to Canada to take part

Troops and marines landing at Montevideo in 1807. The National Maritime Museum

in the war against America. A third battalion was formed at the same time. They saw much service before being returned home in 1815.

St Marcou, off the coast of Normandy, held by marines from 1795 to 1801. From the Naval Chronicle

The Royal Marine Artillery

Ever since bomb vessels had been first added to the fleet in the 1680s, it had been normal for their weapons to be operated by officers and men of the Royal Artillery. The mortars were used for shore bombardment, which required a totally different technique from that used for ordinary naval gunnery, while the explosive shells required extremely careful handling — better done by disciplined and professional soldiers than by seamen. However, the use of soldiers on board ship caused problems, brought to a head in 1795 when soldiers had been used as marines for a time, and there were disputes about how far naval authority extended over them. In 1804, there was further difficulty, when artillerymen aboard bomb vesels off Havre de Grace 'refused to do any other duty than simply that of attending mortars in time of action, and keeping them prepared for service; their officers supported them in this determination, and the commanders of the bombs appealed to the Admiralty.'[10]

The Admiralty's response was to form the Royal Marine Artillery, to replace the Royal Artillerymen serving afloat. Since the operation of mortars was skilled and scientific work, it was ordered that 'the officers and men to be selected from the most intelligent and experienced then belonging to the respective divisions'.[11] Three companies were formed, at Portsmouth, Plymouth and Chatham, and later another was added at Woolwich. By 1805, each artillery company consisted of one captain, three first lieutenants, five second lieutenants, eight sergeants, five corporals, eight bombardiers, three drummers and sixty-two gunners. This gave a much higher proportion of officers and NCOs to men than in other companies, and reflected the more technical nature of the work.

Marine artillery was later included in the battalions formed for service in the Peninsula and in America. They were equipped with their own howitzers, which were landed in support of the troops and seamen.

3 Marine Equipment and Uniforms

Muskets

The basic weapon of the marines was the musket. Essentially, it was a version of the 'Brown Bess' musket, the standard weapon of the British army for more than a century. Compared with the weapons used by the army, the sea service musket was slightly shorter — the barrel was 36 to 38in long, compared with 42in or more for the land weapon. This obviously made it easier to handle in the crowded space aboard ship. The lock of the marine gun was slightly simpler than that of the army, with a flat lock plate instead of a rounded one, and with considerably less decoration. In general the sea service gun was plainer, with less finish — this tended to make it less susceptible to salt water corrosion. It had a steel ramrod, stored under the stock of the weapon, through the ramrod pipes. The musket had rings for a sling, and could take a bayonet. Like nearly all guns of the period, the musket was fired by means of a flint striking against the pan cover, forcing it forward and igniting powder in the pan, which transmitted the fire to the chamber inside the gun. It fired a lead ball of about $\frac{3}{4}$in in diameter, and the barrel was smooth bored. The bore of the sea service barrel was usually slightly larger than the land service one, perhaps because it was subject to more wear and tear at sea; in any case, accuracy was low, and, at a range of more than 100yds, few shots ever hit their mark.

Muskets were supplied by the Ordnance Board, who ordered them from private contractors. Specifications were not fully detailed, and, as a result, there is a certain amount of variation, even within guns of the same period. Guns were either 'bright sea service' or 'black sea service' — the barrel was made either shiny or black during manufacture. In general a ship was issued with equal numbers of each type. The bright guns were used by the marines during parades and as sentinels, while the black ones were for operations where the glint of the sun on a barrel might reveal the presence of a raiding force.

Ammunition was usually made up in cartridges. Both the ball and the gunpowder were wrapped up in greased or waxed paper. The paper at one end was carefully folded over, and at the other it was tied to hold the ball in place. Gunpowder used for muskets was considerably weaker than that used in great guns.

Other Weapons

The standard sea-service bayonet had a triangular blade, with a socket to fit on the muzzle of the musket. Often, the fit was not very good, and had to be modified to be held in place. It was usually about 17in long, and $1\frac{1}{4}$in maximum height. It was triangular in cross-section. Officers and sergeants wore swords, of established patterns. Traditionally sergeants had carried halberds. These were weapons fitted on a long pole, with a head shaped like a combined hatchet and spear. After about 1797, orders tend to refer to pikes rather than halberds, and this may have been a slightly different weapon, with a spear-like head, a bar to prevent it being driven too far, but no hatchet-like part as on the halberd. If so, this would conform to army practice, for they had got rid of the halberd in 1792. Probably neither weapon was much use in action, but served merely to show the sergeant's status, and perhaps to help him check whether ranks of men were straight. Hand grenades were issued to the ship's gunner, and were sometimes used by the marines.

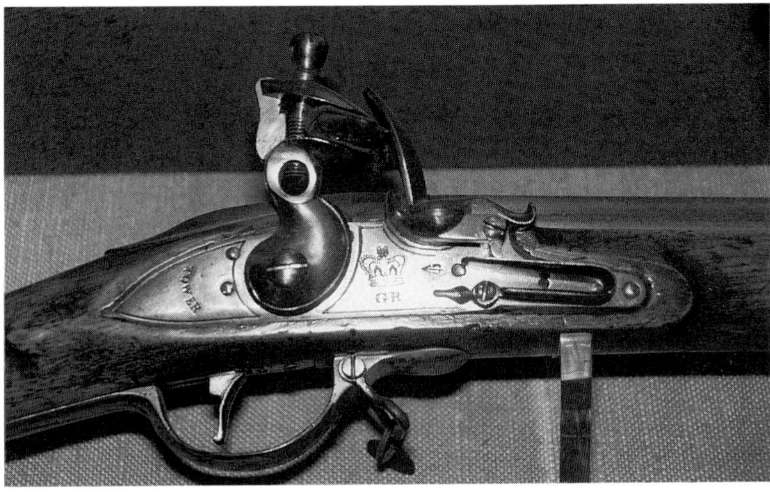

Details of the lock of a sea service musket. Author's photograph, courtesy of the National Maritime Museum

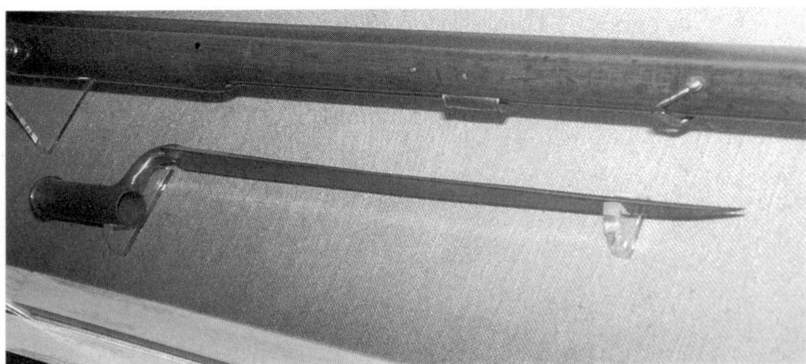

A marine bayonet. Author's photograph, courtesy of the National Maritime Museum

The standard sea service musket. Royal Marines Museum

Uniforms

In general, the uniforms of the marines followed those of the army, though they often lagged behind by several years. According to Grose's *Military Antiquities*, published in 1801, 'The marines are clothed and armed in the same manner as His Majesty's other corps of infantry; their uniform is scarlet, faced with white. They also wear caps like those of the fusilier regiments.' This however changed in the following year, when the marines were awarded the title 'Royal'. Like all royal regiments they were entitled to wear blue facings, and new uniforms were issued, or the old ones modified.

Marine uniforms were supplied by the Navy Board. According to the regulations of 1785, each non-commissioned marine was issued annually with 'A red cloth coat with white cloth waistcoat and breechs; One shirt, with one black stock; One pair of stockings; One pair of shoes; A hat; conformable to the sealed patterns lodged at the Navy Office, and at the headquarters of each division.'[1]

The other ranks' jacket of the 1790s, like that of the army, was descended from the full-length coat which had been worn in the early part of the century. It still had a tail, but the long lapels of the front were usually folded back, to show the facing colour. The two sides of the coat met only in front of the breast, where they were hooked together. A white waistcoat was worn under the coat.

In the early nineteenth century marines wore a different type of jacket, which closed completely above the waist. There were twelve buttons, arranged in pairs, with strips of white tape leading outwards from them. The facing colour was shown on collars, shoulder straps and cuffs; the last also had buttons on them. It is not quite clear exactly when this uniform was introduced; whether in 1797 when the army made a similar change, or in 1802, when the corps was completely re-equipped on becoming a royal regiment. The latter seems the most likely, as the marines generally followed the army by about five years, and in 1802 the corps was at its peacetime strength, which would have made the initial re-equipment quite inexpensive. It was said that the new uniforms were 'by the King's express command, the pattern of the First regiment of Foot Guards',[2] which suggests they would have used the 'closed jacket' of the army. The Admiralty was cautious about the expense involved. The new uniforms were ordered to be issued to all ranks for the King's Birthday parade of 1802, but after that they were to be worn only 'on particular duties, on days on which it is particularly expected the battalion to be perfectly uniform.'[3] The older uniforms were to be worn for working dress for the moment. During the American War there had been a lighter type of uniform, known as 'light clothing'. According to a letter of 1798, 'The marine light clothing was lined with linen instead of wool. The waistcoats and breeches made of raven duck instead of cloth, and thread stockings instead of yarn. Only 500 suits have been supplied this war, and there is no pattern suit.'[4] Presumably, it was obsolete because there was much less action in the hot climates of the West Indies.

In 1797, the men of the grenadier company in each division were to wear an embroidered fuze on each epaulette, while those of the light companies had bugles in the same positions. The grenadiers had 'wings', raised projections on the shoulder. All these distinctions went out of use when the flank companies were abolished in 1804.

Marines generally wore white breeches, of variable quality. In 1802, there was a complaint about them. 'They are generally too tight in the fork, and are so tight that men who are at all muscular in their make find it difficult to get them on, and being sewed close to the edges of the cloth it is impossible to make them larger; the consequence is that it becomes necessary to use those marked 5ft 8in and 5ft 9in for men of 5ft 6in and 5ft 7in, and it often happens that none can be found sufficiently large for grenadiers.'[5] They wore white gaiters for parade, black ones for action.

In the late eighteenth century marines had worn the standard light infantry hat, with a large plume over the top (except for grenadiers,

A marine officer at the battle of Camperdown, wearing the open jacket with white facings. The National Maritime Museum

A marine private, c1805. The National Maritime Museum

who wore fur caps with a regimental badge in front). By the early years of the next century, this had evolved into a hat without a feather, cocked up on each side by two tapes. The hat was made of glazed leather, and tapered slightly towards the top.

In 1796, marine NCOs and men were ordered to wear their hair powdered white; this was soon rescinded, as the king had already ordered that only officers in the army were to powder their hair. In the eighteenth century, marines, like all soldiers, wore their hair tied up in a 'queue' at the back. This was abolished by an order of 1808.

From 1801, men serving on ships in the North Sea were allowed to purchase woollen 'pantaloons' for cold weather wear. Watch coats were supplied for the men on guard.

Officers wore jackets of similar style to the men, but of much better quality, and in scarlet rather than red. One ordered for a lieutenant in 1803 was described as follows:

> 'S' fine scarlet coat cut as regulation. Ten [holes] in lapel by twos. Four blue long holes on to top of lapel, and the rest of the holes on the forepart scarlet. Lapel full four inches at top. Blue lapels, cuffs and stand up collar with one hole and breast button on each side. Two of a side behind ... four [holes] on flaps and cuffs by pairs — White casimere turnbacks and skirts lined with casimere. Embroidered. Skirt ornaments a heart — gold epaulette. Gilt buttons of whatever division they are of whether Plymouth or Chatham.[6]

Officers had to provide their own uniforms to a sealed pattern, and used tailors such as Welch and Stalker, and Buckmaster. Officers wore cocked hats; three-cornered in the eighteenth century, and two-cornered in the nineteenth.

Distinctions of Rank

Until 1807, sergeants were distinguished by the knots on their right shoulders, and by the lace trimmings on their jackets and hats (silver until 1802, and gold after the title 'Royal' was conferred). Corporals had only the knot. In 1807, five years after the army, sergeants were given three chevrons on the right sleeve, and corporals two; the lacing and knots were no longer used. Sergeants had a red sash, which was worn over the left shoulder after 1797.

Officers wore epaulettes on their shoulders. In conformity with the army, captains and subalterns had one, on the right shoulder. Field officers had two. In 1797, majors had one gold star on the strap, lieutenant colonels had two, and colonels had three. By an order of 1810, captains were to be distinguished from subalterns by a bullion fringe on the epaulette, while subalterns had plain fringes. Majors had stars on their epaulettes, lieutenant colonels crowns, and full colonels both crowns and stars. Officers wore red sashes round the waist, and a metal gorget was hung from the neck.

Equipment

The rank and file marine wore two leather straps, pipeclayed to make them white. They were crossed over in the centre of the breast, and a plate, bearing the marines' badge, joined them together. One strap supported a black leather cartridge box on the right hip. The other supported the bayonet frog. Marines could be issued with knapsacks, to be slung over the right shoulder, though it seems that haversacks and water canteens were not normal issue, as there is no sign of them among standard store lists.

Working Dress

The full marine uniform was worn for guard duty aboard ship, and for landing parties. It is not clear how much it was worn in battle, by those marines who were helping to operate the great guns.

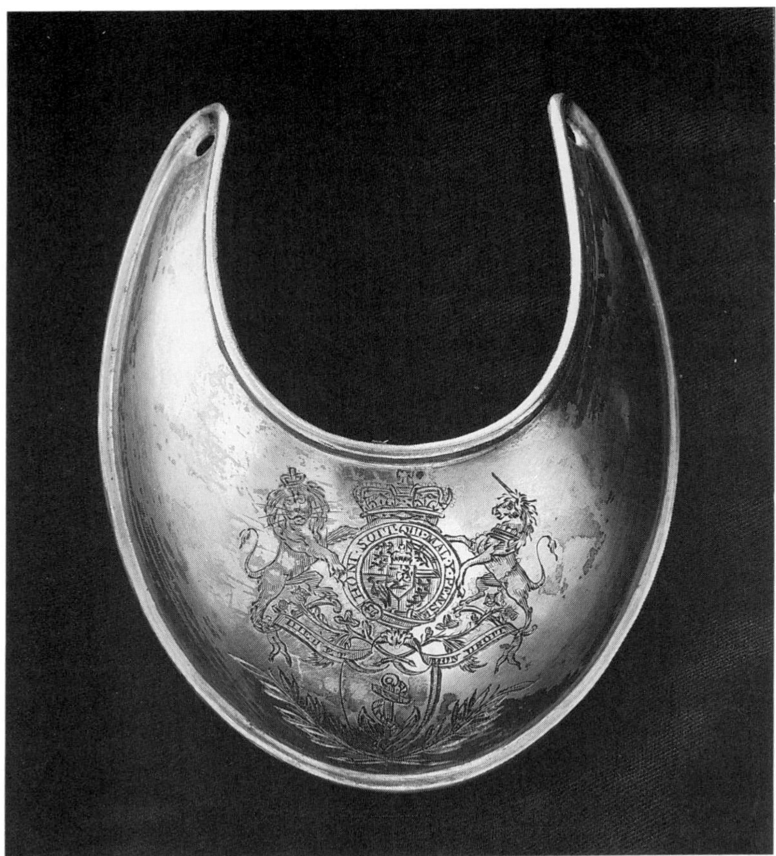

A gorget. This was worn from the neck, and was the main distinction of rank of army and marine officers. Royal Marines Museum

According to one account of Trafalgar, 'In the excitement of the action the marines had thrown off their red jackets, and appeared in their check shirts and blue trousers, there was no distinguishing marine from seamen, all were working like horses.'[7] This seems to suggest that the marines were expected to wear uniform in these circumstances, but did not do so in practice.

There is no doubt that uniform was not worn for ordinary working about the ship. Marines bought slops from the purser in the same way as did the seamen, and an examination of the records shows that they exercised this right fully. The 'marines clothing room' in the orlop was used for storing the uniforms of those marines not allocated for guard duty. Nevertheless, attempts were made to keep the marines differently dressed from the seamen. According to the orders issued on the *Blenheim*, 'The white jacket and trousers to be worn every day by the marines in fine weather between the hours of eight in the morning and eight at night... The new canvas caps given them by the admiral are continually to be kept clean with pipe clay, and never to be worn but with their white jackets.' It was also ordered that 'No NCO or private shall ever appear on deck without his hair being properly combed and tied, his hands and face clean, and his dress as much so as possible.'[8]

Colours

Each of the marine divisions had a set of colours, similar to those of army regiments. In 1801, they had to be replaced because the union with Ireland changed the national flag, and the following year they had to be replaced again, because the facing colour was altered from white to blue. They were mostly used for peacetime parades, but there is some evidence that the Portsmouth colours were carried by the Second Battalion in Spain in 1812.

Part VIII
TECHNIQUES

1 Basic Seamanship

Rope

Most naval rope was made in the ropeworks in the dockyard. Each piece included a single strand in a different colour, either tarred or untarred, to identify it as government property and prevent theft. Most rope, known as 'hawser laid', was three-stranded, but cable-laid cordage was 'made with nine strands, that is to say, the first three stands are laid slack, and then three of them closed together, to make a cable or cablet'. Shroud-laid rope, used for the standing rigging, was four-strand. It had an extra strand known as a 'goke' in the centre of the others; this was one eighth of the strength of the others.[1]

A seaman had several tools to handle the rope. A knife was essential, for obvious reasons. A fid was 'made according to the size of the rope it is intended to open, and is tapered gradually from one end to the other... It is commonly made of hard wood, such as brazil, lignum vitae, & co.'[2] A marline-spike was a smaller version of the same thing, made in iron. Both were used for separating the strands of a rope for splicing. A marline-spike was the sailor's own property, whereas large fids were issued by the boatswain. Another tool issued by the boatswain was the serving mallet. This was shaped like a conventional mallet, but with a groove in the top of the head. It was intended to control the light line used in serving a larger rope.

Running rigging was kept as flexible as possible, and had no tarring or other preparation. Minor ropes of the standing rigging were simply 'well tarred with Swedes, or Stockholm tar, and laid short, so as the tar will sprout out to fill the secret cavities and, after stretched, when in use, to keep the cavities filled with Stockholm tar is the best means of keeping out the tar and not injuring the materials'.[3] More important ropes were 'wormed, parcelled and served'. A light line was twisted round the main rope, filling the gaps between the strands. It was parcelled by wrapping it in paper, coiled round it in the opposite direction. Finally, it was served by wrapping another light line round it, using the serving mallet.

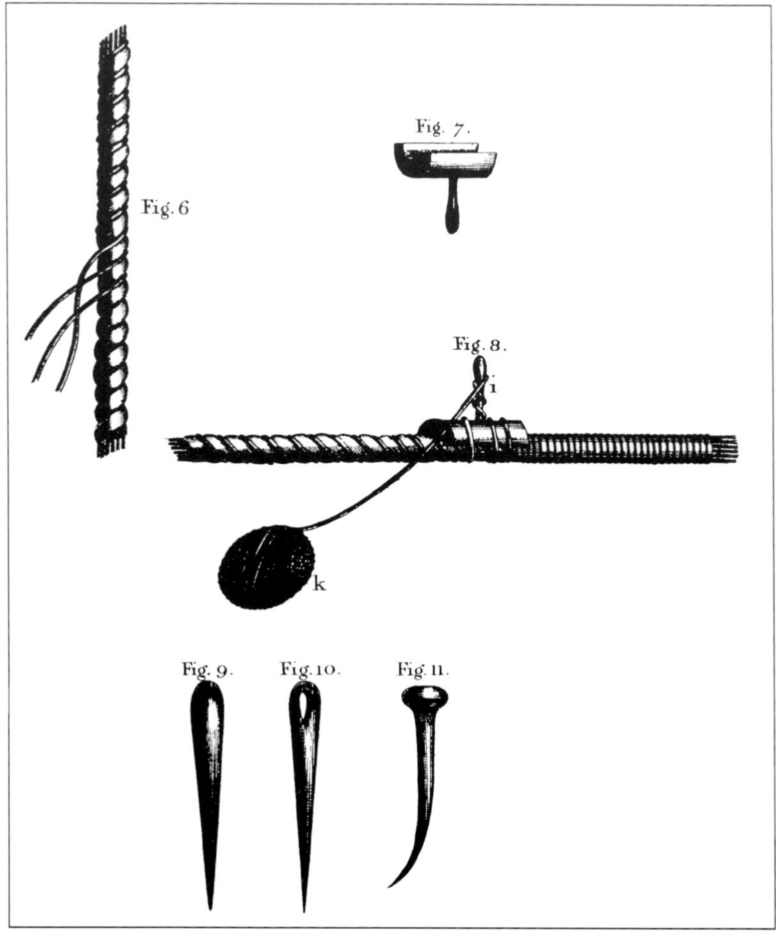

Fig 6, a rope wormed. Fig 7, a serving mallet. Fig 8, serving a rope. Fig 9, a fid. Fig 10, a fid with an eye. Fig 11, a marline spike. From Darcy Lever's *Young Sea Officer's Sheet Anchor*

Knots and Rope Work

Ropework was an essential skill of every seaman. To a large extent,

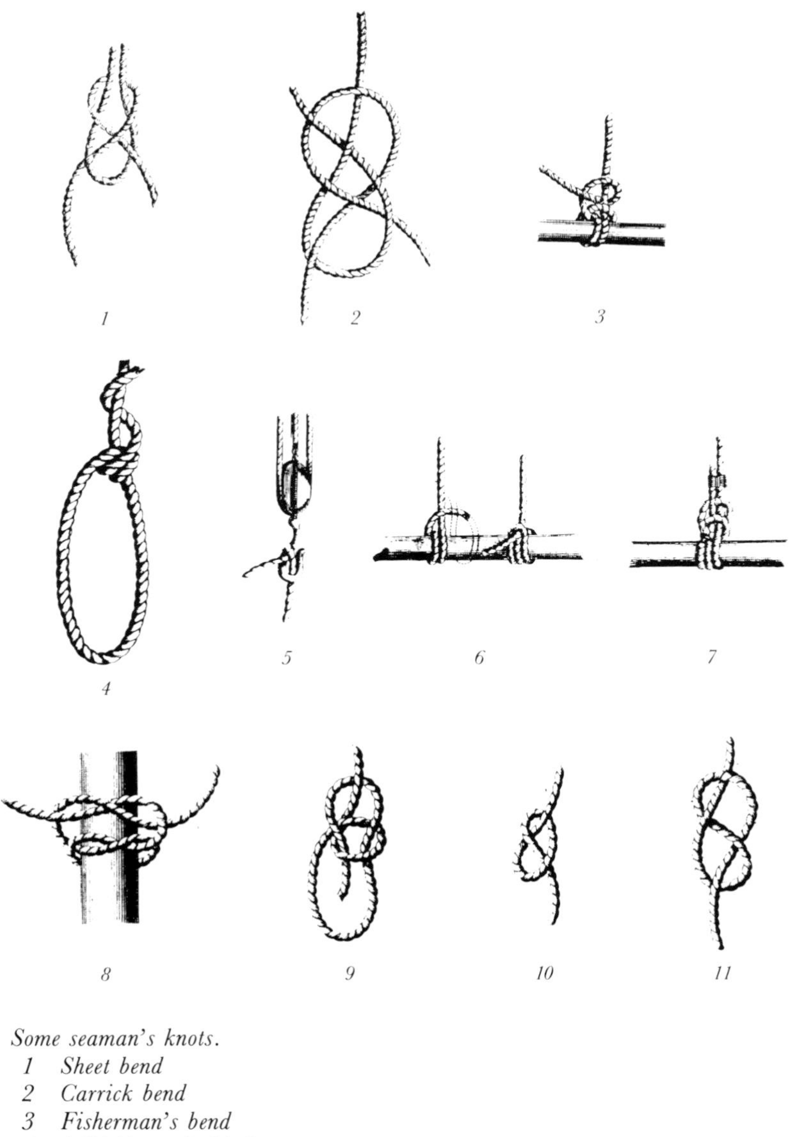

Some seaman's knots.
1 Sheet bend
2 Carrick bend
3 Fisherman's bend
4 Midshipman's hitch
5 Blackwall hitch
6 Magnus hitch
7 Rolling hitch
8 Reef knot
9 Bowline
10 Overhand knot
11 Figure of eight
From Darcy Lever's *Young Sea Officer's Sheet Anchor*

it was taken for granted, and the ability to tie knots or make splices was not specified in the abilities of an able seaman. However, it is quite clear that a skilled mariner could use a wide variety of techniques. Knots can be divided into bends, which are used to tie two ropes together, and hitches which are used to attach a rope to another object. Of bends, D'Arcy Lever and Burney list only the sheet bend and the carrick bend; the fisherman's bend was rather different from the present-day knot of the same name, and in a sense it was misnamed, as it was essentially two half hitches, used to attach a cable to an anchor ring. It could also be used for attaching a rope to a spar. Steel also describes a hawser bend, and a temporary bend.

Hitches were used for attaching a rope to another object, and were slightly more numerous than bends. The best known ones included the midshipman's hitch, used as a tail tackle to augment the purchase of a rope; the Blackwall hitch, used to attach a rope to the hook of a block, and to secure the lanyards of the shrouds; the magnus hitch; and the rolling hitch (which had nothing in common with the modern knot of the same name, and was simply two half hitches used for attaching a rope to a spar). Other knots included the reef knot, which took its name from its use in reefing sail; the bowline knot, used to form a loop in the end of a rope, and originally used in attaching the bowline bridles to the cringles of the sail. Various knots could be used to form a knob in the end of the rope, to prevent it running through a block. The simplest was the overhand knot, followed by the figure of eight.

More permanent knots were formed by unlaying the strands of the rope and fixing them together again in complex ways. Methods of doing this included the wall knot, single or double, with or without a crown; the stopper knot; and the Matthew Walker. The diamond

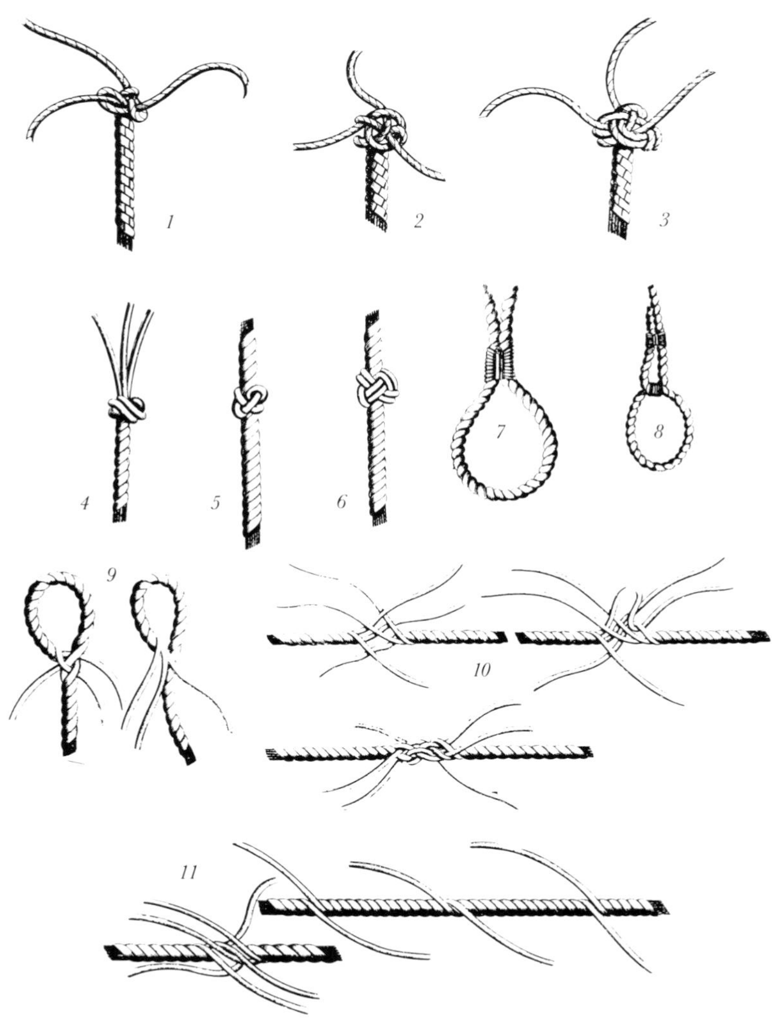

Seizings, splices, etc
1 Single wall knot
2 Wall knot with crown
3 Double wall knot
4 Matthew Walker
5 Single diamond knot
6 Double diamond knot
7 Round seizing
8 Throat seizing
9 Eye splice
10 Short splice
11 Long splice
From Darcy Lever's *Young Sea Officer's Sheet Anchor*

knot, single or double, formed a knob in the middle of the rope instead of the end; it involved splicing two similar ropes together. If the end of a rope was not intended to have a knob, it was whipped — light twine was turned round it, and secured.

Splices were used to join two pieces of rope together, again by unlaying the strands. The most common was the eye splice, which formed a loop in the end of a rope, and was often used for attaching blocks. A short splice used a similar technique to join two pieces of rope together. A long splice also joined two pieces of rope, by unlaying one strand of one, and twisting a strand of the other in its place. It had the advantage that, unlike the short splice, it did not increase the thickness of the rope, thus allowing it to run through blocks.

A loop could also be formed in a rope by seizing; the two parts of the rope were held together, and a light twine twisted round them. In a round seizing, the two parts of the rope ran parallel to one another; in a throat seizing, a bight was formed in the rope, and seized. The loose end was then taken up to the standing part of the rope, and seized to that.

The seaman was also expected to be acquainted with numerous other kinds of ropework; making boarding or hammock netting; making rope ladders for the sides or stern; various works such as gaskets, mats and dolphins. He knew how to fix a running rigging line to the belaying point by means of a system of figure-of-eights, and to coil down its end.

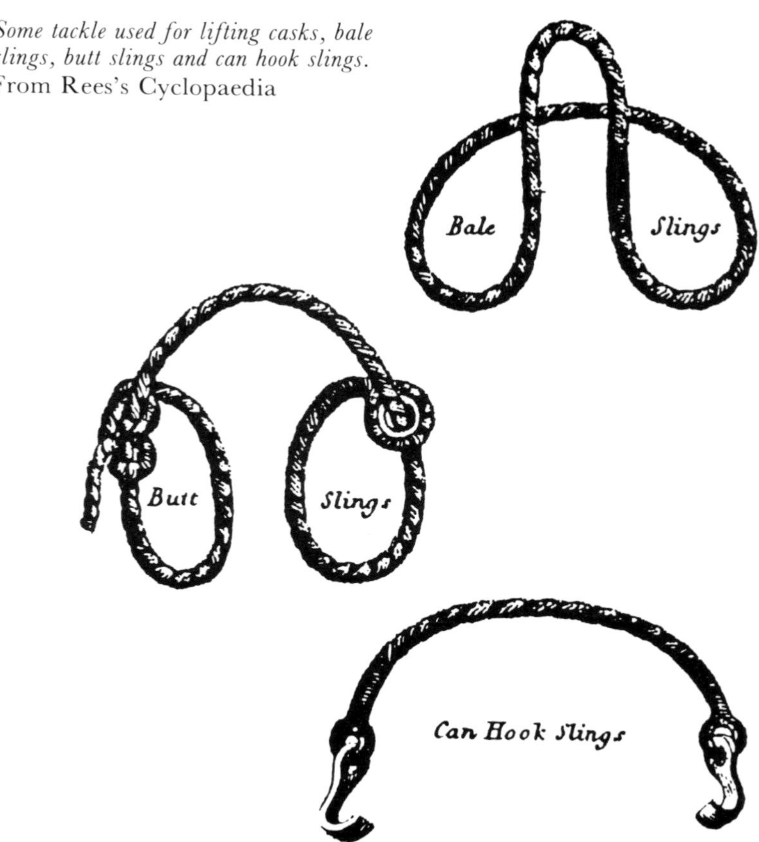

Some tackle used for lifting casks, bale slings, butt slings and can hook slings. From Rees's Cyclopaedia

Lifting Weights

Lifting heavy weights was part of the technique of seamanship, and Captain Gower wrote, 'It is extremely necessary that every seaman should be so far acquainted with the mechanical powers as to be able to calculate the force of those purchases he is continually applying.'[4] The seaman used the handspike as a lever to traverse guns, and the capstain bar as another kind of lever. A simple whip purchase used only one single block attached to the object to be lifted. The men hauling it had to be at a high level, and this gave a mechanical advantage of two — in other words, it doubled the power of the men hauling on it. More complex arrangements were used more often; a single and a double tackle, known as a gun tackle, was also used for lifting weights, and gave a mechanical advantage of four. As with all systems of this sort, it increased the time needed in the same proportion as it increased mechanical advantage. Hauling on a rope attached to an arrangement of blocks was known as bowsing, or hoisting.

Sailors normally hauled on rope by passing it from hand to hand. When more strength was needed, men would reach up the rope with both hands, and then lift their feet off the deck so that their full weight was applied. If yet more strength was needed, 'swigging' was used. According to Gower, 'What is called swigging off, that is pulling at right angles to a rope, is at first a very great power, but it decreases as the rope is pulled out of the straight line.'[5] The technique was for one man to hold the rope tight, turning it under a belaying pin or some such object; another man, or group of men, would pull the rope out from its straight line, and then place their weight on it to bring more of it down to the belaying pin.

Heavy weights could be brought on board, or lifted out of the hold, by rigging tackles from the mastheads (using the pendants provided as part of the standing rigging), or from the yardarms. Another way of raising or lowering casks was by the use of a 'parbuckle' — this was 'formed by passing the middle of a rope round a post or ring, or under a boat's thwart; the two parts of the rope are then passed under the two quarters of the cask, bringing the two ends back again over it, which both being hauled or slackened together, either raise or lower the barrel, and co, as may be required.'[6] The cask had to be hauled against a reasonably flat, smooth surface, and two vertical rails were provided on the sides of most ships.

One of the more difficult tasks was hoisting in live animals, especially large ones, such as bullocks. Captain Griffiths recommended 'Embarking them may be facilitated much, by *mild* means. Do not drive, or hoot, or make a noise with them, but be as quiet as possible . . . Always sling them; to hoist them in by the horns is a bad way.'[7]

Raising and Lowering Yards

Yards were hoisted by the seamen of the ship, and the upper yards were often taken down again in bad weather, to reduce topweight. The fore and main lower yards were quite simple. They were hoisted by means of their jeers, and rarely taken down again at sea. The spritsail yards were slightly more difficult, and had to be carefully manoeuvred into position, but, again, they did not have to be taken down at sea. The upper yards, for the topsails, topgallants and royals, had to be lifted almost vertically to pass them through the rigging. One man stood on the crosstrees, another in the shrouds, to guide the yard through. It was then levelled in position, and attached to the mast by means of its truss. Upper yards were designed to slide up and down the mast, but this only brought it to the level of the head of the mast below. If an upper yard had to be sent down in a hurry, the sail was furled rather than un-bent, and the yard was lowered down through the rigging.

Care of Sails

Though there were specialised sailmakers on board all ships, able seamen were expected to help when necessary, and the ability to 'sew a seam' was one of the qualities expected of an able seaman aboard the *Blake*.[8] The care and repair of sails demanded specialised tools — the sailmakers' palm, which as 'a flat round piece of iron . . . It is sewed on to a piece of leather or canvas, having a hole for the thumb to go through, which encircles the hand so that the iron, when used is against the palm.'[9] Other tools included the thimble, which served the same purpose, but was not fixed in canvas; a hook for extending

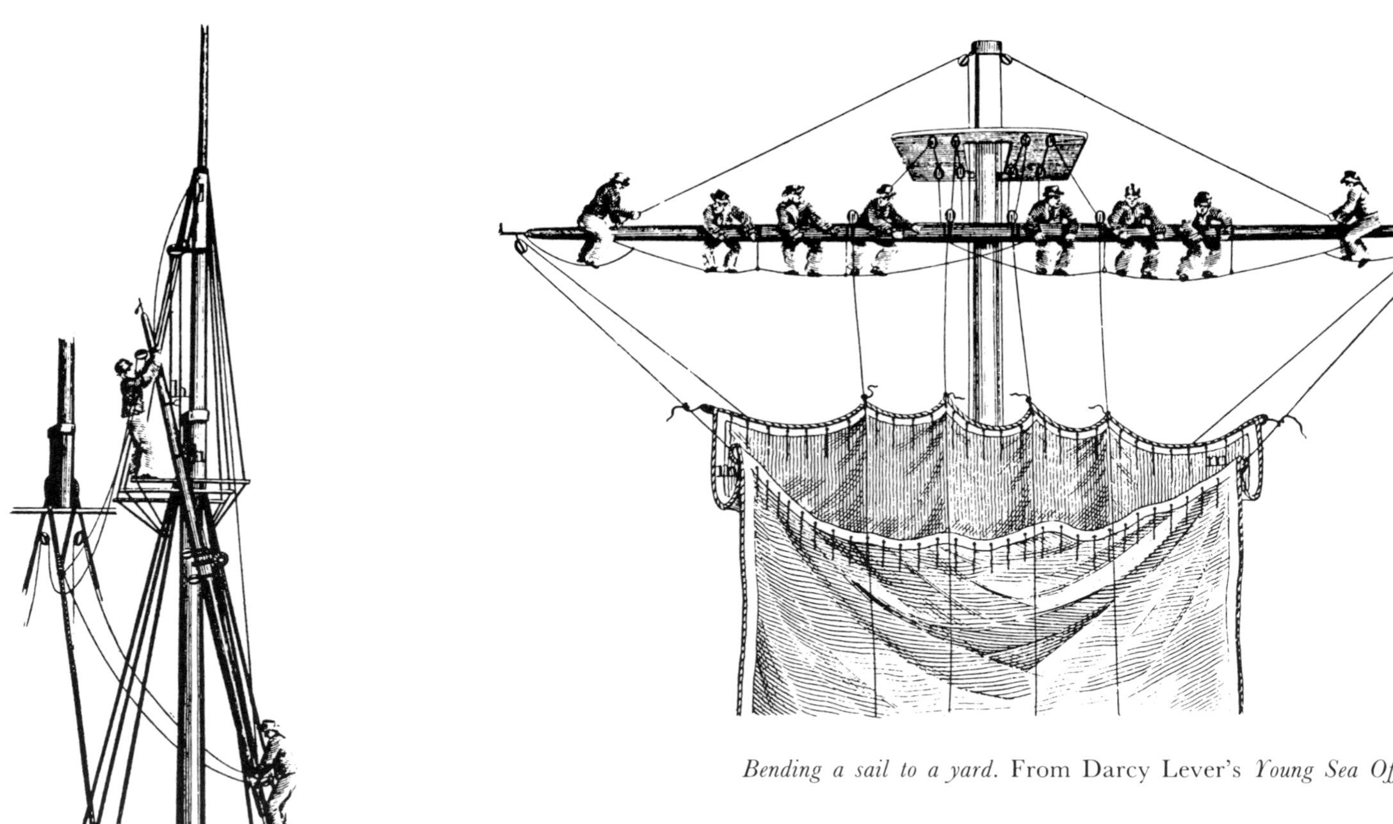

Bending a sail to a yard. From Darcy Lever's *Young Sea Officer's Sheet Anchor*

Raising a topgallant yard. From Darcy Lever's *Young Sea Officer's Sheet Anchor*

the relevant part of the sail and various needles for different kinds of work.

Sails were sewn with 'the best English-made twine of three threads, spun 360 fathoms to the pound, and made from one hundred and eight to one hundred and sixteen stitches in every yard in length.'[10] Sails were not normally covered with any preservative, though there were some who recommended this. When not in use, they were stored in the sail rooms on the orlop deck, carefully dried and protected from damp.

Bending Sails

Yards were usually hoisted without the sails attached. When it came to fit or bend a lower sail to the yard, a line of men was stationed along the yard, ready to receive the sail. The weight of the latter was taken up by means of ropes attached to its reef cringles, head earrings, and along the leech of the sail, and then passed through blocks on the mast and yard. Men on deck hauled on these ropes, until the head of the sail reached the level of the yard. The men aloft then tied the sail to the yard, by means of the ropes provided. For upper sails, it was usually necessary to put the sail into some kind of bundle, with the head showing. This was passed up through the rigging, and attached to the yard. Sometimes it was hoisted up in a bundle, and then laid out in the crosstrees.[11]

Setting Sails

When setting square sails, the topmen took off the gaskets which held the sail furled to the yard. The men on deck below hauled on the sheets to extend the sail, while the topmen overhauled the clewlines, buntlines, etc, through the blocks along the yard. If it was an upper sail, this would have the effect of hauling the clews of the sail out to the ends of the lower yards. The topmen could then get off the yard, and the men on deck would haul on the ties and halyard (in the case of an upper sail) to bring the yard up to its working height. The sail was then 'sheeted home' — the sheets were pulled tight, and then the braces were adjusted to give the sail the optimum angle to the wind. In stronger winds it might be necessary to raise the yard before letting the sail out, as there would be too much pressure on the sail otherwise.

Staysails were set rather differently. They ran like curtains along a stay, and were furled at the mast ahead, or on the bowsprit in the case of jibs. The downhaul was freed off, the men at the crosstrees or on the bowsprit unfurled the sail, while men on deck hauled on the halyard to raise it. The sheets were tightened, and the sail began to draw. The mizzen sail, usually a gaff sail in this period, was different again. The brails which held it up to the gaff and mast were let off, and the sheet was hauled out, and then set at the appropriate angle.

Taking in Sail

A sail could be furled, or taken in completely; or it could be reefed, to reduce its area. Reefing was intended to 'reduce the surface of the sail in proportion to the increase of the wind'.[12] The weight of the upper part of the sail, above the line of reef points, was taken up by the men on deck hauling on the reef tackles of the sail; these were attached to the leeches of the sail, at the level of the various bands of reef points. The topmen were spread along the yard, and took hold of the reef lines of the sail as they came into reach. If a man was working in the middle of the sail, and it was intended to go straight to the second or third reef without using the first, he might have to grab the first reef to haul part of the sail to him, and then reach for the second reef. Having got hold of one of the reef lines on the appropriate level, each man would then find its other end on the other side of the sail. He would tie the two together over the top of the yard, using a reef knot. Meanwhile, the reef tackle would be pulled tight, serving to stretch the head of the sail along the yard.

If a sail had to be taken in completely, it was furled. The men on deck hauled the sail up to the yards by means of clewlines, buntlines, and slablines. If the job had to be done quickly, for example when coming to anchor in light winds, the sail might be left there for some time, as it would not have much effect. However, it would eventually have to be furled properly; topmen would be spread along the yard, each holding a light, short piece of rope known as a 'gasket'. Together the topmen would pull the loose portions of the sail towards themselves, and bundle it up as tightly as possible. They would then tie the gaskets round the sail and the yard, to hold it tight.

There was some controversy about the best way of taking a sail in

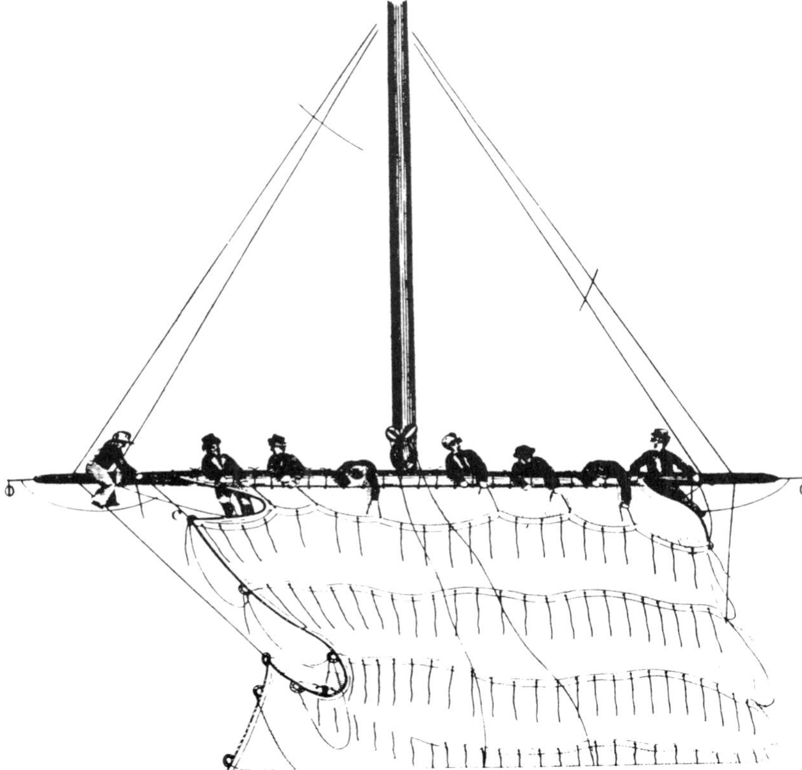

Seamen on a yard taking in sail. From Darcy Lever's *Young Sea Officer's Sheet Anchor*

Taking in a studding sail. From Darcy Lever's *Young Sea Officer's Sheet Anchor*

Men working on a yard. The studding sail boom has been lashed up to keep it out of the way of the seamen. The National Maritime Museum

quickly in a strong wind. William Falconer wrote, 'And he who strives the tempest to disarm/Will never first embrail the lee yardarm.' In other words, the brails on the weather side of the ship had to be pulled tight first, in order to take more of the wind out of the sail. However, there were some who disagreed with this, and it was suggested that it was quicker to brail the lee side first in an emergency, though often at risk to the sail itself.[13] Taking in sail could always be helped by turning the ship slightly into the wind; according to Captain Griffiths, 'A judicious luff at the precise moment of giving the order 'shorten sail' will materially facilitate the performance.'[14]

Setting Studding Sails

Studding sails were used only in very light winds, to give the ship steerage way. They were extended by means of booms pivoting from the ships sides, and from other booms which extended from the yards, passing through rings above the yards. Once the booms were rigged out, the four corners of the sail were put in position by hauling on the appropriate lines. A studding sail was taken in by slacking off these lines, and then hauling the lower inner corner, the clew, of the sail towards the deck, or the top or crosstrees. It was then folded up and sent below.

Going Aloft

The only way of going aloft was via the shrouds, standing on the ratlines attached to them. A seaman would climb out onto the channels, which required some exertion in itself on many ships. He would invariably choose the windward side, as the shrouds on that side were tightened under pressure, and the wind would tend to blow him onto the shrouds, rather than into the sea. He would next climb up the futtock shrouds, for the 'lubber's hole', in the centre of the top, was 'so termed from a supposition that a *lubber*, not caring to trust himself up the futtock shrouds, will prefer that way of getting into the top'.[15] He then climbed up the topmast and topgallant shrouds as necessary, and when he reached the appropriate yard he placed his feet on the foot rope under it, and held onto the yard itself.

Captains took pride in the speed with which their topmen could go aloft, and expected them down quickly after completion of the exercise. Seamen could find other ways of getting down, besides the shrouds — perhaps sliding down a backstay, or finding another route among the rigging ropes.

Steering

All able seamen were expected to be able to steer the ship, and ordinary seamen were trained to the required standard. Usually, two men operated the wheel; the main helmsman, who stood on the weather side and controlled the movement; and the lee helmsman, who was much less skilled, and applied his strength only, standing on the lee side. There were three ways of steering the ship, according to the circumstances as decided by the officer of the watch — by compass, by a visible object such as a landmark or another ship, or 'by the wind'. Compass courses were used when the ship was out of sight of land, or strong tidal streams had to be taken into account. According to Gower, 'The helmsman must not pore over the compass, but alternately watch the compass, and the motion of the vessel's head passing the clouds, the sea, or any objects more fixed than the compass, which may happen to present themselves to view.'[16] Steering on an object was often easier, except that the helmsman's view was quite restricted; in such cases it was sometimes necessary for a quartermaster or pilot to stand in the rigging shouting helm orders.
Steering by the wind was done when the ship was sailing as far as possible into the wind. The helmsman did his best to keep all the sails filled, keeping a careful eye on one of the sails, usually the topgallant or royal, which would begin to rustle first if he sailed too close. In these circumstances, the helmsman controlled the course, and reported what he was able to achieve to the officer of the watch. If he came too close to the wind, and failed to correct it in time, he could put the ship in quite serious difficulties. Likewise, if running before the wind in heavy seas, inattention by the helmsman could cause the ship to 'broach to', and risk being struck broadside on by strong winds and heavy seas.

The helm was probably quite slow to react, and there would be several seconds before moving the helm and the ship starting to turn. Once started, the turn had to be stopped by moving the wheel some way in the opposite direction. A well-trimmed ship had a natural tendency to head up into wind, unless corrected by the rudder — that is, she carried 'weather helm'. The helmsman did much of his steering by feel. 'As the vessel comes-to against the helm, it will feel heavier; and the wind coming more forward will appear stronger; on the contrary, as she goes off and gives way to the power of the helm, it eases in the hand but by the winds drawing aft, it appears to lessen. These circumstances, to an attentive and nice observer, mark the motion of the vessel sooner than the compass.'

2 Ship Handling

Principles of Sailing

The theory of sailing was studied by men such as Bougier in France, who published his major work in 1757; and by Gower of the East India Company, who published his *Treatise on Seamanship* in 1806. Such theoretical works were known to some of the more intellectual officers, but they had relatively little effect on actual practice. Works by Steel and D'Arcy Lever were more practical, and had more influence on the training of young officers.

According to modern theory, a sail operates like an aeroplane wing. The wind strikes it at a certain angle to the yard (about 35 degrees in the case of a sail of 1800), and passes at different rates on each side of the sail. This produces a force which can be divided into two components — one at right angles to the yard, the other parallel to the yard, and therefore having no effect on the ship's motion. The force at right angles, can in turn, be divided into two forces: one pushing the ship forward, the other pushing her sideways, and causing 'leeway'. The effect of the leeway would be much greater if the yard was braced round to about 45 degrees or less to the line of the keel; it would be equal to the forward force in strength.

If the wind was directly behind the sail, the position was rather different. The aerofoil of the sail was now stalled, and it operated in a rather different, and slightly less efficient way. On the other hand, this only happened when the wind was more or less directly behind the ship, and there was, therefore, no leeway.

The centre of effort of a single sail is the point at which the effect of that sail is felt — usually in the centre of the sail. The centre of effort of the whole rig is the summation of these sails, depending, of course, on which sails are set. The centre of lateral resistance is that point in the underwater hull where the effect of the sidways movement

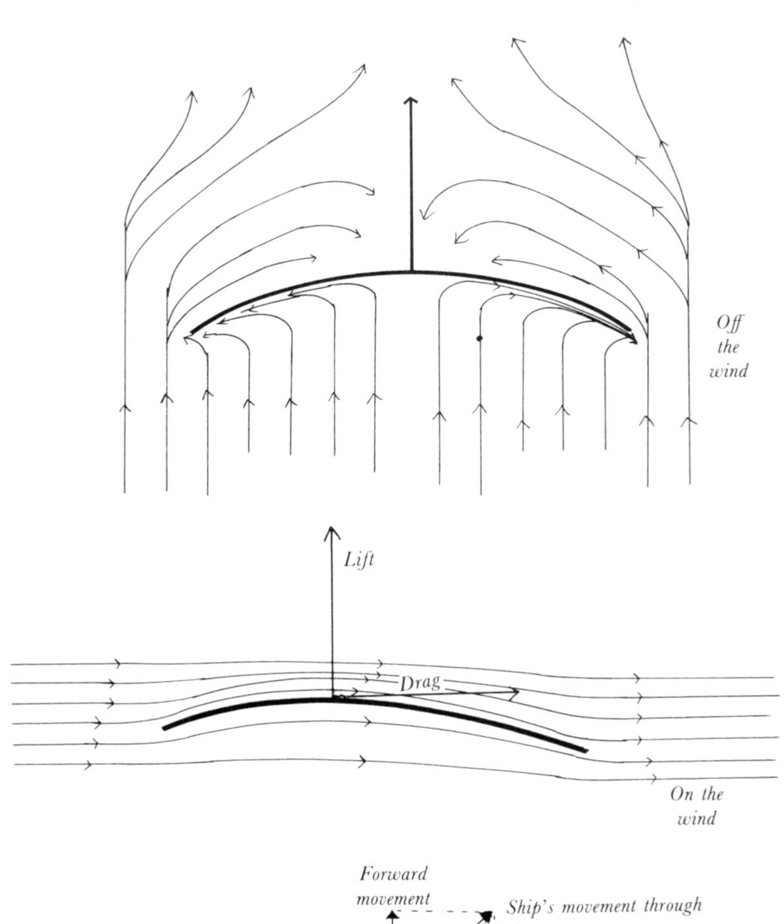

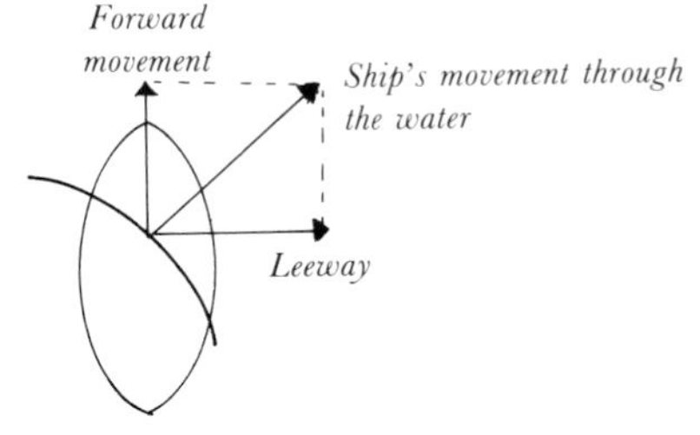

The principles of sailing. Off the wind, there is greater pressure behind the sail than ahead of it, and this creates the forward motion. On the wind, the sail acts like an aircraft's wing, creating a force approximately at right angles to itself, which divides into leeway and forward motion.

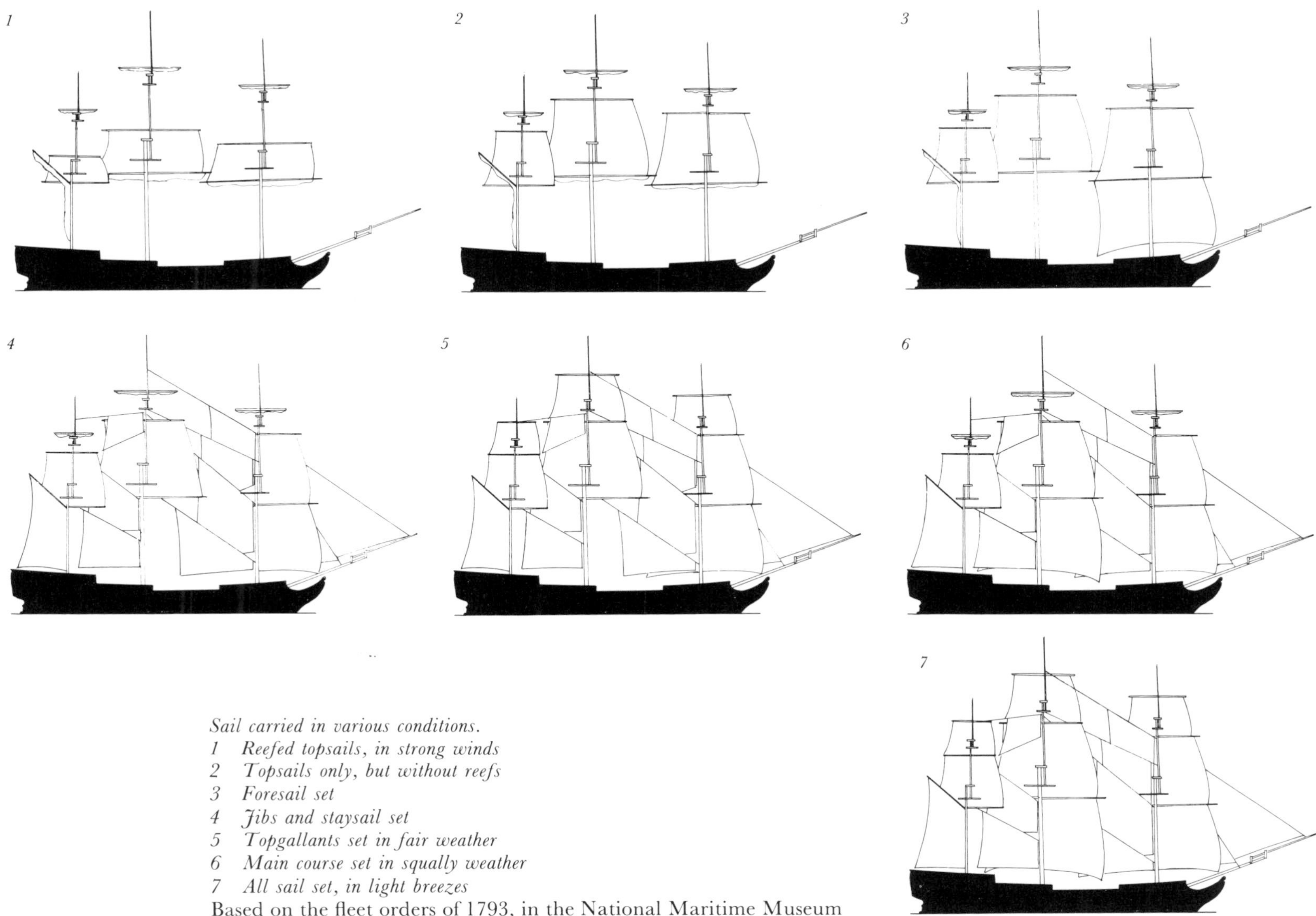

Sail carried in various conditions.
1 Reefed topsails, in strong winds
2 Topsails only, but without reefs
3 Foresail set
4 Jibs and staysail set
5 Topgallants set in fair weather
6 Main course set in squally weather
7 All sail set, in light breezes
Based on the fleet orders of 1793, in the National Maritime Museum

produced by the sails is felt. Seamen of the time did not use these terms, though the concepts were understood by the more scientifically minded. If the centre of effort was directly over the centre of lateral resistance, then the rig would be perfectly balanced and no helm would be needed to keep her on course. If the centre of effort was just ahead of the centre of lateral resistance, then the head of the ship would be pushed off the wind. The converse, with the centre of effort behind the centre of lateral resistance and the bows tending to turn into the wind, was far more normal. The helm had to be continually turned slightly to keep the ship on course, and this was known as weather helm. Part of the art of the seaman was to keep the rig balanced in different circumstances, with sails being set or taken in, sheeted in or braced round, according to circumstances.

Amount of Sail Carried

According to Admiral Beaufort, a man-of-war in this period needed light airs — perhaps 2 or 3 knots — to give steerage way. When the wind reached about 4 knots (about Force 2 in the Beaufort scale), 'a well conditioned man-of-war with all sail set and 'clean full' would go in smooth water', 1 or 2 knots. A gentle breeze of 7 to 10 knots would give the ship 3 or 4 knots of speed, while a 'moderate breeze' of up to 16 knots would give the ship 5 to 6 knots. In a 'fresh breeze' of 17 to 21 knots, there would be 'moderate waves, taking a more pronounced long form; many white horses are formed. Chance of some spray'. A ship in a chase would still keep all set in these conditions, including royals; but, in other situations, sail would be reduced slightly. If the wind increased to a strong breeze of over 22 knots, the royals would certainly be taken in, and the topsails and topgallants would be single reefed. Above 22 knots, a 'near gale', 'Sea heaps up and white foam from breaking waves begins to be blown in streaks along the direction of the wind'. The topgallants would be furled, and the topsail and jibs would be double reefed. In a gale of 34 to 40 knots, the topsails would be triple reefed, and above that, in a strong gale, the ship would carry close reefed topsails and courses. A storm of 48 to 55 knots was 'that which she could scarcely bear with close reefed main topsail and reefed foresail'. By this time, there would be 'very high waves with long overhanging crests. The resulting foam in great patches is blown in dense white streaks along the direction of the wind... The tumbling of the sea becomes heavy and shock like.' Sail would be reduced to close reefed main topsail and reefed foresail, and any idea of making progress to a specific destination would be abandoned. With winds of 56 to 63 knots, the ship would carry only her storm staysails, and in a hurricane of 64 knots or over, the ship would carry no canvas. In these circumstances, 'The air is completely filled with foam and spray. Sea completely white with driving spray; visibility very seriously affected.'[1] However, practical sailors did not learn these circumstances by rote; they reduced or increased sail according to the feel and performance of the ship, attempting to predict squalls and storms.

Another scheme for matching sail to the wind was provided in the fleet orders of 1793. Ships would start off in heavy weather with topsails only. As the wind reduced, they would then set the foresail, and next the jib and staysails; then the topgallants in fair weather, or the main sail in squally weather; then the main, if not already set, or the topgallants.[2]

One important effect of stronger winds was the amount to which the ship made leeway. According to Burney, a ship close hauled with topsails close reefed would make two points, or $22\frac{1}{2}$ degrees, of leeway. If the wind caused the topsails to be taken in, she could make four points, or 45 degrees. In extreme conditions when the ship had taken in all her canvas and was 'trying a-hull', she would make up to seven points of leeway, or nearly 80 degrees.[3] In such circumstances, there was little control over her course, and she was in grave danger if the wind was pushing her towards the shore.

Points of Sailing

When a ship was sailing as near as possible to the direction of the wind, she was said to be 'close hauled'. The yards were braced up so that the yardarms were as far aft as possible on the leeward side, and as far forward as possible on the windward side. The tacks were used to hold the weather clews of the courses forward, and the bowlines did the same job for the leeches of the larger square sails. The shrouds limited the extent to which the yards could be braced round, and the sails would not operate efficiently at an angle of less than about 35 degrees to the true wind; so, at best, a square-rigged ship was expected to sail six points, or $67\frac{1}{2}$ degrees, from the direction of the wind. Even so, the wind was pushing the hull sideways so that she was making at least a point, or $11\frac{1}{4}$ degrees of leeway, and she was only progressing seven points off the wind. She would make slow speed, unless the helmsman was ordered to keep her 'full and bye'. 'The situation of a ship with regard to the wind, when she is close-hauled, and sailing in such a manner as to steer neither too nigh the direction of the wind, nor to deviate to leeward . . . ' To bring her too close to the wind would cause the wind to come mainly on the fore side of her sails, cause them to shiver, and 'render the effort of the wind precarious and ineffectual'.[4]

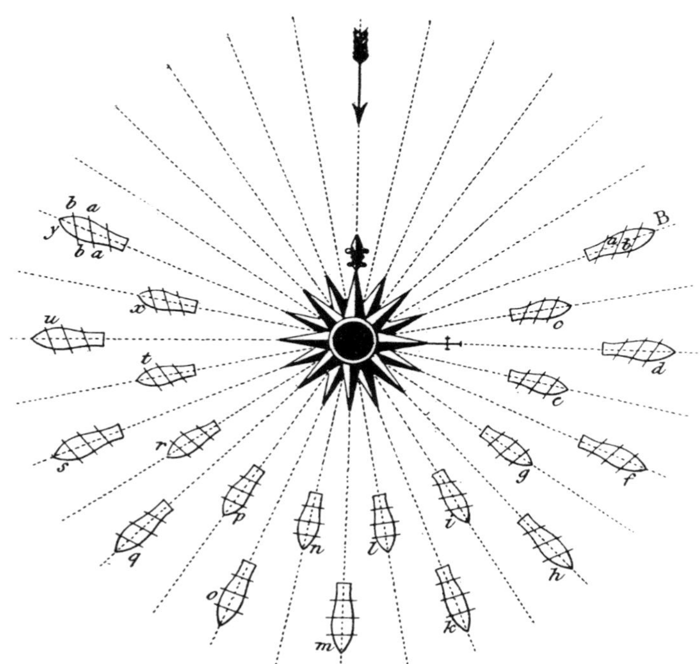

Points of sailing. The direction of the wind is shown by the arrow at the top. The ships marked b and y are close hauled. Then they are, in order, one point large (c and x); two points large, or wind on the beam (u and d); three points large, or one point abaft the beam (e and t); four points large, or two points abaft the beam (f and s); four points large, or two points abaft the beam (r and g); six points large, or on the quarter (q and h); with the wind three points on the quarter (p and i); two points on the quarter (o and k); one point on the quarter (n and l); sailing before the wind, or with the wind right aft (m). From Burney's Dictionary

If the wind was more favourable, the ship was able to sail 'large'. The tacks and bowlines were no longer needed, and the yards were braced round, so that they became closer to right angles with the line of the ship. Sailing with the wind on the quarter was the best point of sailing with most ships; little or no leeway was made, and the sails did not mask one another, as they did when the wind was directly aft.

When the wind was coming from behind, the ship was said to be 'sailing before the wind'. 'In this position the yards are laid at right angles with the ship's length; the staysails being entirely useless, are hauled down, and the mainsail is drawn up in the brails that the foresail may operate; a measure which considerably facilitates the steerage, or effort of the helm.'[5] Even so, the fore topsail and topgallant were masked and had had little effect, except to prevent the ship from 'broaching to', or deviating too far from her course.

Conning the Ship

The officer of the watch was responsible for trimming the sails of the ship, by ordering the seamen to operate the sheets, tacks, braces and bowlines as required. He might take further responsibility, though most captains would prefer to take charge themselves if major alterations of course were required, or tacking or wearing were necessary. The direct supervision of the helm was in the hands of the quartermaster, a petty officer. Both he and the officer of the watch issued various orders to the helmsman as necessary; *Hard-a-port* was 'the order to put the helm close to the larboard, or left side of the ship'; *Hard-a-lee* was the order 'to put the helm close to the lee side of the ship', while *Hard-a-weather* or *Hard-up* meant the opposite: to *bear away* from the wind.[6] Other orders were *Down with the helm*, which also meant putting the wheel to the lee side; *Ease*, or *Bear up the helm*, to cause the ship to go more large, with wind more behind her; and to *Port* or *Starboard helm*.[7] Orders could also be given in relation to the wind. For example, to *Luff* was to sail the ship closer to the wind, perhaps to take some wind out of the sails and make it easier for the men on deck to set them. *Keep your luff* was 'The order to the helmsman to keep nearer to the wind'.[8] *No near* or *No nearer* was the order 'to steer the ship no higher to the direction of the wind than the sails will operate to advance the ship in her course'.[9] *Thus* was 'an order to the helmsman to keep the ship in her present situation when sailing with a scant wind; so that she may not approach too near the direction of the wind, and thereby shiver her sails, nor fall to leeward, and run further out of her course.'[10]

Tacking

Tacking has two slightly different meanings. In a general sense it can mean the whole process of working the ship to windward, zig-zagging into the wind — this technique was also known as 'beating

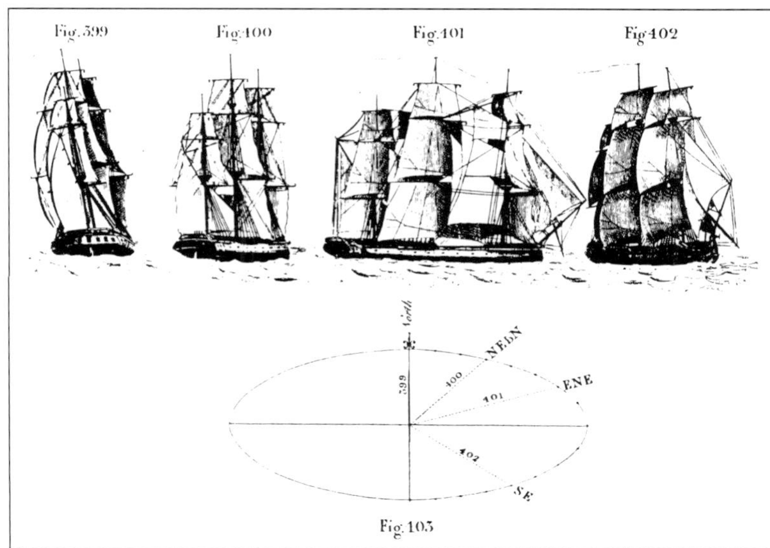

Tacking by the old method, according to Darcy Lever.

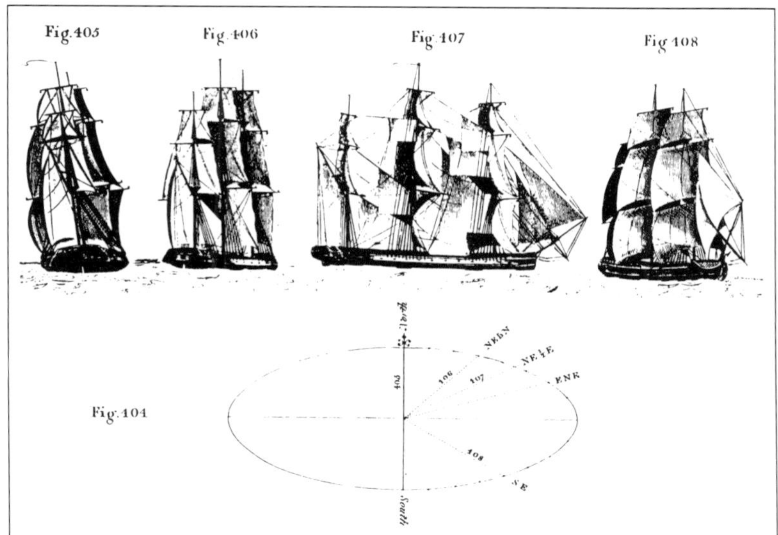

Tacking by the speedier method.

to windward'. More specifically, it refers to the actual process of turning the ship so that the wind is on the other side, by pointing her head into the wind. Also, a ship could be said to be on a specific tack — if the wind was coming over her port side she was on the port tack, and on the starboard tack if it was coming from the other side.

Tacking through the wind began with the officer in command ordering the seamen to prepare the various ropes — having 'the weather braces stretched along, the lee tacks, weather sheets and lee bowlines hauled through the slack'. The order was given to turn the helm to bring the ship windward, and the officer shouted 'The helm's a-lee, fore sheet, fore top bowline, jib and staysail sheets let go.' The jibs would contribute nothing to the manoeuvre, so they were either taken down, or allowed to flap about. As the ship came closer to the wind, the foresails tended to push the head of the ship in the desired direction. Next, the order was given, 'Off tacks and sheets' for the sheets and tack of the mainsail to be let go, along with the sheets of the staysails, so that the sails were allowed to flap about. As the ship faced the eye of the wind, the officer ordered, 'Mainsail haul', and the yards were braced round to the other side. The main and mizzensails were now tending to push the stern in the opposite direction from that of the bow, and thus aiding the turning motion. At this stage, the wind was possibly pushing the ship astern, and the helmsman often had to alter the helm to the other side. When the ship had passed through the wind, the order was 'Let go and haul' for the foresails to be braced round, and the ship to begin to sail on its new course. The tacks, braces and sheets were trimmed to find the optimum position on the new tack, and the helmsman tried to find how close he could sail to the wind.

A more modern method, recommended by Lever in 1808, began in the same way, with the appopriate ropes being prepared and the helm put over; though, in this case, the ship was turned more gradually into the wind, as the old method of putting it hard over had caused too much drag and slowed the ship down. When the ship came close to the wind, the sheets and tacks of the main and mizzensails were let go, to reduce sternway. Just before passing through the wind, the order 'Mainsail haul' was given, rather earlier than in the old method; it was easier to haul in this position. The order 'Let go and haul' was given when the wind was about 45 degrees off the bow, and soon afterwards the ship was able to sail on the new tack.[11]

Wearing

Tacking was only possible when the ship had enough speed to carry her through the wind, and the waves were not large enough to force her head off. Otherwise, wearing (or 'veering') was used as an alternative. Wearing differed from tacking in that the ship's stern, rather than her head, was put through the wind. It had the advantage that it could be done in almost any conditions of wind and sea; its disadvantage was that it needed much more time and space than tacking.

Wearing began with the helm being put hard over to turn the ship away from the wind. On a standard three-masted rig, the main course was useless and was brailed up to the yard, though the main topsails and topgallants were kept set. The gaff mizzensail was also brailed up, and the mizzen staysails were taken in. The mizzen topsail was kept up, but it was shivered; that is, it was continually turned as the ship came round, so that the yard was pointing directly into the wind, which passed on both sides of the sail, causing it to have no effect. Thus all the effort of the sails came from forward of the centre of effort of the hull, and helped to bring the ship around. When the wind was astern it was time to fill the mizzen topsail again,

A ship wearing, with the fore sails braced round to provide most of the drive. From Serres's, *Liber Nauticus*

One method of heaving to, with the fore sails backed to counteract the main and mizzensails. From Serres's, *Liber Nauticus*

Another method of heaving to, with the main topsail backed to counteract the fore and mizzen topsails. From Serres's, *Liber Nauticus*

and the ship was then brought round further towards the wind on the other tack. The yards were braced round as appropriate, and the mizzensail and staysails were re-set. A ship would have to turn through 20 points of the compass when wearing, or 225 degrees; compared with 12 points, or 135 degrees, when tacking.

Heaving-to

Heaving-to, or lying-to, was a means of holding a ship relatively stationary in water. It was done for various reasons: to allow other ships to catch up, to heave the lead, to launch boats or communicate with other ships, to keep station on blockade service, to ride out a storm, or to engage an enemy. Sail was often reduced to some extent, perhaps with the courses being clewed up, or the royals taken in. The other sails were arranged so that some were backing and filling. The sails on one mast were therefore braced round to the other tack; either the foresails or the mainsails could be braced round in this way, according to which tack the ship was to be put on after it resumed its course. The helm was put down, tending to turn the ship into the wind. The most common method was to take in or brail up the courses, topgallants and royals, and to back the main topsail, with the mizzen and fore topsails filled.

Station Keeping

Keeping a fleet in close order was always difficult, especially under sail. In fact it was not attempted very often. Convoys sailed in quite open order most of the time, as did fleets. In general, the officer of the watch was not expected to keep his ship continually a few feet from the next ship, especially at night, after the watch was set, when it would have been even more difficult and wearing on the crew. Line of battle was formed for exercise, or on the immediate onset of battle. Under the more daring admirals, especially Nelson, the line was still not a fetish, and station keeping was not so important. However, under an older admiral, such as Howe, things were different, and as the fleet sailed into action on the First of June many ships had to take great care to sail trim to avoid falling behind, or running into the ship ahead. The *Culloden* 'made and shortened sail occasionally to keep our station in the line. Backed the mizzen topsail occasionally.' The flagship *Queen Charlotte's* log recorded 'Up mainsail and backed the mizzen topsail to keep our station, the ships ahead shortening sail. Filled and backed occasionally, as did the ships ahead.'[12] Backing the mizzen topsail, by bracing it round to the opposite tack, was a common method of slowing a ship down slightly, and it was perhaps one of the most important functions of that sail. When tacking, a fleet in close order went about in succession; each ship tacked one after the other, on reaching a certain point.

The fleet orders of 1793 gave some guidance on station keeping. Close order meant: 'From 1½ to 2 cables length, or a quarter of a mile, according to the state of the weather, that the ships are to keep asunder.' Open order meant: '3 to 4 cables or half a mile distant, according to the state of the weather.' Ships sailed under topsails alone when before the wind in close order, and the general principle guiding the fleet leader was 'to suit the proportion of sail he carries, that the worst sailing ships of the fleet may be enabled to preserve their stations, and the best sailing ships always kept under command'. In order to find the sails needed in any situation, captains were to 'endeavour to obtain, by repeated observation and experiment, a perfect knowledge of the proportion of sail required for suiting their rate of sailing respectively, to that of the admiral's ship, under the various changes of circumstances and weather incident to cruising service'.[13]

Working in a Narrow Channel

Sailing warships spent most of their time at sea or in relatively open anchorages, and rarely entered narrow harbours; there was always a danger of being wind-bound there for a long period, during which the ship was tactically useless. However, it was necessary for ships to enter dockyards from time to time, including those such as Deptford, Chatham and Woolwich which were some way up river. Ships making such journeys would certainly wait for a favourable time, which would involve a delay of only a few hours. They might also wait for a favourable wind, which could take weeks, especially since both the Thames and the Medway were winding rivers. A ship could be towed or kedged, using boats or anchors. Alternatively, a ship could use the tide, and what wind was available, to make the best possible progress. A ship could drift down with the tide, dropping anchor when it was unfavourable, but steerage way was necessary for this, which required some wind. If it was unfavourable, the sails could be backed to give some control over the ship's course. A ship could also drift with her broadside to the current, using some of her sails, especially the jib and spanker set at the extremities of the ship, to control her movement. In a slightly wider channel, a ship could tack, though she would require help from the tide to make real progress.

3 Boat and Anchor Work

The Uses of Boats

As well as transporting men and stores, ship's boats were used to move the ship itself. Large ships had no motive power apart from the wind itself; there were no tugs, and only relatively small ships were equipped with oars or sweeps. This meant that the boats were essential to the actual movement of the ship: to lay out anchors so that she could be hauled off, to tow the ship, to pull her head round when she would not tack in very light winds, to attach ropes to fixed objects in a process known as warping (see page 171), and to help take the mooring lines ashore or to a buoy, when it was difficult to sail the ship in on the wind.

Lowering and Raising Boats

The largest boats, such as the launch and the pinnaces, were stored in the waist, and had to be hauled out by means of a complicated system of tackles. The pendants from the mastheads of the fore and main were rigged, and tackles, suspended from these, were used to lift the boat off the deck. Another pair of tackles were rigged from the ends of the yardarms, and these took the weight next, allowing the boat to be swung out over the water. After that, it could be lowered into the sea. All this caused a certain amount of strain on the spars, and Captain Griffiths warned that 'The weight of a 46-gun frigate's launch [ie, a 38-gun frigate by the pre-1816 classification] is 3 tons 15 cwt. Add to this, the weight of two men, the water in her, the sand, her being water soaked, two boat-hooks, painter, slings, rudder, fenders and co, and the whole cannot be less than 4 tons 2cwt.'[1] He therefore advised that the yards be 'topped up', by having extra lifts fitted to strengthen them. Smaller boats, such as cutters and jollyboats, were often hung from davits at the stern and quarter. They were kept suspended from a tackle, which could also be used for raising and lowering them. This made their operation considerably simpler, and they could be used in emergencies, such as 'man overboard'.

A boat rowing single banked, off Old Harry Rocks in Dorset. From Serres's, *Liber Nauticus*

When the ships were in harbour, the boats were often hoisted in at night, partly to prevent damage from banging against the ships sides, but largely to prevent their theft by deserters. If they were kept out, then reliable men were stationed in them as 'boatkeepers'. When not in use in the daytime, the boats could be dropped astern, where the current could keep them clear of the ship. Otherwise, one of the studding sail booms could be put out, and the boats moored to it; this would prevent them from banging against the ship's side.

Rowing and Sailing Boats

Most ship's boats were designed for both rowing and sailing, though some were better at one than the other. Pinnaces and barges were primarily for rowing, while cutters were best at sailing. Boats could

A boat rowing double banked, with an awning in the stern for the comfort of the passengers. From Serres's, *Liber Nauticus*

be either single or double banked for rowing; if they were single banked, the men sat on the opposite side of the boat from the thole pins, and were, thus, given more leverage; if double banked, two men sat on each thwart and used thole pins on the same side. Obviously more men could be employed on a double-banked boat, and this was more appropriate for pinnaces and barges, where smart rowing was considered highly desirable. Orders to oarsmen included, 'Get your oars to pass', which meant to prepare the oars for use; 'Lay on your oars' was to 'order the men to cease rowing for a short time, in order to speak, or pay homage to a superior when passing'. To feather the oars was to put the blades in a horizontal position so that they would not catch the wind. To 'ship the oars' was 'to place them in the rowlocks ready for rowing'. 'Boat your oars' was 'the order to the men to cease rowing, and lay the oars in the boat'.[2]

Boat sails varied with the type of boat, but in general launches and longboats were sloop rigged, with a single mast, a gaff mainsail, bowsprit and two headsails. Barges and pinnaces had two masts and lateen sails, cutters had two masts with lugsails, and yawls had two masts with spritsails.[3] The detailed techniques of handling sail varied; the lateen sails of the pinnaces were probably the most labour intensive. However, all were fore and aft rigged, and could therefore sail rather closer to the wind than the parent ship, which was square rigged. Captain Griffiths warned of many accidents in ship's boats, largely from 'men standing up and even upon the thwarts, to haul the sail down'. He commented, 'Men-of-war's boats seldom have ballast, the men sit *on* the thwarts, and are in fact injurious to the boat carrying sail; surely they ought not to make it worse by standing up, and as you frequently see them on the thwarts.' 'In taking in a lug or lateen sail', he also recommended, 'haul down by the fore leach, let the after leech alone, as by hauling upon it, the sail keeps full, stands more fore and aft, endangers upsetting the boat, and makes the traveller bind against the mast, which prevents or impedes the sail coming down.'[4] When actually under sail, the boat was

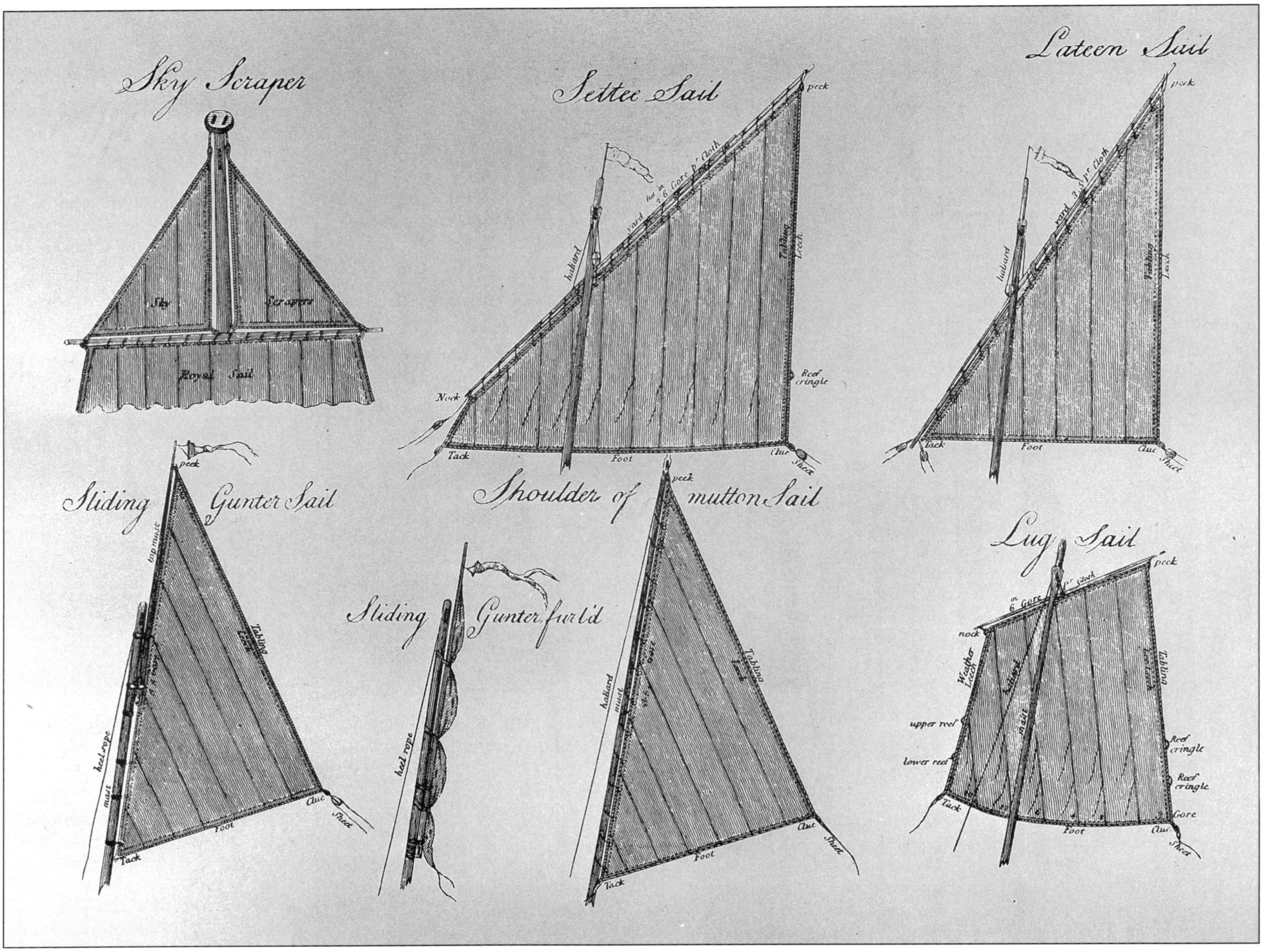

Sky Scraper
Settee Sail
Lateen Sail
Sliding Gunter Sail
Shoulder of mutton Sail
Lug Sail
Sliding Gunter furl'd
Royal Sail
peek
Nock
Tack
Foot
Clue
Sheet
Reef cringle
Tabling Leech
halliard
heel rope
mast
upper reef
lower reef
Weather Leech
Gore

Main
Fore
Mizen
Jib
Foresail
Peek
Head
Gores
Nock
Mast
Halliard
Tabling
Leech
After Leech
Fore Leech
Gromet
Tack
Foot
Clue
Sheet
Reef Holes

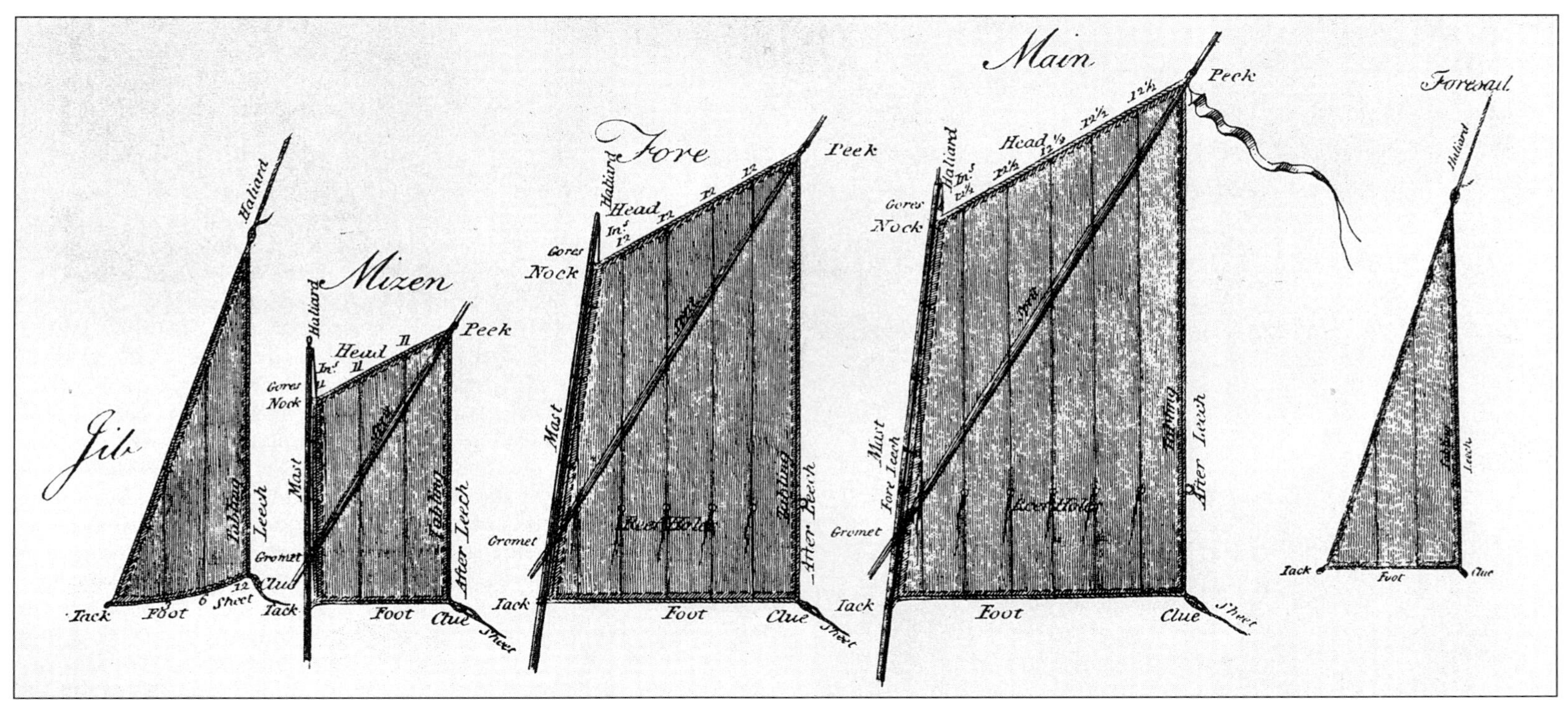

◁ *Types of boat sail.* From Steel's *Mastmaking, Sailmaking and Rigging*

operated like any fore- and aft-rigged craft; the sheets were let out when off the wind, and taken in when close to it. Sloop-rigged craft could often be difficult to sail before the wind, but they made up for it by their good windward performance.

The Principles of the Anchor

An anchor was so designed that when it reached the sea bottom one or other of its arms would bury itself in the bottom, resisting any horizontal pull on it. The most effective part of this effort was caused by the spade-like fluke. The other fluke, and its arm, were of course out of the sea bottom, and were making no contribution. As a result, an anchor of this period had a relatively low efficiency for its weight. Anchors were not effective on rocky bottoms, where they would not bury themselves, nor in very soft mud, where they would meet little resistance against the pull of the ship. To make the pull on the anchor ring reasonably horizontal, a considerable length of cable had to be let out — at least three times the depth of the water, but more was needed in most cases, especially when the wind or current were strong. It was not normal to anchor in more than 40 fathoms, and most anchorages were much shallower than that.

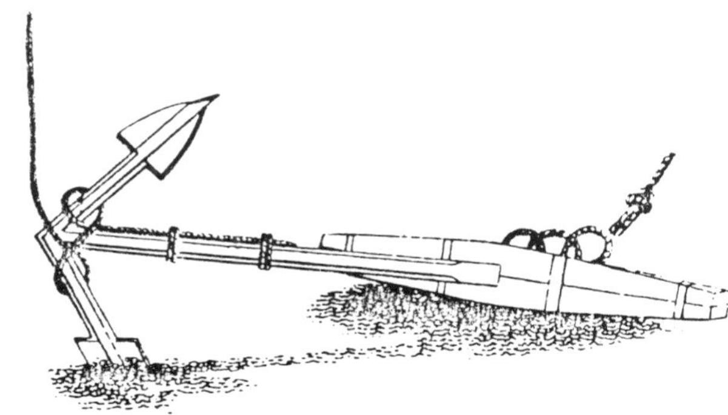

An anchor on the bottom, with the fluke about to bury itself in the sand. It has a buoy rope attached to the crown. From Burney's Dictionary

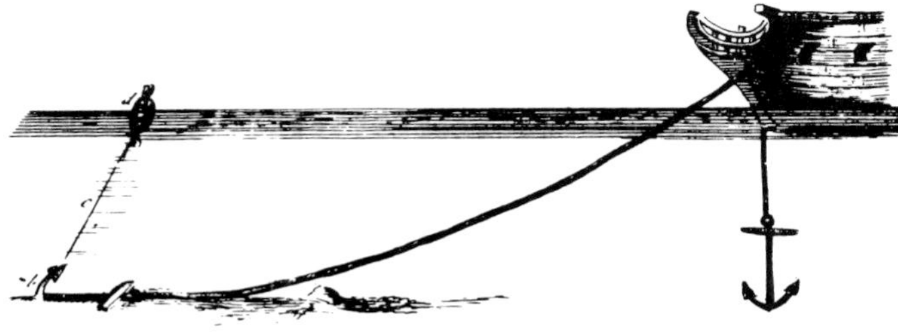

An anchor in use. From Falconer's Dictionary

Dropping Anchor

To prepare an anchor for dropping, it was freed from the cat tackle and fish tackle which held it horizontal against the forecastle. It was left hanging vertically from the cat head, held by a single rope, known as the stopper. The cable had probably been taken off while at sea, and this was led through the hawse hole and re-attached. The chart had been consulted, and estimates made of the depth of water the ship would anchor in. A suitable length of cable was hauled up from the orlop deck and laid out in lines on the lower deck (or upper deck of a frigate). The inboard end of the cable was secured to the bitts, leaving enough to hold the ship effectively in the planned depth of water. The leadsmen in the chains constantly called out the depth of water as the ship got closer to the anchorage.

The approach was sometimes made slowly, under reduced sail — perhaps topsails only, though if the captain wished to impress the observers in other ships, he might come under full sail and take it in very quickly with a skilled crew. If possible, the ship would be steered into the current, and on reaching a suitable point, the sheets would be let fly, and the sails brailed up to the yard. The ship would stop, and slowly gather stern way as the current pushed her back. If necessary, the mizzen topsail would be set and backed, to help with this. The stopper would be let go, and the anchor allowed to fall to the bottom of the sea. After that the cable would be let out slowly in time with the ship's movement astern; this would prevent the cable piling up on the bottom. There were many variations according to the relative directions and strengths of wind and tide, but the essence of the manoeuvre was to have the cable paid out as the ship moved slowly astern.

The cable was attached to the bitts by passing figure-of-eights over the end of the bitt pin and the crossbar. Short ropes known as stoppers (not to be confused with those which held the anchor under the cat head) were attached to ringbolts just aft of the bitts. Lighter ropes led from the ends of the stoppers, and were entwined round the cable, to prevent it slipping.

Single and Double Anchor

When moored by a single anchor, a ship would tend to swing with the changes of the tide, in a wide circle, almost equal to the length of cable let out. A single anchor had relatively weak holding power, and would not be sufficient in strong wind or tide. It would tend to 'come home', or 'drag' along the bottom of the sea. Ships stayed at single anchor for short periods, either when warping, or when making short stops. However, single anchor could also be useful in heavy weather, with several cables joined together to make the pull horizontal.

A ship held by at least two anchors was said to be 'moored'. Two or more anchors could be laid out in line in heavy weather, but mooring normally meant that one anchor was up-tide of the ship at any given moment, and the other was directly down-tide. The first anchor was dropped up-tide, the ship was allowed to fall back and the other anchor was dropped down-tide. The cable on the first anchor was hauled in, so that the ship was approximately midway between the two. Mooring meant that the ship would swing much less with the tide, and was the normal method in such places as Spithead and Torbay. It had the disadvantage that, as the ship swung with the tide, the two cables would tend to become entangled, causing a 'foul hawse'. To prevent this, it was necessary to take care

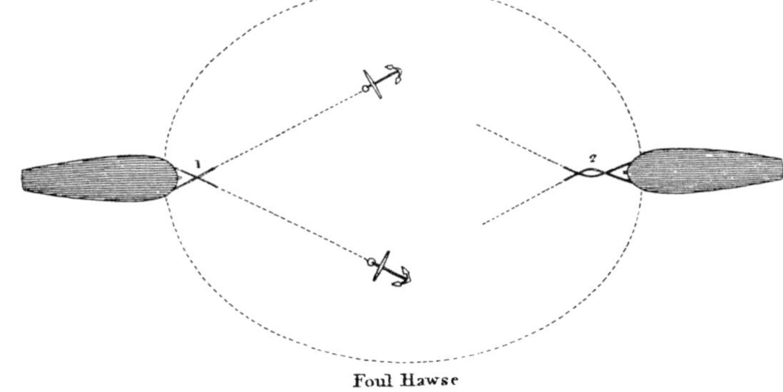

Two forms of foul hawse. From The English Encylopaedia, 1802

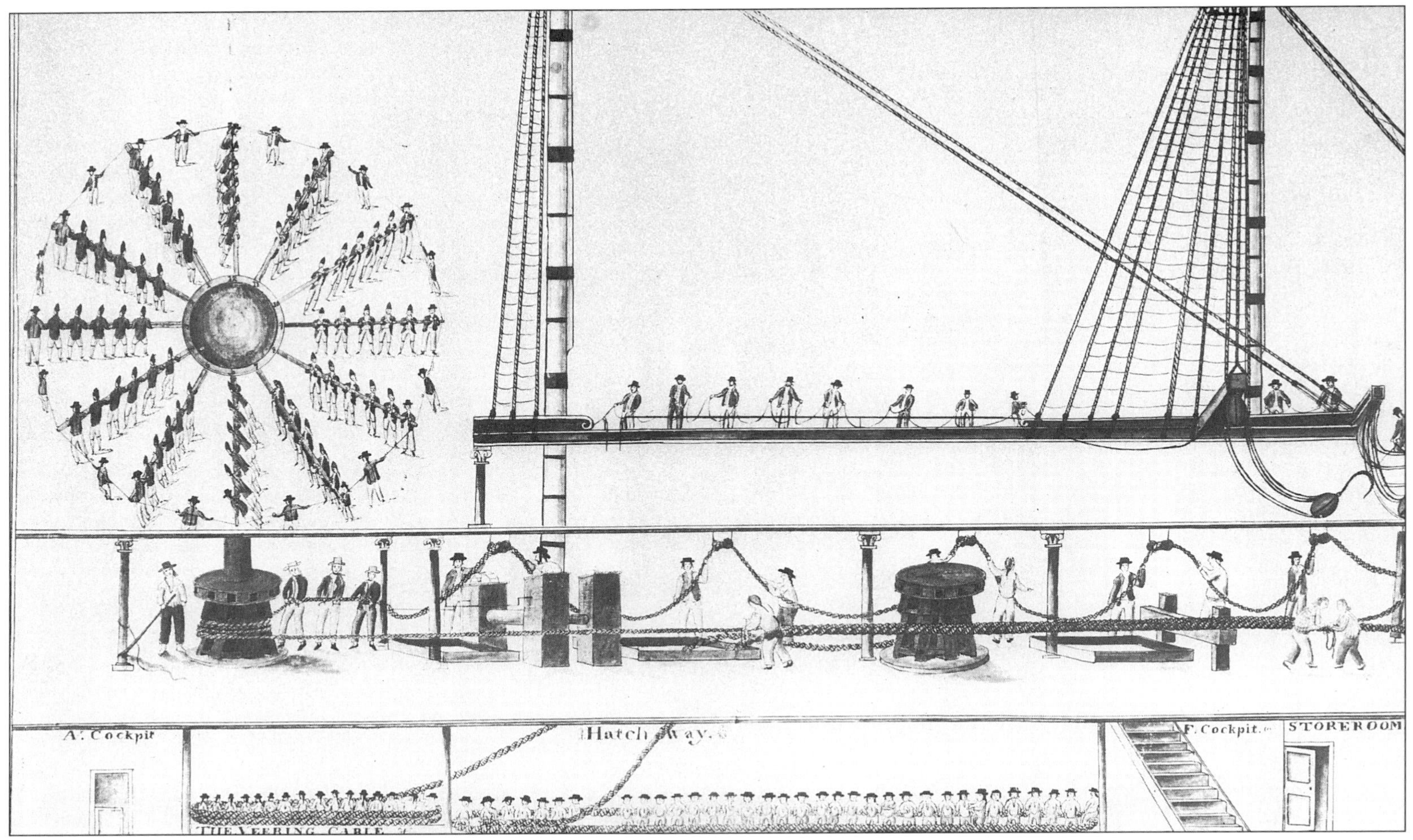

Raising the anchor. Eighty-four men, mostly marines, operate the capstan. The lower part, on the gundeck, is used only to receive the messenger, which passes through rollers on its passage forward from the capstan. At the centre right, two men can be seen attaching the messenger to the cable by means of nippers. The cable is passed down through the hatchway, and on the orlop deck a large party stands by to stow it. On the forecastle, another gang is ready to cat and fish the anchor. The National Maritime Museum

to manoeuvre the ship carefully at each turn of the tide, using the sails if necessary. If the hawse nevertheless became foul, it was often necessary to take off the bitter end of one cable from the bitts, and untangle it from the other cable, using a tackle rigged under the bowsprit.

There were many dangers while riding at anchor. In shallow water the ship might be damaged by the uppermost fluke of her own anchor or one belonging to another ship. In a cross wind or tide a ship might find one cable passing under her bows, the other under her stern, being 'girt by her cable', and unable to swing with the wind and tide. It was not unknown for ships to suffer damage by collision while at anchor, as two ships reacted differently to the conditions, or the radius of the swing round the anchor was misjudged. The anchor itself could become fouled by having the cable twisted round it; this would make it less efficient in holding the ship, and harder to raise when necessary; it would also cause a risk of cutting the cable. It was the duty of the anchor watch to prevent any of these things happening. When coming to anchor, compass bearings were taken on several objects, and these were checked regularly to see if the anchor was dragging.

Buoys

The anchor buoy was attached to the anchor, usually at the crown. It served to indicate the position of the anchor under the sea, giving warning to any ship likely to drift over it and be damaged. It could also be used to 'trip' an anchor stuck fast in the bottom. Hauling on the buoy rope would operate the crown rather than the ring of the anchor, and would tend to loosen the arms from the mud. When not in use, anchor buoys were kept stowed against the foremast shrouds. They were normally made of wood in the same way as a barrel, and lashed with ropes to protect them, and provide points at which a boat-hook could get a grip of them.

A mooring buoy served a different function. It was much bigger, and was securely anchored to the bottom, usually with two anchors and chain cable. It served as a mooring for a ship, which secured its bow to the buoy. Such moorings were common near the main dockyards, especially for ships laid up in ordinary, or those awaiting entry to a dry dock. A 'swinging mooring' was designed to allow the ship to swing with the tide, without becoming fouled. Ships staying for longer periods were moored both head and stern to buoys.

When coming to a mooring buoy, it was possible for the ship to sail up slowly and a man be sent down to attach a rope to it. However, this required highly skilled seamanship, and it was probably more common to use other methods. One was to anchor nearby, send a boat out with a line to the buoy, and haul the ship onto it. Another was to hold the ship hove-to near the buoy, send out the boat with the line, and haul the ship up in the same way.

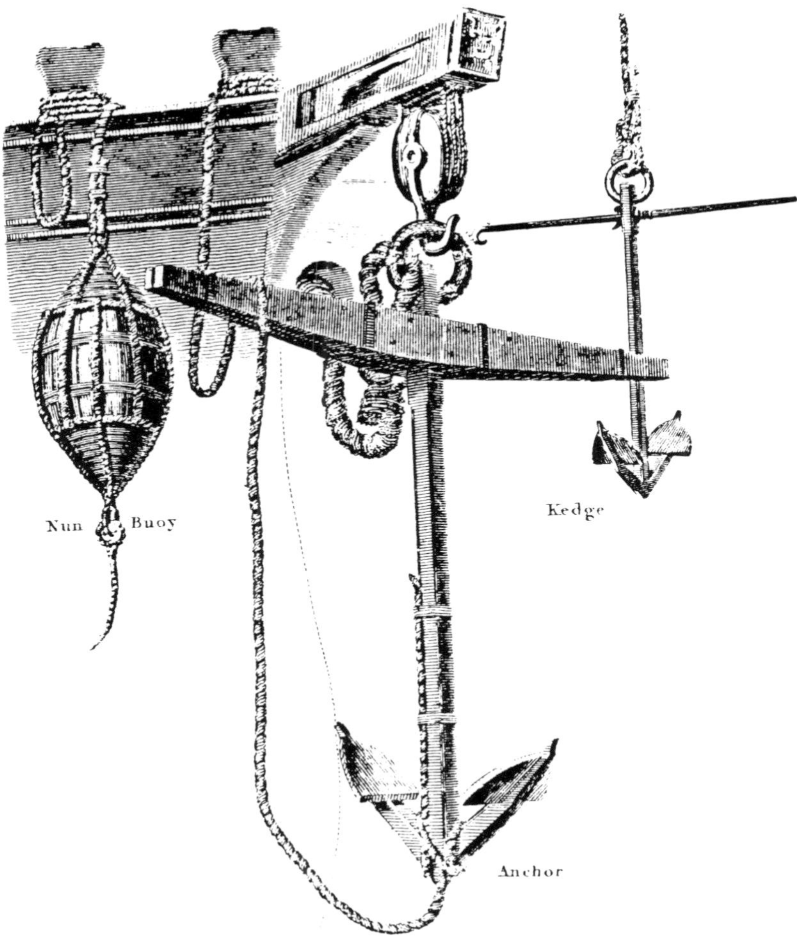

An anchor hung from the cathead, with a buoy attached. In the background, a kedge anchor, with an iron stock. From The English Encyclopaedia, 1802

Raising the Anchor

The anchor was raised by hauling in its cable, by means of the ship's capstans. On ships of any size, the cable was too thick to be turned round the capstan, and the messenger was used instead. This was an endless rope about half the circumference of the cable. It was turned a few times round the lower whelps of the main capstan, and then led forward. Part of it was fixed to the anchor cable as it came in through the hawse hole, by means of temporary lashings known as 'nippers'. The strain was taken up on the capstan, as ship's boys (later known as 'nippers') walked aft holding the ends of the lashings. As each part of the cable reached the main hatch, its nipper was taken off, and the cable passed down into the tiers on the orlop deck. The messenger continued round the capstan, then back through a system of rollers to the area of the hawse holes, where a seaman put a nipper to re-attach it to the cable.

The capstan was usually manned at upper deck level only, unless the strain on the cable was particularly heavy. This allowed the messenger a free run round the lower whelps of the capstan, and prevented the men at the capstan from having to step over it. On many ships, the capstan was manned by marines, and up to ninety-six men could operate a single head — six at each of the twelve bars, plus two more on each 'swifter', a rope which joined together the ends of the bars.

On the orlop deck, another party worked at manhandling and stowing the incoming cable. Another group stood by on the forecastle, operating the cat tackle from the cathead. As soon as the ring of the anchor broke surface, the hook of the cat tackle was put through it, and the anchor was hauled up by the cathead, keeping it clear of the ship's side. The fish tackle was then engaged on the shank of the anchor, and used to haul it up until the shank was horizontal. The cable was often taken off the anchor, and the hawse hole plugged up to keep sea water out.

Kedging

In calm weather or unfavourable winds, a ship could be moved using boats and anchors. The smallest anchor, the kedge, was attached to a light cable and slung under the longboat or launch of the ship. The boat was rowed out in the appropriate direction, the anchor was dropped, and then hauled in by the capstan of the ship. For the system to work over any distance, two anchors had to be employed in tandem, with one holding the ship while the other was being laid out. Burney suggests that this method was used only for moving a ship short distances across a harbour; however, it was occasionally used at sea in a chase, and in 1812 the *USS Constitution* used it to escape from a British squadron. Kedging also had another meaning — to drop the kedge anchor as a means of bringing a ship's head round, when moving with the tide in light winds.

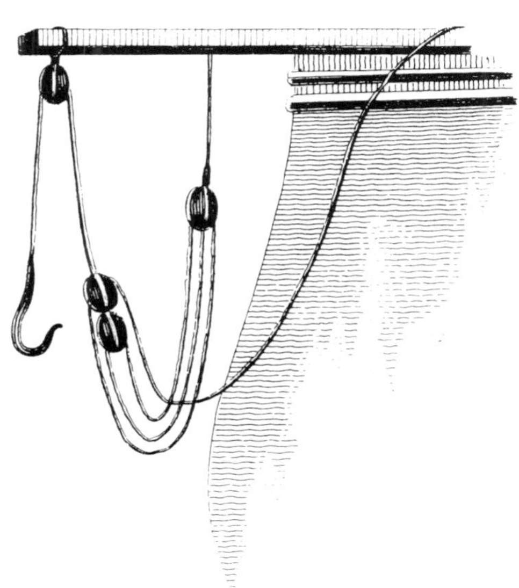

The fish tackle. From Serres's, *Liber Nauticus*

Warping and Towing

Warping was another way of moving a ship in unfavourable conditions, especially in a narrow channel. A rope was taken from the ship to one of the boats, and rowed out to a fixed object; a tree on the land, or a specially sited post in the water, or a buoy. The rope was hauled in by the capstan pulling the ship forward.

When the water was too deep for kedging, and no objects were available for warping, the only alternative to keep the ship moving without wind was by towing by the ship's boats. This was extremely tiring on the crews, and the ships made only slow progress, so it was rarely used — for chasing, or when the ship was being driven into danger by the tide, for example.

4 Gunnery and Fighting

The Role of Gunnery

Gun power was the *raison d'être* of the sailing warship, but naval officers generally paid little attention to the science of gunnery. Mathematicians had made some study of the subject in the last fifty years, but very little of this had penetrated the consciousness of the average naval officer. Army artillery officers were highly trained in ballistics at Woolwich, but naval officers, though not entirely unschooled in mathematics, had little idea of scientific gunnery. Ballistics formed no part of the lieutenant's examination, and ship's gunners were not expected to have any mathematical or scientific knowledge. When Sir Howard Douglas, of the Royal Artillery, watched the ships of Popham's squadron bombarding shore positions in 1812, he 'felt . . . scandalised at the bad gunnery, which made him tremble for the laurels of the navy.'[1] The navy relied heavily on Nelson's dictum that 'no captain can do very wrong if he places his ship alongside that of an enemy'. Close action was the order of the day, and there was doubt about whether mathematical calculation of range and trajectory was relevant on an unsteady platform like a ship. British gunnery was better than French, Spanish or Dutch, and good enough to win its battles. It was only in shore bombardment that its inaccuracy was demonstrated. In close action, the rate of fire was far more important than accuracy, and that was what gun crews were trained in.

Even so, there was no established system of gun orders, according to Sir Howard Douglas, until 1817, when the Admiralty appointed a committee to enquire into the matter. This is somewhat contradicted by Burney in his dictionary of 1815, when he writes, 'The exercise of the great guns in our navy is as follows', and gives a series of fifteen gunnery orders,[2] which were almost identical to those printed in Falconer's Dictionary in 1769, and probably introduced by Anson in the 1750s. Perhaps Burney meant that these orders were quite common, but were not officially sanctioned, as Douglas demanded.

Preparation

The first stage in gunnery exercise, according to Burney and Falconer, was for the officer to call 'Silence'. According to the orders used aboard one ship, this was important. 'Conversation of no kind whatsoever can be admitted, and directions by officers and captains of guns to the different men are to be given by no louder than whispers so that when a loud and general order comes from the mouth of the captain, every man may hear and comprehend.' The gun was normally kept loaded in wartime, with a lead 'apron' over the touch hole to prevent accidental ignition. This was removed, and the tompion was taken from the mouth of the gun. It was either stowed away, or allowed to hang from the muzzle. The other items were laid out as necessary. 'The shot, wads, matches, match tubs, powder horns, lanterns and co, should be placed in amidships, and co, under tubs between every two guns, breechings middle seized, guns hanging by the train tackles, handspikes, sponges and worms down by the guns.'[3]

If it was merely an exercise with a limited number of guns, it was not necessary to 'clear for action' — the particular guns were merely 'cast loose' by taking off the muzzle lashing. The quoin was pushed in to depress the gun barrel and allow it to clear the port, and the gun was run out using its tackle. For a general exercise, it was necessary to take down the partitions of the cabins, especially on the upper deck. In preparing for battle, many items were often thrown overboard to expedite the process. As the *Ajax* sailed into the Battle of Trafalgar, she jettisoned six wooden ladders, ten cot frames, six stanchions, a grinding stone, a set of screens for berths, four weather sails, 30ft of copper funnelling for the galley stove, and many other items.[4]

The quarterdeck of the Venerable *cleared for action, with the bulkheads of the cabins taken down, and a* sauve-tete *netting rigged above, to protect the crew from falling splinters.* The National Maritime Museum

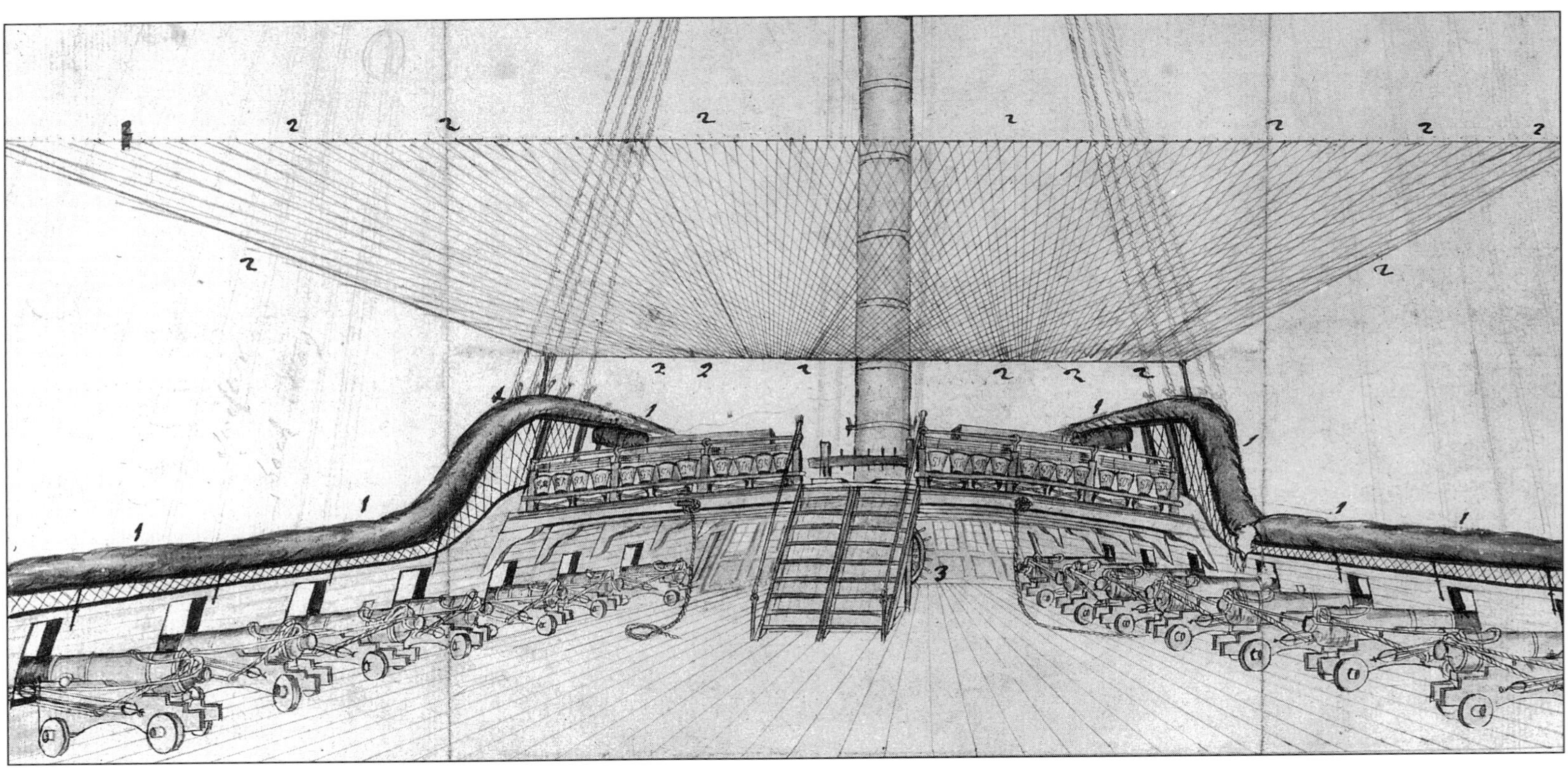

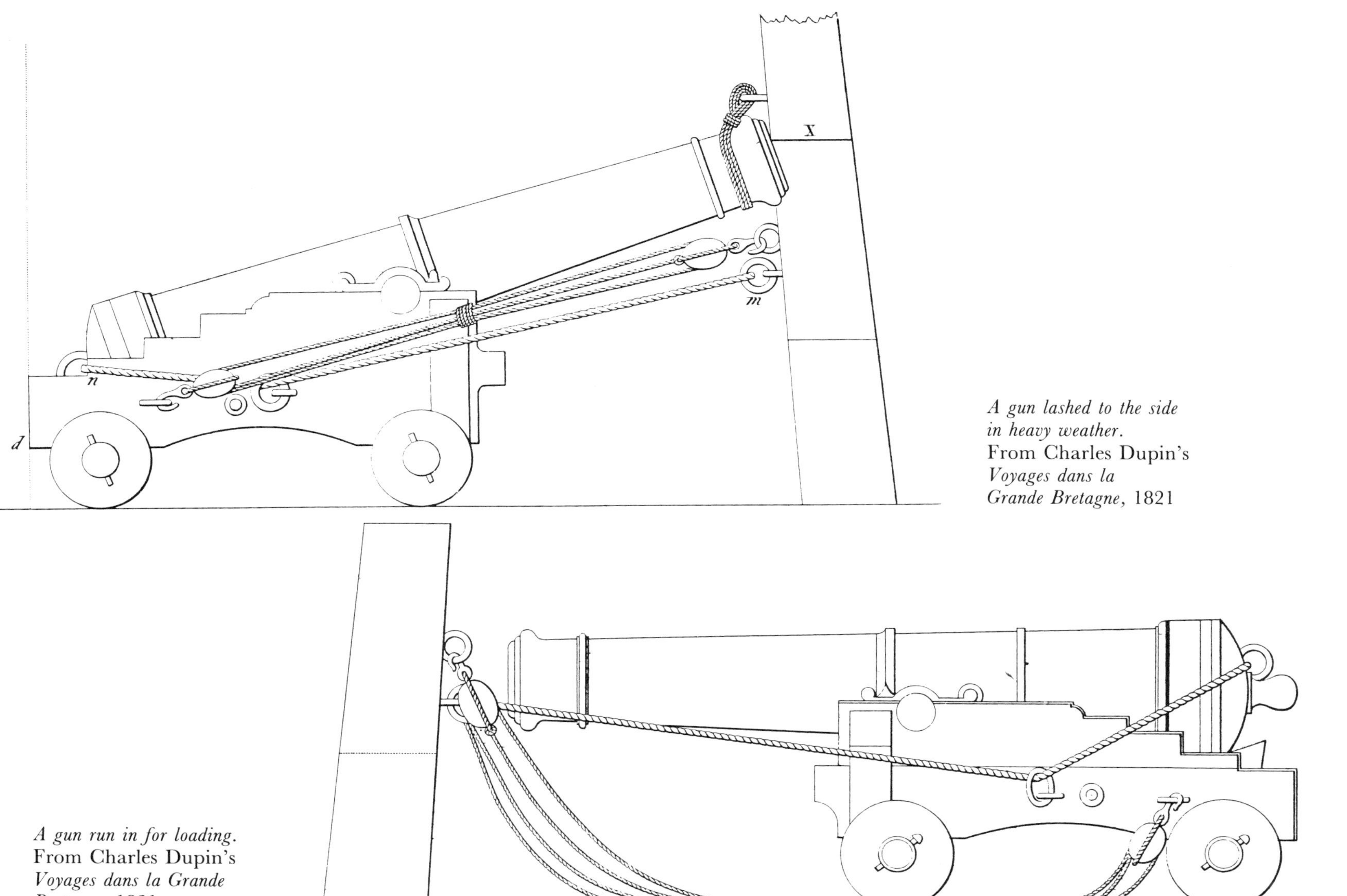

A gun lashed to the side in heavy weather. From Charles Dupin's *Voyages dans la Grande Bretagne*, 1821

A gun run in for loading. From Charles Dupin's *Voyages dans la Grande Bretagne*, 1821

The Supply of Powder and Shot

Ready use supplies of round shot were kept about the decks, resting in holes drilled in the coamings of hatchways. Other types of shot were brought up when preparing for action, and were placed near the guns, with grape shot kept in boxes. Obviously powder was far too dangerous to store in this way, it was brought up round by round, only when immediately needed. Made-up cartridges were passed up from the magazines and powder rooms, with the after guns being serviced by the after powder rooms, and so on. Often, a screen was erected round the magazine or powder room hatch on the lower deck, to protect it from sparks. The junior member of each gun crew, either a boy or a marine, was given a wooden or metal cartridge case to protect the powder from sparks while it was carried to the gun. Obviously, the boys from the upper deck guns had further to travel than those on the lower decks, and it is possible that two boys were appointed to these guns, so that the rate of fire would not be reduced. On the other hand, there is no sign that extra cartridge boxes were issued for the upper guns.

Loading and Firing

The first stage in reloading a gun after firing was to 'worm and sponge'. It was necessary to neutralise any traces of the burning cartridge of the last shot, in case it ignited the new one.

> The sponge is to be rammed down the bottom of the chamber, and then twisted round, to extinguish effectually any remains of fire; and when drawn out, to be struck against the outside of the muzzle, to shake off any sparks or scraps of the cartridge that may have come out with it and next its end is to be shifted ready for loading.[5]

The other end was used as the rammer for the cartridge. Meanwhile, the cartridge was taken out of the wooden or metal container used to protect it from sparks, and inserted in the muzzle.

> The cartridge (with the bottom end first, seam downwards, and a wad after it) is to be put into the gun, and thrust a little way into the mouth, when the rammer is to be entered; the cartridge is then to be forcibly rammed down, and the captain, at the same time, is to keep his priming wire in the vent, and feeling the cartridge, is to give the word 'home' when the rammer is to be drawn, and not before.[6]

Then the shot was put in, and another wad after it. These two were rammed home in the same way. The first wad, between the cartridge and the shot, served to separate the two and was believed to have a useful effect in ballistics; the second wad was to prevent the shot from rolling out with the movement of the ship.

The gun was prepared for firing by pricking the cartridge; a sharp

Run out for firing. From Charles Dupin's *Voyages dans la Grande Bretagne*, 1821

Guns from above. The National Maritime Museum

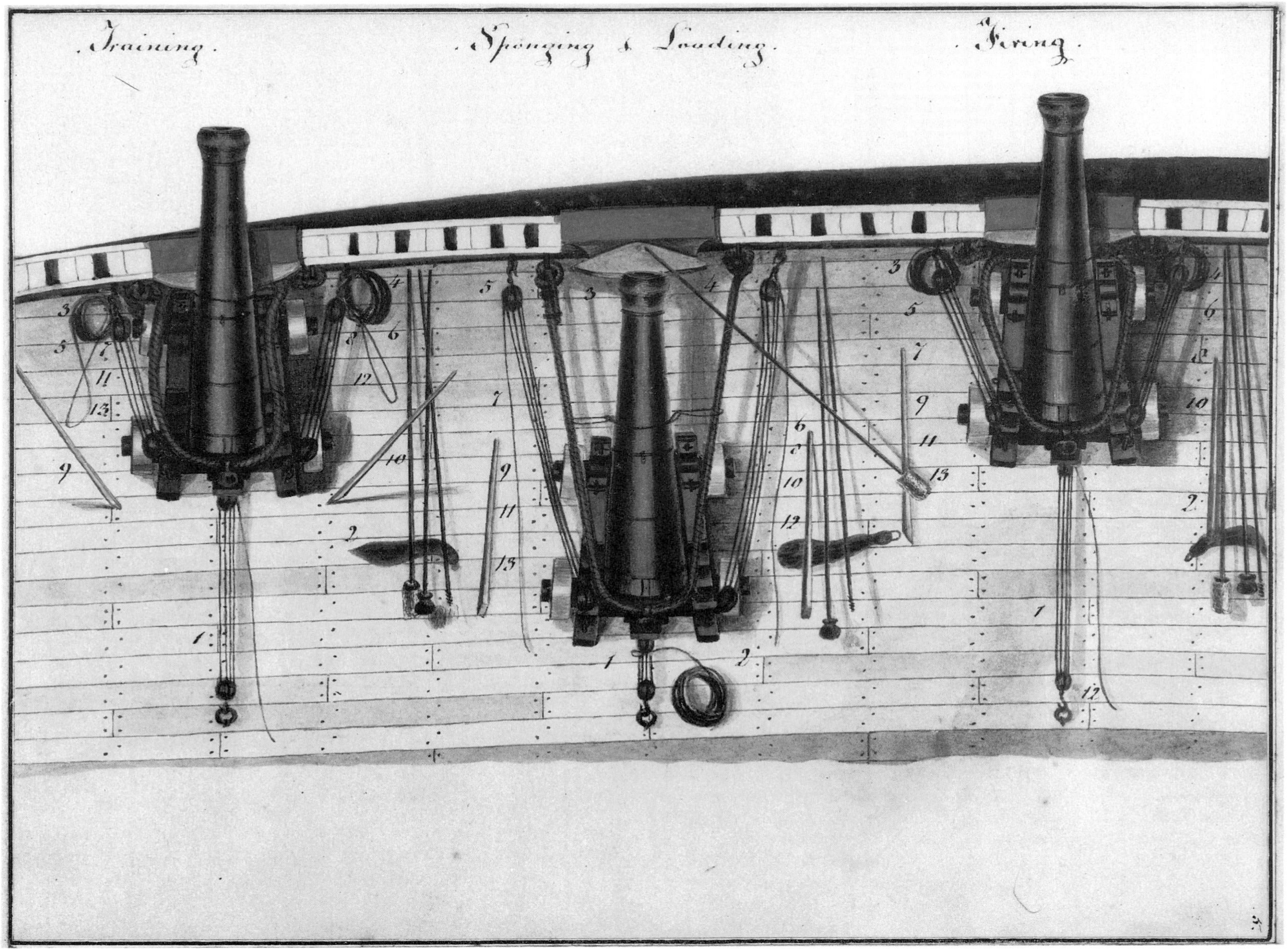

instrument was inserted down the touch hole. More powder was then poured down the touch hole from the captain's powder horn. In the old days, this had been enough, and a lighted match was applied to the hole to ignite the gun, but this system had several disadvantages: in particular, the lighted match, kept on the end of a piece of wood known as a 'linstock', had to be kept handy for use, with obvious dangers. It became more common to use gunlocks for firing.

The gunlock was similar to that used on a musket, though heavier. The spark was carried down to the chamber by way of a quill tube inserted in the touch hole, and the lock was operated by a lanyard held by the gun captain, allowing him to stand clear of the recoil of the gun.

Duties of the Gun Crew

The normal custom was for seven men to be allotted to each 32-pounder, six to an 18-pounder, and so on. If the ship was engaged on one side only, then the crews of two opposite guns could be combined at a single gun. The first captain was in overall charge when both crews were combined, while the second captain, or captain of the opposite gun, was second in command. Often, the men from the gun on the starboard side of the ship operated the starboard side of the gun when both crews were combined, while those of the port gun were on the port side. The various members of the gun crew were distinguished by number, though some officers objected to this. According to Sir Howard Douglas in 1829

> The principle of numbering off the crew of a gun, as practised very properly in the land service, has of late been a good deal followed in the navy... Though fully impressed with the advantages of such an arrangement for the land service, I more than doubt the expediency of adopting it generally in the naval service. Artillery soldiers numbered off to a gun, are not liable to be called away suddenly, in the heat of action, to the performance of other duties assigned to them also by numbers.[7]

In general, the higher numbers did the less skilled work, though on some ships this was complicated by the division between two sides of the ship. According to one set of instructions for an 18-pounder, the first captain should be the best seaman of the gun crew; he 'points and elevates, primes, cocks, fires, stops vent, pricks cartridge'. The second captain was number 7 in the joint crew; he 'trims with handspike, takes in the second best hack, and attends relieving tackle, and runs out'. Number 2 was the first loader, who 'sponges, rams home, runs out.' He was expected to be a 'steady man'. Number 8, the second loader, 'worms every third charge, puts charge in gun, attends apron, runs out'. Number 3 'trims with handspike, runs out', and was a 'stout man'. His opposite number on the starboard side of the gun was number 9, who 'brings shot to number 8, [the second loader] coils side out'. Numbers 4, 5 and 6 on the starboard side were to help with running out, while number 9 on the starboard side was also to bring a wad to number 8. Number 12 was the powder boy, who brought the powder from the magazine and gave it to the second loader.

When fighting on both sides at once, there were fewer men on each gun — often not enough to handle the tackle effectively. Since the next gun on the same side was closer than that on the opposite side, it was common for the higher numbers, who worked mainly at running the gun out, alternated between two adjacent guns, rather than going from one side of the ship to the other.

Aiming

To a certain extent, the gun could be traversed as it was run out, by different pressures on each side of the gun tackle. 'Take hold of the training tackle [ie, the gun tackles] and fall, your eyes fixed on the captain of the gun, always ready to run out and point the tackle as

A gun crew at work. The National Maritime Museum

A gun aboard the Victory *at Trafalgar, with a seaman using a handspike to traverse it.* The National Maritime Museum

Carronade crews at the bombardment of Algiers in 1816. A marine, wearing a type of forage cap, is passing case or grape shot from a box on deck, while a seaman rams home the powder. The adjacent carronade is being run out by its crew. The National Maritime Museum

he shall direct.'[8] After 1779, additional eyebolts were fitted some distance apart on the sides of the ship, to allow some leverage when attempting to aim. However, this method was often ineffective: 'In running a gun out by the side tackles, it seldom occurs when it is out, that it points to the object, owing to its not being possible to equalise the exertions of the men at the two tackles, and from the pitching motion of the ship throwing the gun out of place.'[9] Crowbars and handspikes were therefore used as levers to traverse the gun. This was a slow process because the wheels of the carriage gave no assistance at all. 'The crowbar and handspike are then to be resorted to to train it, which operation necessarily occupies much time.'[10]

Elevation of the gun was rather simpler. The wedge, or quoin, at the breech could be pushed in or pulled out to lower or raise the muzzle. The rolling of the ship could also assist in this. Traditionally British gun crews fired on the downward roll, so that any delay caused the ball to hit the water, and perhaps ricochet into the enemy hull. British gunners aimed for the hull, and French for the rigging; as a result, French ships tended to suffer far higher casualties in action.

The Blomefield pattern gun was designed to be fitted with sights, but these were intended for field and fortress artillery, not for naval use. 'To applications made during the past war with America, except in the case of two or three favourites at the board, for "sights" to the guns, the only reply vouchsafed was "it was not according to the regulation of the service, and could not be complied with." '[11] A few captains, such as Sir Phillip Broke, bought them out of their own pockets, but they were rare in the service.

Types of Charges and Shot

In battle, the size of the charge of powder, and the type of shot used, was generally decided by the captain on the basis of the tactical situation. Orders were conveyed to the magazines and the various decks by runners, and communicated by the officers and midshipmen in charge of the sections of guns. Since the cartridges were made up by the gunner of the ship, the captain had a certain latitude in deciding what to use. Aboard the *Egmont* in 1797, three types were used for the 32-pounder carronades — full allowance, first reduced allowance, and second reduced allowance. The other guns had only full and reduced allowance. With old-fashioned corn powder, the proportion of the maximum charge to the weight of the ball varied somewhat; 40 per cent for a 42-pounder, 50 per cent for an 18-pounder, and 66 per cent for a 9-pounder. With cylinder powder, 33 per cent of the weight of the ball was standard in all guns. Full charge was used in long-distance firing, reduced charges at short range.

The captain had a choice of several types of shot. Round shot was by far the most common, and was used for penetrating the enemy's hull. Grape was used against the men on the decks, mainly by the guns and carronades on the upper works. Double-headed or chain shot was used against the rigging. According to Admiral Parker's fleet orders of 1797, ships were to enter action with their guns loaded in different ways. Those on the quarterdeck and forecastle where to have 'round and grape shot pointed at the gunwale of the enemy's ship'. The first seven guns of the main and middle decks were to have similar loads and targets, while the others were to have 'round shot pointed at the bends [presumably, the sides] of the enemy's ship'. The first and second divisions on the lower deck were to have 'round shot pointed at the bends of the enemy's ship', while the third division was to have 'round and double-headed shot pointed at the gunwale'.[12] A gun could also be double shotted, to fire two balls at once. This increasing hitting power, but the interaction of the two balls inside the barrel led to very inaccurate aiming, so it was useful only at very short range.

Performance

The range of smooth-bore artillery was never very great. Experiments in 1813 showed that the point-blank range of a 24-pounder long gun was 200yds, while, with 9 degrees of elevation, it could reach 2213yds before hitting the ground for the first time. The point-blank range of a 32-pounder carronade was rather more — 340yds. Surprisingly, the full range of such a carronade, with 11 degrees elevation, was not much less than that of the long gun, at 1930yds.[13] Sir Howard Douglas gives quite similar figures, with 2020yds for a gun at 7 degrees elevation, single shotted, with a charge of powder of a quarter of the weight of the shot.[14] However, all these were attained with land-based guns under practice conditions; ranges at sea would be rather less. Accuracy would be very poor at more than a few hundred yards. The penetrating power of a gun at short range was quite high; in the experiments of 1813, the 24-pounder was capable of penetrating a target 2ft 6in thick, made from old ship's timbers.

The speed of the gun crew in reloading the gun was just as important as the capabilities of the gun, especially in close action. There are no detailed figures for this, but it was said that in action with the American *Chesapeake*, the *Shannon* fired $2\frac{1}{2}$ broadsides in six minutes. Broke's biographer implies that this was quite a slow rate

Gun crews on the Victory. *In the foreground, a gun captain primes with the powder horn. Behind, another is about to pull the lanyard to fire.* The National Maritime Museum

of fire, and feels it necessary to explain. 'To account for the cannonade lasting six minutes and yet these guns not having been fired oftener than appears by the above statement, it is necessary to remember that the *Chesapeake* approached the *Shannon* very broad aft, upon the quarter, sailing past the *Shannon*, about 40 feet from her . . .'[15] This leads to speculation that a considerably higher rate of fire might have been possible in ideal conditions, perhaps one round per minute. In the circumstances, the *Shannon* scored twenty-five hits out of thirty on the enemy's hull and masts; but she had a very well-trained crew and few in the fleet could have equalled her in such respects.

Gunnery Exercise

The Admiralty Regulations demanded that crews be trained and practised at the great guns, and the log books of ships confirm that this was done quite regularly. However, most gunnery practice was carried out without actually firing the gun. 'It is customary in many ships in a general exercise to go through the motions without loading or firing once in a year, and in others to exercise a few guns every day, and seldom to have a general exercise or to fire the guns.'[16] On one ship it was ordered 'For the attainment of a perfect knowledge of the use and exertions in the management of great guns the gunner is every afternoon (Sundays excepted) if nothing extraordinary intervenes, to exercise a part of the watch upon deck by one gun at a time, taking the men by turns from the quarter bill . . . not one sham motion is to be made, excepting those of priming, loading and firing.'[17] Captains were often reluctant to use up powder and shot in real firing, though there were exceptions. The gunners' accounts of the *Victory* in 1792–3 include lists of powder, shot and wads expended in gunnery practice.[18]

Improvements in Gunnery

During the American War of 1812–14, it became clear that British gunnery was inadequate against a skilled enemy, and captains like Sir Phillip Broke and Sir John Pechell tried to find ways to improve it. Gun captains were trained in aiming the gun on a rolling deck, by means of a bar inserted into the barrel of the gun and moved up and down to simulate the movement of the ship. Attempts were made to co-ordinate the fire of the guns so that their fire could be concentrated on one point. Means were found for estimating the distance away from an enemy ship, for example, by taking a sextant angle on the height of his masts. A special chock was developed for placing under the slides of carronades, for firing on the windward side. A few years after the war, Sir Howard Douglas applied the more scientific skills of an artillery officer to naval gunnery, and in 1830 HMS *Excellent* began to be used as a gunnery training ship at Portsmouth. However, all this had little effect on the conduct of the great war, and until 1815 the bulk of naval gunnery remained relatively primitive.

Mortars

The mortar, as carried exclusively by the specially designed bomb vessels, was the only type of naval gun which required scientific skill in its operation. It was, therefore, left to trained artillerymen, of either the army or the Royal Marines. The first difference was that the explosive shells had to be treated differently from the solid shot of ordinary guns. They were carried aboard a separate tender, and only issued when about to be used. When taken on board the bomb vessel, elaborate precautions were used to keep the shells safe. Secondly, the mortars were used against town or fortresses ashore, and often a considerable distance away; accurate aiming was much more necessary in these circumstances. The distance from the target had to be measured reasonably accurately, as the length of fuse attached to the shell controlled the time at which it would explode. Too short and the shell would burst over the target; too long and it would allow time for it to be pushed into the sea, or doused with water. Bomb vessels usually chose calm weather for their operations, and were protected by a screen of conventional vessels.

Small Arms

Small arms fell into two types — long-barrelled muskets which were mostly used ashore, or to fire volleys into an enemy ship's decks in close action; and pistols, which were mainly used in boarding, or in repelling boarders. Pistols were supplied in pairs, and sometimes a man could carry two, as reloading in action was virtually impossible. In other cases, each man carried only one, along with a cutlass or other edged weapon. One officer wrote, 'According to the custom prevailing from the earliest period of naval history to the present day, in boarding or opposing boarders, the pistol is held in the right hand, and in the attempt to board is fired and thrown away to enable the boarder to draw his cutlass, which yet remains in the scabbard or left hand.'[19] Some officers now advised a reversal of these tactics. 'A man armed with a pistol ought to reserve his fire to the last extremity if his life is to depend on the discharge of his pistol killing the man opposed to him.' It was recommended that he fire at not more than 3 or 4yds range.[20]

A sea service pistol. Royal Marines Museum

Edged Weapons

The cutlass was the traditional edged weapon of the seaman, and was still in common use. There was no standard system of drill until 1814, but some were devised by individual officers. Lt W P Green suggested the following sequence: 'guard the left side', and 'thrust or parry'.[21] Officers, trained in formal swordsmanship, tried to encourage their men to use the point rather than the edge of the weapon.

> Eagerness and heat in action, especially in a first onslaught, ought never to be the cause of a man putting himself so much off his guard . . . as to lift his arm to make a blow with his cutlass . . . But on the contrary, by rushing sword in hand straight out and thereby the guard maintained, and watching his opportunity of making the thrust, the slightest touch of the point is death to his enemy.'[22]

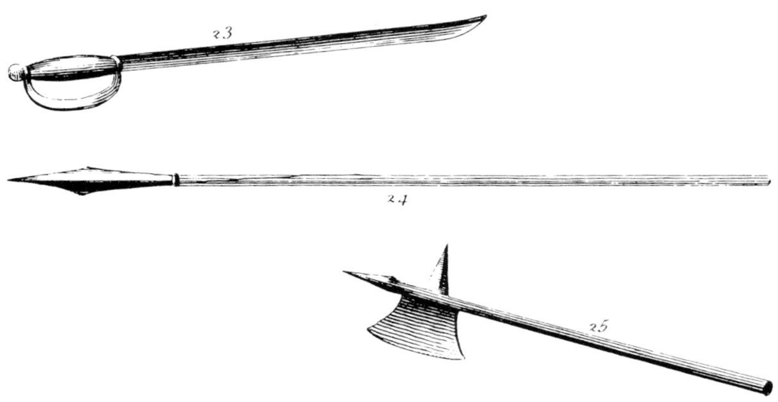

A cutlass, pike and tomahawk. From Serres's, *Liber Nauticus*

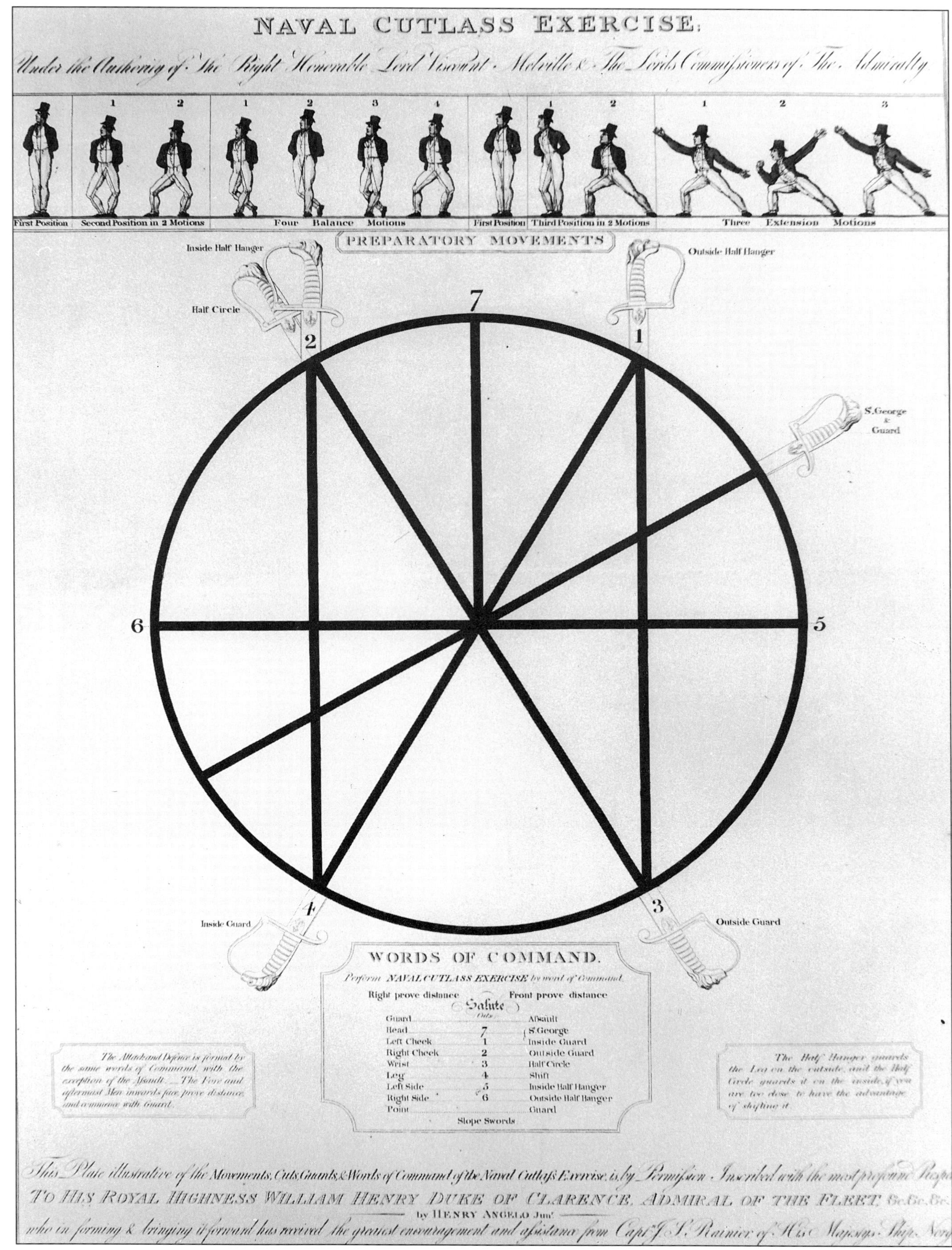

A proposal for cutlass exercise, 1814. Royal Navy Museum

Nelson leads the boarding of the Spanish San Nicolas *at the Battle of St Vincent.* The National Maritime Museum

Other weapons included pikes and tomahawks. 'The pike well managed in the hands of a cool and resolute man is a very dreadful weapon. Armed with it, either for attack or defence, he is to keep it on his right side, directed at the heart of the enemy.' The tomahawk, on the other hand, was not really a man-killing weapon. It was 'a weapon that when sharpened is of great service in cutting rigging', but it was 'inferior to thrusting weapons, such as the musket and bayonet, pike and cutlass'.[23]

Boarding

According to Burney, boarding 'is seldom made use of in ships of war'.[24] However, crews were generally trained, equipped and organised for boarding, and Nelson used it to decisive effect at the Battle of St Vincent. Usually, one man was detailed from each gun crew to act as a boarder, but more elaborate organisations were used in other ships, with several divisions of boarders equipped with different combinations of weapons. The boarding party was put under the command of younger and more active lieutenants, though it was not unusual for more senior officers, such as Nelson and Broke, to lead the charge themselves. Cautious advice suggested that boarding should mainly be used when the enemy was already on the defensive, but Cochrane was able to reverse this in his action with a Spanish frigate in 1800, and use the advantage of surprise.

Boarding began when the two ships came alongside one another, and grappling hooks were thrown aboard the enemy to keep the two ships together. Hand grenades, smoke bombs and 'stink pots' were thrown from the yardarms of the attacking ship, and the men swarmed aboard with musket and bayonet, pike, cutlass, pistol and tomahawk.

Rockets

The rocket was an ancient Chinese invention (like gunpowder), but its military possibilities were first exploited by William Congreve of the Royal Artillery, who formed two rocket companies in 1809. The rockets were carried into action during an attack on the French base at Basque Roads in the same year, aboard the transport *Cleveland.* They were fired from the rigging of various fireships, but unfortunately they proved to be very inaccurate, and endangered British boats and landing craft as much as the French fleet.

5 Navigation

The Importance of Navigation

Navigation was vital to the running of the fleet. It was an essential skill for every sea officer, from midshipman to admiral. It was precisely this skill which separated the sea officers from the petty officers and common seamen, for navigation required basic literacy and a high degree of numeracy. Perhaps more men would have risen from the lower deck to the quarterdeck had this not been so.

The government also recognised the importance of navigation. It did little to support the sciences in the eighteenth century, but the Astronomer Royal and the Royal Observatory at Greenwich were funded precisely because of their importance to navigation. The Board of Longitude had been formed in 1714, to find a solution to the most difficult problem of navigation. Its work had been completed by 1793, and two methods of finding the longitude were in common naval use. Voyages of exploration had been funded throughout the century, notably by Cook, Byron, Vancouver and Flinders. Seas were charted and astronomical observations made in all these expeditions. The essential problems of navigation were now capable of solution, but in individual cases the picture was not so hopeful. The chart coverage of the world was still piecemeal, and many channels and hazards were still inadequately buoyed.

Charts

Until the late eighteenth century, production of charts was largely done by private enterprise, by firms such as Mount and Page. A hundred years earlier, the Admiralty had commissioned Captain Greenville Collins to survey the coasts of Britain, but these charts were often criticised for their inaccuracy, although they ran into many editions throughout the eighteenth century. A new survey was conducted by Murdoch Mackenzie in the 1780s, and updated by Graeme Spence in the 1800s. Surveys of other parts of the world were irregular, and an Order in Council complained of 'the great inconvenience which has constantly been felt by the officers of your Majesty's fleet, especially when ordered aboard, from the want of sufficient information respecting the navigation of those parts of the world to which their services may be directed'.[1] The availability of charts aboard ship largely depended on the initiative of individual officers; at the Battle of the Nile, the captain of the *Goliath* happened to have a copy of the latest French chart, which enabled him to attack the enemy from inside his line. The master, like any other craftsman, was responsible for his own tools, and according to Admiralty Regulations he was 'to provide himself with such charts, nautical books and instruments as are necessary for astronomical

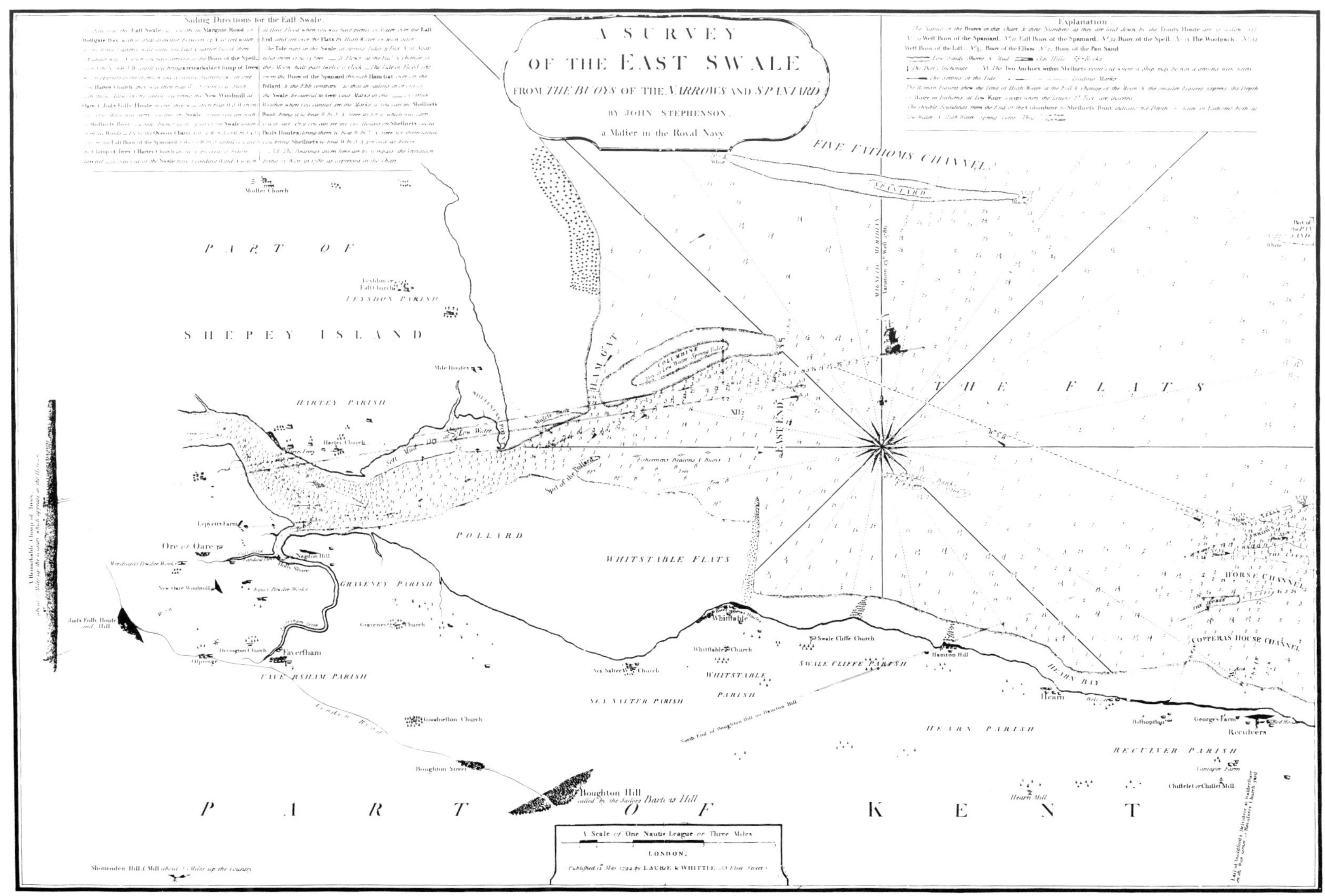

A chart of 1794, showing the entrance to the East Swale, north Kent. It makes extensive use of transits. This chart was produced by private enterprise, based on a survey by a master in the Royal Navy, but the production of official charts was increasing. Author's collection

observations and all other purposes of navigation.'[2] When charts were not available, captains and masters relied heavily on their own local knowledge, or took local pilots on board where possible.

The picture began to change during the course of the wars. In 1795, the Hydrographic Department was set up on a regular basis, with Alexander Dalrymple as the first hydrographer. The department was to produce plans, based on new surveys, or on 'the plans and charts which have from time to time been deposited in this office'.[3] By 1808, boxes of charts for particular areas were made up, and issued to ships. A ship intended for the North Sea would be issued with twenty-eight charts of that area alone, plus four more of the Baltic. For service in the Atlantic and West Indies, the following charts were issued — North Atlantic Ocean, a general chart of the West Indies, Tortuga and the Florida Keys, West end of Cuba and Grand Cayman, and Coast of West Florida and Louisiana, as well as a book of smaller charts of different islands.[4]

Charts were produced using Mercator's projection — the spherical surface of the earth was reduced to a flat surface by increasing the scale near the poles compared with that at the equator, and the lines of longitude were made parallel to one another. Distance, in nautical miles, had to be measured from the latitude opposite the area of operations. The Mercator chart distorted the shape of the earth, as any projection must do. This made little difference in short voyages, but in oceanic travel it could have some effect. Charts gave only essential land detail, with coastlines and prominent features being carefully marked. Depths of water, usually at low tide, were shown in fathoms in spots where soundings had been taken. Compass roses were marked on them at intervals, to allow the navigator to plot courses. Pilot books were mostly produced by private enterprise.

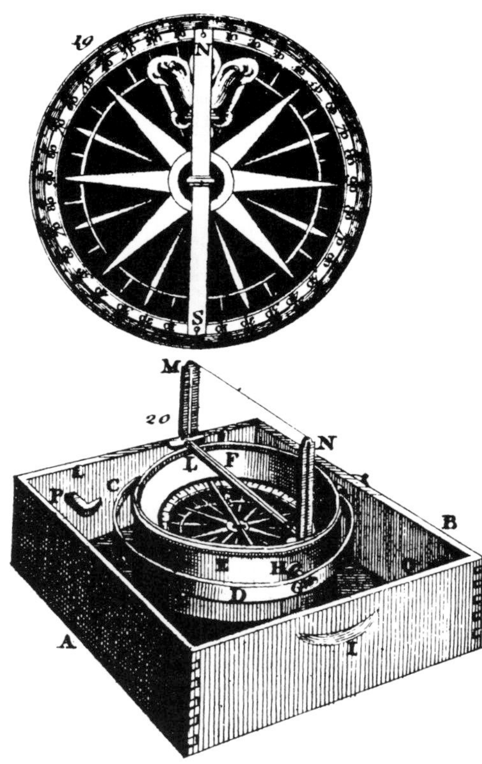

Fig 19, a compass card, showing the needle. Fig 20, a compass fitted with a sighting ring for taking bearings of objects. From Burney's Dictionary

Compass

The compass was essential to all kinds of navigation. Even in inshore waters, it was often necessary to steer a compass course to avoid dangers, and out of sight of land the compass was even more important, especially when cloud or mist obscured the sky. The compass was marked with 32 points: the cardinal ones — north, south, east and west, subdivisions of these — northeast, northwest, etc, and further subdivisions which gave points such as east-northeast, north-north west; and the last subdivision included north by east, southeast by south, and so on. The points could themselves be divided into quarters, so that a helmsman might be ordered to steer 'south southwest $\frac{3}{4}$ south', for example. Some of the more modern compasses were also marked in degrees, as this was often found more convenient for calculation.

The variation of the compass was quite well understood. It was known that the compass needle seldom pointed to true north, but a number of degrees away from this. It was known that this amount varied from place to place, and from time to time. Deviation, the error of the compass caused by factors within the ship itself, was rather less understood, and the importance of keeping iron objects away from the compass was not always appreciated.

Two steering compasses were mounted in the binnacle, just forward of the helmsman, and lighted by oil lamps at night. The azimuth compass was originally designed to measure the position of a celestial body. It was intended to be more accurate than a conventional compass, and was fitted with sights to take bearings. It could be used as part of a system of measuring variation, and also to take bearings on objects on shore. A navigator could take two of these bearings to establish the position of the ship in coastal waters, or preferably three, so that the accuracy could be tested. Such a fix was useful in steering down a narrow channel, and also at anchor, when it could be used to find whether the ship was dragging her anchor or not. It was quite common to note such bearings in the master's log.

Seamarks

While in sight of land, the navigator relied mainly on visual means for keeping the ship away from danger. Buoys could be used to mark channels and dangers, but they were not as common as might be expected, even in the vicinity of a major naval port. Graeme Spence commented on the approaches to Portsmouth in 1805,

> We found that there were not near so many buoys as the safety of men-of-war required, nor did the few that were there lie in the most proper situation . . . No alteration has taken place with any of the buoys . . . since those [surveys] made by Mr Mackenzie in 1784, except that in addition thereto a red buoy has been placed on the wreck of the *Royal George*, a white buoy on the wreck of the *Boyne*, and a black one on the Warren Ledge.[5]

As late as 1815, Burney wrote, 'During a period of upwards of 270 years, very little improvement has taken place in the system of buoyage, though much has been done for every other branch of navigation.'[6] A navigational buoy was usually a 'can buoy', conical in shape, with the pointed end downwards. It was painted one colour and marked as such on the chart, but as yet there was no standard system of marking buoys to distinguish one kind from another.

Lighted buoys were rare, but not unknown, so entry to harbour at night was avoided. Thirty-six different sites in English waters were marked with lighthouses by 1815, and some of these were harbour entrances with more than one light. Some lights, such as Eddystone and the Casquets, marked dangerous rocks and were run by Trinity House. There were also some private lights, paid for by fees from passing ships, and by harbour dues. Some marked dangerous rocks, others showed the entrance to harbours. The actual light was produced by coal fire (mostly on lights built on the shore), candles, or oil lamps. The light could be directed and intensified by means of a system of reflectors. Eddystone, the best known British lighthouse, marked some dangerous rocks off Plymouth. Its light consisted of

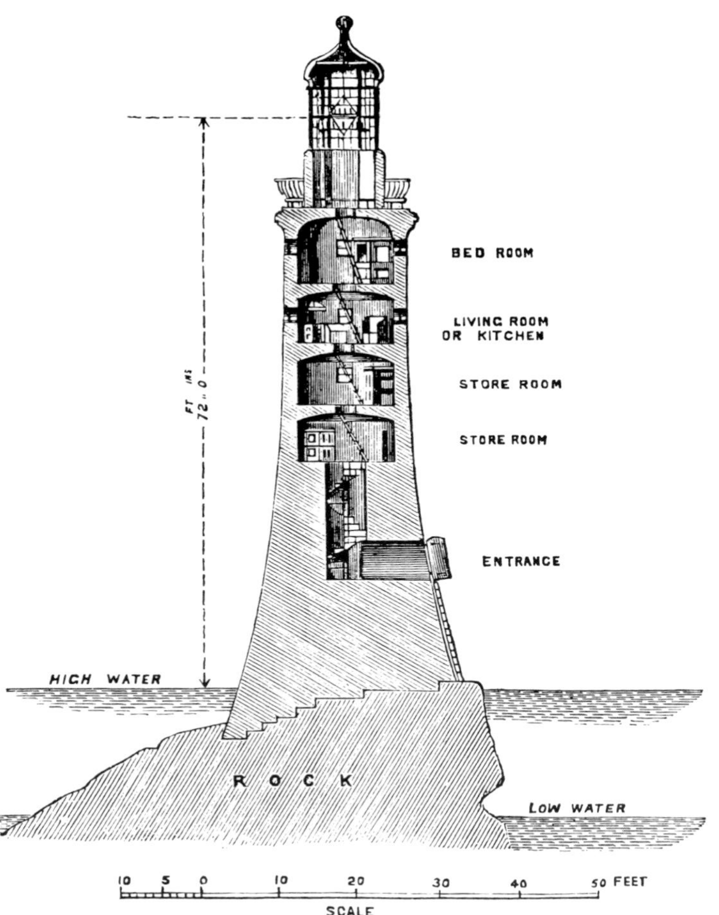

Smeaton's Eddystone lighthouse of 1759. The tower was later re-erected on Plymouth Hoe, and remains there to this day.

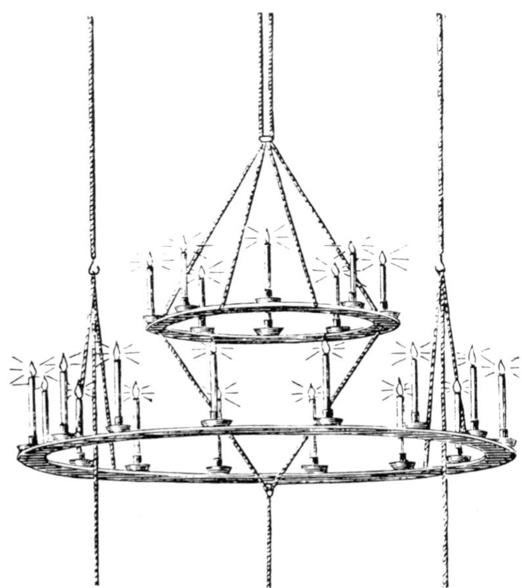

The chandelier of the Eddystone lighthouse.

'three tiers of reflectors, with a neat frame supporting 24 reflectors of silvered copper and brass burners.'[7]

Lightships were relatively rare in 1793 — only three were in use. Several more were established during the wars, especially at sites important to naval operations — in the Solent, Downs and Thames estuary. By the end of the wars, there were ten lightships in use. They mostly used a beacon which could be hoisted or lowered as required, and were not fitted with reflectors.[8]

Pilotage

In the circumstances, ships entering or leaving port relied heavily on pilots with local knowledge. In the River Thames and its estuary they were supplied by the Navy Board and licensed by Trinity House; from the Downs they were supplied by the Society of Pilots at Dover.[9] Pilots were only to be employed 'where it has been the practice to employ one, or in ports or channels which have not been frequented by His Majesty's ships, unless the ignorance of the master shall make it necessary', in which case the pilot's fee was to be deducted from the master's wages.[10] In most cases, a pilot was only taken on for a short period, and paid accordingly. In some parts of the world, it was necessary for a pilot to be taken on as part of the crew, with a cabin in the gunroom, and the rank of warrant officer.

In inshore waters, tides were often strong, and steering directly for the destination could be dangerous. One method was to plot courses on the chart, allowing for the tidal stream and leeway, and ordering the helmsman to steer by the compass. Another was to use 'transits' — two objects on shore which were directly in line. Such transits were marked on the charts, for example,

> To sail into or out of Portsmouth Harbour in the very best of water between the buoys, keep the belfry of Gosport Chapel on with the southmost brick sentry box in Blockhouse battery, which sentry box stands under the rampart on the outside a little to the southward of the flagstaff.
>
> To sail into Langtone Harbour, keep Mr Clerk Jervois's high white summer house, or folly, on with, or rather open to the Westward of Gunnen Point.[11]

Naturally, such navigation was possible only in good visibility.

In some places, off the southwest coast of England for example, coastal passages were quite simple, in good visibility at least. The water was deep and rocks were relatively few. The French side, off the coast of Brittany, had far more rocks, and was difficult to approach except with the best charts, and with good visibility. The *Magnificent* was lost off Brest in 1804, due to the inadequacies of charts. In the southern part of the North Sea, off the Dutch coast or in the Thames estuary, sandbanks were the main problem, and much care was needed with navigation. Local knowledge was usually preferred in such places, and pilots were often taken on if the master of the ship was unfamiliar with the area.

Log Lines and Lead Lines

The speed of the ship, and hence the distance travelled through the water, was calculated by means of the log line. This was a piece of light cord about 150 fathoms long. One end was fixed to a piece of wood shaped like a sector of a circle, which was the log itself; the rest of the line was coiled round a wooden reel, which was held so that the line was free to run out. The line had knots tied in it at fixed intervals, to measure distance. The log was thrown over the stern of the ship and allowed to get clear of the turbulence in the ship's wake. It was then allowed to run out, and timed by means of a small sandglass, for seven or fourteen seconds. The number of knots which ran out in this period measured the speed of the ship. Normally, the log was streamed every half hour, and these readings gave the average speed of the ship over the day's run, though it did not give a continuous read out, and was therefore subject to certain inaccuracies. The 'patent log' gave a continuous reading and measurement of distance travelled through the water, but it was not yet common by 1815.

Accurate knowledge of the sea bottom was essential to the navigator in coastal waters, giving warning of shallower water, and hence the approach of danger. A knowledgeable ocean navigator could tell that he was approaching a continental land mass; on a ship sailing towards Britain, he would enter 'soundings' about 150 miles west of Land's End, when he began to get a reading from his lead lines. A series of readings would give some idea of the profile of the bottom, and this could be compared with the chart. It was also possible to take a sample of the bottom, and find out whether it was sand, mud, weed, rock gravel and so on; the nature of the bottom was also marked on the chart, and could give some help in finding position.

Depth was found by means of the lead line. The lead itself was roughly conical in shape, with a hollow bottom. This could be 'armed' with tallow, which would pick up samples of the sea bottom.

The use of the log line: 14 is the log itself; 15 shows it being run out to measure the speed, and 15 is the reel from which the log line is allowed to run out. From Burney's Dictionary

A seaman heaving the lead, by Cruikshank.

The ordinary lead weighed about 7lb and was attached to a line 20 fathoms long. The deep-sea line was up to 200 fathoms long, and had a lead of 14 to 30lbs. The lead was cast by a seaman standing in the chains, who had to throw it forward so that it would be vertical when it reached the bottom. When the deep sea lead was used, the ship was normally hove-to, but even then accurate measurement was quite difficult. The lead line was marked at intervals of one fathom, using a standard code, which a skilled seaman could read in the dark. For example, a piece of black leather meant three fathoms, and a white rag indicated five.

Tides and Currents

It was well known that tides were caused by the attraction of the sun and the moon, and the state of astronomy allowed reasonably accurate predictions. Tides were particularly strong in southern England and Northern France, and these areas included some of the navy's most important fields of operation, so knowledge of tides was very useful. Tides could affect the navigator in two ways. In the first place, the height of tide at a given moment could allow him to predict whether he would be able to enter a particular harbour, or pass a sandbank. Secondly, the current created by tides had to be assessed for accurate navigation. A cross tide could cause a ship to go miles off course, unless allowed for; conversely, the navigator had to assess the effect of the tide on his day's run in calculating his dead reckoning position. A favourable tide could be used, by planning time of departure to get the maximum benefit from it; an unfavourable one could be avoided by anchoring for its duration, especially in light or unfavourable winds. Since the average tide lasted a little over six hours before reversing its direction, the skilled sailor could use it in many ways. Tide tables were published in the nautical almanacs, and formulae were given for finding the tide heights at different ports. Directions and strengths of streams were marked on charts, though many navigators and pilots relied on local knowledge as much as anything else.

Ocean currents, unlike tides, tended to be more constant in rate and direction. Sometimes, the navigator could shape his course to get the maximum help from a current such as the Gulf Stream. At all times, he had to allow for the estimated strength and direction of the current in finding his dead reckoning position. Such information he could glean from the pilot book, though it was not always easy to find the exact nature of a current.

> In the southern straits, or channels, of the Antilles, the velocity of the current is never under a mile an hour; but its changes are so great, that it is impossible to point out its exact direction, or to establish any general rule for its velocity.[12]

> When the trade wind prevails, a current, often very strong, sets down between Mauger Key and the Northern triangle; there, dividing itself, it sets to the southward between Turneff and Main Key, and to the northward between Triangle Reef and Ambergris Key.[13]

Occasionally, currents could help the navigator to establish his position, with the aid of a thermometer. When approaching the North American coast, a sudden rise in water temperature would show that the ship had entered the Gulf Stream. This had the advantage of 'showing her place upon the ocean in the most critical situation; for, as the current sets along the coast of America, at no great distance from surroundings, the mariner, when he finds this sudden increase in the heat of the sea, will be warned of his approach to the coast, and will thus have timely notice to take the necessary precautions for the safety of his vessel.'[14]

Principles of Celestial Navigation

Celestial navigation gave the seaman a means of establishing the

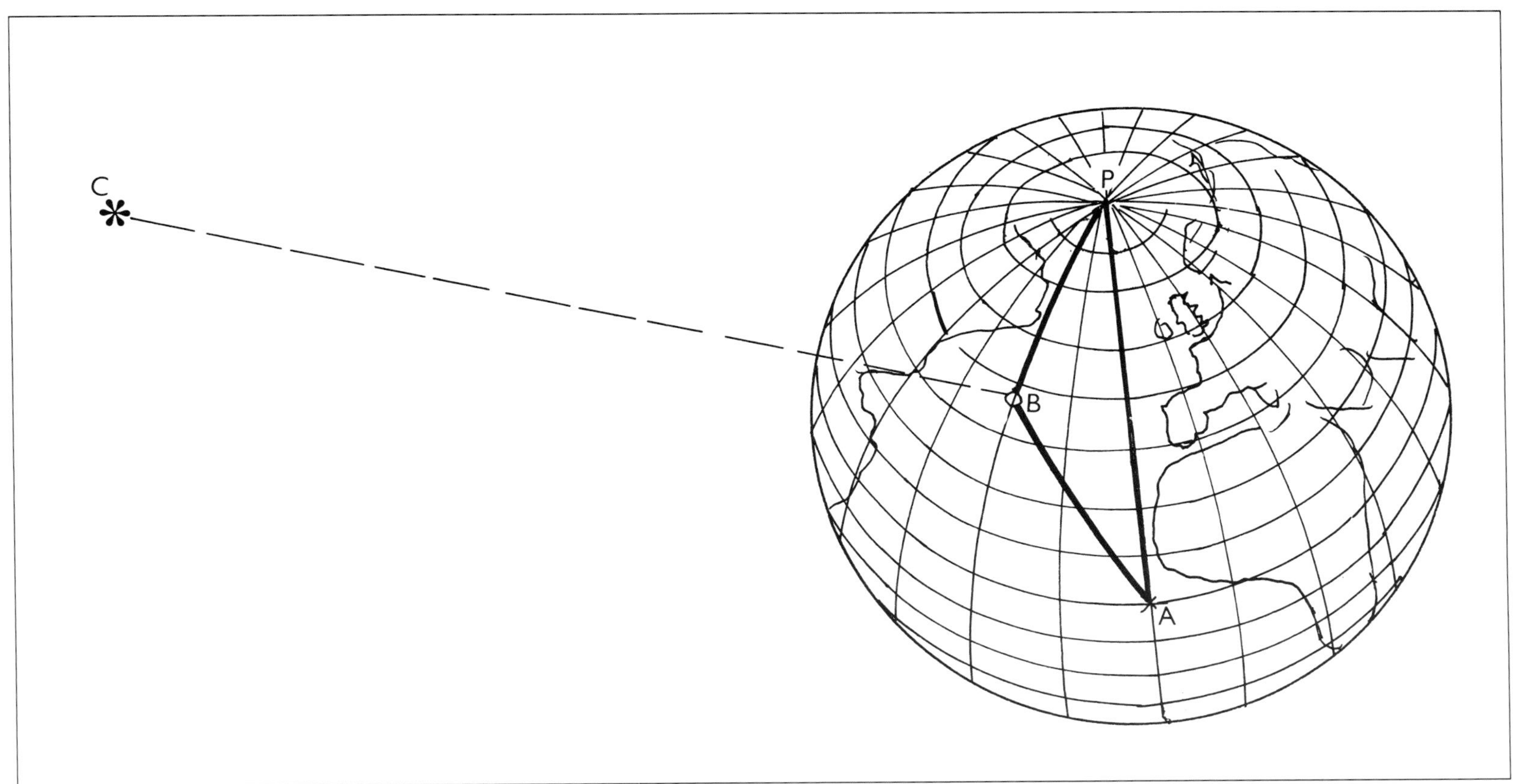

The principles of celestial navigation. C is the celestial body being observed. B is the position on earth directly below it. P is the pole, and A is the position of the ship. Distance AB can be measured using the sextant or quadrant angle, with corrections. PB is known from the astronomical tables, and AP is the latitude of the ship, which is known from the noon sight or other observations. Using spherical trigonometry, the angle APB can be calculated, and added to the known position of the star at that moment to give the longitude of the ship.

position of his ship with reasonable accuracy, though he might not have seen land for several weeks. It was based, of course, on the observation of heavenly bodies: fixed bodies, or stars, which always retained their place in the sky relative to one another; and moving bodies such as the sun, moon and planets. An essential part of the process was to measure, as accurately as possible, the angle between the body and the horizon. Several corrections were applied to this angle, for the height of the observer above the horizon, the inaccuracies in the instrument, and other factors. The nautical almanac gave data on the angles of the body in relation to the equator; and, from complicated calculations, the information could contribute to finding the position of the ship.

The most important proposition in celestial navigation was to solve the celestial triangle; this had one corner at the north or south pole, another at the position of the ship, and the third at a position on the earth directly under the celestial body. The length of one side, between the ship and the celestial body, was known from the measurement of the angle of the body. Another side, between the ship and the pole, was known from the latitude of the ship, which could be calculated by other means. The third side, between the celestial body and the pole, could be found from the nautical almanac, and thus the angle at the pole could be calculated by spherical trigonometry. Added to the known longitude of the celestial body, this would give the longitude of the ship. There was a built-in inaccuracy of the system, which was not always appreciated at the time; the latitude could not always be calculated at the same time as the other observations were made, and any difference had to be made up by dead reckoning, which was not always accurate. But the sailor of 1800 had far better means available than his predecessors. For good navigation, he relied on two important pieces of information; an accurate measurement of the angle of the celestial body with the horizon, and an accurate measurement of the time in relation to a particular place, usually the Greenwich meridian.

Quadrant and Sextant

Hadley's quadrant, invented around 1731, was simply an instrument for measuring angles. It consisted of an arm which pivoted on a frame, in the shape of a sector of a circle, with its rim graduated in degrees. The actual movement of the arm was only through 45 degrees, but a system of mirrors doubled that, to 90 degrees (hence the name quadrant), so that the angle of any celestial body could be measured. It was fitted with shades to protect the observer's eyes from the sun, and sometimes with a tangent screw for easier movement. It was made mainly of wood, with the scale and some other parts in brass. It was a considerable advance on previous instruments, such as the back-staff, in the measurement of angles.

The sextant was simply a more refined version of the quadrant, with modifications to make it more accurate, and to make it more suitable for lunar measurements, which had now become essential to the navigator. However, it never entirely replaced the quadrant during this period, being rather more expensive. The sextant was made of brass instead of wood. It operated through an angle of 60 degrees (hence the name), increased to 120 degrees by mirrors. It was fitted with a vernier scale which allowed measurement to within 10 seconds of arc. It was usually supplied with two telescopes, one showing the objects in their normal position, and the other inverting them. It took a good deal of care to adjust a sextant before use, and the various mirrors had to be set carefully.

The reflecting circle was a further extension, though it never

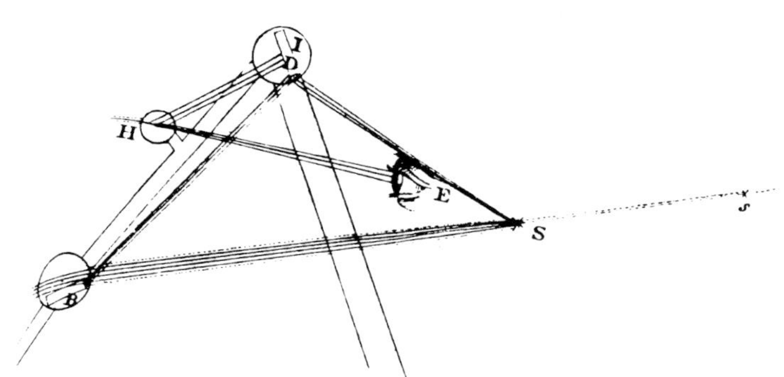

The principles of the sextant. The eye (E) looks through the half-mirror H. It can see the horizon through the part which is not silvered, while some of the light is reflected up to the next mirror, I, and then to the object being observed. As a result, the observer can see the horizon and the object brought into line, and measure the angle between them. From the English Encyclopaedia, 1802

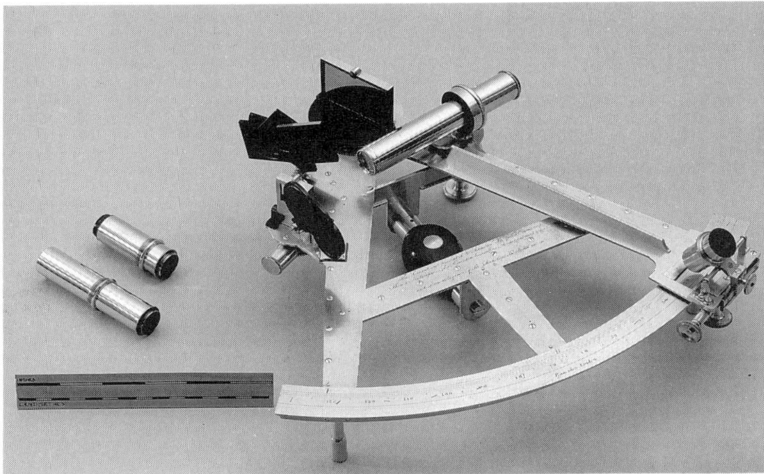

A sextant. The National Maritime Museum

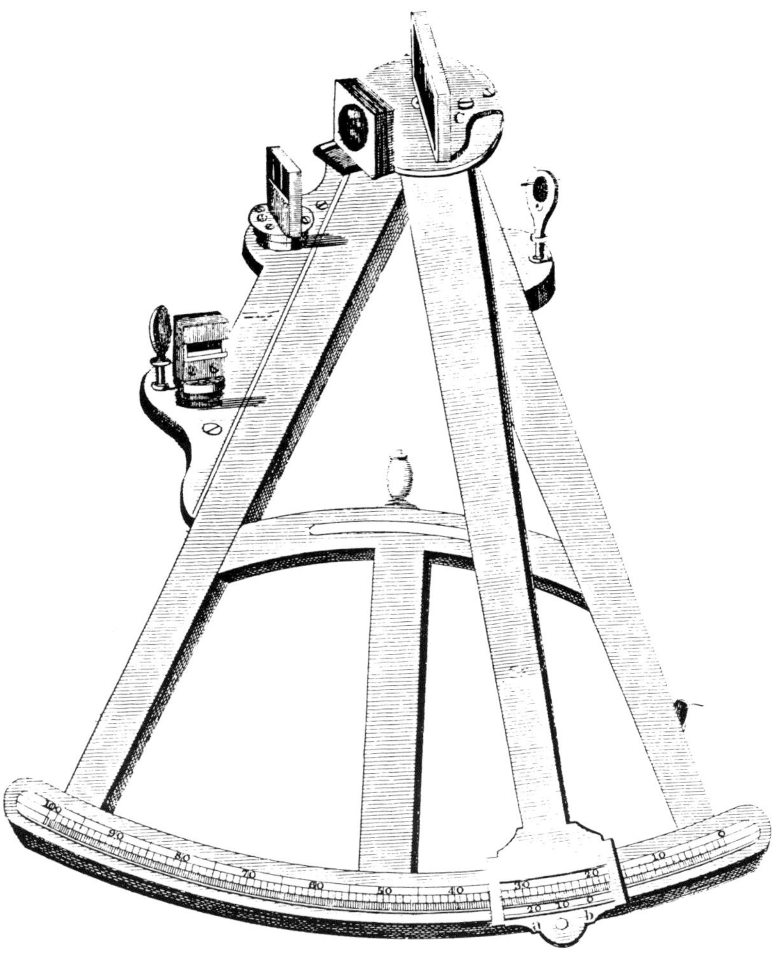

A quadrant. From the English Encyclopaedia

became so general as the other two. It could measure through a full angle of 360 degrees, and was, therefore, useful in lunar observations. Attempts were also made to fit the sextant or quadrant with an artificial horizon, for use when the true horizon was obscured. However, such measurements were never accurate enough to be useful.

Finding the Latitude

The latitude was relatively easy to find at noon, provided both the sun and the horizon were clearly visible. The observer took a series of sextant or quadrant angles, thereby finding the sun's highest position without any need to know the exact time. This angle, the zenith distance, was added to the sun's declination, found in the almanac, to give the latitude. The calculation was much more difficult at any time other than noon, and had built-in inaccuracies. Hence, the taking of the noon sight was an important event aboard ship, and, until 1805, the navigational day, as recorded in the log book, began at noon.

Longitude by Lunar and Chronometer

Longitude was always more difficult to find, but the essential problems had been solved by the 1790s. The first method, refined around 1760, was to measure the angle between the moon and a fixed star, thus giving an accurate indication of the time. Three separate angles had to be taken simultaneously — the height of the moon, that of the star, and the angle between the two. This had to be carefully calculated using spherical trigonometry, and the time was calculated using tables which gave the moon's position for periods of three hours. All navigators were expected to understand lunars, even after chronometers came into use.

The chronometer was simply an accurate clock, with compensating mechanisms to allow for all the variations which might be found aboard ship — temperature, movement of the ship, hard knocks, dampness, dust and many others. It had been developed by John Harrison over many years, and was finally and grudgingly awarded the £20,000 prize by the Board of Longitude in 1774. Chronometers were expensive and far from universal in the 1790s, though any naval ship going on a foreign voyage was entitled to have one, on the captain's application.

Chart Plotting

Chart-plotting instruments included dividers and compasses, and a 'plane scale', or scale ruler. Parallel rules were not yet in use, though they were known to surveyors ashore. Instead, the navigator placed his ruler along the course to be steered, and extended his dividers between the edge of the ruler and the centre of the nearest compass rose on the chart. He slid the dividers along the edge of the ruler, and the other end indicated the course on the compass rose.[15]

When the ship was out of sight of recognisable land and the weather did not permit astronomical observations, the ship was nagivated by dead reckoning. This was defined as

> The judgement or estimation which is made of the place where a ship is situated, without any observation of the heavenly bodies. It is discovered by keeping an account of the distance she has run by the *log*, and of her course steered by the *compass*; and by rectifying these data by the usual allowances for *drift*, *leeway*, & co. according to the ship's known trim. This reckoning, however, is always to be corrected, as often as any good observation of the sun can be obtained.[16]

The strength and direction of the tide was calculated using tables, the information on the chart, or the pilot's local knowledge. Leeway, or 'the lateral movement of a ship to leeward of her course'[17], caused by the effect of the wind, varied according to the strength of the wind, how close the ship was to the wind, and with the state of the sea. There was no method of calculating it except by experience of the performance of the ship, and it tended to be an uncertain element in any dead reckoning calculation. Inaccuracies in steering, reading the log or in estimation of the current could often be cumulative over a long period, so dead reckoning was only used as a last resort when no other means were available.

Captain Basil Hall describes the normal method of chart plotting:

> The ship's place each day, as estimated from the log-board, is noted on the chart; and also the place, as deduced from chronometers and lunar observations. The first is called the place by dead reckoning, the other the true place. The line joining the true places at noon, is called the true track; and that joining the others is called the track or course by dead reckoning. As it happens, invariably, that these two tracks separate very early in the voyage, and never afterwards come together, unless by accident.

He recommended that each day's dead reckoning position be taken from yesterday's true position.[18]

Navigational Procedure

The master's cabin or office, situated on the quarterdeck on the opposite side from the clerk's office, served as the chartroom and centre for navigation. It was fitted with a table for plotting, and the charts were stowed there. Other navigational instruments, such as log and lead lines, were stored in drawers in the binnacle, while instruments like sextants were the property of the officers using them, and were kept in their cabins.

The noon sight was one fixed point in the navigational day. Otherwise, things tended to happen half-hourly, when the log was cast. The officer of the watch recorded the course steered during the last half hour on the log board, which was usually a blackboard situated close to the wheel. Wind directions were also recorded, since these were needed in calculating leeway. All this was eventually transferred to the master's log, which was the basic navigational document of the ship, giving an hour-by-hour record of such details. The other officers also kept logs, though with less navigational information. The noon position was always recorded, whether by bearings on shore objects, or by dead reckoning, or by celestial navigation. There was a column for the wind directions during the day, and another for the 'remarkable occurrences'. This included a summary of the navigational information, but also included other matters, such as floggings, ships sighted, encounters with the enemy and so on. Officers had to submit their logs to the Admiralty before they could be paid, but often the logs of the captain and the various lieutenants show a great deal of similarity, suggesting that they were compiled in collusion.

6 Disaster at Sea

The Hazard of the Sea

No-one doubted that the seaman's life was a hazardous one. John Weatherell claimed to have been shipwrecked a dozen times, and to have been the sole survivor more than once.[1] Ships relied almost entirely on wind power, and often found themselves at the mercy of storms and gales. Many parts of the world were uncharted, and ships could have their bottoms ripped out by hidden reefs. They were made of wood and loaded with explosives, so fire was a constant danger. Rescue services were primitive or non-existent, and the lifeboat was in its infancy. Shipwreck formed the basis of much of English fiction, for example *Robinson Crusoe* and *Gulliver's Travels* (both written by landmen), and the public was well aware of the dangers of the sea.

Yet shipwreck was not the greatest killer of seamen. Disease and individual accident accounted for 70-80,000 men from 1793 to 1815, while shipwreck and fire killed around 13,000; enemy action came as a poor third, with about 6,500 fatalities.[2] Nevertheless, the toll was high; 101 rated ships, including twenty-eight ships-of-the-line and seventy-three frigates and small two-deckers, were lost through accident in these years. The largest was the *Queen Charlotte*, which caught fire in 1800, and was lost with the majority of her crew. In a typical year — 1799 — nineteen ships were lost. The *Apollo* frigate was lost off the coast of Holland, but the crew were saved. The *Weazel* sloop was sunk in Barnstaple Bay, and only the purser was saved. The *Prosperine* of 28 guns was sunk in the River Elbe, with the loss of fifteen lives. The *Nautilus* of 16 guns was lost off Flamborough Head, but the crew were saved. The *Grampus* store ship was grounded and lost on Barking Shelf in the Thames, without loss of life. The *Brave* lugger was run down in a collision with a transport off Beachy Head, and the crew were saved. *Les Deux Amis*, a captured sloop of 14 guns, was lost near the Isle of Wight, without loss of life. The *Contest* gun vessel was sunk off the coast of Holland, though again the crew was saved. The *Trincomalee* of 16 guns was blown up in an engagement with a French ship in the Straits of Babelmandel (at the entrance to the Red Sea), killing all her crew except two. The *Blanche* of 32 guns, was lost in the Texel, Holland, but her crew was saved. The *Fox* schooner sunk in the Gulf of Mexico, and the *Lutine* off the coast of Holland, with the loss of two men from the latter ship. The greatest loss of the year was the *Impregnable* of 90 guns, which went down between Langstone and Chichester, without loss of life. The *Nassau* of 64 guns was the second ship-of-the-line lost, with forty-two of her crew, off the coast of Holland. The *Orestes* of 16 guns foundered in a hurricane in the Indian Ocean, with the loss of all hands. *L'Espion*, a 38-gun frigate, was lost on the Goodwin Sands without loss of life. The *Sceptre* of 64 guns was lost in Table Bay, Cape of Good Hope, with 291 of her crew. The *Ethalion* of 38 guns was lost on the Penmarcks, South Brittany, but her crew were saved.

The Cleopatre *in a storm, 1814.* From the Naval Chronicle

L'Amaranthe, a sloop of 16 guns, was lost off the coast of Florida, and many of her crew died of hunger on shore.[3]

Fire

Clearly, a wooden ship was a highly inflammable object, especially dangerous because the crew often had nowhere to escape. It was impossible to avoid flames on the decks of ships, as they were needed for firing guns, cooking food, for lighting and, sometimes, for heating. 'Captain in the Royal Navy' referred to 'the fatal and shocking effects of fire', and of 'the dreadful mischief that a drunken man might create, where, in many cases, no alternative exists between the fury of the flames and the ocean'. He went on,

> Fire excites, at the moment when it bursts forth, the most violent agitation; and we find that, the example of others, without reflecting on the consequences of the act, has frequently plunged many unhappy victims into a watery grave, at a time when, by a proper degree of coolness and caution, their lives might have been preserved, and the flames overcome.[4]

Bartholemew James describes the fire which destroyed the *Boyne* in 1795:

> The flames were rapidly increasing, the loaded guns going off and multitude of people flying from all quarters to view the awful yet grand catastrophe. At five o'clock in the evening the noble ship... blew up and disappeared in an instant... the accident happened from the marines exercising on the poop, by a cartridge having been blown in the admiral's quarter gallery, which lodging in some packages in the cabin, caught fire at half past eleven in the morning.[5]

He also describes a fire in the steward's room of his own ship, the *Petrel* sloop, in 1796:

> On opening the door, the fire, then receiving vent, flew out with such violence that we were unable for some moments to recollect our state, for it appeared totally impossible to extinguish a fire that visibly made its progress to the bulkhead of the magazine, which we clearly saw was in flames. But the officers I had the honour of commanding were active and attentive, as well as brave and cool, and a quantity of water and wet bedding had been collected.[6]

Eventually the ship was saved.

Captain's orders usually included some regulations aimed at preventing fire breaking out. Smoking was often confined to the forecastle and upper deck; the master at arms was specially charged with seeing that all lights were extinguished at night, and water buckets were placed at strategic points, especially hanging from the break of the poop; the galley fire was put out on the approach to battle. Obviously the most hazardous areas of all were the magazine and the powder room, and special precautions were taken there. Both were kept locked and guarded when not in use, and only opened under the care of the proper officers.

Many captains made careful provisions for dealing with fire once it had started, though Captain Griffiths wrote 'It is not, I believe, yet a *general* practice to have the men stationed in case of fire. Surely there can be nothing more likely to avoid the confusion such as a calamity is calculated to produce, than that every officer and man should have a precise station, and duty assigned to them.'[7] On most ships, one man from each gun crew was a 'fireman', to be called if his services were necessary in action. However, fire could break out at any time, and aboard the *Mars*, there was quite an elaborate system for dealing with it. The men were to go immediately to their quarters. The carpenters were to open the cocks which allowed water into the pump well, and the suction pumps were to convey water to the appropriate decks, by means of hoses. Other men were to fill buckets of water in the cisterns of the chain pumps, and pass them along to the area of the fire. The weather-side gunports were to be closed, if possible, to prevent air reaching the fire.[8] According to 'Captain in the Royal Navy', 'In ships that have not a fire bill, when a fire is discovered, the usual mode is to beat to quarters, that it may detach their minds from viewing the danger, and prevent them from leaping overboard.'[9]

Explosion was a specially violent kind of fire. Naturally, there were few witnesses from ships which had suddenly blown up — survivors were few, and these were usually stationed at the bows and stern of the ship, well away from the explosion. When the *Amphion* frigate blew up in 1796, there were only eleven survivors, including a woman and child. Three officers and a marine guard were in the stern cabins at the time the boatswain was in the cathead and was blown into the water; about thirty persons died in the accident, including women and children visiting the ship.[10] The cause of the accident was not known, but it was conjectured that the gunner, who was under suspicion for stealing powder and had been intoxicated that day, had accidentally left a trail of powder leading to the magazine.

Man Overboard

Seamen often fell from the rigging. If they hit the decks, they were killed or seriously injured; if they hit the water they had some chance of survival, provided they could be got out of the water in time. Life-jackets were unknown, and the seamen of the time would probably have scorned to wear them. A 'life-preserver' had been 'lately contrived by Mr F C Daniel of Wapping, to secure persons from sinking in water when shipwrecked'.[11] It was said that 'if a person were to fall overboard, a trained seaman might almost instantly seize the life-preserver, and be overboard to the assistance of his distressed shipmate, holding him fast until a boat could be lowered from the ship.'[12] However, such items did not become standard issue, and there was no attempt to train seamen to swim — perhaps because this would have aided desertion.

If a man did fall overboard, the ship would be quickly hove-to, and its motion through the water would be stopped. The cutters and yawls suspended from davits on the stern and quarter could be launched fairly quickly, and manned with the sea boat's crew. But sometimes the attempt to rescue a man from the water could lead to much greater disaster. In 1804, the *Venerable*, 74, was raising anchor in Torbay when the fish-hook of the anchor gave way and a man fell into the sea. Preparations were made to lower a cutter, but in the confusion it was let go too quickly, and three men were drowned. Another boat succeeded in picking up the first man, but meanwhile the ship was drifting towards Brixham, and failed to tack to clear Berry Head, so that she was wrecked near Paignton.[13]

Leaks

Wooden ships always leaked to some extent, no matter how strong their construction or good their caulking. The ship was designed so that such water would be directed towards the pump well amidships, and so could be pumped out. The carpenter and his mates had the duty of sounding the well, by dipping a stick into it, to find the depth of water. A regular report was made to the officer of the watch, perhaps hourly in ordinary circumstances or more often in periods of danger. If the water seemed to be gaining, men were sent down in relays to operate the pumps, but pumping was hard work, and unpopular with the men. 'Few officers of any experience must not have known the difficulty with which men are almost drove to return to the pumps of leaking ships, when obliged to keep them going. It strains their loins, affects the muscular parts of their arms like violent rheumatic pains, and galls their hands.'[14] When the ship was seriously damaged, the situation became even worse, and men soon became exhausted by constant exertion.

Attempts, could be made to stop up leaks, even when at sea. In action, the carpenters were stationed on the orlop deck with plugs ready to stop up any shot holes made 'between wind and water'. However, it was more efficient to get at the leak from outside, if possible, as then the water would tend to push the blocking object towards the hole, instead of away from it. One way of doing this was by 'fothering', a form of which was described by Burney.

> A basket is filled with ashes, cinders and chopped rope yarns, and loosely covered with a piece of canvas; to this is fastened a long pole, by which it is plunged repeatedly into the water, as close as possible to the place where the leak is conjectured to lie. The oakum, or chopped rope yarns, being thus gradually shaken through the twigs, or over the top of the basket, are frequently sucked into the hole along with the water, so that the leaks becomes immediately choked, and the future entrance of water is thereby prevented.[15]

Another method was described by Griffiths. 'If part of a sail of number one canvas be doubled, and brought by ropes to cover the leak, though it may not stop it, there can be no doubt that it would materially assist in reducing it.' This method, however, only worked when the leak was 'not too near the keel, or too much in the run; that is, if it be in any part where you can bring a sail in *contact* with it.'[16] This method could be made more efficient by lining the sail with 'chopped rope yarns, oakum, wool, cotton, and co.'[17] Of course this was not always effective, and several ships were lost because of holes in their hull, usually caused by rocks, or by enemy action.

Grounding

Ships were quite often driven aground for one reason or another. Navigational error, especially failure to allow enough for leeway, was a common cause. Strong winds could make a ship uncontrollable, and prevent her from tacking out of a bay or estuary. Loss of gear, especially a rudder, could cause the ship to be driven onto sandbanks or rocks. Grounding was not always disastrous, and, in the majority of cases, the ship was got off without serious damage. On running aground, the captain would usually order all the sails taken in, to prevent the ship driving any further into the sand or mud. If it was before high tide he might simply wait for the water to rise and lift the ship off. Another possibility was to use the boats to lay out the kedge and stream anchor out astern, and haul the ship back onto them. It was also possible to lighten ship by putting heavy items such as stores and guns into the ship's boats or, in the last resort, jettisoning them. A combination of these techniques usually resulted in the ship being floated off eventually.

However, even a grounding on relatively soft sand or mud could cause the loss of a ship, if the circumstances of wind and tide were not favourable. In 1801, the *Invincible*, 74, hit a knoll of Great Yarmouth at a speed of 9 knots, due to navigational error by the pilots guiding the ship through the narrow channels of the area. Believing that she would sail over the knoll at high water, the captain 'ordered the topmasts to be struck and the water started and some of the provisions to be thrown overboard, in order to ease and lighten the ship.' However, the ship had been holed by the violence of her grounding, and the water continued to gain on the pumps. That evening 'the wind freshened greatly, and the swell rose suddenly, and the ship laboured and struck with such violence that I expected she would have broke asunder.' The masts were cut down to save topweight, and 'the ship forged over the bank and became afloat, but she was at this time totally ungovernable (her rudder being knocked off).' She drifted into deep water and was anchored there, but soon sank at her moorings due to the damage already sustained.[18]

The loss of the Magnificent *on an uncharted reef during the blockade of Brest; the seamen clambering up the side are being rescued by boat.*
The National Maritime Museum

Most of the boats were lost, and more than 400 men were drowned.

Hitting rocks was rather more dangerous, even in relatively calm water. The *Magnificent* struck uncharted rocks off Brest in 1804 while weighing anchor, and was totally lost, though her crew was saved by nearby vessels. In bad weather, the position became much worse. Ships could be broken to pieces in a short time, with few survivors. The Royal Navy's greatest disaster of these years was the loss of the *St George* and *Defence*, which were cast away on the coast of Jutland in 1811, with the loss of over 1000 men. This coast was a classic lee shore, with the prevailing winds blowing onto it, and no harbours of refuge.

Storm and Tempest

Ships were built to stand almost any weather, and had to survive all kinds of storms, and even hurricanes, though suitable precautions had to be taken by the crew to ride out the storm. As a result, few ships were lost through weather alone; only seven rated ships are believed to have been lost in this way, and some of these, such as the *Blenheim*, 74, simply vanished without trace.[20] A storm could cause enormous damage to a ship, as Bartholemew James found out in 1791.

> The ship laboured so much and shipped so much water that six hands was constantly employed at the pumps, and the water gaining on us. At daylight of this horrid morning we were reduced to the foresail only, and the ship could hardly stagger under . . . At five in the morning of the 24th, being then under a close reef fore topsail and foresail, scudding at the rate of seven knots, the tiller rope gave way and the ship broached to, which threw her once more on her beam ends and filled her decks fore and aft with water.[21]

She lost most of her masts and threw much of her cargo overboard, but survived.

Many ships were of course driven onto a lee shore by storm, and were destroyed by rocks. Even in the open sea, a sudden squall could lay a ship 'on her beam ends', with the wind pushing her so far over that her deck beams were almost vertical. There was a danger that the guns would break loose and the ballast would shift, causing further damage; however, most ships recovered as the squall ended, though often with the loss of their masts. When a ship was laid over on her side, the sails and rudder lost most of their effect, and she was uncontrollable. One answer to this was to lay a hawser out to windward, with a buoy or spar at the outer end to keep it afloat. This helped to bring her bow or stern to the wind. In an extremity, the masts had to be cut away to reduce topweight. Skilled seamen could detect the approach of a storm by observing cloud and weather conditions. Sail was reduced as quickly as possible, in order to ride out the gale. In such circumstances, a ship would 'lie to', or heave to, meeting the waves at an angle of about 45 degrees, so they could do the least damage. Sometimes this was done under the mizzen staysail, though the ship could not wear without also setting her fore or foretopmast staysail. In other cases ships could ride out a storm under mizzen staysail and mizzen, but this placed a great deal of stress on the mizzenmast. Some ships were better under the main topsail. 'A heavy rolling ship, whose centre of gravity lies low, will require a lofty sail to keep her steady in the water, and to lay her down for that purpose. A close reefed main topsail . . . is generally used for such a ship to lie under.'[22] Another possibility was the main staysail 'for ships which are not so stiff . . . a main staysail . . . is reckoned the most eligible of any *single* sail, as it strains the ship much less than any other, by lying immediately over the greatest cavity, and the power is divided between the main and fore masts.'[23]

A ship scudding before a wind. From Serres's, *Liber Nauticus*

In other cases, the pressure could be divided between all three masts, using three lower staysails and the mizzen. Yet other ships, especially those which were trimmed very much by the stern, lay to under the foresail, as this made them easier to steer.

If a ship had blown out all her canvas, or she was unable to bear any, then she could lie 'under bare poles'. One method of keeping control of the ship's movements in these circumstances was to 'veer a good scope of a hawser or cablet over the lee quarter . . . with a buoy, and co, attached to the end, to keep it from sinking'.[24] The hawser would tend to remain to the windward side of the ship, pulling her stern in that direction and thus allowing the ship to be brought before the wind, when the hawser was hauled in.

Steering was often difficult while a ship was riding out a storm, and she could easily be 'brought by the lee' — the ship was so far off course that the wind came on the wrong side of her sails, and the masts were again in danger. If this happened, the sails had to be trimmed rapidly before any damage was done. If the steering diverged in the opposite direction, bringing the broadside of the ship into the wind, she would 'broach to'. This, too, could put great pressure on the masts and sails, and could result in their loss.

Box and Club Hauling

While trapped in a bay or close to a lee shore, it was essential that a ship be able to tack or wear out of it. This was often difficult in heavy seas, which prevented the head of the ship from coming up to the wind. When a ship failed to tack in such circumstances, she was said to be 'in irons' — unable to pay off in one tack or the other, and therefore immobilised. One way of tacking in unfavourable conditions, when the ship was well manned, was by 'box hauling'. The after yards of the ship were braced round so that they were aback, causing the ship to make stern way. The mainsail and mizzen were brailed up, and the helm was turned to bring the stern round towards the wind. Eventually, the ship would turn through nearly 180 degrees, with her stern to the wind. The yards were then squared and filled, the ship gathered headway, and moved through 90 degrees or more to put her on the opposite tack. This manoeuvre placed considerable strain on the masts and stays, and most seamen would use it only in an emergency.

Club hauling was even more drastic, and was used only when the ship would neither tack nor wear, and was in imminent danger of running aground. It involved dropping the lee anchor as the ship turned towards the wind, with a hawser led to it from the lee quarter. The cable was brought to by the stopper, and this tended to pull the

A ship under trysails. From Serres's, *Liber Nauticus*

Club hauling. From Darcy Lever's *Young Sea Officer's Sheet Anchor*

head of the ship further into the wind. The cable was cut, but the hawser was left on a little longer to help bring the stern round, before it too was cut. Since it involved the expenditure of an anchor, club-hauling was not often done.

Jury Rigs

Having lost all or some of their masts, captains were ingenious in finding ways of replacing them at sea. Ships always carried some spare spars, albeit light ones such as topmasts and topgallant yards. These could be lashed to the stump of the broken mast or, failing that, the remnant of the old mast would have to be removed from the partners, and the spare spar put in its place. Standing rigging would be improvised from spare cordage, and yards would be lashed across to hang a sail from. A temporary sail could be found from among the spare sails issued to the ship, or improvised from tarpaulins or spare lengths of canvas, or even from joining boat sails together. With most jury rigs, the foremast was given priority, for with that mast alone the ship could sail reasonably well with the wind behind her. Damaged ships could also be towed by their companions, until they could be repaired in dockyards.

Seamen abandoning ship. From G Ramsay's *Shipwrecks and Disasters at Sea*, 1812

Damage to the steering gear was equally serious. An extra tiller was issued to ships, and the rudders of large ships had two holes, one above and one below the upper deck so that the spare could be fitted without necessarily removing the remains of the old one from the tenon. Loss of the rudder was potentially catastrophic if the ship was close to danger; and even if there was time available, replacement was difficult because no spare was carried. Emergency chains were fitted to hold the rudder to the ship even if the gudgeons and pintles were broken, but these did not always hold, and many rudders were lost when ships went heavily aground, as happened with the *Invincible* in 1801. One well-publicised way of making a jury rudder, invented by Captain Pakenham, was to place three spars together, cut to the appropriate lengths. Planks were then nailed on both sides of them, producing an assembly of similar size and shape to the original rudder.

Abandoning Ship

As a ship approached her last extremity, discipline tended to collapse, and there was a common myth that the authority of the captain no longer existed in law. Sailors had little religious feeling, and were more inclined to break into the spirit room than to pray if it became apparent that all was lost.

> All hands were now struck with consternation and dismay, and everything was enveloped in uncertainty and gloom. The officers, hoarse by so much exertion of voice, issued their orders hesitatingly, and in vain. Subordination, the first and most important branch in naval discipline, seemed for the time being suspended in every man... In vain did the captain call out for all hands to remain on board till day break, when all would be saved, everyone acted to the best of his own judgement.'[25]

However, discipline usually remained intact while there was some hope of rescue. If there were other vessels nearby and the seas were not too rough, or the ship was near the shore, then the ship's boats could be used to get the men off. Not surprisingly, this in itself was very hazardous.

> The boat it was my fortune to be placed in was a very large boat and had a small pump fixed in her. This was of infinite service in freeing the boat, and also keeping us in motion. We were twenty-eight souls on board... Our foresail, the only sail we had left, was of very much service to us in keeping the boat before the sea and also prevented her from shipping the water she would have shipped by lying in the trough of the sea. We suffered a great deal from the severity of the cold, more particularly in the snow squalls which followed each other successively.'[26]

These tales are harrowing enough, but, for the 13,000 seamen who perished by the sea, the disaster was worse.

Part IX
SHIPBOARD LIFE

1 The Organisation of the Crew

The Need for Ship Organisation

A first rate ship had a crew of over 800 men, and even a large frigate had nearly 300. Many of these were disaffected, unwilling, illiterate or stupid. From time to time, most of them could be disgruntled, homesick, tired, drunk or sick. But all the complex and highly-skilled manoeuvres of the ship had to be carried out. The sailors might spend years at a time on board, relying on the navy for all their material needs. They had to live together in incredibly confined space. To make such a body of men into an efficient team required an enormous degree of discipline and organisation.

We know very little about how ships' crews were organised before the 1750s. Captains seem to have paid little attention to the welfare of their men, and the sailors, themselves, would have resented any interference. Presumably, duties about ship were carried out in traditional ways, as little was written down. But, from the 1750s onwards, the life and work of the crew was increasingly regulated. Ships were now bigger, and a group of several hundred men could not be treated as an amorphous mass; the crew had to be divided up for different tasks and roles. Campaigns were longer, and so were individual voyages; captains were likely to be with their men for longer periods of time, so they became more concerned with their welfare and discipline. Naval warfare was more intense, and a well-trained crew was a great advantage. For all these reasons, the organisations of crews had become much more elaborate by 1793.

According to a midshipman of 1811, 'Every man has his separate station allotted to him according to the service which is going on; consequently as soon as an order is given the proper person is immediately at his post, every officer being in possession of a list of all names and attached to each name the several duties to which the man is occasionally appointed.'[1] A single sailor would have many different roles, according to what the ship was doing at that moment. Aboard the frigate *Bacchante* in 1812, for example, David Munroe was in the first part of the larboard watch. He was one of the crew of the first yawl, and belonged to the division of main topmen. In action, he helped serve the first gun on the quarterdeck, but if necessary he might be called away to work the pumps. In unmooring ship, he would help put on the nippers to the messenger and cable. When all hands were called to make or shorten sail, he was to rig out the main topgallant studding sail boom. When the ship was put about, he was to let go the backstay falls on the quarterdeck, and when this was done in action he worked on the fore and main sheets. When all hands were called to reef topsails, he was stationed on the main topsail yard. When the courses were reefed and the topgallant yards and masts were taken down on the approach of a storm, he helped toggle or untoggle the main topgallant halyards. When all hands were called to furl sail, he was stationed on the main topsail yard. He had a different set of duties when operations were performed with one watch alone.[2] In addition, he would sling his hammock at a particular place in the ship, and stow it in another in the daytime. He would belong to a mess for his meals, and he might have some duties as part of the mess. He would be part of a division for administrative and welfare purposes. In all, he might have twenty-five or thirty different roles about the ship, and he had to be familiar with them all. Aboard most ships, the men were allocated to these roles by the first lieutenant, taking into account their individual capabilities.

Watches

Clearly, the first task of the first lieutenant was to ensure that enough competent men were on duty at any given moment to keep the ship safe. To achieve this, it was normal to divide the crew into two watches. The anonymous 'Captain in the Royal Navy' strongly recommended three watches: 'Captains, prejudiced in favour of old customs, cannot divest themselves of the idea, that their ships would not be safe with less than half the ship's company on deck; and again, it is a very predominant opinion, that a ship's crew, being at three watches, acquires a habit of laziness, which disqualifies them for active pursuits when required.' However, the captain argued that the three-watch system should be used as a reward for an efficient crew. It should be introduced 'after the ship has been some time in commission, and at sea, that it may be considered as an indulgence; and that if, from sickness, desertion, or any other cause of being short of complement, it be necessary to reduce them to two watches again, it should not be considered as a hardship.'[3]

However, it is clear that the majority of ships used the two-watch system, by which the bulk of the crew was divided into two equal parts. Burney's dictionary of 1815 assumed that the two-watch system was standard, and that a three- or four-watch system was used only occasionally, and in harbour.[4] The watches were known as larboard and starboard. When both watches were on deck, the men of the larboard watch were often ordered to operate the ropes on that side. According to a midshipman on the *Gibraltar*, 'The lieutenants in succession take the command of a watch consisting of half the ship's company, and a third of the midshipmen; but as it seldom happens that all the hands in a watch are wanted at the same time, they are not subjected to much fatigue, unless upon extraordinary occasions.'[5]

Idlers

The majority of men were placed in watches, and the remainder were known as the idlers. According to Burney, 'idler' was 'the general name given to all those on board a ship of war, who, from being liable to constant day duty, are not subjected to keep the night watch; but must, nevertheless, go on deck if all hands are called during the night.'[6] The author of *Observations and Instructions* recommended sixty-two idlers on a first rate, or 7 per cent of the total crew; down to twenty idlers (10 per cent) on a sixth rate. These included the master at arms and ship's corporals, the armourer, sailmaker, cooper and their respective mates, the yeoman of the boatswain's, carpenter's and gunner's store rooms; various servants, and the cook and his assistants; butchers, hairdressers, barbers, poulterers, tailors, the pursers steward and the writer to the first lieutenant. Aboard the *San Domingo* in 1812, with a crew of about 590, there were twenty-seven 'idlers exempted from working ship duty', including thirteen men in the band, the master at arms and corporals, the ship's cook and pursers steward, the wardroom servants and officers' cooks, and the 'captain of the head'. There were also thirty 'working' idlers, who went on deck when all hands were called to work ship — the yeoman, artisans, cook's mates, barbers and tailors. Finally, there were twenty marine idlers — two in the band, plus more tailors, shoemakers, painters, bakers and servants. Presumably, some of them had been chosen because of the civilian occupations.

Parts of Ship

For purposes of duty, each watch was divided into several 'parts of ship', reflecting the area in which the men mostly worked. The

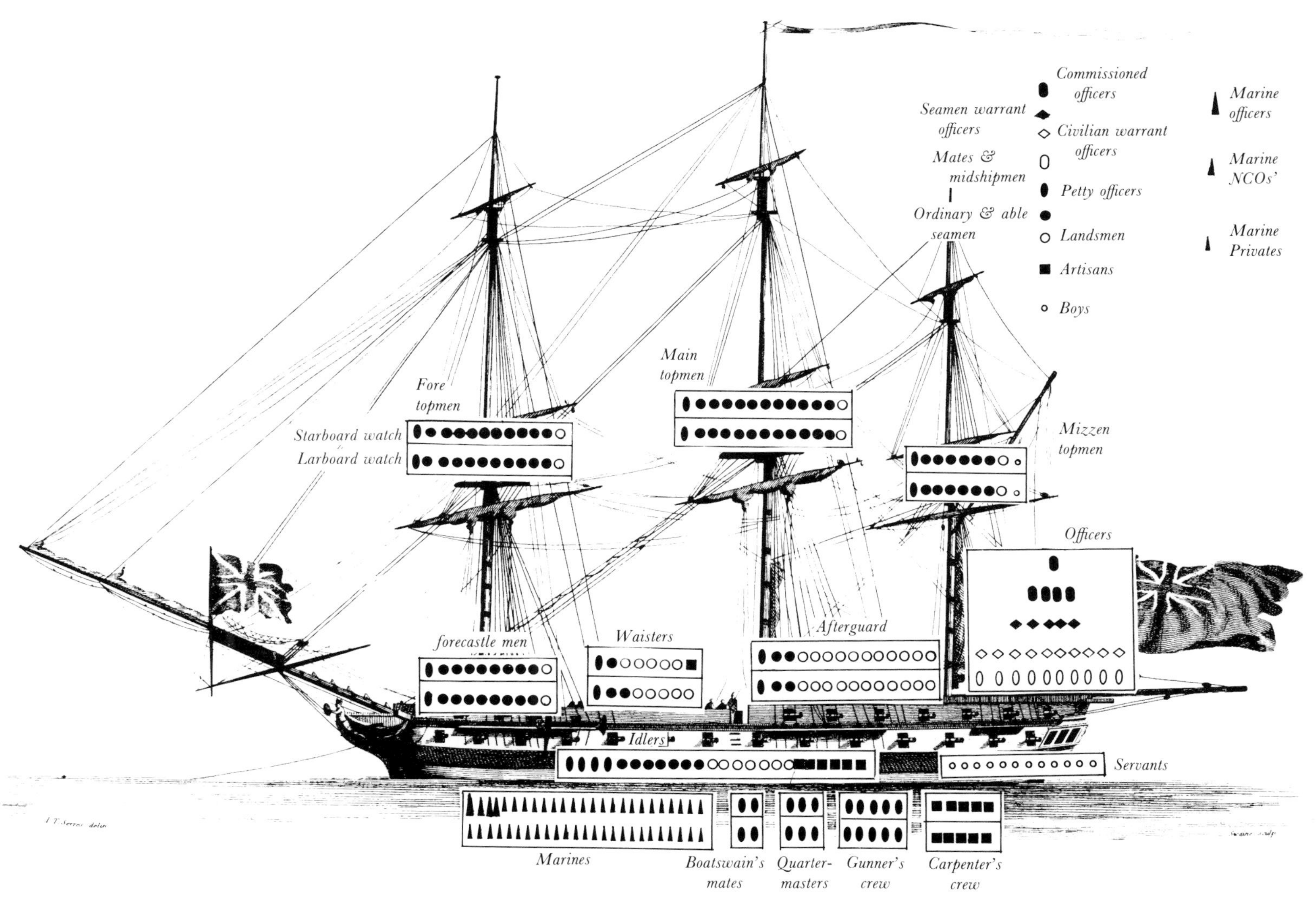

The allocation of the crew of a 36-gun frigate, based on figures given by Marryat in NRS Manning Pamphlets. Background illustration from Serres's, *Liber Nauticus*

topmen were the most skilled seamen. On large ships, there were three groups of topmen, for the fore, main and mizzen; on smaller ships, the mizzen topmen were part of the afterguard. According to Robert Wilson, a seaman of the time, the work of the topman 'not only requires alertness but courage, to ascend in a manner sky high when stormy winds do blow; in short, they must . . . exert themselves briskly. The youngest of the topmen generally go the highest.' According to Captain Marryat, 'the smartest able seamen are, as much as possible, distributed among those classes which go aloft, such as the maintopmen and foretopmen.'[7] He recommended that a 36-gun frigate should have twenty-six maintopmen and twenty foretopmen, all but two of whom were petty officers or able seamen; the others were promising landsmen attached for training. Aboard the *San Domingo* 74, there were twenty-five foretopmen, twenty-seven maintopmen and fifteen mizzentopmen in each watch.[8] Each group was commanded by a petty officer known as the captain of the foretop, etc. Until 1806, they only had the pay of able seamen, but after that they had the same rates as quartermaster's mates.

The other members of the crew rarely went aloft. The forecastle men had to do a certain amount of skilled work with anchors, and according to Wilson they were 'generally allowed in all ships to be the best sailors in the ship', but they were also 'the most elderly and corpulent of the seamen, because their duty is not so urgent as the topmen'.[9] Marryat's 36-gun frigate had twenty of them, of whom eighteen were petty officers or able seamen, under the command of a captain of the forecastle for each watch. The afterguard worked on the quarterdeck and poop. It was 'composed of a description of men who never go aloft, except to furl the mainsail, which is seldom done, and are merely required to pull and haul; out of twenty-eight, six are able seamen, who serve as leading men to the others'. The *San Domingo* had twenty-five forecastle men in each watch, twenty-two in the afterguard, and six more in the poop afterguard. The waisters were the least skilled of the men on deck; they were 'the worst of the landsmen, and are what seamen call neither soldiers nor sailors'; their duty is to do all the drudgery work on the main, or gundeck, and occasionally to assist in working ship'. Marryat allowed five able seamen and eleven landsmen, and the San Domingo had thirty waisters in each watch.

These five or six parts of ship made up about half the ship's seamen, excluding marines, boys, officers and servants. Also included in the watch system were the certain groups of petty officers. Four boatswain's mates served on Marryat's frigate, and six quartermaster's mates. The gunner's crew was quite large, with one quarter gunner to every four guns. There was not always enough work for them in the maintenance of the armament, and they were often employed as an elite division of seamen, for special tasks.

Divisions

For administrative, social and sanitary purposes captains of large and medium-sized ships organised their crews into divisions. This was actually demanded in the Admiralty *Regulations and Instructions*, which in general have little to say about the organisation of the crew. The captain was

> with the assistance of the officers, to divide all the ship's company, exclusive of the marines, into as many divisions as there are lieutenants allowed to the ship; the divisions are to be equal in number to each other, and the men are to be taken equally from the different stations in which they are watched. A lieutenant is to command each division; he is to have under his orders as many master's mates and midshipmen as the number on board, being equally divided, will admit; he is to sub-divide his division into as many sub-divisions as there are mates and midshipmen fit to command under his orders.[10]

The main purpose of the division was to allow the officers to supervise the health and welfare of the men. Clothing and bedding were to be examined; the officers were to prevent 'swearing, drunkenness and every other immorality'. Aboard the *Mars* in 1804, the crew was divided into five divisions, with several squads in each. The petty officer or midshipman in charge of each squad was to keep a list of all his men, with their duties, and the numbers of their hammocks. In port they were to muster their men every evening, and at sea they were to inspect their clothing and persons every Sunday morning.[11]

Stations

Each man was allocated a station for each of the important manoeuvres carried out by the ship. Aboard the *San Domingo*, these included mooring and unmooring, getting under weigh, tacking ship with the watch, wearing ship with the watch, and manning the yards. Groups rather than individual men were allocated to tasks; for example, when getting under weigh, the foresail was to be loosed by the 'forecastle men of the first part of both watches', the main topsail by 'the main topmen of the first part of the starboard and third part of the larboard watch'. The main sheets were to be hauled tight by the 'afterguard of both watches, second and third part of the starboard watch of main topmen, and poop afterguard of both watches'. Marines were included in the station bills, and in tacking ship they were to haul on the main brace.[12] On a smaller ship like the *Bacchante*, individual men were given tasks, except for the less skilled groups such as the afterguard. When all hands were called to shorten sail, for example, the afterguard of the watch on deck was to man the main clewgarnets; when reefing topsails, the first part of the starboard watch of the afterguard was to man the mizzen topsail reef tackles.[13]

A list of around 1800[14] gives the number of men to be employed in various tasks in the different manoeuvres. In mooring or unmooring a 100-gun ship, for example, thirty men were to be on the forecastle, seventy at the heaving tier of cable and sixty at the veering tier. Thirty were to 'light round messenger', thirty to hold onto the messenger, and there were six nipper men. Fourteen were to 'carry forward and hold on' to the nippers, and four to pay the cable down the hatchway. Fifteen were to operate the fish tackle, while ninety-six were stationed at the capstan bars, and twenty-four more at the swifters of the capstan. This took up a total of 383 men, leaving 275 for other duties, such as preparing the sails.

Quarters

In action, most of the crew were stationed at the guns. A first rate of 110 guns had 738 men, exclusive of officers and servants. Fifty-three men were quartered at the guns of the quarterdeck and forecastle, 144 on the upper deck, 192 on the middle deck and 224 on the lower deck — a total of 613, or 83 per cent of the crew. A 36-gun frigate had a total of 232 men, with eighteen on the quarterdeck guns, twelve on the forecastle, and 143 on the upper deck — 173 men, or 74 per cent. A standard number of men was allowed to each gun of a given size — fourteen for a 32-pounder, eleven for an 18-pounder, and eight for a 12-pounder, for example. In fact, this meant a pair of guns, one on each side of the ship; it was assumed that the crew would not often have to fight both sides of the ship at once. Thus a single 32-pounder had a crew of seven men in a well-manned ship, but it would combine with its opposite crew when the ship was engaged on one side only.

Out of these seven, one man would be the gun captain. Most of the others had subsidiary duties, and would be called away in certain circumstances. Aboard the *Goliath* in the 1800s, two men in each pair of guns had 'B' marked against their names. They were boarders, to be called on deck when necessary. Two more, usually the skilled

A page from the station list of the San Domingo. The National Maritime Museum

Mooring or Unmooring continued

WAIST.

Lieut. Lieut.

Mr. Mr.

Topsail Sheets.

Fore. 3rd part of the Starbd. Watch of Fore Topmen, Waisters of both Watches & Idlers of the Larboard Watch.

Main. On the Quarterdeck. Afterguard of both Watches, 2nd & 3rd part of the Starbd. Watch of Main Topmen, and Poop Afterguard of both Watches.

Mizen. On the Poop. 2nd part of Mizen Topmen of both Watches, and Signal men.

Hoisting the Topsails.

Fore. Forecastle men of Starbd. Watch & 1st part of Larbd. Do. Fore Topmen of the Starbd. Watch & Waisters of both Watches. The Captains of the Forecastle to see the halyards stretched close aft to the Quarter-deck.

Main. All the Starboard Watch & 3rd part of Larboard Watch of Main Topmen, Afterguard of both Watches, and Idlers of the Larboard Watch.

Mizen. 2nd part of both Watches of Mizen Topmen, Poop Afterguard and Signal men.

In the event of standing fast Heaving the Men stationed to the Capstan, Cables & Messenger to divide themselves in the following manner to the Topsail Sheets. The Marines to the Main Topsail Sheets, Sailors to the Fore, and Boys to the Mizen, who are also to assist in hoisting the Topsail they Sheet home.

POOP.

Lieut.

Mr. Mr.

IDLERS.

Starbd. Watch. 18 in No. Larbd. Watch 18 in No.

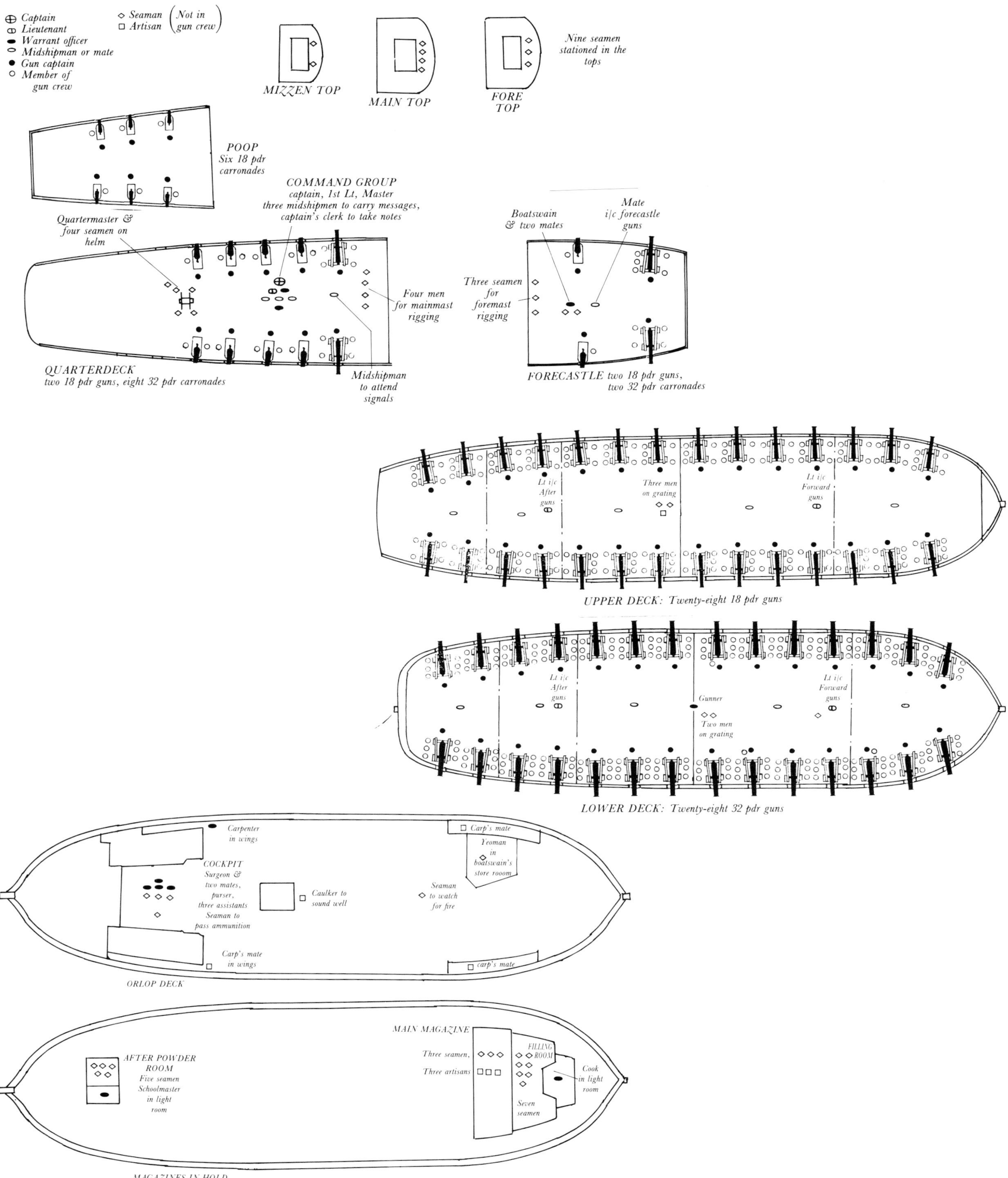

Captain
Lieutenant
Warrant officer
Midshipman or mate
Gun captain
Member of gun crew
Seaman (Not in gun crew)
Artisan (Not in gun crew)
MIZZEN TOP
MAIN TOP
FORE TOP
Nine seamen stationed in the tops
POOP
Six 18 pdr carronades
COMMAND GROUP
captain, 1st Lt, Master
three midshipmen to carry messages,
captain's clerk to take notes
Quartermaster & four seamen on helm
Four men for mainmast rigging
QUARTERDECK
two 18 pdr guns, eight 32 pdr carronades
Midshipman to attend signals
Boatswain & two mates
Mate i/c forecastle guns
Three seamen for foremast rigging
FORECASTLE two 18 pdr guns, two 32 pdr carronades
Lt i/c After guns
Three men on grating
Lt i/c Forward guns
UPPER DECK: Twenty-eight 18 pdr guns
Gunner
Two men on grating
LOWER DECK: Twenty-eight 32 pdr guns
Carpenter in wings
Carp's mate
Yeoman in boatswain's store rooom
COCKPIT
Surgeon & two mates, purser, three assistants
Seaman to pass ammunition
Caulker to sound well
Seaman to watch for fire
Carp's mate in wings
carp's mate
ORLOP DECK
AFTER POWDER ROOM
Five seamen
Schoolmaster in light room
MAIN MAGAZINE
Three seamen,
Three artisans
FILLING ROOM
Seven seamen
Cook in light room
MAGAZINES IN HOLD

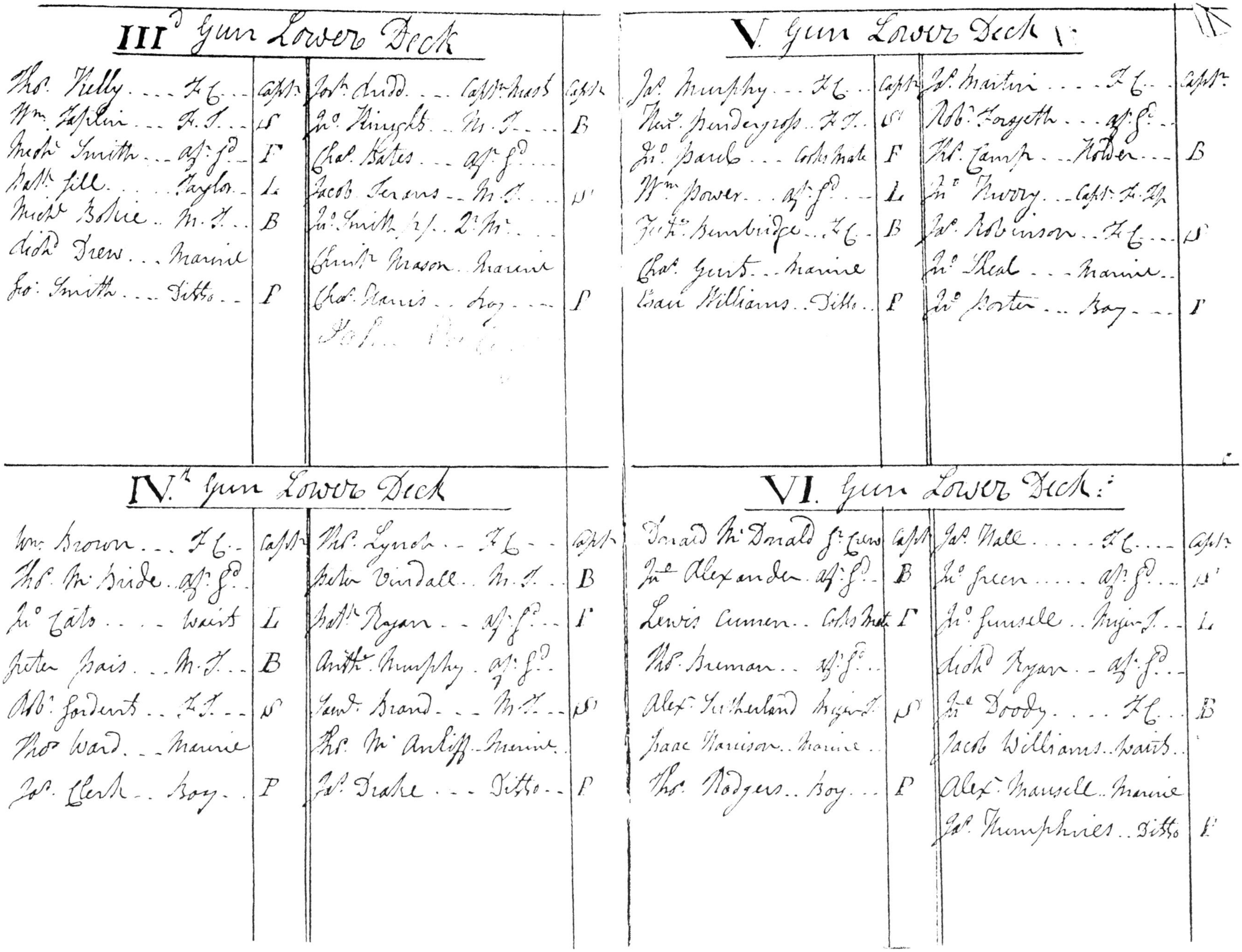

IIId Gun Lower Deck

Thos. Kelly	F.C.	Captn.	Jos. Judd	Captn. Mast	Captn.
Wm. Tapling	F.T.	S	Jno. Knights	M.T.	B
Michl. Smith	afr. Gd.	F	Chas. Bates	afr. Gd.	
Natt. Fill	Taylor	L	Jacob Servens	M.T.	S
Michl. Bolice	M.T.	B	Jno. Smith	2d M.	
Richd. Drew	Marine		Christr. Mason	Marine	
Jos. Smith	Ditto	P	Chas. Harris	Boy	P

V. Gun Lower Deck

Jas. Murphy	F.C.	Captn.	Jas. Martin	F.C.	Captn.
Nichs. Pendergrass	F.T.	S	Robt. Forsyth	afr. Gd.	
Jno. Pauls	Cooks Mate	F	Thos. Camp	Holder	B
Wm. Power	afr. Gd.	L	Jno. Ivory	Captn. F. Top	
Fredk. Bembridge	F.C.	B	Jas. Robinson	F.C.	S
Chas. Guest	Marine		Jno. Sheal	Marine	
Evan Williams	Ditto	P	Jno. Porter	Boy	P

IV.th Gun Lower Deck

Wm. Brown	F.C.	Captn.	Thos. Lynch	F.C.	Captn.
Thos. McBride	afr. Gd.		Peter Vindall	M.T.	B
Jno. Tato	Waist	L	Natt. Ryan	afr. Gd.	F
Peter Pais	M.T.	B	Antho. Murphy	afr. Gd.	
Robt. Fordent	F.T.	S	Saml. Brand	M.T.	S
Thos. Ward	Marine		Thos. McAuliff	Marine	
Jos. Clerk	Boy	P	Jas. Drake	Ditto	P

VI. Gun Lower Deck

Donald McDonald	Fc. Crew	Captn.	Jas. Hall	F.C.	Captn.
Jno. Alexander	afr. Gd.	B	Jno. Green	afr. Gd.	S
Lewis Cunnen	Cooks Mate	F	Jno. Gunsell	Mizen T.	L
Thos. Beeman	afr. Gd.		Richd. Ryan	afr. Gd.	
Alex. Sutherland	Mizen T.	S	Jno. Doody	F.C.	B
Isaac Harrison	Marine		Jacob Williams	Waist	
Thos. Rodgers	Boy	P	Alex. Mansell	Marine	
			Jas. Humphries	Ditto	F

A page from the quarter bill of the Goliath, *showing the subsidiary duties of many of the crew, eg, B means boarder, S means sail trimmer*. The National Maritime Museum

seamen had 'S', and were sail trimmers, who would help with the manoeuvres of the ship. Two had 'P', and would operate the pump. One had 'F', and would form part of the fire party, and another had 'L', and he would fetch and hold a lantern if the ship was engaged in night action.[15] Marines were distributed among the gun crews, though some might remain under their own officers on the poop or quarterdeck as small-arms men. The other seamen — those not manning the guns — were quartered in the tops and rigging, where they fired small arms at the enemy and helped work the sails; in the magazine, to fill cartridges and pass them out to the gun crews; and in the cockpit to assist the wounded. The carpenter and his mates worked in the orlop deck, in areas known as the carpenter's walks, ready with plugs to fill any holes which enemy gunfire caused in the side of the ship.

The captain, first lieutenant and master usually took up position on the quarterdeck, where they directed the action and set an example of coolness under fire. They had a few assistants — aboard the *Goliath* three midshipmen acted as aides de camp, and another as signals officer, while the captain's clerk stood by to take notes of the action. Each of the lieutenants took charge of a section of the ship's guns, and each of the gundecks was divided into two parts. Each of these was further subdivided into two sections, under a midshipman. The surgeon took charge of the cockpit, with the assistance of his mates and the chaplain and purser. The gunner was in charge of the main magazine, and the cook of the light room. The boatswain was in charge of the forecastle.

◁ *The quarters of a 74-gun ship, based on the quarter bill of the* Goliath.

2 The Ship's Day

Timekeeping at Sea

For the efficient management of a large body of men aboard ship, timekeeping was just as important as the allocation of duties. A sufficient number of men had to be available on deck to deal with any emergency, at any hour of the day or night. Duties had to be carried out at specific times, as when the hammocks were brought up in the morning, or taken down at night. Certain men in posts which required high concentration, such as helmsmen, sentries and lookouts, were relieved after quite short periods on duty; those at more gruelling tasks, such as pumping, also had to be replaced regularly. Some activities, such as cooking, had to be begun well in advance, with the raising of food casks from the hold and the issue of provisions to the cooks. Time was even more important for navigational purposes. All this demanded a constant awareness among all hands of the time of day, though few had timepieces of their own, and most would not have known how to use them.

The basic division of time was the watch, lasting for four hours, except for the dog watches. The first watch was from 8pm until midnight; it was so called because it was the first watch to be set in night-time hours, when the rest of the crew had hung up their hammocks and got ready for sleep. It was followed by the middle watch from midnight to 4am, and the morning watch till 8am. The forenoon watch was from 8am till noon, and the afternoon watch until 4pm. After that, there were two dog watches, the first from 4pm to 6pm, and the second from 6pm to 8pm. These divisions were intended to create variety, so that the same watch was not on duty at the same time every day.

A four-hour watch was divided into eight equal periods of half an hour. These were indicated by a number of strokes on the ship's bell — five bells meant that two and a half hours of the watch had elapsed, and eight bells meant that the watch was over; three bells in the middle watch, for example, was half past one in the morning. On large ships, a petty officer, known as the quartermaster of the glass, was appointed specifically for this task in each watch. On smaller vessels, it was done by the sentry to the captain's door.[1] He had two sand glasses, one of four hours to signify when the watch had ended, and one for half hours to time the ringing of the bell. The bell itself was placed at the aftermost beam of the forecastle, in a belfry which was quite heavily decorated, and was a prominent feature of the ship.

Helmsmen and Lookouts

Throughout the day and night at sea, the wheel was manned. An experienced seamen took the weather side, with a landman or ordinary seamen on the lee side, to help with physical effort as necessary. A quartermaster was in charge of the wheel, and, if the wind was strong, more men might be needed to help. The helmsman served for a 'trick' which might last for about an hour, before he was relived. Some captains tried to make sure that all able seamen had a chance to steer occasionally, and the rest had turns as lee helmsman, but this must have been difficult in large ships. In others, the helmsmen were drawn from one part of the ship, probably the afterguard. Lookouts were also relieved regularly, but their duty varied by day and by night. It was said that 'There is always a lookout kept on a ship's forecastle, to watch for any dangerous objects lying near her track, or for any strange sail heaving in sight.'[2] The foretopmen and the maintopmen each supplied one lookout for their respective mastheads; traditionally, the one who first sighted a ship or object was relieved early; if both failed to see it, and it was first seen from the deck, they were given extra duty. Aboard the *Hyperion* in 1811–15, a midshipman was to be sent aloft at daybreak and nightfall, to look round the horizon. By night, men were to be 'constantly stationed on each quarter, gangway and cathead for that purpose.'[3] Aboard the *Mars*, men were also stationed at the gangway, poop and cathead on each side during fog.[4]

Early Morning

On most ships, the decks were cleaned during the morning, though times varied, and there was some controversy about the value of the exercise. In 1802, Lord Keith, in command of the Mediterranean fleet, wrote of 'The custom of washing the decks of ships of war in all climates in every temperature of air, and on stated days, let the weather be what it may, having become almost universally prevalent to the destruction of the health and the lives of valuable men'.[5] The lower deck was to be washed only once a fortnight, and the cockpit never, being brushed instead. The upper deck was only to be washed after sunset.

But most captains preferred to keep their crews employed and their ships smart. On the *Mars* the upper deck, quarterdeck and forecastle were washed and scrubbed daily, and the lower deck once or twice a week; it was to be swept clean every morning before breakfast.[6] Aboard the *Unite*, the upper deck was washed by the watch on deck every morning, before the hammocks were piped up.

A four-hour sand glass, used to measure the length of a watch. Author's photograph, courtesy of the National Maritime Museum

The belfry of a ship-of-the-line, set at the break of the forecastle. The bell was rung every half hour to signal the passage of time, and to allow lookouts, helmsmen, etc, to be relieved. Author's photograph, courtesy of the National Maritime Museum

Water was brought up by the ship's pumps, and the men used blocks, known as 'holystones' because they were of the same shape and size as bibles, to scrub the decks; the gunner's crew cleaned their cannons. Aboard the *Revenge*, cleaning was begun at 4am, during the middle watch.

> They come on deck again, pull off their shoes and stockings, turn up their trousers to above their knees and commence holy-stoning the deck... Here the men suffer from being obliged to kneel down upon the wetted deck and a gravelly sort of sand strewed over it... In this manner the watch continues till about four bells or six o'clock; they then begin to wash and scrub the decks till seven bells, and at eight bells the boatswain's mates pipe to breakfast.'[7]

In practice, the ship's day began when the crew, or at least those who were not on watch, were roused from their hammocks by the boatswain's mates with cries of 'All hands ahoy', followed by 'Up all hammocks ahoy'. The exact time varied slightly from ship to ship and according to circumstances: aboard the frigate *Unité* in the 1800s, it was done 'at six bells, or seven o'clock in the morning; in winter at half past seven, or seven bells.'[8] On the *Superb* in 1804, they were to be stowed 'to admit of piping to breakfast at precisely 8 o'clock.'[9] The time allowed for stowing the hammocks also varied, but all were agreed that it had to be done smartly. On the *Unité* it was five minutes; on the *Superb* twelve, and on the *Pegasus* fifteen minutes. In any case, 'with a rapidity which would surprise a landsman, the crew dress themselves, lash their hammocks, and carry them on deck, where they are stowed for the day'.[10]

After that, the hands were piped to breakfast. As with all meals, it was regarded as one of the high points of the seamen's day, and captains were particularly concerned that it should not be disturbed except in emergency. On the *Mars*, 'The ship's company are never to be interrupted at their meals, but on the most pressing occasions'. Three quarters of an hour was allowed.[11] On the *Unité*, only half an hour was allowed, and 'If the duty of the ship is required to be executed at meal times, so that the hands, or the watch, is disturbed, the time they may want of their allowed duties is made up to them when the duty is done.'[2] However, as far as possible, both watches, plus idlers, ate together, leaving only a few lookouts and helmsmen on deck, with the officer of the watch.

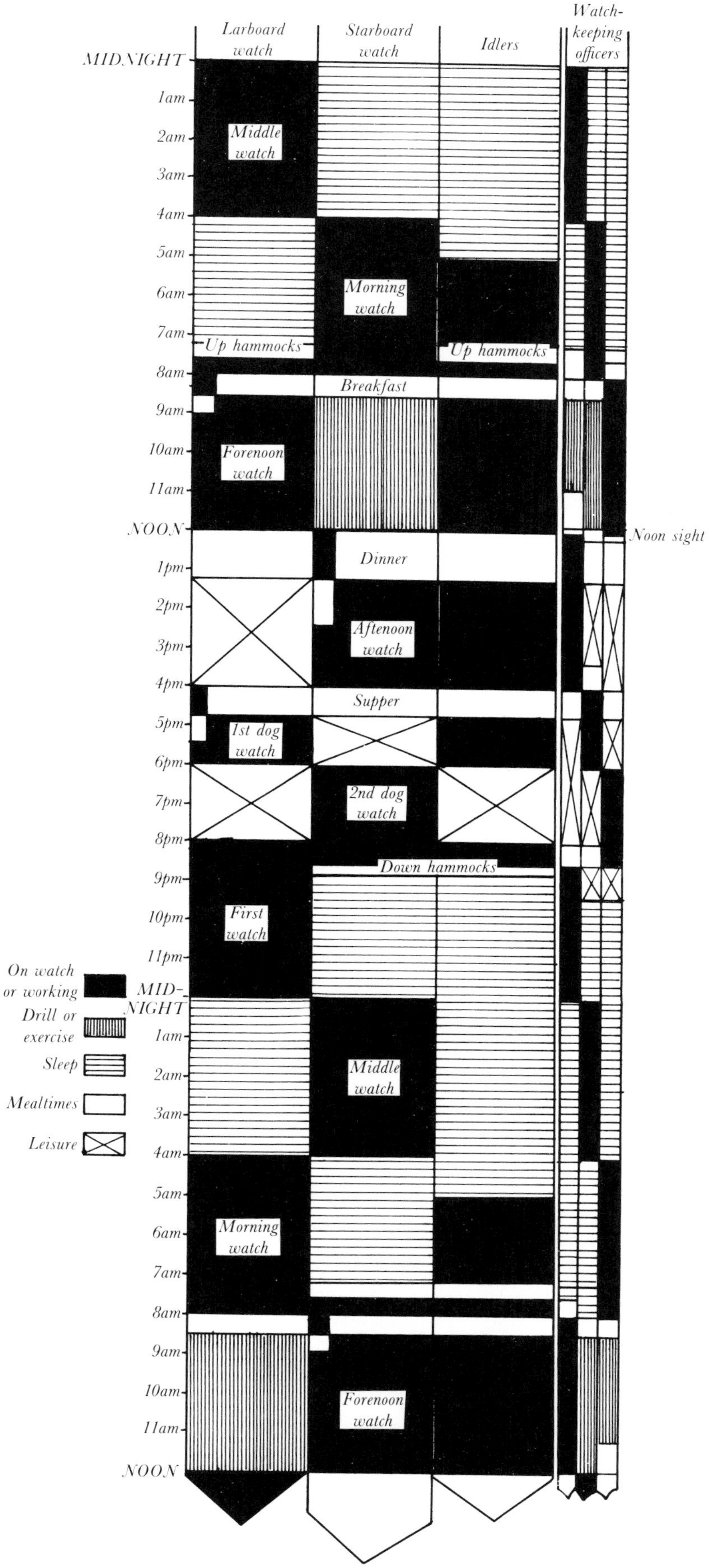

A typical ship's day.

The Daylight Hours

For the rest of the daylight hours, the idlers were at their work on deck and below decks; the watch on deck was fully employed in maintenance duties about the rigging under the direction of the boatswain, or on deck. The topmen of both watches were often exercised in handling the sails, or selected groups of gun crews practised at their guns. Marines were paraded, and some seamen were exercised at the cutlass or small arms — a task which they performed reluctantly and to the amusement of their colleagues, who regarded such training as only fit for soldiers. If the ship was sailing with a fleet, she might be engaged in fleet exercises under the direction of the admiral, with both watches on deck. If on patrol, she might stop many different merchant ships and inspect them. The ship would be cleared for action, and the crew sent to quarters, if there was the slightest threat of an enemy warship.

By about 7am, the holders (who worked in the hold) had brought up some casks of food and drink for daily use, and placed them in the steward's room aft on the orlop deck. Between 7am and 9am the cooks of the different messes went down there to be issued with their daily provisions. At 11am, the hands were called to be inspected by divisions, and any punishment was carried out. After that, the sea officers began to prepare for the noon sight, which would give the best possible indication of the ship's latitude. Midshipmen and lieutenants, as well as the captain and master, were expected to take the sight, for practice. Until 1805, the ship's day officially began at noon, half a day behind Greenwich time, and was so recorded in the log books.

By this time the ship's cook and his mates had prepared dinner. The hands were piped to dinner by the boatswain's mates, and the cooks of the messes went to collect the cooked provisions. The time allowed for dinner was quite long — an hour and a half aboard the *Mars*, and an hour on the *Unite*. For the seamen, it was 'the pleasantest part of the day'.[13]

The Evening

On board the *Revenge*, 'At two bells in the afternoon, or one o'clock, the starboard watch goes on deck and remains working the ship, pointing the ropes or doing any duty that may be required until the eight bells strike when the boatswain's mate pipes to supper.'[14] Three quarters of an hour or an hour was allowed for this meal.

Some time after dinner, preparations began for 'setting the watch', or leaving the ship in the charge of a single watch, while the rest of the men bedded down for the night. This was done at 9pm in winter in northern latitudes, and 8pm in summer. Sometimes, it was necessary to reduce sail during preparations, especially on blockade service, when the ship was in no hurry to go anywhere, or on convoy duty when merchant ship practice was the order of the day. Then the hammocks were piped down — 'The next pipe is "Stand by your hammocks"; everyone lays hold of his own, but at his peril takes it out of the netting until the hammocks are piped down; then everyone

An unglamourous time at sea – the middle watch in bad weather, with helmsman, officer of the watch (with speaking trumpet), midshipmen (feeling the effects of the cold and rain), lookouts, and servant. The National Maritime Museum

shoulders his own, and bundles down below with it and hangs it up in its proper berth.'[15] Aboard the *Pegasus* the routine was different: the hammocks were uncovered fifteen minutes before sunset, and taken down one subdivision at a time.[16] After that, the idlers and the watch below were free to sleep, though the latter would be called again at midnight.

Night Watches

During the hours of darkness, great care was taken to ensure that no lights were kept burning after the crew had gone to bed. A single candle might start a disastrous fire, or reveal the position of the ship to an enemy. On the *Mars*, the master at arms was not to go to bed until after midnight, having first inspected the decks with his corporals, to make sure that no lights were burning and all was in order below decks.[17] On the *Hyperion* and many other ships, a midshipman was to be sent below at least once every hour, to report 'if any lights have been discovered in improper places, or any other irregularity or breach of the orders of the ship.'[18]

Apart from the helmsmen and lookouts, the duties of the watch on deck were light. In bad weather, they would shelter under the half deck, just forward of the wardroom. In warm climates, they were sometimes allowed to sleep on deck, though other captains specifically forbade this, and a distinguished medical officer commented, 'They should never be allowed to sleep on deck during their watches, a custom too prevalent, but which is always greatly injurious to the health of the people, and more particularly so in warm climates, where the dews are more profuse than even in colder latitudes.'[19] The watch changed at midnight, and again at four in the morning; after that, as daylight approached, the ship's day began again.

Weekly Routine

There were some variations from day to day in this routine, especially with regard to washing, and on Sundays. The captain of the *Bellerophon* made up quite a detailed list of the weekly routine. On Monday, the men were to wash their clothes, and in the morning they were to exercise at the great guns and small arms. In the afternoon they would replace any deficiencies in the gun equipment, such as wads and gunner's implements; and more gun exercises would take place in the evening. On Tuesdays, the hammocks would be scrubbed in the morning, the marines would exercise with muskets, and in the afternoon the seamen's bedding would be aired. On Wednesday, the men's bags and the boat sails would be scrubbed, and the marines would pipe-clay their white belts and equipment. There would be an exercise in reefing and furling sails in the forenoon watch, and in the afternoon one division would be exercised at the great guns. On Thursday, the men would clean themselves and their clothes, and be inspected by their divisional officers. The master at arms would tour the decks picking up any stray clothes lying about, and in the afternoon the seamen would mend their clothes. Friday mornings were devoted to washing clothes, and divisions were exercised at the great guns both morning and afternoon. Every second Saturday the fire pump would be used to wash the poop, and in dry weather the lower deck and cockpit would be washed in the forenoon. On Sundays, the men would draw clean hammocks, and dress in their best clothes for muster. After church service, they had some free time, and were disturbed for 'nothing but the indispensible duties of the ship'.[20]

Few captains made such detailed lists, but most allocated some time for washing hammocks and clothes. On the *Mars*, clothes were to be washed on Mondays and Fridays.[21] All authorities agreed that Sunday was different, and the Articles of War demanded that divine service be performed. The Articles of War themselves were read to the assembled crew at least once a month, usually on a Sunday.

Routine in Port

Ships and fleet often spent considerable time at anchor, waiting for repairs, favourable winds, or news of the enemy. This was particularly true of the Channel fleet under Howe, when, for tactical reasons, he preferred to keep large numbers of ships in port. In harbour, the whole routine of the ship was altered. Discipline was largely relaxed, and women were allowed on board. 'Petty warrant' victuals were issued, with soft bread, unsalted meat and fresh vegetables. The seamen had a full night's sleep, though the hammocks were brought up quite early, perhaps at 4am. Only a few men, the anchor watch, were kept on duty overnight. If the captain was agreeable, small numbers of seamen were allowed ashore for twenty-four or forty-eight hours at a time. Officers had a well-established right to shore leave, though orders usually specified that a certain number be on board at any given moment — on the *Mars*, 'The ship when in port is never to be left without three lieutenants and two officers of marines.'[22]

3 The Necessities of Life

Advocates of Uniform

There was no official uniform for common seamen before 1857. Medical officers deplored this, and the great naval physicians, Lind, Blane and Trotter, all advocated a standard dress. The latter wrote, 'A uniform in all situations contributes so much to personal delicacy and cleanliness that we are at a loss to conceive how our officers have neglected it so long.'[1] The Admiralty paid no attention to this, but many individual captains supported it, and sometimes they tried to enforce unofficial uniforms on their crews. According to the captain's orders for the *Mars*,

> As the ship's company in general will have a much better appearance by preserving a uniformity of dress, they are to be discouraged from purchasing any other clothes than blue outside jackets, red, white or blue waistcoats, long white trousers or hats; and it is recommended to the lieutenants to excite as much as possible in the people of their different divisions a spirit of emulation in point of dress.[2]

A few captains paid for special costumes for their men. According to a contemporary newspaper report,

> The *Tribune* frigate ... is no less remarkable for the gallantry than the coxcombry of the crew ... Every man wears a smart round japan hat with green inside the leaf, a gold lace band, with the name of the ship painted in front in capital letters; black silk neckerchief, with a white flannel waistcoat bound with blue; and over it a blue jacket, with three rows of gold buttons very close together, and blue trousers.[3]

Others equipped the men of their personal gigs and barges. Sometimes they used watermen's caps; in other cases, they designed uniforms which reflected the name of the ship. On some ships, seamen wore some kind of uniform for special occasions; aboard the *Unite* in 1808, the men wore 'dress blue jackets and white trousers' to man the yards for the visit of an ambassador.[4] Men at Nelson's funeral were to wear 'Blue jackets, white trousers and a black scarf round our arms, and hats, besides gold medal for Trafalgar, value £7.1s round our necks.'[5]

Seamen's Preferences

Seamen had their own distinctive style of dress, totally different from that of landmen (they wore short jackets and loose trousers, while the landmen wore long coats, breeches and stockings) and, when the seaman Robert Wilson dressed in the 'long clothes' of a landman, it was to disguise himself from the press gang. When taken by the gang despite his disguise, he was mocked by his comrades aboard the tender as a 'Lord Mayor's man'.[6]

Practical considerations dictated much of the seaman's dress. His wide trousers were easy to roll up, and allowed free movement. His short jacket was less restrictive than a long coat, and it had buttoning cuffs, so that the sleeves could be rolled up for working. Check shirts were quite common. The cocked hat of the landman would soon blow away or be knocked off in the rigging, and the seaman preferred a hat with a small brim, or a woollen or fur cap — sometimes with flaps to fold down over his ears. It was becoming fashionable for seamen to paint the names of their ships on their hats.

The seaman also had his indulgences and his extravagances. Rich with prize money, he might well buy 'a silver watch and silver buckles for himself'.[7] Less wealthy seamen could buy colourful clothes from the 'bum boats' which came alongside in port. This was disliked by some captains, who preferred uniformity. 'Flimsy white linen trousers, cloth waistcoats or variegated colours, and various other trash are only brought on board to catch the eye of and cheat the inexperienced boys'.[8]

Slops

Seamen were normally expected to provide their own clothes, but, in practice, their choice was somewhat limited. Men taken up in the streets by the press gang had only the clothes they stood in, and quota men might be dressed in rags. Those taken from merchant ships would normally be allowed to bring their own clothes, but on a long voyage these would wear out. Eventually, most seamen would have to resort to the purser, with his supply of slop clothes. These were issued to the purser of the ship by the storekeeper at the dockyard where the ship fitted out, and kept in the slop room aboard ship, aft on the orlop deck. Naturally, there was a certain amount of standardisation, though this was caused by mass buying, rather than any deliberate policy. Seamen, coming on board for the first time, were allowed to buy slops, for up to two months' pay in advance, but muster books and other documents suggest that some seamen went for considerable periods without buying from the purser. If a seaman died in service, his clothes were sold at the mast for the benefit of his dependants, and often his friends paid extravagant prices for them. Sometimes, captains stipulated a minimum amount of clothing each seaman was to have.

Seamen could acquire clothes in other ways. The Marine Society had a policy of issuing clothes to landsmen recruited for the fleet, partly in order that they would not be ridiculed by other seamen because of their land clothes, and partly for reasons of health. A good seaman could make his own clothes, as Samuel Richardson did aboard the frigate *Minerva* in 1793. Due to a shortage of slops, the men were issued with 'so many yards of dungaree as were required to each man for jackets, shirts and trousers, with needles and thread for them.'[9] Likewise, aboard the *Unite* in 1807, 'Cloth for white trousers was served out.'[10]

Washing

Gilbert Blane, one of the founders of naval medicine, was perhaps a little optimistic when he wrote, 'A true seaman is in general cleanly.' He went on to admit that 'the greater part of men in a ship of war require a degree of compulsion to make them so.'[11] Captain's orders usually made a point of setting days for the washing of clothes, and, to a lesser extent, of the person. However, little was done to make this easy. The issue of soap was left to the initiative of individual captains and admirals, and did not become general. Presumably tubs and buckets were available for washing in, but the water was usually pumped in from the sea. This led to a complaint by the crew of the *Reunion* in 1796: 'Captain Baynham also obliges us to wash our linen twice a week in salt water and to put two shirts on every week and if they do not look as clean as if they were washed in fresh water he stops the person's grog.'[12]

Seamen in 1808, from an engraving by Atkinson. One wears a blue jacket, and the seated man has a check shirt, with a woollen or fur 'monmouth cap', always popular with seamen. The National Maritime Museum

Types of Food

In theory the issue of food at sea was quite carefully regulated by the Admiralty. Each man was to have a pound of ship's biscuit every day; plus four pounds of beef, two pounds of pork, two of peas, one and a half of oatmeal, six ounces of sugar, six of butter, and twelve ounces of cheese a week, spread over the different days. Other provisions could be substituted when necessary: flour and raisins for beef, rice for bread (biscuit), and so on. Obviously there was a lack of fresh vegetables in this diet, but in port the purser was allowed to buy them 'when they can be procured and not at any time exceeding the value of the peas saved, at the purser's credit price.'[13] Whether he did so or not depended largely on the views of the captain or admiral. In port, fresh beef was supplied instead of salt 'when convenient'.[14]

Food was stored in casks in the hold, except for bread or biscuit, which was kept in sacks in the bread room aft. The meat was cut into small pieces, and of course it was salted to keep it in eatable condition. Biscuit was 'a sort of bread much dried, to make it keep for the use of the navy, and is good for a whole year after it was baked'.[15]

Drink

Water was carried in large quantities aboard ship, but it could become quite unpleasant after months in the cask. Seamen were allowed to drink it from the 'scuttle butt', a cask placed on the deck. Sometimes captains found it necessary to put a sentry on it, to prevent wastage. With his meals, the seaman preferred something stronger. The classic naval drink was rum, but it was very far from universal. Beer was generally more common, and when available, usually in home waters, it was issued at the rate of one gallon per man per day. If it was not available, then each man was entitled to 'a pint of wine, or half a pint of rum, brandy or other spirits.'[16] Rum was watered down, with two parts of water to one of rum. It was taken up on deck and mixed in a tub 'by the quartermasters of the watch below, assisted by other leading and responsible men among the ship's company, closely supervised, of course, by the mate of the hold'.[17] The large quantities of strong drink were intended to keep the men contented, but often the drunkenness on board caused mistakes and indiscipline, and was, therefore, responsible for both floggings and courts-martial. Sometimes men were encouraged to take only part of their allowance, and aboard the *Royal William* in 1804, the captain instructed 'in case he is not able to drink it without being intoxicated, he is to take up only a part thereof, and the pursers shall be directed to make him compensation in money for the remainder.'[18] But there was no general move to reduce the supply of liquor, despite the misgivings of some medical officers; it would undoubtedly have inspired disaffection and mutiny, for seamen had become dependent on it, as one of their few pleasures in life.

Seamen at a mess table, presumably on a frigate. They sit on sea chests, and behind can be seen their bags, and racks for the mess's cutlery. From the Log Book, 1830

Messes

For eating and recreational purposes, the crew was divided into messes. The core of each mess was a table. On a two-decker, one was fitted up between each pair of guns on the lower deck, with one end hinged against the side and the other suspended from the deckhead. On a frigate, there was slightly more room, as the lower deck had no guns. On a three-decker, presumably part of the middle deck was also available. A bench was situated along each side of the table, for the men to sit on. The tables were constructed by the ship's carpenter at the beginning of the commission.

One of the few liberties granted to the seaman was the right to choose his messmates, within certain limits. Seamen and marines were not encouraged to mess together, but they had no real wish to mix. Men could only change their mess at a fixed time, perhaps monthly, and had to give notice to the first lieutenant so that the supply of victuals could be rearranged. There was usually some restriction on the maximum and minimum sizes of a mess. Aboard the *Blake* in the 1800s, only even numbers were allowed, from four to ten. On the *Pegasus* in 1786, the minimum was four. According to Captain Basil Hall, 'the number of men in a mess varies from eight to twelve in a frigate, each mess having a separate table... In a line-of-battle ship the tables are larger, and two messes sit at the same table, one on each side. The average number in the mess is the same as in a frigate, and they are under the same regulations.'[19] Both Wilson and 'Jack Nastyface' gave eight as the normal number for a mess. However, according to Samuel Leech, 'It is no infrequent case to find a few, who have been spurned by all the messes of the ship, obliged to mess by themselves.'[20] Captain Anselm Griffiths argued against any restrictions. 'While in command, my crew ever messed as they liked. The berth was allotted to the number it was calculated to hold, and if one, two or three messes were in it, that rested with themselves.'[21]

According to Robert Wilson, some messes were 'well fitted up'. Nastyface is more specific. 'Nearly all the crew' had 'a hook pot in the galley', along with a spoon and knife. 'There are also basins, plates, etc, which are kept in each mess.'[22] All this was at risk in heavy seas. In a voyage back from Newfoundland in 1794, the crew of the frigate *Boston* found that 'the accidents are many, but serious ones befell the platters and earthenware. If we do not get back to England soon the supernumeraries — wooden bowls and spoons — must come in general use.'[23]

The 'cook of the mess' was appointed daily according to Hall, or weekly according to the orders for the *Superb* in 1804. 'The men in the different messes are every Sunday to appoint one of their messmates to keep the berth mess utensils clean, and in proper order for the following week.'[24] The other duty of the cook of the mess was to collect the day's food from the steward every morning, take that which needed cooking to the ship's cook, and get it back in time for the meal.

The Issue and Preparation of Food

The food was issued in the steward's room, in the after part of the orlop, by the steward and his assistant, 'Jack in the dust'. 'The purser's steward, or rather the ship's, is the person that issues out all the different species of provisions and the liquor allowed to the ship's company in general, and keeps an account of the same.'[25] The food which needed cooking was taken to the galley, under the forecastle. There, it would be boiled in the two large 'kettles' provided under the supervision of the ship's cook, but 'The cook's mate does all the drudgery work, the cook inspects him. Every article into which the

A model of a ship's cooking stove, showing the lids for the two compartments of the kettle. The doors to the oven can be seen on the left-hand side, with the rack for the grill just forward of that. To the right of the funnel is the turnspit; the chimney, which carries the smoke clear of the weather deck, is placed to the left. The National Maritime Museum

provisions are put is perfectly clean. The serving of the provisions out of the boilers or coppers is managed entirely by the cook himself, for if there is any deficiency he is answerable for it.'[26] As mealtime approached, the cooks of the messes came to collect their provisions, including a portion of meat of a fixed size for each man in the mess, and the grog. The cook marked them off with a pin as they were collected. The cook of the mess had certain perquisites, such as the spare grog; but he was responsible to his messmates, and if he neglected his duty, he could be tried by a court of the cooks of the other messes.[27]

The Quality of the Diet

Clearly, naval food was neither enjoyable nor plentiful; but in fact there were rather fewer complaints about it than one would expect. The Nore mutineers of 1797 asked 'that our provisions be raised to the weight of sixteen ounces to the pound, and of a better quality; and that our measures may be the same as those used in the commercial trade of the country', and that 'they might be granted a sufficient quantity of vegetables, of such kind as may be the most plentiful in the ports to which we go'.[28] Apart from that, there are very few written complaints. No-one ever praised naval food, but, clearly, the seamen became inured to it, and perhaps a little suspicious of changes in diet. The quantities were minimal, but adequate, and undernourishment was not a major problem.

The great achievement of the late eighteenth-century naval administration was in defeating scurvy, mainly through better feeding of the men. By 1795, large quantities of lemons were issued, causing a great improvement in the health of the Channel fleet. Parsimony caused the substitution of limes for lemons, although they were less effective anti-scorbutics; but the disease became much less common, and in 1797 no case could be found in Haslar hospital.[29]

Hammocks and Beds

Each seaman was issued with at least one hammock, though by 1800 it was becoming increasingly common to issue two, so that they could be cleaned and dried in turn. 'The establishment of two hammocks to each man, so conducive to the preservation of health, is always to be complied with if it is possible.'[30] A hammock was 'a piece of hempen cloth, six feet long, and three feet wide, gathered together at the two ends by means of a clew, and slung horizontally under the deck, forming a receptacle for a bed for the sailors to sleep in.'[31] A clew was 'the combination of small lines by which it is suspended, being formed of knittles, grommets and lanyards.'[32]

A hammock was merely a 'receptacle for a bed', not the bed itself. In addition, each sailor had a mattress to put in the hammock. Whereas the hammock was the property of the government and was only on loan, the bed was brought on board by the man, or purchased from the purser like other slops. Usually, it was filled with flock, or wool; but Blane complained that 'they are frequently stuffed with chopped rags, which, consisting of old clothes, emit a disagreeable smell and may even contain infection.'[33] In addition, a seaman had a blanket, a 'coverlet' and a 'bolster' or pillow.

A hammock, with bed inside, aboard HMS Victory. *There is a stowed hammock to the left.* HMS *Victory*

The Hammock Plan

According to a seaman of this period, 'The great disparity in numbers between the crew of a merchant ship and that of a man-of-war occasions a difference in the internal arrangements and mode of life, scarcely conceivable to those who have not seen both.'[34] This was particularly apparent in the slinging of hammocks. Aboard a 74, for example, about 500 men had to berth in an area of 6000sq ft. Seamen could not sling their hammocks where they wished, for the limited space below decks had to be allocated very carefully by the first lieutenant. Men of the same part of ship were kept together so that they could be mustered in an emergency, but the watches were alternated so that more space was available when one watch was on deck. The decks were so crowded that only 14in width was allowed for each man (though of course this would be doubled at sea when one watch was on duty). Petty officers were placed near the sides of the ship, and were allowed 28in. Hooks were placed under the upper deck beams for fixing the hammocks. Sometimes a man could find himself in a very uncomfortable position. Aboard the *Amazon* in 1799, it was decreed that 'Any man or men who sleep near hatchways or scuttles who feel any draught of wind, or who are subject to be wet in their hammocks from seas or rain, are to acquaint the first lieutenant, that painted canvas screens may be neatly nailed up to make their berths as comfortable as possible.'[35] Some men slept in the cable tier on the orlop. This was considered quite a desirable berth, and was often given to petty officers. Presumably, the lack of disturbance from other activities compensated for the shortage of light and ventilation.

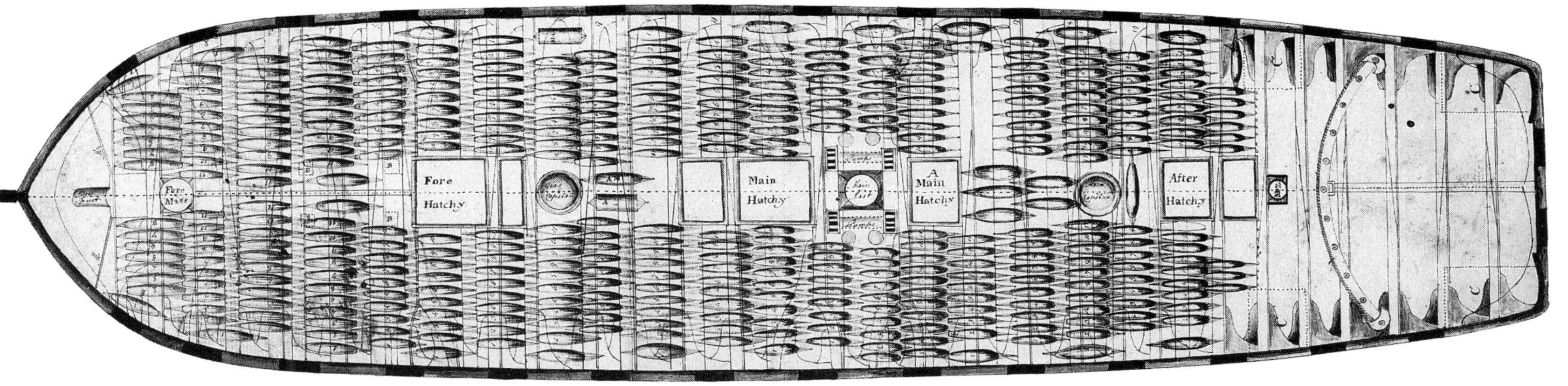

The hammocks on the lower deck of the Bedford, *74. The last three rows are coloured red, instead of blue, in the original, presumably because they were for marines.* The National Maritime Museum

Hammock Stowage

In the daytime, the hammocks were carefully rolled up, with the bedding and perhaps some spare clothes inside them. Aboard the *Amazon* in 1799, 'The boatswain is to pay particular attention that when the hammocks are piped up, they are taut and neatly lashed, so that no bedding appears. No clothes are to be stowed in them.'[36] The hammocks were placed in netting arranged along the sides of the ship, for it was believed that they had some value in stopping enemy fire. In bad weather, the hammocks were lashed up tight and kept below decks, or they were stacked under the half deck, just forward of the wardroom on a two-decker.

Heating, Ventilation and Lighting

The crew spaces on men-of-war had little need of heating, even in the north European winter. The lower deck of a ship was so crowded that the men generated their own heat — 'on the same deck with me, when the crew was complete, slept between five and six hundred men; and the ports being necessarily closed from evening to morning, the heat in this cavern of only six feet high, and so entirely filled with human bodies, was overpowering.'[37] Portable stoves were issued in 1783, at the rate of one for each deck, but it seems that these were intended to dry the ship when she was laid up and empty, rather than keep the crew warm.

Ventilation was more necessary, for it was not always possible to keep the ports open at sea. Ventilators, operated by bellows, had been fitted aboard ships since the 1750s, and Admiralty Instructions demanded that they be worked continually.[38] Aboard the *Superb*, 'The ventilator is to be constantly worked by day in winter, and by night and day in summer in a warm climate.'[39] In hot weather, that was not enough. Men often wanted to sleep on deck, or to sling their hammocks under the boat booms in the waist. Captains had varying opinions about this. In the *Pegasus* in 1786, they could be slung under the forecastle, half deck, boat booms and gangways, but the men were not to sleep on deck.[40]

Light was supplied by candles purchased out of the purser's 'necessary money'. They were placed in lanterns for safety, and extinguished in the evening when the watch was set. Careful patrols were arranged so that this rule was not broken.

Sanitary Arrangements

Toilet accommodation for the commissioned officers was in the quarter galleries adjoining the cabins in the stern; though this was not available to the officers of frigates, who lived in the gunroom. Presumably, they used chamber pots, which were later emptied over the side of the ship. A ship-of-the-line had two small 'round houses' on the foremost bulkhead of the upper deck. These were used by the junior warrant officers until 1801, when one of them was reserved for the men in the sick berth. For the crew, the main toilet accommodation was in the heads of the ship, in the structure behind the figurehead. Seats were placed there, with trunking to carry the waste out into the sea. Some ships also had 'piss dales', small receptacles like basins on the side of the ship, with a pipe leading out through the side. Evidently, this was not sufficient for many seamen, and Admiralty Instructions demanded that sentries be placed by the gratings to prevent men from 'easing themselves' into the hold.

4 Rewards and Pleasures

Shore Leave

A seaman had absolutely no right to shore leave during his service. The Articles of War and the Admiralty Instructions said nothing about it, and the Admiralty itself paid very little attention to it. Because of the fear of desertion, captains were generally reluctant to grant it, and it was quite possible for men to spend years on end without leaving their ship. This was one of the major complaints of seamen in 1797, as at other times. The Nore mutineers asked 'that we may in somewise have grant and opportunity to taste the sweets of liberty on shore, when in any harbour, and when we have completed the duty of the ship, after our return from sea'.[1] In 1803, the marines of the *Mariner* asked to be paid off, as 'The major part of us have served His Majesty upwards of ten years, without having the satisfaction of seeing our friends.'[2] The lack of shore leave led one seaman to write of his five years of 'floating imprisonment' aboard the *Powerful*.[3]

When captains did grant shore leave, it was to small groups at a time, to men with records of good conduct, and often with some kind of guarantee. In some cases the men still on board were held as hostage for the good conduct of the rest. The crew of the *Prosperine* complained in 1797, 'The smallest indulgence of liberty is obtained by one shipmate hazarding himself to the powers of a court-martial or otherwise punished as the captain thinks proper. If the person obtaining liberty does not return, his bondsman suffers the above.'[4] There was an element of bluff here, for the captain had no powers to have a man court-martialled in such circumstances; but there was nothing to stop him having the man flogged. When the *Royal Sovereign*, arrived back at Plymouth after Trafalgar, her crew were allow leave only six at a time, though they claimed that men from other ships were allowed ashore a hundred at a time. They looked, somewhat optimistically, to the 'common privilege and liberty customary in every of His Majesty's ships when in port'.[5] Leave was somewhat more common in overseas ports, where desertion was slightly less easy. John Nicol was allowed to work on shore for a time while his ship, the *Proteus*, was out of service at Quebec.[6]

Recreation

For their amusement on board ship, seamen often turned to handicrafts. Some, according to Robert Wilson, employed themselves in their old shore occupations, such as painters, shoemakers, and hat-makers. Furthermore, 'Those who are not employed sewing and mending, you'll see them either learning to read or write, or cyphering, or instructing others... Others are relating awful stories of what happened in awful times, while their hearers are listening with repectful silence, especially the young sailors.' Ships' cooks, being old seamen, were particularly adept at the latter; 'when their work is finished for the day they'll take their pipes, seat themselves in Copper Alley, and spin you a long yarn about what they have seen and done which, allowing for the language and style it's related in, suffices to pass away a dull hour or two.'[7]

Music

Music played a large part in the seamen's lives. One of the favourite recreations, according to Wilson, was 'playing the violin, flute or fife, while others dance or sing thereto'.[8] A midshipman of 1811 observed, 'It is ridiculous to hear the sailors lie and sing in their hammocks of an evening. They chant the most dismal ditties in the world, and the words be ever so merry, yet the tune is one and the same, namely

A seaman amuses his comrades with a tale, and the rest enjoy their grog. The National Maritime Museum

Seamen and their women dance to a one-eyed, one-legged fiddler, while others gamble or read letters. The National Maritime Museum

"Admiral Hosier's ghost". They never seemed to dance with any spirit unless they had an old black to fiddle to them. He is of the name of Bond.'[9] To Samuel Leech, music was all that kept the sailors from despair.

> Seated on a gun, surrounded by scores of men, he sang a variety of favourite songs, amid the encores and plaudits of his rough auditors. By such means as this, sailors contrive to keep up their spirits amidst constant causes of depression and misery. One is a good singer, another can spin tough forecastle yarns, while a third will crack a joke with sufficient point to call out roars of laughter. But for these interludes, life in a man-of-war with severe officers, would be absolutely intolerable; mutiny or desertion would mark the voyages of each ship.[10]

Elsewhere he writes, 'A casual visitor to a man-of-war, beholding the song, the dance, the revelry of the crew, might judge them to be happy. But I know that these things are often resorted to, because they feel miserable, just to drive away dull care.'[11]

Dancing to a fiddler was quite common, and William Richardson records, 'Every evening, weather permitting, it was customary for the people to have a dance, and one of these evenings the lanthorns were lighted as usual, and hung on each side of the launch, which was stowed in those days on the main deck under the booms, and the fiddler on the topsail sheet bitts began to play away on his violin.'[12]

Ships bands were not unusual, though not recognised by regulation. They may, however, have been intended to perform ceremonial functions and entertain the captain, rather than the crew. 'Jack Nastyface' accused the captain of the *Revenge* of pressing men solely for the band, 'for the captain's amusement, and not to strengthen our force against the enemy.'[13] However, most ships had a share of professional musicians on board. The *San Domingo* had fifteen members of her band in 1812. The *Caledonia* had ten in 1811, and the *Dromedary*, with only 121 men, had one 'itinerant fiddler'.[14]

Religion

Religion played very little part in the life of the seaman. Certainly, the Articles of War started off with the instruction, 'All commanders, captains and officers, in or belonging to any of His Majesty's ships and vessels of war shall cause the public worship of Almighty God . . . to be solemnly, orderly and reverently performed in their respective ships.' But this had been originally written in the Puritan days of Oliver Cromwell, not in the sceptical eighteenth century. Some early nineteenth-century captains were strong supporters of the Evangelical movement, and tried to bring religion to their crews. Admiral Lord Gambier took his faith very seriously, and as a result was known as 'Dismal Jimmie' to his men. Edward Mangin, as Chaplain of the *Gloucester*, 74, perceived that 'nothing can possibly be more unsuitably or more awkwardly situated than a clergyman in a ship of war; every object around him is at variance with the sensibilities of a rational and enlightened mind.'[15] He found that visiting the sick was worse than useless: 'The entrance of a clergyman is, to a poor seaman, often a fatal signal.' He saw that his 'constant efforts to rebuke the seamen, etc, for profane swearing and intemperate language of every kind' had no effect. He found employment in conducting Sunday service, when the men behaved 'with utmost decorum', and in burying the dead, a common enough occupation on a man-of-war. 'To convert a man-of-war's crew into Christians,' he wrote, 'would be a task to which the courage of Loyola, the philanthropy of Howard, and the eloquence of St Paul united, would prove inadequate.'[16]

Drunkenness

The real nature of the nautical sabbath was described by Samuel Leech. 'The sabbath was also a day of sensuality. True, we had sometimes the semblance of religious services . . . but usually it was observed more as a day of revels than worship.' Christmas was even more debauched. 'Drunkenness ruled the ship. Nearly every man, with most of the officers, were in a state of beastly intoxication at night.' Even in normal times, 'To be drunk is considered by every sailor as the acme of sensual bliss.' And 'In our ship the men would get drunk, in defiance of every restriction.'[17] Probably, more than half the courts-martial for mutiny, indiscipline or negligence arose directly from drunkenness, among both officers and men, and drunkenness was the single most common reason for flogging. Deprived of their liquor, the seamen were no less ungovernable, and the crew of the *Royal Sovereign* after Trafalgar petitioned the Admiralty

Women on board a ship in a port, showing one in a hammock, others squabbling, and some dancing to a fiddler in the background. The National Maritime Museum

because their ready-use supply had been lost during the battle.[18] In 1805, for example, George Mason refused to obey an order, commenting 'it was a damn shame he could not get any beer, and sooner than work on such a bugger of a ship, he would go to a yardarm first, and if everyone was of his mind they would do the same.' He was sentenced to 300 lashes.[19]

Sex

Though seamen were rarely permitted ashore, women were allowed to come on board, and to stay with them for several days if the ship remained in port. In the past, the Admiralty Regulations had been quite restrictive about this: 'No women be ever permitted on board, but such as are really the wives of the men they come to; and the ship be not too much pestered even with them. But this indulgence is only tolerated when the ship is in port, and not under sailing orders.'[20] This clause was never rigidly enforced, and the 1806 rules only demanded that women were not taken to sea.[21] Captain Keats ordered his officers to fill in a form as the women came on board, asking such questions as 'Woman's name', 'With whom', 'Married or single', and 'Conduct'.[22]

Samuel Stokes records that aboard the *Dreadnought* of 98 guns 'we had on board thirteen women more than the number of our ship's company, and not fifty of them married women.'[23] 'Jack Nastyface' says that aboard the *Revenge* in 1805, 450 women came on board for a crew of 600. 'On the arrival of a man-of-war in port, these girls flock down to the shore, where boats are always ready; and here may be witnessed a scene, somewhat similar to the trafficking in slaves in the West Indies.' The women themselves were mostly prostitutes. 'Of all the human race, these poor young creatures are the most pitiable; the ill usage and degradation they are driven to submit to, are indescribable, but from habit they become callous, indifferent as to the delicacy of speech and behaviour, and so totally lost to all sense of shame, that they seem to retain no quality which properly belongs to women but the shape and name.'[24]

Aboard ship, the women slept with the men, despite the total lack of privacy on the decks. According to one disapproving officer, 'The whole of the shocking, disgraceful transactions of the lower deck it is impossible to describe — the dirt, filth, and stench; the disgusting conversation; the indecent beastly conduct and horrible scenes; the blasphemy and swearing; the riots, quarrels and fighting.' The men and women were 'squeezed between the next hammocks and must be witnesses of each other's actions.' They were accused of 'giving way to every excess and debauchery that the grossest passions of human nature can lead them to.'[25]

Homosexuality was not unknown aboard ship, though it was punishable by death. Few cases ever came to light among seamen, and memoirs and accounts are largely silent on the subject. In any case, it would have been very difficult on the crowded gundecks. Courts-martial show quite numerous cases of child molesting by officers. In the first few months of 1808 alone, there were three such cases. A boatswain was tried for 'taking improper familiarities with the persons of two boys'. He was dismissed and imprisoned. A lieutenant took 'indecent liberties' with a boy, taking him into his

Crossing the line. The National Maritime Museum

cabin and committing a sexual offence with him in his cot, on more than one occasion. A sergeant of marines was acquitted of indecency with a drummer.[26]

Personal Belongings

A seaman had few personal possessions apart from his clothes and bedding. However, he did occasionally buy a few luxury items, such as watches or gifts for his relatives and girl-friends. There was not space aboard ship for each man to have his own sea chest, so invariably one was shared between several men. More chests were allowed on a frigate, for there was more room on the lower deck, without any guns. On the *Amazon* in 1799, 'in a frigate, where many chests are permitted, one is to be allotted to a certain number of men, according to its size and the number of men in a mess.'[27] On such a ship, the chests were kept on deck, and it was suggested that care should be taken to have the deck cleaned under them.[28] In 1795, the crew of the *Blanche*, 32, complained that because of frequent washing of the lower deck, 'every day our chests and bags is ordered on deck and not down till night.'[29] On ships-of-the-line there were fewer chests, and they were not allowed to clutter up the gundecks. Often they were put down in the hold or on the orlop when the ship was at sea. In such cases, the seaman kept his clothes in a bag which was hung against the side of the ship beside his mess. Sometimes men were paid large amounts of money in back pay or prize money and had nowhere to keep it; they put it in their chests, or sometimes sewed it in the linings of their jackets. In 1798 aboard St Vincent's flagship, some seamen 'had jumped off the foreyard with all their clothes on'. One of them 'had forgotten that all he possessed in the world was in his trousers pocket in bank notes, and that the exertion of swimming had reduced them to a useless pulp, and that now the man was in despair, for the sum was considerable'. St Vincent made up the £70 from his own pocket.[30]

Tobacco

Until 1798, seamen were allowed to buy tobacco from the purser, the price being deducted from their wages. After that, it was issued free, at the rate of 2lb per month for seamen who wanted it. Some men had clay pipes, though smoking was not allowed below decks because of the danger of fire, and was generally permitted only on the forecastle. Others chewed it. Tobacco was issued to the ships at the main victualling ports.

Crossing the Line

Seamen enjoyed a kind of saturnalia on crossing the equator. The custom of a visit by King Neptune, followed by shaving and ducking of those who had not crossed the line before, was already well established.

> This figure, with his train of sea gods, advances to the quarterdeck — salutes, with true marine politeness, the captain of the ship, and all his officers. Enquires of each, whether he has ever before been in this part of Neptune's dominions. If he has, no more is said to him; but if he has not, he is then desired to do homage to the briny deep — which is being dipped in a bathing tub of seawater, or pay a fine of a bottle of rum to escape this sometimes very unmerciful ducking.[31]

5 Medicine and Health

The Importance of Naval Medicine

There can be no doubt that the health of crews was one of the most important factors governing the success or failure of naval operations. Nelson himself wrote 'The great thing in all military service is health.'[1] In the eighteenth century, many campaigns had failed dismally because of disease, especially in the West Indies. Hosier's campaign of 1727 and Vernon's Cartagena campaign of 1741 were the most notorious examples; thousands of lives were lost. As late as 1809, the Walcheren expedition cost the lives of 4000 men and caused 11,000 invalids. Keeping ships on continuous blockade service, as St Vincent did in 1800, could be hard on men as well as ships, and only drastic improvements in medicine made it possible. Even so, disease and accident did far more damage to the fleet than enemy shot. It has been estimated that 50 per cent of the navy's casualties in 1810 were caused by disease, 31 per cent by individual accident, and 10 per cent by foundering, wreck, fire or explosion; compared with 8 per cent caused by enemy action.[2] Over 5000 men perished in that year alone. Other sicknesses, short of death, could incapacitate the crews of ships for considerable periods. But naval medicine had made considerable advances over the years, and by the 1790s the worst problems of keeping fleets at sea had been solved. Thanks to great physicians like Lind and Blane, fleets and ships were able to stay at sea much longer than ever before, and the navy was able to expand.

The Role of the Surgeon

In theory, a ship was well provided with medical personnel. The Admiralty Regulations allowed a surgeon and three mates for a three-decker, two mates for a two-decker, and one mate for a frigate. This gave an average of about one qualified surgeon to 200 men. In practice, the position was much less satisfactory. In the first place, naval surgeons were not always easy to come by. At Camperdown in 1797, the surgeon of the *Ardent* had no mates to help him treat the wounded of the battle.[3] One surgeon complained that 'The medical profession in the navy was never duly estimated nor renumerated properly' at this time.[4] Reforms in 1806 improved the position, and surgeons benefited from increased pay and better conditions. There seems to have been more improvement after that.

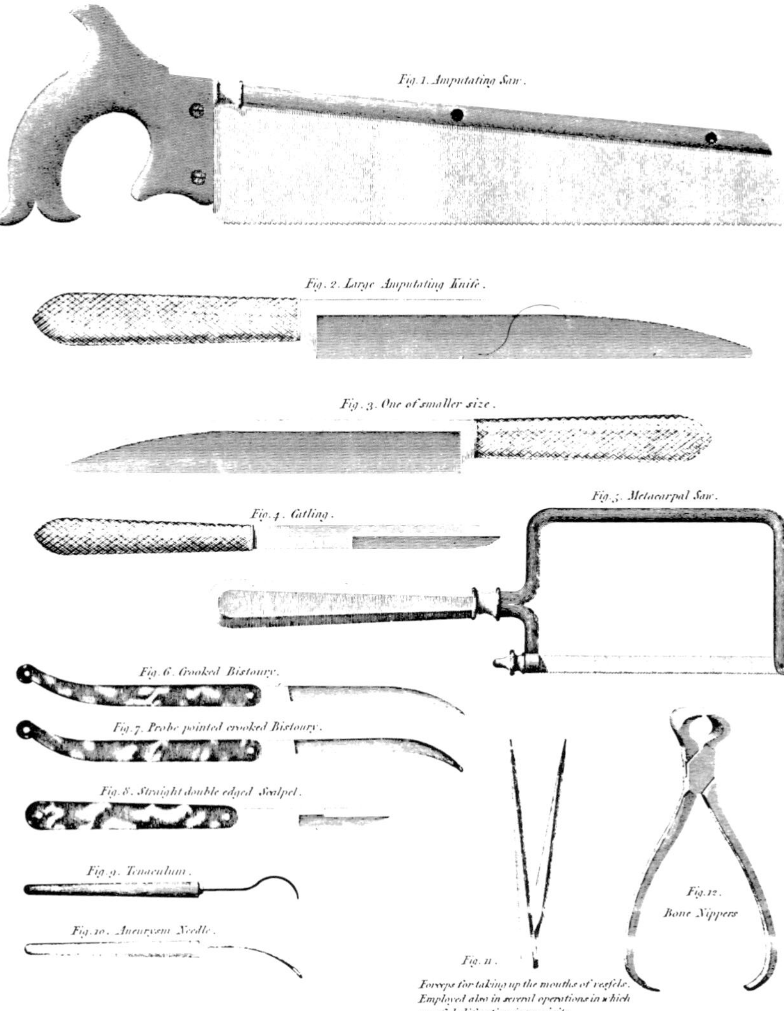

Surgeon's instruments. From the English Encylopaedia, 1802

A surgeon's medical chest, showing bottles of drugs, etc. The National Maritime Museum

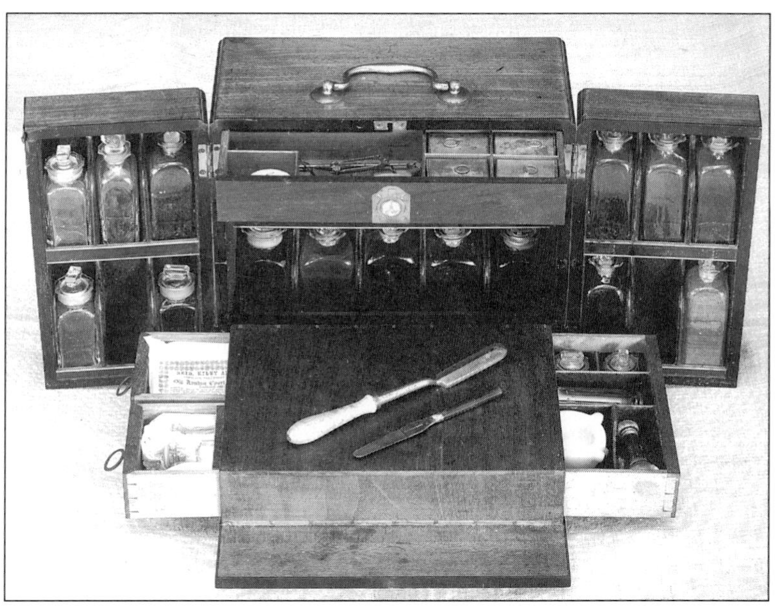

Secondly, the status of the surgeon was still quite low, as anaesthetics were not in use and no kind of delicate operation was possible. Physicians had much higher status, but were rarely employed in naval service. In 1797, there were only fifteen in the fleet, including those on half-pay. Physicians were employed as senior officers in the naval hospitals, or in supervisory and advisory roles as physicians of the fleet to the major commands. The surgeon was skilled at amputation and bleeding, and little else. Furthermore, many naval surgeons had poor qualifications, or bad characters. The Spithead mutineers complained of one surgeon, 'for inattention and ill treatment of the sick and wounded and not being qualified, as we can judge by several accidents happening in the ship. And for not visiting the sick for two or three months together, and when visiting has often been observed in liquor'.[5] However, other surgeons earned praise from their patients: 'My countenance is certainly altered, but it would have been much more so had it not been for the surgeon's mate.'[6] Even in 1797, the mutineers made complaints about individual surgeons, but not about the medical corps as a whole.

In spite of all his faults, the naval surgeon had heavy responsibilities. He was 'at once physician, surgeon and apothecary, upon whom in

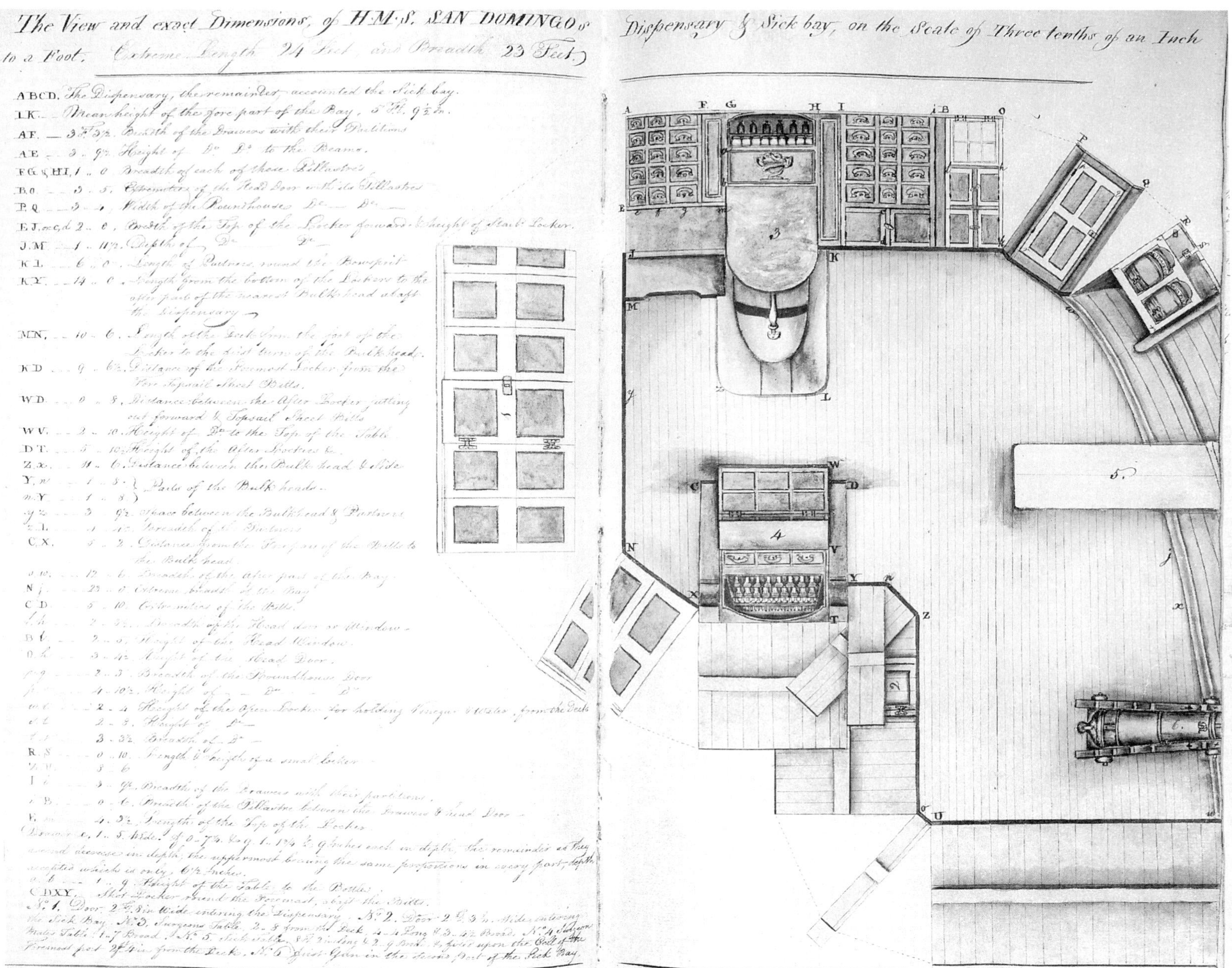

The sick bay of the San Domingo. The National Maritime Museum

these characters, the health and lives of so great a number of valuable subjects of the state are often solely depending.'[7] The Admiralty Regulations demanded that the surgeon provide himself with appropriate instruments, and a medicine chest, though, after 1804, the drugs were paid for by government. The surgeon was to visit the sick twice a day and present a sick list to the captain daily. He was to keep a detailed journal, in two parts. One dealt with disease, the other with surgical operations. The actual work varied according to circumstances. The *Gladiator* had 103 men sick at one time or another during the year up to February 1798, out of a crew of about three hundred. Of these, one died, nine were sent to hospital, and ninety-three were successfully treated aboard ship. On average, about five men were sick on any given day. The *Albion*, with about 600 men on board, had twenty-eight sick during a period from 1797–8. However, the surgeon had recently had to deal with a major outbreak of yellow fever, which had decimated the crew.[8] Aboard the *Victory* early in 1805, there was only one sick man out of 840.[9]

Another duty of the surgeon and his mates was to examine new men who came on board, especially those raised by the press gang or the Quota Acts. He was to 'discover whether they have any disease, or are in any other respect unfit for the service'. He was also to take care to find out about any past diseases, or whether he had been in contact with any infectious illnesses.[10]

The Sick Berth

Until the end of the eighteenth century, there was no general rule about the placing of the sick berth; the Admiralty Regulations merely demanded 'the most airy part of the ship'. There had been a fashion for placing it near the galley, because it was believed that smoke could be helpful for certain diseases; but this view was largely discredited by 1793. The most common type of sick berth was simply a row of hammocks on the lower deck, where the sick were so crammed together that the air was foul, and the medical attendants could not reach them. Many surgeons preferred to avoid the sick berth altogether. 'There is seldom occasion to remove the sick in ship, from their proper beds, into one place; and it is done only, when their number is increased, so as to make it inconvenient for other men to attend them when separate.' It should be 'a proper berth between decks, or in the hold'.[11]

A new type of sick berth was invented by Captain Markham of the *Centaur* in the late 1790s. He moved it away from the lower deck, and had the starboard side of the upper deck under the forecastle partitioned off to isolate the sick. In 1798, St Vincent ordered that this was to be copied throughout the Mediterranean fleet. 'The commander-in-chief positively directs that no sick are to be kept below the upper deck in any line-of-battle ship under his command, and that a sick berth is to be prepared in each [ship] under the forecastle, on the starboard side, with the round-house [or toilet] enclosed for the use of the sick.'[12] In 1800, this arrangement was extended to the Channel fleet and became common, but it was never universal.

The new type of berth had many advantages. It allowed plenty of light and air and also the heat of the galley stove, when necessary. It kept the men apart from the others, and allowed direct access to the round-house for toilet accommodation. The space for it was cleared by removing the pigsties from under the forecastle, and placing them elsewhere. However, there were some captains who did not follow the spirit of St Vincent's orders. The crew of one ship complained of their captain 'breaking up the hogsty and suffering the swine to range the main deck to the annoyance of the men'.[13]

The sick berth was provided with a dispensary. The ship's carpenter made cradles for the men who had broken limbs or other injuries. The rest of the men presumably lay in hammocks.

The Cockpit

Below decks in the airless orlop, the surgeon had his cabin, and his mates shared the midshipmen's berth. Medical stores were also kept there, in the dispensary. However, the main medical role of the cockpit was in action, when it was converted to the ship's operating theatre. It had the advantage that it was relatively free from enemy shot, but wounded men had to be brought down there by ladder, and this must have caused much additional pain. Often, there were too many sick for the cockpit, and they overflowed into the cable tiers, or even the gunroom and wardroom above. The surgeon's untrained assistants, known as 'loblolly boys', helped with the operations and brought the men forward for treatment. On most ships, the casualties were treated in strict order according to their time of arrival in the cockpit, regardless of rank.

In action, one man in ten was issued with a dressing to be used as a tourniquet. Wounded men were brought below to the cockpit by their comrades, though marine sentries were placed on the hatchways to prevent other men from taking refuge from enemy shot.

Sea Diseases

Of course, the best known of sea diseases was scurvy, caused by a

Nelson is treated in the cockpit of the Vanguard *after the battle of the Nile. As usual, the decks are shown much higher than they were in reality.* The National Maritime Museum

lack of fresh vegetables in the diet. Apart from some outbreaks in 1793 and 1794, the disease had largely been conquered by 1795 with the issue of lime and lemon juice. Though it was better diet rather than medical treatment which caused the improvement, medical men take most of the credit. Sir Gilbert Blane and Dr Thomas Trotter were instrumental in having fruits and juices made available. Better education and awareness among captains and admirals also helped.

Infectious diseases could be a terrible problem aboard a crowded ship, and typhus was the most serious and prevalent. Though medical opinion was divided about its causes, doctors were aware that dirty clothes, bad water and foul air contributed to its spread. Captains, therefore, issued orders on cleaning and ventilation, and there was some improvement. But the disease was not conquered. No men were admitted to Haslar hospital for scurvy in 1809, but 219 were admitted for fevers, of which typhus was easily the most common. This was reflected aboard individual ships. During 1797–8, the surgeon of the *Gladiator* treated seventeen men for fevers, and none for scurvy. His colleague on the *Alfred* treated twelve for fevers in a much shorter period.

Yellow fever was also common on tropical stations. Many officers avoided service in the West Indies because of it, but the seamen had no choice. An epidemic in 1794–6 killed thousands in the army and navy. Aboard the *Vanguard*, 120 of the 500 men aboard died.[14] There was no known cure, though some surgeons favoured bleeding. Smallpox was relatively rare at sea, and innoculation was available, though it was never compulsory.

Many other complaints were caused by the hardships of the seaman's life. Hernia was common, and trusses were issued to sufferers. Rheumatism was caused by damp conditions on deck and below deck, and other illnesses were caused by exposure to cold. Captains were aware of this, and on the *Audacious* in 1795 it was ordered that 'The men are not to go into their hammocks with their clothes on, nor to sleep anywhere without clothes on, as there can be nothing more prejudicial to their health — and a seaman in the king's service is too much consequence to his country to be allowed to risk his life by such means as saving himself a little trouble.'[15] Insanity was prevalent, and it is suggested that one man in a thousand was seriously affected — seven times the rate in the population at large. It was attributed to the fact that intoxicated seamen often hit their heads against deck beams. Victims were sent to the hospital at Bedlam, where they were confined in inhuman and degrading ways.

The seaman's lifestyle made venereal diseases very common. For a long time, the Admiralty believed that such diseases were virtually self inflicted, and the men who had to be treated by the surgeon were fined 15s. This practice was abolished in 1795, largely at the instigation of Dr Trotter, who pointed out that it prevented men coming forward for treatment.[16] The cure itself was unpleasant enough.

Casualties and their Treatment

It was estimated that 1630 men died in individual accidents in 1810 alone, and presumably thousands more were injured. Such cases made up 15 per cent of the sick list of the *Gladiator*, and 10 per cent on the *Alfred*. Naval surgeons were generally adept at treating fractures. Control of bleeding was another speciality, but amputation was the most impressive of the surgeon's skills, and was often used on shattered limbs. The contemporaneous image of the old sailor with one limb missing had some basis in fact.

In battle, the cockpit of a ship of war presented a scene of horror. According to one seaman, 'The surgeon and his mate were smeared with blood from head to foot. They looked more like butchers than doctors... The task was most painful to behold, the surgeon using his knife and saw on human flesh and bones as freely as the butcher

No. 30.

SICK TICKET.

To the Commissioners appointed to take Care of Sick and Wounded Seamen, or their Agent, at

WHEREAS we have sent on Shore the Person mentioned in the within Ticket, being afflicted with we desire that Care may be taken to promote his Cure, and to provide him Quarters, according to the Methods of the Navy.

He has taken the following Necessaries on Shore with him.

Beds	Chests	Bags	Coats	Waistcoats	Jackets	Breeches	Drawers	Trowsers	Pair of Sheets	Pair of Stockings	Shirts	Handkerchiefs	Pair of Shoes	Hats	Caps	Wigs	Books	Watches	Rings	Buttons	Silver Shoe Buckles	Silver Knee Buckles	Tickets			Cash

Captain
or
Lieutenant.
Surgeon.

HOSPITAL DISCHARGE,

THESE are to certify, that the within-mentioned was sent to this Place upon the Day of 18 for the Cure of and being cured, was discharged hence this Day of 18 to go forthwith to

He has received in Cloaths to the Value of········£
And in Conduct Money ······················

Amounting to Pounds Shillings and Pence.

Witness my Hand,

Appointed to take Care of Sick and Hurt Seamen.

The form of a sick ticket, issued to men sent to shore hospitals or a hospital ship. Admiralty *Regulations and Instructions*, 1808

at the shambles.' Hardened surgeons were no less affected, and one wrote,

> Ninety wounded were brought down during the action. The whole cockpit deck, cabins, wing berths and part of the cable tier, together with my platform and my preparations for dressing were covered with them... Melancholy calls for assistance were addressed to me from every side by wounded and dying, and piteous moaning and bewailing from pain and despair. In the midst of these agonising scenes, I was able to preserve myself firm and collected, and embracing in my mind the whole of the situation, to direct my attention where the greatest and most essential services could be performed.[17]

Shore Hospitals

The two home naval hospitals, at Haslar near Portsmouth and at Plymouth, were built in the 1740s and '50s. In building them, the government's motive was not entirely philanthropic. In the past, men had been sent ashore to private houses for treatment, but this led to desertion, drunkenness and corruption. The naval hospitals had high walls round them, with marine sentries. The patients were the only men in the navy to be provided with an official uniform — to prevent desertion. Haslar was situated on a narrow marshy peninsula, to make escape difficult.

In 1794, it was recommended that Haslar hospital should have a medical staff of one physician, one surgeon and six assistants, one visiting apothecary and four dispensers. In the following year, naval officers — a captain and three lieutenants — were appointed to supervise 'the proper discipline and subordination' and 'the interior arrangement and economy of the said hospitals' at Portsmouth and Plymouth.[18] By this time, Haslar was treating 15,000 patients per year, with a capacity of 1200 at one time.

Smaller hospitals were built on important naval stations — at Deal to service the Downs anchorage, Paignton for Torbay, Sheerness for the Nore, Yarmouth and Dartmouth. On overseas stations, the navy was quite well equipped with shore hospitals, and these were situated at Malta, Gibraltar and Port Mahon in the Mediterranean; Barbados, Jamaica and Antigua in the West Indies; Halifax and Bermuda in North America; and at the Cape of Good Hope and Madras.

Nursing had not yet become a profession, and the women nurses in naval hospitals were often rather disreputable. Many were dismissed for drunkenness, prostitution, or for helping sailors to desert. According to a rather puritanical seaman in the hospital at Plymouth, 'Being accustomed to the manners and associations of sailors, those ladies are exceedingly bold and audacious, and without concern to make use of the most indecent observations and actions in their common conversation. I had a great deal to do to repulse the temptations I met with from these sirens.'[19]

Hospital Ships

In places where shore hospitals were not available, old ships were used instead. The projected hospital at Chatham was not finished until much later, and the old 74 *Arrogant* served instead for most of the period of the wars. She was commanded by a lieutenant, with a purser, boatswain, gunner and carpenter, but no master. There was a surgeon and his assistant. She had a total crew of sixty-seven including seamen who were largely employed in maintenance, in loading stores, and in manning the boats to ferry the sick back and forth. She also had twenty-five marines, to prevent desertion.[20] At Falmouth, the hospital ship *Chatham*, an old 50-gun ship, was not in good condition. 'She has sprung a leak three times, but is very tight in smooth water.'[21] Nevertheless, she was ordered to be placed so that she could assist in the defence of the harbour if necessary, because there was very little naval presence in the port. Because of the western situation of Falmouth, the *Chatham* was well placed to receive casualties from the Channel fleet. A hospital ship was also situated at Plymouth, to take the overflow from the shore hospital. Mobile hospital ships were used occasionally, to follow the Mediterranean fleet, for example.

6 Discipline

The Articles of War

The Articles of War provided the legal basis for naval discipline. They had originally been drawn up in the 1650s, and were adopted by Charles II's government at the Restoration. A slightly different version was passed by parliament in 1749, and more amendments were made a few years later, changing the notorious clause which had sent Admiral Byng to his death in 1757. Altogether there were 36 Articles, defining the major crimes which could be committed in the fleet, and giving sentences. One contemporary divided the articles into four different groups. First, offences 'against God and religion' — the articles demanded that divine service be held on the Sabbath, and they banned profanity and swearing; these were relatively minor offences, and their punishments were left undefined. Second, 12 articles defined crimes against 'the executive power of the king, and his government.' Such offences included espionage, holding communication with an enemy or rebel, as well as naval crimes such as false muster or neglect of duty. Many of these crimes were punished severely — with the death penalty being available in most cases. Third, there were articles against actions which 'violate and transgress the rights and duties which men owe to their fellow subjects'; they included the clauses against murder, theft, and assault, and, again, the death penalty was available in most cases. Finally, there were military offences such as 'Yielding and crying for quarter', 'Withdrawing or keeping back from fight', and 'Forbearing to pursue an enemy'. The six articles in this category were particularly severe, and all provided for the death penalty, often without any other option for the court. 'Every person in the fleet who through cowardice, negligence, or disaffection, shall forbear to pursue the chase of any enemy, pirate, or rebel, beaten or flying; or shall not relieve and assist a known friend in view to the utmost of his power, being convicted of such offence by the sentence of a court martial, shall suffer death.' In all, death was mandatory for eight crimes, and optional for eleven more.[1]

The Articles of War did not define many of the duties and roles of sailors and officers; they had many gaps, and there was no clearly defined offence of fraud, while some of the punishments were obviously too severe, and little used. The articles did increase the power of the captain by a catch-all clause: 'All other crimes, committed by any person or persons in the fleet, which are not mentioned in this act, or for which no punishment is hereby directed to be inflicted, shall be punished according to the laws and customs in such cases used at sea.'[2]

Admiralty Regulations and Instructions

Regulations and Instructions Relating to His Majesty's Service at Sea was a thick volume. The 1806 edition had 440 pages of instructions, plus additional orders recently issued, samples of forty-seven forms to be used by the captain, and twenty-eight more for the use of the purser. Mostly, the regulations consisted of rules for the conduct of the ship's officers, especially the captain and the purser. They dealt largely with matters of accountancy and storekeeping, though there were also clauses dealing with the cleanliness and health of the crew, and with fire safety. There were several different editions, dating from 1787, 1806 and 1808. The later editions tended to reflect greater concern with health. They said very little about the detailed organisation of the ship, except to demand that the crew be put in divisions, and quarter and station bills be made out.

Captain's Orders

The lack of a 'uniform system of discipline' throughout the fleet was often lamented, and at the end of the American War, Admiral Howe had attempted to rectify this by issuing instructions for the ships under his command. But, in general, each captain was left to draw up his own set of instructions to his officers and crew, and to fill in the many gaps left by the Articles of War and the Admiralty Regulations. There was no obligation for captains to draw up such instructions, and it is not certain that all did. The Admiralty paid no attention to this matter, and did not collect sets of instructions, so only a few have survived. However, it must have been difficult to administer a large ship without them.

Surviving instructions show a great deal of variety. According to Robert Wilson, 'most officers have plans of their own which the crews over which they command do follow and it's a common saying "different ships, different rules", for it must be considered that every commanding officer of a vessel of war is like unto a prince in his own state.'[3] Admiral Duncan wrote in 1797, 'Many things should now be thought of as fixing the internal regulations of ships on one plan. Of late years, every captain has taken upon him to establish rules for himself.'[4] In a few cases, it is clear that captains copied from one another but, more often, they seemed to have asserted their own authority, and followed their own ideas on how a ship should be run. In a few cases, captains merely continued the instructions of their predecessors, with a few small amendments. This happened when Captain Duff of the *Mars* was killed at Trafalgar, and Captain Oliver took his place.[5] Crews could be put to some inconvenience if new captains insisted on changing everything.

Captain's instructions usually contained detailed orders to the officers, in particular, the officers of the watch and the departmental officers. They gave details about the ship's daily and weekly routine, about such matters as washing days and when the hammocks were to be taken down and brought up. Often, the captain made each officer sign to show that he had read them. Important orders were read out to the crew, and posted 'in the usual places of the ship' — under the half deck.[6]

Courts-martial

The most serious punishments — death and imprisonment for all ranks, floggings of more than about three dozen lashes for lower ranks only, and cashiering, dismissal and reduction in rank or seniority for officers — could only be awarded by court-martial. The procedure was normally initiated by the captain of the ship, who submitted a request to the commander-in-chief of his station. A court had to consist of at least five, and not more than thirteen captains or admirals. Often, prisoners were held in confinement for weeks until such a number could be assembled. The commander-in-chief convened the court-martial, so he could not serve on it himself. The second in command on the station normally presided, with the next most senior officers making up the required number. In cases where the ship was not under a commander-in-chief, the commander of a detachment could call a court-martial, or any five ships meeting could send their senior officers to form a court. A court-martial was automatic when any naval ship was lost. All the officers and crew were tried, though in the great majority of cases they were all acquitted. Occasionally, even admirals were tried, as in the cases of Calder in 1805, and Gambier after the Basque Roads affair in 1808.

Even legal experts recognised that there was a built-in bias in courts-martial, in that a seaman was certainly not tried by his peers.[7] Seamen themselves were aware of this, and one commented that he would have been acquitted 'had I been tried by a jury of seamen.'[8] The trial itself was no more unfair than could be expected in the circumstances. The 'prisoner' was allowed a counsel, and the verdict was reached by a vote, not necessarily unanimous, among the members of the court. Many prisoners were acquitted, and, in general, the evidence seems to have been heard fairly. The judge advocate to the fleet, or one of his deputies, attended to advise the court on legal matters.

Courts-martial were held aboard ship, usually in the great cabin of the flagship. They sat in the forenoon only, and some courts, especially those on captains and admirals, lasted for many days. Those on seamen were much shorter. Courts-martial became quite common in the later years of the wars; 337 were held during 1812.[9]

The Death Penalty

For seamen, petty officers and marines, the death penalty was carried out by hanging. By tradition this was carried out aboard the offender's own ship. A gun was fired to give warning, and the other ships in the port each sent a boat with an officer and a full crew to witness the punishment. The victim stood on the cathead with a bag over his head. A rope was passed through a block at the fore yardarm, and the noose was put round the man's neck. A gang of sailors hauled smartly on the other end of the rope, pulling the man up to the yardarm, where he was allowed to hang for an hour. According to one account, 'About twenty stout fellows seized each of the ropes. One instant's, and only one instant's, pause occurred, for the boatswain piping 'hoist away', the executioners ran with all speed towards the poop; and the unfortunate culprit, hurried aloft with the rapidity of thought, died in an instant ... it seemed to me the most humane execution I had ever witnessed.'[10] It was normal for the men hauling the rope to come from the different ships on station; but, in 1797, St Vincent insisted that the crew of the *Marlborough* should hang one of their own number, convicted of mutiny.[11]

Before it was carried out, any sentence in home waters had to be confirmed by the Admiralty, and was subject to the Royal prerogative of mercy. Reprieves were quite common, and in cases where large numbers were sentenced to hang, they were sometimes ordered to draw lots to decide which one it should be. In cases where pardons were given, it was to be 'kept extremely secret, until the offender is, on the day appointed for execution, brought upon deck, and everything prepared for his execution, agreeable to the custom of the navy; and then only to make known to him His Majesty's pleasure, and to release him from his confinement'.[12] Convicted officers normally suffered death by shooting.

Flogging Round the Fleet

In theory, death was the severest punishment that could be imposed, but many held that flogging round the fleet, when between 100 and 1000 lashes could be awarded by a court-martial, was much worse. Three hundred lashes was the normal for deserters convicted by court-martial, unless there were mitigating circumstances. One seaman begged to have death instead, but was told that the flogging was what the court had decided.[13] Another said, 'I am sure I cannot go through with this torture; I would rather have been sentenced to be shot or hung from the yardarm.'[14]

An offender was sentenced to have part of his punishment opposite each one of the ships in port at the time — perhaps twenty-five lashes at each. He was tied to capstan bars erected in the ship's launch, and rowed from one ship to another, accompanied by a drummer playing the Rogue's March, as well as officers and marines from his ship, a boat from each ship, and a surgeon who would feel his pulse and stop the punishment if his life seemed in danger. 'It was a dreadful sight; the unfortunate suffered tied down on the boat and rowed from ship to ship, getting an equal number of lashes at the side of each vessel from a fresh man ... He was rowed back to the *Surprise*, his back swelled like a pillow, black and blue; some sheets of thick blue paper were steeped in vinegar and laid to his back. Before, he seemed insensible, now his shrieks rent the air. When better he was sent to the ship, where his tortures were stopped, and again renewed.'[15] Many men died under such punishment.

Other Punishments

Up to two years' imprisonment could be given by a court martial, and officers could be reduced in rank or seniority. Some classes of warrant officer, such as boatswains and masters at arms, could be degraded and ordered to serve before the mast. This happened to Midshipman Richard Parker, who later became the leader of the Nore mutiny. Commissioned officers could be dismissed the service, losing all rights to pay; or dismissed their ship, with or without a proviso that they never be allowed to serve again, but retain their half pay. They could be reduced in rank, or put at the bottom of the seniority list within their rank, and perhaps debarred from rising in the list. For relatively mild offences, they could be reprimanded.

Trial by the Captain

Minor offences were tried by the captain of the ship. Usually a man would be reported by an officer or petty officer, and brought before his commanding officer. On one ship at least, such affairs were held in public. The crew was mustered, the marines drawn up in ranks,

> The ship's corporal brings forward the prisoners. A grating is fixed up for them to be siezed on. They are called before the captain one by one to make their defence; they are allowed a fair trial. If any officer speaks in their favour, they are acquitted or their punishment is mitigated; if they can clear themselves, well and good. In short, it's like a court of judicature.[16]

Probably, it was more common for such trials to be held in the privacy of the great cabin, and not all seamen were so optimistic about the standard of justice. According to 'Jack Nastyface', 'nineteen out of twenty men that are punished, suffer without being conscious that they have violated any law; and in many instances they are the most expert and able seamen.'[17] There was no right of appeal from a captain's sentence, and a seaman who refused to strip for punishment, saying he would have a court-martial instead, was eventually awarded 300 lashes by the latter body.[18]

A flogging. The offender is lashed to a grating, and a boatswain's mate stands ready with the cat. The boatswain stands behind with his cane. A single marine guards the offender, and the rest are drawn up on the poop with fixed bayonets, under their officer. A young drummer is ready to beat the roll (though this is possibly inaccurate, as the marines tended to use adults rather than boys as drummers). The crew is drawn up on the right, while the officers, including some very young midshipmen, are on the left. In this case, the convicted man is reprieved, because another has owned up to the offence. The National Maritime Museum

Offences and Punishments

The most tyrannical punishments, such as flogging the last man off the yardarm, were very rare; the only known instance was aboard the *Hermione* in 1799, and that inspired a very savage mutiny. In a more typical case of severe punishment, thirty-one men of the *Alfred* were flogged for separate offences in one day in 1810.[19] A more general picture of ship's discipline is shown from the punishment book of the *Blake* from 1810 to 1814.[20] It gives some idea of the frequency of punishment: 135 floggings took places in a year. Of course there were a few persistent offenders. The worst was Patrick Purcell, who was flogged seven times from June 1809 to December 1812. His offences included drunkenness (four times), disobedience, neglect of duty, and fighting. Drunkenness was by far the most common offence, and was usually awarded twelve lashes, or more for repeated offences. Other crimes included 'theft' (usually given thirty-six lashes), filthiness (eighteen), 'having wet clothes below' (twelve), 'sleeping when on duty' (six) and 'pissing on the poop' (twelve). The most severe punishment of all was forty-eight lashes, plus two months' confinement, for 'attempting an unnatural crime with a boy'. Some men were forgiven on their first offence, and petty officers were usually disrated without any flogging.

The Admiralty Regulations allowed the captain to award a maximum of twelve lashes, but this rule was often ignored, as the punishment book of the *Blake* shows. Sometimes, they made the excuse that the man had offended several times at once, by disobeying an order as well as being drunk, for example. It was suggested that 'It is justifiable *only* from the ancient practice and usage of the navy, and may even be deemed leniety in a commander to punish, occasionally, offenders with two or three dozen lashes, rather than bring them to a court-martial.'[21] In 1797, the crew of the *Prosperine* complained of 'the severest of punishments for the severest of offences, by two, three or four dozen lashes without any court of enquiry'.[22]

Captains could award other punishments — disrating was common for petty officers, and a man's grog could be stopped for several days. This was regarded as a serious hardship by many men, as it deprived them of one of the few pleasures available on a man-of-war.

Flogging

Flogging was carried out by the 'cat-of-nine-tails', made up from one piece of thick rope as the handle, and the appropriate number of pieces of light line, knotted in places. The boatswain's accounts of the *Victory* show that every few days four log lines were 'used in making cats for punishment'.[23] For theft, an even more painful instrument, known as the thieves' cat, was used. This had 'larger and harder knots upon it than those generally employed'.[24] In 1808, one of the charges against Captain Corbet of the *Nereide* was that he used the thieves' cat for normal punishments.[25]

The crew was assembled to witness the punishment, and marines stood by with muskets and fixed bayonets. A grating was taken up from its position over one of the hatches, and placed upright in the waist. The wrists and ankles of the offender were tied to it, and his back was stripped. 'The boatswain's mate is then ordered to cut him with the cat-o'-nine'tails; and after six or twelve lashes are given, another boatswain's mate is called to continue the exercise.'[26] According to Robert Wilson, 'When a poor fellow is being punished, his agonising cries pierce you to the soul. The scene is awful! Hot boiling lead poured on a criminal's back would be but in comparison to the suffering of those who come under the lash of the unrelenting boatswain's mates.'[27]

Flogging round the fleet. The offender is lashed to capstan bars. A boatswain's mate stands guard over him, and a drummer kneels in the bows. The boat is towed by another, and each ship has sent a boat and crew to witness the punishment. The National Maritime Museum

Running the Gauntlet

The punishment of running the gauntlet was awarded for theft, and since it was carried out by the crew themselves, its severity partly depended on the feelings of the men. The prisoner was dragged round the decks on a seat placed on top of a tub. 'The cavalcade starts from the break of the quarterdeck, after the boatswain has given the prisoner a dozen lashes, and the ship's crew are ranged round the decks in two rows, so that the prisoner passes between them, and each man is provided with a three yarn knittle; that is, three rope yarns tightly laid together and knotted. With this, each man must cut him, or be thought to be implicated in his theft.'[28] The practice was abolished in 1806, by Admiralty order.[29]

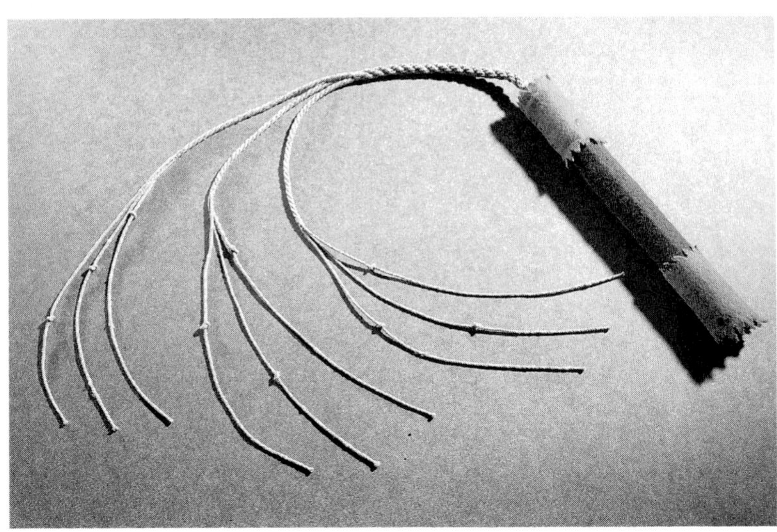

A cat-of-nine-tails. The National Maritime Museum

Informal Punishments

Many other punishments could be awarded by the junior officers or the petty officers, without the formality of a trial, or an entry in the ship's log. Of these, the most common was 'starting'. On some ships, every petty officer carried a rope's end, which he used to lash seamen, either on the orders of his officer, or on his own initiative. 'Some of the men's backs have often been so bad from the effects of the starting system that they have not been able to bear their jackets for several days.'[30] Petty officers also carried canes and sticks for striking the men. On his first introduction to naval service, William Richardson was appalled by the injustice and inefficiency of the system. 'Soon after I got on board we had to cat the anchor, and in running along with the foul, boatswain's mates were placed on each side, who kept thrashing away with their rattans on our backs, making no difference between those that pulled hard and those that did not.'[31] Aboard the *Terpischore* in 1800, 'the Boatswain now carries a stick cut of rawhide plaited and served all over, and tarred twine, with which he cuts and slashes all he comes near.'[32] Some captains attempted to abolish starting, and Captain Cumby of the *Hyperion* decreed, 'The highly improper practice of what is called starting the men is most peremtorily forbidden.'[33] It was held that it had been abolished generally as a result of a court-martial on Captain Robert Corbet in 1809, but it is doubtful if this had much effect.

Another common punishment was to gag a man, usually for insolence of blasphemy. In one incident aboard the *Impeteux* in 1808, a petty officer reported, 'I clapped the bolt into his mouth, and kept it there for about ten minutes, when he was peaceable.' The man's hands had already been tied behind his back.[34] According to 'Nastyface', 'The man is placed in a sitting position, and his hands secured behind him. His mouth is then forced open, and an iron bolt put across, well secured behind his head.'[35]

Aboard the *Prosperine* in 1797, the men complained that 'The smallest absence from your watch, forced to drink half a gallon of

A midshipman is seized up to the shrouds as a punishment. The National Maritime Museum

salt water, if refused, punished directly or spread on the weather rigging in the inclemency of the weather.'[36] Offenders were seized up to the rigging on other ships, and sometimes started while they were there. In 1795 one Lt McKinley was accused of 'making us strip and lashing us up to the rigging, and beating us with the end [of] a rope till we almost expire.'[37]

'Confinement' could be used as a punishment, but it was more commonly used as a way of keeping offenders waiting trial. There were no cells aboard ship, so prisoners were kept 'in irons' instead. Shackles were fitted to the deck and to an iron bar, so that the leg contained would be almost totally immobilised. Either one leg or two could be locked in the 'iron garters' or 'bilboes', according to the severity of the punishment or the demand for space. A marine stood guard over any men in the bilboes, and they were usually placed aft on the lower deck, near the gun room. Captain Anselm Griffiths asked, 'Is there no wrong done to an innocent man, robbing him of his exercise, degrading him, obliging him to sleep on deck with his leg in irons, the worry of his feelings (for seamen have feelings) and the loss of his grog?'[38]

Undoubtedly the severity of punishments varied greatly from ship to ship, and from officer to officer. The Admiralty made some attempts to mitigate the worst punishments, and some officers were court-martialled for cruelty; but the rights of the seaman depended very much on chance and on the whims of his commander.

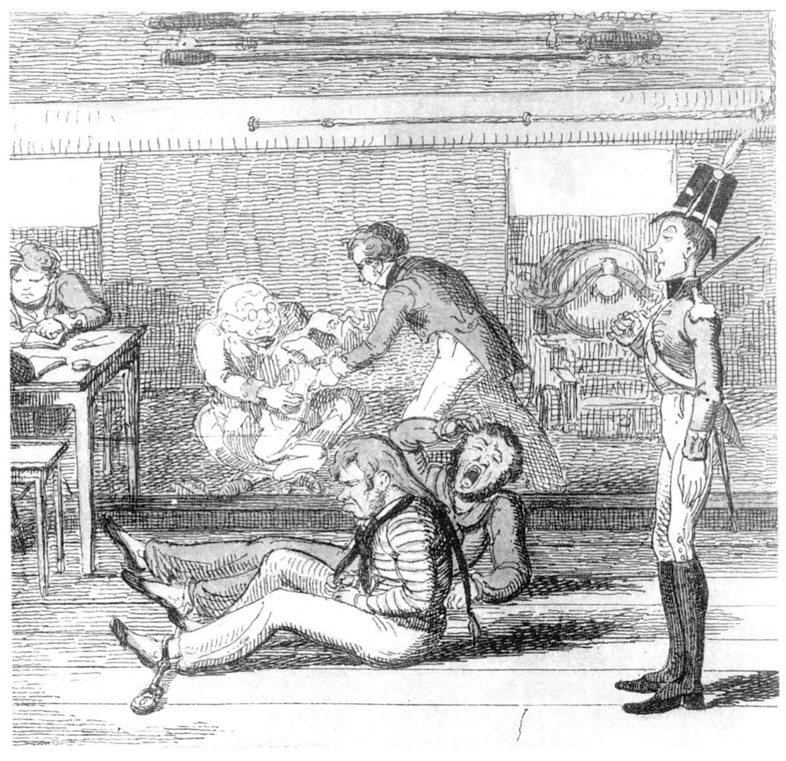

Two seamen in irons. A marine sentry stands guard over them with drawn bayonet. In the left background, two midshipmen sit at a table learning navigation, with the ship's tailor to their right. The National Maritime Museum

Part X
DOCKYARDS AND BASES

1 The Work and Facilities of the Dockyards

Ship Maintenance

It is often said that ships of the age of sail could last for long periods without maintenance. This belief is largely based on the fact that the *Victory* was forty years old at the time of Trafalgar, and that other ships such as the *Royal William* and the *Britannia* also lasted for long periods. In fact, such experience was far from typical, and the *Victory* was only kept afloat at great expense, amounting to several times the cost of her original building. Other ships had far shorter careers, and were often scrapped after about fifteen years. Even to keep them at sea for that long required considerable expenditure, and this was the task of the Royal dockyards.

A dockyard was intended to service the ships themselves, and was only part of a naval-base complex. The needs of the men were looked after by the victualling yards, hospitals and marine barracks which were often situated nearby, and the ordnance depots were responsible for the armament of the ships. The dockyards were responsible for building the ships in some cases, or supervising their building in others. They carried out nearly all the navy's ship repair, and supplied the thousands of items required to keep the ships operational. They looked after the reserve ships of the ordinary, and manufactured many items, such as blocks and anchors, on their premises. The Royal dockyards were easily the largest civilian employers in the country, and in 1814 they employed over 15,000 men in the home yards alone.[1]

Shipbuilding

Private enterprise was mistrusted in the eighteenth century. Attitudes had moderated since 1742, when the Navy Board declared, 'We should judge it the best economy to perform all His Majesty's works in his own yards, on account of the goodness of them.'[2] But private shipbuilders were still treated with suspicion, and often blamed for failures, such as the 'Forty thieves' class of 74-gun ships. They were accused of bad workmanship, and of trying to form rings to fix prices.

Peacetime shipbuilding was done almost entirely in the dockyards (though at the end of a war the private yards often had a backlog of naval work which might last for years). But the dockyards, which had only twenty-six building slips between them in 1800,[3] were no longer adequate to the task of wartime shipbuilding. The dockyards concentrated on building the larger types of ships, and all three-deckers were built there, partly because few private yards had facilities for such big vessels. Two-deckers were built approximately equally in the dockyards and merchant yards, with the result that 52 per cent of ships-of-the-line were produced in the merchant yards, and almost exactly half the tonnage of ships of this type.[4] Frigates and smaller vessels were much more likely to be built in the merchant yards. From 1793 to 1815, 627 ships 'under the line' were built in the merchant yards, compared with 78 in the dockyards.[5]

A sawpit for cutting timber, with a ship being built in the background. The Naval Chronicle

The masthouse at Chatham. The loft was used as a mould loft for drawing out the lines of ships. Author's photograph

Though they did not build all the ships themselves, the dockyards remained responsible for those built elsewhere. The Navy Board took good care to place its contracts with yards close to the dockyards — especially in the Thames, the Solent, and the West Country — and the expanding industry of the north of England was little exploited for naval purposes. A naval overseer was appointed to each contract-built ship, with responsibility to ensure that there was no bad workmanship or inferior materials. An overseer was a trusted shipwright of the dockyard, often a foreman or quarterman. Their work was reinforced by periodic visits from the master shipwright of the dockyard, but there was always the danger that an overseer could be bribed to ignore bad construction.

Types of Repair

Ship repair was carried out almost entirely within the dockyards, for 'The repairing ships in merchant yards has never been resorted to, but in cases of absolute necessity, and confined to frigates only.'[6] The scope of a repair might vary enormously, from replacing a few items of rigging, to stripping a ship down almost to her keel, and rebuilding her. The first stage of the process, after the ship had arrived at the dockyard, was the survey, carried out by the master shipwright and his assistants. For minor repairs, ships could be surveyed afloat, with most of their guns and stores still in. If greater defects were suspected, the ship had to be totally emptied and put into a dry dock. There, the surveyors would bore into the wood, or remove some of the planking to look at the state of the timbers below, and a report on the condition of the ship would be sent to the Navy Board, with an estimate of how much it would cost to put her in good condition. The latter body, in consultation with the Admiralty, would decide whether the ship was worth repairing, or should be broken up.

At the upper end of the scale was the 'large' or 'great repair'. This involved major structural work, stripping off most of the planking and replacing much of the timbers. It was mostly done to valued ships with good sailing qualities, especially large ones, such as the *Victory* in 1801–3. The 98-gun *Prince* was taken apart for rather different reasons, and a 17ft section added amidships, to lengthen her. Of such repairs, it was complained 'No ship ever received a thorough repair without costing more than when she was built'[7] and this is largely borne out by the figures. The large repair of the *Bedford*, 74, cost £52,317 in 1805–7, while the 'very large repair' of the *San Josef* cost £89,308 in 1807–9.[8] A 'middling repair' involved some structural work, and was estimated to take about ten months on a 74, though some took much longer. The repair of the *Queen Charlotte* cost £44,219, and that of the *Ville de Paris*, £39,289.[9] A 'small repair' was expected to take about a quarter of that time,[10] but the cost might vary enormously. The repair of the *Bellona* cost £588 in 1805, while that of *Bellerophon* cost £18,082.[11] There were some additional categories such as 'very large repair', 'between large and middling repair', and so on. However, the majority of repairs were relatively minor, and described by the terms 'made good defects' or, if only work on the rigging and fitting was required, 'refitted'. Refitting had not yet taken on its modern meaning, which can include very extensive repairs.

During the course of the Napoleonic Wars there were several special programmes of repair, in order to get ships into service as quickly as possible. The most important of these was the 'doubling and bracing' programme on the eve of Trafalgar. Twenty-two ships-of-the-line and eleven frigates had diagonal braces fitted across their hulls, and the planking doubled on the outside, to prolong their lives. It was recognised that this was an emergency measure not to be repeated, but some of the ships had quite successful careers after that.

The introduction of coppering had reduced much of the need for routine docking. Fast ships no longer had to be docked and cleaned every four months or so, and, on average, ships were put into dock about once in two years, though many lasted for much longer; ships on foreign stations sometimes had to go for five years or more without docking. On average, ships needed a middling repair or larger about once in three or four years.[12] Repairs often took much longer than the original estimate, as new defects were discovered, as the system of survey and estimate was often found to be inadequate.

Coppering and Fitting

New ships, whether merchant of dockyard built, were coppered after launching. Those from merchant yards were towed into the dockyards, and then put into dry dock for coppering. After that, the copper was cleaned and repaired every time the ship was put into dry dock, perhaps once in two years. A certain amount would wear away, or be knocked off in accidents, so the repair of the copper was the most common element in all dockyard repairs. Sometimes, the whole of the copper had to be taken off, and the ship recoppered; this happened to the *Bellona*, 74, in 1797, 1798, 1801, 1805 and 1809.[13]

The fitting out of a ship with masts, rigging, sails, and certain types of stores was largely the responsibility of the dockyard. Though much of the work was done by the ship's crew, the dockyard had to issue all the requisites, and yard craft or hired vessels, were used to convey them to the ship, which was generally anchored off the dockyard. In particular, the sheer hulk of the dockyard was needed for getting the lower masts in.

The Ordinary

In peacetime, most ships of the navy were laid up 'in ordinary'. In wartime, a few ships still remained in this state, perhaps because of outdated design or because not enough men were available to man them. Ships in ordinary were kept moored bow and stern to buoys in the rivers or harbours close to the yards. Their guns, stores and upper masts were removed, but they were sometimes rigged with windsails to help to air the lower parts of the hull, in an effort to prevent timber decay. A ship in ordinary was manned by her standing officers, the gunner, carpenter and boatswain, and by the purser and the cook. In addition, a small number of servants was employed — four on a 74-gun ship and one on a fifth rate.[14] Parties of shipwrights and labourers went round the ships carrying out routine maintenance, and pumping out the bilges when necessary. The work of a warrant officer of a ship in ordinary was quite easy compared with his service afloat. 'We are now no more (thanks be to God) summoned on deck with the cry of "all hands, hoy!"... The *Caesar* never went to sea after this, being completely worn out... In order to amuse myself, I bought some elm board and built myself a little boat about eleven

Chatham Dockyard from the River Medway. The National Maritime Museum

feet long, and rigged her with mast and sails. Many pleasant excursions I had in her.'[15]

At the beginning of 1784, when the navy had practically returned to a peacetime footing after the American War, there were 243 ships in ordinary compared with 159 in commission. Larger ships tended to see less service in peacetime, and 105 out of 130 completed ships of-the-line were in ordinary.[16] By the time the war ended in 1801, there were only 81 ships in ordinary, out of a fleet of 945 ships and vessels. The ordinary included 29 ships-of-the-line, 18 frigates and 20 sloops.[17]

Guardships

Unlike ships in ordinary, guardships were ships in commission, though not completely ready for sea. They were kept fully rigged, and partly armed, stored and manned. They formed the first line of reserves, as ships that could be prepared for action in a few days, once the press gangs had brought in enough men to make them up to full strength. Guardships were mostly 74s or 64s, though a three-decker sometimes served at each of the major ports, as flagship for the port admiral. In 1784, Portsmouth had the strongest force of guardships, with one 90, seven 74s, a 64 and a 50.[18] A few guardships were also kept on in wartime. In 1801, there were eight, from 80 to 26 guns.[19] When serving as a guardship, a 74 had a crew of 400, with four lieutenants, 47 marines, 245 seamen, and other officers in proportion.[20] At night the men took it in turns to row round the dockyard, checking the ships of the ordinary for security, and looking into the creeks and inlets for smugglers and spies.

St Vincent was first lord of the Admiralty during the peace of 1802–3, and he had a prejudice against guardships; they were 'So infamously rotten and corrupt, as to have sown the seeds of all the theft, false musters, and general departure from the regulations of the service; and the men in them made idle and profligate.'[21] Very few were fitted out in the peace of 1802–3, and ships in full commission were used instead; but the idea was revived after 1815.

Dry Docks

In a sense, the dry dock was the core of the dockyard, and gave it its name. It was essential to the fulfilment of its primary function of repairing ships. When Plymouth dockyard was founded in 1690, it consisted almost entirely of a single dock plus houses for the officers. In view of the reluctance to entrust repair work to outsiders, the naval dry docks were kept constantly busy in wartime. Despite the growth of the fleet, the number of dry-docks did not increase greatly;

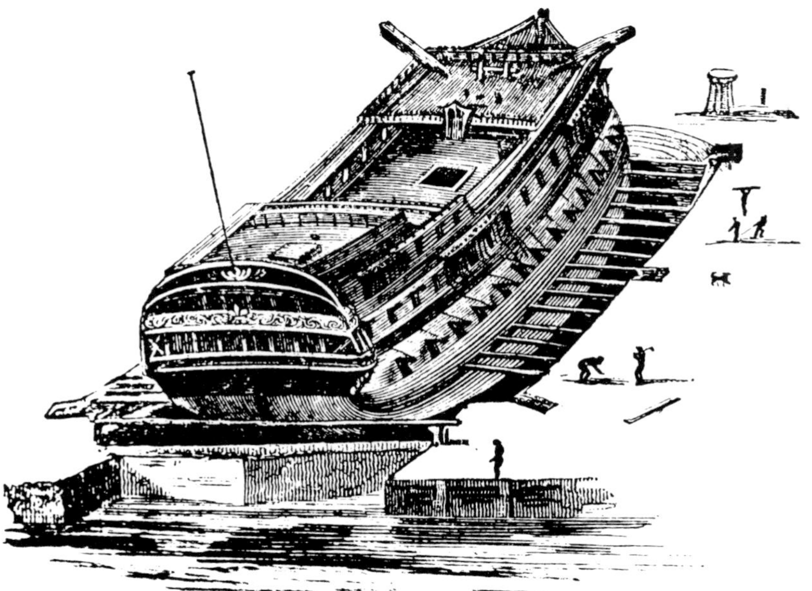

A ship in dry dock, with shores to support it in position. From the Naval Chronicle in 1753, there was capacity for nineteen ships in the yards, and, by 1815, this had risen only to twenty-five.[22] However, ships needed rather less docking than in the past, because they were coppered.

The largest dry-docks, capable of serving first rates, were about 200ft long. The docks were built in stone with steps round their sides, and these helped to provide a base for the shores which supported the ship upright after the water was taken out. The dock had either a pair of flood gates or a caisson; the latter floated while there was water in the dock, and was therefore easier to manoeuvre into position to close it; it was constructed in a single piece, reducing the likelihood of leaks. The ship was put into the dock at high tide, and the falling tide could therefore be used to empty the dock. The rest of the work was done by men operating chain pumps.

The largest ships could only be docked at spring tides, which occurred fortnightly. A ship could be put in and taken out in the course of two tides if a hurried repair of the bottom was needed. Otherwise, she would occupy the much-needed dock for two weeks until the next spring tide. This created a cyclical pattern in dockyard work, and spring tides were so valuable that even Lord Barham, an Evangelical and a strong opponent of Sunday work, had to concede that such a tide could not be missed.[23]

Wet docks were less useful, though one was completed at Portsmouth in 1805, with some of the dry docks leading off from it. It was used to keep ships out of the tidal flow, allowing them to be worked on without any rise and fall, though of course it did not allow any access to the underwater hull. The use of the dry dock in conjunction with the wet dock was described as follows:

> When a ship-of-the-line is to be taken from the harbour into dock, the flood gates of the wet and a dry dock are opened at high water. The ship is hauled into the dry dock, the gate of which and that of the wet dock are shut. A sluice is hauled up in the dry dock and the water let off into the basin. When the repairs of the ship are finished in a dry dock, she cannot be taken out into the wet dock by letting water from the latter into the former because if that was done the ship would still remain aground in the dock; for there is not water sufficient in the wet dock to float a ship although only one dry dock has been filled from it; but to get the ship out, the flood gate of the wet dock next the harbour must be opened at high water and the flood gate of the dry dock also when the ship is immediately taken thence to the harbour.[24]

Building Facilities

All the dockyards had slips for building ships of war—Deptford had five, Woolwich and Plymouth four, Chatham and Portsmouth six, and Sheerness two.[25] All the yards except Sheerness had the facilities to build at least one first rate, and Chatham could build three simultaneously if necessary. Sheerness was capable of building nothing larger than a 38-gun frigate, though the yard could repair larger ships. Slips were of course placed on the water's edge, and angled slightly downwards to allow the completed ship to slide into the water.

As well as the building slips, the main yards also had mould lofts where full-size plans of the ship could be drawn out. At Chatham, the mould loft was situated above the mast house.

Hulks

Apart from the ordinary and guardships, numerous other ships were stationed off the main dockyards, at permanent moorings. The navy used hulks for various purposes. Receiving ships held recently recruited men, and the crews of ships which were in dry dock. Prison ships were stationed at all the dockyards, largely for prisoners of war, but hospital ships were only needed at yards where there were no shore facilities. The navy used old ships for these purposes, rather than buildings on land, for various reasons: because they were cheap and available, because they were difficult to escape or desert from, because they allowed a certain flexibility of operation, and because of restricted space and investment in the dockyards. They were usually commanded by lieutenants, and, like guardships, they were warships in commission.

A sheer hulk lifting a mast into a two decker. From Serres's, *Liber Nauticus*

Support Craft

Many other vessels were operated by the dockyard, in support of its operations. The largest of these were the sheer hulks; in 1807 there were two of these each at Portsmouth, Plymouth and Chatham, and one each at Woolwich, Deptford and Sheerness.[26] A sheer hulk was 'an old ship of war, cut down to the gun or lower deck, having a mast fixed in midships, and fitted with an apparatus consisting of sheers, tackles & co, to heave out or in lower masts of His Majesty's ships.'[27] Each one was manned by a boatswain, boatswain's mate and six seamen in 1807, though other men were probably drafted in when heavy work was in progress.[28]

Each yard also had at least one buoy boat, used for repairing and moving the mooring buoys near the yard, and fitted with heavy lifting gear for the purpose. Other sailing vessels included sailing lighters for carrying stores, well boats for carrying men and stores to ships under repair, and hoys or small transport vessels. In addition, each yard had several yachts, for the use of the officers. For example, the *Plymouth* yacht of 96 tons, used by the officers of that yard, was 64ft long and carried six guns.[29] In 1813, Woolwich had four transports, two lighters, two longboats and a yawl for the use of the

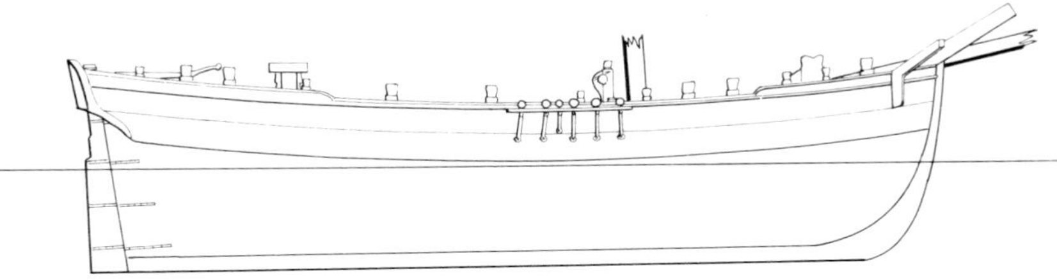

The Tamar *buoy boat, used at Plymouth. It has two windlasses and a capstan.* Based on a drawing in the National Maritime Museum

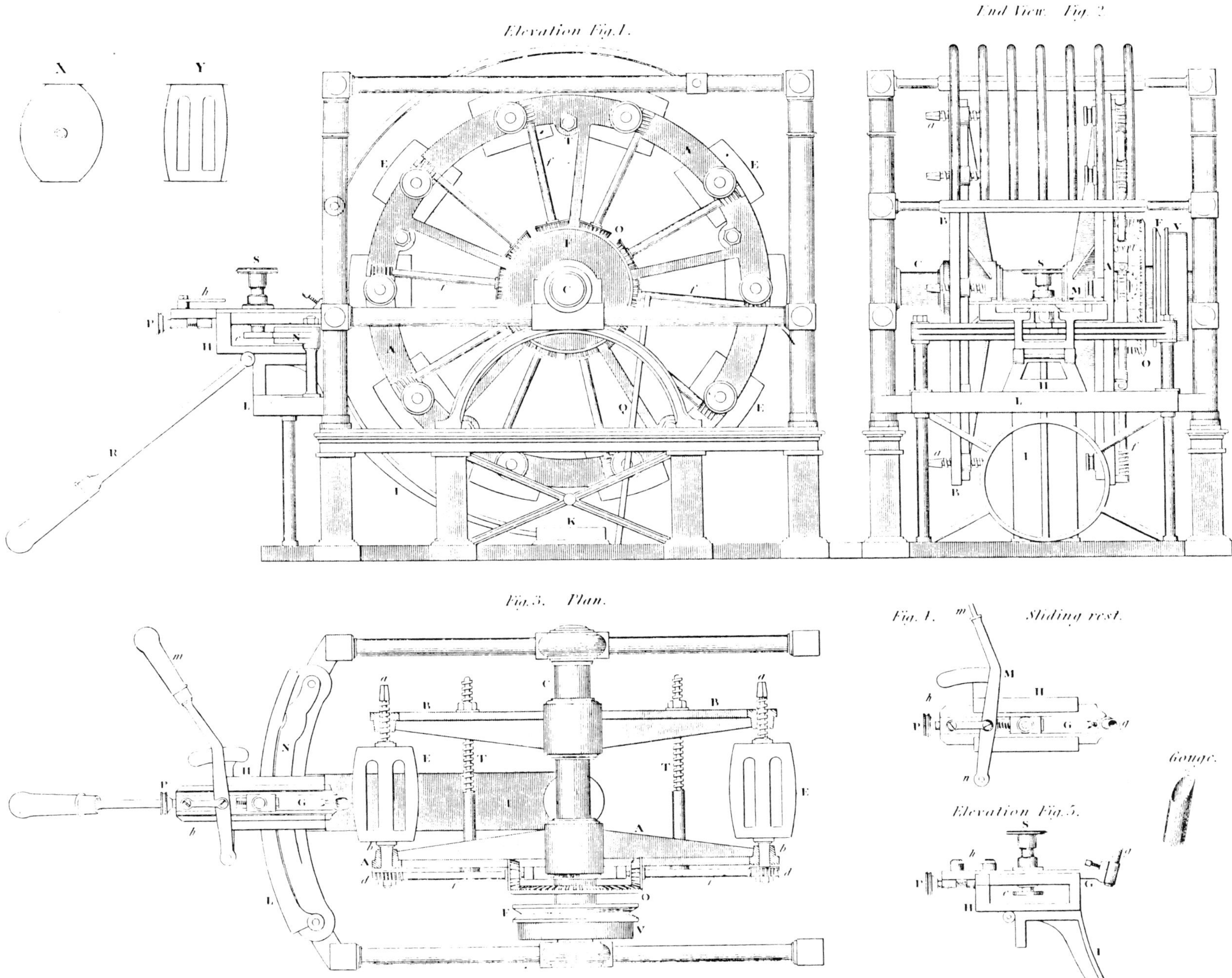

A shaping engine, part of the blockmaking machinery at Portsmouth. From Rees's Cyclopaedia

master attendant, a wherry and a gig for the commissioner, a wherry each for the clerk of the cheque, master shipwright and assistant master shipwright, a gig and a cutter, three launches 'for transporting and navigating ships', two harbour boats, three dirt boats 'for taking dirt [ie, ballast] from ships in ordinary, taking off and loading anchors from ships'.[30]

Manufacturing

Besides the ships themselves, many of their fittings were also made in the dockyards. Four of the yards, Woolwich, Chatham, Portsmouth and Plymouth, had ropeyards, employing a total of 1169 men between them in 1806.[31] They produced the majority of the navy's cordage, though by this time some was also produced by private contractors. Anchors were also made at all the yards, requiring quite heavy investment in capital equipment; though, again, the naval facilities did not keep up with the growth of the fleet, and anchors of up to 71 tons, suitable for 74-gun ships were being bought from contractors by 1803.[32] Rigging blocks had originally been made by contractors but in 1802, Marc Isambard Brunel (father of the great Victorian engineer) installed a set of very advanced machines at Portsmouth, and these produced hundreds of thousands of blocks every year for the navy. The yards also had sail lofts, and more than 200 sailmakers and apprentices worked in them. Each of the main yards had a boatbuilding establishment under a master boatbuilder, though these tended to specialise in carvel building; clinker-built boats, such as cutters, were usually built by contract.

Naval Stores

Thousands of different items were needed to keep the ships and yards running. Contracts were made for them by the Navy Board, demanding that the various private contractors supply amounts of certain articles to the dockyards as requested. Among the items delivered to Chatham in 1807 were copper sheets, Petersburg hemp, casks and wooden hoops, coal, Stockholm and Archangel pitch and tar, iron ballast, candles, camp forges, lightning conductors, stone-

A storehouse at Chatham, with the clock tower above. Author's photograph

ground glass, bedding, sails and blocks. Timber of various kinds was also delivered, according to specification, for example straight and compass oak, Norway fir, larches, spars, deals, Dantzig fir and ash, partly completed masts, oak knees and thick stuff.[33]

Timber was by far the largest item kept in the dockyards. Most of it was stored in the open, in stacks in every available space in the yards. Storehouses were provided for all the other items — the large square building at Deptford was one of the distinguishing features of the yard. Stone buildings were preferred, because of the risk of fire. As well as the major warehouses, the dockyards also had 'cabins' or huts, where a ready supply of materials such as tar and oakum were kept, under the control of 'cabinkeepers'.

Houses

The main dockyard officers were provided with houses, with orders that 'The several officers shall reside in their houses, allotted for their use by the establishment of the yard, and shall enjoy the gardens and offices respectively attached to them.' They were not to spend the night away from them without permission, in order to 'be in readiness to receive and execute all directions as may be given by us, or the resident commissioner.'[34] As with other government building of the day, the standard of architecture could be very high. Plymouth had a very imposing terrace with houses for twelve senior officials, including the commissioner at the centre. The Commissioner's House at Chatham had been built in 1702–3, and was decorated with a painting originally fitted in the cabin of the *Royal Sovereign* of 1701. Churches were built inside the walls of most of the yards, for the officers and their servants, and the yard watchmen and porters.

The gatehouse at Chatham. Author's photograph

Security

The security of the yard was a constant concern of the Navy Board and the dockyard officers. The defence of the area from foreign invasion was the province of the army, and covered an area beyond the dockyard itself. But, on a much smaller scale, there was the danger of penetration by spies or saboteurs (such as 'John the Painter', who was hanged for starting a disastrous fire at Portsmouth in 1777), and of theft or negligence of the dockyard workers. High walls were built round all the yards, with a limited number of gates, guarded by gatehouses. Pumps, often similar to those used aboard ships, were provided for use against fire, and mobile fire engines were also introduced.

2 The Dockyard Workforce

The Commissioner

Until 1806, the role of a dockyard commissioner was rather ambigious. One was appointed to each of the major yards, except Deptford and Woolwich, which were near London and therefore regarded as being under the direct supervision of the Navy Board. They were technically members of the Navy Board, though they hardly ever went to London to attend its meetings. Many of the Navy Board's orders to the yard were addressed to the individual officers such as the master shipwright, and did not necessarily pass through the hands of the commissioner. Much depended on the personalities of individuals, and on the local situation. At Chatham, for example, the commissioner did oversee most of the business, whereas at Portsmouth he did not. At Plymouth, the commissioner had 'authority over all persons employed in the yard, but he has no power to reward, promote, or even to cause a man to be entered in the service'. He appeared to have 'less influence over the workmen than any other officer'.[1] The commissioner's power was also restricted by the fact that the seamen of the navy, and the ships in commission, were under the authority of the port admiral. The commissioner was merely a liason officer with the Navy Board. He reported on ship movements and on work in the dockyard, and attempted to co-ordinate the work of the other officers of the yard. A commissioner was usually an experienced naval captain. Some, such as Charles Cunningham, had quite distinguished careers in action before retiring from the navy to take up the appointment. Others were well connected, such as George Grey, son of Earl Grey, sometime first lord.

The commissioner's position was considerably changed by orders of 1805. A single commissioner was appointed to supervise both Deptford and Woolwich, and the powers of all the commissioners were clarified. 'The resident commissioner shall have full authority over all officers, and other persons whatsoever, employed in the dockyard and ordinary, and is to control every part of the business carried on therein.' Orders and warrants from the Navy Board were to be 'sent open to the resident commissioner', and the principal officers of the yard were to 'attend every morning at his office, when respectively summoned by him; and he shall cause the public orders, warrants, and letters to be read, and that such discussions may be immediately had upon the circumstances, as may be necessary, to prevent any delay in carrying the same into execution.'[2]

The Master Shipwright and his Assistants

Since the main work of the dockyard was shipbuilding, fitting and repair, it is not surprising that the master shipwright of each yard was a pre-eminent figure. He was invariably an experienced shipwright, whose career had been given a flying start by an apprenticeship to a master shipwright or his assistant, rather than to an ordinary workman. Robert Seppings was by far the most innovative of the master shipwrights of these years, but in many respects his career path was quite typical. He entered as an apprentice to the master shipwright at Plymouth in 1782, and finished his apprenticeship in 1789. He served as shipwright, quarterman, foreman and master mastmaker before becoming assistant master shipwright in 1797. He became master shipwright at Chatham in 1803, and then surveyor of the navy in 1813. Other master shipwrights moved from one yard to another in advancement of their careers. Edward Sison held the post at Plymouth from 1793–5, at Chatham until 1801, and at Woolwich until 1816.[3]

The master shipwright was no longer responsible for the actual design of the ships, but he was in charge of most of the labour force of the yard, and of most of its fixed and running capital, in the form of docks, slips, timber and other stores. According to Burney, 'He has the direction and superintendence of nearly the whole operative business of the dockyard to which he is appointed.'[4] He had several assistants, of similar background and training — up to three in the largest yards. From 1801, some of the assistants in the various yards were known as timber masters, and had special responsiblity for buying and controlling that essential commodity. Others were known as master caulkers. The master shipwright and his assistants were essentially naval architects, schooled in the principles of ship design and construction, and separated from the common herd of shipwrights. They had quite a well established promotion path, rising

The commissioner's house at Chatham, the oldest intact naval building in the country. Author's photograph

from one yard to a larger one, and ending at the office of the surveyor of the navy.

The Other Officers

There were five other 'principal officers of the yard', directly under the commissioner and the Navy Board. The master attendant was 'answerable for the general care and management of the ships in ordinary'. He was 'to see that the several warrant officers keep their ships clean, and otherwise perform their duty; that, in the proper season, the awnings be spread, and the windsails daily made use of; that they be, in all respects, kept well aired and dry.'[5] He was to supervise the work of the 'supervising masters', each of whom was in charge of a division of the ships in ordinary at the port. He was also responsible for the mooring and navigational buoys in the area of

Dockyard organisation, before the 1806 reforms. After that, orders from the Navy Board passed through the commissioner

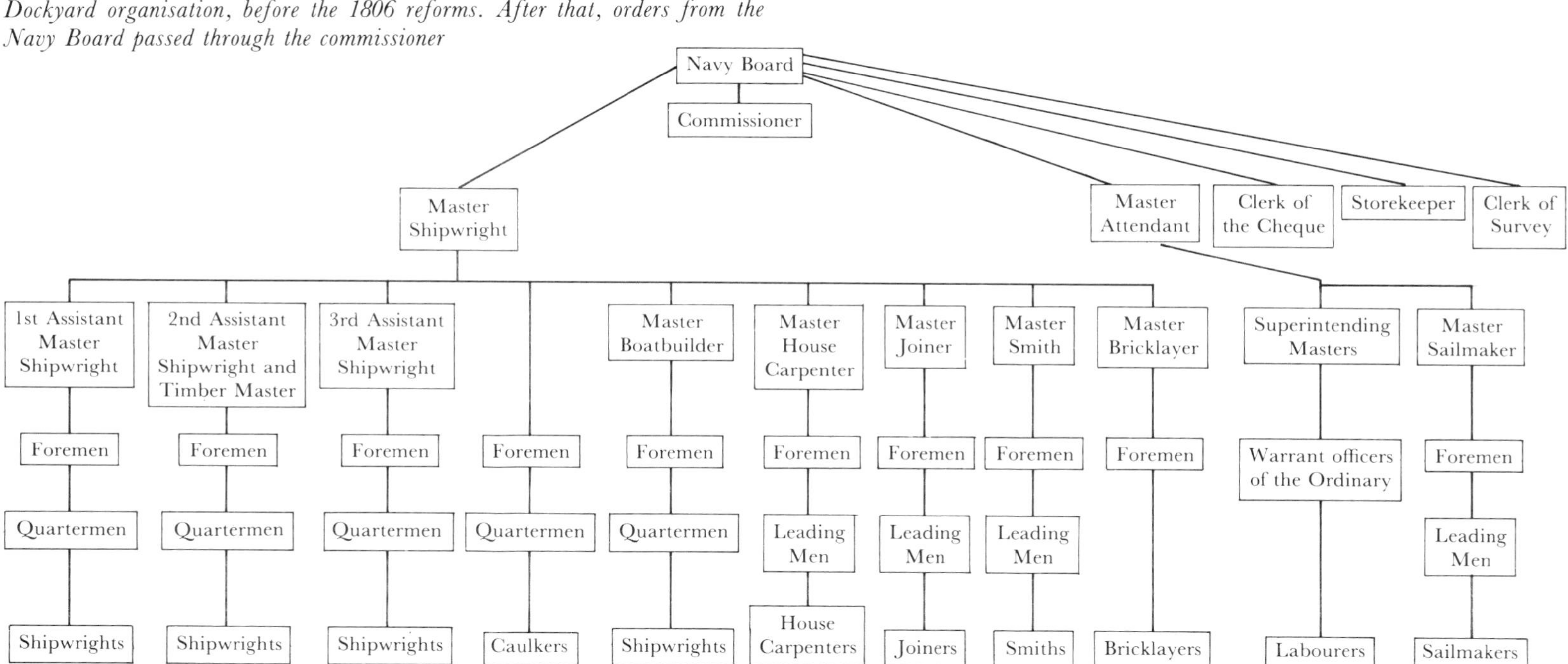

the yard, and had general responsibility for navigation and pilotage into the yard. At Chatham, for example, he was expected to take charge of each ship and navigate it as far as Long Reach, which took a whole day even in good conditions. The master attendant was an experienced master, now employed in a civilian capacity.

The other officers were in control of the material and finances of the yard. They had overlapping responsibilities, arising from a system of checks and balances which had been established centuries ago and was intended, without much success, to prevent embezzlement. The clerk of the cheque was responsible for mustering the employees of the yard and the ordinary. He was 'To keep books of the entry and discharge of all artificers and co.... to transmit a weekly return of artificers and co',[6] to check the names of the men as they entered and left the yard, and to supervise the payment of ships in commission. The storekeeper was 'invested with the charge of the principal naval stores, as the sails, anchors, cordage, etc; it is likewise his duty, in rotation with the clerk of the check and clerk of the survey, to attend the survey and receipt of all stores from contractors, and the delivery of lots of old stores from the purchasers; and to check the certificates made out by the clerk of the cheque, for stores received upon contract.'[7] The clerk of the survey 'with the master shipwright and master attendant',

> Directs the issue of all stores to the warrant officers of ships, and for the use of the yard, and keeps a charge against the persons to whom they are issued it is his duty to survey all articles returned to store, and with the clerk of the cheque and the storekeeper, to attend the receipt of all stores from contractors, and the delivery of lots of old stores to the purchasers; and to examine the certificates made out by the clerk of the cheque, of the stores received, by which the contractors obtain payment. He is also to survey all the remains of stores of boatswains and carpenters, at the returns of ships from sea, and passes their accounts.[8]

The clerk of the ropeyard 'musters the people in that department, upon their coming to and quitting work; and he is charged with the hemp, tar, and other articles used in ropemaking, of the expenditure of which he keeps an account'.[9]

It was quite normal for an administrative officer to move from one type of job to another. In 1801, for example, there was a general promotion in which the storekeeper at Woolwich became clerk of the cheque at Plymouth; the clerk of the survey at Woolwich became storekeeper at the same yard; the clerk of the ropeyard at Chatham became clerk of the survey at Woolwich; and a clerk in the Navy Office in London became clerk of the ropeyard at Chatham.[10]

Clerks

Each dockyard officer had one or more clerks to help him with his accounts and correspondence. At Chatham, the commissioner and master shipwright had three each, the master attendant and clerk of the ropeyard one each, the clerk of the cheque seven, the storekeeper four, the clerk of the survey four.[11] Until 1801, the basic pay of a dockyard clerk was from £30 to £40 per annum, with extra fees and gratuities which might raise it to over £200 per year for a senior clerk. Clerks had to be at least sixteen years old, and each had to be 'examined in the presence of the commissioner touching his qualifications; and the commissioner, in case of his approval, is to sign a certificate of examination, which certificate shall be sent to this board with the nomination'.[12] But despite this, appointment as a dockyard clerk depended more on personal connections than anything else. John Dickens, father of the novelist, is believed to have been appointed because his mother was a servant at the house of Lord Crewe. A clerk's salary would allow him middle-class status, with perhaps a servant or two.

Supervisory Staff

Apart from the main body of shipwrights, there were various specialised gangs in the yard, each supervised by a master craftsmen. Under the master shipwright were the master boatmaker, master caulker and master mastmaker, as well as the master joiner and house carpenter, master bricklayer and mason, and master smith. The shipwrights themselves worked under foremen; at Chatham in 1806 there were two 'foremen afloat', who looked after repairs of ships in commission and in ordinary, including those in the dry-docks; and two 'foremen of the yard', or 'foremen of new work', who supervised ships under construction. Under the foremen, were quartermen, each in charge of a gang or 'company' of about ten men; there were twenty of these in Chatham in 1806.[13] According to regulations, each had to be at least four years out of his apprenticeship as a shipright. The master craftsmen of the other departments also had one or two quartermen to assist them; except for the smiths, who worked in small gangs of about four men, each under a quarterman; there were seventeen of these at Chatham in 1806. Other groups were headed by the master sailmaker and master rigger, under the master attendant; and the master ropemaker, who was part of a separate establishment.

The distinction between the foremen and quartermen on one hand, and the workmen on the other, was not very great. Samuel Bentham commented that the former

> Being little raised above the artificers themselves, either in point of emolument or rank, living amongst them and thence being continually liable to feel the momentary effect of their ill will, it cannot be expected that he should be very ready to stand forward in enforcing regulations which in many instances must bring upon him the resentment of hundreds of those whose interests he thwarts.[14]

Shipwrights

In 1814, there were nearly 5000 shipwrights in the Royal dockyards, almost a third of the total workforce. They were all skilled workers, who had served an apprenticeship of seven years in either the dockyards or private yards. The right to have an apprentice was a privilege granted 'as a reward for merit and industry to the most deserving of the artificers'.[15] The workman was allowed the keep the pay, including the extra, of his apprentice. As there was no provision for entry to the trade besides apprenticeship, the supply of shipwrights was inelastic; they could also be hard to come by, since the pay in merchant yards tended to be much higher in wartime. However, the dockyards offered some security, in contrst to the merchant yards which took on men for the duration of a single contract only. Reliable men could be allowed a pension at the end of their service, and all were, of course, protected from impressment. Like all workers, the shipwrights in the dockyards were paid quarterly, at least one quarter in arrears.

Shipwrights at work on a rudder of a 74-gun ship. From Pyne's *Microcosm*

Other Workers

In 1814, the dockyards employed 433 caulkers, 888 house carpenters, 465 joiners, 596 riggers, 299 sailmakers, 934 sawyers, 182 bricklayers, and 770 smiths. Smaller groups of tradesmen included painters, carvers, coopers, glaziers, masons, locksmiths, plumbers, and wheelwrights. Unskilled and semi-skilled workers were also employed in large numbers. There were 500 scavelmen, who dredged for ballast, 130 bricklayer's labourers, 12 warders, and nearly 3000 yard labourers. The latter were also employed in the ordinary, and it was recommended 'that men who have served in Your Majesty's fleet shall at all times have the preference, in being entered as shipkeepers in all the classes for which they may be qualified'. This was intended to 'afford a retreat to able seamen, who, having passed their best days at sea, in the service of their country, may be inclined to serve in a less laborious situation'.[16]

The Working Day

Before the reforms of 1815, the working hours varied in the different yards. At Plymouth, the men worked from 7am to dusk in December and January; in February, from 6.30am to 6pm; from March to October, 6am to 6pm; and in October and November, 6.15am to 6pm, daylight permitting. Dinner lasted two hours in the summer, and 1½ hours in the winter.[17] In 1805, standard rules were laid down for all the yards.

> The common working hours, for both the yard and ordinary, being from six in the morning to six in the evening, the bell will ring at those hours, when the workmen are to repair to or leave the yard. This rule is to be observed when the daylight will admit . . . The common allowance of time for breakfast shall be for eight in the morning to half past eight; and for dinner, from twelve to half past one, during the summer months.[18]

In winter, the men were to have their breakfast before they came to work. Often the men were paid overtime, in the form of 'nights' and 'tides'. A night lasted for five hours, and earned an extra day's pay. A tide lasted 1½ hours, and was paid a third of a day's pay.

Before starting in the morning, the men were to be mustered by the officers of the yard. At Woolwich, it was complained that 'The duty of mustering the men does not appear to have been strictly attended to — the weather being rainy, the absence of the clerks, or their being busily employed, were assigned as reasons for the neglect of it occasionally.'[19] At Plymouth, the men were mustered by two clerks, and it could take up to half an hour before the men were allowed to start work.

Task and Day Work

Since 1775, the naval administration had tried to employ shipwrights and other craftsmen on a system of piecework, known as 'task work', or 'job work'. All the various jobs which might be done were to be paid at specific rates — a rigging gang was allowed £98 for a first rate ship and £71 for a 38-gun frigate; sailmakers were expected to carry out a certain amount of work in five hours; anchor smiths were allowed 4d extra per day when working on anchors of more than 20cwt; sawyers were paid for different sizes and types of wood, for example 'all under 18in in depth', or 'cross cuts, all under 12in, as slab or pink'; shipwrights were paid according to a complex system.

Not all workers could be employed on task work, as it was difficult to assess the performance in certain jobs. Those working in the mould lofts, or as cabin-keepers, were paid by the day, as were gangs of older or inferior men. Other men were paid by the day when bad weather interrupted their work.

The Organisation of the Workforce

Around 1800, there was an attempt to 'shoal' the workforce. The more skilled or more active men were taken into elite gangs, and these did the task work, with the opportunity to earn higher wages; of the twenty gangs or 'companies' of shipwrights at Chatham in 1806, six were on task work and fourteen on day work.[20] At Deptford in 1813, 'There are five companies generally employed in new works, a selection is made from all the shipwrights in the yard as are considered most eligible for this service. The remainder are shoaled, the quartermen alternately selecting man for man in the presence of the master shipwright and his assistants and foremen.'[21]

Labour Relations

Labour relations in the dockyards were bad throughout the eighteenth century, and strikes (or 'riots' and 'mutinies' as the authorities insisted on calling them) were endemic; there had been major outbreaks in 1739 and 1775. Like the seamen, dockyard workers remained on wages that had been fixed more than a century previously, but price rises — especially of bread in 1799–1800 — caused a considerable fall in their real value. The Combination Acts of those years made strikes and trade unions illegal, but a strong and efficient organisation was built up by the dockyard workers. Matters came to a head after St Vincent became First Lord of the Admiralty; his authoritarianism and hatred of inefficiency caused a series of outbreaks at several yards. At Plymouth, there were riots, and troops had to be called out. Despite this, the dockyard men successfully demanded the release of some of their comrades. At Sheerness, Commissioner Coffin was physically assaulted by a mob shouting 'Throw him over, kill him.' However, St Vincent restored order in the yards, and eventually dismissed 340 men. This was not difficult, because it was peacetime and the workforce was being run down in any case. However, the workforce became depleted when war broke out again soon afterwards, and it was difficult to attract men in the face of competition from the merchant yards. After that, there were many small strikes, and some improvements in labour conditions.[22]

Crime and Corruption

It was widely believed in government circles that both officials and workmen in the dockyards were regularly involved in embezzlement and corruption. St Vincent, never one to understate his case, believed that the yards were filled with 'shameful and fraudulent practices', that 'the artificers are all thieves', and that all the clerks should be pensioned off on condition that 'they should reside fifty miles from any dockyard'. Captain Thomas Troubridge went further, and suggested 'all the master shipwrights should be hanged, every one of them, without exception'.[23] However, very few dockyard officers were ever dismissed or prosecuted for embezzlement, even under St Vincent, and the real scale of the problem was never discovered. This was an age when the distinction between government and private property was not completely clear, and when nineteenth-century ideas of integrity were just beginning to emerge. Dockyard officials tended to rely on ancient privileges and perquisites to make up their salaries, and this conflicted with the new age.

At the lower end of the scale, the issue of 'chips' was a constant bone of contention. Shipwrights had the ancient privilege of taking home scraps of timber which were no use for shipbuilding. In theory, these should be small enough for a man to carry under his arm, and probably only good for firewood. In practice, it was claimed, men took out much larger pieces, and often sacrificed good pieces of timber to make chips for themselves. The practice was abolished in 1801, and the men given 3d to 6d per day 'chip money' instead.

3 Home Anchorages and Naval Bases

The Siting of Naval Bases

Of the six home naval bases, only Plymouth had been founded in relatively recent times — in 1690. The others were much older, and suffered many disadvantages.

> The naval arsenals of Great Britain having been established at a period when her commerce was in its infancy, and the art of navigation but little understood, when her colonies were unimportant and the naval force necessary to protect her dominions were equally inconsiderable with that of the surrounding states, it was natural to choose situations adapted to the security, number and small dimensions of her ships of war and to lay out their establishment of docks, quays and storehouses upon a corresponding scale.[1]

Another writer commented, 'England, the first naval power in the world, and equal to all the rest united, is the most deficient in proper accommodations for its navy. Her dockyards have risen from small beginnings to their present state, by a series of expedients and makeshifts.'[2] A small yard was set up at Milford Haven in the 1800s, and an attempt to set one up at Northfleet on the Thames came to nothing; otherwise, the yards remained in their old sites, often chosen three hundred years earlier. Most suffered from the silting up of their rivers and harbours, and were ill adapted to the increased size of modern ships.

But, from a strategic point of view, the yards were quite well placed. It was important that a yard be situated on a reasonably sheltered river or natural harbour which had to be close to an anchorage. Harbour mouths were narrow, and often had difficult navigation in unfavourable winds; if large numbers of ships were kept in harbour in wartime, there was a real danger that they could be trapped for weeks or months, while the enemy might have a free hand. Ships in commission rarely entered harbour except for essential and major repair, and remained at anchor outside to take on stores and men. Large anchorages were needed to assemble fleets and convoys, and those within range of the dockyards clearly had an advantage. The anchorage has to be considered as part of the wider naval base. In practice, there were two types of anchorages: those immediately outside the harbour, such as those at the Nore, Spithead and Plymouth Sound; and those further away and more open, such as the anchorages at the Downs, St Helens and Torbay. The outer anchorages were used by merchant ships as much as warships, and provided areas where ships of every kind could shelter from storms. The characteristics of a good anchorage were described by Graeme Spence in 1812: 'As the properties of a good roadstead which ought to be six according to my definition of a good one; namely capacity, shelter, depth of water, good ground, easy access and little tide.'[3]

Harbour engineering was still in its infancy in 1815; the harbour at Ramsgate was the greatest such project of the later eighteenth century, and the breakwater at Plymouth was not completed for many years after the wars. Apart from that, navies relied almost entirely on natural harbours and anchorages. Britain was well provided with these, and this gave her some decisive advantages in the French wars. The French, on the other hand, had no natural harbour west of Brest; it is impossible to tell if such a harbour would have altered the course of the wars, but it is significant that the building of the artifical harbour at Cherbourg in 1860 caused panic in Britain.

The Nore

The Nore anchorage was situated in the Thames estuary, just off the

Naval facilities in the Kent area, including four dockyards, two anchorages, two minor bases, and gunpowder mills. Based on Morden's map of Kent

entrance to the River Medway; it was fed by ships coming down from the Thames from Deptford and Woolwich, and by Chatham. It was the main assembly point for ships coming out of these yards, and for the squadrons blockading the Dutch coast, and protecting the Straits of Dover. It was largely protected from easterly winds by the sandbanks of the estuary, but there were few fortifications. The difficulty of entrance to the estuary without expert pilotage was probably enough to deter any attack, and in any case there were no fixed assets situated there, only the ships themselves.

The Downs

The Downs was an area of sea off the east coast of Kent, protected from westerly winds by the land, and from easterlies by the Goodwin Sands. It was between the Straits of Dover and the Thames Estuary, so merchant ships awaiting an easterly wind to take them down the Channel or up to London gathered there, often for quite long periods. Sometimes many hundreds of merchant ships could be seen in the Downs. It could be quite a dangerous area. The Goodwin Sands were constantly shifting, and were not always adequately marked. Storms could also cause ships to be driven onto the shore, or onto the sands. In February 1807, several merchantmen were lost in this way, while three men-of-war lost their masts and suffered damage to their hulls.

There was no natural harbour in the vicinity of the Downs, since Sandwich had silted up centuries before. Ramsgate Harbour had been extended after 1749, at great expense, and served mainly as a refuge for merchant ships, especially in southerly winds. It was completed at the end of 1792, and had capacity for up to 200 merchantmen. Warships were supplied from the town of Deal, where boats landed on a steep shingle beech.

From a naval point of view, the Downs served as a permanent base for ships patrolling the North Sea. In the early stages of the Napoleonic Wars it contained the headquarters of the whole North Sea fleet, though that was based on shore at Walmer Castle. At all times, the Downs Squadron was quite a significant force, responsible for the blockade of the southern Dutch ports. There were always some warships in the area, either part of the squadron or passing through. There were relatively few landward defences in the area; Henry VIII's three forts at Sandown, Deal and Walmer were not supplemented, though the fortress at Dover Castle was constantly expanded and updated.

Spithead and St Helens

Spithead was probably the best-known anchorage of the British fleet, and it had much in its favour. It was closer to a dockyard than any of the others, and this was a major factor in the expansion of Portsmouth. It was well sheltered, with the mainland to the north, the Isle of Wight to the southwest, and various sandbanks to the east. It was relatively easy to get out of, though only small ships used the Needles Passage to the west; most dropped down to St Helens to await a favourable wind.

Spithead was the main assembly point for fleets based at Portsmouth. On mobilisation, individual ships were sent out to the anchorage as soon as they were manned and fitted, and stayed there as other ships gathered. During Lord Howe's command of the Channel fleet, his ships spent a great deal of time there, awaiting news of French movements. Spithead also served for naval reviews, for example during the 'Spanish Armament' of 1790, when the king came down to inspect his ships; and in 1814, when the Tsar of Russia and the King of Prussia were rowed round. Spithead was also an important assembly area for large convoys of merchant ships. As a result of all this activity, it could sometimes become very crowded. In 1794 when the *Gorgon* came in, 'a large fleet of men-of-war were assembled. Before we came to an anchor we had run foul of several ships, and I remember the *Invincible*, 74, hailing us, saying, 'You have cut my cable, sir.' This was not all, for we shaved the old *Royal William*'s quarter gallery, which some shipwrights were repairing — who had barely time to save themselves. We were not allowed to anchor at Spithead, but proceeded to Mother Bank [between Spithead and Cowes].'[4]

St Helens was an advanced anchorage to Spithead. Ships bound to the westward, including the majority of those leaving Portsmouth, ran down there in a westerly wind, or tacked down in an easterly, as necessary. They remained at St Helens until an easterly wind allowed them to sail down the channel. The whole area of the eastern Solent was quite well defended by land fortifications — Southsea Castle and Fort Cumberland on the northern side, with smaller forts between them, and Fort Blockhouse on the western side of the harbour entrance.

Torbay

Torbay is a large bay in south Devon, well protected from south, west and northerly winds, with a suitable depth of water, good holding ground and low tidal streams. Its situation made it an assembly point for fleets intended to blockade Brest — it was a safer anchorage than Plymouth Sound and Cawsand Bay, and unlike Spithead and St Helens, ships there could reach Brest without having to battle against the prevailing westerly winds. On mobilisation of the fleet, ships generally fitted out at their home bases and then went round to Torbay, and stayed there until sufficient numbers had been assembled.

Torbay was also useful to the Western squadron in that they could use it 'when driven off their station by westerly gales of wind'. However, Torbay was an anchorage where 'the chance of being caught by an easterly wind, which is the most favourable wind for the enemy to put to sea; the risk of the ships lying in an anchorage so open and exposed; the inconveniencies and delays and expense of bringing supplies and stores and provisions from the other ports, all contribute to make Torbay a very ineligible rendezvous for the Western squadron.' Ships had to get out of Torbay as soon as the wind showed signs of swinging eastward, otherwise they were in danger. According to Captain Brenton, 'With the wind in the position it then was (between west and southwest), [Torbay] offered a most friendly and acceptable shelter; but I must again warn my naval readers of the risk they incur of being caught there with an easterly wind, by which, with a convoy, very serious injury and delay to our trade has been experienced.'[5] In February 1795, Howe's fleet of thirty-four ships-of-the-line and sixteen frigates was caught in Torbay when 'there happened a heavy gale of wind at southeast, which blows right into the bay. The danger to which the fleet was exposed is inconceivable; the swell of the sea was tremendous; many of the ships were driven into the shallow water and some parted their cables'.[6] The *Venerable*, for example, was lost in Torbay in 1804. It was generally uncomfortable, and in 1805 Cornwallis wrote, 'In the middle of last month we put into Torbay, where we were a week, but the being in Torbay is no great relief, for no person or boat goes on shore. We visit our friends and neighbours in the fleet, but have no communication with the rest of the world.'[7] Torbay was useful because 'the same wind, a WSW which would drive the English fleet for shelter in Torbay, would prevent the French from coming out of Brest. Admitting, however, that a shift of wind occurred, and that the French were thus enabled to effect their escape; the same shift of wind would also be fair for the British fleet to sail from Torbay in pursuit of them; and, though the enemy would have the start, it is not unlikely that they might be overtaken, or indeed find themselves between two fires.'[8]

The land around Torbay was almost entirely rural in the early

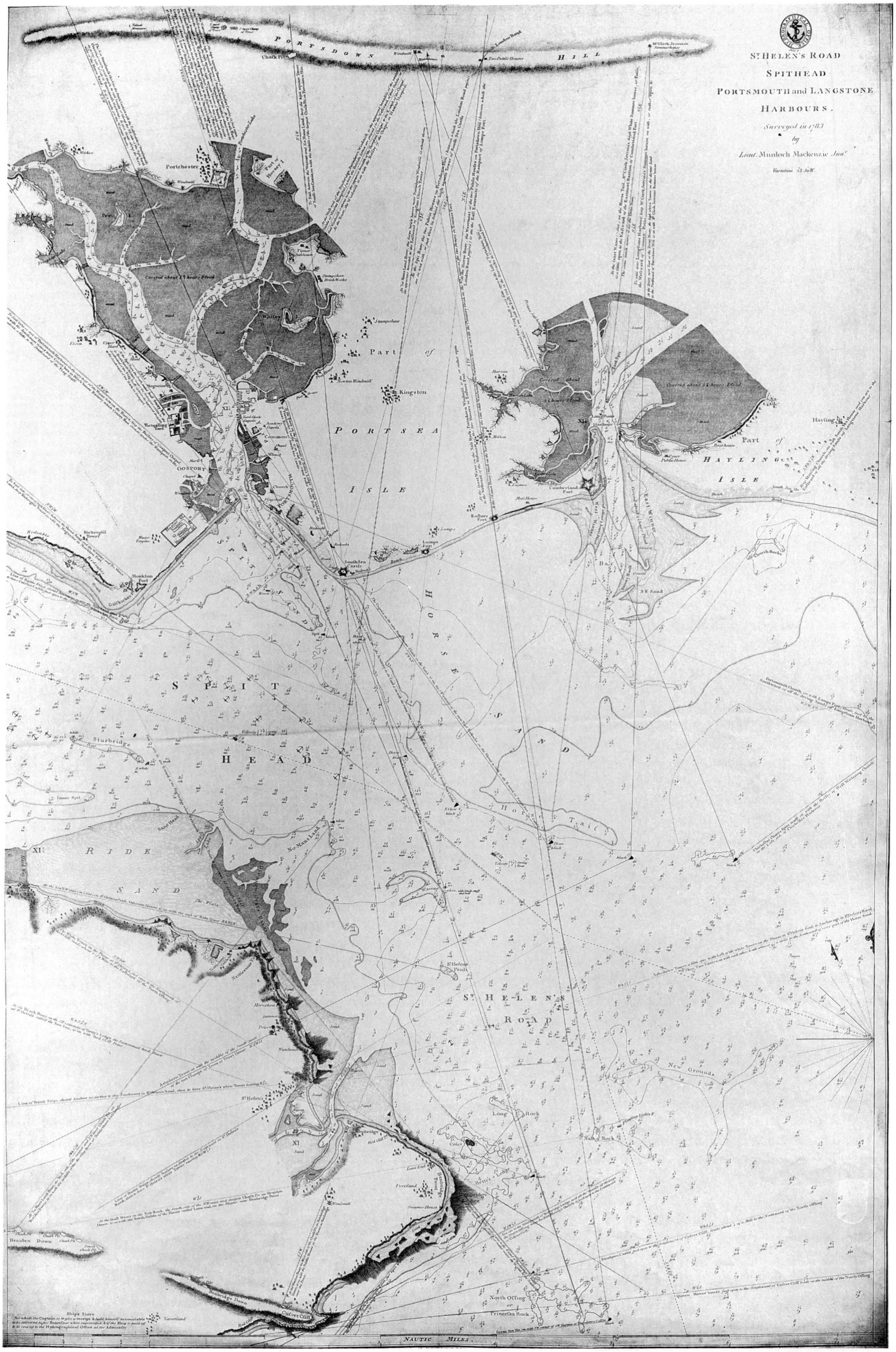

The Channel Fleet entering Torbay
From the Naval Chronicle

Plymouth Sound, showing the propos
breakwater, which radically altered
the nature of the anchorage.
From the Naval Chronicle

A chart of the Portsmouth area, shov
the harbour, Spithead and
St Helens, along with the victualling
yard at Gosport, the Gunwharf,
Haslar Hospital, and other installat
in the area. It also illustrates the us
of transits in navigation. The
National Maritime Museum

nineteenth century, with small harbours at Brixham and Torquay, suitable only for small boats. The naval presence led to very little building effort; only a hospital at Paignton and a small store and watering station at Brixham. Permanent fortification came quite late, with batteries being constructed at Berry Head and Hope's Nose in 1803-4.

Plymouth Sound and Cawsand Bay

Plymouth Sound was, of course, very close to a major dockyard, but it was completely open to southerly winds, and could be highly dangerous. 'The very exposed situation of Plymouth Sound, and the heavy swells that roll in, particularly when the wind blows in fresh from the southwest to the southeast, render it so unsafe an anchorage that the ships of war employed in blockading the enemy in the port of Brest have of late years deemed it more expedient... to bear up for the more distant anchorage of Torbay.'[9] Ships awaiting repairs anchored in the sound, because a favourable wind was needed to get into the dockyard in Hamoaze. Other ships took refuge occasionally, but generally in small numbers.

Cawsand Bay, at the southwest entrance to the Sound, was only slightly better. It did not cut very deep into the land, so it was quite open and exposed. The water was not deep enough close inshore, and ships sometimes found themselves striking the bottom when the waves were large. It was quite small, and in 1803 Cornwallis wrote, 'I beg to observe that there are now ten sail of the line at this anchorage, which crowds it very much.'[10] There were attempts to use it as an alternative to Torbay, but it was not really suitable, and it was used only as an occasional refuge, or for ships victualling or awaiting repair at Plymouth.

Because of the inadequacies of these anchorages, construction of the breakwater across Plymouth Sound began in 1812. This was one of the greatest civil engineering projects of the age, but it was not completed until 1840, under the direction of John Rennie. Some of the breakwater had begun to show above the surface of the sound by 1815, but it was not enough to make Plymouth Sound a completely safe anchorage. When this finally happened, Torbay was obsolete for these purposes.

Other anchorages

There were minor anchorages all round the British coast, and some of these served the fleet on occasion. Scapa Flow had been noticed as a possible fleet base by 1812, but it was a century later before it sprang to prominence. Leith Roads in the Firth of Forth was the most important Scottish base, though far from the main activities of the enemy fleets, and chiefly used for the assembly of convoys. Yarmouth Roads, off the Norfolk coast, was protected by the shore to the west and sandbanks to the east. It was used to assemble fleets for the Baltic, and had a small stores depot and hospital. Dungeness Roads was in the Eastern Channel, protected from westerlies by a triangular promontory. It could be used as an anchorage by ships guarding the Channel or the French Channel ports, and in 1803, for example, it was to be used as a station for one 50-gun ship, four frigates, four sloops, and several gunboats. It had no shore facilities, but was close to Dover. Ships further west in the channel could sometimes take refuge behind Portland Bill, but this was not one of the main naval anchorages.

Deptford and Woolwich

The two Thames yards, Deptford and Woolwich, were extreme examples of the outdated situation of the British bases. Both had been founded in the early sixteenth century, and were placed well up the River Thames, so that they could be close to London and protected from foreign invasion. Such a policy was antiquated in the days when the British fleet controlled the seas, but both yards still served as maintenance and building yards — and, as storehouses, they had some advantages in being near the London markets.

Of Deptford, John Rennie commented, 'Ships-of-the-line which are built there cannot as I am informed with propriety be docked and coppered. Jury masts are put into them and they are taken to Woolwich, where they are docked, coppered and rigged, and I have been told of an instance where many weeks elapsed before a fair wind and tide capable of floating a large ship down to Woolwich occurred.' The Thames was silting up, ships were bigger than they had been in Henry VIII's time, and Deptford was declining as a dockyard. Its proximity to London gave the yard certain advantages, but it was a building and repair yard, not part of an advanced naval base like Portsmouth or Plymouth. The Deptford complex, built on the south bank of the Thames, included a great victualling yard, but it never had a marine barracks or hospital, and of course it had no need for an ordnance depot.

Woolwich was only slightly better. Unlike Deptford, it had been extended during the French wars, but 'It is too far up the river, and there is not sufficient depth of water to carry ships-of-the-line down to Gravesend with their guns and stores on board.' Ships had to be taken to Northfleet or Gravesend to receive their guns. The River Thames was winding, and generally ran easterly, so a passage up to Deptford or Woolwich was against the prevailing winds. Like Deptford, Woolwich was built on the south bank of the Thames. It had a marine barracks after 1805, and was close to the main Ordnance Board depot.

Chatham

According to Rennie, the base at Chatham was 'of great magnitude' in 1809. Its greatest problem was its situation on the River Medway. Like the Thames, that river was silting up, and the channel of the Medway was no less difficult. 'The navigation of the Medway, from the Thames or the Nore, is intricate, the river being very crooked, and the water in the upper part shallow.' Large ships had to be taken down to Sea Reach, on the Thames, to be fitted with their guns.

The shallowness of the water also created problems in docking ships. 'The cills of the dry docks are all too high. In the first or southmost dock, there are only 15ft 4in on the cill at spring tides, and 13ft 10in at neaps.' First and second rates could only be docked at high spring tides. However, Chatham, built on the east bank of the river Medway, was a complete naval base. It had a marine barracks, and there was an ordnance depot in Upnor Castle just across the river, though it had only a hospital ship instead of a regular hospital. It was the third largest yard, after Portsmouth and Plymouth, and employed 2672 workmen in 1814.[11] The dockyard was well fortified, with the 'lines' protecting it on the eastern, or landward side. Ships were moored outside the yard in the River Medway.

Sheerness

It was said that 'Sheerness as a refitting port must always be considered from its eastern situation and proximity to the sea as a place of very considerable importance and almost indispensable utility.'[12] On the other hand, 'every sailor knows the inconvenience to which Sheerness is subject, with strong northwesterly winds, particularly with spring tides, when the ships are coming in and going out of dock. There is often so much sea going on the jetties and walls, that work is entirely suspended; while, on the other side, the water is perfectly smooth.'[13] The yard was built on a rather restricted site, on reclaimed land and marshy ground, and away from major centres of habitation. It was often difficult to attract workmen, and they had to be accommodated in hulks because of the shortage of housing. Ships up to the third rate could be repaired there but none as large as that were built there; it catered mainly for frigates and smaller vessels. Its greatest advantage was its proximity to the anchorage at the Nore, and its accessibility from the sea. It was well fortified to landward, and had a small ordnance depot, but no victualling yard, marine barracks or hospital.

Portsmouth

Portsmouth was generally agreed to be the most important yard in the country by the end of the eighteenth century. Samuel Bentham wrote of 'The pre-emminent importance of the port of Portsmouth', and concentrated most of his innovative work there.[14] It had an excellent anchorage at Spithead, far closer to the dockyard than the Nore was to Chatham, Deptford or Woolwich, and far safer than the Sound at Plymouth. It had a forward anchorage just a few miles away at St Helens. It had all the facilities needed for a base, built on both sides of the entrance to the harbour. On the eastern, or Portsmouth side, was the dockyard itself; the gunwharf was to the south, with the marine barracks just inland from the dockyard. On the western, Gosport, side, were the hospital at Haslar, the Weevil victualling yard and Priddy's Hard Ordnance Depot — each situated on a separate peninsula. Both sides were fortified, with seperate defences round the town of Portsmouth and round the yard, and round Gosport and Priddy's Hard on the other side, to prevent landward attack. To seaward, there was a chain of forts facing into the Solent, including Southsea Castle and Fort Cumberland. Portsmouth Harbour divided into two channels just inside the entrance, each with enough water for large ships of the ordinary, and those awaiting repair. The only real problem with Portsmouth was that it was too far to the east to serve the Channel Fleet off Brest.

> Portsmouth, though called by some a western establishment, has no claim to the appellation, being only half the distance from the North Sea on the east, that it is from the ocean on the west; and that from the prevalence of westerly winds in the Channel of England, it has at least three times the opportunities of sending ships any where into the sea eastward, than it can find of sending them westward half the distance to the ocean.[15]

Plymouth

Plymouth yard was very well situated, in the sense that it was the most westerly in the country, and closest to the French base of Brest. It had fewer problems with silting than other yards, as Rennie agreed: 'Perhaps Plymouth has suffered the least decay. The receptacles into which the tide flows and ebbs are greater, and the shores of Hamoaze and the Cattewater as well as the banks of the rivers emptying into the Sound are more rocky and of harder materials than those of any of the others.'[16] However, the very rockiness of the ground created problems. The yard had been built on difficult ground, and any extension was costly, as the levelling of the site had to be undertaken first. Plymouth also lacked a suitable anchorage nearby; the Sound and Cawsand Bay were too exposed, and Torbay was thirty miles away over hilly ground and poor roads. Finally, the route into the Hamoaze, through the Cremyll passage, was often extremely hazardous: '....a sea in the passage like a boiling pot, in which a helmsman can scarcely command the steerage of his boat from the run of the tide.'[17] Only the building of the breakwater was to solve these problems.

Plymouth dockyard was situated in the Hamoaze, on the eastern bank of the River Tamar, several miles from the town of Plymouth itself. As a result, a separate town of Dock grew up around the yard. The ordnance depot was to the north of the yard, and the marine

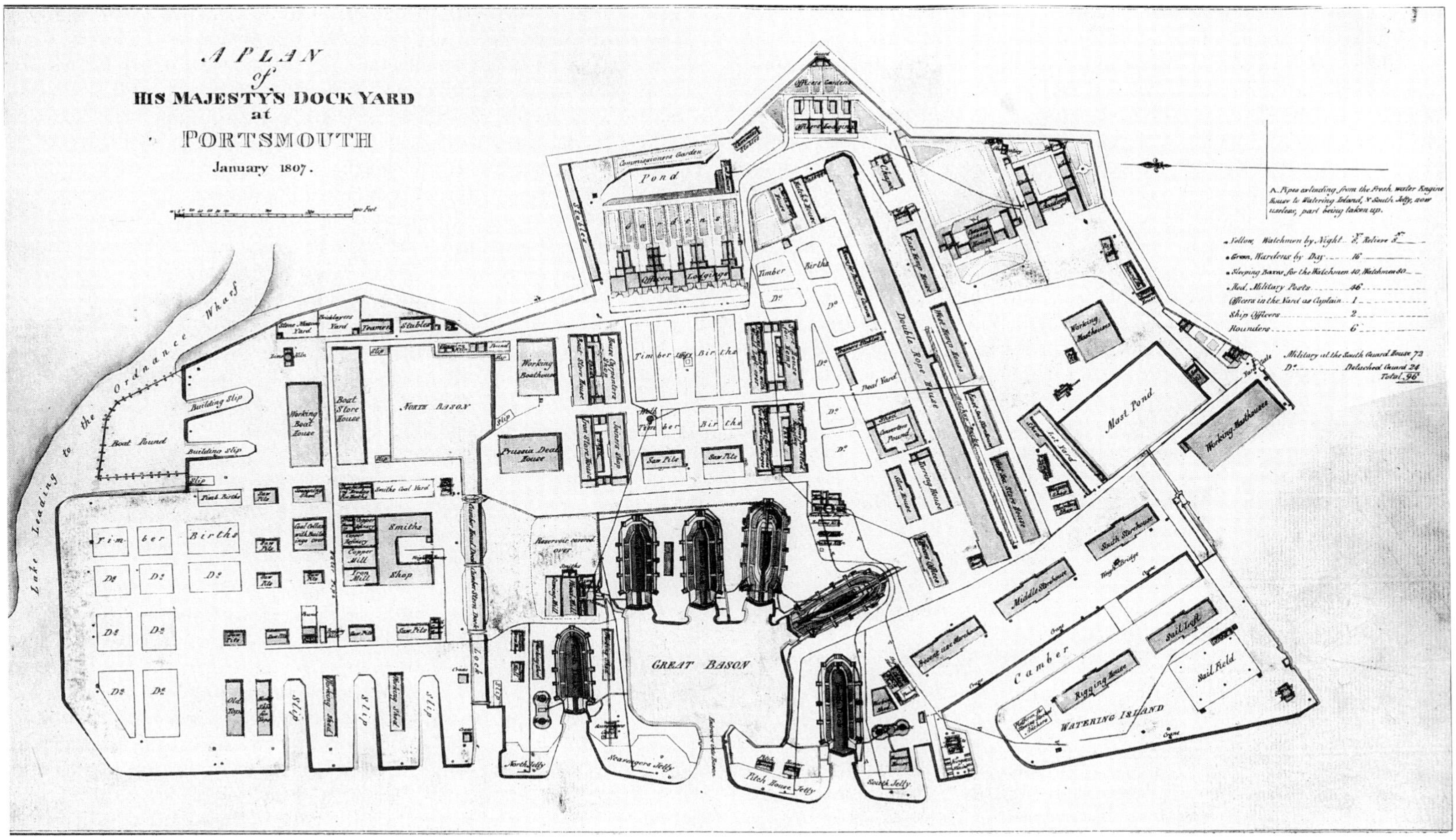

Portsmouth dockyard in 1807. Public Record Office

Plymouth Dockyard in the 1790s, as painted by Pocock. The National Maritime Museum

barracks and hospital at Stonehouse were on a separate peninsula, on Plymouth Sound itself. The victualling yard, and the marine barracks and hospital at Stonehouse were on a separate peninsula, and was situated in the town of Plymouth. The whole area was defended by the Plymouth citadel, south of the town; by the batteries on Drake's Island, Mount Edgecombe and Devil's Point at the entrance to the Hamoaze, and the yard itself was protected by landward fortifications.

Minor Bases

There were several minor naval bases round the coasts of Britain and Ireland, close to the major and minor anchorages, or to large natural harbours. None had dry-docking facilities for ships, but some had small-scale repair facilities for work on ships afloat. Most had stores and victualling depots, and sometimes hospitals. Each yard was headed by a 'naval officer', who was not in fact a commissioned officer of the navy, but was a civilian representative of the Navy Board. Deal yard was probably the most important, and it had served the anchorage in the Downs since 1672. As well as the Naval Officer, it had a master shipwright and a master attendant. Nearby was a hospital, employing six medical and other officers in 1814, and there was an ordnance depot and a small victualling yard nearby at Dover. Harwich had a naval officer and a master attendant, and Leith had a master shipwright, in addition. There was a base on a similar scale at Kinsale, on the south coast of Ireland, which was tranferred to Haulbowline Island in 1811. Nearby was a victualling yard at Cork. Of similar status was Great Yarmouth, servicing the anchorage at Yarmouth Roads from 1803 onwards. It also had an ordnance depot, but there was no victualling yard nearby. The base at Milford Haven was often proposed for expansion into a full dockyard, though St Vincent wrote, 'I do not conceive it probable that any ship-of-the-line will ever resort to it, except by stress of weather or accident. In the latter event, a dock might be useful, yet I have doubts whether it would be beneficial to the public to fix a large establishment at Milford Haven.'[18] Several ships-of-the-line were built there, until the establishment was transferred across the harbour to Pembroke Dock in 1813. In addition to the bases already mentioned, there were ordnance depots at Gravesend (serving the Nore), Hull, Purfleet on the Thames, and at Pendennis Castle near Falmouth.

4 Overseas Bases

Bases and Naval Strategy

The wars with France were all colonial wars to some extent, and the French Revolutionary and Napoleonic Wards were fought in all the seas of the world. As well as capturing and protecting colonies, the navy had to contain the French and other enemy fleets, wherever they were. For this, it could perform much better with bases near the scene of the action. In this respect, the most important overseas base would be one close to the French Mediterranean port of Toulon. The other French ports were covered by the home dockyards, while the Spanish bases at Cadiz and Cartagena could be blockaded by fleets serviced at Gibraltar. In the last years of the eighteenth century, Toulon was well covered by bases on Corsica and Minorca, but these were lost at the peace treaty of 1801. The other Mediterranean bases, at Malta and Gibraltar, were too far away to perform this task well. Another major group of bases was in the Caribbean and North America. The third group was in India and the sea route round the Cape of Good Hope.

The security of overseas bases was always important. Preferably, they should be situated on small islands, which could be defended by naval forces, or in colonies which were reasonably well established, such as Nova Scotia, where there was a base at Halifax. Easily defended land situations, such as Gibraltar, were also good situations for bases.

The number of overseas bases increased quite considerably during the wars. There were only four in 1793, at Gibraltar, Halifax, Jamaica and Antigua. By 1814, Cape of Good Hope, Malta and Bermuda had been added to the list, with store depots at Barbados, Minorca, Martinique, Lisbon and San Domingo. Ajaccio and Alexandria had also served as bases at one time or another during these years. Bombay and Madras, owned by the East India Company, each had a strong naval presence.

Facilities and Workforce

None of the overseas bases had facilities which approached those of a home dockyard. There was no manufacturing in any of them, and no overseas dry-dock until the completion of one at Malta in the mid nineteenth century. One was proposed there in 1807, but ran into serious geological problems, and a double dock proposed at Antigua in 1796 never materialised. Some dockyards, such as Antigua, had facilities for careening ships — hauling them down on one side to clean them. All had fairly extensive warehouses, for ships stores, ordnance supplies and victualling. Some had water tanks for the use of ships. In captured bases such as Malta and the Cape, the original buildings were often adapted for British use.

Most of the skilled workers in the overseas bases — shipwrights, caulkers, house carpenters and coopers — were recruited from the home dockyards and sent out. Where the situation permitted, men were also recruited locally. At Malta, the entire labour force of the victualling yard was of native workers.[1] At the Cape of Good Hope, the commissioner had six black Africans taught to caulk, and was very satisfied with their work.[2] In the West Indies, slaves were bought for menial work, and they could sometimes earn promotion to more skilled labour. According to the instructions to dockyard officers, they were to buy 'able healthy boys of 12–14 years of age', place them under the care of individual white artisans, and after three years they were allowed to qualify for 3s a week as an incentive.[3]

New bases were often started simply by the local commander-in-chief appointing the purser of one of his ships as storekeeper, and perhaps a carpenter as master shipwright. Soon the situation would become regularised, and the Navy Board would take over the appointment of officials. In 1793, only Halifax and Gibraltar had commissioners, but they were appointed to most of the other yards between 1803 and 1808. Every yard had a 'naval officer', or naval storekeeper, a well as a master attendant and a master shipwright. The latter was usually a ship's carpenter, who had spent more time afloat than in the dockyards. By the 1800s, a commissioner usually had two clerks, a storekeeper had up to four, and a master shipwright and master attendant had one each.

Gibraltar

Gibraltar had first been captured in 1704, and British possession was confirmed by the Treaty of Utrecht in 1713. Obviously, the rock was a prime site, at the entrance to the Mediterranean, but it was a long way from the French bases, and therefore less well regarded than

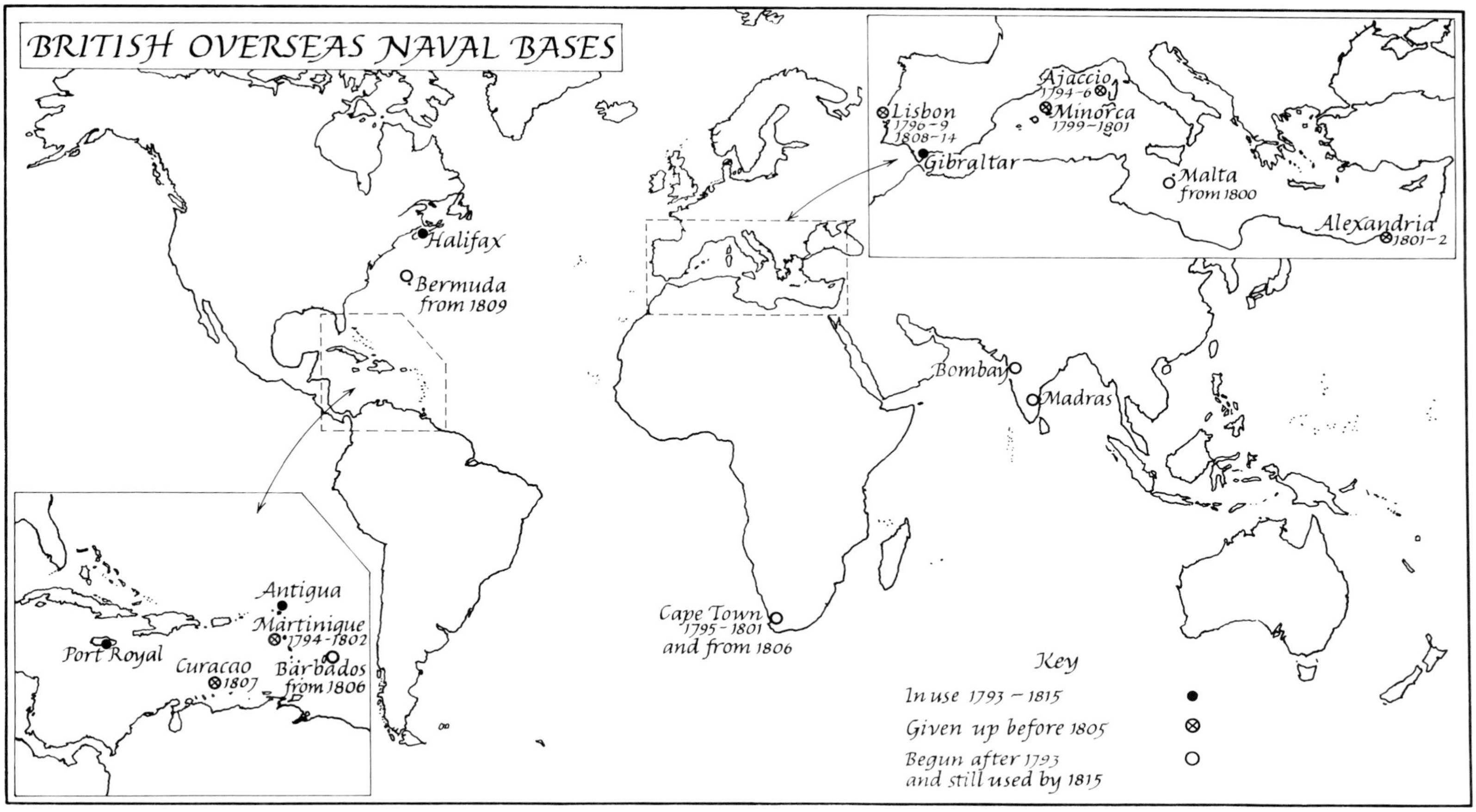

BRITISH OVERSEAS NAVAL BASES

Halifax
Bermuda from 1809
Lisbon 1796–9 1808–14
Gibraltar
Ajaccio 1794–6
Minorca 1799–1801
Malta from 1800
Alexandria 1801–2
Bombay
Madras
Cape Town 1795–1801 and from 1806
Antigua
Martinique 1794–1802
Port Royal
Curacao 1807
Barbados from 1806

Key
In use 1793 – 1815
Given up before 1805
Begun after 1793 and still used by 1815

British overseas naval bases.

Minorca in the eighteenth century. Gibraltar's harbour was largely unprotected from southerly winds, and it was not a particularly satisfactory anchorage. It was heavily besieged by Spain from 1779 to 1783, and this reduced its effectiveness in the American War. However, after 1793 it was never under serious threat, because British naval supremacy made a siege unlikely. Its importance was shown by the fact that two of the major battles of the war, St Vincent and Trafalgar, took place within two hundred miles of Gibraltar, while two squadron actions were fought within sight of the rock in 1801.

Gibraltar had a commissioner, storekeeper, and master shipwright in 1793; a master attendant and boatswain were added in 1796. It employed 170 artificers and labourers in 1814.[4]

Corsica

The island of Corsica was captured from the French republicans by Lord Hood's fleet in 1794, soon after it had evacuated Toulon. It provided an ideal base for the blockade of that port: the harbour of Ajaccio, in the west of the island, was chosen, and Isaac Coffin appointed commissioner. By 1796, he was proposing to move the base to St Florent in the north, but, later in the year, the British fleet evacuated the Mediterranean, and all the stores and provisions on Corsica were moved to Lisbon, with the officers and artisans.

Port Mahon

Minorca was first captured by the Royal Navy in 1708. It was lost in 1755, and Admiral Byng was shot for his failure to relieve the

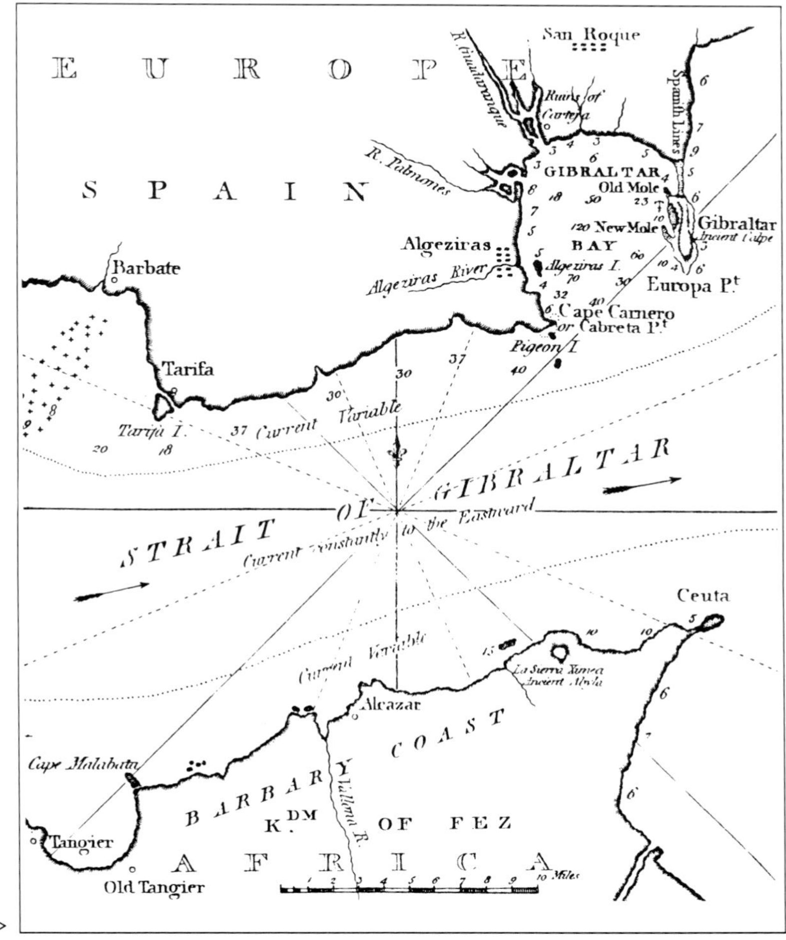

The Straits of Gibraltar. From the Naval Chronicle ▷

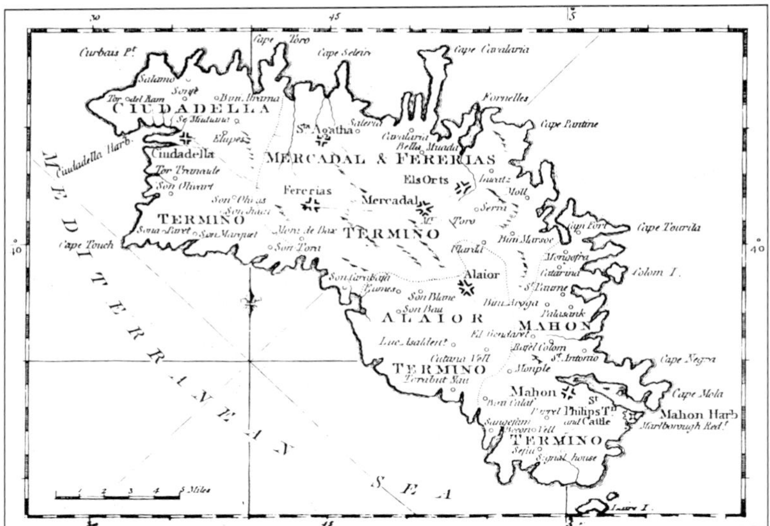

Minorca, with Port Mahon in the southeast corner. From the Naval Chronicle

The naval hospital at Port Mahon. From the Naval Chronicle

island. It was regained at the end of the Seven Years' War in 1763, but lost again in 1782. It was captured by British forces in 1798, without the loss of a single man. The stores, officers and artificers of the old Ajaccio base, under Commissioner Coffin, were transferred from Lisbon (see below) to Minorca early in 1799. The base had a naval storekeeper, a master shipwright and a master attendant.[5]

The main harbour, at Port Mahon, was sufficiently large to contain any fleet, 'and it is sufficiently deep too, but narrow at the entrance. There is convenience for careening three ships at a time, and much more could be made of the port as might be required. There is plenty of water at St Johns... The arsenal is small but sufficient for the supply of a fleet of twelve sail of the line and frigates and proportion.'[6] Minorca was given up at the peace treaty in 1801.

Malta

Since 1530, a religious and military order, the Knights of St John, had ruled Malta, using it as a galley base for campaigns against the Ottoman empire. Most of the Knights were of French origin, and had some loyalty to the French Crown, which of course ended with the revolution. In 1798, Napoleon, on his way to Egypt, occupied the island. The British blockade of Malta began a few months later, and lasted for two years, until September 1800. The Treaty of Amiens stipulated that Malta be handed back to the Knights, but the British retained possession and this was one of the main causes of the resumption of war in 1803.

There was considerable controversy about the value of Malta as a base, even among naval officers. In favour of it, Lord Keith wrote,

> Malta has the advantage over all the other ports that I have mentioned, that the whole harbour is covered by its wonderful fortifications, and that in the hands of Great Britain no enemy would presume to land upon it, because the number of men required to beseige it could not be maintained by the island... At Malta all the arsenals, hospitals, storehouses, etc, are on a grand scale. The harbour has more room than Mahon and the entrance is considerably wider.[7]

Sir Ralph Abercrombie wrote, 'As a military station, Malta may be pronounced to be the most complete in His Majesty's dominions and the harbour, which is capacious and safe, is perhaps the best port in the Mediterranean.'[8]

At first, Nelson was not impressed with Malta as a base, and compared it unfavourably with Minorca. Later, he partly modified these views, and wrote,

> My opinion of Malta as a naval station for watching the French at Toulon is well known and my present experience of what will be a three weeks passage fully confirms it. The fleet can never go there if I can find any other corner to put them in; but having said this, I now declare that I consider Malta as a most important outwork to India, that it will give us great influence in the Levant and indeed all the southern parts of Italy. In this view I hope we shall never give it up.[9]

In other words, Malta was little use in the immediate tactical situation, which was dominated by the need to blockade the French in Toulon; but it had enormous strategic potential, which would be developed later.

The facilities of Malta, as originally captured, were quite extensive but not fully adapted to the needs of a sailing navy. They consisted mainly of the houses, stores and galley sheds built by the Knights of Malta.[10] In 1806, it had an establishment of four officers with five clerks, a 'working foreman of shipwrights' and ten shipwrights 'who must likewise be caulkers', along with house carpenters, smiths, sawyers, labourers gate keepers and watchmen, giving a total workforce of 40.[11] By 1814, this had been increased to 378.[12] The navy used French creek, off the main harbour of Valetta, as its base.

Lisbon

Lisbon was never a British possession, but Portugal was a British ally, and the men and equipment of the base on Corsica were transferred

Valetta Harbour. From the Naval Chronicle

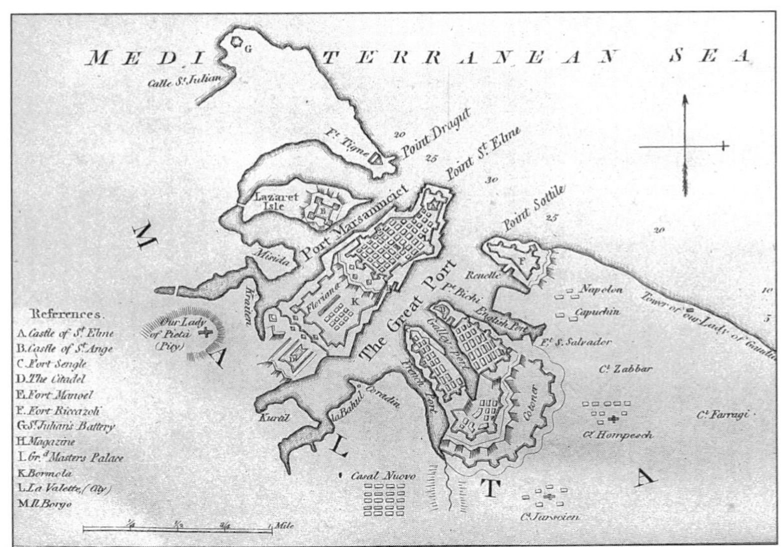

there in 1796, before being removed again, to Minorca, in 1799. Lisbon has a good natural harbour, making it suitable for the British fleet which had abandoned the Mediterranean. In 1808, the Peninsular War began, and Lisbon became the base for Wellington's army. As such, it sometimes came under attack from French forces, but Wellington's lines of Torres Vedras always held, and Lisbon was safe. A naval officer was appointed at Lisbon in 1808, but the yard never expanded beyond that.

Port Royal from the sea. The National Maritime Museum

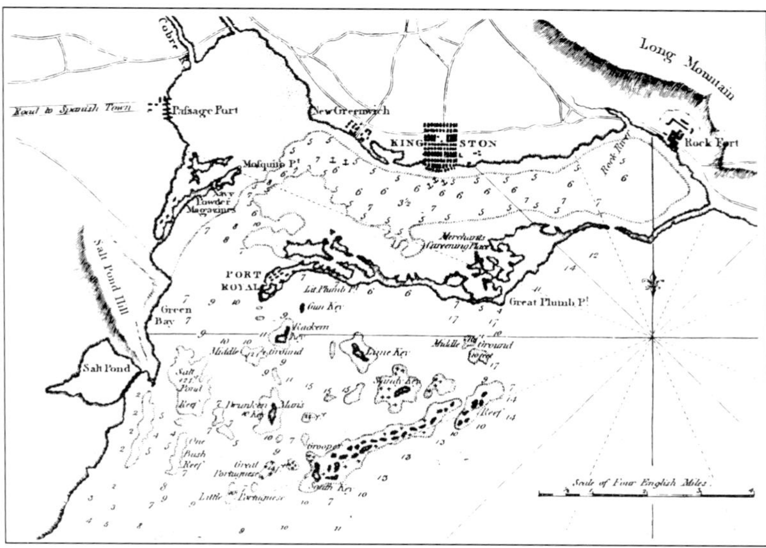

A map of the Kingston area, showing Port Royal. From the Naval Chronicle

Bermuda

Bermuda had been first colonised in 1609, with the wreck of the *Sea Venture* on its way there. It was well sited for watching the coasts of North America, and had occasionally been used by fleets before it was decided to build a dockyard there in 1809. Convict labour was brought in for the heavy work, and by 1814 the yard had a storekeeper, master attendant, master shipwright, and forty-seven manual workers.[13] According to Captain Brenton, Bermuda was 'admirably calculated either for an advanced post, or a port of equipment in time of war, to guard our West India trade from the enterprises of the enemy's cruisers, and particularly those of America. Here our naval arsenal is now established.' But, he went on, 'I fear much British money has been expended in making a dockyard contiguous to one of the worst, or most unpleasant, roadsteads I am acquainted with.'[14]

Antigua

The West Indian island of Antigua had been settled by the English in 1632. It is one of the most northerly of the Leeward Islands, and this gave it a certain advantage, as the prevailing winds allowed attack on most of the other islands in the Caribbean. It was a good anchorage and refuge from hurricanes. The naval base originated in 1728, and a careening wharf was built there. It expanded considerably during the war of 1739–48, as the main base for the Leeward Islands squadron. It had a naval storekeeper, master shipwright and master attendant by 1793, and its first commissioner was appointed in 1803. By 1814, it had 327 manual workers.

Port Royal, Jamaica

Jamaica had been captured by the English in 1655, and was the largest British island in the Caribbean. Port Royal, near the capital, Kingston, on the south side of the island, was situated on a large natural harbour, and it was chosen as the site for a naval base in 1735, in preference to Port Antonio on the north side of the island. Port Royal was sheltered from the prevailing winds, and from much of the rain that fell in the area in winter. The yard had a commissioner, first appointed in 1782, a master shipwright and storekeeper from its earliest days, and a master attendant after 1804. In 1814, it employed 309 artisans and labourers.

English Harbour, Antigua. From the Naval Chronicle

Cape Town

The Cape of Good Hope was originally a Dutch colony, founded in 1651 and used as a port of call on the sea route to her colonies in Indonesia. It was captured by the British fleet under Elphinstone in 1795, but returned to the Dutch at the Treaty of Amiens in 1801. It was recaptured in 1806 by a fleet under Sir Home Popham, and remained British after the peace treaties.

Like Malta, the Cape was not entirely approved of by naval strategists. The base was a very long way from the main scenes of conflict, and was taken and held chiefly for the benefit of the East India Company, and to prevent the French from using it. According to one of the directors of the East India Company in 1795,

> The importance to the Cape, with regard to ourselves consists more from the detriment which would result if it was in the hands of France, than any advantage we can possibly derive from it as a colony. It commands the passage to and from India as effectually as Gibraltar doth the Mediterranean; and it serves as a granary for the Isles of France; whilst it furnishes no produce whatsoever for Europe, and the expense of supporting the place must be considerable.[15]

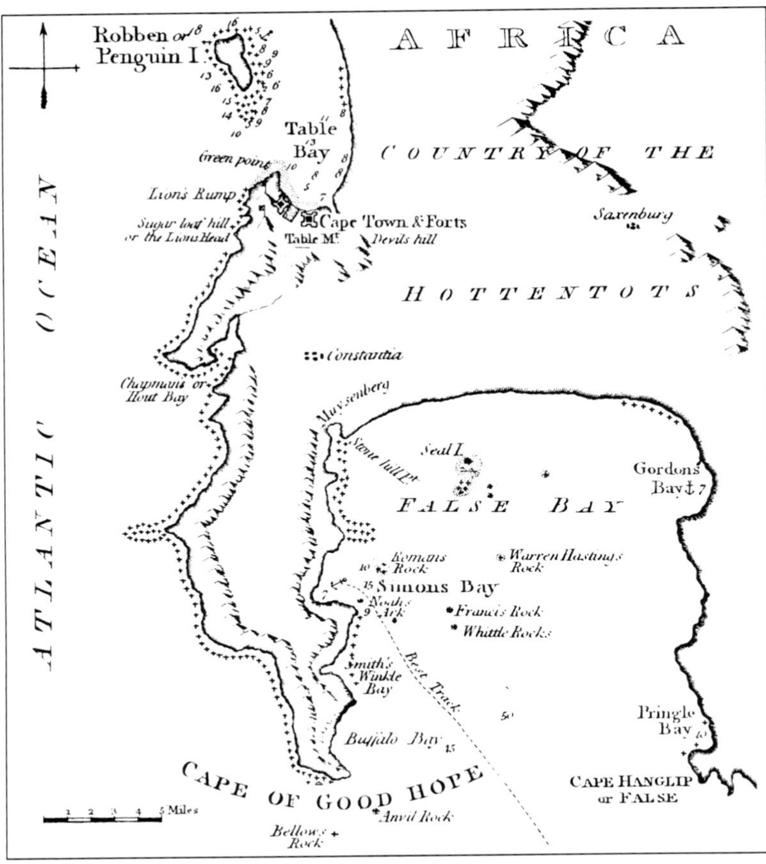

The Cape of Good Hope. From the Naval Chronicle

In 1801, the secretary of state for war and the colonies considered that it was 'a peculiarly expensive, insecure and extremely inconvenient port of refreshment.'[16] However, after its second capture, it became quite an important base for the attack on the French islands in the Indian Ocean, and for the general policy of sweeping them from the Eastern seas.

The Cape had no safe anchorage. Table Bay was 'an infernal one; it is safe against no wind, and its sea is worse than the wind.'[17] It was usable only in the summer months. In winter, ships were taken round to Simon's Bay, about thirty miles away by sea. In 1813, the naval establishment was moved from Table Bay to Simonstown; but its harbour facilities were still primitive even after that, and its defences were 'very incomplete' some years later.[18] Supplies in the area were often short and, in 1796 for example, there was a 'total want of bread and grain which obliged the admiral to unload by force the neutral Danish ship *Count Schuellan* to procure some rice stowed at the bottom of the cargo.'[19]

After its first capture in 1795, the Cape Town base had the usual complement of master attendant, master shipwright and naval storekeeper. After 1808, these were headed by a commissioner, and a boatswain was appointed in 1795, and again in 1806. In 1810, the commissioner wrote that he employed eight shipwrights, six ships' carpenters, and seven caulkers, 'including six black men'.[20] By 1814, the total labour force was up to ninety-two.[21]

Bombay and Madras

Bombay had been occupied by the British East India Company since 1626, and served as a dockyard for the Company's ships. Its first dry-dock was built in 1750, and several more were built over the years. One fit for a 74-gun ship was partly completed in 1806, and another in 1810. The yard also had a ropewalk, smith, hospital, gaol, storehouses and houses for the officers. It employed a mainly native workforce, under the joint master builders Framjee Maneckjee Wadia and Jamsetjee Bomarjee Wadia. From 1801, it built several ships for the navy, including the 74-gun *Cornwallis*, completed in 1813; several more were being built when the war ended.

Rather than rely solely on the company's resources, the navy also appointed officers to superintend its affairs in Bombay. In 1814, there was a commissioner, naval storekeeper, master attendant and master shipwright. Madras was rather less important to the navy, but it had the same set of officials.

Other Bases

Several small bases were occupied for short times during the wars, usually under a storekeeper or naval officer. Barbados was the most windward of the West Indian islands, and this gave it some tactical advantages. It was used as a stores base after 1806, though it was considered subordinate to Antigua. There was a short-lived appointment of a naval storekeeper during 1807, in the former Dutch West Indian possession of Curaçao. The French island of Martinique was occupied from 1794 to 1802, and a storekeeper, master shipwright and master attendant were in office during these years.

An acting naval officer was appointed at Alexandria in 1801, but this post ended with the campaign in Egypt, in the following year. The harbour at Trincomalee, Ceylon, was surveyed in 1811, and considered to be sufficient for forty ships-of-the-line, but it was not developed until later years. The island of Heligoland, off the German coast, was taken from the Danes in 1807, and a naval harbourmaster was appointed.

The naval hospital at Madras. From the Naval Chronicle

5 The Victualling Organisation

Feeding the Fleet

The task of feeding a fleet of up to 145,000 men was by no means easy, yet the Victualling Board which undertook the work was not a high-profile organisation. It attracted relatively little attention from the various parliamentary commissions of the time, and not much more from subsequent historians. This cannot be taken to mean that all was well with the victualling arrangements, or that naval food was always good and wholesome. Yet there were no complaints like those of the 1750s, when it was claimed that men made trouser buttons out of their cheese. Dr Thomas Trotter went as far as to say,

> This is a department where great improvements have been made of late years. The salted beef and pork are excellent; and the bread, till the high price of corn rendered a mixture necessary, was as good as could be desired. Equal attention has been paid to other branches of provision. Our officers are not a little vigilant in taking care that all articles are in due preservation, and of the proper quality.[1]

It would be rash to say that there was no corruption or incompetence in the victualling department, but things had certainly improved in the second half of the eighteenth century.

In theory, the Victualling Board was allotted by parliament 19s out of every £4 paid per man per month before 1797, and 38s out of £7 after that. In practice, the Victualling Board spent £1,354,945 in 1798, and £1,676,987 in the following year.[2]

The Victualling Officers

The Victualling Board consisted of seven officials, each in charge of one branch of the service. The chairman was head of the cash department, and the deputy chairman also acted as chief storekeeper. The other members of the board were, respectively, in charge of transport hoys, brewhouses, cutting houses (ie, slaughterhouses), dry stores, and cooperage. The board met daily at its offices in Somerset Place, London, to discuss contracts and issue orders to the yards. The three senior officers had houses at Tower Hill, where the board had formerly met. There was quite a large staff at the office, with about a hundred and twenty clerks by 1810.

Deptford was the main storehouse and depot for victualling, and was directly under the eye of the Board in London, only three miles away. The organisation at Deptford was slightly more elaborate than at the other yards. There was an agent victualler, clerk of the cheque, storekeeper, master brewer, master cooper, and superintendent of the wharf. At local level, the agent victualler was the main representative of the victualling board. He was 'an officer stationed at a royal port, to regulate the victualling of the king's ships, under the direction of the commissioners for victualling the navy. He receives all the provisions from the victualling office in London, and distributes them to the ships in the harbour. He also receives into his storehouses such as may be returned by ships after the expiration of their cruise.'[3] He also supplied the pursers with their 'necessary money', and any 'short allowance money' that might need to be paid. Other officers at local level were the storekeeper, clerk of the cheque, and master cooper. Where appropriate, there was also a master brewer.

Contracting

All the items needed to victual the fleet had to be bought in some form — either as raw materials, such as wheat to make biscuit, or as articles ready for use, such as coal. There was no power to requisition goods, and all had to be bought at market prices, reflecting seasonal fluctuations, good and bad harvests, and shortages brought about by storm or enemy action. The board in London made most of these contracts, and the terms varied according to the article in question. Contracts were made by placing tenders in a sealed box on the appropriate date. This was opened later, and the opinion of the relevant officer, such as the master brewer or master miller, was taken into account, and the contract awarded to the lowest bidder.[4]

The quality of the items was described to a certain extent; for example, biscuit was to be 'made from biscuit stuff, arising from wholemeal, ground from good sound wheat and dressed through a cloth not coarser than a patent cloth no 4, and shall be equal in goodness to the biscuit baked at His Majesty's bakehouses at the port of Plymouth.' Peas were to be 'kiln dried English . . . of the best quality.'[5] 'Petty warrant bread' was to be 'in loaves weighing 32oz each, in all respects good and fit for His Majesty's service'.[6] Sometimes, a single merchant agreed to provide all the supplies of a certain commodity to one or more victualling depot — for example, peas to

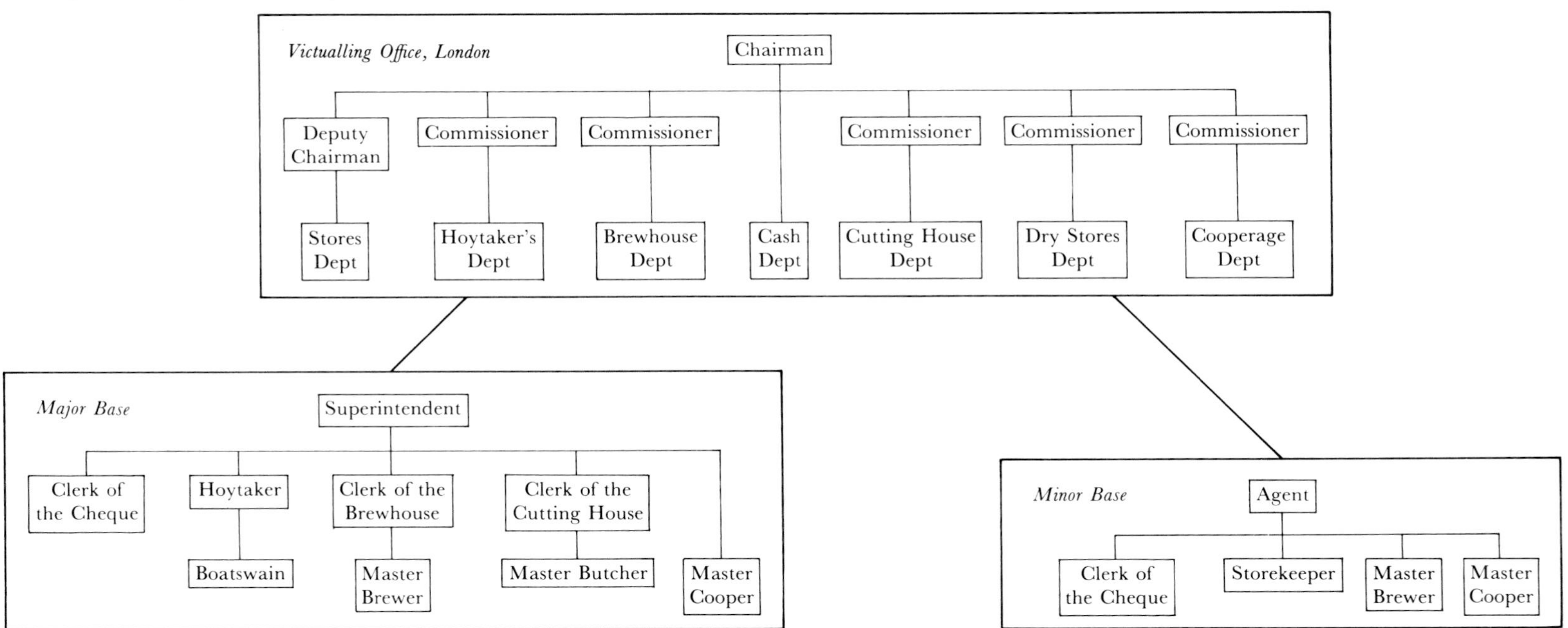

The organisation of the victualling department.

Smithfield Market, London, where cattle were bought for the navy. The Museum of London

London, at a commission of 9d per quarter, from 1794 to 1803, or beef to London and Portsmouth, 1797 to 1808, at 7d per hundredweight above the purchase price.[7] More often, short-term contracts for specific amounts were made with the merchants. Cheese and butter contracts were for deliveries as demanded, not for fixed quantities. Hops, for making beer, were contracted for single deliveries only, or for deliveries over a short period. Flour, for biscuit, was bought in quantities from 30cwt to 3000cwt, with the larger amounts usually being bought in London. Up to about 1797, a certain amount of beef was bought from Ireland, already slaughtered, cut up, salted and put in casks. Most was bought as either whole carcasses or live animals, to be slaughtered in the victualling yards. Biscuit was sometimes bought ready made, but most was produced in the yards. Coal was bought either as a single amount immediately available, or for quantities to be supplied on demand over a period.[8]

Slaughtering cattle. From Pyne's *Microcosm*

In the case of overseas yards, a single merchant often undertook to supply a whole theatre; for example, during the war of 1813, Mr Andrew Belcher was to supply the North American station, including ships as far apart as Halifax and Bermuda, with 'sea provisions, rum, wine, spruce beer, and tobacco'.[9] These goods were of course delivered to the victualling officers at the various yards.

Manufacturing

In view of the general distrust of private enterprise, it is not surprising to find that the main victualling yards were equipped to produce the main items of naval victualling — biscuit, salt beef and pork, and beer. Cattle and pigs were slaughtered at the yards, then cut up into 8lb pieces, rubbed with salt and saltpetre, and put into casks, with a layer of salt between each layer of meat. Other meat remained unsalted, and was issued daily to the ships actually in port. Deptford yard received up to 260 oxen per day in the season, bought at Smithfield Market, London.

The main yards all had bakeries producing ships' biscuits, and received supplies of wheat for the purpose. There were breweries at Plymouth, Portsmouth and Deptford. The master brewer in charge of the Plymouth brewery 'inspects cargoes of malt hops and coal and brewing at Southdown; and taking care of such quantities of beer as the service may require'.[10] At Deptford in 1813, 'the various operations of grinding the malt, pumping the beer from the vats with the coolers and co', were performed by a 10-horsepower steam engine.[11]

In 1808, the master bakers were issued with instructions on the making of biscuit:

> To take particular care that the dough be properly mixed, well kneaded or braked, and that none shall be left in the kneading troughs in the evening, after the last suite of biscuit is made, in order to avoid any loss to the public from its becoming sour. You are also to take care that the biscuits be made thin, properly baked, and of such a size as not to be less than five to a pound.[12]

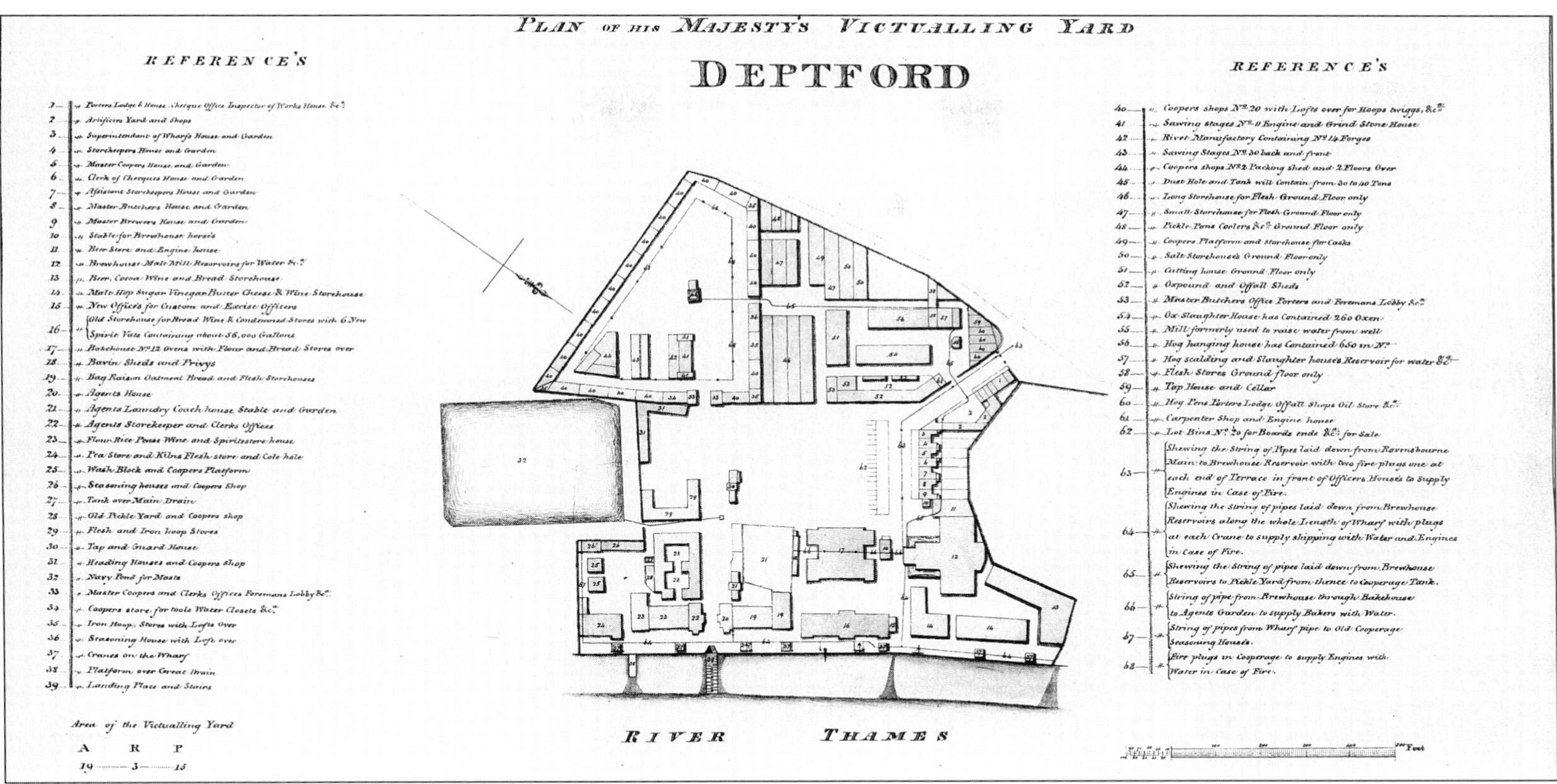

Deptford Victualling Yard in 1813. Public Record Office

At Portsmouth in 1813, 'About thirty men are constantly employed making biscuit for the navy... The quantity baked in a day is said to be about a hundred bags, each weighing a hundredweight. The biscuit baked here is considered as superior to that which is supplied by the contractors and is therefore issued to ships going on foreign stations.'[12] The Plymouth bakehouse had capacity to make biscuit for 16,000 men a day.

Storage and Cooperage

Nearly all the items at the victualling yards, with the major exceptions of biscuit and coal, had to be put into casks as soon as possible in order to preserve them. The cooperage establishments at each yard were quite large, and the expenditure on casks was quite high — the only major scandal in the victualling establishments during this period was about the embezzlement of casks from the Plymouth victualling establishment. Coopers were either 'block coopers' paid on piece work, or 'day coopers', paid by the day. The cooperage work at Weevil yard in Portsmouth was one of the few well-planned victualling board buildings on the South Coast, having being built according to a plan of 1766. Casks served for perishable items such as beer and foodstuffs; other goods such as coal and biscuit were kept in canvas bags. All goods were kept in large warehouses in the victualling yards until needed. Those at Portsmouth and Plymouth were considered inadequate because of their small sizes, and because their wharves could only be used at high tide. The Plymouth storehouses had capacity for rations for 25,000 men for 112 days, including 25,000cwt of biscuit, 240,000 pieces of pork, 600,000lb of flour and 175,000lb of lemon juice.[14]

Transport

Water transport was much easier and cheaper than land transport in 1800, and this suited the Victualling Board quite well, as all its establishments were naturally close to navigable waterways. The one exception to this was livestock, which could make its own way to market. Other goods were generally delivered to the victualling depots by sea. As a rule, the ships of the navy were expected to come to the victualling yards for their supplies, rather than have the supplies sent out to them; it was too difficult to find a fleet at sea, and in any case the ships had to come in to the dockyards by rotation for routine repairs. However, supplies often had to be sent long distances to the overseas bases. The goods might well be bought and prepared by the victualling yards in England, though the conveyance was arranged by the Transport Board. The Victualling Board had its own fleet of small ships for movement within the estuaries and harbours of the main naval bases. At Plymouth in late 1803, there were three small vessels; the *Supply* sloop, crewed by a master, a mate, two able seamen and an apprentice, the *Relief* sloop, with a master, an able seaman and a boy, and the *John* sloop, with a master and an able seaman. These were for 'carrying provisions for victualling His Majesty's ships at Plymouth and Torbay.'[15] It was about forty miles by sea from Plymouth to the Torbay anchorage, and the yard's vessels were obviously very small. Presumably if the whole Channel squadron was at Torbay, extra transports would have to be supplied. However, this was not always done, for example in December 1794, 'The Channel Fleet, having put into Torbay from contrary winds, experienced much cold weather and a dangerous gale of wind from the southeast... While the fleet lay in Torbay, no fresh beef was served to the people, but mutton for the use of the sick only; by which means we were full five weeks on salt provisions, when fresh meat was allowed at Spithead.'[16] At Chatham in 1813, there were three hoys, each with a crew of a master, mate, and two seamen or apprentices.[17] Dover had no hoys, but goods were transported to the Downs by vessels hired under contract.

Employees

The Victualling Board could not rival the Navy Board as an employer of labour, though the numbers in the various depots were quite

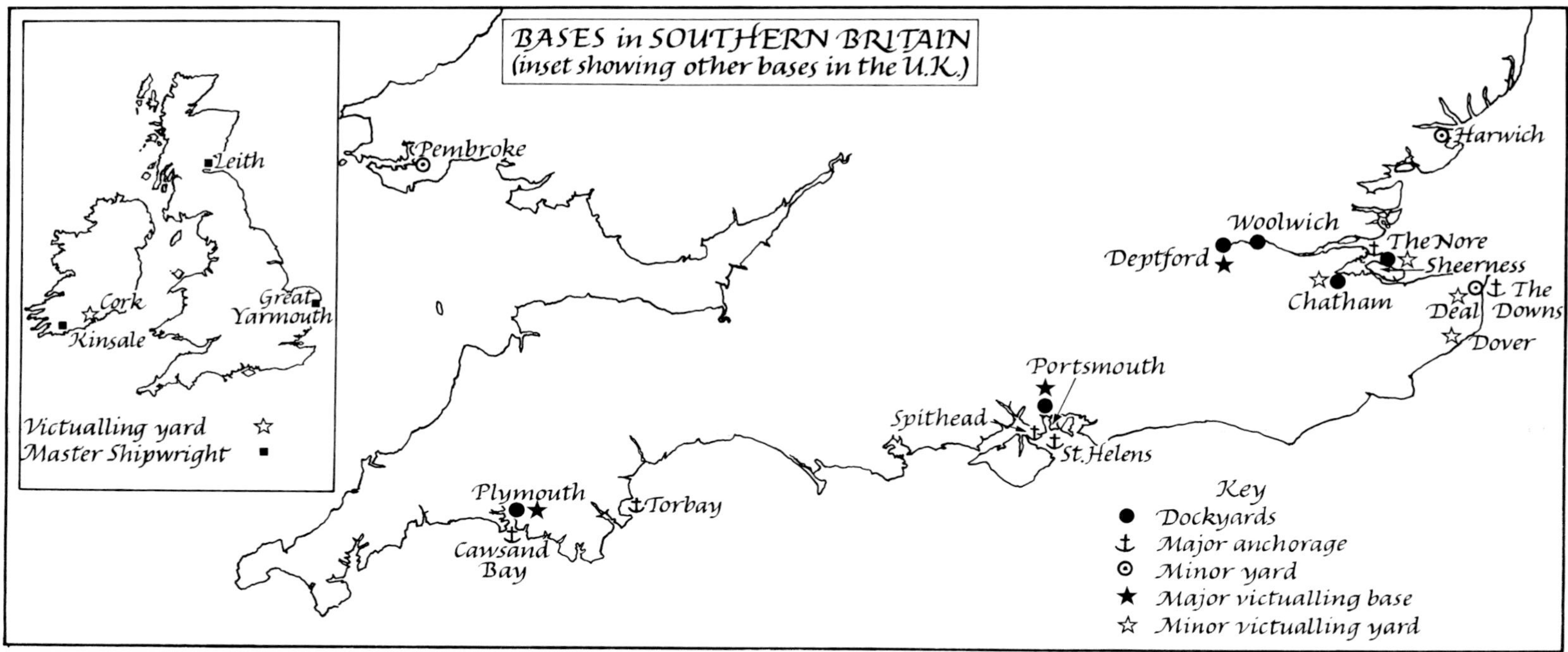

The home victualling bases.

substantial by contemporary standards. At Plymouth on a war footing in 1803, the Agent Victualler employed eight clerks, the storekeeper six, and the clerk of the cheque five. There was a foreman of coopers, with a second foreman, and store-cooper and his assistant; between them, they had six apprentices. In addition there were eleven day coopers, and eight block coopers, and two sawyers for sawing staves. The bakery was headed by a foreman, whose duties were 'superintending and conducting the baking of biscuit'. There were forty bakers and three assistant bakers; a boatswain of the wharf, who was also in charge of 111 labourers; a granary man, a miller and his assistant, four pastry men, five warders and a gatekeeper. The brewery at Southdown had another cooperage, with a master cooper, three clerks, seven apprentices, six day coopers and forty-four block coopers. The master brewer was assisted by the clerk of the brewhouse and three clerks. There were three stokers, two millers, three tunmen, 119 labourers, a gatekeeper, six wardens and twelve sawyers.[18] In 1813, the victualling yard at Portsmouth employed 210 men under the agent victualler, including eighty-eight labourers and thirty coopers, with 319 more at Weevil on the other side of the harbour entrance. Plymouth employed 436 men, while Deptford had 526 on day work, and 1251 on piece work. Dover had fifty five men.

Home Bases

In general, the Victualling Board's buildings were much less distinguished than those in the dockyards. The exception was the main yard at Deptford, which was 'perhaps the most complete establishment of the kind in this or any other country. Unlike our dockyards it is not made up of a succession of makeshifts, but has been laid out with a view to the expectation of what was to be expected from it'.[19] The yard had been rebuilt in the 1780s, with purpose-built storehouses and other features.

At the other naval bases, the Victualling Board buildings were much more dispersed, and the board tended to rent them rather than build them specially. At Plymouth the victualling premises, including a brewery and a flour mill, were situated in the old town of Plymouth, several miles from the dockyard, and in 1813, 'it was obvious that much inconvenience must be felt from the dispersion of the victualling premises in the neighbourhood'.[20] At Portsmouth the Weevil yard was self-contained on the western side of the harbour entrance, and was the main storehouse, and an important workshop for coopers. The brewery was also situated on that side of the entrance, but the bakery was in Portsmouth town, as was the slaughterhouse and flour mill. The mill was situated between Portsmouth and Portsea, and was driven by water power from the receding tide passing through the moat between the two towns. At Chatham, there was virtually no manufacturing or production, as it was more convenient to supply ships at the Nore from Deptford. 'From the depot, the ships in the Medway are principally supplied with provisions and water; but no articles of store are manufactured here, but are received from the other yards, chiefly that of Deptford.'[21] There was a small slaughterhouse at Chatham; the yard as a whole had ninety-four employees in 1813.

In 1799, there was only one small victualling station, apart from the larger ones at Deptford, Chatham, Portsmouth and Plymouth. That was at Dover, and was used for supplying ships in the Downs. It had its own brewery. By 1810, two more yards had been set up — at Deal and Sheerness, each under storekeeper. By 1814, there was also one at Cork.

Overseas Bases

In 1799, there was only one overseas victualling base, at Gibraltar, and on other stations the commander-in-chief took responsibility for finding supplies for his ships. The Gibraltar station had a clerk and a storekeeper, and received its supplies from Deptford. By 1810, there was also agent victuallers at Malta, the Cape, Rio de Janeiro and Heligoland. During the Peninsular War, there was also a yard at Lisbon, employing five clerks, ten coopers with a foreman and an apprentice, thirteen labourers, a porter and five carpenters.[22] The yard at the Cape had three storehouses in 1797.[23]

Part XI
FLEETS

1 The Distribution of Fleets

The Navy in the World

The great bulk of British naval force was to be found in the main fleets, distributed round the world. Some ships were devoted exclusively to convoy escort, and a few captains sailed directly under Admiralty orders, but most ships were part of these fleets. Each was headed by a commander-in-chief, who was an admiral of considerable seniority — Nelson was a commander-in-chief only for the last two years of his life; he fought the Nile and Copenhagen as a subordinate admiral. Some squadrons were formed for specific purposes, and usually known by the names of their commanders, but the principal fleets always had geographical denominations. These were not always exact — the area of the Mediterranean fleet extended as far as the coast of Portugal, while the Channel fleet operated as far south as Spain. The real strategic importance of fleets varied quite considerably, as did their size. The Channel fleet was always kept strong, while the West Indies fleets tended to decline after the French had been defeated in the area. The Newfoundland and Nova Scotia fleets were nearly always weak and unimportant, except during the war of 1812. Usually there were seven or eight main fleets with geographical titles, plus port admirals, detached squadrons, and single ships.

The Channel Fleet

The Channel fleet (also known as the Western squadron, and occasionally as the Atlantic fleet) was the main keystone of British defence. In 1755, Anson had written, 'The best defence for our colonies, as well as our coasts, is to have a squadron always to the westward as may in all probability either keep the French in port, or give them battle with advantage if they come out.'[1] The idea was not new then; it had originated in the 1690s, when naval superiority over France had first been achieved. Anson, of course, referred to the blockade of Brest, whether open or closed, but this strategy was always the main priority of the Channel fleet, and according to Keith's orders of 1812 it was to be supervised personally by the commander-in-chief.[2] When resources allowed, the other ports were blockaded as well. Rochefort was the second most important, and the French ports of L'Orient and Cherbourg, as well as the Spanish base of Ferrol, were also blockaded. To the eastward, the responsibilities of the Channel fleet extended as far as Selsey Bill, just east of Portsmouth, so Le Havre had to be taken into account. In 1804, it was planned to have twenty ships-of-the-line off Brest, directly under the commander-in-chief, seven off Rochefort under a subordinate admiral, seven more off Ferrol, and a detachment of three more forming the 'Straits mouth squadron . . . instructed to range the coasts of Portugal and Spain from Lisbon to Cape Trafalgar, and from thence to Cape Spartel, so that scarce anything will be able to come out or go into the Mediterranean without being discovered or intercepted'.[3] Later, the west coast of Spain and Portugal was taken away from the commander of the Channel fleet, and his responsibilities ended at Cape Finisterre.

The Channel fleet had twenty-six ships-of-the-line in 1795, including seven three-deckers. It also had seventeen frigates, a hospital ship and two fireships.[4] In 1800, it had three first rates, eleven second rates, and thirty-three other ships-of-the-line. It had nineteen frigates, four sloops, a cutter and a fireship, a total of seventy-two ships and vessels.[5] In 1805, it had thirty-five ships-of-the-line and sixteen frigates.[6] In 1812, when Admiral Keith took over, the fleet had fifteen ships-of-the-line, fourteen frigates, three sloops, four gun brigs, and

The Channel fleet, led by the Ville de Paris *flying St Vincent's flag, sails from Spithead.* The National Maritime Museum

three cutters.[7] Because of the number of ports to be blockaded, the fleet needed plenty of flagships, and subordinate admirals. In 1799, it had a full admiral in command, and another as second in command; and five rear-admirals, including the captain of the fleet.[8]

One reason why the Channel fleet remained important was that the French fleet at Brest was never put out of action. It engaged in only one full battle — with Howe's Channel fleet on the First of June 1794. It lost six ships, so it was never annihilated in the way the French Mediterranean fleet was destroyed at the Nile and Trafalgar. The main bases of the Channel fleet were Portsmouth and Plymouth, where its ships were fitted out, victualled and repaired. It used the anchorages of Spithead, St Helens, Cawsand Bay and Plymouth Sound on occasion, but its main rendezvous and shelter was Torbay.

The commander-in-chief of the Channel fleet was always one of the most important figures in the navy. From 1790, the post had been held by Lord Howe, sixty-seven years old at the beginning of the war. He had a great deal of experience, which caused him to use the fleet with caution — opting for open rather than close blockade, with the ships spending most of their time at Spithead or Torbay, unless they were warned that the French had come out. In 1799, Howe died and was succeeded by Lord Bridport, but the policy did not change greatly. St Vincent took command in 1800, and immediately adopted the strategy of close blockade. This continued till the end of the war, and was adopted by Cornwallis in 1803, at the beginning of the next one. Close blockade remained the main strategy after that, while the Channel fleet was successively under the command of St Vincent (1806–7), Gardner, Cotton, and Lord Keith, after 1812.

The Irish and Channel Island Squadrons

The Irish squadron, based mainly at Cork, was intended for the protection of trade to the westward, and to help protect the island from invasion or unrest; though it was never big enough to do either effectively without the support of the Channel fleet. In the crisis of 1805, it was given a slightly different role in the scheme of defence. 'From Cape Clear to Finisterre, Admiral Lord Gardner at Cork had been furnished with all the means, and directed to establish a line of frigates for the sake of a direct communication between those points.'[9] In 1797 the squadron had sixteen ships, including one of the line (as a stationary flagship), ten frigates and three sloops. Two years later, it had only twelve ships. In 1805, it had twenty-three ships, including twelve frigates and eight sloops. By 1812, it had been reduced to thirteen ships, none larger than frigates.

The Channel Islands, or Guernsey, squadron was also quite small, and served to prevent a French invasion of these islands, and to keep some check on the privateers of St Malo. In 1812, it had eleven ships, including three frigates and three sloops. Commanders on the station included Samaurez, who had personal connections with the area.

North Sea Fleets

The other major home command was the North Sea fleet, though again the title was rather misleading, as the area extended to Selsey Bill, and therefore included about half of the English Channel. It became quite important in blocking invasion, particularly when the enemy held Holland and Belgium. In 1797, it had fifty-six ships, including twenty of the line,[10] under the command of Duncan; this fleet won the Battle of Camperdown in that year.

In addition, there was a Downs squadron, intended to protect the entrance to the Channel; Lord Keith wrote, 'I have ever held a squadron of stout ships in the Downs to be of essential consequence, because I can hardly believe that the French troops will ever embark unless covered by a squadron proceeding into the Channel, either straight up or north about; both are difficult and dangerous, but not impracticable.'[11] There was a small force at Leith, which was the main naval presence in Scotland, and was largely engaged in convoy escort.

At the outbreak of war in 1803, these separate squadrons were combined into a single fleet: 'The eastern command, now under Lord Keith, extends from Selsey Bill, near Portsmouth, to the Shetland Islands, comprehending a space of between two and three hundred leagues. There are six flag officers usually employed under his lordship and near 150 pennants [ie ships] great and small.'[12] In fact, Keith's fleet had eighty ships in 1805, including eleven of the line and twenty frigates. These were, at that time, divided into five squadrons, including a new one at Dungeness, for blockading Boulogne and Etaples. In 1804, this squadron had two 64-gun ships, two 50s, four 38s, ten sloops and various bomb vessels, gunboats and smaller ships.[13] The headquarters was ashore, at Ramsgate.

Lord Barham was against the unified command for the North Sea, claiming that it was too complicated for one man to handle, and should be divided into separate units, each under the Admiralty. However, changes were not made until after Barham's retirement, when it was divided into the Downs, Yarmouth, and Leith squadrons, with another for blockading the Texel and Scheldt, the main entrances to the Dutch ports. In 1807, there were thirty-four ships in the Downs squadron, including one of the line; eight at Yarmouth, none larger than a sloop; seven at Sheerness all small; and fifteen at Leith, including a third rate and two frigates. Another force was the North Sea fleet proper, with fourteen ships, including a third rate, a fifth rate and five sloops.[14] In 1812, there were thirty-one ships in the Downs squadron, with no ships-of-the-line or frigates, but sixteen sloops. At Yarmouth, there were eight ships, including four sloops. The Texel and Scheldt force was much larger, with fifty-three ships, including twenty-seven of the line, five frigates and twelve sloops. At Leith there were fourteen ships, including two frigates and four sloops.[15]

The Baltic Fleet

The Baltic was always important to British naval strategy, but the presence of a fleet there was only intermittent, and depended on the strategic situation. In 1801, the formation of the League of Armed Neutrality caused a strong squadron to be sent under Sir Hyde Parker. It included Nelson as second in command, two second rates, nineteen third rates, eleven frigates and 50s, seven bomb vessels, nine

George Elphinstone, Viscount Keith, commander in chief in India, 1795-7, Mediterranean Fleet 1799-1802, North Sea 1803-7, Channel Fleet 1812-14. From the Naval Chronical

Sir John Jervis, Earl of St Vincent, commander in chief in the Leeward Islands 1794-5, Mediterranean 1795-9, Channel Fleet 1799-1801, 1806-7. The National Maritime Museum

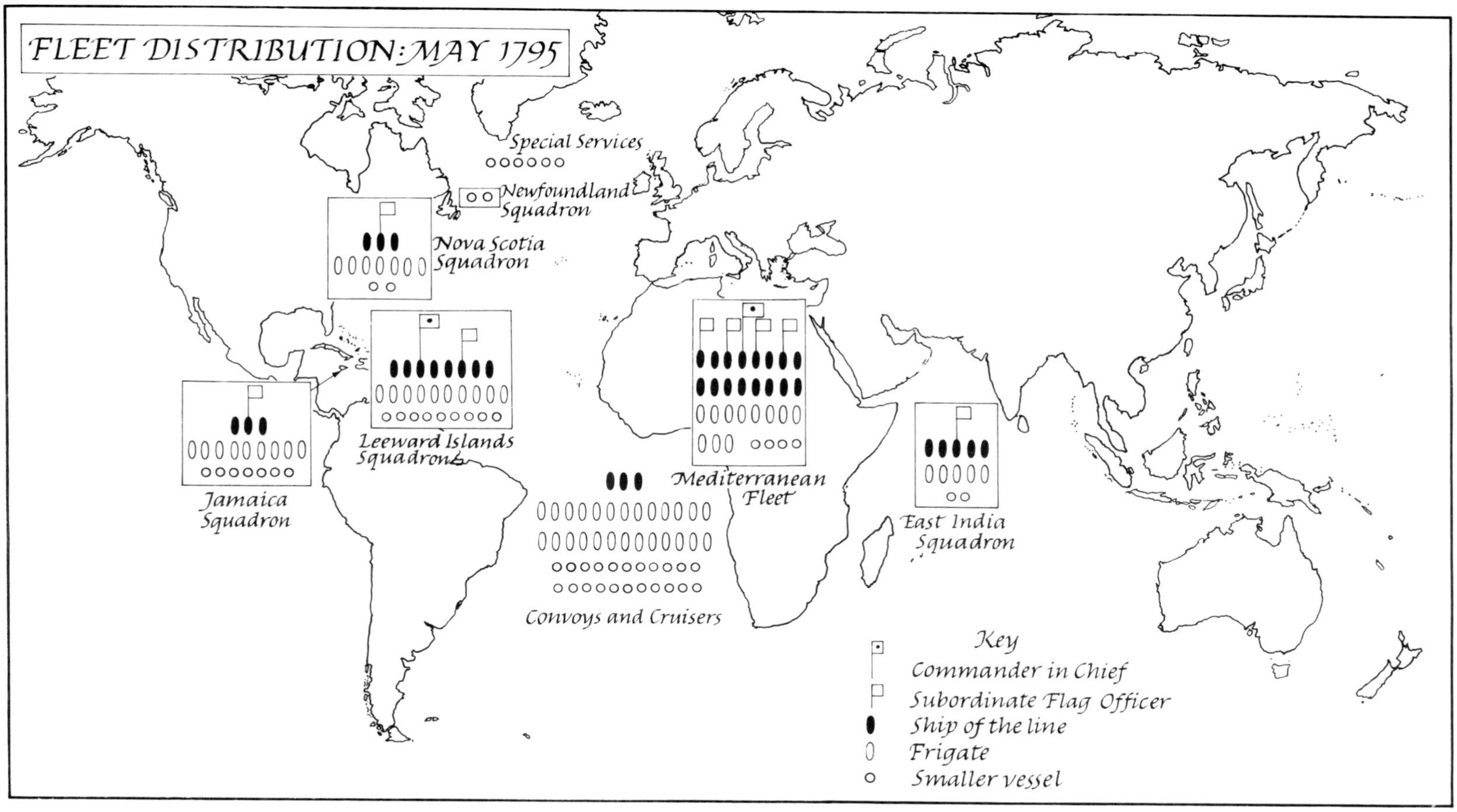

The distribution of the fleets, May 1795 and June 1808. Based on the Adm 8 series in the Public Record Office. These show the numbers of ships actually allocated to the fleets, not necessarily those on station. There are some differences in accounting between the two periods, for example more ships are described as 'unappropriated' in 1808, whereas in 1795 they would have been described as fitting for specific fleets. See also pages 248–49

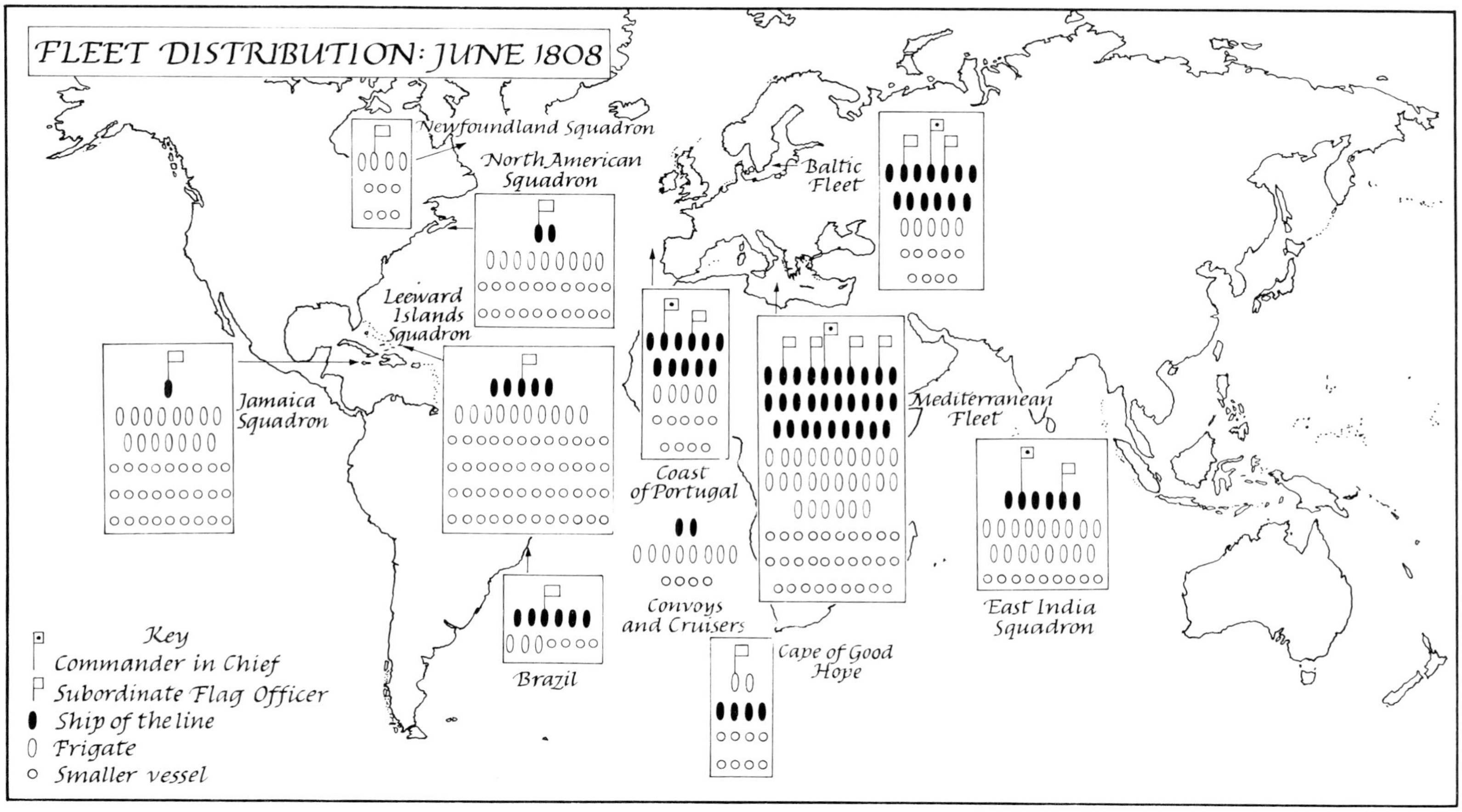

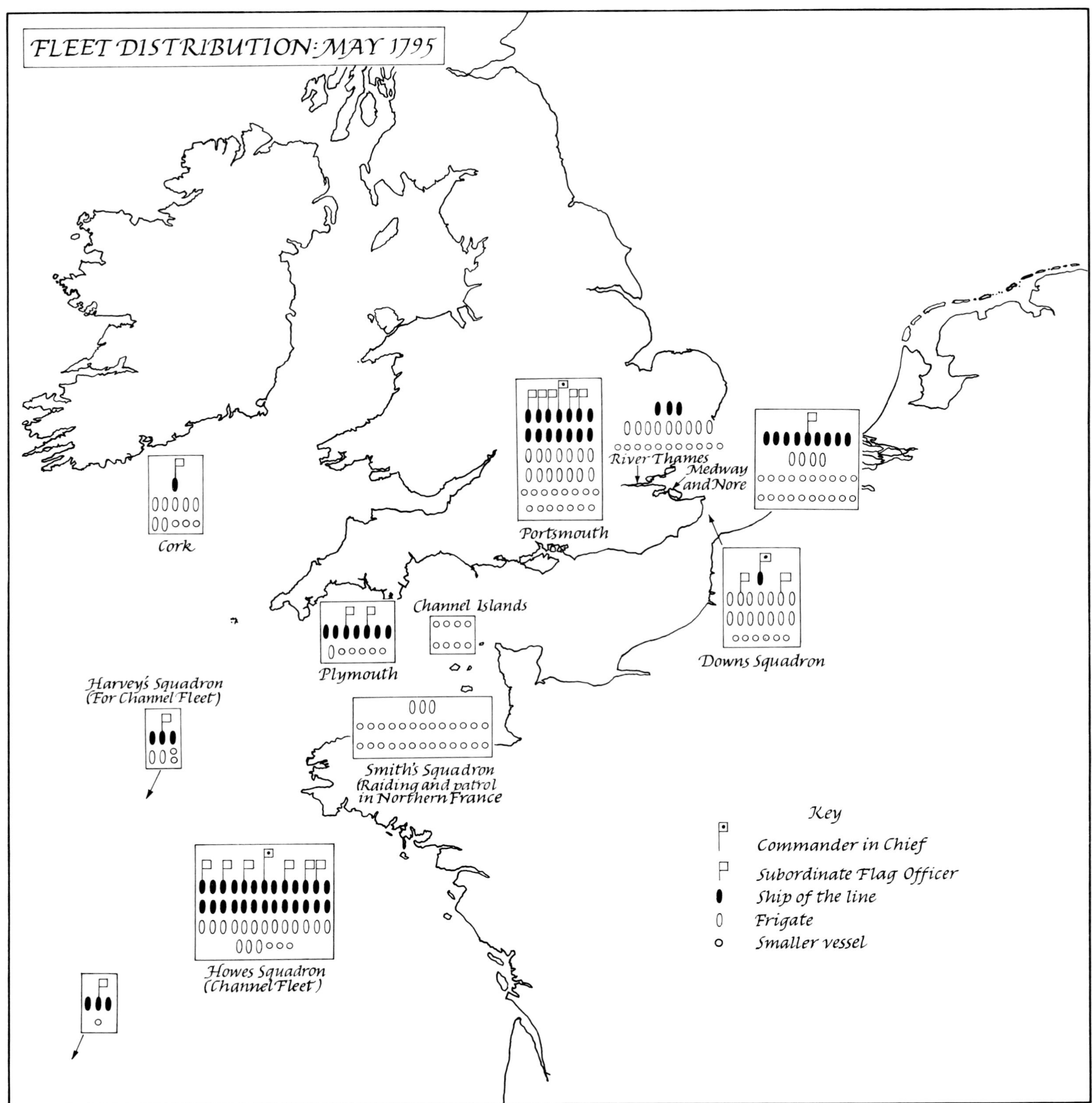

gun brigs, two cutters, a schooner and two luggers.[16] It was a squadron for a special service, rather than a geographical fleet; it won the Battle of Copenhagen in April of that year.

The next intervention came in 1807, when Admiral Gambier was sent with a fleet of seventeen ships-of-the-line, to demand the surrender of the Danish fleet. This was refused, Copenhagen was bombarded, and the fleet taken. The permanent Baltic fleet was formed in the following year, under Sir James Saumarez, in reaction to the Continental System and the hostility of Denmark and other powers. By 1812, it has a strength of thirty-nine ships — including ten of the line, six frigates, and fourteen sloops. The commander-in-chief was involved in complicated diplomacy with the various governments, in an area where Britain had no base of her own. He organised enormous convoys of merchant ships, largely carrying naval stores for British warships and merchant vessels. He masterminded a system of deception intended to evade the Continental System among powers, such as Sweden, which were not ready to enter open conflict with the French. Throughout most of this period, Saumarez had his headquarters aboard the *Victory*, moored in Wingco Sound, off the Swedish western coast, protecting the entrance to the Baltic. The

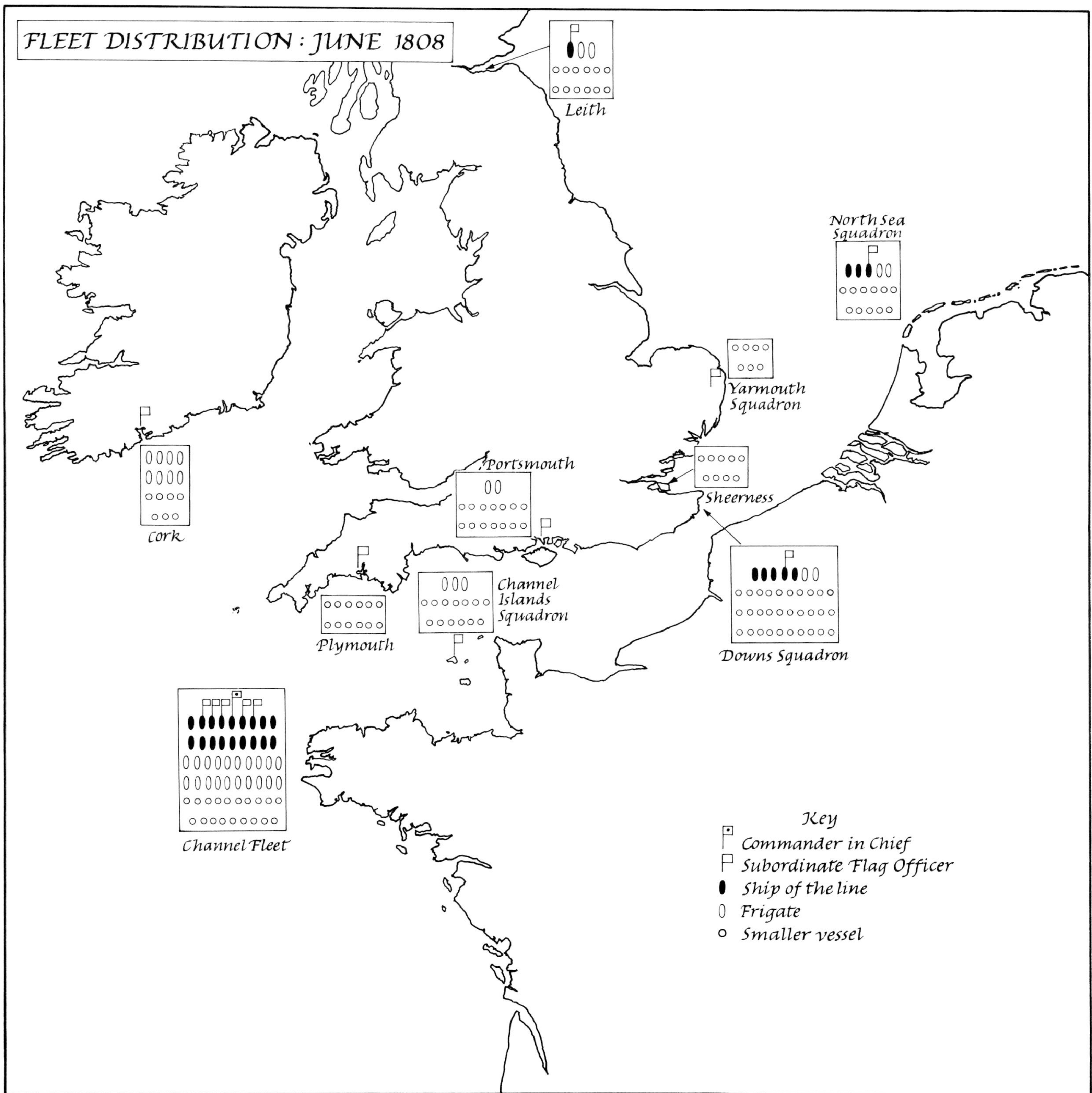

fleet was withdrawn in the winter of each year, and returned in the spring.

The Mediterranean Fleet

The Mediterranean fleet was one of the most important commands in the navy, overshadowed only by the Channel fleet. It was always headed by a senior and well-tried admiral —Hood from 1793 to 1794, during which period Toulon was captured and abandoned; Admiral Hotham to 1795, followed by St Vincent to the middle of 1799. During this period, the Battle of St Vincent was fought, the Mediterranean abandoned for a time, and re-entered by St Vincent's subordinate, Nelson, in a campaign which led to the battle of the Nile in 1798. Late in 1799, St Vincent resigned the command, and Lord Keith took over till the subsequent peace. Nelson took command in May 1803, and after his death at Trafalgar he was succeeded by Collingwood who died in March 1810, and was succeeded by Sir Charles Cotton. Pellew had the command from 1811 to 1814.

Clearly, the Mediterranean command was a very gruelling one. The fleet fought three of the six major battles of 1793 to 1815; Nelson died in action, where Collingwood died of natural causes, and St Vincent was worn out by his experiences. Though the Mediterranean is a clearly defined geographical area, the ships of the command often found themselves some way outside it. The limits of the station extended as far as Cape St Vincent, but under Nelson the fleet found itself going even further from base, chasing the French fleet across the Atlantic to the West Indies and back. The priority was to blockade or destroy the French Mediterranean fleet from Toulon, and the Spanish fleet at Cadiz. However, the commander-in-chief could find himself involved in much wider activities; negotiating with the small states of Italy, finding escorts for convoys for British trade in the region, corresponding with the British diplomats in the area, gathering intelligence, and supporting friendly forces in the Mediterranean, especially after the beginning of the Spanish revolt in 1808.

The Mediterranean fleet always had plenty of subordinate flag officers. In 1801, it was commanded by a full admiral (Keith), supported by a vice admiral and two rear admirals. In 1814, it was commanded by Vice Admiral Sir Edward Pellew, supported by two more vice admirals and six rear admirals.[17] The Mediterranean fleet had thirty-one ships in 1795, including five three-deckers, eleven third rates, and eleven fifth and sixth rates.[18] In 1797, it was the biggest single command, with sixty-two ships — twenty-three of the line, twenty-four frigates and ten sloops.[19] In 1812, it was even stronger, with ninety ships — twenty-nine of the line, the same number of frigates, and twenty-six sloops.[21]

The West Indies

The West Indies never became quite so important as it had been in the later stages of the American War of Independence, when the main bodies of the French and British fleets had fought the Battle of The Saintes there. The Caribbean was divided into separate commands, one for Jamaica and one for the Leeward Islands. Jamaica had a good harbour at Port Royal, and because of the prevailing winds was well situated for an attack on the Spanish mainland colonies from Venezuela to Mexico. Such schemes had little priority between 1793 and 1815, so the Jamaica station concentrated on convoy escort and on defeating privateers and pirates in the western Caribbean. At the beginning of war in 1793, the Jamaica squadron was a typical peacetime colonial force. It was headed by Commodore John Ford, with his flag in a 50-gun ship. He also had three 32-gun frigates, four sloops and a schooner.[22] In 1795, there were nineteen ships on the station, including three ships-of-the-line, two fourth rates, six fifths, a sixth and three schooners.[23] In 1797, it had thirty-one ships, including seven of the line, fifteen frigates and seven sloops.[24] In 1805, it rose to fifty-one ships, including three of the line, fourteen frigates and twenty-four sloops.[25] In 1812, when Britain was in alliance with Spain, it had only nineteen ships, including one of the line and eight frigates. [26]

In the early stages of the war, the Leeward Islands squadron was commanded by Rear Admiral Gardner, with nine ships-of-the-line and fourteen smaller ships and vessels.[27] In 1794, St Vincent (or Sir John Jervis, as he was then) arrived with three more ships-of-the-line and seven other vessels, as well as a large convoy of troops. Jervis became commander-in-chief, and began a campaign which resulted in the capture of various French possessions in the area.

The Leeward Islands squadron had twenty-six ships in 1795, comprising eight third rates, ten frigates, six sloops, a schooner, hospital ship and store ship. In 1797, it had forty-four, with nine of the line, sixteen frigates and eleven sloops. After 1797, the fleet was progressively reduced, as most of the important enemy possessions were captured. By 1801, it had fallen to twenty-six ships and vessels, including one of the line, nine frigates and seven sloops and post ships.[28] Many of the captures were restored at the Peace of Amiens, and by 1805, the fleet had built up again to a total of forty-one, including six of the line, thirteen frigates and the same number of sloops.[29] By the end of 1810, the French, Spanish and Dutch islands had again been occupied, and by 1812, the fleet had again been reduced, to a total of twenty-seven, including one of the line, five frigates and thirteen sloops.[30] The main British bases in the area were at Antigua and Barbados, but when the islands of Martinique, St Lucia and others were in British possession they also provided useful anchorages.

North America

Since the loss of the American colonies, two squadrons had been kept off the American coast, based at Halifax (Nova Scotia) and Newfoundland. Both areas were regarded as backwaters, and their commanders-in-chief combined their naval duties with the governorships of their respective colonies. In 1792, the Halifax station had only four ships and vessels, none larger than 32 guns, and in 1793 the Newfoundland squadron had one 64-gun ship, three frigates and five sloops.[31] It never became very large, for it had a total of five ships in 1797, seven ships in 1799, thirteen in 1805, twelve in 1812. The Halifax (or North American) squadron had ten ships, including three third rates, in 1795; and thirteen ships, including two third rates, in 1800. In 1805, it was rather smaller, with only eight ships, none larger than frigates. However, the American War of 1812 brought the station into some prominence. By July 1812, it had twenty-five ships, including one of the line, eight frigates and seven sloops. By the middle of 1813 the North American station had sixty ships, including eleven third rates, sixteen fifth rates and twenty-five sloops.[32]

East Indies and the Cape

There was constant land and naval warfare in the East Indies, based on the subcontinent of India, and on the raiding and protection of convoys on their way back to Europe. Britain had the ascendancy in these battles, and Wellington extended British rule in India, while the East India squadron protected her trade. However, the French fought back, especially with Admiral Linois's cruise to the Indian Ocean in 1804. The East India Squadron had only four frigates and three sloops in 1792. By the middle of the following year it had expanded to thirteen ships, including five third rates, under George Elphinstone, later Lord Keith. It expanded even more in the next two years, and by 1797, it had thirty-two ships, including ten of the line, seventeen frigates and four sloops. It declined in the later stages of the French Revolutionary War, with seventeen ships under Admiral Rainier in 1799, and twenty-three, including seven of the line, at the end of the war. In 1805, there were twenty-nine ships, including eight of the line; and in 1812 there were twenty-four, including one of the line.

Fleets for Special Services

Fleets and squadrons intended for special tasks — the invasion of an enemy colony, or the interception of a fleet or convoy — were usually named after the commander; for example, Sir William Smith's squadron was a force of twenty-nine ships, including frigates, sloops, and eighteen gunboats, intended to raid French shipping off Brittany and Normandy in 1795. This force succeeded in taking the island of St Marcou. Sir Richard Strachan's squadron, formed in 1797, had nine ships, including four frigates. Popham's squadron took the Cape of Good Hope in 1806, and then took part in an abortive expedition to South America. Such squadrons were often commanded by a senior captain, or by a commodore or junior rear admiral.

Even in official records, the main geographical fleets were also known by the names of their commanders in some cases — the Channel fleet as Lord Howe's squadron, and the North Sea fleet as

Duncan's squadron. In other cases, small squadrons were formed and sent out as a unit to reinforce the main fleets — for example Harvey's squadron was formed of a second rate, two third rates and three smaller ships, and sent out as a group to join the Channel fleet in 1795. In the same year, Blankett's squadron (three third rates and a sloop) was formed to join Elphinstone at the Cape.[33]

Ships under Admiralty Orders

Some ships were not under the command of an admiral at all, but sailed directly under the orders of the Admiralty. This was a considerable advantage to the captain, who would then get a larger share of any prize money won, as there was no flag officer in command. Such ships might be convoy escorts (though these were often provided by the main fleets as well) or they might be ships on a 'cruise' — sent out to raid enemy commerce, with the prospects of large sums in prize money.

Port Admirals

Port admirals were appointed for all the main bases — Portsmouth, Plymouth, Deptford and Woolwich, Chatham, the Downs, and the Nore and Sheerness. A port admiral was responsible for 'the speedy and perfect equipment of all ships, and for the punctual execution of all duties at the port where he commands'. He was in charge of all ships in commission in the harbour, and at the anchorages outside, 'except those which, not being in harbour, shall be under the orders of a senior flag officer who is present'.[34] He supervised the fitting out of ships, and the distribution of men from receiving ships, and from ships going out of commission, onto those getting ready for sea. He could order men to be lent from one ship to another to help in refitting, or to make up her crew. In wartime, he was also 'to keep a sufficient number of frigates and small vessels under his command cruising in proper situations to prevent any ships of war, privateers, or other vessels of the enemy, from approaching the port without being discovered.[35] He had no responsibility for the dockyard or any of the other shore facilities of the base, which were under the charge of the civil officers. Therefore, relations with his colleagues were sometimes strained, and a good port admiral needed some of the characteristics of a diplomat. It was a post usually occupied by older men, of no great fighting distinction. By 1814, most ports had a vice admiral in charge, with a rear admiral as subordinate.

2 Fleet Administration

Powers of the Commander-in-Chief

The commander-in-chief of a fleet took his orders direct from the Admiralty. He might hold any rank from commodore to admiral-of-the-fleet, but usually he was at the higher end of the scale. His power tended to rise the further his command was from London, for of course it might take months to receive instructions in the Mediterranean or Indian Ocean. This gave him a great deal of initiative in dealing with hostile or neutral powers, and considerable responsibility in keeping his command well maintained and disciplined, and his men well fed. A major command might have up to sixty ships, and several thousand officers and men. It might operate in a largely hostile environment, such as the Baltic. The commander could find himself faced with very difficult decisions about the movements of the enemy, as Nelson did in 1805. Probably, there is no-one in the modern world who can appreciate the burden on such a commander, isolated from his superiors and often faced with an awesome dilemma. It is not surprising that occasional admirals such as Calder and Gambier fell by the wayside and lost popular esteem; it is much more surprising that so many commanders — including St Vincent, Keith, Saumarez, Cornwallis, Collingwood and of course Nelson — could bear such a strain over the years and, eventually, defeat the enemy.

Admiral's Instructions

The instructions to commanders-in-chief do not appear to have been issued on the appointment of a new officer to the post. In 1818, for example, it was noted that no new set of instructions had been issued since Lord Keith had been appointed to the command of the Mediterranean fleet in 1799. Instead, the old admiral was ordered to pass on any standing or unexecuted orders to the new one. The orders which governed the conduct of the fleet were not reviewed regularly, but were often largely a matter of tradition.

Judging by Keith's orders of 1799, the admiral was given little guidance about his strategic duties, though these were sometimes outlined in individual letters from the Admiralty. Keith's instructions had fifteen clauses. He was

to correspond with the governors of Gibraltar and Minorca, and all British consuls in the Mediterranean;
to give every assistance to the governor of Gibraltar;
to appoint such of His Majesty's ships and vessels under your command to convoy the homeward bound trade, as are the least fit to remain abroad, as you shall judge sufficient for their protection;
to detain and keep under his command any ships sent out to him, except storeships, which were to be sent back when unloaded;
to send surgeon's mates to help in Gibraltar hospital if needed;
to have his ships apply for provisions at Gibraltar;
to notify the Admiralty of any stores and provisions lacking;
if purchasing any ships and vessels, to get Admiralty permission, and to have them surveyed by the commissioners at Gibraltar;
to conform to the established rules and customs of the navy;
not to appoint any victualling officers on shore, but to apply to the Admiralty for permission;
to visit ships and muster men, and see that they were rated properly, and to look to the cleanliness and economy of ships under his command;
to have his ships refitted at Gibraltar and Minorca;
to order his captains to take good care of rigging, stores and so on;
not to allow his ships to come home except in cases of necessity;
and to keep a journal, and send regular reports to the Admiralty.[2]

Subordinate Admirals

A commander-in-chief might have up to six junior admirals under his command, or he might appoint senior captains to lead squadrons, especially of frigates. If the fleet was kept together as a body, the subordinate admirals would head divisions and squadrons of it, and take responsibility for supervising such ships. Each would lead his division in action, and be responsible for seeing that his ships performed according to the orders of the commander-in-chief. One of the admirals would be expected to take over on the death of the commander-in-chief in battle, though the orders were still to be given from the fleet flagship until the battle was over, and the second-in-command was merely to be informed privately of the death of his superior.

A subordinate flag officer might also find himself leading a detached squadron on a mission of considerable responsibility. Thus in 1798, Nelson was detached from St Vincent's fleet; he took his squadron into the Mediterranean to seek out the French fleet, resulting in the Battle of the Nile. He was still a subordinate flag officer, second in command to Sir Hyde Parker, at Copenhagen in 1801 — which is why he found it necessary to put his telescope to his blind eye to ignore Parker's recall signal.

The Flagship

When appointed to a command, the admiral's orders usually specified which ship he was to use as a flagship, though it is not unlikely that he had already told the Admiralty which one he preferred. The ship, usually a three-decker, was fitted out as such, with extra cabins for the Admiral and his staff. The admiral lived aft on the upper deck, below the captain on the quarterdeck and above the wardroom officers on the middle deck. He was allowed about twice as much space as the captain, with a large 'admiral's apartment' opening onto the quarter galleries and the stern gallery, a 'state room' or sleeping cabin on one side and a general-purpose room on the other; and a

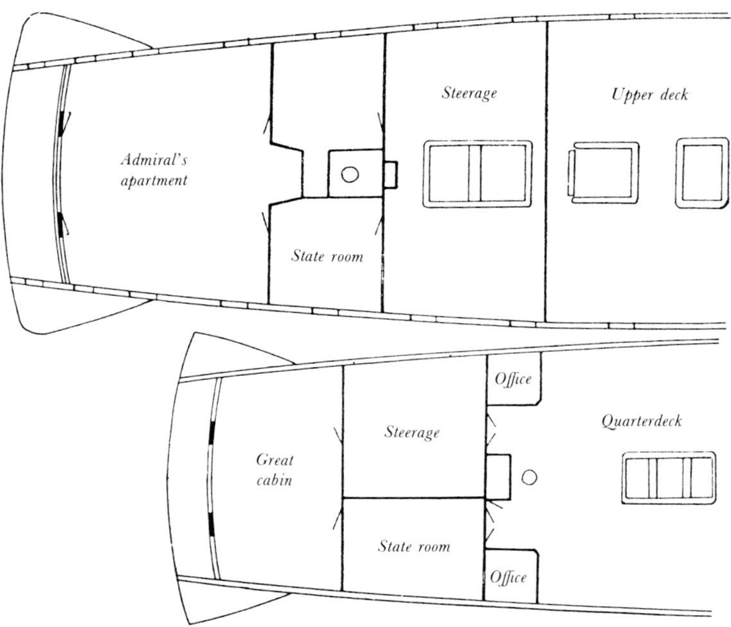

The admiral's apartments aboard a 100-gun ship, 1784, compared with the captain's quarters, below. Public Record Office

large area known as the 'steerage' forward of the mast. He would provide his own furniture for the cabin, and some officers seem to have had quite luxurious tastes.

It is not clear where the officers of his staff lived; possibly they had cabins in the wardroom, but it seems more likely that they had light cabins built on the upper deck, similar to those in the wardroom. Possibly, the steerage was used as the admiral's office, or perhaps small cabins were used by the secretaries and clerks, on the model of that for the captain's clerk on the quarterdeck.

The Admiral's Allowances

The basic pay of a full admiral was £3.1.0, per day, while that of a rear admiral was £1.15.0, and these figures remained constant throughout the wars. In addition, an admiral or commodore commanding in chief was allowed 'table money'. In theory, this was to cover expenses in 'keeping a table', or feeding official guests on board ship. This was paid at the rate of £1.10.0 per day. From 1795, compensation was paid for the loss of servants, from £56 per annum for an admiral of the fleet, to £15.10.0 for a rear admiral, commodore or captain-of-the-fleet.[3] Commanders-in-chief were also given money to pay the expenses of the stationery used in running their commands — £47 per annum for the North Sea, increased to £70 in 1806; £35 for the Mediterranean, rising to £60; and £25 for the Halifax station, rising to £30.[4]

Captain-of-the-Fleet

Since 1747, a first captain had been allowed to each squadron of twenty ships or more. In 1795, one was allowed a fleet of fifteen or more, and in 1805, this was further reduced to ten ships 'when the Lords of the Admiralty see the occasion.'[5] The title was slightly ambigious, as the captain-of-the-fleet often held the rank of rear admiral, or, if he did not, he ranked ahead of all the other captains, and had the pay and privileges of a rear admiral. He was the chief-of-staff to the commander-in-chief, and acted as his main adviser. He could issue orders in his name: 'All orders and instructions issued by the captain-of-the-fleet are to be given as the orders and co of the commander-in-chief, and they are to be obeyed by all persons to whom they are addressed, as well as by those who are senior to, or of higher rank than, the captain-of-the-fleet, as by others.'[6] He was to assist the commander-in-chief 'in regulating the details of the fleet, in making the necessary distribution of men, stores, provisions, and in such other duties as he shall think fit to direct.'[7] Sir Thomas Byam Martin took over the job temporarily under Saumarez in 1808, and wrote 'I have been here about a week in the capacity of captain-of-the-fleet, having left the *Implacable* to engage in a much more arduous duty than I expected.'[8] As captain-of-the-fleet under St Vincent, Sir Robert Calder soon lost the trust of his admiral. 'I hope Sir Robert Calder will have more confidence than when he served with me; his dread of approaching the shore was at that time truly ridiculous, and I was under the necessity of instructing the master not to pay the smallest regard to his influence.'[3]

The Flag Captain

In contrast to the captain-of-the-fleet, the flag captain was a relatively junior captain, and often had command of a larger ship than his seniority would normally have entitled him to. Captain Hardy had only seven years in the rank at Trafalgar, and this would normally have entitled him to command a small ship-of-the-line or a large frigate. He was responsible mainly for the running of the flagship, though he might on occasion give advice to the admiral. The regulations allowed the flag captain to a full admiral the pay of the captain of a first rate, no matter what size of ship he commanded. The flag captain to a vice admiral was allowed the pay of a second rate, and the flag captain to a rear admiral, a third rate — unless the ship he commanded was larger than the one stipulated, when he was given the appropriate pay for the ship.[10]

The Flag Lieutenant

The flag lieutenant was essentially the signal officer aboard the flagship. There were no specific rules governing the appointment, and custom seems to have varied somewhat. He might be a protégé of the admiral; in 1812, Sir Thomas Byam Martin wrote, 'It would give me much pleasure, if I should ever be employed, to have Mr Smith as flag or first lieutenant, whichever he may prefer, and if he should think such a situation better than the one he at present holds.'[11] Sometimes, a flag lieutenant could follow an admiral from ship to ship, as Thomas Mansell followed Saumarez from the *Diomede* into the *Hibernia* and then to the *Victory*.[12] However, Nelson treated the post differently. It was his custom 'to make the officer first on

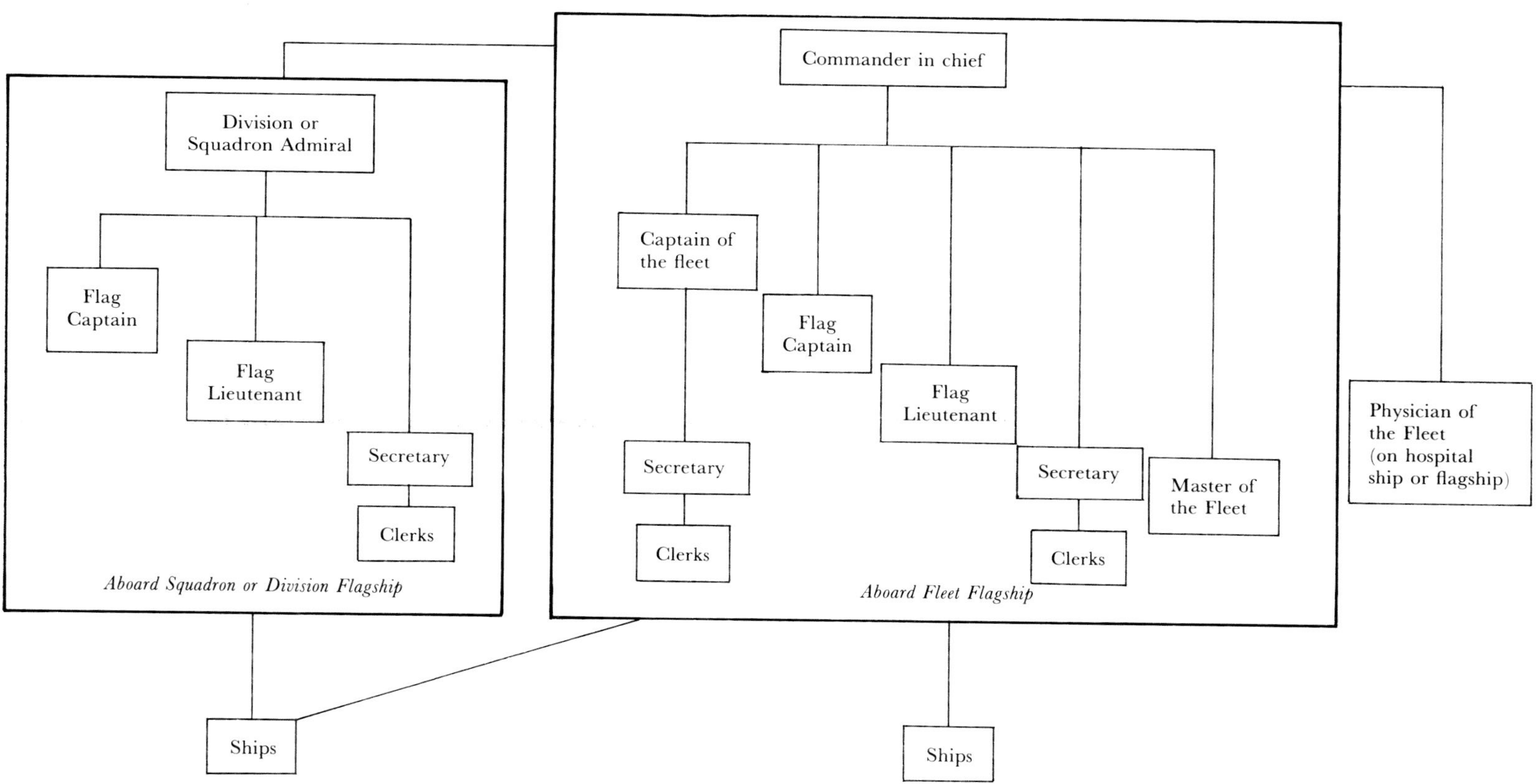

Fleet organisation.

the list for promotion [ie, on the flagship] do the duty of signal officer, and the junior that of first lieutenant'.[13] Richard Pasco, his flag lieutenant at Trafalgar, was unhappy about this, and intended 'to have represented to him that he considered himself unfortunate to be doing duty in an inferior situation instead of that to which his seniority entitled him'.[14] His fears were justified, and his promotion was delayed because of this. However, most flag lieutenants eventually reached high rank, largely because of the admiral's patronage.

The Admiral's Secretary

The correspondence connected with the command of a major fleet was quite extensive. On a rather busy day in June 1807, the commander of the Mediterranean fleet, Lord Collingwood, issued the following letters:

> To the Foreign Secretary relating to the Barbary States. To the Secretary of the Admiralty on the same subject, acknowledging receipt and in reply to their lordships secret order of 2nd June with intelligence received from the *Bittern* from Sicily and Egypt, on the general services of the state. To the ambassador at Lisbon, relating to the violence committed by the Gibraltar privateers at Villa Real, and to forward my dipatches and co. To the governor of Gibraltar on the subject of the complaint made by the Spanish general Castanos. To the several public officers at Gibraltar on their department, and to the senior officer to hasten ships out.[15]

As well as letters dealing with both ends of the Mediterranean, he had to issue orders to individual ships and standing orders to the fleet; he had to supervise the accounts of the standing officers of the various ships, and keep a journal of the fleet's movements. If he had the power to promote officers, the work was even greater. In three months of 1793, Lord Hood issued 138 commissions; for example when one of the senior lieutenants of the flagship was promoted, each of the junior ones needed a new commission moving him one place up. There was a great deal of paperwork involved in running a fleet, and most of it was the responsibility of the flag officer's secretary.

An admiral's secretary was definitely a protégé of the admiral, and tended to follow him throughout his career. St Vincent's secretary, Benjamin Tucker, even followed him to the Admiralty and became second secretary there. An admiral's secretary usually started his career as a purser, though in 1804, it was ordered that pursers of ships in commission were not to serve simultaneously as secretaries.[16] Secretaries complained in the same year of 'the inadequacy of their salaries to the laborious and important services required of them'. Each was assisted by a clerk, who was paid only at the rate of an able seaman, and 'they are consequently maintained at the expense of the said secretaries'. The Admiralty agreed to pay the secretary to the admiral-of-the-fleet £450, while those to commanders-in-chief were allowed £400 or £300, and those to other admirals, £150. Clerks were given £50 per annum.[17]

The Admiral's Retinue

Until 1795, a flag officer had an enormous number of servants — and admiral-of-the-fleet was allowed fifty, a vice admiral twenty, and a rear admiral fifteen. Only a small number of these — sixteen for the admiral-of-the-fleet and ten for vice and rear admirals — were actually 'borne on the ship's books as servants'. The admiral could pocket the wages of the rest if he wished. From 1795, admirals were given compensation for the loss of most of their servants, and each was allowed a retinue on a fixed scale — twelve men for commanders-in-chief, down to five for rear admirals not commanding in chief. This figure included the flag lieutenant, the secretary and his clerk, so that aboard the *Victory* in 1808, bearing Saumarez's flag as commander-in-chief, there were eight servants in the commander-in-chief's retinue. In addition, the captain-of-the-fleet was aboard with his own retinue — a secretary, clerk and three servants. Including the admiral and the captain of the fleet, eighteen officers and men were borne as 'supernumeraries for wages and victuals' aboard the flagship.[18]

William Mark describes the work of an admiral's clerk in the

Nelson's cabin aboard the Victory. Author's photograph

1800s. 'Despatches arrived, copies were to be made to be sent home, others came and others went, and thus we not only worked all day, but often all night... I had many kind visits in my office. The captains and other officers had business there about surveys, states and conditions, promotions & co.'[19]

The Physician-of-the-Fleet

Though he was not formally part of the admiral's staff, the physician often acted as chief medical adviser. Thomas Trotter, for example, had such a relationship with Howe. 'When consulted by the admiral on the propriety of taking the *Valiant* to sea, I gave it as my opinion that in the present declining state of the contagion she was fit for service.'[20] He argued against the charge of 15s for a man cured of venereal disease, and 'His lordship though the subject of sufficient importance to engage the attention of the Lords Commissioners of the Admiralty and laid it before them.'[21] The physician-of-the-fleet was based in the squadron's hospital ship, if there was one. Otherwise, he was 'to be on board such ship as the commander-in-chief shall direct'. He was to 'visit the ships of the squadron frequently and enquire into the health of the ships' companies and the treatment of the sick'.[22] Compared with surgeons, physicians were much rarer at sea, and had higher status. A surgeon was trained by apprenticeship, but a physician had a medical degree. In the early 1790s there were only four such men in the fleet. Physicians who had considerable influence on the development of naval medicine included Blane, Gillespie and Trotter. In 1814, there were only two physicians-of-the-fleet in service; Dr William Beatty with the Channel fleet, and Dr Alex Denmark with the Mediterranean fleet.

Other Warrant Officers

Obviously, the master of a fleet flagship would have considerable responsibilities, in that he would navigate for the whole fleet rather than just his own ship. This was partly recognised by an order of 1805, which created the office of 'first master'.

> The commanders-in-chief of His Majesty's fleets who are allowed a first captain [ie, captain-of-the-fleet] are in future to be respectively allowed an additional master to be borne on the books of the ships on board which their flags may be flying, to be called the First Master, whose duty will be to attend to the navigation of the fleet... And the person so appointed First Master to a commander-in-chief must be qualified for, and will be allowed the pay of a ship of the first rate.[23]

The other heads of department aboard ship were not represented on the admiral's staff. The secretary was probably an ex-purser, so he would perhaps be able to help supervise the victualling of the fleet, if he had the time. There was no 'carpenter of the fleet', or 'gunner of the fleet', but occasionally the warrant officers of the flagships could be put in charge of their counterparts on other ships. In 1796, for example, St Vincent ordered each ship to send 'a complete, steady sober shipwright' to go ashore during the fleet's stay in Gibraltar, and their names were to be given to the carpenter of the *Victory*, who would presumably supervise them.[24]

Responsibility for Other Ships

Every admiral had responsibility for ships under his command, and this included inspecting them, and supervising their administration. Keith's orders of 1799 demanded that he visit his ships, muster their men, see that they were properly rated according to their abilities, and look into the cleanliness, order and economy of the ships. This was reinforced by the 1806 and 1808 editions of the Admiralty Instructions.

> He is to direct commanders of squadrons and divisions to muster frequently the crews of the ships under their orders, to enquire into the qualities of the men and their fitness of the stations in which they are rated... The degree of attention paid to cleanliness, and other means of preserving the health of the crew... And when other duties of the fleet will admit of it, the commander-in-chief is to visit the ships, and enquire into these things himself.[25]

Some commanders did not pay much attention to what went on in the ships under their command, and log books and journals show very few instances of admirals actually visiting their ships. However, many admirals gave regular attention to the running of their ships. St Vincent constantly issued orders on the discipline of his ships, and sometimes enforced them quite ruthlessly. In 1796, for example, he demanded, 'that the strictest attention by paid by the surgeons of the squadron to the sick on board their respective ships'.[26] Two years later he issued a general order 'to apprise the warrant and petty officers of HMS *Marlborough*, that they will lose the high ground they stand on with him, if they do not exert themselves with vigilance and activity to prevent drunkenness among the people'.[27] Sometimes he would punish all the officers of a ship for its 'disorderly state', by forbidding them to go on shore.[28] Lord Keith was much less of a martinet, but he did issue orders to his squadron on washing of decks, the powdering of hair and many other matters.[29] In a rather different vein, Nelson's mistress could sometimes moderate discipline aboard his flagship. 'The men, when threatened with punishment for misconduct, applied to Lady Hamilton, and her kindness of disposition, and Lord Nelson's known aversion to flogging, generally rendered the appeal successful.'[30]

Relations with Shore Bases

Commanders-in-chief at home had no authority in the dockyards within their station, but abroad they had 'command over the dockyards, and all other officers employed in the naval service', provided there was no commissioner of the navy within the limits of the station. 'When there is no commissioner resident, he may suspend from his employment any officer, in any department, whose misconduct shall make it necessary for him to do so, and he may appoint another to act in his stead until the pleasure of the Lords Commissioners of the Admiralty shall be known.'[31] Some new yards, such as Ajaccio, were initially founded by the commander-in-chief appointing a storekeeper. However, by about 1810, most overseas yards of any size had a resident commissioner, and the power of the commander-in-chief was much reduced.

3 Fleet Tactics

Fleet Battles

The Royal Navy fought only six decisive fleet battles in twenty years of warfare between 1793 and 1815, and none after 1805. Yet fleet battle was the ultimate aim of every ship-of-the-line, and it was the most important decider of naval warfare. Not only did ships have to be trained in gunnery to be ready for fight; whole fleets had to be exercised in complex manoeuvres under sail, to be ready for the day, if it ever came, when the enemy fleet was engaged.

Four major enemy fleets were defeated in these years; the French at the Glorious First of June, the Nile and Trafalgar; the Spanish at St Vincent and Trafalgar; the Dutch at Camperdown and the Danes at Copenhagen. All these battles resulted in British victories, more or less crushing. Only the French would remain as a major naval power in the nineteenth century; the Danes, Spanish and Dutch never recovered from their losses.

It is significant that nearly all naval battles were named after adjacent points of land, because, apart from the First of June, they were all fought inshore. At the Nile and Copenhagen, indeed, the enemy fleets were actually at anchor, within positions they mistakenly regarded as secure. Battles could only be decisive if the enemy's retreat was in some way cut off. The exception, the First of June 1794, occurred because the French fleet had to protect an important grain convoy.

British fleet tactics developed over the years, and each battle was more decisive than the last, and was fought against greater odds. At the First of June, the British fleet had twenty-five ships-of-the-line, and the French had one more. Six French ships were captured, and one sunk. At Trafalgar eleven years later, the combined Franco-Spanish fleet had a superiority of thirty-three to twenty-seven; fifteen enemy ships were captured on the day, and six more within the next two weeks. Nelson's greatest achievement was to break completely with the rigid, formal tactics which had dominated British naval thinking over the last century, and develop highly aggressive techniques of his own. He was not the first of the tactical innovators of the eighteenth century, but he carried the process to its logical conclusion.

The Broadside and the Line of Battle

A ship is naturally long and relatively narrow, and if it is to carry a large number of weapons, most of these have to fire from the sides rather than forward and aft. A sailing ship of war was, therefore, not able to fire on the enemy and advance on him at the same time. The bows and sterns of ships-of-the-line had few if any guns, and the sterns were very weakly constructed. It was natural that ships should fight in a single line, so that nearly half their guns could be brought to bear in a single direction, and they would not mask one another. It was equally natural that the line of battle became essentially a defensive formation. If the enemy had plenty of sea room and declined to fight against such a fleet, there was very little that could be done about it. If two fleets did engage, and neither abandoned the line of battle, it was unlikely that the fight would be decisive.

All this was essentially known by the beginning of the eighteenth century, and battle tactics became totally rigid. British admirals were expected to follow fighting instructions drawn up around 1690, and any officer who neglected to form line of battle, like Admiral Mathews off Toulon in 1744, was likely to find himself before a court-martial. Individual initiative was debarred by Article 20 of the permanent instructions, which stated, 'None of the ships of the fleet shall pursue any small number of enemy's ships till the main body be disabled or run.'[1]

There was a strong connection between battle tactics and signalling. While signal codes were primitive and simple, the number of orders which could be given was limited — the permanent instructions of 1703 had only thirty-three articles, though more articles (up to twenty-nine in some cases) could be added by individual admirals.[2] Signals became far more sophisticated in the last quarter of the eighteenth century, and this aided the development of tactics, though it is not the whole story. Just as much depended on the attitude of the commander — how much he was prepared to trust his subordinate captains — and on the growing tactical superiority of the British fleet over its enemies.

The Weather Gage

British tactics were always more aggressive than those of the French, even in their most conservative days. The Royal Navy always entered battle with the aim of destroying the enemy fleet, while the French looked for ways to escape with their ships undamaged and ready for the next task. As a result, the British invariably favoured the weather gage, while the French generally preferred the lee gage.

The weather gage was defined as 'the situation of one ship to windward of another, when in action & co'.[3] It had several immediate advantages. The smoke of battle soon cleared from that side and blew onto the enemy; fireships could only be used by ships holding the weather gage, though this was perhaps no longer relevant. More important was the principal disadvantage of the lee-gage. 'It cannot decide the time and distance of the action, which may commence before it is sufficiently formed.'[4]

However, the arguments were not all in favour of the weather gage. Ships heeled in the wind, and this could make it difficult for ships with the weather gage to open their lower deck ports in rough weather. The heel also tended to expose the men on their decks to enemy musket shot. Most important of all, the ships of the lee line could retreat easily, either as individual damaged vessels, or as a defeated fleet. This option was not open to the weather line, which could not escape without fighting its way through the enemy fleet. The weather gage was preferred by the more aggressive fleet, the lee gage by the defensive; hence the Royal Navy always found itself with the weather gage in all the major battles of the French Revolutionary and Napoleonic Wars.

Theories of Naval Warfare

As a rule, British admirals were not greatly interested in the theoretical study of naval tactics, and at first the ideas tended to come from France. The best-known early treatise had been produced by Paul Hoste in 1697. The author was a Jesuit who had served as a chaplain with the leading French admirals of the day, and his book *L'Art des Armes Navales*, outlined some quite daring tactical ideas, such as 'doubling' and 'breaking the line', which were further developed in the late eighteenth century. As a result, Hoste's work was published several times in English from 1750 onwards. It was extensively quoted by many authors, down to Ekins in 1824.[5]

The most influential British writer was John Clerk of Eldin. He was a Scottish merchant who studied naval tactics as an amateur, without ever going to sea. His work, *Essay on Naval Tactics* was first printed privately in 1782, and published eight years later. He argued strongly in favour of breaking the enemy line, and caused Adam Smith to remark 'The only thing which tempts me to entertain a doubt with respect to your system is, that the beneficial effects are so manifest, that one wonders they should not have occurred to professional men'.[6] This remark caused considerable resentment among naval officers. Nevertheless, Clerk had a great deal of influence at sea. It was believed by many that Rodney's successful tactics at the Battle of the Saintes in 1782 was a direct result of his theories,

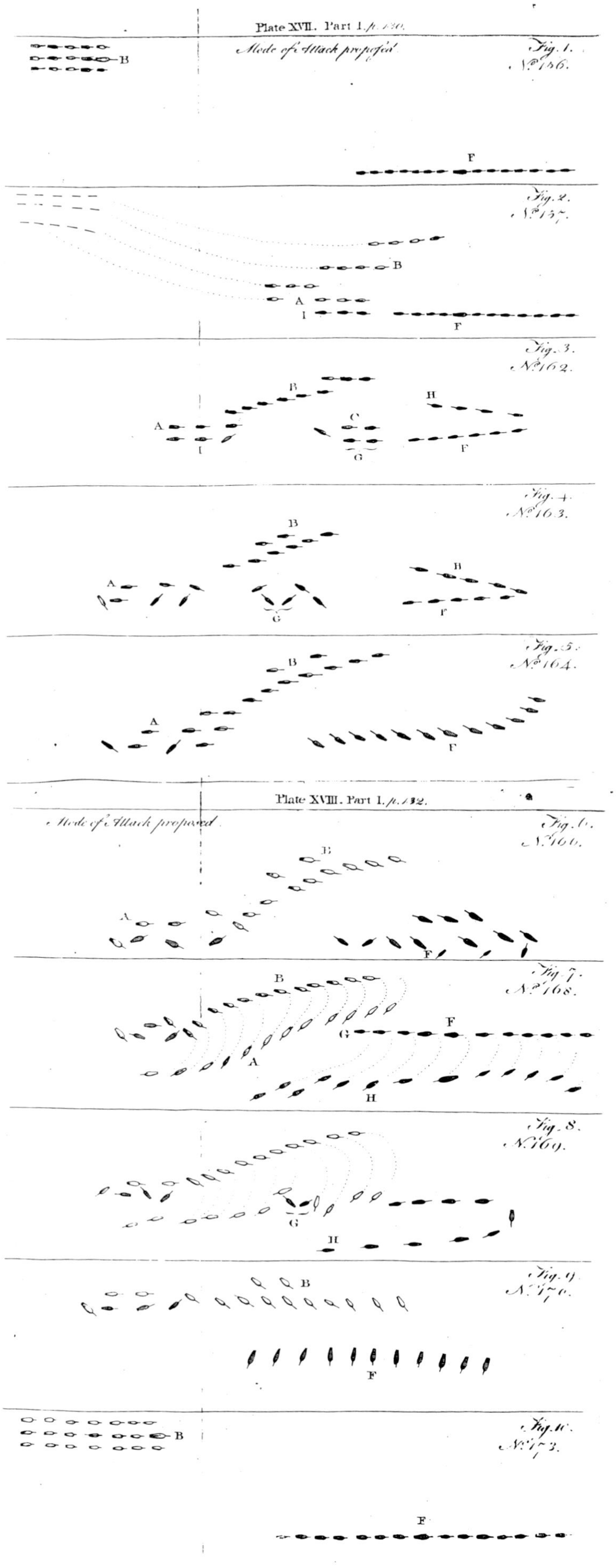

◁ *Theoretical naval tactics, from Clerk of Eldin. Top, breaking the line; bottom, concentration of force.*

and, certainly, some later sets of fighting instructions, such as those issued by Admiral Cochrane, in command at the Leeward Islands from 1805 to 1814, show strong signs of being copied from him.[7] The exact effects of his writing was controversial at the time, and remain so; but certainly he provided some theoretical basis on which the practical admirals could act.

The Decline of the Permanent Instructions

By the 1740s, some commanders were already beginning to write 'additional instruction' to the standing instructions. These tended to allow for more aggressive tactics in certain situations; for example, when the enemy fleet was retreating, or of inferior strength. 'In case of meeting any squadron of the enemy's ships whose numbers may be less than those of the squadron of His Majesty's ships under my command, and that I would have any of the smaller ships quit the line', the admiral was to make a signal to this effect.[9] Over a series of battles — the two Battles of Finisterre in 1747, Quiberon Bay in 1759, and the Saintes in 1782 — British tactics became increasingly daring, and the line of battle was used less. In 1790, Lord Howe, in command of the Channel fleet during the 'Spanish Armament', took the process yet further with a new set of fleet instructions, which were to remain the basis of the rules by which the navy fought. Much more scope was allowed for individual initiative. If the fleet was larger than that of the enemy and some ships found themselves without an opponent, they were 'to distress the enemy, or assist the ships of the fleet, in the best manner that the circumstances will allow.'[9] In certain circumstances, ships were allowed to pursue their beaten opponents out of the line, and above all, provision was made for breaking the enemy's line, in a highly effective manner, on the orders of the commander-in-chief. The new instructions, renewed and modified in 1799, were highly successful, and caused Nelson to call Howe 'the first and greatest sea officer the world has ever produced'.[10]

Practical naval tactics; Howe breaks the French line in his flagship, on the First of June, 1794. From James's *Naval History*

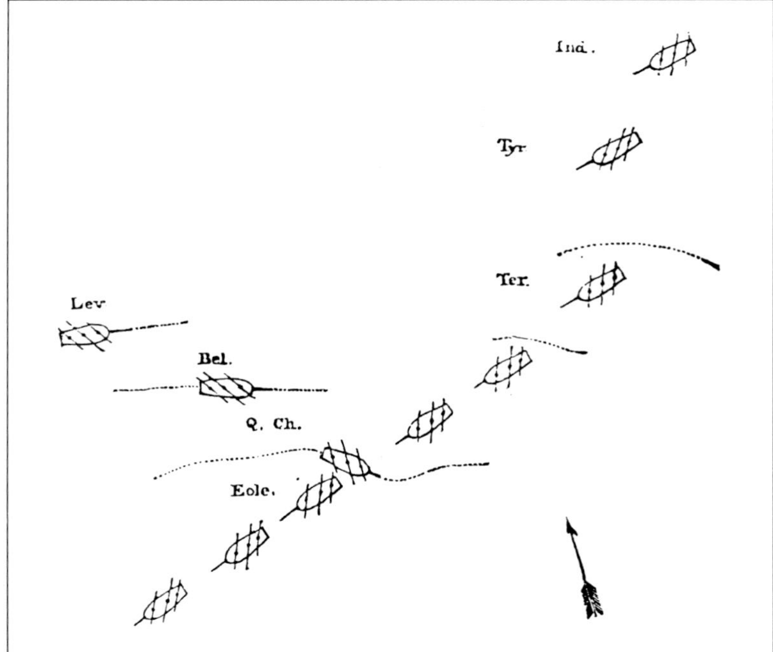

Nelson's fleet sails into action at the Battle of the Nile. The National Maritime Museum

Breaking the Line

Breaking the enemy line could be a very risky manoeuvre. A ship had to turn towards the opposing line, so that her guns would be largely ineffective while the enemy was at full strength. The structure of her bows was weaker than that of her sides, and she could suffer much damage on the approach. However, once she was passing between two ships of the enemy line, she could use both her broadsides, and the enemy could use none. Having passed through, she could engage the enemy on the other side, which was probably unprepared. If she had started with the weather gage she would now have the lee gage, and thus cut off the enemy's retreat. Breaking the line was a tactic which could win battles, and it did at the Saintes, St Vincent and Trafalgar. Perhaps it would have been too risky if the gunnery of other fleets had been as good as that of the British fleet; but in the given circumstances it was highly successful.

In fact, there were two ways of breaking the enemy line: as a fleet, or by single ships. The first was practised by Rodney at the Saintes, largely on the urging of his captain-of-the-fleet. He simply turned his flagship towards the enemy and had the rest of his fleet follow him through the gap he thus created. It was successful, but the manoeuvre was not in itself decisive.

Much more devastating was the system devised by Howe, and used in his fleet orders. Signal number 34 was 'When, having the wind of the enemy, the admiral means to pass between the ships in the line for engaging them to leeward; or being to leeward, to pass between them to obtain the weather gage.'[11] This was used at the First of June Battle, when various ships penetrated the line at different points, resulting in victory. At the Battle of St Vincent, Nelson took the initiative and broke through the Spanish line without orders,and was supported by only one other ship; again, this resulted in victory.

Concentration of Force

The concentration of force on a single part of the enemy fleet was another method of winning a decisive battle. Perhaps the most striking example of this was at the Battle of the Nile. On approaching the anchored French fleet in Aboukir Bay, Captain Foley of the leading ship, the *Goliath*, noticed that there was room between the first French ship and the shoal water ahead of the French fleet. He took the ship through the gap, and was followed by several others, while the rest of Nelson's ships remained on the outermost side of the French. The ships at the head of the enemy line were attacked on both sides, those at the rear not at all; they were unable to manoeuvre because they had started the battle at anchor, and the British ships moved up to them after eliminating the first ships. The Battle of the Nile was perhaps the most decisive ever; eleven out of thirteen enemy ships-of-the-line were destroyed or captured.

The Nelson Touch

Nelson's great contribution to the Royal Navy was in battle tactics — not writing about them, but in practical application. The signal books available to him were rather more extensive than those

The approach to the Battle of Trafalgar. The National Maritime Museum

The Mediterranean fleet in sailing order, 1797. From a drawing in the National Maritime Museum

available to his predecessors, but this was not the basis of his system. He relied little on written orders, or on signals during the battle. He much preferred to call together his captains — his 'band of brothers' — and brief them on what was expected. Individual enterprise was allowed a good deal of scope. At the Nile, it was Captain Foley's initiative which made the battle so decisive. At Trafalgar, every captain was virtually on his own after the approach to battle, and the truth of his famous dictum was illustrated: 'No captain can go far wrong if he places his ship alongside that of an enemy.'

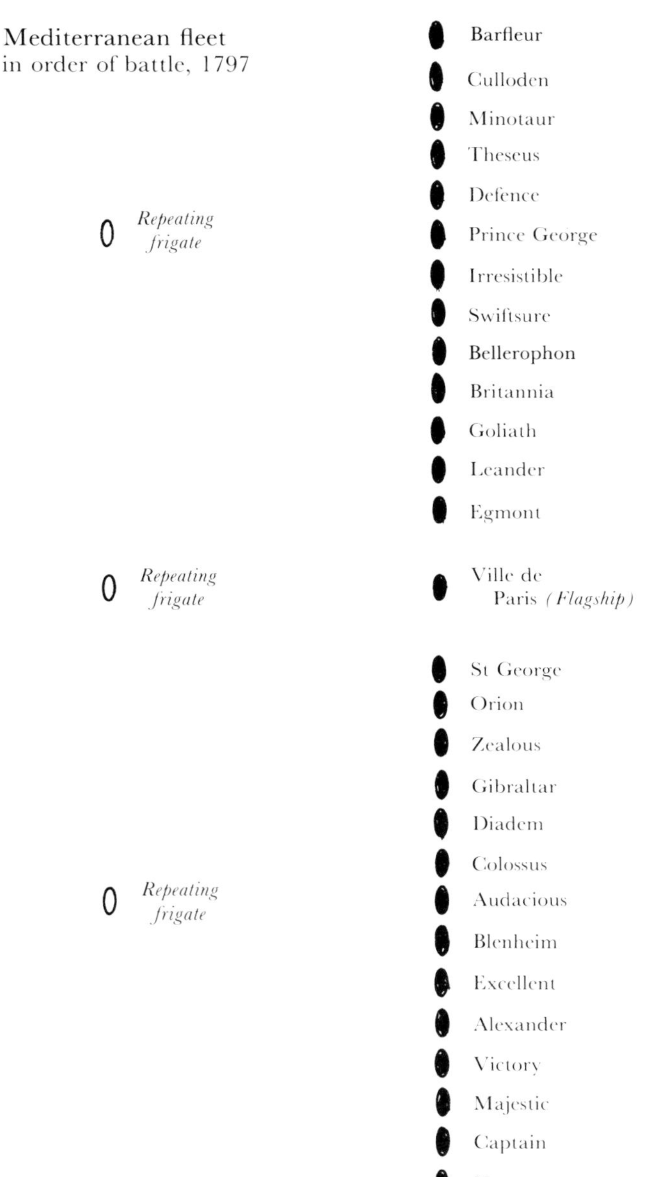

The Mediterranean fleet in order of battle. From a drawing in the National Maritime Museum

Nevertheless, the tactics of Trafalgar were quite sophisticated. Nelson had originally planned to attack in three columns — one to cut the enemy's line about a third of the way from its head, another to engage the ships thus cut off, and a third 'which I shall always keep to windward or in a situation of advantage, and I shall put them under an officer who, I am sure, will employ them in the manner I wish, if possible. I consider it will be always in my power to throw them into battle in any part I choose'.[12] In practice, he had only thirty-three ships instead of forty, and he had to do without the third squadron. In the event, Collingwood led the lee line with half the fleet, intending to cut the line; while Nelson led the other half, which would engage the cut-off section of the enemy. Again, the tactics were daring, but they were successful because of the enemy's demoralisation and lack of experience.

Division and Squadron Organisation

Fleets did not usually fight in divisions, except at Trafalgar. Normally, a fleet was formed into a single line at the beginning of a battle, and ended up in no particular order. In such circumstances, the role of the subordinate admiral, in charge of a division or squadron of the fleet, was not a major one. According to the Admiralty Instructions, he was to 'be particularly attentive in observing that the ship which carries his flag, and all the squadrons and divisions under his orders, preserve very correctly their station in whatever line or order of sailing the fleet may be formed'. His responsibility could even be extended outside his own division. He was instructed to 'correct, by signal or otherwise, the mistake or negligence of a ship in another squadron or division, whenever it is probable that, from their relative positions, that ship cannot be distinctly seen by the flag officer commanding the squadron or division to which it belongs'. In battle, he was 'very attentively to observe the conduct of every ship near him, whether of the squadron or division he commands, or not, and he is, at the end of the battle, to report it to the commander-in-chief, that every officer may be commended or censured as his conduct shall really deserve'.[13] These were not very responsible duties for officers of such high rank. Unless he took his own initiative, as Nelson did at St Vincent, or was left in command through the death of his superior, like Collingwood after Trafalgar, a subordinate admiral had little chance of distinguishing himself.

However, fleets were almost invariably put into divisions, of roughly equal strength and according to the number of flag officers available. In 1807, for example, Admiral Gambier had three equal squadrons of ten ships, and each of these was divided into two divisions, under a rear admiral or commodore. When cruising out of sight of the enemy, fleets did not normally maintain the line of battle. In 1797, St Vincent's fleet, of twenty-seven ships-of-the-line, cruised in two parallel lines of ten ships each, a mile apart, with 2½ cables between the ships, and the flagship, the *Ville de Paris*, just ahead of the starboard column. The remaining seven ships-of-the-line sailed line abreast, two leagues to windward of the others. Look out and repeating frigates were placed all round the fleet.[14]

Fleet Exercises

Fleet battles were rare, but the fleet had to be regularly trained in its conduct in action — not only in gunnery but also in fleet manoeuvres. This was demanded by the Admiralty Regulations, which ordered the commander-in-chief 'to take every opportunity, which the service he may be employed on will admit, to exercise his ships under his command, in forming orders of sailing, and lines of battle, and in performing all such evolutions as might be necessry in the presence of an enemy'.[15] Most commanders executed these orders quite thoroughly, if only because there was little else to do on blockade service.

4 Signals

The Importance of Communication

Signalling between ships of the fleet became increasingly important during the wars of the eighteenth century, as tactics became more sophisticated, and as naval officers became more and more involved in complex political and diplomatic problems. It is no coincidence that two of the most famous incidents of Nelson's life — putting his telescope to his blind eye at Copenhagen to ignore Parker's recall signal, and the famous Trafalgar signal, 'England expects that every man will do his duty' — both involved the use of signal flags. Ship to ship communication developed rapidly in the last ten years of the eighteenth century, but there was more to communication than that; telegraph systems were developed for land-based signals, and others were placed round the coasts to warn of enemy action. In a world without any telecommunications, as they are known today, messages could nevertheless be sent hundreds of miles in a few minutes.

Flags and Ensigns

Warships used flags to identify their nationality (or to conceal it by flying false colours); flags could also identify the rank of the senior officer on board the ship, and help to identify its place in the fleet. The main British flag was the ensign, whether red, white or blue. The white ensign was not yet identified with the Royal Navy, and ships flew the ensign according to the rank of the admiral commanding their division — thus ships under an admiral of the blue would fly the blue ensign, and so on. It was an obsolete system based on the nine-part division of the fleet in the mid-seventeenth century. Often, it had to be modified in practice; if there were two divisional admirals of the same colour in the fleet, the admiral might order one of the divisions to change its flag, so that the divisions could be distinguished in action. In other cases, ships of the whole fleet wore the same ensign. Ships sailing under Admiralty orders wore the senior flag, the red ensign.

The ensign consisted of the union flag in the upper corner of a red, white, or blue background. The white ensign also had the red St George's cross on the white background. The union flag itself changed in these years. Until 1801, it incorporated the St George's cross of England and the St Andrew's cross of Scotland. In 1801, Ireland joined the union, and St Patrick's cross was added. The ensign was flown from the flagstaff at the stern, except when the spanker boom prevented the flagstaff being rigged. In that case, it was from the halyard leading to the peak of the gaff.

Nelson's famous signal is hoisted at Trafalgar. The National Maritime Museum

The union flag was flown from a staff projecting upwards from the bowsprit of the ship, and in this position it was known as the jack. When placed there, it interfered with the jibs and forestaysails, so it was not normally used except in harbour. Other flags served to indicate the rank and status of officers and officials on board the ship. A private ship, carrying no individual of higher rank than her own captain, flew a pendant. This was 'a long, slender streamer, having St George's cross on a white field in the upper part next the mast, with the fly, or tail, either red, white and blue, or entirely of the colour of the particular ensign worn by the ship... The pendant being hoisted shows the ship is in commission, and this part of the colours is never hauled down day or night'.[1] It was flown from the head of the main mast. Around 1794, the pendant of a 90-gun ship was 32yds long, while that of a 74 was 30yds, and frigates had 24yds to 28yds.[2]

The broad pendant was worn by a commodore. It was much shorter than the 'commissioning' pendant of private ships, and could be red, white or blue. If the commodore commanded the ship himself without a captain under him, the pendant had a large white ball near the staff. Admirals of the various ranks were distinguished by rectangular flags, red white or blue according to the colour of the admiral, and flown from the head of the mainmast by full admirals. The admiral of the fleet flew a union flag from the mainmast. The flags of the Admiralty, Navy Board and Victualling Office used the symbol of anchors in various ways, and were hoisted when members of these bodies were on board. The royal standard, combining the lions of England and Scotland with the arms of Hanover and the harp of Ireland in a rather complex system of quartering, was worn only when a member of the royal family was on board.

Flags were smaller than they had been in past years, but still very large. At the First of June, 1794, the *Brunswick* carried an ensign 20ft by 40ft, while the union flag of Lord Howe was 12ft by 17feet. Jacks were considerably smaller than ensigns. In 1802, a commissioning pendant could be up to 24yds long. Flags were made in the royal dockyards, or by contract; on occasion the ship's sailmaker could put one together when required. Judging by the crude shape, this was the way Howe's union flag was made. A 74-gun ship was issued with three ensigns, one of each colour; a red foul weather ensign; three jacks; two pendants of 26yds each; one each of the French, Dutch and Spanish jack, ensign and pendant; a set of signal colours; and 35yds of spare bunting.[3]

Early Signal Flags

Naval signalling systems had already been in use for centuries, and the earliest known English ones date from the time of Henry VII. By the late seventeenth century quite sophisticated systems had developed, but as yet there was no special set of signal flags. Instead, ships used their ordinary flags hoisted in peculiar positions, gun signals, letting fly particular sails, or anything else that was convenient. 'If the admiral would have the van of the fleet to tack first, he will put abroad the union flag at the staff on the foretopmast head, if the red flag be not abroad; but if the red flag be abroad, then the foretopsail shall be lowered a little, and the union flag shall be spread from the cap of the foretopmast downwards.'[4] Clearly, the scope was limited; and as more additional instructions came into use, extra flags were needed to cope with them. By the 1750s plain flags of different colours were used, along with flags with two to seven horizontal stripes in different colours, with crosses in different colours, and with checks. Twenty-three different flags were available to the admiral of 1762, in addition to the royal standard, union flag and red ensign, also used as signal flags on occasion.[5]

There were two main faults in the old system: It had grown up

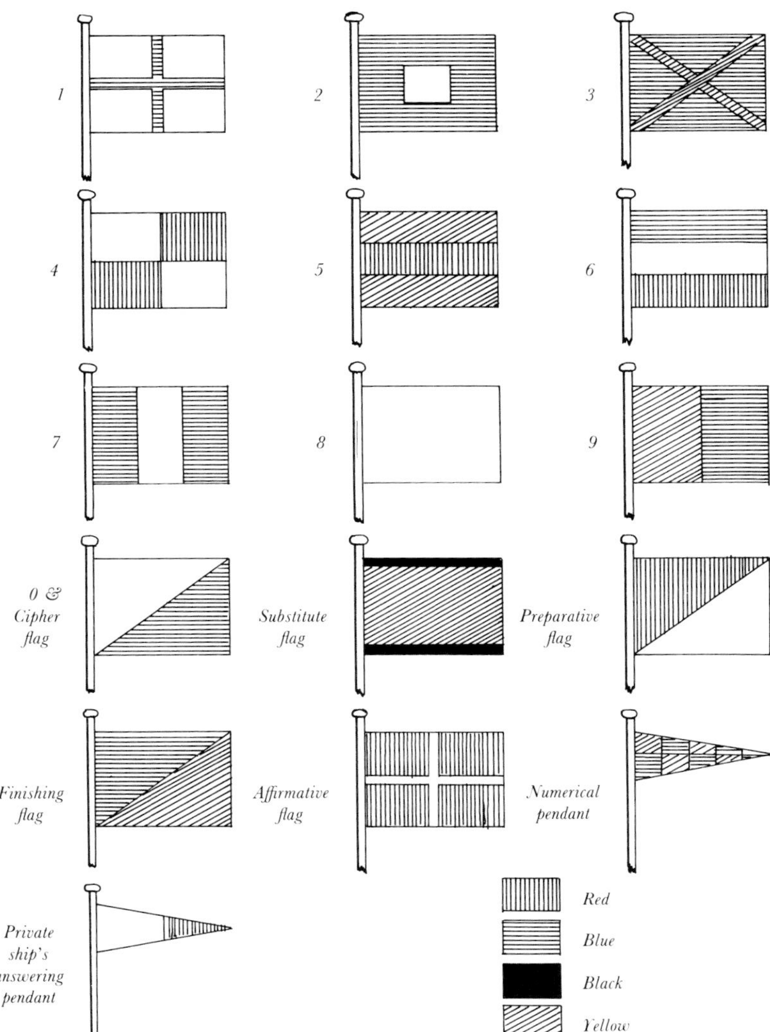

The flags used in the Howe code.

piecemeal, and, therefore, often used flags inefficiently; second, it used too many flags, which could not always be distinguished in the prevailing visibility. With the sun behind the flag, it was not easy to tell a cross of one colour from that of another. If the flag hung limp from the halyard in a calm, it was not easy to tell whether it was red and white stripes, or a check. Towards the end of the American War of Independence, several officers began to look at these problems, and develop new signal codes. Three admirals — Kempenfelt, Knowles and Howe — worked independently on the problem, and came up with different codes. Howe became the first lord of the Admiralty from 1783 to 1788, and commander-in-chief of the Channel fleet from 1790. This allowed him full scope to apply the new methods, the culmination of which was his signal book of 1790.

The Howe Code

Howe's code was based on a system of ten numeral flags, 1 to 10, combined with a substitute flag, a preparative flag, and assent and dissent flags, making a total of fourteen. Other flags were used for specialised meanings. For example, the union flag was hoisted to call officers, and a blue and yellow chequered flag signified a rendezvous. Each of the numeral flags had a meaning of its own: 1 was 'Enemy in sight', 2 was 'Form in order of sailing by divisions' and so on. Flags could also be used in combination for more complex messages: 6 and 3 meant 'Anchor as soon as convenient'. Some of the features of the old code still survived, and 'Prepare for sailing' was denoted by loosing the foretopsail. The design of the flags was much more careful than in the past, and several of Howe's original flags have survived to become part of the modern International Code of Signals. There was only one flag with a dark cross on a light background, one with a dark upper half and a light lower half, one with a light square inside a dark edge, and so on. The original code of 1790 allowed about 260 messages to be sent, while the revised version of 1799 allowed 340.

The actual flags of the code were changed in 1799, 1803 and 1810. In 1799, with the expanded version of the code, the numeral flags largely remained intact, except that number 1 was changed from a plain red flag to a red horizontal stripe on a yellow base; in addition, the substitute and dissent flags were altered. In 1803, the schooner *Redbridge* fell into enemy hands, and her commander, Lt Lempriere, neglected to throw his unofficial copy of the signal book overboard. Nelson, therefore, had all the flags in the signal book changed round, so that number 1 became number 5, 0 became 2, and so on. The order of the signals was again altered in 1810.

The Popham Code

In 1800, Sir Home Popham found himself in command of the *Romney*, conveying signals between the British diplomats in Copenhagen and the fleet off Elsinore. He soon found that diplomatic messages were more complex than naval ones, and devised a new code to cope with them. Hence his signal code included such unexpected messages as 'Change of ministers is about to take place' (181). Popham first published his work in 1800, but the revised edition of 1803 was much better known. He continued to refine his work, and another version of the code was published in 1812, and issued to the fleet in the following year.

Popham used the same numerical flags as the Howe code. Letters could be formed by using numeral flags to indicate the position of the letter in the alphabet; for example, 3 was C, and 12 was M. J was not yet fully recognised as a letter of the alphabet, and was combined with I as number 9. Words could thus be spelled out when necessary. However, Popham also supplied an extensive vocabulary for words and sentences which could be made up from a single hoist of up to four numbers. In effect, the signal book was divided into three parts. The first consisted of simple or common words, made with two flags; thus under A there was 'Able' (26), Admiralty (42), and Active-ly (38) for example. Less common words needed four flags, always beginning with number 1: under T there was 'Tedious-ly-ness' (1857), 'Thus' (1871) and 'Tolerable-ly' (1873). The third part included place names and complete sentences, made with four flags, beginning with number 2: 2461 was 'Madeira'; 2480 was 'I have my complement of men'; and 2529 was 'She sailed in the night'. Popham's code could produce an infinite number of messages, if enough flags were available. It could also transmit a large number of common messages very quickly. In its developed form, the Popham code consisted of 'nearly 6000 primitive words, exclusive of inflexions of verbs, & co, making in all upwards of 30,000 real words; the sentences have also been extended to about 6000, with about 1500 syllables, a geographical table, a table of technical terms, a table of stores and provisions, and a spare table for local significations.'[6] Words were used independently of speech or inflexion. Thus number 1046 could mean 'admonish', 'admonished', 'admonishing', or 'admonition', for example, and the recipient of the message was left to work it out from the context.

The Popham code did not entirely supersede the Howe system, which was retained for operational and tactical messages. At Trafalgar, Nelson's second most famous signal 'Engage the enemy more closely' was made in the Howe code — number 16. His 'England expects . . .' signal was made in the Popham code, and it was both

VOCABULARY
A 1

First Part, or original Edition.

26 Able
27 Above
28 About
29 Abreast
30 Absence-t-ed-ing-tee
31 Absolute-ly
32 Accept-ed-ing-ance
33 Accident-ally
34 Accompany-ied
35 According-ly
36 Acquaint-ed-ing-ance
37 Act-ed-ing-ion
38 Active-ly
39 Add-ed-ing-ition-al
40 Adjourn-ed-ing-ment
41 Admiral
42 Admiralty
43 Advance-d-ing-ment
44 Advantage-ous-ly
45 Advise-d-ing
46 Africa-n
47 Aft, abaft, after-wards
48 Again-st
49 Agree-d-ing-ment-able
50 Aid-ed-ing, assist-ed-ing
ance, abet-ed-ing
51 All
52 Alone
53 Also
54 Alternative-ly
55 Am
56 America-n
57 Amicable-ly
58 Ammunition
59 An

Second Part.

1026 Aback
1027 Abate-d-ing-ment
1028 Abrupt-ly
1029 Abundance-tly
1030 Accommodate-d-ing
1031 Accomplish-ed-ing-ment
1032 Account-ed-ing
1033 Accurate-ly
1034 Accuse-d
1035 Acknowledge-d-ing-ment
1036 Acquire-d-ing
1037 Acquit-ed-ing-al
1038 Across
1039 Actual-ly
1040 Adapt-ed-ing
1041 Adequate-ly
1042 Adhere-d-ing
1043 Adjacent, adjoining
1044 Administer-ed-ing-ration
1045 Admit-ed-ing
1046 Admonish-ed-ing-ition
1047 Adrift
1048 Advice-s
1049 Afar-off
1050 Affair-s

1051 Affect-ed-ing-ly
1052 Affirm-ed-ing-ation
1053 Afford-ed-ing
1054 Afloat
1055 Ago
1056 Aground
1057 Alacrity, alter-ness
1058 Alarm-ed
1059 Allot-ed-ing-ment

c

VOCABULARY
A 1

Third Part

2026 Action. Shall I leave off action
2027 I have been in action
2028 I have not seen any action
2029 I have heard of an action
2031 I am clear for action
2032 Shall I commence action?
2034 In coming into action, do you lead?
2035 Admiral's Office. Go to the Admiral's Office
Admiralty, see Sail
2036 Algiers
2037 Anchor. May I anchor?
2038 I must anchor
2039 I am in want of an anchor
2041 I have lost an anchor
2042 I can spare an anchor
2043 I cannot spare an anchor
2045 Anchor-stock. Can you spare an anchor-stock?
2046 I can spare an anchor-stock
2047 I cannot spare an anchor-stock
2048 Anchorage. I have anchorage
2049 I have not anchorage
2051 April
2052 Assit ships specified in action
2053 Assistance. I want assistance
2054 Do you want assistance?
2056 I do not want assistance
2057 Shall I give assistance?
2058 I cannot give assistance
2059 I can cut them out without any assitance
2061 Attempt. Shall I attempt to burn or destroy them?
2062 Attention. Pay particular attention

Pages from the Popham signal book, showing how combinations of numeral flags are used to send single words, and complex messages.

facilitated and altered by it. His original intention was to send 'Nelson confides . . .', but his signal officer pointed out that neither of these two words was in the code, whereas 'England' and 'expects' both were. Only 'duty' had to be spelt out in full.

Night Signals and Fog Signals

At night, light signals had to be used instead of flags. Coloured lights were not yet in use, so the signaller had three main means of transmitting: 'false fires', or flares, guns, and combinations of white lights, arranged in frames and hoisted up the yards. A special frame was constructed for this by each ship's carpenter, and in 1793, Lord Howe enforced some standardisation: each frame was to consist of 'two battens, each 12ft long, 1½in thick and 2½in broad. Each batten has five 3in mortices equally distant from the holes.'[7] The frames were so arranged that up to five lights could be placed in line, or shapes such as triangles, diamonds and squares could be formed. Many signals used a combination of guns, false fires and lights: 'Seeing strange ships, to chase and examine them' used two lights of equal height, and one false fire; 'To alter course to starboard' used four lights in a square, with three guns fired slowly, or three false fires.[8] Up to seventy different signals could be made at night, in the 1799 code.

In fog, the range of signals was rather smaller, as only guns, horns and bells could be used. The signal to tack was made by firing two guns in succession, followed by two more half a minute later, and it was answered by the ringing of bells. 'To alter the course to starboard' was signalled by four guns, then, after an interval of half a minute, one gun for every compass point to be altered. Twenty signals were available in fog.[9]

The Techniques of Signalling

In a flagship, the flag lieutenant was in charge of signals, but on a private ship the job usually fell to a midshipman. 'Captain in the Royal Navy' suggested that four midshipmen and clerks should take care of signals and take minutes on a flagship, and two on a private ship-of-the-line. Six seamen were allotted to signal duty in each type of ship. On the *Goliath*, one midshipman was quartered 'to observe signals', and presumably some of the afterguard helped him by hoisting and lowering signals.[10] A flagship needed many halyards to hoist signals, and in 1794, the *Royal George* had fifteen on each side, not counting the ensign halyards. The mainmast alone had a halyard on each side from the truck of the main topgallant mast to the deck; a pair from the same truck to the top; from the maintopmast crosstrees to the top; from the maintopgallant yardarm to the top; and from the maintopsail yardarm to the top. In all, the signal halyards needed 973 fathoms of rope, and allowed many positions for hoisting signals, so that they could be seen from any desired angle. To help spread the message, repeating frigates were stationed on one side of a fleet in line of battle, to show the signals being made by the admiral.[11] A 74-gun ship needed to make fewer signals, and had 339 fathoms of halyards.[12]

The flag lockers at the break of the poop on the San Domingo, *74. Each compartment is painted with the flag it contains. It was probably more common to have the flag locker right aft, at the taffrail.* The National Maritime Museum

Vocal and Written Communication

Despite their increasing sophistication, visual signals had their limitations. Detailed standing instructions for the fleet had to be issued in writing, and the normal way of doing this was to hoist a flag for each ship to send a boat — commanded by a petty officer or an officer according to the importance of the order — to the flagship, where written orders would be issued. For tactical planning, the admiral often summoned his captains aboard the flagship. This was a special feature of Nelson's system of leadership, and his personality was able to convey his intentions far better than any written order. Hailing from ship to ship was also necessary, especially for non-naval vessels. It could not be assumed that merchant ships outside convoys would carry the naval signal books, especially if they were foreign. Patrolling ships came close to them (firing a gun across their bows if necessary) and spoke to them through speaking trumpets.

Telegraph stations and coast signal stations, 1814. Based on the information in the 1814 Navy List

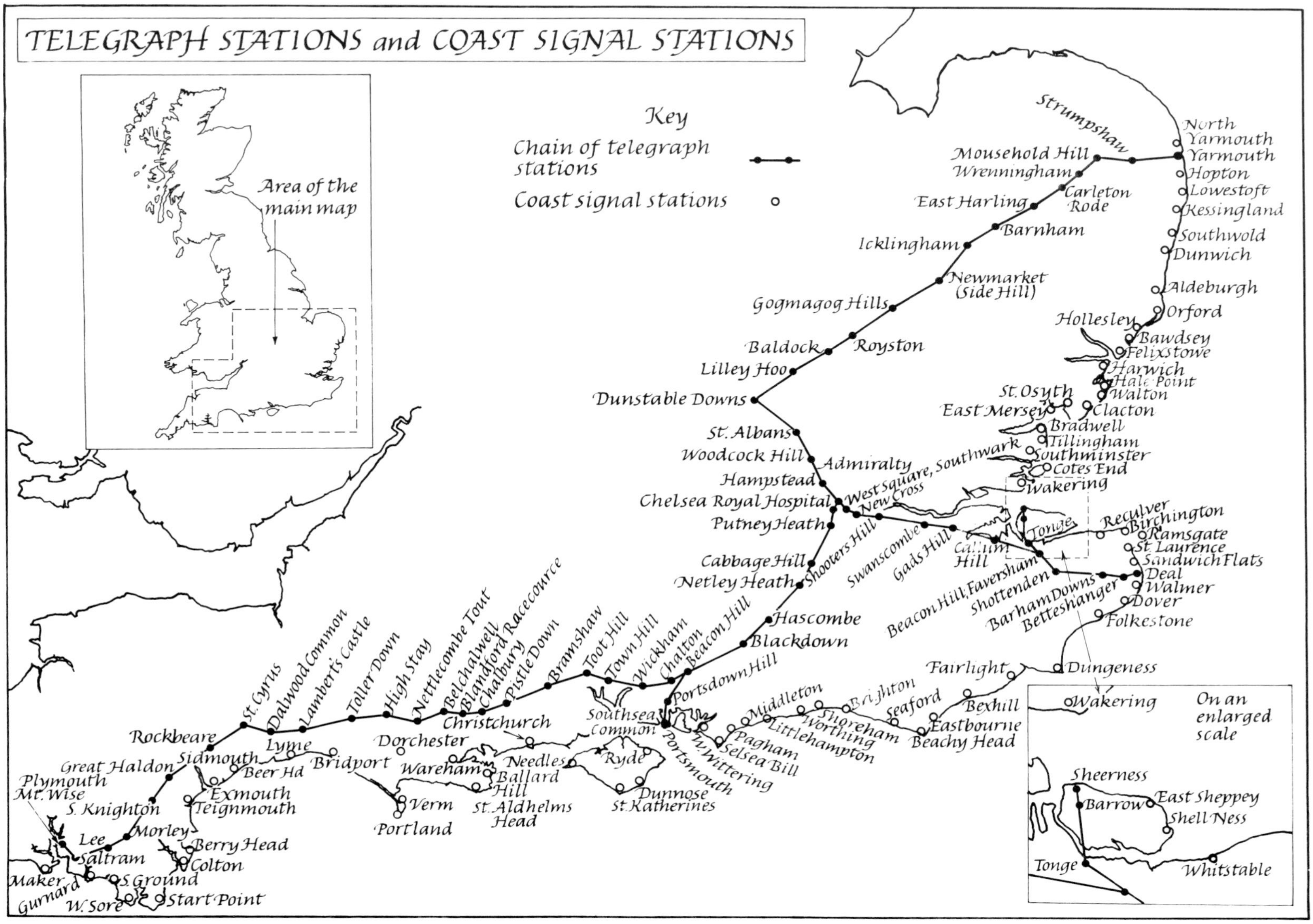

Despatch Vessels

The Admiralty telegraph was to make long-distance communication possible over land, and improved signal flags made for easier communication between ships in sight of one another; but for longer distance over the sea, there was no other way than to send a ship with a message. Small fore and aft rigged vessels, mostly cutters and schooners, were attached to the main fleets for this purpose. They could sail closer to the wind than the ships of the fleet, and maintain their way in very light winds. Furthermore, they were designed for sailing rather than fighting, with only light guns, and a well streamlined hull. For long-distance communication frigates were preferable, as they could keep the seas in rougher weather. The Admiral also sent his despatches on ships which were returning home for repairs, or for other reasons. He usually sent at least two copies in separate ships, in case one was lost.

The most famous despatch carrier of these years was the schooner *Pickle*, which brought the news of Trafalgar to London. She left the fleet with Collingwood's depatch on 26 October, five days after the battle. She took eight days to reach Falmouth, from where her commander took the mail coach to London, arriving thirty-seven hours later.

Coast Signal Stations

In 1795, the Admiralty set up a series of signal stations on prominent points round the British coast. These were intended to observe ships' movements in the adjacent seas, to warn any merchant ships in the area of enemy movements, and to inform the local militia in case of an attempted landing. A few were in Scotland, for example at Carlton Hill, Edinburgh, but naturally most were to be found on the south and east coasts of England, where the threat was much greater. They were erected on many notable coastal features, such as Land's End, Manacle Point, North Foreland, St Catherine's Point (Isle of Wight), Needles Point, St Aldhelm's Head and St Anthony's Head. Each station was manned by a lieutenant, paid 7s 6d per day in addition to his half-pay; a midshipman, at 2s per day and the pay of a fourth rate; and two seamen at 2s per day. Two dragoons from a local cavalry regiment were attached, to carry messages to the military head-quarters or to the militia, and the tower was also equipped with a signalling system. It had a mast with a gaff, and could hoist a combination of flags and balls to make various signals. Each station was supplied with a large and small red flag, a white flag, union flag, red, white and blue pendants, twelve balls, and a frame to use a beacon, for night signals. There were also eighty-one stations in Ireland, under an admiral.[13] There was no standard design for coastal stations; some used existing buildings, such as the old lighthouse at St Catherine's, Isle of Wight.

James Anthony Gardner was appointed to the signal station at Fairlight, near Hastings, in 1806. He had 'the strictest orders to be on the look-out day and night, in consequence of the threatened invasion'. In addition,

> Whenever the wind blew strong from the westward, so as to occasion the cruisers to take shelter under Dungeness, the French privateers were sure to come over and pick up the struggling merchantmen before the men-of-war could regain their station off Beachy Head. We had also to be constantly on the watch to give notice in case of smugglers being on the coast, and to prevent prisoners of war making their escape from the vicinity of our station.[14]

He found the work surprisingly hard, and 'suffered more anxiety at this station than I ever did on board a man-of-war'.

A model of a shutter telegraph station. Royal Naval Museum

The Admiralty Telegraph

In 1796, the Admiralty began to set up a separate signal system, to allow it to communicate directly with its bases. The system was devised by Lord George Murray, and consisted of a large rectangular frame, with six 'ports' or shutters, arranged three on each side. All shutters were open when the station was at rest. To prepare to transmit, they were all closed. After that, a code of letters was used — one shutter open for A to F, one closed for G to M, and so on. Telegraph stations were placed in lines, with each at the top of a hill or other prominent feature. The first two lines were opened in 1796. Two signalling mechanisms were built on the roof of the Admiralty building in Whitehall, one facing east and the other south. One line ran to Portsmouth, via eight intermediate stations. Another ran east via four stations, to Gadshill in Kent. There, the line divided, with one branch going to Chatham. The Sheerness branch led across the Isle of Sheppey by way of one more station, and the Deal branch went through three stations to reach the east coast. In 1806, another line was opened to Plymouth. It followed the first seven stations of the Portsmouth line to Beacon Hill, in Hampshire. After that it turned westward, and reached Mount Wise, Plymouth, by way of twenty-one stations. The final line, to Yarmouth, was opened in 1808. It had a total of eighteen stations.[15] Initially, each signal station was manned like a coastal station, but it was later found that lieutenants were not needed. In 1812, some of the coastal stations were converted to semaphore so that they could communicate with one another.

Part XII
THE SEAMAN'S WORLD

1 Winds and Currents

The Seaman in the World

Probably, no-one in history has been more dependent on the weather than the seamen of the age of sail. It was a source of both danger and motive power, and a calm or a storm could easily become a matter of life or death. The wind patterns of the world were known to all long-distance sailors, and were of crucial importance to navigators and strategists as well as merchants and colonists. The trade winds were aptly named.

The knowledge of the world's winds was handed from one man to another, like all lore in past ages. It was assumed that a good seaman would know that the best way from Britain to the West Indies was not to set a direct course, and that it was dangerous to round Cape Horn in Winter. Little of this was written down, though scientists, including Newton, Halley, Kepler and many others, had studied the winds. The basic theory of winds — that they were caused by the rotation of the earth and by differential heating and cooling of various parts — was already known to students such as George Halley and Major John Rennell, one of the leading geographers of the age, was beginning the study of ocean currents. The theory of the tides was also well known, and this was most useful, for it allowed their accurate prediction. Not all of this scientific knowledge was available to the average master or captain in the navy, and he may have preferred to do without it; his experience gave him many useful tools for finding the best winds around the world, predicting the weather, calculating the height or strength of the tide, and, to a lesser extent, this experience equipped him to estimate the currents of the oceans.

Tides

Tides were vitally important to the navigator in the English Channel and the southern North Sea, where they are very strong; the north coast of Brittany and the Bristol Channel have the second and third highest tide ranges in the world, after the Bay of Fundy on the other side of the Atlantic. In other areas, tides are less important. In the great oceans, they tend to be subsumed among the long-distance currents, while inland seas such as the Mediterranean and Baltic are virtually tideless. But since a great deal of naval effort was concentrated in the North Sea and the Channel, tidal prediction was an essential skill of the mariner.

The link between tides and movements of the sun and moon had been more or less correctly understood for centuries. The moon, being much closer to the earth, has the greatest effect, and high tides occur twice a day, just after the time when the moon is closest or furthest away from the spot in question. 'The mean daily period is 24 hours 49 minutes, during which there are two flood tides and two ebb tides. This interval is the time in which the moon performs her mean apparently daily revolution round the earth.'[1] The sun also has some effect on tides, and when the moon and sun were either in line or opposed, once in two weeks, there were extreme tides known as 'springs'. The high water was very high, and low water very low. The range of tides gradually declines after that, until the 'neap tide' occurs when the sun and moon are not operating together. As well as the daily and fortnightly cycle, there are much longer-term cycles, with very high springs occurring twice a year, just after the spring and autumn equinoxes.

The range of tide in a particular place depended largely on geographical circumstances. Where the incoming tide was forced into a narrowing bay or estuary, the range could be very high — 50ft near Bristol in November 1813, or 54ft at Mont St Michel off Britanny.[2] More typically, the maximum range was between 10ft and 20ft at springs — 16ft at Portsmouth Harbour, the same in Plymouth Sound, and 14ft at the Nore. The Solent has a peculiar tidal pattern, with a double high tide, the second one being about two hours after the first.

Tides, if used properly, could be immensely useful to seamen. Times of departure could be chosen to get the maximum benefit from the tide; rise and fall of the water could greatly aid the emptying of dry docks; a high tide could lift a ship over an obstruction, and was often worth waiting for. On the other hand, there were also dangers. A ship going aground at high spring tide would be 'neaped', unable to lift off until the next suitable tide, which might be six months later. Tides, unlike north European weather, were almost completely predictable, and therefore could be used by the skilful navigator.

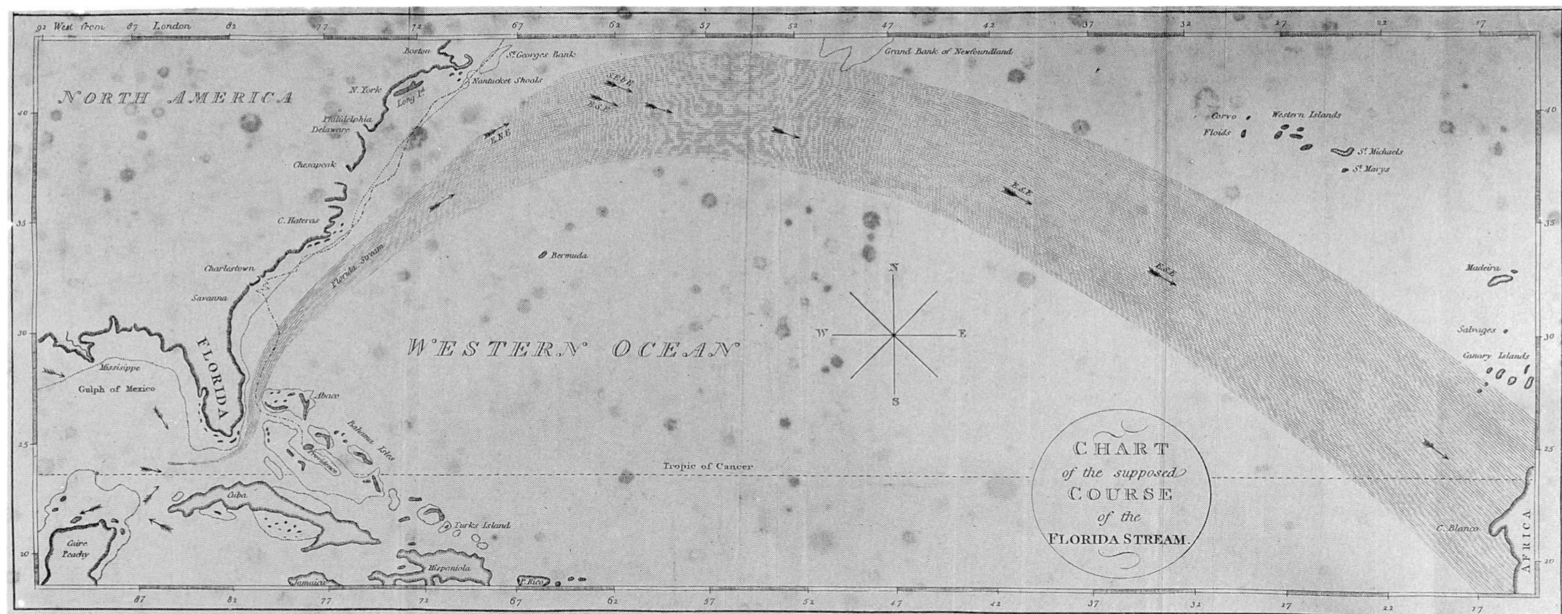

The Gulf Stream as it was believed to operate in 1804. From the Naval Chronicle

Ocean Currents

The currents of the ocean were less well known and understood, mainly because in the days before the chronometer, it had been difficult for ships to calculate their real progress across the ocean, and hence the effects of the currents. The actual movement of water caused by tidal forces, is quite small in comparison with the size of the oceans, and most of the currents were caused by other factors, particularly the effect of the wind in moving the water. Lack of knowledge of ocean currents caused many navigational errors, as captains did not know how much to allow for it in their calculations.

One current which was easily observed was that into the Mediterranean. It was debated whether this was caused by the evaporation of the water in that sea, or by a counter current running beneath the surface. Another current of some importance was the Gulf Stream, or Florida Stream as it was known. This begins in the West Indies, sweeps past Florida, and then up the North American coast before crossing the Atlantic and dispersing across the west European coasts. By contemporary estimates it was 100 miles to 200 miles wide, with a speed of 2 knots to 4½ knots.[3] It was considerably warmer than the surrounding water, which gave the navigator an indication that he was approaching the North American coast, and guaranteed some warmer weather in which his crew would recover after the hazards of the transatlantic voyage. It also provided a useful impetus for ships homeward bound from the West Indies.

Other currents were less understood. Major Rennel found a current setting north across the entrance to the English Channel, and attributed the loss of many sailing vessels on the Scilly Isles to this. The general circulatory nature of the currents, in the North Atlantic for example, was not known to the majority of seamen. Since the currents usually follow the direction of the winds, this ignorance did not necessarily affect his choice of route; but he tended to make too little allowance for them in his dead reckoning.

Trade Winds

The trade winds blow between the latitudes of 30 degrees north and 30 degrees south. They are perhaps the most basic winds on the globe, constant throughout the year, largely unaffected by the presence of land masses, and caused by the heating of the air in the region of the Equator, and by the rotation of the earth. In the north Atlantic, the trades blow consistently all the year round, from the northeast. In the south Atlantic they blow from the southeast, converging just north of the Equator.

> The two trade winds in the Atlantic have different characters. The northeast is sometimes strong, particularly in its northern part, and far from the eastern continent. The south seas trade was 'more regular', and 'more severe', and reached some way north of the equator in summer, with an average limit of 2½ degrees north.[4]

The meeting of the trade winds just north of the equator created the infamous doldrums, where sailing ships could wait for days or weeks for a wind to carry them back into the trades.

> At the eastern end of the interval, between the NE and SW trade winds, there is a continual succession of calms, terrible thunder, lightning, water-spouts, and such frequent rains, that this portion of the ocean has been denominated 'the rains'. Ships have here, it is said, been detained for months, in passing between the latitudes of 1 and 4 degrees.[5]

Ships often cross to the western Atlantic to avoid this region.

The Pacific has broadly similar winds to the Atlantic in these latitudes. The Indian Ocean is dominated by the land mass north of the Equator, and there the pattern of winds is rather different.

The Westerlies

North or south of the trades, the weather is dominated by westerly winds, though these are not nearly as steady and predictable as the trade winds. The theory of the travelling depression, so familiar to modern weather forecasters, was not yet known, but it was fully understood that winds in British waters, though mainly southwesterly, could be highly variable. Observation showed that strong winds often began approximately southerly, then veered quickly to the west, accompanied by cloud and rain; and then veered more to the north, with further wind and rain. Easterly winds also occurred, and these were most useful to the seaman wanting to go down the English Channel or up the Thames. In some respects, the variable winds around Britain helped to create the pattern of trade, for almost any wind is available if it is waited for.

In the same latitudes on the other side of the Atlantic are Newfoundland and Labrador. They have different climatic conditions; colder, because they are not warmed by the Gulf Stream,

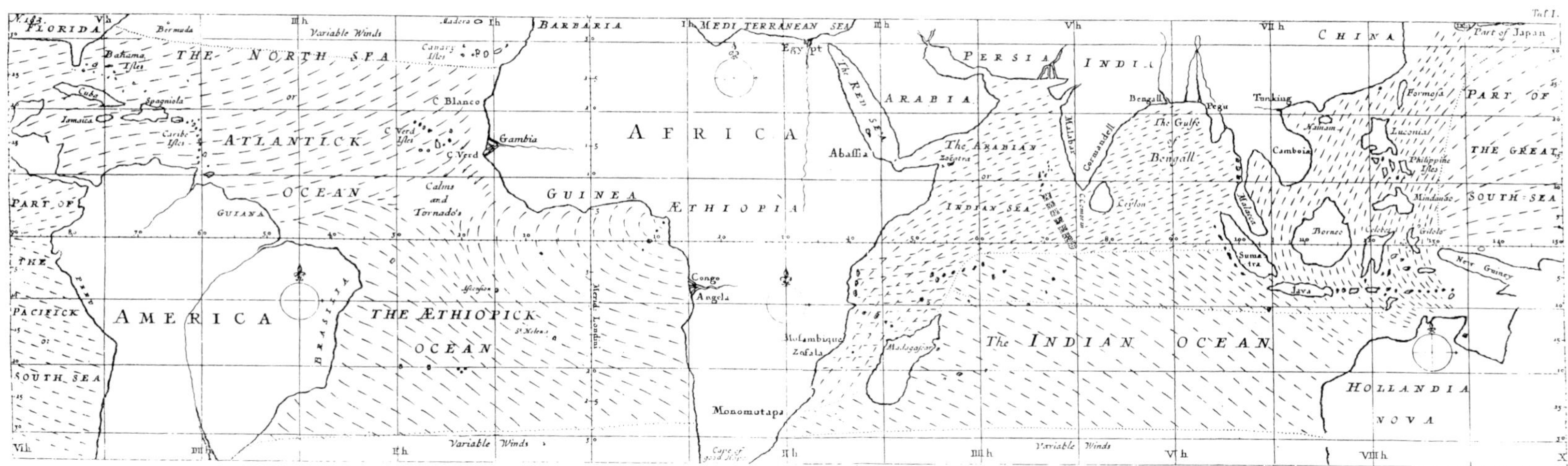

The trade winds, according to Halley.

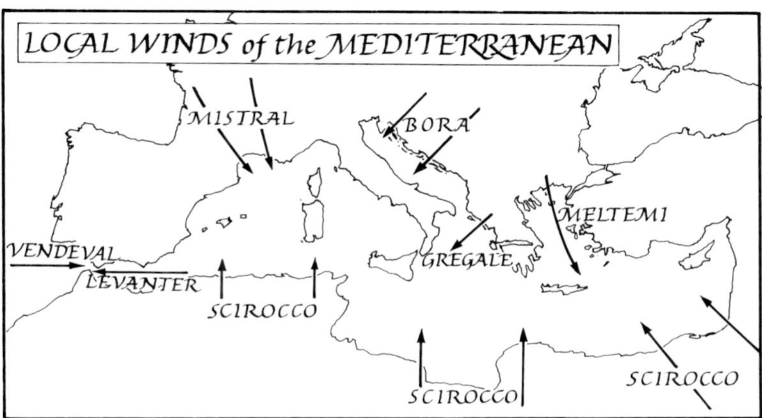

Local winds in the Mediterranean.

and with less wind because they are partly sheltered by the North American continent. The area is notorious for fogs, especially in summer.

The Monsoon

In the Indian Ocean, the northern land mass is much greater than that in the Atlantic, and this creates a different pattern of winds. In the southern part, a southeasterly wind similar to the trades blows throughout the year. However, in winter its effect is not felt north of about 10 degrees south. Strong northeasterly winds, created by the cooling of the land mass of India and Asia, blow from September to April, and reach well south of the equator; these are called the northeast Monsoon. In summer the situation is reversed, the land heats up more quickly than the sea, and the wind blows strongly towards it – the southwest Monsoon. This turning of the Monsoon was crucial to the trade and navigation of India, and its effect was felt throughout Asia.

Local Winds

The Mediterranean feels little or no effect from the trade winds or westerlies, and is quite often calm, interrupted by sudden storms. However, there are many local and seasonal winds, created by the land and mountains all around. At the straits of Gibraltar, the easterly wind known as the Levanter blows most of the time, though a westerly wind (the Vendeval) sometimes blows. The Mistral blows from the northwest, from the southwest coast of France, when certain conditions of pressure prevail, though mostly in winter. The Scirocco blows north from the deserts of North Africa, from Egypt to Algeria. Again, it was more common in winter, and the conditions which created it were not predictable to the seaman of 1800. The Gregale blows southwest from the Balkans; the Meltemi, or Etesian, blows throughout the whole year, southwards through the Aegean Sea between Greece and Turkey. Few of these winds were entirely predictable, or available for the whole year, and, as a result, Mediterranean navigation had some dangers.

The general pattern of wind was always modified by the proximity of land, and even the trade winds were only fully effective forty miles or so from the continents. In other areas, sea and land breezes had much effect. The land warms up much more quickly than the sea after sunrise, and this creates a draught of air towards the land. Typically, this would last from about 9am to 3pm. Land breezes are created by the converse forces, as the land cools down during the night. They tend to be weaker than sea breezes, but could be quite important in the tropics, particularly in the West Indies, where they might create a danger to ships anchored off a shore protected from the trade winds.

Tropical Storms

Hurricanes in the northwest Atlantic and the northeast Pacific, typhoons in the northwest Pacific, and cyclones in the Arabian Sea, Bay of Bengal and southern Indian Ocean, are all essentially similar phenomena, known by different names in different parts of the world. They are similar to the depressions of the more temperate latitudes, in that they consist of winds revolving round a centre which moves across the surface of the earth. However, the tropical storms are much more concentrated, and therefore more dangerous, producing winds of up to 130 knots. All are seasonal; hurricanes in the northwest Atlantic occur from May to December, with a maximum frequency in September, and about six to ten hurricanes in an average year; cyclones in the South Indian Ocean take place from May to December, with a peak in January or February, and four to six cyclones per year. Hurricanes in the north Atlantic generally originate in mid-Atlantic, at latitudes around 20 degrees. They often head towards the West Indies, and then curve northwards and pass along the coast of North America. The hurricane was the dread of every seaman.

> On the approach of a hurricane the sea and air become perfectly calm and motionless, without a breath of wind stirring either. Soon after this the sky is darkened, the clouds accumulate, and the light of the day is replaced by terrible flashes of lightning. During the continuance of this general calamity, the vessels which were anchored in the roads frequently cut their cables and put to sea, where they are driven at the mercy of winds and waves, having struck their yards and topmasts.[6]

If possible, ships avoided the hurricane areas during the season, though this was not always possible for warships.

Weather Forecasting

Weather forecasting depended entirely on the observations of the men aboard a single ship, since there was no way that advance warning of bad weather could be telegraphed to ships. Skilled seamen, especially fishermen, were noted for their accumulation of weather lore, based on their observations. Some held that celestial bodies, especially the moon, had considerable effect on the weather, as on tides. the influence of the moon on the weather 'has, in all ages, been believed by the generality of mankind'; it was also attracting the attention of some scientists.[7] However, most observations of the moon depended on its colour or visibility, rather than its position on the sky. Since these gave some indication of the state of the atmosphere, they may have had some real value. Observations of other celestial bodies were less useful. 'In Cornwall . . . the fishermen never presume to remain out when the signal is given by the eruption of certain meteors, which immediately presage a tempest.'[9] This belief gave its name to the modern science of meteorology, but it has never been proven.

Observations of the state of the sea or the atmosphere were much more valid. An increase in the size of the waves, without a corresponding rise in the wind, might indicate a storm some distance away on the ocean. The well-known 'red sky at night' did indeed show that an area of high pressure was approaching from the west, and weather was likely to improve. 'Mares tails', or cirrus cloud, did often indicate the approach of a front, and therefore bad weather. 'Mackerel sky', or stratocumulus clouds, indicated some turbulence in the atmosphere. 'If the sky, after being a long time serene and blue, become fretted and spotted with small undulated clouds not unlike the waves of the sea, rain will speedily follow.'[9]

The seaman's best means of forecasting was the barometer, which had been invented in the late eighteenth century. This gave reliable indication of the pressure of the atmosphere, though this information was not a great deal of use in itself. More important, it showed any rapid fall in the pressure, which was a reliable indicator of the approach of bad weather.

Trade Routes

Seamen knew well enough that a straight line was not always the quickest route between two points. For transatlantic voyages from east to west, it was usually best to follow the trade winds far south, to about 20 degrees north. Ships confirmed their position from the Canaries or Cape Verde Islands, and turned west to follow the winds. If they were headed for the West Indies, this route would take them straight to their destination; if going to North America, they would find the Gulf Stream and then turn northwest. In the opposite direction, the transatlantic voyage was quite simple and direct, using the westerlies. Ships from the Leeward Islands would head northwards, getting the trade wind forward of the beam. Those from Jamaica had to head round the western end of Cuba in summer, and even through the Florida straits, thus getting the benefit of the Gulf Stream, to carry them up to where they could pick up the westerlies. In winter, ships headed east, keeping close to the islands of San Domingo and Haiti to pick up a current and using land and sea breezes.

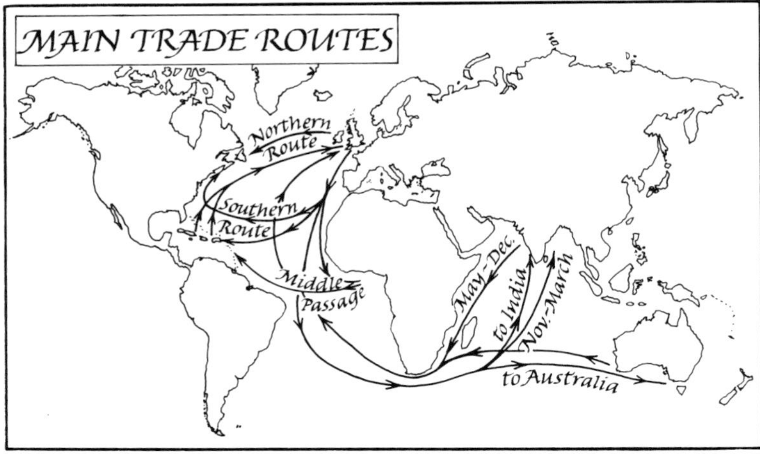

The main trade routes.

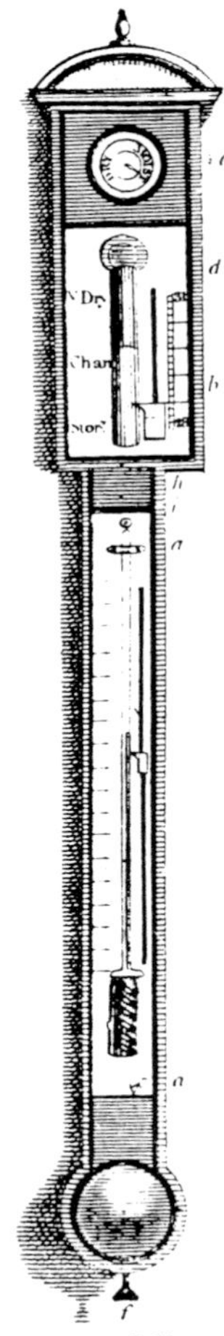

A contemporary barometer. From the English Encyclopaedia, 1802

Ships heading south to round the Cape of Good Hope generally passed about ten leagues to the westward of the Cape Verde Islands. After that, they continued to the southwest, almost crossing the Atlantic to the coast of Brazil, so that the southeast trades would be on the beam. Having reached the latitude of about 3 degrees south, they picked up the westerlies and began to follow them in the direction of the Cape. For the homeward voyage, ships headed northwest with the trades behind them. After crossing the equator they continued on the northwest course, with the trade winds on the beam, until they entered the westerlies at about 30 degrees north.

The passage to and from India was largely determined by the monsoon. Ships had to leave England in the spring to get full use of the southwest monsoon. On reaching the Indian Ocean, there was a choice of several routes; inside or outside Madagascar for ships bound to Bombay, and further west for ships heading for Calcutta and eastern India. Ships bound for Australia headed almost due west, as this would take them to the south coast, where the British colonies were situated. The other route, round Cape Horn, was dangerous and not much used at this stage, as Britain had relatively little trade, and few interests, in the Pacific. However, the eastbound passage was possible for much of the year, and was assisted by winds and currents.

2 The Merchant Marine

The Navy and the Merchant Marine

The Royal Navy had a very ambivalent attitude to the merchant service. It depended for its existence on foreign supplies of timber and other naval stores, and it was paid for out of the taxes which a strong commerce generated. Merchant ships were also needed to transport troops, and to supply the navy itself with food and other necessaries. The merchant interest was quite strong in parliament, and this too helped to ensure that much of the Royal Navy's effort was spent in convoy escort. In the longer term, the navy was dependent on the merchant marine for its supply of trained seamen, especially at the beginning of the war. But this was also the root of another problem. Naval officers often saw merchant ships as prey, from which they could recruit their crews. The seamen themselves, once into the navy, became jealous of the merchant seamen, and delighted to see them pressed.

British merchant shipping was easily the greatest in the world. It has been calculated that Britain and her dominions had 16,079 merchant ships in 1792, of $1\frac{1}{2}$ million tons, employing 118,286 men in that peacetime year.[1] War did not interrupt trade enough to stop expansion, and in 1800 there were 1.8 million tons of merchant shipping. Its importance was emphasised by Charles Whitworth MP 'It was a mistaken notion (says a celebrated writer) which obtained almost to the present times — that war alone determines the superior power of nations. It is now more than half a century that the balance of power has depended more upon commerce than upon war.'[2]

Government Control

The commercial system of 1800 was a long way from the Victorian idea of free trade. The Navigation Acts, first passed in 1651 and modified several times after that, created a protected market for British shipping. The acts demanded that all trade with British colonies be carried out via British ports, in British ships, with at least three quarters of the crew being British subjects; this ensured that sugar from the West Indies, for example, was often brought to Britain and then re-exported to other European countries. Secondly, the acts demanded that most goods imported into Britain had to be carried by British ships, or ships belonging to the countries from which the goods originated; this was highly damaging to nations such as the Dutch, who had tried to become carriers for the trade of Europe. Certain kinds of goods, such as tobacco from Holland or Germany, could not be imported 'upon any pretence whatever',[3] and fish and other products of the sea could only be imported on paying heavy duty. The acts were mitigated in many ways; by treaties with individual countries, by relaxation in emergency, and not least by smuggling; but they largely served their purpose in protecting British merchants from foreign competition.

Even among British ships, trade was restricted in several ways. The East India Company had a monpoly of commerce with the east, and worked hard to maintain this, prosecuting any 'interlopers' found in illegal trade. Ships setting out for certain areas, such as the Mediterranean, needed licences from the government, and had to pay for them. Most ships were compelled by law to travel in convoy in wartime, unless they were considered fast or well armed enough to travel on their own. Above all, trade was given priority by issuing protections from impressment. These controlled which trades could operate free from naval interference. In general, the government regarded the merchant marine as something which the state was entitled to mobilise for warfare, rather than as a group of independent traders.

The Long-distance Trades

Most oceanic navigation was carried out between Britain and her colonies, especially the most profitable ones in India and the West Indies. The East India Company had been founded in 1600, purely for trading. It soon began acquiring territory, and this process continued with Wellington's campaigns in the 1790s, so that the company controlled a large part of the sub-continent. The company came increasingly under government control throughout the years, as its power increased, though it was still technically a private corporation in many respects. It maintained a fleet of ships, each far larger than the general run of merchantment, as well as soldiers and civil servants in India. Only about sixty voyages a year were made to India, carrying a total of about 50,000 tons; but the trade in tea, spices, ivory, silk and muslin was highly profitable. In 1784, the Company imported £4,962,126 worth of tea for home consumption, and £1,539,784 for re-export.[4] In 1800, imports from Asia totalled nearly £5,000,000.[5]

Another profitable trade was the triangular trade between Britain, West Africa and the West Indian colonies. Ships carried manufactured goods to trade with the local rulers in Africa, and purchased slaves. These were taken on the notorious 'middle passage' to the West Indies, where they were sold. The ships loaded up with locally produced goods, especially sugar, and returned home. In 1798, forty-

An East Indiaman on its launching ways. From Rees's *Naval Architecture*

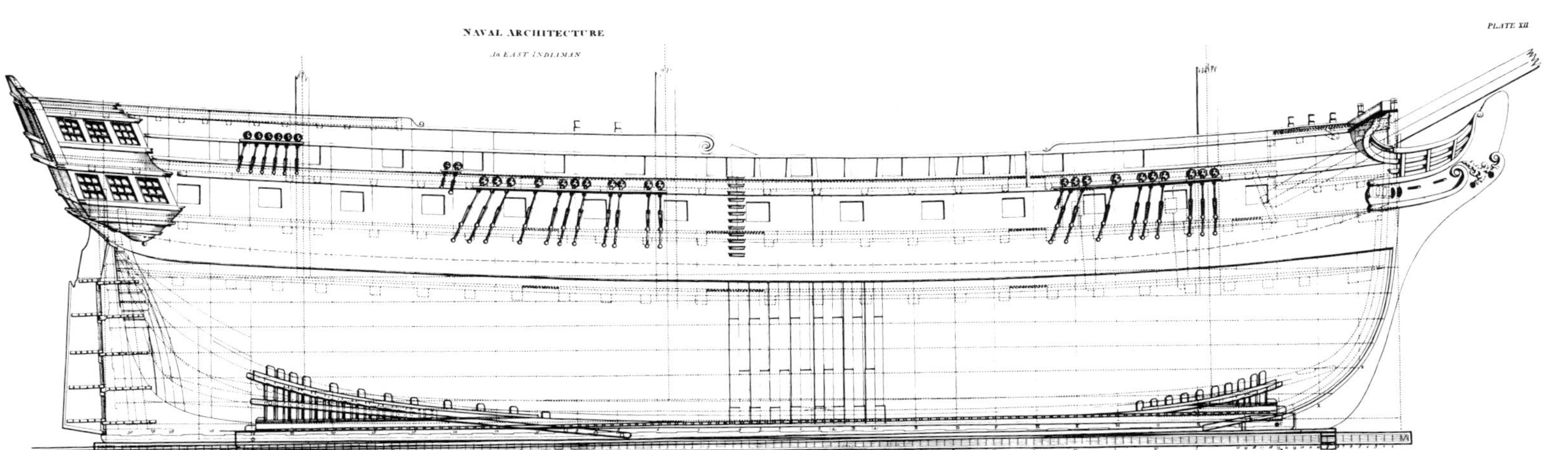

nine ships brought slaves to the West Indies. The largest, the *Elliot*, was of 371 tons and had a crew of ten. She carried 303 male negroes, 201 females, and one child. The smallest was the *Flora*; 39 tons, six crew, with fifty two males, eighteen females and two children.[6] In 1799, under pressure from the abolitionists, certain conditions were imposed on ships involved in the slave trade. The space between decks was to be not less than 5ft, with a false deck for extra accommodation, and the space was not to be encumbered with merchandise and stores. No vessel was to carry more than ten slaves for every free person on board, and no cargo was to consist of more than 400 slaves. Slaves lost in the voyage, including those thrown overboard because of ill health, were not to be compensated by insurance.[7] It was not until the beginning of the nineteenth century that the slave trade was abolished by Britain. But in wartime the navy had few resources to stop it effectively, and it continued illegally for many years.

British trade with northern Europe was less one-sided than some of the colonial commerce. The Baltic was a very important source of naval stores, such as tar, timber and cordage. Imports from Russia amounted to nearly £2,000,000 in 1800.[8] Sweden was a source of iron, and Poland produced much timber. Wine was imported from Spain and Portugal, along with wool and fruit; trade with these two countries came to about £1½ million in 1800. Trade in the Mediterranean was less extensive, though imports from Turkey amounted to nearly £200,000, and there was substantial trade with Italy.

A Thames barge loading on a beach after the tide has gone out. From Pyne's *Microcosm*

Coastal Shipping

The sea was by far the cheapest form of transport, especially before the railways, and in the days when the turnpike road system was not fully developed. As far as possible, goods were carried along the coast and up the river estuaries, to towns such as London and Bristol, quite a long way from the sea. Coastal trade involved all kinds of commodities — manufactured goods, agricultural produce, raw materials and passengers.

The largest coastal trade was in coal, from the ports of the northeast of England to London. In 1799, there were said to be 597 ships from Newcastle, alone, carrying coal to London, though it is possible that some of these operated other routes as well. Other ports included Sunderland, Hartley and Blythe. The typical ship was of 200 tons to 220 tons, with a crew of about eleven, including apprentices. Such seamen were highly regarded by the navy, being 'superior to seamen from other trades . . . the active employ they have in the coal trade, with the difficulty of navigation, soon bring them to perfection.'[9] Despite this, the navy offered no regular protection to men in the trade, and there were often difficulties with manning.

A collier. From Serres's, *Liber Nauticus*

Trade with Ireland was also conducted on a large scale, from Whitehaven, Liverpool, Swansea and Bristol. Coals, worth about £360,000, were exported annually, and 32,152,399yds of Irish linen were imported legally in 1800.[10]

Estuaries and Inland Waterways

The Thames estuary had a flourishing trade, using spritsail rigged barges, simply constructed and able to load and unload on beaches. They operated from ports as far away as Harwich and Dover, carrying agricultural produce, including hay for horses, into London; they took out manufactured goods. Above London Bridge, a very angular type of barge was used. It was open except for a canvas awning at the stern. It carried a large single square sail when running before the wind, and was hauled by horses or men when the wind was unfavourable. It took coal and manufactures up the river, and carried foodstuffs and timber down. In the Tyne estuary, there was a substantial fleet of 'keels', used in carrying coal down river to Newcastle, and loading it on to the collier brigs. In 1799, there were 319 of these vessels based at Newcastle, and 520 at Sunderland.[11] Various types of local craft were used in other rivers and estuaries; keels and sloops in the Humber, gabbarts in the River Clyde, and so on.

The rivers and estuaries linked up with the inland waterway system, then in the middle of its greatest phase of expansion. From 1790 to 1800, forty-eight new canal acts were passed by parliament; new canals included the Grand Junction, begun in 1793, the Kennet and Avon in 1794, the Rochdale Canal and the Huddersfield Canal in 1794, the Gloucester and Berkeley Ship Canal in 1793, and the Crinan Canal in the same year. Most of these canals were used only by specially designed narrow boats but the Caledonian Canal, begun in 1803, would eventually provide a means by which small ships could pass through the north of Scotland.

Fishing

The fishing industry was a major employer, and source of food. The type of fishing varied, from line fishing to harpooning of whales, and from small coastal open boats to ships which could cross the Atlantic to Newfoundland. One of the biggest trades was the herring fishery, largely based in Scottish ports. Standard Irish herring boats were of 30 tons, with a crew of eight, and used 40 lines of 54 fathoms each, with 1,000 hooks attached. Vessels of Campbelltown in Scotland were of 20 tons to 70 tons. 'They haul in one of their lines every morning, and at the same time they set another, the rest of the day they are cruising and lying to . . . splitting and cleaning their fish, baiting their lines for the next morning.'[12] Herring were gutted and dried, then put in barrels marked with the official stamp, and exported as far as the West Indies. In 1798, there were reported to be 1096 Scottish vessels fishing for herring.

Other ports pursued different trades. In the Thames estuary, small peter boats had wells in which fish could be kept alive for the market. At Hastings, there were seventy boats employing 210 men. The thirty-two largest boats were used for mackerel, from April to July, and caught 350,000 fish per year. The rest trawled for flat fish, such as brill, turbot and sole.[13] At Yarmouth, the typical boat cost £500 to £600, and had two masts and twelve crew. The ships made voyages of three to six days, catching red herring in the North Sea. At Brixham in Torbay, the boats were specially designed to help the crews avoid impressment. 'Each of these vessels is in general navigated by four persons, that is by the master, one man and two apprentices, which of course protects them under 2nd Geo III.' This was necessary in an area which was 'frequented by men-of-war, and every vessel continuously boarded by their boats.'[14]

A large amount of fish found its way to London. It was sold at Billingsgate, where there was a wholesale market from 3am to 10am, and a retail market after that. Ports such as Hastings and Brixham sent their fish by road, as sea transport was considered too risky for these purposes. More came up the Thames to Gravesend, where it was trans-shipped into wherries for the last part of the journey.

There were two important long-distance trades. In peacetime, small ships, mostly from West Country ports such as Dartmouth and Plymouth, crossed the Atlantic to Newfoundland; these were from 40 tons to 130 tons, and had crews of ten to fifteen men. They stayed on the Grand Banks for three or four weeks, catching and curing their fish, and then returned home. In wartime the nature of the trade changed, mainly because single ships could not cross the Atlantic for fear of privateers. The fish were caught by local open boats, cured on shore, and sold to ships for transport.[15]

Typical merchant ships – brigs unloading at a small port. From Pyne's *Microcosm*

The other long-distance trade was the Greenland fishery. Whale oil was essential for many purposes, including lighting and for paying the sides of the ships. As a result, it was encouraged by the government, by a bounty of £4 per ton. By 1788, there were 216 English shps involved in whaling, and 31 Scottish — a total of 71,579 tons, and an average of about 290 tons each. Most were based at Hull, and other ports included Newcstle, Sheilds, Sunderland, Leith, Aberdeen and Whitby. The trade could be quite profitable — the *Lady Jane* of Newcastle killed thirteen whales in 1813, to make a record profit of £12,000.[16]

Ships

Sea-going merchant ships were generally built on the same principles as warships, with the same system of framing and planking, and similar principles of rigging. Since naval construction was concentrated in the South of England, the ports of the Tyne, Mersey, Humber and many other rivers were free to concentrate on merchant-ship building. Merchant ships tended to have a rather square midship section, and bluff bows. The classic examples of this type were the north east colliers, which were almost box-shaped in comparison with men-of-war. Most merchant ships were quite small. In 1796, there were only 157 ships of more than 500 tons, out of 15,996 on the register. More than 11,000 of these were less than 100 tons.[17] By 1807, the officially registered merchant fleet had increased to 22,646 vessels, with a total of 2,324,818 tons; 259 of these were over 500 tons, and 14,000 were of less than 100 tons.[18]

Square rig was preferred for vessels of any size, because fore and aft rig had not yet been fully developed. Vessels of more than about 250 tons were generally ship rigged, with three masts. For vessels of between 250 and 80 tons, the brig rig was favoured, and this was very common among Newcastle colliers, and in certain transatlantic trades. Smaller vessels generally used the sloop rig, with a single fore and aft-rigged mast, and often a bowsprit and more than one headsail. The schooner rig, fore and aft and with two or more masts, was not yet widespread among merchant ships. The largest ships in the merchant marine were the East Indiamen; they fell into three broad classes, of 1200 tons, 800 tons or 500 tons. The 1200-ton ships were of similar size to naval 64s, though longer and narrower; and, indeed, several were taken over by the navy in the 1790s. In East India service, they carried about thirty-eight 18-pounder guns. The 800-ton class was the most numerous by this time, and carried thirty-two 18-pounders.[19]

Officers

The officers of the merchant service were masters, mates, and carpenters. The social status of masters varied considerably. Those who worked in short-distance trade relied on local knowledge rather than theoretical navigation, and needed little education. Those who went further out to sea were much better educated. Such men were often the sons of the merchant class, advanced through the influence of their fathers. They had quite high social status, and considerable power over their crews.

First mates, like captains, were protected from impressment. They needed all the skills of the captain, as they might have to take over in the event of his death. Second mates were not protected, and often of less education; they were capable of taking charge of a watch, but little more, of supervising the seamen at their work, but not of navigating the ship or making out the accounts. East India Company officers were regarded as a cut above the rest of the profession. It was written of a case involving embezzlement of cargo in 1798, 'The mates of the East India ships are wholly excepted from this charge.

The new London docks. The National Maritime Museum

Their rank and generally their education and circumstances, place them above the temptation of committing such acts of turpitude.'[20] Mates of other vessels did not have to undergo any kind of examination, and were selected entirely by the masters and owners.

Seamen

In many ways, the seamen of the merchant navy were indistinguishable from their colleagues aboard warships. They remained in merchant ships mainly because they had succeeded in evading the press gangs, either by protections or by more devious means. In the Newcastle coal trade it was said that there were four types of seamen in wartime: apprentices, foreigners ('not so numerous'), men 'rejected for the king's service who are generally known by the description of protected seamen', and men bearing protections from the Greenland whale fishery, who found extra work in the autumn and winter. It was said that such men were 'the ringleaders of all disturbances for raising wages.'[21]

Merchant ships carried far smaller crews than warships. Newcastle colliers had one man for every 20 tons, compared with one for about 3 tons on a warship. The Transport Board specified five men and a boy for every 100 tons for its hired ships. This did not necessarily mean that merchant ships were less crowded than warships, as the owners tended to fill up any available space with cargo when possible. Owners had to pay quite high wages to lure seamen because of the threat of possible impressment, and conditions in the merchant service were expected to be better than in the navy. On joining a merchant vessel for the first time after service on the king's ships, Robert Hay found 'those of the seamen on board who were better acquainted than I with the general usage of merchant vessels and who consequently had fared better, relished their treatment very indifferently, and complained much, but the treatment and the fare we received being much better than I had been accustomed to in the king's service, I had no reason to complain.'[22]

Owners

Although shipping was operated by large companies, such as the East India Company, ownership was spread quite widely among the middle classes. Even the East India Company did not own the ships it used, and the ownership of smaller vessels was even more dispersed. Traditionally, a ship was divided into a number of shares, usually sixteen or thirty-two. A few larger-scale shipowners were beginning to emerge, for example, Henley and Sons. The founder of the firm began as a waterman on the Thames, and bought his first ship in 1775. He supplied coal to the dockyards, and chartered vessels to the Transport Board. Between 1775 and 1814 he owned or part-owned at least 123 ships and vessels.[23]

Ports

London was by far the biggest British port, and 13,949 ships entered it in 1794. The trade of London was greatly restricted by the antiquated nature of its quays, and the lack of any modern docks. By a system established in the time of Queen Elizabeth, ships had to unload at the 'legal quays' between London Bridge and the Tower of London, which had only 1,464ft of space, or in certain 'sufferance wharfs' nearby. As a result, the river became crowded with shipping, and up to 775 vessels were sometimes moored to await unloading. One pilot testified, 'at times the river is so filled up with shipping, that a boat cannot pass; that ships often run foul of each other; that he himself has been delayed for seven days together, by the crowded state of the river, from moving up from Deptford.'[24] From 1800, steps were taken to improve this position, and the first wet docks, the West India Dock on the Isle of Dogs, the London Docks near the Tower of London and the East India Dock at Blackwall, were opened in the 1800s.

Elsewhere, there were some improvements to facilitate navigation. The port of Glasgow was developing, because the River Clyde above Dumbarton was deepened by building piers to restrict the river. As a result, the city became less dependent on its satellite town of Port Glasgow, twenty miles down river. Liverpool was better provided for by nature, and it grew rapidly in the eighteenth century because of its connections with the slave trade, which employed 132 ships in 1792. In that year the city imported more than a quarter of a million tons of goods.[25] Both Liverpool and Glasgow sent their ships round the north of Ireland, and this gave them advantages in avoiding French privateers. The port of Bristol was declining for the same reason, though it, too, was involved in the slave trade. The other major ports were Yarmouth, which exported corn and fish, and Newcastle, the main centre of the coal trade. Sunderland and Whitby were also important in this trade. Hull, on the river Humber, was the centre of an extensive inland navigation feeding into the river, and a dock 500 x 83yds had been dug out there.[26]

There were hundreds of small ports round the country. Some were river ports, with natural harbours. Others were simply open beaches, where flat-bottomed vessels could be grounded at high tide and unloaded at low. A few, such as Ramsgate, had totally artificial harbours. Some ports which had once been great, such as Hythe and Sandwich, had declined because of the silting up of their rivers. Others had been developed in recent years, and were at the peak of their trade. Whitehaven in Cumberland was the principal port for the coal trade with Ireland, and exported 167,231 chaldrons per year in 1797.[27] The main characteristic of a major port was the presence of a customs house, which allowed legal foreign trade; there were seventy-five such ports in England in 1807.

War and Shipping

In many ways, war was disruptive to the shipping trade. Men were taken up for the navy, and the merchant owners were forced to pay high wages, and to take on foreigners, landmen or boys to make up the numbers. Privateers played havoc with commerce, and the convoy system slowed everything down, as convoys took considerable time to assemble, and then had to travel at the speed of the slowest ship. Insurance rates soared because of the risks. Many markets were closed, especially in the years of the Continental System.

Yet the expansion of the British merchant marine continued, though perhaps at a slower rate. The war itself stimulated some business, including the transport of troops and naval stores, which sometimes took up about 10 per cent of British shipping. British industry was undergoing a transformation, and the Industrial Revolution allowed the country to produce coal and textiles far more efficiently than ever before, while the iron industry expanded, partly because of government orders for cannon. British goods were in demand abroad, despite Napoleon's attempts to ban them from Europe. The Continental System soon developed some notable gaps; Sweden from the beginning, Portugal and Spain after 1808, and Russia after 1812. As a result, cotton exports soared from £16.5 million in 1793 to £22.5 million in 1815. The government received £13.57 million from customs duties in 1793, and £44.89 million in 1815; thus the growth in trade financed the war.[28]

3 Other Naval Services

The Transport Service

Since the navy was successful in preventing the invasion of Britain, almost all of the army's fighting was done abroad. Troops had to be taken to the West Indies, Iberia, and many other places — and supplied once they had arrived. The effort was not so great as in the American War of Independence, when the army was heavily committed in North America, but it was substantial all the same; in 1809, 980 ships, of nearly a quarter of a million tons, were in use for the transport of troops and stores.[1] This was more than 10 per cent of total British merchant tonnage.

Until the early years of the French Revolutionary War, the Navy Board had been responsible for such ships, but the Transport Board was formed in 1794, to organise the hire of merchant ships for naval and military purposes. Its responsibilities were not only for troopships; it was charged with 'the hiring and appropriating of ships and vessels for the conveyance of troops and baggage, victualling, ordnance, barrack, commissariat, naval and military stores of all kinds, convicts and stores to New South Wales, and a variety of miscellaneous services.'[2] In practice, its ships fulfilled four main functions — troopships (77,400 tons in 1810, plus 17,617 tons of 'cavalry ships', fitted for horse transport); army victuallers (3690 tons); navy victuallers (16,534 tons); and naval storeships, mainly supplying the overseas dockyards (32,754 tons).[3] The Ordnance Board still hired its own transports.

The Transport Board consisted of six commissioners, mostly naval captains. It employed resident agents at some of the major ports — Deal, the Isle of Wight, Portsmouth, Leith, Plymouth, Liverpool, Dublin, Gravesend, Dublin and Cork. The most important post was at Deptford, where many of the transports were first hired. The resident agents were usually naval lieutenants, but the most important posts, at Deptford and Portsmouth, were held by captains. They were responsible for hiring ships, and surveying them to see that they were suitable. In addition, the Board employed 'agents afloat', also naval captains and lieutenants. They took command of fleets of transports, directing their movements and ensuring that they obeyed naval orders. An agent flew a broad blue pendant from the transport he chose to sail in; 8ft by 20ft for a principal agent, and smaller for subordinate agents. The masters of the various merchant ships were directed to obey his orders.[4]

Hired transports were fairly typical merchant ships, with an average of about 250 tons; though troopships were bigger than average, at around 350 tons. They were manned at the rate of five men and a boy for every 100 tons, and carried troops at the rate of one man for every two tons. The rate of hire varied, and coppered ships were at a premium; until 1807, they were paid at 19s per ton per month, which was later increased to 25s. Under the new rates, wood sheathed vessels were paid 21s per ton per month, and unsheathed vessels, 20s.[5] In 1807, 171 out of 214 troopships were coppered.[6] Ships were usually chartered for periods of three or six months, with the possibility of an extension. The service had certain advantages to both owners and crews, in that the seamen were protected from impressment.

When fitted as troopships, transports had their lower decks divided into cabins. The men slept in hammocks, and stowed them in hammock nettings in the daytime, in the same way as did seamen. Troops were not always well behaved aboard ship. 'The soldiers' cabins on board transports being frequently broken or destroyed by the troops when embarked, so as to require much repair upon the return of the ships to port', the officer in command of the troops was directed to put one of his sergeants in charge of the cabins.[7] The troops were fed at two thirds of the allowance for seamen, while their wives had three quarters of that, and children had half that of the women.

Hired transports were spread around the world, but most were concentrated in the major military campaigns. In 1810, at the height of the Peninsular War, 234 ships were operating to and from the coast of Portugal; 86 from the coast of Spain; 120 to Gibraltar and the Mediterranean; 15 for the Baltic and Heligoland; 19 for other areas — the coast of Africa, Cape of Good Hope, North and South America, and the West Indies; 54 more were in home waters, either preparing for service, unloading, or carrying out miscellaneous services.[8]

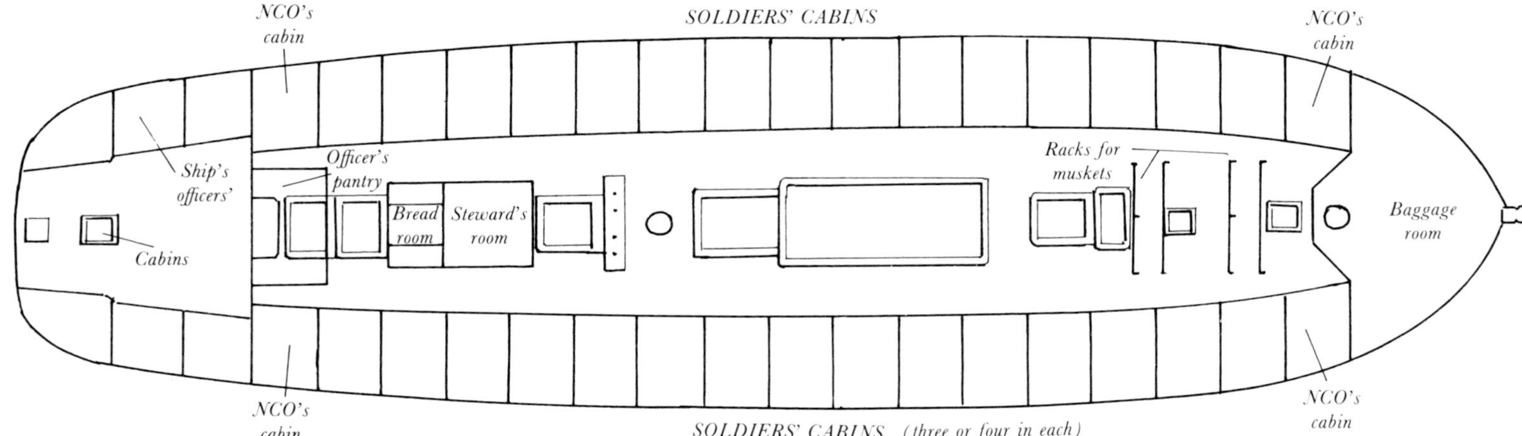

The deck plan of a transport, showing the cabins for troops. From a drawing in the National Maritime Museum

'Armed transports' were different from ordinary hired transports. They too were chartered from merchant shipowners, but without officers and crews. They were commanded by naval lieutenants, and were capable of sailing independently of convoys, or acting as escorts to groups of transports. They must also be distinguished from 'hired armed vessels', which had naval crews, but did not carry troops, and served as patrols and escorts.

The Revenue Services

Smuggling was endemic throughout the eighteenth and early nineteenth centuries; even the most respectable people obtained supplies of smuggled liquor, while whole communities in the seaports and coastal districts were heavily involved in illegal trade. One source estimates that 12 million out of 18 million pounds of tea consumed between 1773 and 1782 were smuggled.[9] Much of government revenue depended on import duties, which were quite difficult to enforce. Inadequate organisation of the services was partly to blame, because different government agencies had overlapping responsibilities. Direct conflict between naval ships and those of the revenue services was not unusual: in 1806, an officer from the naval brig *Sentinel* was sent on board the revenue cutter *Eagle* to haul down her flag.[10] Nevertheless, the Royal Navy was sometimes asked to send ships to help prevent smuggling.

The revenue service was divided into two parts, largely independent of each other. The Board of Customs was responsible for duties levied on imported goods, and therefore did the main work against smugglers. The Board of Excise raised revenue mainly from inland taxes, such as stamp duty and a tax on bricks. It also collected taxes on drinks, such as imported cocoa beans, tea, and imported spirits such as rum and brandy. Since the latter items were among the smugglers' favourites, the Excise Board had its own coastal patrols. there were separate Boards for Customs and Excise in Scotland while in Ireland there was a joint Customs and Exercise Board. As a result, there were five separate organisations dealing with smuggling, in addition to the Royal Navy.

The English customs service was headed by the board in London. It had customs houses in seventy-five ports in England and Wales, each supervised by two collectors. At the local level there were numerous officials and employees, such as tide-surveyors, tide waiters, and watermen, who helped inspect ships coming into the port. Riding officers commanded bands of men who patrolled the coastline, seeking out the small craft used by smugglers. The Excise Board also had collectors spread around the country, in inland towns as well as seaports.

The sea-going element was provided by a flotilla of cutters, stationed round the coast. There were thirty-three such vessels in the customs service in 1797, plus three more building. Those in the north of Britain each had quite a large area to cover from Milford to the Solway firth on the West Coast, or from Berwick to Spurn Head in the east. The cutters in the south tended to be more concentrated, and some had quite small areas to cover — from the Downs to Long Sand, or between North and South Foreland; others covered slightly larger areas, such as Dover to Brighton.[11] They varied in size from 28 tons to 153 tons, with crews of eight to forty-three men, and up to 16 guns. Most were around 130 tons, with 14 guns and thirty to forty men, headed by a commander and two mates. The Excise Board had fewer cutters, only seven in 1784, though they were generally considered to be more efficient.[12] The Irish cruisers were more uniform than the English ones, and most had a commander, first mate, second mate who also served as gunner, boatswain, carpenter, steward, and fourteen seamen.[13] The officers of cutters wore uniform similar to that of naval officers, though they were refused permission to wear silver epaulettes in 1804, lest they 'should interfere with His Majesty's naval service'.[14] In 1809, there was a major reorganisation of the revenue services, with the establishment of a unified 'Preventive Water Guard'. England and Wales were divided into three districts, covering the south, east and west coats, each under an inspecting commander, with one cutter and two tenders under his immediate control. In addition, there were thirty-nine cutters and sixty-two boats spread around the coasts.

The revenue cutter was usually built by contract, and its design was based on that of the vessel originally used by smugglers. It had a flush deck, with all accommodation below. It had a very lofty rig on its single mast, including both square and fore and aft sails. It had a long bowsprit, which gave it some advantage over non government vessels, which were banned by law from having bowsprits of more than a certain length. According to Captain Marryat, the revenue cruiser was all too recognisable. 'She is a cutter, and you may know she belongs to the Preventive service by the numbers of gigs and galleys which she has hoisted up all round her... You observed that she is painted black, and much more lumbered up... her bulwarks are painted red.'[15]

Revenue cutters were sometimes diverted to the service of the navy, for example, in support of the Walcheren expedition of 1809. In general, they had some success against smugglers from 1793 to 1815, despite the increasing ingenuity of their opponents. However, the proportion of smuggled goods remained high throughout the wars.

Sea Fencibles

The word 'fencible', a corruption of defensible, usually meant a part-time soldier, liable to service in his home area, for defence against an enemy invasion, and trained in his spare time. In the late 1790s, with the increasing threat of French invasion, it was decided to set up a corps of Sea Fencibles, able to defend the coast by either land

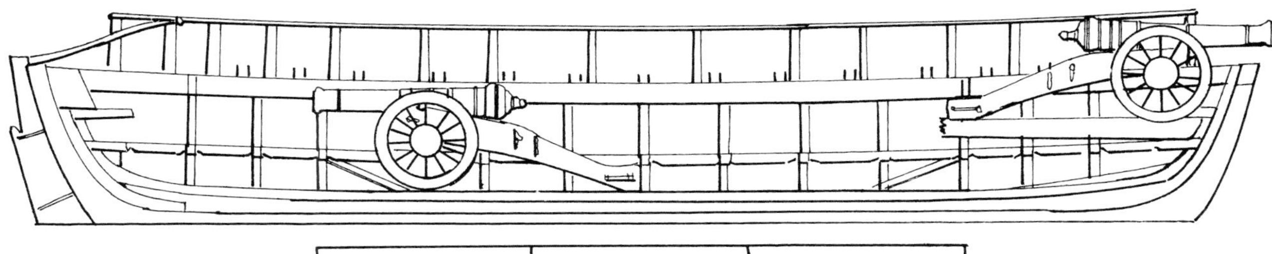

Longitudinal section of the Smith/Parkin gunboat of 1796. Variations of this type were to be used by the Sea Fencibles in later years. From a drawing in the National Maritime Museum

or sea. It was established by Order in Council in May 1798, and it was decided to enrol 'under the denomination of Sea Fencibles all such of the inhabitants of the towns and villages of Great Britain as shall voluntarily offer themselves for the defence of the coast'. They were to learn the use of the cannon and pike, and to help man the Martello towers already being planned. They were to assist the coastal signal stations, help the revenue services, and eventually they were given small boats and gunboats to harass the enemy barges while a landing was in progress. The men were to be paid 1s a day while on service, but perhaps a greater incentive was immunity from impressment, and from the ballot for the militia. This must have been attractive to fishermen and others. The fencibles of each port were put under the command of a naval lieutenant, with captains supervising districts.

From the beginning, the Sea Fencibles attracted their share of criticism, from inside and outside the navy. Captain Schomberg, in command of the Dungeness Fencibles, complained, 'Notwithstanding the number of men who volunteered to go afloat, it is inconceivable the difficulty I find when the time arrives to persuade them to embark... The people, who are mostly smugglers and wreckers, object to go on board the revenue cutters.' Nelson, in command at the Downs, was a little more favourable. 'The men, I believe, will come forth when the country prepares for fighting and all business stands still; but they are no more willing to give up work than their

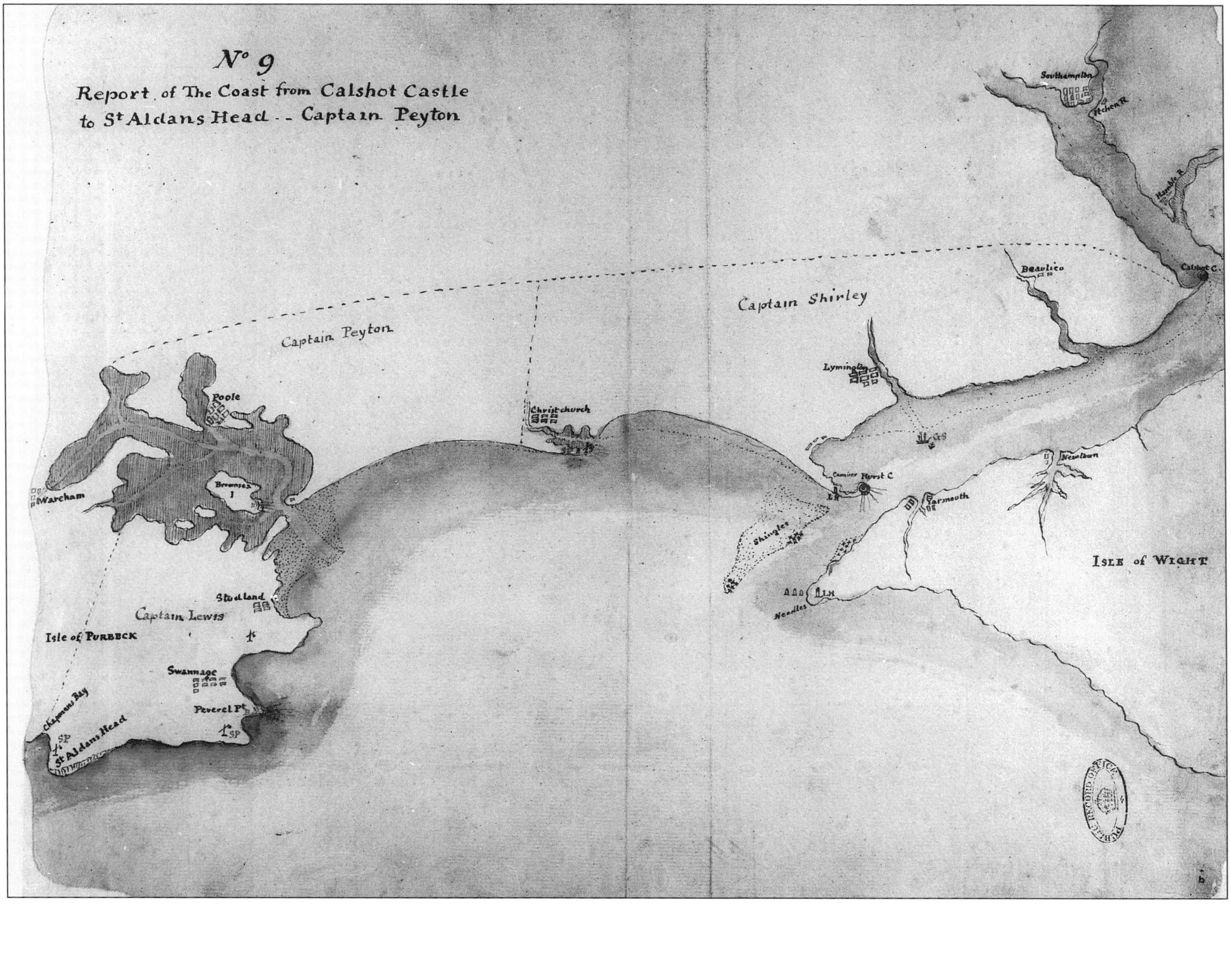

A map showing the Sea Fencible areas in Dorset, Hampshire and the Isle of Wight. It also shows signal stations, and defensive batteries. Public Record Office

Trinity House, on Tower Hill, London. From Lambert's *History of London*

superiors.'[16] William Cobbett's *Political Register* commented on 'the immense cost of the Sea Fencibles'. It was questioned 'if any benefit has accrued to the naval service of Great Britain, by the institution of the Sea Fencibles', and if 'the abolition of them would not greatly contribute to the manning of our ships of war'.[17] They were disbanded at the peace of 1801, but in 1803 St Vincent revived them, despite many doubts. They were not to be raised until the impress service had had some time to recruit men for the fleet.

The Sea Fencibles were now placed under the command of Lord Keith, who was also in charge of the North Sea fleet. By the end of 1803, they were quite a substantial force — there were 941 men between Emsworth and Beachy Head, 'all perfect in the boat and great gun exercises', with fifty-nine boats; 250 men from Sandown to North Foreland, with seventeen boats, and 'every boat in the district is in perfect readiness'.[18] In South Devon, the force was rather uneven. At Dartmouth 'The Sea Fencibles amount to 250, and consist chiefly of shipwrights.' At Start Point 'The Sea Fencibles in this bay... amount to forty-six, the greatest part of these are clearly liable to the impress, as they are all fishermen in boats which do not allow more than one man being protected.' At Bigbury, 'The Sea Fencibles in this place are 146, they are mostly bargemen who are employed in open boats to dredge for a particular sort of sea sand for the purpose of agriculture.' At Plymouth there were 239, but 100 of these were employed by the customs, and exercised with the Sea Fencibles. The rest were mostly fishermen.[19]

The Sea Fencibles grew to a maximum strength of 23,455 in 1810.[20] They occasionally exchanged long-range fire with small enemy forces, as in 1804, when the Hastings Fencibles fired their battery guns at

An East India Company officer's uniform. Author's photograph, courtesy of the National Maritime Museum a French privateer, and lamented the lack of any armed vessel with which they could have pursued it.[21] However, the invasion did not materialise, and by 1810 it was clear that it would never come. The Sea Fencibles were disbanded that year.

Trinity House

The Corporation of Trinity House had been founded in the reign of Henry VII, and was headed by a committee of masters, wardens and elder bretheren. Since the demolition of its hall at Deptford in 1787, it had been based at Tower Hill in London. It had many duties connected with the sea — the examining of masters for the navy, the appointment of pilots for the River Thames, the control of ballastage and dredging in the river, for example. It was also responsible for the setting up and maintenance of lighthouses, light-ships and other sea marks around the coasts of England, and this caused it to create a small fleet of vessels. The flagship was the *Trinity* yacht of 100 tons, built in 1791 and used to take the Elder Bretheren on tours of inspection, as well as more mundane duties. Other vessels used from 1793 to 1815 included: the *Argus* of 1791, the Wells and Yarmouth tenders of 60 tons, a Yarmouth survey tender of 20 tons, the *Antelope*, a cutter of 36 tons for servicing the Eddystone lighthouse, and an unnamed buoy yacht.[22] Cutters were also used to take pilots out to incoming vessels, and take them off those departing; but these were not owned by Trinity House. The size of such vessels could vary considerably according to local conditions.

During the invasion scare of 1805, Trinity House made a contribution to the defence of the Thames. At the expense of £10,000, it raised a force of 1200 men, to man blockships moored across the entrance to the river at Lower Hope. They were a mixed body, including 'seamen, landmen, volunteers, pilots, lascars, harbour volunteer marines, river fencibles, Greenwich pensioners and East India Company pensioners'.[23] Elder Bretheren assumed the military rank of captain, while the senior warden became a major, and the deputy master became a lieutenant colonel in command of the force. The blockships were mostly old frigates, and the *Trinity* yacht served as a tender. The force was disbanded after two years.

Privateers

Unlike the other auxiliary naval services, privateers were neither paid for nor controlled by the government. They were privately owned men-of-war, sponsored by merchants and allowed to prey on enemy merchant vessels. Each privateer was issued with a letter of marque, signed by the Lords of the Admiralty. Without this, it was merely a pirate, and its crew, if captured, were liable to be hanged as pirates rather than treated as prisoners of war. Privateering had no role in British naval strategy, and apart from the issue of letters it was virtually ignored by the government. Letters of marque of the Napoleonic Wars came under an act passed by parliament soon after the outbreak of war, giving privateers' licences 'for apprenhending, seizing and taking the ships and vessels and goods belonging to the French Republic'. Captured ships were to be brought before prize courts, and if it was decided that the vessel was legal prize, the whole value of it was divided among the owners and crew of the ship.

It is difficult to believe that British privateering was very profitable, since enemy commerce was usually confined to its harbours from quite early in the war. Nevertheless, quite large numbers of letters of marque were issued — 300 by the end of June 1803, and a further 561 by the end of that year. The rate slowed down quite considerably after that, and in 1810 only 167 were issued for the whole year. Some ships were quite large. The *Marquis of Ely*, for example, was almost equivalent to a naval frigate — 1316 tons, thirty-six 18-pounder carronades, and 130 men. More typical ships were around 200 tons, such as the *Cornwallis* snow of 184 tons, with 10-pounders, 12-pounders and 6-pounders and thirty men. Some were much smaller — the *Mary and Ann* schooner was 62 tons, and had four 4-pounder guns, with a crew of ten.[24]

The island of Guernsey fitted out eighty-eight privateers from 1793 to 1805, though only twelve were in service in 1800, carrying 148 guns and 670 men between them.[25] In previous wars, many privateers came from ports such as Bristol, whose own trade suffered from French raiders, but which did not share in the work created by having naval bases nearby. However, Bristol privateers were less active by this time, and only a dozen or so are known from these years. Liverpool privateers began their work early, and took their first prize on 5 April 1793. That port continued to fit out many privateers in the next twenty years.

The East India Company

As well as its fleet of ships carrying goods between Europe and Asia, the East India Company had a small navy to protect its interests in the east. It was based at Bombay, and in 1807, it had thirteen vessels; the ship *Mornington* of 24 guns, three brigs of 12 to 20 guns, four snows of 12 to 14 guns, three ketches of 14 to 20 guns, a schooner of six guns, and a small vessel of unidentified rig and gun power.[26] Most of its vessels were built in the Bombay dockyard, and more were added in later years — the *Thames*, a bomb vessel of 102 tons in 1814, the *Aurora* sloop of war of 14 guns and 247 tons in 1808, for example.[27] Its officers were divided into senior captains, captains, first lieutenants, second lieutenants, midshipmen, and volunteers. The rank of commodore could be created for special purposes. The force operated mainly against pirates, or in support of land operations against Indian princes, though it also took part in several fights with French privateers. Ships were sometimes sent in support of naval operations, such as the attack on Java in 1812.

The Packet Service

The Post Office maintained a small fleet of vessels for carrying mails over the seas. Its ships were of different sizes, according to the route they were designed for. The most important port was Falmouth, the base for services across the Atlantic and to Spain, Portugal and the Mediterranean. The transatlantic packets had originally been planned to be 150 tons each, but the masters had protested about this, and they were increased to 170 tons. They had been designed by Marmaduke Stalkaart, author of a well-known textbook on naval architecture. They were 61ft long, with a crew of twenty-eight. Each had six passenger cabins, and cabins for the captain, master, mate, surgeon, boatswain and carpenter. They were ship rigged, and in 1807 there were five of them operating to Lisbon, fourteen more to the West Indies and North America, as well as four non-standard ships of 180 or 220 tons, with thirty-six men each.[28]

Smaller vessels were used on other routes. The Harwich to Holland service used six 70-ton vessels, apparently schooner rigged, with seventeen men each. The Dover vessels were of 50 or 60 tons, with ten or sixteen men. Three more, based at Weymouth, were of 50 tons and sixteen men, and carried mail to the Channel Islands. There were ten vessels at Holyhead and Milford for the Irish services, of 70 or 80 tons, with eleven men each. Other boats were hired for services within the West Indies, from Whitehaven to the Isle of Man, and at Dongahadee in Ireland.[29] The packet services suffered quite heavily from storm and enemy action during the wars. Forty-six vessels were lost in the French Revolutionary War, mostly taken by privateers. Thirty-five more were taken in the Napoleonic Wars, including a large number taken by the Americans during the war of 1812.[30] Several others were sunk, including the *Lady Hobart* which struck an iceberg off Newfoundland in 1803.

Part XIII
FOREIGN NAVIES

1 The French Navy

History

The French navy was the main rival of the British fleet from 1689 onwards, and it was the second largest navy in the world for most of this period. It was often said that France was not really a maritime nation in the same way as Britain or the Netherlands were — that her merchant fleet was relatively small, that her navy always took second place to the army, and that she was less dependent on sea transport than other countries. Nevertheless, the French fleet remained prominent throughout the eighteenth and nineteenth centuries. It suffered many defeats, and a few disasters — at Barfleur in 1692, Quiberon Bay in 1759, and Trafalgar in 1805. It always recovered from them within a few years, and began to threaten British supremacy yet again.

The modern French navy had its origins with Jean-Baptiste Colbert, who held office as navy minister between 1669 and 1683, under Louis XIV. He produced a regular system of administration, recruitment and training, and built up a fleet of 199 ships and vessels by 1677, making it the largest fleet in the world for a time. He encouraged several new types of vessel, such as the bomb ketch, used initially against the Mediterranean corsairs. This fleet won the Battle of Beachy Head against combined Dutch and English forces, but was heavily defeated at Barfleur and La Hogue in 1692. After that, the main battlefleet was neglected, and the government concentrated on the *guerre de course* — sending privateers against English and Dutch shipping. This was the golden age of privateering, and men like Jean Bart and Duguay Trouin, based in ports such as St Malo and Dunkirk, built up great reputations for themselves. There was considerable panic in British commercial circles, though it is unlikely that the privateers really had the means to defeat British sea power.

France was engaged in several major wars with Britain after that; Spanish Succession, Austrian Succession, the Seven Years' War and the War of American Independence. The French fleet was always a decisive factor, until it was destroyed in battle — at the Battles of Finisterre in 1747, Quiberon Bay in 1759, and the Saintes in 1782. The *guerre de course* remained a central part of policy, and caused the British to make much use of convoys and cruisers to protect merchant shipping.

Administration

The French navy was controlled by the Ministre de la Marine et des Colonies. The powers of the ministry were defined by a decree of 1795. They included control over the officer corps, the Inscription Maritime, naval schools, crews of ships, health of seamen, hydrography, dockyards, shipbuilding, fisheries, and many other naval matters. The period produced no great naval ministers at the level of Colbert, but some served with considerable competence. Admiral Truguet, appointed in November 1795, regained control of the fleet from the revolutionaries, and began to return it to pre-revolutionary standards of administration. Under Napoleon, the most important navy minister was Decres, appointed in 1801. He enjoyed considerable support from the emperor, but was generally timid in his conduct of strategy.

Ships

The French navy built very fine ships, and many of these served as models for British construction after their capture. The French relied less than anyone else on outside influences for their design — they never copied captured ships, or employed emigré shipwrights. Instead they depended on scientific training for their builders, who were taught at a special school in Paris. Though the positive effects of this can easily be exaggerated, there is no doubt the French naval architects were highly competent. However, ship design was almost static by this time. In 1786 the naval administration imposed standard

A model of the 74-gun ship Eole *of 1789. She was damaged at the First of June, and took part in the campaign in the West Indies in 1806.* The National Maritime Museum

Craft of the 1803 invasion flotilla.
1 A vessel of the 1st class, a prame
2 A chaloupe – a gun vessel of the 1st class
3 A 2nd class gunboat, type 'Muskin'
4 A 2nd class gunboat, type 'Carlin'
5 A 2nd class gunboat, of the Dutch type
6 A vessel of the 3rd class, a peniche
7 Another type of peniche
8 and 9 Caiques
Based on drawings in Desbrière's *Projets et Tentatives de Debarquement aux Iles Britanniques*, vol II, 1901

designs, by Jacques-Noel Sané, on the fleet. Thus all 80s or 74s, for example, were built to the same draught, and the naval architects in the dockyards were allowed little initiative.

The French navy tended to concentrate on the larger classes within each number of decks. Three-deckers were of 120 guns, and two-deckers of 80 or 74. Construction of the 64 ceased quite early, and by 1786 there was only one left in the fleet; the 90 or 98-gun ship was never common in France. With frigates, the standard type was the 'fregate de 18', with twenty-six 18-pounders on the upper deck, and ten carronades on the quarterdeck and forecastle; equivalent to the British 36. Older frigates had thirty-two guns, with only 12-pounders on the gundeck, while in 1806 the 44-gun frigate was recognised, with twenty-eight 18-pounders as the main armament. Corvettes (equivalent to British sloops) increased greatly in numbers in the early nineteenth century, and these usually had twenty guns.[1] Various types of flotilla craft were developed, in support of the projected invasion — 'tartanes', each carrying a single 36-pounder gun with a single lateen rigged mast, and brig or lugger rigged gunboats, for example.

In 1792, the French navy had 241 ships and vessels, including eighty-three of the line and seventy-seven frigates. The number of ships-of-the-line was reduced over the years, largely because of defeat in battle. In 1800, there were only forty-six in the fleet, though by 1804 this had risen to fifty-one. Defeat at Trafalgar reduced the number quite considerably; in 1807, the navy reached its nadir at

The decorations of the Bucentaure, *the French flagship at Trafalgar.* British Library

thirty-five ships-of-the-line. However the post-Trafalgar building programme built up its strength again, and by 1813 it was almost back at its pre-war strength, with seventy-one ships-of-the-line, and forty-two more under construction. The number of frigates reached its peak in 1795, with 101 on the list. It fell drastically after that, and was never more than forty between 1801 and 1813. The number of smaller craft increased greatly during the wars, partly because of the building of the invasion flotilla in the 1800s. In 1793 there were only 187 small craft in the fleet, but then numbers reached a peak in 1795, at 551; and another in 1811, at 922.[2]

French ships shared a common technology with the British, and captured ships from one fleet could serve quite easily in the other. However, there were certain differences in construction and fitting. French ships were of slightly lighter scantling. They did not use cant frames near the bow and stern, but instead their timbers went straight from ordinary frames to hawse pieces at the bows. The deck layouts were slightly different. French two-deckers stowed their boats on the upper deck in the waist, not on booms at the level of the quarterdeck and forecastle; the main capstan was placed aft between the lower and upper deck, as on British ships; but the fore capstan was much smaller, and placed well forward, between the upper deck and forecastle deck. The sternpost tended to be straighter than on British ships, and therefore the rudder was more upright.

The gun arrangement of the French 74 was slightly different from the British one. Both had fourteen ports per side on the lower deck, but the French ships had one more on the upper deck, with fewer guns on the quarterdeck. Even in the most egalitarian days of the Revolution, the French preferred to keep the captain's cabin free of guns, and this had some influence on gun arrangements. The French pound was slightly heavier than the English one, so that the French 18-pounder, for example, was larger than its equivalent in Britain. The 36-pounder was the standard weapon of the French battlefleet, and this gun fired a ball actually weighing 39 English pounds — almost as heavy as the 42-pounders which the British were discarding from their first rates. Perhaps this contributed to the slow rate of fire of French ships.

The interior of Brest harbour. From the Naval Chronicle

The entrance to Rochefort Dockyard. Author's photograph

Bases

France had no large natural harbour on her north coast; Boulogne, Le Havre and Cherbourg all served the navy to some extent, but provided no anchorage comparable to those at Portsmouth and Plymouth on the opposite side of the Channel. The main northern French base was at Brest, near the western tip of Britanny. Its position had many advantages — it allowed the fleet to choose between an attack across the Atlantic, or southwards, or to Ireland or even an invasion of England; the coast outside was exposed and rocky, making the blockade all the more difficult. On the other hand, Brest was some way from the more industrial regions of France, and it was difficult getting supplies to the port, either by land or sea. Brest had extensive storehouses, barracks, building slips and docks, and all the facilities of a main dockyard. Brest Roads provided a large and safe anchorage.

Brest harbour. From the Naval Chronicle

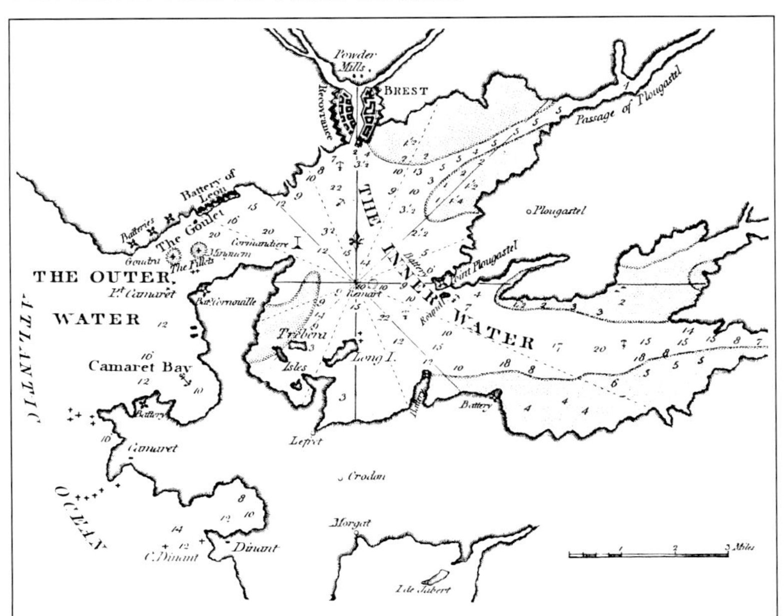

Rochefort was the main base on the French Atlantic coast. It had been founded by Colbert in the late seventeenth century, and was close to the anchorages of Aix and Basque Roads, sheltered by the islands of Re and Oleron, but it was some way up the narrow and winding River Charente. Even more than Chatham and the Thames yards, it suffered from contrary winds and unfavourable tides. It was one of the few planned dockyard towns in Europe, with full facilities, including a foundry for the manufacture of cannon. The navy also used the port of L'Orient, further to the north along the Atlantic coast. This port had originally been developed by the East India Company.

The main Mediterranean base was at Toulon. According to Captain Brenton, 'The great and only naval arsenal of France in the Mediterranean is Toulon; a place that has been called one of the finest ports of maritime equipment in the world, though it falls infinitely short of Portsmouth, either as a harbour or depot, or of

The Tonnant, *80 guns, badly damaged at the Nile, but not yet ready to surrender.* The National Maritime Museum

◁ *A seaman-gunner of the Corps d'Artillerie de la Marine.* From the *Ordonance* of 1786

Spithead as an anchorage.'[3] In addition, several important foreign bases came under French control during the wars, particularly in the Netherlands and northern Italy. Flushing in the Netherlands was seen as 'a pistol pointed at the heart of England', while Genoa, Venice and Spezzia were also under French control for long periods.

Officers

The officer corps was perhaps the greatest weakness of the French navy. The pre-revolutionary officers had been aristocratic, well trained and professional, but the Reign of Terror had caused many of these to flee the country, while those that remained were often distrusted by the government. Promotion was very fast for some, and Villaret-Joyeuse went from lieutenant to commander-in-chief in three years. Revolutionary fervour was enough to make good soldiers, but sailors needed technical skills which could not be learned without long years of experience. The government tried various expedients to find officers for its ships. Merchant captains were allowed to become lieutenants and captains, but this did not solve the problem, for they were trained in navigating their ships from one port to another, but not in fighting. The experiment of placing revolutionary agitators to keep an eye on the officers worked no better. Jean-Bon St André, a member of the Committee of Public Safety, gained no respect at the First of June battle, when he retired to the cockpit at the beginning of the action. A naval officer requires a peculiar blend of technical skill, fighting ability, and loyalty to the state. Merchant captains, soldiers and revolutionary organisers each had some of these attributes, but they were not combined in a single person. The French navy of the early 1790s was not well run. Subsequently, efficient training programmes were organised for officers, and naval schools were formed in the 1800s.

Officers began their careers as *aspirants*. This title was created by the republicans, to replace the old one of *garde marine*; after 1814, they were renamed *élèves de la marine*. The lowest rank of commissioned officer was *enseigne de vaisseau*, followed by *lieutenant*; roughly similar in duties and status to a British naval lieutenant. Captains were divided into two classes. The *captaine de frégate* was of less than three years seniority, while the *captaine de vaisseau* was equivalent to a senior captain in the British establishment. Above the captains, was a hierarchy of *contre-amiral*, *vice-amiral* and *amiral*. The old grade of *chef d'escadre* had been replaced by *contre-amiral* in 1789.

Seamen

It is estimated that there were about 60,000 French seamen at the beginning of the wars,[4] so the base from which the navy was recruited was about half that available to the British. To get these seamen into the navy, the government had long since used the *Inscription Maritime* — a system of conscription. The *Inscription* had been founded by Colbert in 1681. Seamen were registered by the state, and called to service in the navy when needed. By a law of '4 Brumaire An IV' [1796] in the revolutionary calendar, seamen were divided into four classes; unmarried men, widowers without children, married men without children, and fathers of families. They were also divided into divisions, round the main bases at Brest, Toulon, Rochefort, L'Orient and Le Havre. Sailors of more than fifty years of age were exempt from conscription, but the others were called up by class and division when necessary. From 1808, ships' carpenters and caulkers were also subject to the *Inscription Maritime*. The French system of conscription was, on paper at least, far more efficient than the British press gang, though the results were not always as successful as they might have been. In a state where men were regularly conscripted into the army, the drafting of seamen excited less comment than did the press gang in Britain.

The French navy had a corps of regular long-service men, known as the *Corps d'Artillerie de la Marine*. It consisted of seamen gunners, who served as dockyard guards in peacetime and as the nucleus of crews when the ships fitted out for war. The corps also included specialised bombardiers, trained in the use of the mortars of bomb vessels. The corps was abolished in 1793, as part of a drive against élitism by the revolutionary government; it was re-established in the 1800s.

In the early stages of the Revolutionary War, the seamen were a somewhat disruptive force. The discipline of ships had largely broken down, and seamen often joined rioters ashore. Unpopular officers were hounded out, while crews agitated for better conditions. Order was restored in the 1790s; in any case, the French seaman remained reasonably efficient when actually at sea.

Napoleon attempted to rebuild his navy after Trafalgar, using methods more akin to those of a contemporary army, or indeed of a modern navy. Fifty battalions of the Imperial Marine were formed in 1808 with uniforms and shakos (though the stiff leather hats worn by soldiers were not retained at sea). They were trained in musketry, and each crew was given an eagle standard, like an army regiment. A group of Marines of the Guard was formed, on the model of the Imperial Gurd which was made up of the élite soldiers of the army. However, none of this could compensate for the fleet's demoralisation and lack of real sea training.

Strategy and Tactics

Since the defeat at Barfleur in 1692, French admirals had come to recognise that they were unlikely to gain control of the seas from the British, even when they were allied with Spain and the Netherlands, and had numerical superiority. The French fleet made little impression on the colonial wars of the 1790s and 1800s, or contribution to the defence of the French coast — but the strength of the French army made it extremely unlikely that the British would invade by sea. The main task of the French fleet, in co-operation with its allies, was to act as a threat to the British — as a 'fleet in being', which might be doing very little at the moment, but would be ready to strike anywhere when the chance came. In particular, the fleet threatened an invasion of Britain. The French never attempted 'commando' raids on the British coast, for this would have been difficult without some measure of control of the seas. However, full-scale invasion was on the agenda every time France and her allies had numerical superiority — in 1779–80, 1796 and in 1804–5. At a slightly lower level, there was always the possibility of French support for rebels within the British territories. The Scottish Jacobites had been defeated half a century before, but the threat of rebellion in Ireland was always present, and came to a head in 1798. In practice, French support for such insurrections was always ineffective.

The French fleet tended to concentrate on specific tasks, whereas the British one was designed for the more general control of the seas. British ships would seek battle when there was any prospect of victory, but the French tended to avoid it unless it was absolutely necessary — their role was to carry out a specific mission, and a sea battle would cause delays, or even the abandonment of the objective. Because of this, they received the scorn of the Mahan school of naval historians, but it could be argued that they were using sea power in the best way available to them.

It was well known that in battle the French aimed at the rigging rather than the hulls of their opponents. This, it was hoped, would allow them to escape from pursuit. It seems that there was no official policy to encourage these tactics, but they were certainly used, with the result that British casualties in action were often remarkably light compared with those of the French. In fleet battles, the French showed little tactical sophistication, mainly because their captains were trained in no manoeuvres other than forming a line of battle. Had their tactics been more sophisticated, Nelson's victory at Trafalgar would have been much more difficult.

Privateers

Ever since the 1690s, the French had used privateers against British commerce. It is doubtful if this was ever more than a nuisance against a determined British State, but the *guerre de course* cost the state nothing, as it was financed by private enterprise. Legend suggests that it was highly profitable to its participants, but a more sober analysis shows that, on average, it barely broke even. Shipowners and sailors often had no other way of making a living in the face of the British blockade.

St Malo, in Britanny, was one of the premier corsair ports. By 1796 it was sending out twenty-eight ships, which captured thirty-eight vessels during that year (though nine of the privateers were themselves captured). Other Breton ports included Morlaix, Brest, Quimper, Port Louis, and Nantes; the last port fitted out sixteen privateers in 1793. Other privateering ports including Bayonne and St Jean-de-Luz on the southern Atlantic coast, and Dunkirk in the English Channel. In the Mediterranean, privateers were based at Marseilles and other ports.[5]

The golden age of French privateering was long past by 1793, but some captains made names for themselves — L'Hermitte, Soleil, Leduc, Troude and Lamarre-Lameillerie, for example. Privateering effort tended to decline over the years. Between 1803 and 1814, 178 privateers were active from St Malo, and 77 of these were captured. A mere nineteen ships were sent out in 1809, only nine of which were more than 100 tons. By 1810, France still had 195 corsairs, employing 9923 men.[6] By 1812, less than half these numbers were active.[7]

Merchant Shipping

French commerce was hard hit by the wars. Apart from privateers, which used their speed or their gun power to take care of themselves, French merchant ships were almost driven from the high seas. Some coasters continued to operate, by sailing under the protection of shore batteries; without them, it would have been very difficult to supply ports such as Brest with victuals and materials.

2 The Spanish Navy

History

The Spanish navy, like the Spanish empire, reached its zenith in the sixteenth century. Phillip had ruled the Netherlands, the Phillipines and most of America, while other members of his family ruled Austria and parts of Italy. The decline of the empire started with the Dutch revolts which began in 1572, and was accelerated by the failure of the 'Invincible Armada' sent against England in 1588. The naval defeat was not fatal, and the war continued for another fifteen years after that; but in the following century, under weak kings, Spain gained no new territories, while her navy was completely overshadowed by those of England, France and Holland. After the War of Spanish Succession (1702–14), there was a family alliance between the kings of Spain and France. The fleet had a major setback in 1718, when it was defeated by the British at the Battle of Cape Passaro, with the loss of twenty-two ships.

The Spanish navy, like the French, began to revive in the 1730s, and some new ships were built. The War of Jenkin's Ear began in 1739, and, for almost five years, the Spanish were alone against the British fleet; they acquitted themselves quite well, and suffered no major defeats except the loss of Portobello at the beginning of the war. The Spanish joined the Seven Years' War rather late — in 1761. The war was disastrous for both the empire and the navy; Havana and Manila were both taken, with the loss of many ships. Spain joined the American War of Independence in 1779, and her ships formed part of the Franco Spanish fleet which dominated the Channel for a time. However, nothing was achieved, partly because of the poor administration of the Spanish navy. Spain had no major victories, and her ships were defeated at the Moonlight Battle of St Vincent in 1780. At the peace treaty, she regained Minorca and Florida, but not Gibraltar, which had withstood a siege for several years.

Administration

The Spanish navy had been reformed in the early part of the eighteenth century, under Patino. It was changed from a federation of local forces into a single national one. A shipbuilding programme introduced modern types using the best principles of French and British design. The old aristocratic officer corps was replaced by a more modern one, and the dockyards were developed, and concentrated in fewer places.

From 1787 until 1796, Antonio Valdés was navy minister. He was himself a former naval and marine officer, and therefore acquainted with the problems of the service.[1] The biggest difficulty of this period was lack of money. The Spanish economy was not expanding at the same rate as the British and French ones, and the riches of the Indies were no longer enough to support a modern fleet. Valdés's administration saw a considerable amount of shipbuilding, but though the ships of the navy were of good quality, other resources were in short supply. After Valdés, the naval administration was less efficient, and the Prime Minister Godoy was no advocate of naval power.

Ships

Like many navies, the Spanish were not afraid to use the shipbuilding ideas of others. The Spanish navy took ideas and practices from both France and Britain, usually in the form of immigrant shipbuilders. These included Richard Rooth of England and Matthew Mullan of Ireland, who directed the naval yard at Havana, and built the *Santisima Trinidad*. The leading French shipbuilder was Jean François Gautier, who had learned his trade in the dockyard at Toulon and went to Spain in 1765. He designed many ships, including the

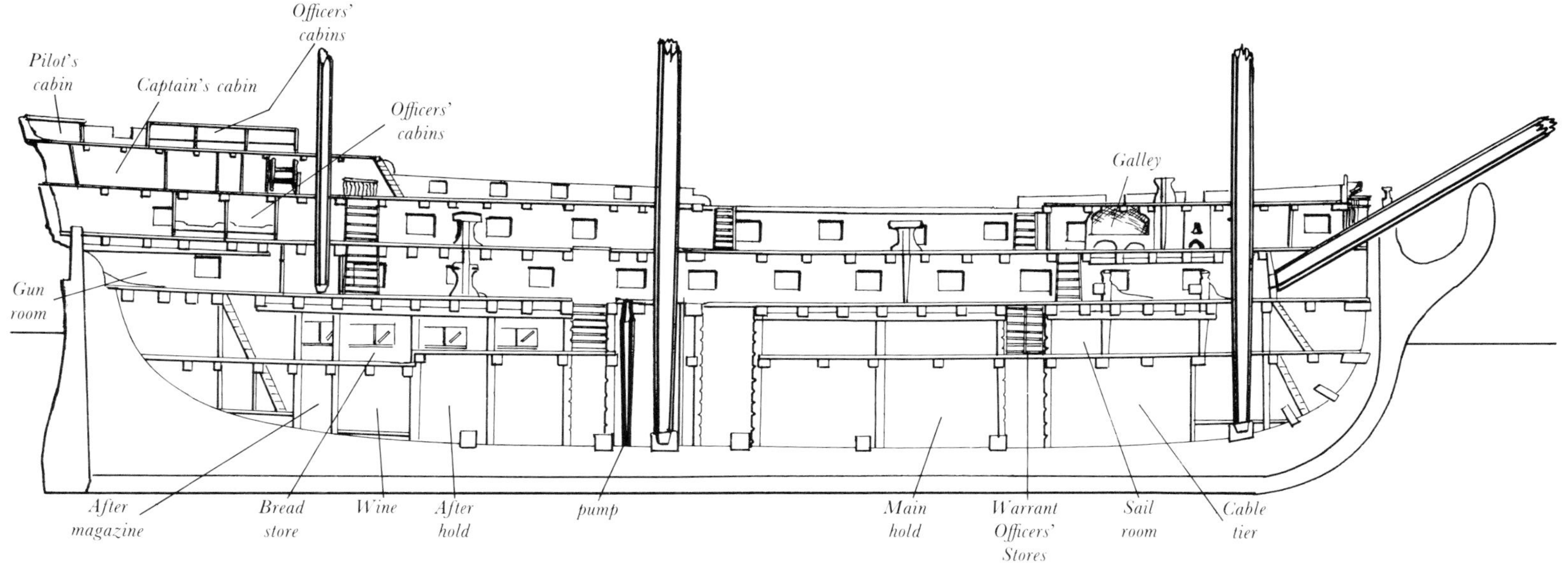

A longitudinal section of a Spanish 74. Based on a drawing in the Museo Naval, Madrid

74-gun *San Juan Nepomuceno*, which was launched in 1767 and lost at Trafalgar. Despite the alliance with France, the Spanish tended more towards British style construction. They still had a large overseas empire, and to defend it they needed sturdy ships which could survive long periods away from dockyards. The most important of the native Spanish designers was José Romero y Landa, who served as director of engineering from 1792 to 1794. He produced the *San Idelfonso* class of 74s.

Scale model of the hull of San Juan Nepomuceno, *captured at Trafalgar. She served in the Royal Navy as the* San Juan *until 1808.* Museo Naval, Madrid.

The Spanish navy had forty-seven ships-of-the-line in 1796. It tended to favour large ships, including three-deckers. The pride of the fleet was the *Santisima Trinidad*, built at Havana in 1769. This ship was a four-decker, with 130 guns, and the largest ship in the world at the time. In fact she represented a very old fashioned idea of ship design, which put height of battery before sailing qualities. Many naval officers were fully aware that she sailed badly, and before Trafalgar, Admiral Mazarredo recommended that she be used only for the defence of Cadiz harbour.[2] Nevertheless, she put to sea, was captured by Nelson, and lost after the battle. Three-deckers were more common; eleven ships of 112 guns were built between 1779 and 1794, though no more were built after that; five 80-gun two-deckers were also built from 1795 to 1803. As with all major navies, the 74 was the backbone of the line of battle, and eight of them fought at Trafalgar. As with other navies, the 64 was obsolete, but retained in service because nothing else was available. Spanish ships-of-the-line were much respected by the British, though none was ever copied. Spanish frigates were less admired, but there were fifty-three in the fleet in 1794. The navy also had some purely Mediterranean types, such as the xebec, copied from the North African Corsairs and armed with 14 to 36 guns.

◁ Santisima Trinidad, *the largest ship in the world when she was built at Havana in 1769.* Museo Naval, Madrid

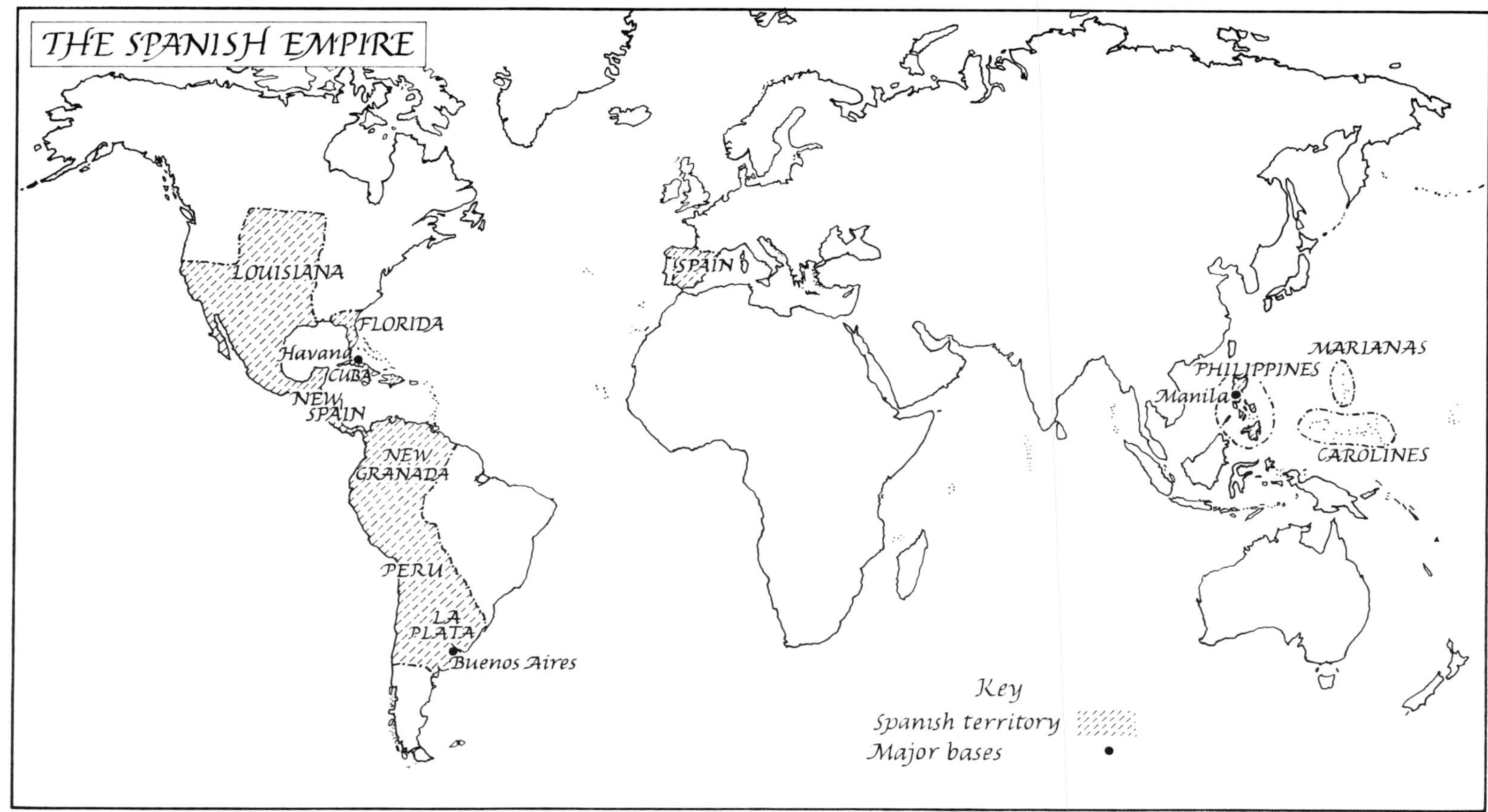

Spanish bases around the world.

Bases

There were four major home naval bases — Cartagena in the Mediterranean, La Carraca near Cadiz, El Ferrol in the northwest corner of the country, and Guarnizo near Santander, on the northern coast. The Spanish went much further than any of the other European powers in the development of their overseas facilities, with bases in South and Central America, the Caribbean and the Phillipines. The dockyard at Havana was the best-developed naval port outside Europe, and, unlike the British and French, the Spanish were prepared to build large warships away from the homeland, using supplies of American timber. Havana built seventy-four ships-of-the-line during the eighteenth century, including the *Santisima Trinidad.*

Officers

Officer ranks in the Spanish navy generally followed those of the French. The highest rank was *capitan general de la armada*, equivalent to admiral of the fleet. There were *amiralantes* (admirals) and *teniente generales* (sixteen in 1795). The *jefe de escuadra* was equivalent to a rear admiral, or a *chef d'escadre* in the old French system. There were fifteen in the fleet of 1795. A *brigadier* was not equivalent to a commodore, but was merely a senior captain, who did not necessarily have any ships but his own under him. Other captains were divided into three grades — *capitan de navio*, *capitan de fregata* and *capitan de corbeta*; in 1795, there were 110, 143 and 221 officers in the respective ranks. A *teniente de navio* was equivalent to a lieutenant in the Royal Navy, and there were 224 of these in 1795.[3] Below these, were the *alferez de navio* and *alferez de fregata* — titles based on old administrative ranks in local government, and similar to ensigns in the French service. the *guardia marina* was equivalent to a midshipman, and below him was the *aspirante*, or naval cadet. In all, there were 1324 officers of midshipman rank or above in the navy of 1795.

There is no doubt about the personal courage of Spanish officers. At Trafalgar, men such as Churucca fought their ships bravely, and in some cases lost their lives. They did not entirely lack sea experience, for some had made important voyages of exploration before the wars, but they — like their crews — had little training in the techniques of handling ships-of-the-line in battle.

Men

More even than the British and French, the Spanish found that the size and efficiency of their fleet was limited by the number of experienced seamen they could recruit. A report of 1787 showed that the country had only 53,147 registered mariners, whereas 89,350 would be needed to man the fleet fully. It was pointed out that only 5800 of these were deep-sea sailors; the rest were from the coastal or fishing trades.[4] Seamen were raised for the navy by a form of conscription known as *la leva*. When this failed to produce enough men, landmen were taken. The Spanish ships-of-the-line spent little time at sea, so it was not possible to drill these men to become effective seamen.

It is often said that the Spanish navy relied too heavily on soldiers in the fleet, and army officers were given too much prominence afloat. The problem was not just numerical. A Spanish 74-gun ship had a total crew of 510, with 112 marine infantry and thirty-eight marine artillerymen — about 30 per cent of her crew were military. This compares with a British 74 of around 1810, in which about 20 per cent were marines. The Spanish had a regular marine corps, known as the *Compania Real de Guardia de la Marina*, though like the British they often used soldiers from the army aboard ship. However, the status of the army officer was much higher in Spain, and he was more likely to interfere in the running of the ship.

The remnants of the French and Spanish fleets off Cádiz after Trafalgar. Manuel Gómez Moreno

Strategy and Tactics

As a rule, the Spanish navy did not produce many original strategic ideas, but preferred to follow the policies of its main ally, usually France. The Spanish battlefleet had actually sailed with the French in the American War, and the combined fleet had dominated the Channel, though to little effect. It was to come under French orders again at Trafalgar. Apart from that, one important task of the Spanish navy was the defence of the empire, which was still large, and included most of Latin America, except for Brazil and the Guyanas, several large islands in the Caribbean such as Cuba and Hispaniola, parts of North America such as California, and the Phillipines. Ships were stationed to protect these territories, especially at the great base at Havana. However, such ships had to be spread very thinly, and the main burden of defence was land based. In a sense it was quite effective, and British attacks on the Spanish possessions were only successful in the case of small islands, such as Trinidad, where sea power was at its most effective. The larger islands were mostly left alone; and the only major attack on the mainland, at Buenos Aires in 1807, was both unauthorised and unsuccessful.

The Spanish empire in America was a great source of wealth for the home government, in the form of gold and silver. Traditionally, this had been carried to Spain by convoys, which sailed on regular routes at fixed times of the year, bringing the bullion to Seville. By the 1790s, the old system had largely been abandoned, and the new one was much less rigid. However, Spanish frigates still had the task of bringing home the wealth of empire, and the capture of such ships was still the dream of every British officer and seaman. In 1804, while Britain and Spain were still at peace, a squadron of four British frigates attacked a similar number of Spanish frigates which were known to be carrying a large consignment of treasure from Montevideo. The Spanish ships defended themselves, but one blew up and three were captured. This precipitated Spain's declaration of war on Britain, though she had already decided to begin hostilities before the attack.

Vice Admiral Frederico Gravino, the Spanish Commander at Trafalgar. Musee Naval, Madrid

The End of the Spanish Sailing Navy

During the wars, the Spanish lost seventy-nine ships-of-the-line. Twenty-two were lost in action, and ten more by accident at sea. Thirty-nine were condemned because of their bad condition, and eight more fell into French hands.[5] The Spanish revolt began in 1808, when Napoleon attempted to send an army through the country to invade Portugal. Meeting resistance from the Spanish people, he deposed the king and put his own brother on the throne. Over the next six years the Spanish fought against the French on land, mainly by guerrilla action, until the enemy was driven from the country. However, that part of the Spanish navy which had survived Trafalgar disappeared. The French held the main ports, including Cadiz, and took control of the ships there. This was not fatal to the cause, and the Peninsular War was supported by the British fleet, but Spain had no navy of her own until it began to revive after 1825.

3 The American Navy

History

The United States Navy had originated during the War of Independence, and was first established by Congress in 1775. After the peace of 1783, it was decided to disband the force, and by 1785, its ships had been sold off. However, American merchant ships were left without protection, either from the press gangs of the British fleet or the corsairs of the Barbary States. By 1794, there was trouble with the Dey of Algiers, and merchant ships had to be bought and hired for a campaign against that port. Congress passed an act authorising the building of six frigates, and the navy was reborn. Agreement was reached with Algiers before the ships were ready, but by 1798 there was conflict with France over the rights of American merchant ships. This led to a 'quasi war', in which the *Constellation* captured the French frigates *L'Insurgente* and *La Vengeance*. From 1801–5 there was another conflict with the Barbary corsairs, this time with Tripoli. The frigate *Philadelphia* grounded off that port in 1803, and was captured; in the following year, a landing party from the *Constitution* entered the harbour and destroyed the ship.

Conflict with Britain developed slowly over the years, due to the interruption to American trade caused by the British blockade, and to the British custom of boarding American ships to search for alleged British citizens or deserters. Americans found it very difficult to prove their nationality to a press gang, even with certificates from their consuls and State governors. In 1812, the American State Department had records of 6257 Americans impressed into the Royal Navy, and there were perhaps twice as many unrecorded cases.[1] When the war broke out, 2548 Americans in the British fleet refused to serve and were imprisoned. Even before 1812, there had been conflict between British and American warships, when the *Chesapeake* was fired on by the *Leopard* in 1807, and the British *Little Belt* was attacked by the USS *President* in 1811.

The public saw the war as a series of single-ship actions, but there were also amphibious operations against Washington and New Orleans, an extensive war against trade, and a campaign on the Great Lakes. In the frigate actions, the Americans had great success in the early stages, and caused changes in British policy. The honours were more even in the latter part of the war, and peace was made at the end of 1814, though it took six months for hostilities to cease in all parts of the world. The United States Navy began the war with a force of seventeen warships, none larger than a frigate. By the end, it had launched its first ship-of-the-line, and quadrupled in size.

Administration

The administration of the United States Navy was, and is, headed by the president, who is designated by the constitution as the commander-in-chief of the armed forces. During the war of 1812, the president was James Madison. Under the president was the Navy Office in Washington, set up in 1798. This was headed by the secretary of the navy, an office first held by Benjamin Stoddert. Congress also had a certain amount of control over the fleet. According to the constitution, only Congress could declare war. It voted funds for the navy, and passed acts which regulated its growth. Such an act caused the building of six frigates of 1794, though even that was conditional — if the conflict with Algiers was resolved, the building of the ships was to be stopped. In fact, an extra act was needed to continue their building.

Strategy

As late as 1812, Americans as a whole were still uncertain about whether they needed a sea-going navy at all. Under President Thomas Jefferson (1801–9), construction concentrated on small gunboats for coastal defence, and it was argued tht these would be enough to protect the major ports from invasion, while the militia could defeat any landing. It was also felt that privateers would be enough to deter any opponent on the high seas. However, the conflicts with Algiers and Tripoli had already undermined these views. The Barbary States had no significant merchant fleets of their own, and privateers were no use against them. America, on the other hand, now had a large merchant fleet, and only regular naval ships could be relied on to protect it, and avenge any attacks on it. The frigate victories of the war of 1812 created enormous interest, and made the public aware of the need for a fleet.

American ship design was closely related to her strategic policies. There was no prospect of a navy which could dominate the seas, but there were abundant naval resources — seamen, commanders, ship designers, timber and other assets. It was possible to build ships which were superior to those of their class in other navies — frigates which could outsail anything they could not outfight. These would distract the British (or any other naval power) from their blockade of the American coast, and would raid enemy commerce far more effectively than privateers. In some senses, the American strategy was an extension of the French one, of building for quality rather than quantity, and sending ships out on raids rather than to dominate the seas; but the American policy was executed with rather more daring, and, in its own terms, it was highly successful.

The USS Constitution *chased by a British squadron.* The National Maritime Museum

Frigates

The most famous ships of the US Navy were the three large frigates of the *Constitution* class. They had been ordered by the act of 1794, and were designed by Joshua Humphries of Philadelphia, with the assistance of Josiah Fox. They were nearly 175ft long on the gundeck — about as long as a contemporaneous British 74 — and were rated at 44 guns, though they had ports for up to 62. They were virtually flush-decked, as the waist was closed by gangways creating a 'spar deck' — though the *President* later had a small poop. They had the pick of the timber from the American forests, so that the *Constitution* became known as 'Old Ironsides' after her fight with the *Guerriere* in 1812. They were armed with thirty long 24-pounders, twenty or twenty-two 32- or 42-pounder carronades on the quarter-

a. The frigates of the Constitution *class, as originally built.*
b. The Constellation *and* Congress, *rated at 38 guns.*
c. The New York *of 36 guns, built in 1799.*
d. The Boston *of 32 guns, also of 1799.*
e. A British 38-gun frigate to the same scale.
Based on the drawings in H I Chapelle's *The American Sailing Navy*

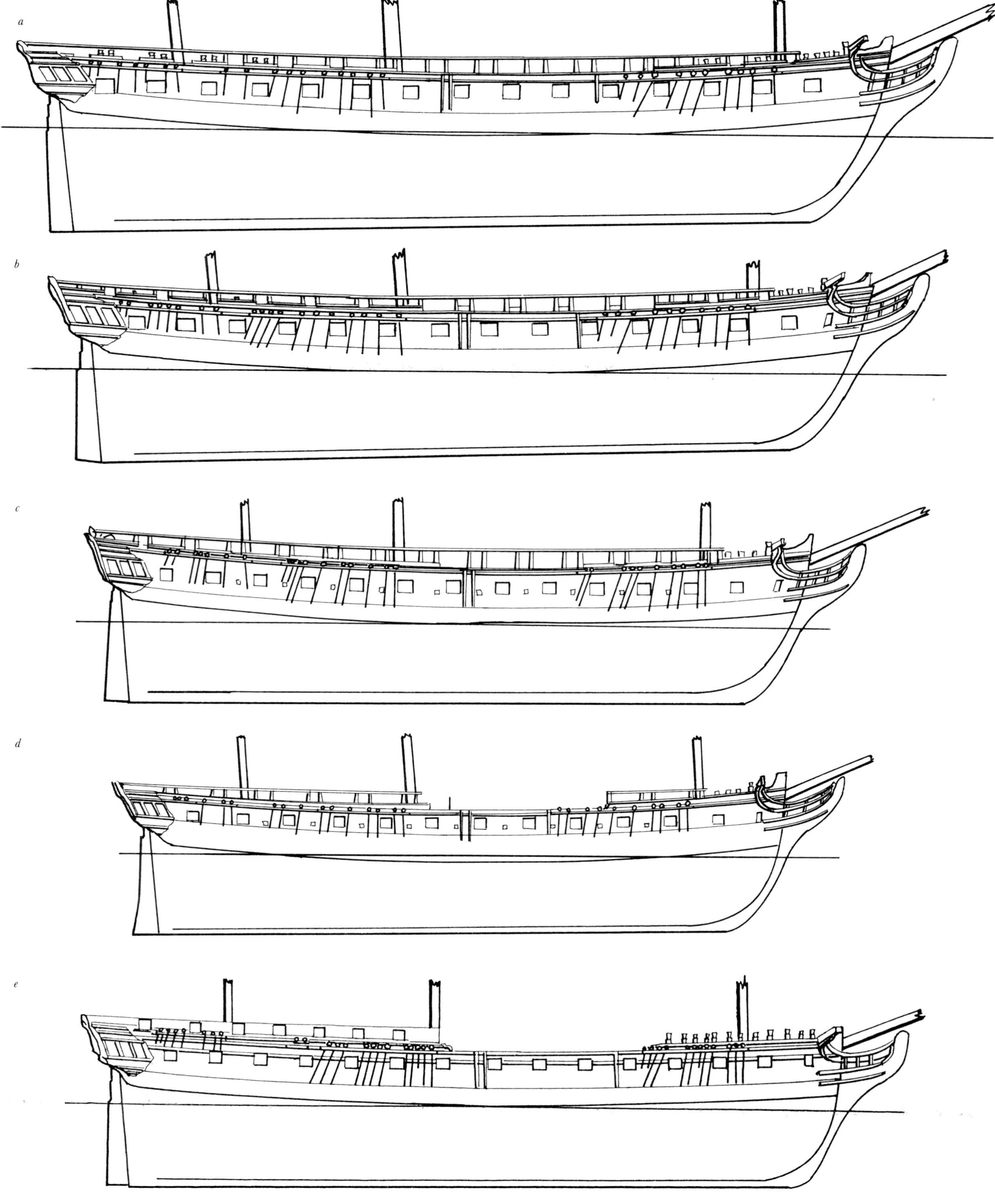
a
b
c
d
e

a. The Wasp, *an 18-gun sloop of 1806.*
b. A 10-gun brig of 1815.
c. The Oneida, *a schooner used on Lake Ontario.*
Based on drawings in H I Chapelle's *The American Sailing Navy*

Officers of the war of 1812 – Macdonough, Perry and Decatur. From J F Cooper's *History of the Navy of the USA*

deck and forecastle. The *United States* and *Constitution* were launched in 1797, the *President* in 1800.

The three smaller ships of 1794 were the *Constellation* (1797), *Congress* (1799) and *Chesapeake* (1799). They were rated at 36 guns, though they were pierced for 58. They were virtually reduced copies of the 44s, and were 164ft long (compared with a British 38 of 146ft). During the quasi war with France, five more frigates were built by subscription of different states — the *Philadelphia*, *New York*, *Essex*, *Boston* and *John Adams*. The largest of these, the *Philadelphia*, was 157ft long, and eventually rated as a 36-gun ship — though she had originally been planned as an improvement on the 44-gun class. The smallest was the *John Adams*, launched at Charlestown in 1799; she was 136ft long and rated as a 28-gun ship. The captured British ships *Macedonian* and *Alert* were added to the fleet during the war; the *Guerriere* and *Java* were also captured, but too damaged to be of any use.

Sloops and Smaller Vessels

During the last years of the eighteenth century, when the US Navy found itself very short of ships, various merchant sloops and brigs were acquired for service. These included the *Baltimore* (ex *Argus*), of 20 guns, acquired in 1798; the *Ganges* of 26 guns, bought in 1799; and several other ships which were quickly sold because they were found to be unsuitable as warships. At the outbreak of the war in 1812, the navy had eight ships below the status of frigate, ranging from the *Hornet* of 18 guns and 480 tons, built at Baltimore in 1805, to the *Viper* of 12 guns and 148 tons, purchased in 1810. During the war of 1812, several more smaller vessels were acquired for the navy. These included the schooners *Carolina* and *Nonsuch*, and nine revenue vessels, all schooner rigged, which were put into naval service. The best documented of these is the *James Madison*, of 94ft and pierced for 16 guns. Several other small vessels were purchased, but there was no uniformity among these craft, because of their varying origins.

In the war of 1812, Lake Champlain and the Great Lakes, especially Lake Ontario, became important scenes of conflict. The British, under Captain James Yeo, built several sloops and gunboats near the site of modern Toronto, while the Americans started the war with only the *Oneida*, a brig of 14 guns, on Lake Ontario. They purchased a few small schooners, mounting 2 to 9 guns; and began to build some more at Sacket's Harbour, New York.

Ships-of-the-Line

The Americans had built their first ship-of-the-line, the 74-gun *America*, during the War of Independence. She was launched in 1782, but given to the French on the same day. There was a further plan to build ships-of-the-line during the quasi war with France, and in 1798 Stoddert recommended a fleet of twelve 74-gun ships. An Act of 1799 authorised six 74s, but not enough money was provided, and the ships were never built. The outbreak of the war in 1812 led to another plan, and the four ships of the *Independence* class were laid down at Boston. Portsmouth, Philadelphia and Washington. None actually took part in the war of 1812, but the *Independence* first put to sea in July 1815, very soon after hostilities had ceased, while the second ship, the *Franklin*, was launched in the following month. It is interesting to speculate how they would have fared against British ships. Like the American frigates, they were much bigger than equivalent ships in other navies, and more heavily gunned than their nominal rating would suggest. The *Independence* was 190ft long, about 14ft longer than a typical British 74. The American ships were to cause considerable re-thinking of British ship design in future years, but they took no part in the war of 1812.

Officers

The American officer corps was largely modelled on the British, and the ranks were similar. However there was no regular rank above captain, though commodores could be appointed on a temporary basis. The best known of these were Truxtun, who was in command during the campaign against Tripoli; and Prebble in the war of 1812. The rank of master commandant was equivalent to the British rank of master and commander. The officer corps remained quite small, even during the war of 1812. Down to the rank of midshipman, the navy needed only 269 sea officers for ships fitting out or in service late in 1812. In addition to a captain, surgeon and chaplain, a large frigate of the *Constitution* class had five lieutenants, two surgeon's mates and sixteen midshipmen. A smaller frigate of the *Constellation* class had the same number of lieutenants and surgeon's mates, but only twelve midshipmen. A sloop generally had two lieutenants, one surgeon's mate and four to six midshipmen.[2] With the proposed building of ships-of-the-line, the officer corps of the navy would have been doubled; but of course that programme was not completed when the war ended. But allowing for officers on half pay, there were exactly 500 in the navy in 1812; twelve captains, ten masters commandant, seventy-three lieutenants, fifty-three masters, 310 midshipmen, and forty-two marine officers.[3] By 1815, this had increased to 936, including marine officers. The largest increase was in midshipmen, and there were 510 of these by 1815.

Warrant and petty officers grades were also similar to those used in the British service, and a 44-gun frigate had two masters, two masters' mates, seven midshipmen, a purser, surgeon (with two mates), clerk, carpenter (and two mates), boatswain and two mates, gunner, yeoman of the gun room, eleven quarter gunners, one coxswain, sailmaker, cooper, steward, armourer, master at arms, cook and chaplain.[4]

American and British bases of the war of 1812.

Men

The American navy was almost unique in the world, in that it did not need conscription to man its ships in wartime. Its merchant fleet was quite large compared with the size of the navy, and conditions in the latter were relatively good. Seamen were attracted by means of recruiting posters, and were offered two to four months' wages in advance; officers were allowed to give \$10 or \$20 bounty 'should you find it absolutely necessary'. Men enlisted for two years, and an able seaman was paid \$12 per month, an ordinary seaman \$8 to \$10.[5] British authorities have suggested that the US Navy owed its success to the presence of large numbers of British deserters in its ranks. Americans deny this, and point out that there were many British trained seamen in the US Navy, but these were actually Americans who had been impressed into the British fleet at one time or another. American estimates suggest that between 5 and 10 per cent of the sailors in the US Navy were of British origin.[6] There is little doubt that the seamen were of high quality, and most earned the rating of 'able seaman'. On her later cruises, the *Constitution* had a crew of 440, which included 218 able seamen, ninety-two ordinary seamen, twelve boys and forty-four marines.[7]

Marines

The United States Marines was first founded in 1775, when Congress voted to form two battalions, but they were disbanded at the end of the war. The corps was re-formed in 1798, and its headquarters was established in Washington in 1800. It was largely modelled on the British marines, and at this stage it served mainly to provide shipboard detachments, without any of the broader roles undertaken by the modern Marine Corps. However, in 1814, when the British invaded Washington, a company of marines from the headquarters helped in the defence of the city. In 1813, the captain of marines of the *Essex* was put in charge of a prize, which was commissioned as the USS *Greenwich* — perhaps the only occasion in modern times when a marine officer has commanded a warship. Even earlier, marines had taken part in the campaign against Tripoli.

A 44-gun frigate carried sixty marines as part of its complement — two lieutenants, three sergeants, three corporals, a drummer, a fifer and fifty privates. A 36-gun frigate had one lieutenant, two sergeants, two corporals, a drummer and a fifer, and forty privates.[8]

Bases

By 1801, the US Navy possessed six bases — as many as the British had home yards. All were deep-water ports, because the large frigates had deep draughts, and all were in good natural harbours. However, not all of them were well developed by this time. The most important was the New York Navy yard, at Brooklyn, which employed 102 men. Gosport (or Norfolk) yard in Virginia soon became important as a base for ships going to and from the West Indies. Facilities were best at Washington yard; the others were still relatively primitive, especially Portsmouth, New Hampshire. The remaining yards were at Charlestown (Boston) and Philadelphia.

Privateers

Privateering formed quite a large part of American naval effort, as might be expected from a nation which had a large merchant marine, and a mistrust of government authority; 515 ships were issued with

A schooner – a characteristic American type at this period, and often used as a privateer. From Serres's, *Liber Nauticus*

letters of marque during the war of 1812, and at least 1345 vessels were captured by them. Most of the coastal states fitted out a few, but large numbers came from the states of Massachusetts (150), Maryland (112) and New York (102). Among individual ports, New York fitted out the largest number. The privateering effort began early in the war, and on 1 July 1812, soon after the war was declared, a newspaper reported, 'The people in the eastern states are labouring almost night and day to fit out privateers. Two have already sailed from Salem and ten others are getting ready for sea.' By the middle of October, New York had fitted out twenty-six privateers, mounting 300 guns.[9] The majority of the early privateers were small — often local pilot boats, hastily converted to carry a single heavy gun mounted amidships, and a few lighter weapons. Such ships frequently had large crews — the *Dash* of Baltimore had one gun and forty men, for example. They did well enough when the British merchantmen were unprepared for them, but something larger was demanded in the later stages of the war. The schooner rig was still favoured, including the *Decatur* of Charleston, which carried six 12-pounders, one long 18-pounder and a complement of 103 men, and was engaged in a successful fight with the British schooner *Dominica* in 1813.

4 Other Foreign Naval Forces

The Netherlands

In the seventeenth century, the Dutch navy had some claims to be the greatest in the world. At one time or another, it had inflicted defeats on the Spanish, the English and the French, and for much of the century it was as large as any of the others. However, several factors had combined to cause the relative decline of Dutch naval power. The country was open to invasion by France, and this meant that a large amount of resources had to be devoted to land defences. Ships tended to get bigger over the years, but the Dutch fleet was restricted by the shallowness of its home waters. The old Dutch navy had relied heavily on the country's extensive merchant fleet for men, officers and ships; but the warship became increasingly specialised over the years, and the Dutch were left behind. By the late eighteenth century the Dutch navy was definitely in the second rank, though it maintained its traditions of efficiency and fighting skill.

The Netherlands, or 'United Provinces' as the state was officially called, was a federation of several provinces, with a rather complicated republican system of government. Naval administration was equally complex, as the main maritime provinces — Maas, Amsterdam, Noordkwartier, Zeeland and Freisland — each had their own fleets, which came together in case of war. Dutch ships tended to be small because of the difficulties of navigation. There were no three-deckers, so the largest flagships were of 74 or 76 guns. The standard ship-of-the-line was the 64, supplemented by ships of 68 or 60 guns, and substantial numbers of 54-gun ships. Later some two-decker 80s were built. The Dutch fleet raised its men by conscription as did all navies except the American. Its officers often had strong links with the merchant service. The main Dutch naval bases were at Hellevoeutsluis, in Zeeland, and at Amsterdam. The exit to the latter port was

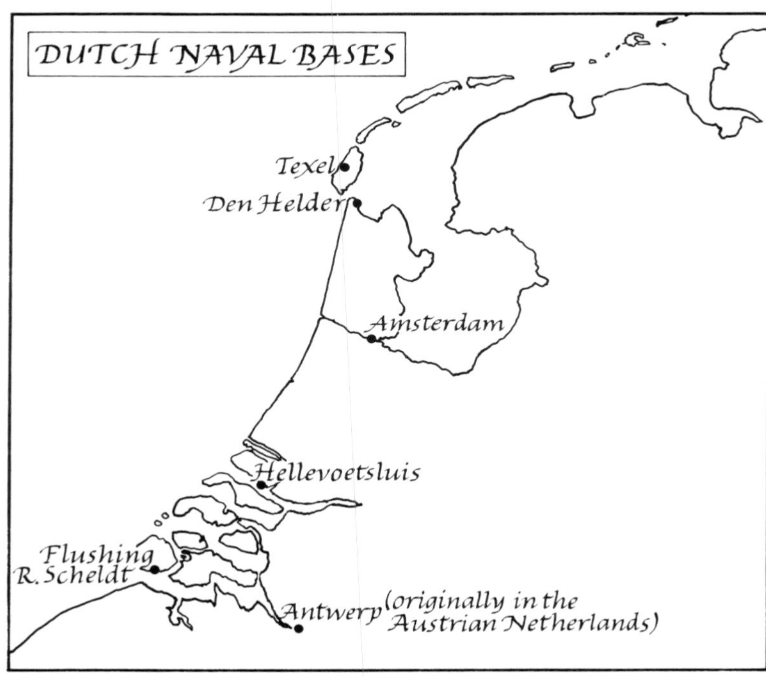

Dutch naval bases.

through the Texel Channel, and this was one of the key blockading stations for the British North Sea fleet. The harbour of Vlissingen, or Flushing, in the south of Zeeland, was also important.

The Dutch entered the first coalition against France, but were quickly invaded by France, with much support from the Dutch people. The Batavian Republic was formed, and the fleet was defeated at Camperdown in 1797. The French connection remained throughout the peace of 1801–3. Napoleon's brother became king in

European and North African naval bases.

1806, and in 1810, the countries were merged. British attacks were made on the Netherlands several times — by the Duke of York in 1794, and with the Walcheren expedition of 1809. Much more successful was Admiral Duncan's campaign of 1799, in which he captured twelve ships-of-the-line and thirteen Indiamen, without firing a shot.

Denmark–Norway

The Danish fleet had never attempted dominance of the seas, but it

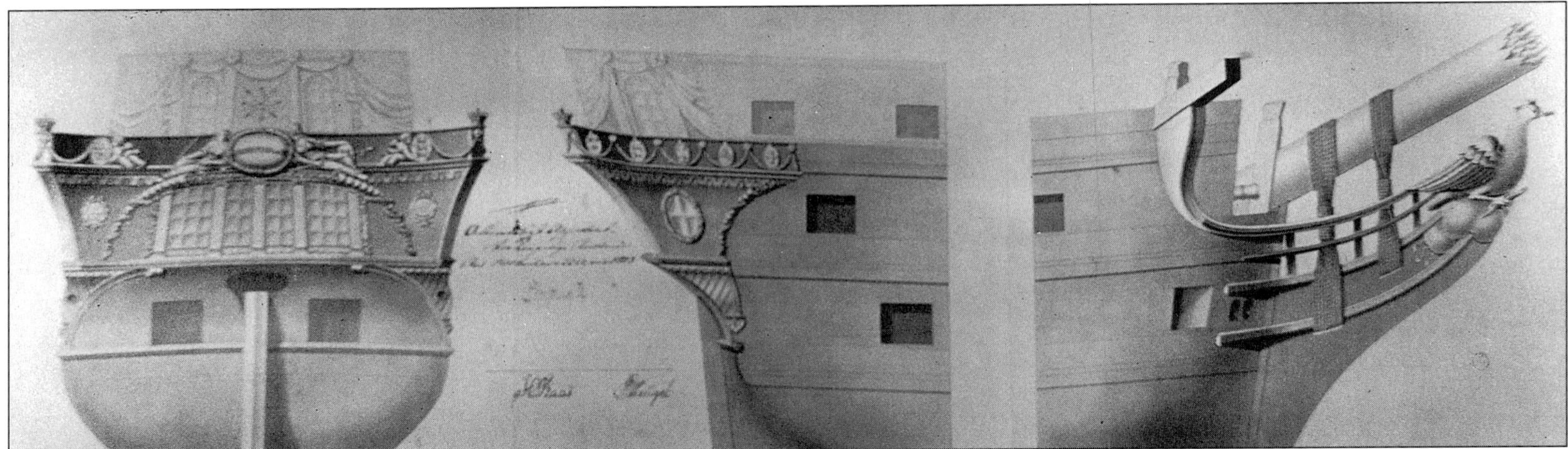

The stem and stern of the Danish ship Christian VII. *Captured at Copenhagen in 1807; the stern may have had some influence on Seppings's design for his circular stern.* Riksarkivet, Copenhagen

had been built up in the course of the eighteenth century to become quite a substantial force. Like the Spanish navy, it used features of both French and British design for its warships; though, since they had few colonies to protect, the Danes tended to favour the French practice. Instead of recruiting foreign builders to serve in their yards, the Danes sent parties of trainee shipwrights abroad, mainly to France or Britain, to study their methods and get hold of plans of their ships. Danish ship design was quite successful, and rather innovative. Like other navies, they used the 74-gun ship quite extensively, based on the *Fredericia*, designed by Gerner in the 1770s. About one ship a year was built after that, and the fleet had twenty-three ships-of-the-line in 1801.[1] Under Chief Constructor Hohlenberg, there were some original designs, and the *Njaden* 74 was the first ship to carry a new type of stern, designed to allow all-round fire. Such a stern was fitted to the *Christian VII*, and attracted the attention after that ship was captured by the British. Since 1772, the fleet had been standardised with ships of 74, 64, 42, 36 and 24 guns. By 1801 there were plans to standardise it yet further, with only one design for frigates, ships-of-the-line, and so on. It was planned that a ship-of-the-line could be converted to a frigate simply by removing one deck. All this was interrupted when Nelson defeated the Danes at Copenhagen in 1801, destroying and capturing several old ships used as static defences. Construction of major warships ceased after that, and the more modern ships of the navy were mostly lost after the second Battle of Copenhagen in 1807. A large fleet of gunboats was built after that, mainly for raiding British commerce in the channels at the entrance to the Baltic. In 1813, it had four ships-of-the-line, two frigates, and 120 gunboats.[2]

Sweden

The ships of the Swedish navy had been rationalised and improved by one of the most innovative naval architects of the eighteenth century, Fredrik Henrik af Chapman. Typically, he was the son of an English immigrant from Yorkshire. He had spent considerable time travelling around the shipyards of western Europe. Between 1782 and 1785, he designed ten 60-gun ships, and the same number of 40-gun frigates. Around 1790, because of the threat of large Russian ships, he produced designs for ships of 66, 74, 80, 94 and 110 guns. None of these was built, though he did produce the *Konug Gustav IV Adolf* of 76 guns. She had a displacement of 2700 tons, with thirty 36-pounders, thirty 24-pounders and sixteen 12-pounders.[3] The Swedes had developed a gunboat navy far earlier than most, and from 1760 Chapman had designed four different classes of gunboat, from 90ft to 140ft long, and armed with heavy guns mounted on swivelling carriages. These were not entirely successful, and by 1789, the Swedish navy used gun sloops and gun yawls, with a maximum length of 66ft.[4] At the beginning of 1813, the Swedish navy had twelve ships-of-the-line, with two more building; eight frigates, with three building; plus cutters and gunboats.

Swedish naval officers were considered as part of the military, and expected to wear spurs, a fact which caused some comment from British seamen. The main naval base, especially for the wars against Russia, was Carlscrona, in the Baltic. Other major ports were Stockholm and Gothenburg.

Russia

The Russian navy had been founded by Peter the Great, in the late seventeenth century. As the Muscovite State expanded into the Baltic it came into conflict with Sweden, and a fleet became necessary. Soon afterwards, the state expanded into the Black Sea, and another fleet was built there to fight the Turks. Peter had visited Holland and Britain to learn more about shipbuilding, and the policy of learning from others continued over the decades. Many foreign officers, including Sir Charles Knowles, Sir Samuel Bentham and John Paul Jones, served with the Russians at one time or another. They introduced some quite advanced ideas, and the Russian navy was using steam power in its dockyards before the British. Under Czar Paul I (1796–1801), officers were ordered to wear a green uniform.

The main base in the Baltic was at Kronstadt, near the capital of St Petersburg, with another base at Reval, further west. As well as conventional warships, the Baltic fleet — like other navies in the area — relied heavily on galleys and rowing gunboats. The Black Sea fleet was based at Sebastapol in the Crimea. There was also a squadron based at Archangel in the north.

The Russian fleet was large, though not all ships were effective. In 1801, it had eighty-two ships-of-the-line, but only thirty-one of these were available for service.[5] By the later stages of the Napoleonic Wars, the Russian fleet was quite substantial. According to one report, the Baltic fleet had fifty-nine vessels, carrying 2260 guns, with a galley fleet of forty-one ships and 705 guns. In the Black Sea, the sailing fleet had forty-one ships with 1225 guns, supported by forty rowing gunboats. There was also a small flotilla at Ochozk in Siberia, with eleven vessels carrying 36 guns, and another in the Caspian Sea, with six vessels carrying 70 guns. Ten ships-of-the-line were building.[6] The Russians operated several three-deckers at one time or another, especially in the Baltic. These included the *Apostolov*, *Knyaz Vladimir* and *Sv. Nikolai* of 100 guns each; 74-gun ships were also common, as were ships of 66 guns.[7] Ships based in the Black Sea tended to be smaller than those in the Baltic.

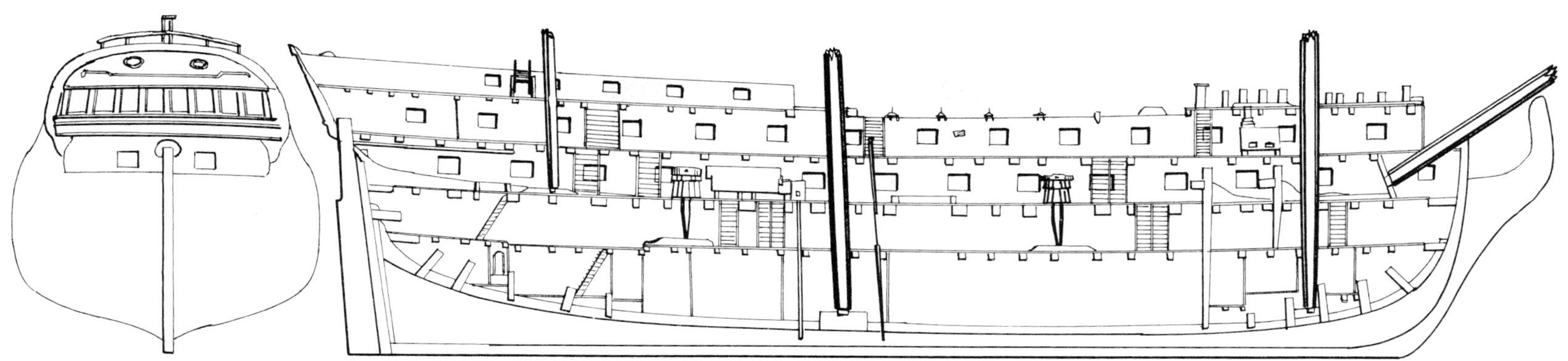

Longitudinal section of the Russian 64-gun ship Ratisvan, *drawn in 1796. Compared with western European ships, it has several unusual features – it has a large cistern on the gundeck, presumably for the pumps; swivel guns are mounted in the waist; the floors rise rather steeply for a ship-of-the-line; it has no poop and a single stern gallery; and it has only single capstans.* Based on a drawing in the National Maritime Museum

The Russian fleet had already begun to break out of the confines of the Baltic and Black Sea, and was operating fleets in the North Sea and Mediterranean. In 1795, when Russia entered the war against France, a fleet of twelve ships-of-the-line and eight frigates was sent by Catherine the Great to serve with the British in the North Sea. They took part in some operations against the Dutch, and helped maintain the blockade during the Nore mutiny. In 1798, the Russians and Turks operated against the French in the Mediterranean, and helped to take some of the Ionian Islands from France. Russia made peace with France in 1799, but joined the campaign against Napoleon in the 1800s. The Mediterranean fleet, with a strength of nine ships-of-the-line and six frigates, operated from Corfu. In 1807, Russia joined the war in support of Napoleon, and in 1808, they were blockaded by the combined British and Swedish fleets in the Baltic. Some Russian ships, including an 80 and six 74s, were trapped in the River Tagus in 1808. An agreement was reached between Britain and Russia, whereby the crews were to be returned home, and the ships sent to England 'as a deposit by His Britannic Majesty', and released at the end of the war. After 1812, when the Russians were invaded by Napoleon, another fleet was sent to the North Sea.

The Russian navy had several grave weaknesses. Its ships were poorly constructed, of inferior timber, and its men were inexperienced and badly trained. One British officer wrote of 'poor miserable Russian recruits, who come to a new element from their peaceful habitations in the depth of the wilderness'. He went on,

> The lives of men are beyond imagination valueless here and deaths so common as to excite no observation... in the sea hospitals from the beginning of spring hardly less than twenty have in any day departed for the other world. The rest are so dispirited that they die from no other cause, like Swiss soldiers, who sing melancholily of the charms of their native mountains and die regretting them.[8]

Russia's geographical position made it difficult for her fleet to operate outside the Black Sea and Baltic, as it could not pass the Dardanelles

Russian ships. From the Naval Chronicle

A xebec in the Mediterranean. This type was developed by the Barbary corsairs, but adopted by the other Mediterranean states. From Serres's *Liber Nauticus*

and the Sound without support from other powers. Added to which, its northern ports were liable to ice up in the winter.

Turkey

The Ottoman Empire, based at Constantinople, was the nominal ruler of much of the Mediterranean, from Greece, through Palestine and Egypt, as far west as Algeria. In practice, its African provinces were largely independent, with only nominal rule from Turkey. However, the Turkish fleet was quite substantial in numbers. In 1787 it had an active force of twenty-two ships-of-the-line and eight frigates, mounting 1700 guns.[9] There was continual conflict with Russia over the control of the Black Sea, though Turkey was generally successful in this. At the Battle of Athos in 1807, the Turks had a force of six 84-gun ships, three 74s, four 50s, a 44 and five frigates and sloops. In 1810 they operated off the Crimea with a force of three 100-gun ships, six two-deckers, six frigates and three smaller vessels.[10] At that time, its total force was said to be three three-deckers, twelve two-deckers including five 74s, three more sail-of-the-line building, seven frigates, seven corvettes, two bomb vessels and two brigs.[11]

Italy and the Adriatic

Venice had once had a great navy, and her galleys had played a considerable part in the Christian advance against the Turks in the early modern age. By the 1790s, the galley was obsolete, and the Venetian navy was moving towards the sailing warship. It had ships of 70 and even 74 guns, such as the *Aquilea Valliera*, but large ships had to be raised up by lighters, to allow them to enter the Venetian lagoon. Venice had a notable arsenal, a dockyard with large supplies of naval stores.

In 1797, northern Italy was conquered, and the Venetian navy came under the control of the Austro-Hungarian empire. That power had had a small beginning as a naval power, based on the Adriatic port of Trieste. The navy was revived by Joseph II in 1786, but consisted only of two 20-gun cutters, built at Ostend. It was combined with the old Venetian navy after 1797, though the two forces were administered separately. The combined force was thirty-seven vessels, with a total of 111 guns and 787 men. This became the Imperial Austrian navy in 1804, but in 1809 the empire was cut off from the sea, and the navy was taken over by France. It was restored in 1814, and the Venetian fleet (still under Austro-Hungarian control) had five ships-of-the-line, two frigates, one corvette and several smaller vessels. This was the nucleus of a force which was to gain some distinction in the nineteenth century.[12]

In the south of Italy, the Kingdom of Naples had begun with a small but quite effective fleet; in 1795, she had three ships-of-the-line. A British chaplain observing two 74s — the *Saminte* and *Guicsardo* — co-operating with the British fleet, described them as 'very fine ships'.[13]

The Barbary States

The Barbary States, the forerunners of the modern countries of Morocco, Algeria, Tunisia and Libya, were a constant nuisance to the European maritime powers, and to the United States of America. They regarded themselves as legitimate controllers of the seas around their coastline, and claimed the right to prey on merchant shipping in the Mediterranean, unless the countries involved entered into agreements with them, and paid them substantial sums of money. Seamen captured by the Barbary corsairs could be enslaved — often for many years. Britain kept in alliance with the Barbary States during this period, mainly because she needed the ports of North Africa for provisioning the fleet. Other countries, such as Denmark and the United States, fought wars against them. The Barbary corsairs developed a very efficient type of vessel known as a xebec. It was lateen rigged with two masts and a well-faired hull. It was equally at home under oars or sail, and was ideal for the waters of the Mediterranean; indeed it was copied by some of the European powers such as France and Spain, and used as a kind of frigate. Other Mediterranean craft, such as feluccas and tartanes, were also used by the Barbary States, as well as some craft of European and American design which had been either captured or paid as part of the tribute demanded of certain states. For example, the United States gave the Dey of Algiers a 32-gun frigate, a brig and two sloops as part of the settlement of the war which began in 1802. The Americans took some care with the design of these vessels, and the frigate was produced by Josiah Fox, one of the country's leading naval architects.[14]

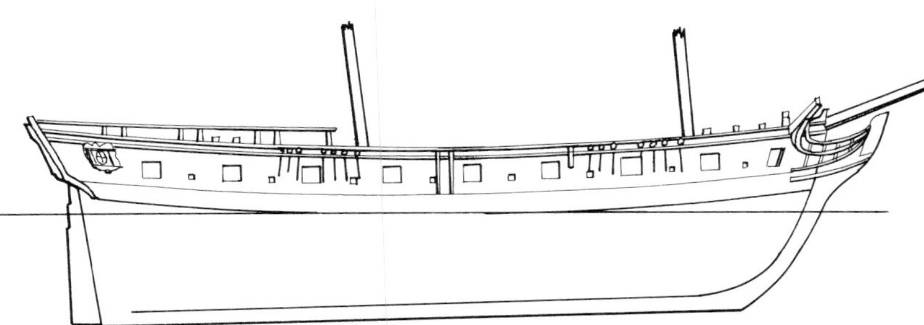

The Skjoldebrand *of 1798 – a ship given by the American government to the Dey of Algiers, as part of the settlement of the war with that state.* Based on a drawing in H I Chapelle's *The American Sailing Navy*

Morocco was the most powerful of the Barbary States, though she had few good ports, and little timber. Around 1815, she was said to have about fifteen frigates, some xebecs, and twenty or thirty galleys. Algiers had five frigates of 34 to 24 guns, three xebecs of 10 to 21 guns, four 'half galleys' and three 'galliots', while Tunis had three of four large barks of 20 guns and twenty men each, as well as xebecs of 10 to 14 guns, and some feluccas and galliots, to a total of about fifteen vessels.[15] Even such small forces were able to cause considerable disruption in European trade, largely because the powers were divided about how to deal with the problem. In 1816, the British and French combined to bombard Algiers, and in 1821 the French occupied the country, bringing the issue to an end.

Part XIV
TACTICS

1 Fighting Tactics

Single-Ship Action

Single-ship action was regarded as a microcosm of the conflict between fleets and nations, and as a unique test of the character of officers and seamen. According to a contemporaneous naval writer, 'An engagement between two adverse ships is in some measure an epitome of an engagement between two fleets.'[1] Victors in action between two frigates gained little in prize money, as the captured ship was likely to be seriously damaged and without a valuable cargo; but the officers of the victorious ship gained much more in terms of acclaim, promotion and honours. For capturing the *Cleopatre* in 1793, Captain Pellew of the *Nymph* was presented to the king, and knighted; for taking the *Hermione* in 1797, Captain Hamilton of the *Surprise* was knighted, granted the freedom of the City of London, and presented with a sword valued at 300 guineas by the Jamaica House of Assembly. As a rule, a successful captain could expect to be knighted, while the commander of a sloop would be promoted captain, and the first lieutenant, or senior surviving lieutenant, would be promoted commander. Successful frigate captains became national heroes, and were widely publicised (by the standards of the time). Conversely, a succession of defeats at the hands of American frigates sent shock waves through the navy and the country.

Attitudes to Battle

There is no doubt that British seamen relished the prospect of battle. 'Our men were in the highest spirits and too eager to engage', wrote a chaplain in 1795.[2] On the approach to Trafalgar, Jack Nastyface wrote, 'I will say that could England but have seen her sons about to attack the inhabitants of Spain with an inferior force ... from the zeal which animated every man in the fleet, the bosom of every inhabitant of England would have glowed with indescribable patriotic pride.'[3] Another seaman wrote, 'A serious cast was to be perceived on every face; but not a shade of doubt or fear. We rejoiced in a general action; not that we loved fighting; but we all wished to be free to return to our homes, and follow our own pursuits. We knew there was no other way of obtaining this than by defeating the enemy. "The hotter the war the sooner the peace" was a saying with us'.[4] Perhaps months of being cooped up in overcrowded conditions made the seaman pugnacious. Perhaps he thought a decisive victory would end the war, and hasten his own release. Perhaps he wanted another opportunity to show his superiority over foreign seamen, or to demonstrate his fearlessness to his comrades. Perhaps the lure of prize money still attracted him, even in fleet battles; or perhaps the rum and beer ration inspired him to great feats of daring. In any case, his attitude is well documented, and contrasts with the trepidation shown by the men of other countries' navies as they approached battle.

Chasing

As with fleet action, it was often possible for a squadron or single ship to decline action, and escape. There were many circumstances when this was not possible — when a convoy had to be protected, or the ship was close to a lee shore, or when the two opposing forces were of similar gun power, and honour demanded that battle be joined. Occasionally, challenges were issued by the captain of one ship, and taken up by another. The most famous example of this was the battle between the HMS *Shannon* and the American *Chesapeake* in 1813, but there were others. A similar challenge had been issued from the *Boston* to the French *Embuscade* in 1793. It was taken up, but the British ship suffered heavy damage and casualties, and was forced to retreat.

In other cases, one side or the other decided to retreat in the face of superior force. In an open sea, an escaping vessel would choose its best point of sailing, and in such a case a fore and aft rigged vessel stood a good chance of escape from a square rigged ship, by sailing closer to the wind. Otherwise, both ships would put on as much sail as the wind allowed, though if too much were put on, and masts or spars were carried away, then the race was lost. There was no point in pursuing a ship of equal sailing ability. 'A vessel that chases another ought to have the advantage of sailing because, were the ship chased as good a sailer as the chaser, she could never come up to her, if they manoeuvred equally and at the same time'. When chasing a vessel to windward, it was advisable to tack as soon as the chase was directly on the beam. 'The chaser heaves about as soon as

Cornwallis's retreat, From the Naval Chronicle

the vessel he is in pursuit of is on his beam; because she is, at this time, the shortest possible distance, if she chases on the same tack and steers on the same course with the vessel chased.'[5] When being chased by a vessel of superior sailing qualities, it was better to stand on one course rather than tack, as the chaser would be able to tack better. When pursuing a vessel downwind, it was considered best to steer a course which would intersect with the chase, rather than steer exactly the same course. The chased ship would hope to loose her opponent in darkness or bad visibility.

When a fleet or squadron was being chased by a superior force, it was suggested that it should sail *en echelon,* two lines at an angle of 135 degrees and the flagship at the apex of the angle, and all ships sailing the same course. The best-known escape from overwhelming force was 'Cornwallis's retreat' of 1795, when a force of five ships-of-the-line and two frigates escaped a French fleet of twelve ships-of-the-line and eleven smaller vessels. Cornwallis was inhibited by the poor sailing qualities of two of his ships, but was eventually able to persuade the enemy that the rest of the British fleet was over the horizon, by having his frigates make signals to imaginary ships.

Handling the Ship in Action

Once in action, ships usually carried topsails only.

> When the adverse fleets approach each other, the courses are commonly hauled up in the brails, and the topgallant sails and stay sails furled. The movement of each ship is chiefly regulated by the main and fore topsails, and the jib; the mizzen topsail being reserved to hasten or retard the course of the ship, and, in fine, by backing or filling, hoisting or lowering it, to determine her velocity.[6]

This applied equally to single-ship action. Obviously, in such a case, the ship was not hampered by the need to keep station with others, but the three topsails gave her a good deal of manoeuvrability, without the need to keep large numbers of men on deck to handle them.

Heaving-to was always a useful manoeuvre. If a ship had decided to accept battle from an approaching enemy, it allowed a steadier gun platform from which to fire on the opponent as he approached. During close-range combat, both ships were often hove while firing into each other. Tacking was a difficult operation, especially under reduced sail; ships in action were more likely to wear. This often allowed one ship to bring a full broadside to bear on the bows or stern of another — with devastating effect. Otherwise, the ship was handled in action by altering the helm and trimming the sails, using the sail trimmers detached from each gun crew as laid down in the quarter bill. The master was in charge of the handling of the ship in action, though the captain would normally decide the actual tactical movements.

Fighting Range

Action often began with long-range cannonading, especially if one ship was hove-to in order to await the other. However the ships were very close together once the main action had begun. An extreme example of this was in Lord Cochrane's fight with the vastly superior Spanish frigate *Gamo* in 1801.

> My orders were not to fire a gun till we were close to her; when, running under her lee, we locked our yards amongst her rigging, and in this position returned our broadside, such as it was... My reason for locking our small craft in the enemy's rigging was the one upon which I mainly relied for victory, *viz,* that from the height of the frigate out of the water, the whole of her shot must necessarily go over her heads, whilst our guns, being elevated, would blow up her maindeck.[7]

In the action between the 74s, *Mars* and *Hercules,* it was said that the ships were so close together that it was not possible to run out the guns properly, and they had to be fired with the muzzles inboard.[8]

In general, captains favoured a slightly greater range in more equal encounters. The *Shannon* fought the *Chesapeake* at a range of about 40yds. Campbell suggested 'point-blank shot, so that the guns may be levelled with some certainty of execution'.[9] In this case, point-blank range can be taken to mean 'the distance a ball goes in a straight line direction', rather than its alternative definition of 'the distance the shot goes before it strikes the level ground, when discharged in the horizontal or point-blank direction'.[10] The latter definition would give a range of 300yds for a 24-pounder carronade,[11] while point-blank range by the other definition — though not easy to calculate — was certainly much shorter. In 1815, Captain Maitland of the *Bellerophon* described his tactics to Napoleon after his surrender: 'In working out we passed within about a cable's length [240yds] of the *Superb*. He asked me if I considered that was near enough for a naval engagement; I answered that half the distance, or even less, would be much better; as it was a maxim in our navy, not to be further from the enemy than to give room for working the yards, and manoeuvring the ship.'[12]

Raking

Everyone knew that a man-of-war had nearly all her strength, both offensive and defensive, on her sides. Her bows carried few guns, and the structure there was relatively weak, especially in the case of a ship-of-the-line before the round bow was introduced. The stern was even weaker, in both frigates and ships-of-the-line. There was at least one row of glass windows, and perhaps even galleries. At best, the structure was very light, with little of the strength and thickness of the timbers which formed the sides. Therefore, the most effective move in any combat between two ships, whether alone or part of a fleet battle, was 'raking'. To rake a ship was 'to cannonade her on the stern, or head, so as that the balls shall scour the whole length of her decks; which is one of the most dangerous incidents that can happen in a naval action.'[13] Raking shot would pass all along the deck, until it met some obstruction. It would kill men, dismount guns, and wreak carnage as long as it continued.

One way to rake a ship by the bows was to wear as the chasing ship approached. To rake by the stern, it might be possible to let the enemy pass a little ahead, and then wear under her stern. When passing the bow or stern, it was best to let each gun fire as it bore on the enemy ship. Thus the raking fire was continuous, and devastating. Raking required skilful manoeuvring; if it went wrong, the advantage could go to the other side. 'The *Caesar* was nearly up with their van ship, when she, luffing up too much in the wind to rake us, came about on the other tack, which put them, in great confusion, and we peppered them well during this time.'[14]

Broadside-to-Broadside

If neither ship was able to manoeuvre into position so that one could rake the other, both would settle down to a long broadside-to-broadside duel. Such battles were fought at close range, and accuracy of aim was less important than rate of fire; though the British policy of firing into the hull was far superior to the French practice of firing at the rigging. According to Campbell, 'The firing is seldom performed in volleys, as that would shake the ship too much, but the guns are loaded and fired one after another, with as much despatch and as little confusion as possible, care being taken to fire only when each gun is properly directed to its object.'[15] During the action with the *Chesapeake*, Captain Broke is said to have directed 'Throw no shot away. Aim every one. Keep cool. Work steadily. Fire into her quarters. Don't try to dismast her. Kill the men, and the ship is

The action between the Pilot *sloop and the French 28 gun ship* La Légère *in 1815, here being fought at relatively long range. This proved to be the last action in the wars with France.* From the Naval Chronicle

yours.'[16] This was simply a concise statement of normal British gunnery policy. Though less devastating than raking fire, well conducted broadside fire could have horrific effects, as the crew of the *Macedonian* found against the *United States* in 1812.

> By and by, I heard the shot strike the sides of our ship; the whole scene grew indescribably confused and horrible; it was like some awfully tremendous thunderstorm whose deafening roar is attended by incessant streaks of lightning, carrying death in every flash, and strewing the ground with victims of the wrath; only, in our case, the scene was rendered more horrible by the torrents of blood which dyed our decks.[17]

The Role of Boarding

According to Burney, 'Such is now the practice of naval war, that the necessary order of battle and the fabric of our ships very seldom permit the assault of boarding, unless in single actions.'[18] However, in the latter case, it was quite commonly employed. Cochrane used it with great effect against the *Gamo* in 1801.

> The doctor, Mr Guthrie, who, I am happy to say, is still living to peruse the record of his gallantry, volunteered to take the helm; leaving him therefore both commander and crew of the *Speedy*, the order was given to board, and in a few seconds every man was on the enemy's deck — a feat rendered the more easy as the doctor placed the *Speedy* close alongside with admirable skill.[19]

As a result, he was able to overcome a ship which carried 320 men, with a crew of 50. More conventionally, boarding was used against an enemy who was already partly beaten by gunfire.

Squadron Tactics

Between the single-ship action and the great fleet battle was the squadron action, between equally balanced forces of about half a dozen frigates or ships-of-the-line. It was possible to fight a squadron

The Battle of Lissa. The National Maritime Museum ▷

action formally, like an old fashioned fleet battle, but this rarely happened; if anything, squadron tactics were slightly more daring than fleet tactics of the period. At Lissa, the largest frigate action of the wars, the British did indeed begin with a line of battle consisting of four small frigates, but it was soon abandoned to defeat a Franco-Venetian squadron of six frigates and four smaller vessels. At Strachan's action, when the commodore of that name led a squadron of ships-of-the-line against some French survivors from Trafalgar, the line of battle was soon abandoned. 'Our captain, being impatient to begin the battle, hailed the *Hero*, and told them to hail the *Courageaux* and to inform that he would begin the action immediately without waiting for the *Namur* to come up, and their answer was three hearty British cheers.'[20]

Frigate versus Ship-of-the-Line

A frigate captain who avoided battle with a ship-of-the-line would certainly not be accused of cowardice, as the force of the larger ship was totally overwhelming. In fleet actions ships-of-the-line did not normally fire on frigates, unless the latter fired first. For example, at the Battle of the Nile the 74-gun *Goliath* was manoeuvring into position alongside the French line when the frigate *Serieuse* opened fire on her; the *Goliath* fired back, and with a single broadside dismasted her, shattered her hull, cut her cable, and caused her to drift away and, eventually, sink. Even several frigates were not normally expected to take on a single ship-of-the-line, though

The action between the Terpsichore *and the French* Vestale *in 1796, with the two ships battering each other broadside to broadside.* From the Naval Chronicle

Boat action. The crew of the Quebec *frigate and other vessels boarding some gun brigs off the French coast.* From the Naval Chronicle occasionally this could be done with good effect. In 1797 the French 74, *Droits de l'Homme*, was intercepted by the 36-gun *Amazon* and the 44-gun *Indefatigable* (cut down from a 64-gun ship, and carrying 42-pounder carronades and 24-pounder long guns). The frigates used their manoeuvrability to rake the French ship by turns, and damaged her rigging so much that she was driven onto rocks and wrecked. The *Amazon* was also wrecked, and the *Indefatigable* was seriously damaged.

Boat Action

As well as landing operations, ships' boats could be used to attack, or 'cut out', ships which were anchored close inshore, or were in harbour, or under the protection of shore batteries. Such actions mostly took place at night, and were usually conducted by junior officers; so they gave a considerable scope to lieutenants and midshipmen. In 1800, for example, Lt Beaufort of the *Phaeton* persuaded his captain to let him lead an attack on a Spanish polacre moored under the guns of Fuengirola.

> I went away with the pinnace, two five-oared cutters and the launch with carronade... At 3 o'clock, arrived in shore in smooth water, where I intended laying by a few minutes to rest the people's arms after so fatiguing a pull... But the alarm being given on the beach, and fires, muskets, etc, communicating our station to the ship, I had no time to hesitate but pushed on directly... When, within about two cutters' lengths, she fired a few shots but without other effect than as a signal for us to rush on and giving inspiring cheer, I soon found myself under the starboard main chains. She was soon carried as the officers and sailors had deserted the deck and nobody remained upon it but the marines, who indeed defended it bravely.[21]

Many such actions took place, successful and unsuccessful; bars to the Naval General Service Medal were awarded for fifty-four separate boat service actions from 1793 to 1815.

Another type of action involving boats was an attack on British frigates or other ships by swarms of enemy gunboats, especially in the Mediterranean or Baltic. At the entrance to the latter sea, Danish gunboats were a serious hazard, and could often outfight sloops and brigs in a calm. It was necessary to station two ships-of-the-line 'anchored for the mutual support of each other', and four of these were needed for the protection of the vital convoys passing into the Baltic.[23]

2 Blockade

The Threat of Invasion

Sea power can never be absolute. The sea occupies just over 70 per cent of the world's surface, or 139 million square miles. From the masthead of a ship it might, in good conditions, be possible to see about 1200 square miles. At its peak during the Napoleonic Wars, the Royal Navy had less than 800 ships in commission, so even if they were dispersed evenly they would be able to see less than a hundredth of the sea surface. In practice, the ships were not evenly dispersed, for most of the larger ones were concentrated in the main fleets. Allowing for poor visibility, it seems likely that about one thousandth of the world's sea was visible at any given moment. Obviously, ships and fleets had to be placed in the most critical places, where they could do the most good.

British naval strategy had evolved slowly over the years, and a number of aims had been formulated. Trade had to be protected, the colonies guarded, and at the same time, the war had to be taken to the enemy, in the form of offensive action of one kind or another. But in every one of the eight wars against France between 1689 and 1815, the most important single task was the defence of the British Isles, including Ireland, against invasion. Until Wellington crossed the Pyrenees in 1814, the British army never seriously contemplated the invasion of France except in support of French Royalists, shortly after the Revolution. The French army was too large, and until the eve of the Revolution there were no large disaffected groups who might support a rebellion. Only when war became total enough to demand the overthrow of Napoleon was the complete defeat of France necessary — all the other wars had been settled at the conference table.

The French, on the other hand, often planned the invasion of the British Isles. After 1692, the Royal Navy was always large enough to defeat the French, but they often had allies in Spain and Holland to assist them. Even when they did not, as in 1803–4, they tended to hope for a temporary local superiority which might allow them to land their armies without interruption. In other cases, they tried to exploit disaffected elements within the British Isles — Scottish Jacobites up to their defeat at Culloden in 1746, and Irish nationalists after that. In practice, the full-scale invasion of southern England was often threatened but never launched. When it came to supporting Scottish or Irish rebels, the French fleet might have stood a better chance, for the coast of Ireland, in particular, was difficult to guard; but in general the actual rebellions had to rely on their own resources, without large-scale outside help, and thus they were invariably defeated. But although the French never achieved a successful invasion of either kind, they did achieve some of their aims. French strategists knew full well that the very fear of an invasion was enough to divert British resources from other tasks.

The Role of Blockade

Blockade was the cornerstone of British naval strategy, and the routine job of the typical ship-of-the-line. For every hour spent in action with the enemy, the average sailor spent several weeks, or perhaps months, on blockade service. Such work seemed unglamorous at the time, and crews on the blockade of Brest were known as 'Channel gropers'. Yet history has invested the blockade with a good deal of drama, largely inspired by Alfred Thayer Mahan's famous description of 'Those far distant, storm-beaten ships, upon which the Grand Army never looked', which 'stood between it and the dominion of the world'.[1] In the absence of a decisive victory over the enemy, it was clearly necessary to restrict his movements, and prevent him from doing damage to British colonies or trade, or invading the homeland itself. Yet over the years there was little agreement about how this was to be done — whether to keep him confined permanently in his ports, or to entice him out into battle; whether to keep the enemy fleet bottled up and impotent, or to take the risk of allowing him out, and hoping to catch him and force him into a decisive battle. The close blockade, so beloved of Mahan and his followers, became established relatively late in the day, though it was not a new idea in itself. Blockade had been attempted in the Dutch Wars of the seventeenth century, but the English rarely had sufficient superiority to carry it out effectively. It had been used against Brest in the 1690s, though it was never effective until the Seven Years' War, when Anson began the policy of continuous blockade. In the American War it proved impossible to implement, as the British fleet was heavily outnumbered. It did not reach its full development until

The blockading squadron at anchor off Cadiz in 1797. From A Anderson, *Journal of the Forces in the Mediterranean,* 1802

the late 1790s, and it was made possible by several improvements, including better ship design, and the use of anti-scorbutics.[2]

Open Blockade

At the beginning of the war in 1793, Lord Howe, then aged 66, was put in command of the Channel fleet. Despite a clear naval superiority, he did not revive Anson's policy of thirty years earlier, of close blockade. Instead, he began a system of 'open blockade', or 'observation'. The main fleet was to remain at Spithead, ready to put to sea but protected from the dangers of storm and shoal. A squadron of frigates was to remain off Brest, and send cutters or schooners with news of any French attempt to leave. Other frigates would try to follow the French, and report on the direction of attack — to Ireland, the West Indies, India, or towards the British mainland. The main fleet would thus be guided onto the French.

This policy was severely criticised by Mahan and his followers at the end of the nineteenth century, and it has often been suggested that it was timid, defeatist and ineffective. In fact, it had several clear advantages: the material of the fleet was protected from harm in port, and the French were more likely to be enticed out to defeat than by a policy of close blockade. The disadvantages were that the French could often escape to launch an expedition, and they attempted several during these years; and that the British fleet, confined to port, tended to become bored and mutinous.

Close Blockade

The idea of close blockade was re-established by St Vincent, when he took command of the Mediterranean fleet off Toulon in 1795. St Vincent gave remarkably little thought to naval tactics and strategy, and it is more likely that he was trying to find a way to keep his ships and officers better disciplined. He wrote of keeping the fleet in 'constant movement', and in 'perpetual motion',[3] in order to keep the crews busy and unable to communicate with the shore, or with other ships. St Vincent took close blockade with him to the Channel fleet in 1800, and by the resumption of war in 1803 it had been accepted as standard doctrine. Strategic as well as disciplinary reasons were given for adopting it; Lord Melville wrote, 'The system of our enemy remaining in their ports while our force is constantly at sea, must operate substantially in our favour, in so far as it adds to the skill and alertness of our seamen, while at the same time the seamen of the enemy are making no additional acquirements in that respect'.[4]

Coastal Blockade

The blockades of the main enemy ports were intended to keep the enemy fleet in port, but there was always the possibility that it might escape, or that an invasion might be mounted by light coastal ships and gunboats from minor ports, without the support of the main fleet. To counteract this, lines of blockade were established on both sides of the Channel, off both the French and English coasts, during the invasion scare of 1803–5. In 1803, Keith's North Sea fleet was made responsible for most of this, with cruisers stationed at important points. On the English side, much of the work was to be carried out by gunboats, manned by Sea Fencibles, and by hired vessels. On the French side of the Channel, four frigates and four sloops were to be stationed off Le Havre, while a squadron of one 50-gun ship, four frigates, four sloops and several brigs and cutters was to be based at Dungeness, to keep an eye on Boulogne, Dieppe and Fecamp. A force of three frigates, six sloops and ten smaller vessels was based in the

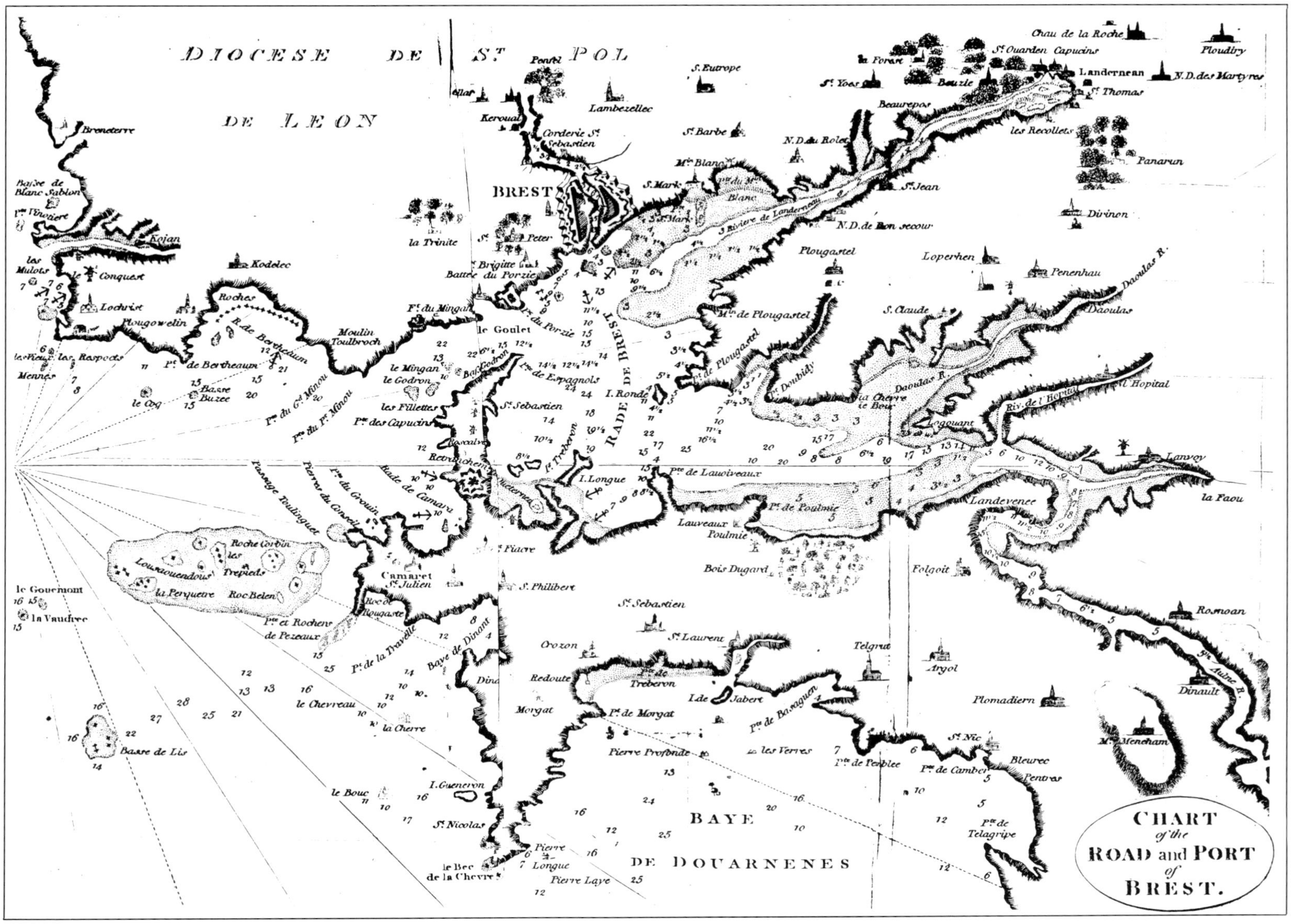

The Brest area, showing the many dangers to ships on blockade. From the Naval Chronicle

Downs to patrol off Calais and Dunkirk; while a 50-gun ship, three frigates, four hired merchant ships and six smaller vessels patrolled the entrance to the Scheldt, thus covering Flushing and Antwerp. Three frigates, three sloops and three cutters were to be based off the next Dutch port of Helevoetsluis, and two ships of two decks, two frigates, two sloops and three cutters were placed off the Texel, based at Yarmouth Roads. Another small force was to be placed at the mouths of the Elbe and Weser, though these were not expected to keep on station throughout the winter.[5] By July 1804, Keith was recommending that

> The whole line from Havre to Ostend should be declared in a state of blockade, and as Flushing, Dunkirk, Boulogne and the ports of the Seine may be considered from the number of HM ships stationed before them to be blockaded already *de facto*, I am of opinion that with the addition of a few more small vessels the blockade of the intermediate ones may be easily effected.[6]

After 1808, the purpose of these small squadrons changed; they were now intended to enforce a total economic blockade of the French coast, rather than prevent an invasion. They tended to be spread more thinly, and to cover even smaller ports.

The entrance to Brest harbour. From the Naval Chronicle

Blockade Stations

Brest was always the most important blockade station of the British fleet. Not only did it neutralise the main French fleet and base; it also provided a force which could control the western end of the English Channel. In practice, the main body of the blockading fleet kept a position about ten miles northwest of the island of Ushant. It might move ten or twenty miles north of this spot to show its presence in the Channel, and it sometimes went south to cover the main entrance to Brest more closely; but on average the fleet seems to have spent about half its time within quite a small area off Ushant. In normal circumstances, the Brest squadron was directed by the commander-in-chief of the Channel Fleet in person, even though he had many other forces under his command.

The French base at Rochefort was, according to Keith's instructions of 1812, 'next in importance to Brest',[7] especially after a large French force took refuge there in 1808. It was blockaded from within the outer anchorage at Basque Roads, though Keith decreed that the squadron was to operate outside the Roads 'in certain winds'. The French fleet remained further in, protected by the batteries of the Ile d'Aix, and those on Oleron and the mainland.

At Toulon, the main French Mediterranean base, the blockading force was normally situated approximately south of the port. Nelson had command of this force in 1803–5, and his dispositions were criticised by Captain Whitby.

> First, then, he does not cruise upon his rendezvous; second, I have consequently repeatedly known him from a week to three weeks, and even a month, unfound by ships sent to reconnoitre . . . thirdly, he is occasionally obliged to take the whole squadron in to water, a great distance from Toulon; fourthly, since I came away the French squadron got out in his absence, and cruised off Toulon several days, and at last, when he came out, he only got sight of them at a great distance, to see them arrive at their own harbour. From all this I draw one general conclusion — that it is very possible for them to escape him.[8]

Whitby hinted that Nelson's temperament was unsuited to blockade service, but it must be remembered that his bases, at Malta and Gibraltar, were a long way from Toulon, and that in some senses Nelson preferred to lure the enemy out of port and into battle.

At Cadiz, the main body of the fleet was kept close inshore.

> We were tacking and wearing ship continually as the blockading service required us to keep as near the harbour's mouth as possible, and consequently, when the wind was blowing on the land, we were obliged to beat off; and when it was blowing off the land, then to beat up to the harbour's mouth as near as we could, to prevent the escape of the enemy.[9]

At other times, the fleet of Cadiz was kept at anchor. In 1797, the inshore squadron, under Nelson, was anchored in a crescent formation close to the harbour mouth, while the main body, under St Vincent, anchored a little further off. It was only necessary 'to keep out of gun shot from St Sebastian's light', because 'the *Namur* of 90 guns when under weigh was struck with a shot from thence.'[10]

The blockade of the Dutch bases, in the Texel and Scheldt, was carried out by the North Sea fleet, based at the Downs and Yarmouth. In the 1790s, Admiral Duncan used open blockade, but with cruises to the north of the Dutch ports during periods of Dutch activity. While attempting to follow Dutch fleets or convoys, the fleet ranged over quite a wide area, though of course the waters of the North Sea are relatively narrow, and it would be much more difficult for the Dutch to escape completely. The system was generally successful — a small inshore squadron spotted the Dutch fleet leaving port in October 1797. Duncan, refitting at Yarmouth, was informed, and defeated them at the Battle of Camperdown.

The Fleet on Blockade

One of the disadvantages of close blockade was that it required a large number of ships, as a proportion of the fleet was constantly being sent back to port for repairs and replenishment. Melville suggested that 'the portion of the Channel fleet appropriated to the blockade of Brest ought to be double of what is requisite for the actual blockade.'[11] Captain Phillip Patton was rather more optimistic. 'In my opinion, these British squadrons should consist of such a number of ships as would admit that a fourth, or third, part of each of them should be able to go into the nearest port to refit, to victual, or to store; and the remaining three fourths, or two thirds, sould be of such force as still to have a decided superiority over the enemy.'[12]

Routine on blockade could sometimes be rather tedious. 'We put to sea again and cruised off Toulon, as usual, doing nothing but tacking back and forward, from and to the land, watching the manoeuvres of the French fleet, which sometimes came out of port to plague us, to make sail, and clear for battle and then run away from us like wild geese, giving us a wild goose chase after them beneath their batteries.'[13] But, in general, blockade service was better for morale than lying in harbour for month after month, as had happened with open blockade. As a result, there were no major mutinies among the fleets on blockade service.

Many officers spent their time devising ways to bring the enemy to battle, or to find ways of attacking him in harbour. One scheme which was actually attempted was the attack in Basque Roads in 1809, using rockets and fire ships. This attack failed because the commander-in-chief was not prepared to press it home fully, but many other projects did not even get that far. Another scheme, put forward by Captain Peter Puget in 1804, was for fire-brigs to enter Brest Roads and attack the French at anchor there; this was never attempted. But in many ways, these expeditions should be considered as amphibious operations, rather than as part of blockade service.

In general, blockade service was less boring than might be imagined. Ships were constantly detached to stop and search passing merchant vessels or chase privateers, frigates made reconnaisances, the inshore squadron made intricate passages through the shoals and rocks of the harbour mouth, while the bulk of the fleet carried out gunnery and fleet exercises.

Reconnaissance and Intelligence

The commander of a blockading squadron had to use any means available to find out all he could about the enemy forces, and especially about their intentions and readiness for sea. The most obvious way was to send frigates and sloops as close into the harbour as possible, to observe the preparations. In 1805, Lt Beauman of the frigate *Aigle* reported to Admiral Cornwallis,

> In obedience to your signal of this morning, I . . . reconnoitred the enemy's force in Brest harbour at 3pm; had a favourable opportunity of getting a very distinct view of the fleet, and found them to consist of twenty-one sail-of-the-line, four of which are three-decked ships, four frigates, two corvettes, two brigs and one cutter, with one admiral and two rear-admiral's flags flying.[14]

Frigates could also report on harbours not yet fully covered by the blockade, and later in the year Beauman reported,

> I proceeded with His Majesty's ship *Aigle* and reconnoitred the harbours of L'Orient and Port Louis on the 31st, and finding none of the enemy's squadron in the above harbours, except a man-of-war brig in Port Louis, proceeded immediately to Rochefort, which port I reconoitred this day at 3pm, and found lying here an 80-gun ship nearly unrigged; being anxious of gaining information on the French squadron, stood into Basque Roads, and brought to a French sloop, loaded with firewood, the master of which informed me that the French squadron was at Rochefort.[15]

The inshore squadron exercising off Cadiz. The National Maritime Museum

Neutral ships were also a useful source of information:

> The information which has been received of the enemy was by an American vessel from Rochefort spoken by the *Acasta*, who states their squadron at anchor near the Ile d'Aix to be six sail-of-the-line — one having joined them from Rochefort — and by a small vessel taken by the *Pickle* which had been a fortnight from L'Orient.[16]

Spies could be useful, though their chains of communication tended to be rather long, often through British consuls and agents ashore, and then via the Admiralty in London. Skippers of enemy merchant ships and fishing boats seem to have been rather garrulous, and had little conception of state security.

The Inshore Squadron

The inshore squadron was a force of ships-of-the-line, employed closer to the enemy base than the bulk of the fleet. The need for such a force was demonstrated December 1797, when the French fleet escaped from Brest through the frigate squadron on observation duty. An inshore squadron of ships-of-the-line might have been able to disrupt the exit of the French from the port and wreck the expedition, or perhaps follow the enemy while the frigates went to inform the rest of the fleet. Inshore squadrons became standard in the 1800s. Under Cornwallis off Brest in 1803–5, the squadron consisted of two-deckers, mostly 74s, as they had better sailing qualities than three-deckers. When first formed at the outbreak of war, it had three ships-of-the-line and two frigates, out of a total fleet of twenty-five sail. By 1804, it had increased to five of the line. A relatively young and active admiral was generally put in command of the inshore squadron — Nelson commanded it off Cadiz in 1797 — and suitable ships were usually attached to it by rotation, as the work involved considerable strain on officers and crew. At Brest, the squadron operated off the entrance to the harbour itself, while the main fleet was about thirty miles away off Ushant.

Supply and Replenishment

Ships of the blockading fleets usually had to go into port for replenishment about once every two or three months — hence the need for large numbers of ships to be available, and the occasional weaknesses when too many ships were off the station. Ships on the Brest blockade went to Cawsand Bay, Torbay or St Helens to take on supplies, and entered Portsmouth or Plymouth for repairs. In the Mediterranean, fleets had to find their supplies where they could. Alliances had to be forged with the Barbary States, especially since Gibraltar was very short of water and foodstuffs. Ships from the Toulon blockade often had to put into the port of Tunis. 'Our squadron used to water near the Goletta, a small channel leading to the ancient harbour of Carthage, fortified on each side and a chain across.'[17] Likewise, the Cadiz squadron, though 'anchored seven or eight miles from Cadiz', was 'compelled from time to time to leave our anchorage for the purpose of procuring water and cattle from the neighbouring coast of Africa.'[18]

Bad Weather Procedure

Most blockading stations were dangerous in bad weather, and this was especially true of Brest. Gales tended to come from the west, and such weather would create a highly dangerous lee shore, which ships would find it difficult to escape from. This of course was even more of a problem for the inshore squadron, which might be trapped inside the entrance. The main fleet was off Ushant, and could easily retreat to Torbay, where it was safe as long as the wind remained westerly. Meanwhile, the French were trapped inside their harbour by the same wind which had driven the British off station.

In other instances, ships might merely be separated from the main fleet by bad weather, or detached on special service. To allow for such cases, a rendezvous would be appointed where the ships would meet when possible. Upon his reappointment to the command of the Channel Fleet in 1806, St Vincent wrote, 'I cannot approve of the rendezvous of my predecessor, "seven leagues southwest of Ushant", and intend to change it to "well in with Ushant during an easterly wind" '.[19]

The Men on Blockade

Both officers and men tended to dislike blockade service. Off Brest in 1810, Captain Broke had 'another tiresome, useless week! The only variety a little foul weather to tear our sails and make us swear at the wind'.[20] Blockade service was never popular, and that off Brest was especially thankless. 'We soon found we had become Channel gropers, a term given to the Channel fleet in wartime, which is destined to hover about Brest when the wind is fair, for the French fleet to come out', wrote 'Jack Nastyface'. This was,

> A fresh-beef station [which was] neither being abroad nor at home. One reason why they have a dislike of it is that they are open to the ridicule of seamen who may be coming from foreign stations, as well as by the girls and people in the sea-port towns, by cantingly telling them they would never have the scurvy or that they might as well be by their mothers' fireside and tied to the apron strings, as merely running in and out of harbour; and nothing hurts Jack's feelings more than being taunted of anything unmanly or inferior.[21]

Of course, this was grossly unfair, and took no account of the dangers of gales, lee shores, and uncharted rocks, such as that which destroyed the *Magnificent* in 1804. On the spot, Admiral Collingwood saw things very differently.

> I am lying off the entrance to Brest harbour, to watch the motions of the French fleet. Our information respecting them is very vague, but we know they have four or five and twenty great ships, which makes it necessary to be alert and keep our eyes open at all times. I therefore bid adieu to snug beds and comfortable naps at night, never lying down but in my clothes.[22]

3 Convoys and Cruisers

The System of Convoys

The convoy system had been developed and refined by the navy, ever since the early days of the French privateers. By the 1790s, it was quite complex and sophisticated, for it had to cater for a merchant fleet trading all over the world, and employing 16,000 ships. It did not use an unduly large proportion of naval resources — in 1808, for example, only fifteen ships were employed full time as 'convoys and cruisers' — two third rates, one fourth rate, seven fifth rates, one sixth rate, three sloops and a brig.[1] In addition, there were ships being sent out to overseas stations, which might escort a convoy on the way; ships appointed as escorts by local commanders-in-chief in the Mediterranean or West Indies; and hired armed vessels which were employed to escort coastal convoys.

Merchants had many objections to convoys, as they slowed up trade and subjected their ships to the attention of the press gang. To prevent them being tempted to take the risk of sailing without convoy, the system was enforced by Act of Parliament. As soon as war broke out in 1793, ships were embargoed in port 'until the usual preparations now carrying on at the various ports shall be sufficiently advanced to afford them adequate protection'.[2] Ships were sent out to meet homecoming vessels, which might not have heard of the outbreak of war; escorts were got ready for the ships in harbour; and of course the press gangs began to recruit crews for the navy. In 1798 the system was strengthened by a Compulsory Convoy Act which imposed a tax on vessels to pay for the cost of convoy. The act was renewed in 1803, but without the tax. Any vessel attempting to sail without convoy, or without Admiraly permission, was liable to a fine of £1000. Furthermore,

> Every master is liable to a penalty of £200 for not having painted on board, and affixed to some conspicuous and convenient part of his ship or vessel, so much of the act of 33 Geo III c66 as makes captains under convoy liable to be articled in the court of Admiralty for disobeying signals, or deserting the convoy without notice given and leave obtained for that purpose [and] every such master is liable to a penalty of £100 who, in danger of being boarded or taken possession of by the enemy, shall not make signals by firing guns, or otherwise to convey information of his danger to the rest of the convoy, as well as to the ships of war under the protection of which he is sailing and, in case of being boarded or taken possession of, shall not destroy all instructions confided to him relating to the convoy.[3]

Standing Convoys

Water transport was far cheaper and more efficient than land transport in the days before the railways, and a large proportion of British trade was along the coast. The most notable example of this was of course the Newcastle coal trade, though there were many other local commodities which were carried around the country by sea. In addition, trade with Ireland took up a large amount of shipping. All this was protected by the navy, by means of regular coastal convoys known initially as 'standing' convoys. Major ports, such as Exeter, St Ives, Swansea, Plymouth, Bristol, Dartmouth, Yarmouth, Falmouth and Leith, each had a small vessel — gunboat or hired armed vessel — permanently attached. The captain was under orders to respect the wishes of the mayor or chief magistrate of the port, and to assemble convoys and escort them to the next major port, in either direction. The divided command, between the magistrates and the navy, led to many problems, and in 1797–8 the system was changed, so that Admiral Duncan, the commander-in-chief in the North Sea, was in charge of all convoys in that area, while the port admiral at Plymouth commanded those in the Channel and west coast.[4] They were now known as 'coastwise' rather than 'standing' convoys. There was a regular fortnightly service, from the Nore and the Downs via Yarmouth, Hull and Leith, and then across the North Sea for ships which required it. In the opposite direction, a service operated from the Downs via St Helens, Portland,

An East India convoy, escorted by a frigate. The National Maritime Museum

Torbay, Plymouth and Falmouth, to Cork, Waterford and Dublin in Ireland, or to the Severn, Swansea, Liverpool, Belfast and the Clyde. Anchorages, rather than specific ports, were now the focus of the convoy system.

Long-distance Convoys

Long-distance convoys were also well established, though less frequent than coastal convoys. Around 1808, convoys from Longhope Sound, Orkney, to Gothenburg were run monthly, with feeder convoys from Liverpool and the Clyde to Longhope. Other Baltic convoys were run every fourteen or twenty-one days; those to and from Greenland and the Davis Straits, supporting the whaling trade, operated from time to time. There were monthly convoys to North America, Newfoundland and Quebec, during March to September. Those to the West Indies, Surinam, Demerera, Berbice, Portugal, Spain and the Mediterranean also sailed monthly, with extra convoys when the situation demanded. Yet more monthly convoys sailed to the East Indies, China, Cape of Good Hope, St Helena and the South Seas. Military convoys to support the British forces in the Peninsular War were operated 'as necessary'.[5]

The East India convoys were among the most important. In this case, organisation was not difficult, as all the ships belonged to a single company. Bombay and China ships set off early in the year, as they had the longest distance to cover. About four ships left the Downs in January or February of a typical year. Ships for Bombay and St Helena sailed monthly for the rest of the year, with six to nine in a typical convoy. Ships for China were escorted all the way, but for convoys bound for India the naval escort sailed only as far as St Helena, except when a man-of-war was being sent out to join the East India squadron. Despite the relatively good discipline of the East India captains, there were plenty of disputes with naval commanders. Admiral Troubridge complained, in 1805, of 'the great negligence of many of the convoy', and of 'the pointed tendency to neglect to signal by many of the ships by day', and of 'omissions and neglect' by the East India officers.[6]

Escorts

There was no specialised design of convoy escort, though it was the main task of many small vessels such as sloops and brigs. All kinds of ship could escort convoys from time to time, and large military convoys sometimes had enormous escorts. For St Vincent's expedition to the West Indies in 1794, a fleet of 200 transports was escorted by 34 ships-of-the-line.[7] In 1795, another convoy consisted of 200 sail of merchantmen, escorted by thirteen ships-of-the-line, three frigates, one 44-gun ship, two cutters, one brig and one fireship.[8] However, a typical convoy had a much smaller escort, with fewer and smaller ships. Many had only a single sloop, perhaps with an even smaller vessel to keep the merchant ships in order and act as 'whipper in'. In September 1793, for example, a convoy of 158 homeward-bound West Indiamen was escorted by a single ship. A coastal convoy was usually escorted by a single hired armed ship, under the command of a lieutenant. In 1804, eighteen such vessels were allocated to convoy duty in the North Sea under Lord Keith, and ten more were

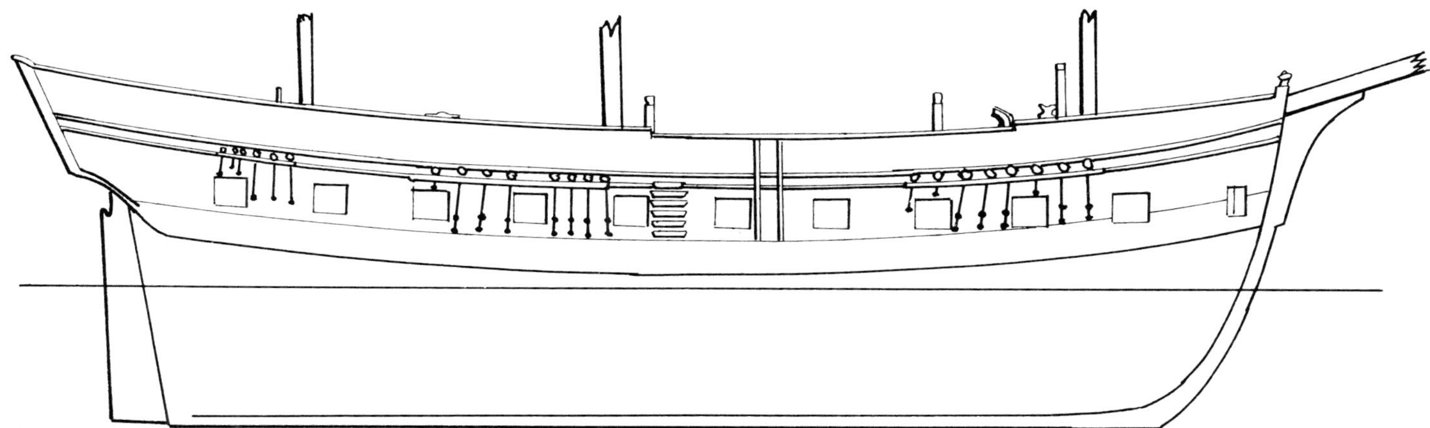

The Albion, *an armed ship of 14 guns hired in 1798 as a convoy escort.* Based on a drawing in the National Maritime Museum

under the Plymouth command.[9] A typical vessel of this type was the *Lady Taylor*. She was surveyed at Deptford in 1793, and was found to be eleven years old, and of 379 tons, ship rigged and copper sheathed. During the following year she escorted convoys from the Nore to Cuxhaven and Ostend, and then between Dublin and Cork.[10] William Richardson describes the work of a 'whipper in':

> Another affair of a different nature happened soon after this, which was that of a Scottish brig which sailed so badly that she, being always astern, detained the whole fleet very much. One day, she being far astern, our signal was made to tow her up to the fleet . . . When we got her ahead of the fleet we cast her off, but she had got such a twisting that she wanted no more towing during the passage.[11]

Convoy Organisation

The basis of convoy organisation was the convoy signal book. Copies of this were printed by the Admiralty, and issued to the commander of the escort in accordance with the number of ships expected. The convoy gathered at an anchorage; in a large one such as Spithead, convoys heading in different directions were identified by their signal flags flown from the men-of-war. Those heading northwards or eastwards had a red pendant under a triangular flag, those bound for the Elbe had a blue and yellow flag, those for the West Indies flew the Union flag, and so on.

On arrival at the anchorage, each merchant ship captain would send a boat to the lead ship of the escort to receive a copy of the instructions. These gave considerable detail about how the convoy was to be run. There were signals for 'Land discovered', 'Alter course to starboard one point', and for many other manoeuvres. Much attention was paid to keeping the convoy together, with signals for 'Ships astern to make more sail', 'The convoy to close nearer together', and 'The ships to leeward to make all sail possible to windward, and get into the body of the convoy', for example. There was no numerical code for convoys as yet, and much communication had to be made by other means. There were signals for 'The ships of the convoy to pass within hail of the commander thereof', in order that verbal messages might be passed. There were night and fog signals, to be made with guns, flares and lights, as with fleet signals.

In addition to these, each commander issued instructions relating to his own convoy, and according to need and his prejudices. He issued an order of sailing for the merchantmen, normally placing them in a rectangle made up of columns of ships, or occasionally in a diamond formation.[12] A large convoy would be divided into two

A typical convoy, with escorts and pennant ships all round. Public Record Office

The convoy to the West Indies which sailed under the escort of Admiral Jervis and several ships-of-the-line, November 1793.
Based on a drawing in the National Maritime Museum

A heavily escorted convoy, protected by the Channel fleet in April 1794.
a. Sailing by the wind
b. Sailing large
Based on a drawing in the National Maritime Museum

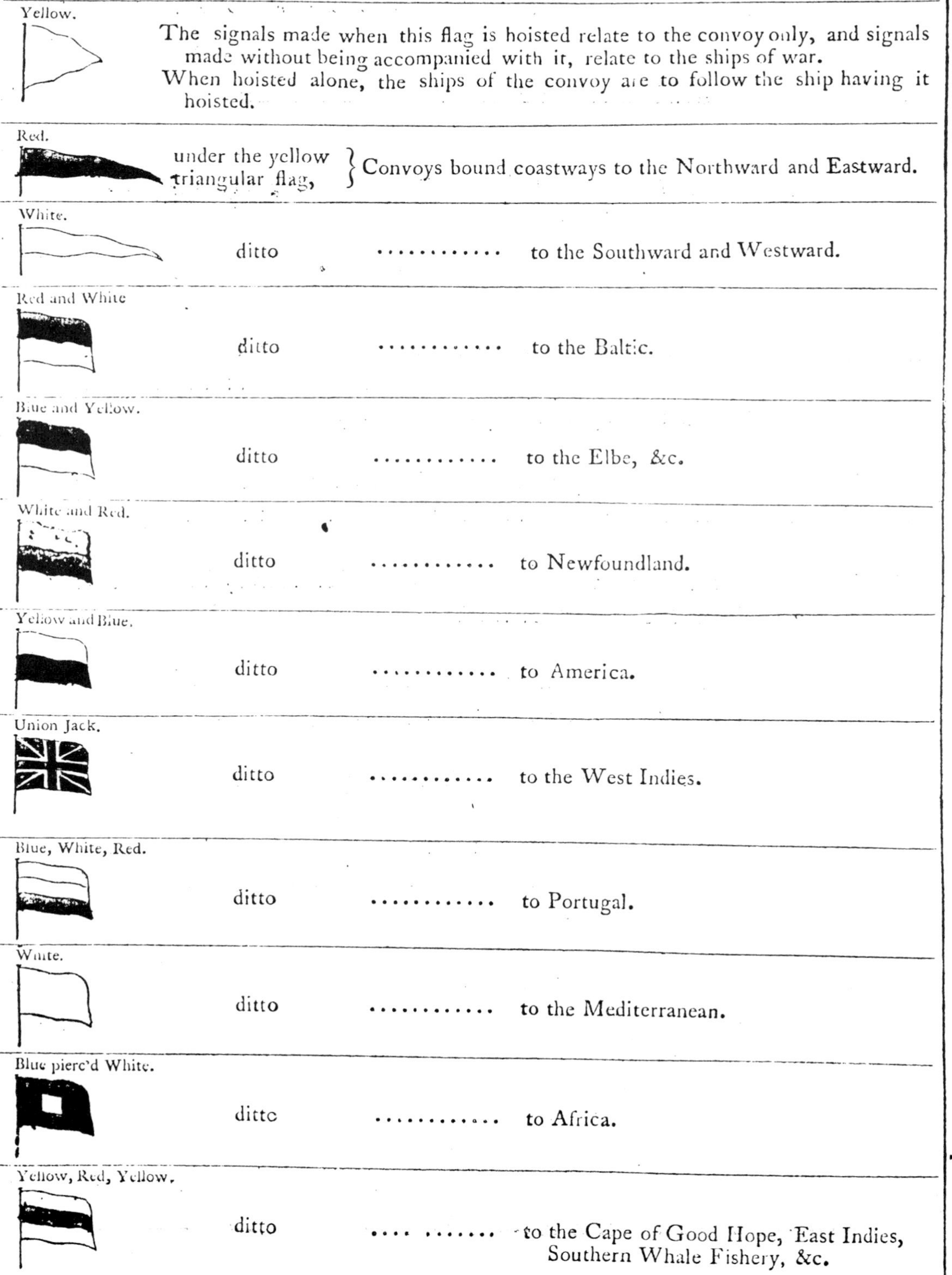

DISTINGUISHING SIGNALS to be made by the King's ships, at Spithead or at any other anchorage, when appointed to take the charge of convoy, and occasionally to be carried at sea, that the Masters of merchant vessels may know to what ship they are to apply for protection; to distinguish the different convoys when more than one may sail together, and point out their proper ship when the convoys may separate for their places of destination.

Flag		
Yellow.	The signals made when this flag is hoisted relate to the convoy only, and signals made without being accompanied with it, relate to the ships of war. When hoisted alone, the ships of the convoy are to follow the ship having it hoisted.	
Red.	under the yellow triangular flag,	Convoys bound coastways to the Northward and Eastward.
White.	ditto	to the Southward and Westward.
Red and White	ditto	to the Baltic.
Blue and Yellow.	ditto	to the Elbe, &c.
White and Red.	ditto	to Newfoundland.
Yellow and Blue.	ditto	to America.
Union Jack.	ditto	to the West Indies.
Blue, White, Red.	ditto	to Portugal.
White.	ditto	to the Mediterranean.
Blue pierc'd White.	ditto	to Africa.
Yellow, Red, Yellow.	ditto	to the Cape of Good Hope, East Indies, Southern Whale Fishery, &c.

A page from a convoy signal book.
Public Record Office

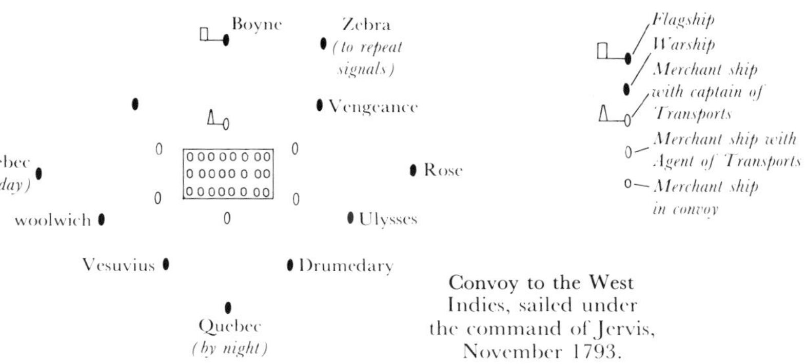

Convoy to the West Indies, sailed under the command of Jervis, November 1793.

or more rectangles, with escorts or 'pennant ships' between them and around them.[13]

Sometimes the larger merchantmen could be called on to help defend the convoy, or at least try to bluff the enemy. According to orders issued from the sloop *Arrow* in 1805, 'Should the commander find it necessary for its protection to form a line of battle, with the men-of-war and vessels having guns on board, he will shew a flag striped blue and white at the main to prepare them for the same.' The rest of the convoy was to keep on one side or another of the line, away from the enemy force. Merchant ships could be called on to help the organisation of the convoy in other ways. One such was the *Lady Ann*, and it was attested that

> During the whole time she acted as a pennant ship the master paid every possible attention to the orders of the commodore of the convoy in collecting the scattered vessels of the fleet, in boarding strange vessels, protecting the convoy, in rendering every other service in his power, and that he contributed very much to the safety and order of the fleet.[14]

Relations between convoy and escort were not always good. A signal book privately printed by Captain Maxwell of the *Arab* in 1804 included signal number 465, which ordered one of the ships of the escort to 'Enquire the reason for the ships astern, or those whose distinguishing signal is shown herewith, why they do not make sail agreeable to their situation. NB Impress a man from each.' Even more severe was numbeer 468: 'Fire into the ship, or ships, lying

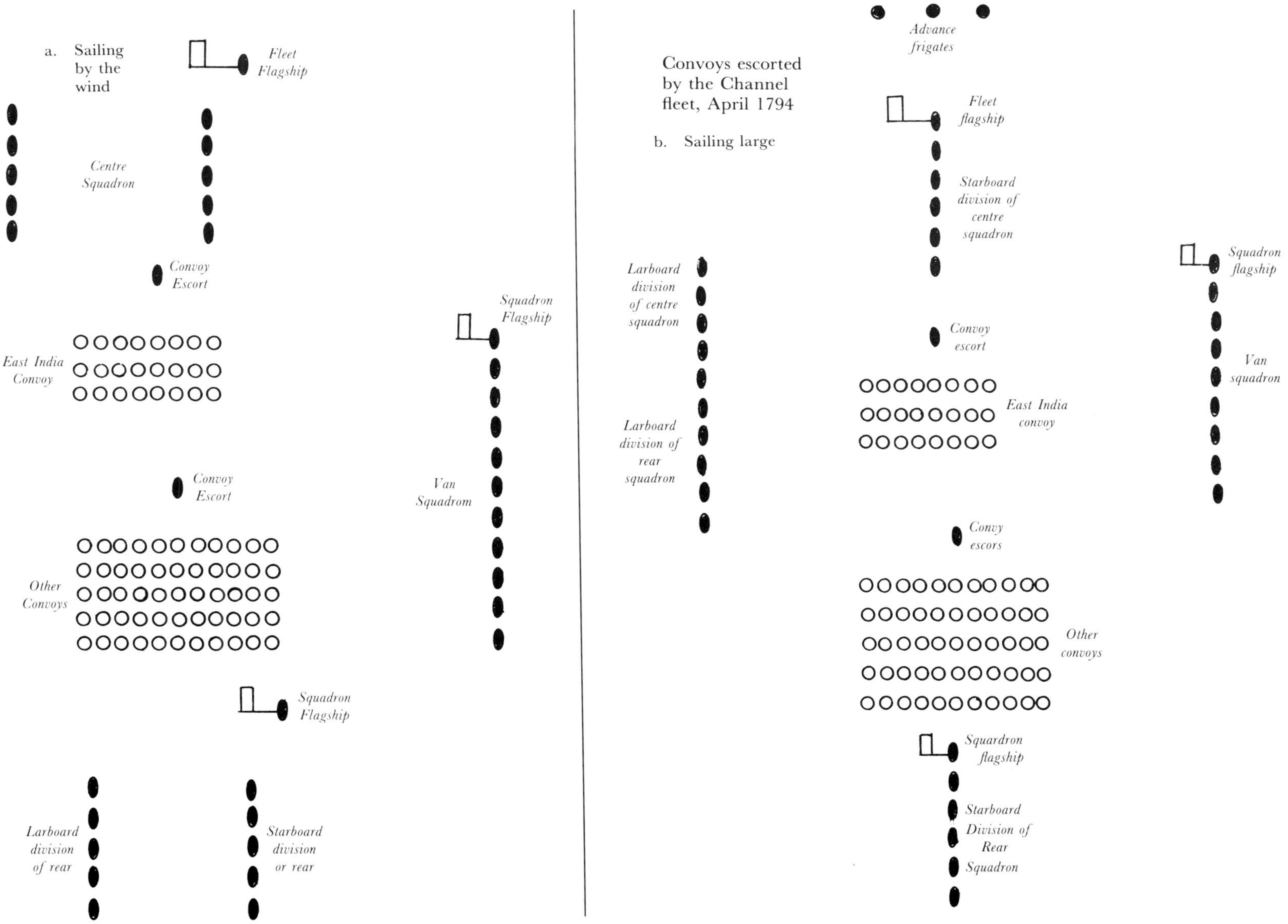

Convoys escorted by the Channel fleet, April 1794

a. Sailing by the wind

Fleet Flagship

Centre Squadron

Convoy Escort

East India Convoy

Convoy Escort

Other Convoys

Squadron Flagship

Larboard division of rear

Starboard division or rear

Squadron Flagship

Van Squadrom

b. Sailing large

Advance frigates

Fleet flagship

Starboard division of centre squadron

Larboard division of centre squadron

Larboard division of rear squadron

Convoy escort

East India convoy

Convy escors

Other convoys

Squardron flagship

Starboard Division of Rear Squadron

Squadron flagship

Van squadron

astern, or those whose distinguishing signal is shown herewith.'[15]

According to Steel, 'There should be in the convoy a number of frigates, which are to be distributed ahead, astern and on the wings of the fleet, which is always to be kept in the order of convoy of 3, 4 or 6 columns.' The men-of-war were to be ahead and to windward of the weathermost column, 'because in that position they will be able with promptitude to attend wherever their presence may be necessary.' Small sloops and similar ships were placed between columns to maintain order. 'Their particular business will be to get the tardy ships to make more sail, and oblige those that may be out of their post to resume it.'[16] If sufficient escorts were available, they were distributed round all four sides of the convoy. If there was only one it would stay to windward, as that was the most likely direction of attack, and it would allow the escort to reach any part of the convoy under threat. Likewise, a large escort would have the bulk of its force to windward. The large West Indies convoy of 1794 had two alternative formations, according to whether the fleet was sailing close to the wind, or large. In the former case, there was a van squadron of frigates, with two columns of ships-of-the-line ahead of the convoy, another to windward, and two more astern. If sailing large, four columns of ships-of-the-line were placed around the fleet, with an advance squadron of frigates in line abreast.[17]

Success and Failure of Convoys

In general, the convoy system was highly successful. About 7000 merchant ships were captured by the enemy from 1803–15, though this is only a small proportion of voyages undertaken; it is estimated that only about 0.6 per cent of ships actually in convoys were lost, though 6.8 per cent of stragglers were taken.[18] Convoy losses could often be quite spectacular when they occurred. In 1794, a convoy from the Channel Islands to Newfoundland was attacked by a French squadron, and fourteen vessels were captured. One of the most disastrous convoys was that captured off the Naze of Norway in August 1810, with the loss of forty-eight ships out of 200, at a cost of £425,000.[19] Sometimes, a convoy could be disrupted by the neglect of the captain of the escort. In 1804, the frigate *Hebe*, escorting a convoy across the Atlantic from the West Indies, carried full sail without any regard to the sailing qualities of the merchant ships, and simply left most of them behind. In a similar case in 1795 the captain of the *Medusa* sailed from Jamaica with the *Triton* under his command, and a convoy of 130 sail. The captain put on all possible sail, and sometimes logged as much as 184 miles a day. The convoy was left behind, and only twenty ships, mostly copper sheathed, could keep up with him. Sixteen of the others were captured by privateers. Following a complaint by a committee of West India merchants, the captain of the *Medusa* was court-martialled and put on half-pay for the rest of his life.[20]

Runners

Some ships, known as runners, were allowed to sail without convoy. The Admiralty issued passes to such ships, and kept a record of their particulars, including the name, tonnage and rig of the vessel, the number of carriage guns, and the number of men and boys on board. Licences were issued to vessels which were considered fast or well armed enough to avoid capture. To qualify, a vessel had to carry one carriage gun or swivel for every twenty tons of her burthen, along with one musket or blunderbuss, a pair of pistols and a sword for each person on board; this was later reduced because armaments were in short supply.[21]

Cruisers

Every naval ship had the duty to hinder enemy commerce, and to inspect merchant ships met on the high seas. Naturally, enemy ships tried to disguise themselves as neutrals, and officers had to be skilled in detecting such deception. In cases of doubt they boarded the suspected ship, where they were advised to examine the 'sea brief or title' of the vessel, its muster book, clearance from the last port, bills of lading, comparing these with the log book of the ship. This was not always easy in the case of a foreign ship from a minor country: Was she carrying strategic goods to France while pretending to go elsewhere, or was she French owned with a neutral crew, or was she practising some other deception? An officer often had to play detective to find out. 'Alteration to dates is a very great key to the detection of frauds, every word in every paper should be read again and again, and if there is any suspicion, the people should be examined separately, and cross-examined on their different stories.'[22] It is not clear how the language barrier was overcome in such cases, though there was some kind of *lingua franca* among seamen.

Many ships were stationed in particular areas specifically to intercept enemy vessels, and to protect British and allied trade. Orders to such ships were of several different kinds. Some were to patrol between specific limits of latitude and longitude. Others were to cruise off an enemy port, while yet more were to be stationed off the English coast — either off a particular headland, where merchant ships might rendezvous, or between two headlands.

4 Amphibious Operations

The Importance of Amphibious Operations

Some writers on the army in the Napoleonic Wars suggest that landings and amphibious operations were rare. In fact, there were at least sixty-eight major landing operations during these years,[1] and dozens of small ones. All the main French islands in the Caribbean were captured twice — once during each war. Cape of Good Hope was also captured twice, and Ceylon, Surinam and Curaçao were taken from the Dutch, along with the French colonies in the Indian Ocean. Wellington's army was landed in Portugal, and naval forces co-operated with the Spanish guerrillas. Two of the three main French bases, Toulon and Rochefort, were subjected to major attack, with only limited success. The Dutch Island of Walcheren was attacked by an army of nearly 30,000 men, and in 1807, an army was landed near Copenhagen which bombarded the town and forced it to surrender. Amphibious operations had a decisive effect on the wars, especially on Wellington's campaign in the Peninsula, as he himself recognised.

Ships and Armies

The sailing warship was undisputed master of the seas, but when it came within gun range of the land, its strength was rapidly diminished. Compared with land forces, a ship-of-the-line had massive gun power; only the very largest fortresses would be able to mount 74 guns, and bring up to 37 to bear in one direction. But the ship also had very grave disadvantages. It did not provide a steady platform for aiming. While close inshore, it was often in danger of striking the bottom. It was too dangerous for a ship to use explosive shells or red-hot shot, while these very projectiles, fired from the land, could be fatal to a wooden ship. As a result, ships tended to avoid conflict with land fortifications. Since these protected important positions such as the entrances to harbours, other means had to be found to attack fleets in port, or to land troops.

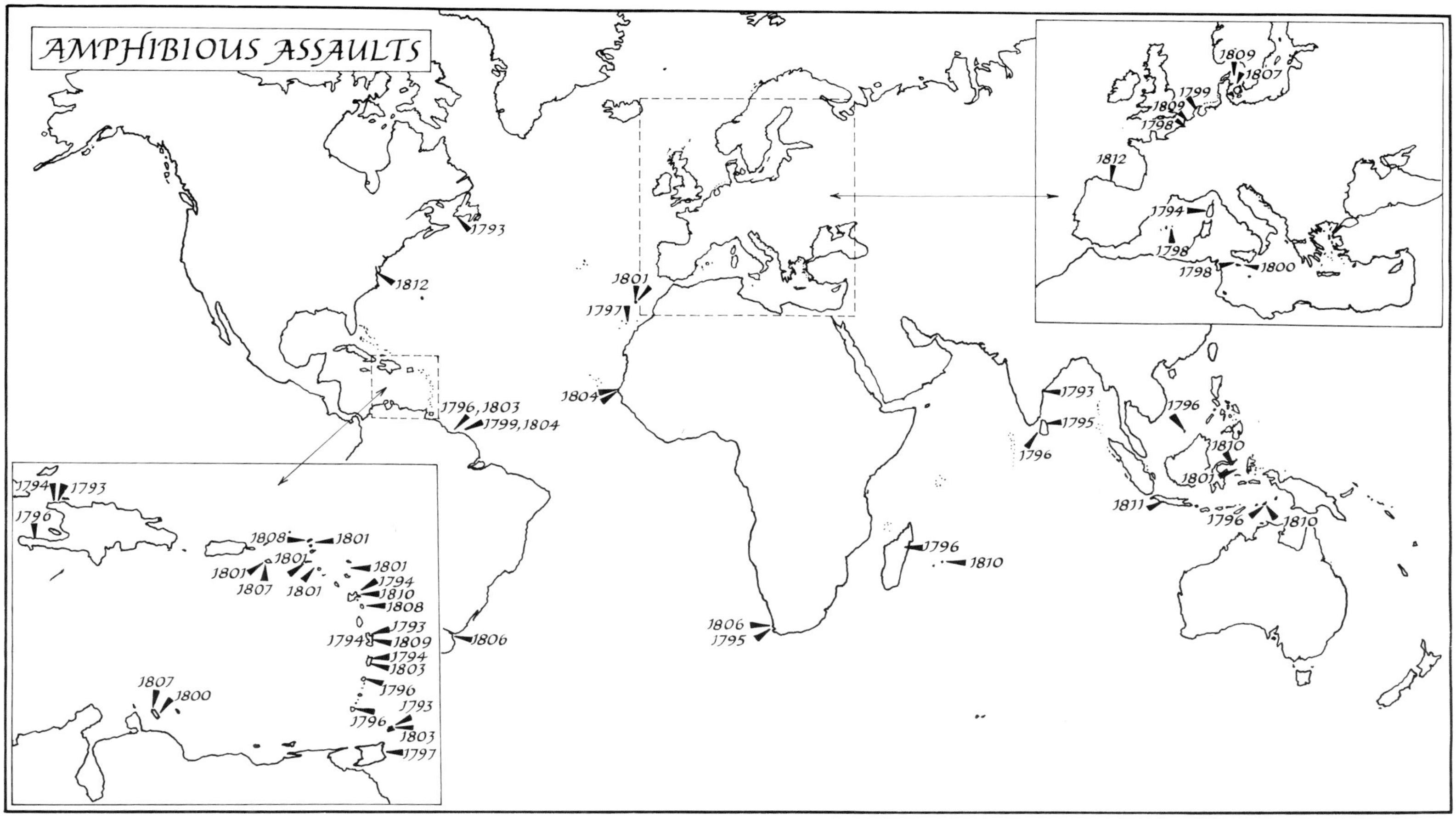

AMPHIBIOUS ASSAULTS

Major amphibious operations, 1793–1815. Compiled from James's *Naval History*

The tower at Mortella in Corsica. From the Naval Chronicle

The landing at Curaçao in 1807. National Army Museum

One exception which tended to prove the rule was the attack on the tower at Mortella, in Corsica, in 1794. This was heavily attacked by naval forces in 1794, but resisted strongly, although it was a comparatively small fort. 'The walls were of prodigious substance, and the upper part, where two 18-pounders were, was lined with junk and filled with sand — but our batteries above it set fire to the junk yesterday by some hot shot, and the enemy not being able to extinguish it, surrendered.'[2] Thus the fort was captured by the use of guns mounted on shore, and not by naval power alone. The affair made a great impression on British officers, and the later 'martello' towers were inspired by it.

Conversely, ships had a great advantage over troops when operating along a coastline, especially one indented by estuaries and rivers, or dominated by mountains. Popham's campaign on the north coast of Spain was a success because of this. On the other side of the peninsula, Cochrane ranged along the coast causing havoc with the defences.

> Lord Cochrane, during the month of September 1808, with his single ship the *Imperieuse*, kept the whole coast of Languedoc in alarm — destroyed the numerous semaphoric telegraphs, which were of utmost consequence to the coasting trade of the French, and not only prevented any troops being sent from that province into Spain, but even excited such dismay that 2000 men were withdrawn from Figueras to oppose him, when they would otherwise have been marching farther into the peninsula. The coasting trade was entirely suspended during this alarm; yet with such consummate prudence were all Lord Cochrane's enterprises planned and executed, that *not one of his men were either killed or hurt*, except one, who was singed in blowing up a battery.[3]

Provided he avoided enemy strongpoints, a naval commander could use his mobility to tie up large land forces.

Types of Operation

There was no specific Admiralty policy to carry out small coastal raids, as they very much depended on local circumstances, and on a commander taking any opportunity which might present itself. Cochrane was one who excelled at such operations, but there were others.

Attack on an enemy colony, especially an island, was perhaps the most common form of large-scale amphibious warfare. Often, it was not very difficult. Islands could be cut off by sea power, or attacked before the home government had time to reinforce them. The French army, despite its great strength, could not be everywhere at once, and colonial defence had relatively low priority in an age of European war. Often a colony had a small European population among large numbers of black slaves or native peoples. A naval force could concentrate on one island at a time, and reduce them one by one. Jervis's campaign of 1793–4 resulted in the capture of Guadeloupe and Martinique, along with several minor islands. In the case of Martinique, an unsuccessful attempt was made in co-operation with French royalists in 1793; in the following year, it was attacked by another force, and it was eventually found that the whole island was defended by 600 men, including 400 militia. Nevertheless, the battle was hard fought, and it took several landings in different places, and five days of fighting, to take the island. Most of the West Indian conquests were given back at the Peace of Amiens, and had to be recaptured later. In 1809, it took a force of six ships-of-the-line and twenty-two smaller vessels, and a fleet of transports with 10,000 troops on board, to recapture Martinique. French forces included 2400 regular troops and about the same number of militia. Again, several landings were made in different places, guns were set up to bombard the French strongholds, and the enemy surrendered.

Colonial expeditions were not always successful. Sir Home Popham succeeded in capturing the Cape of Good Hope in 1806, but was misled by intelligence reports that the Spanish colonists of Buenos Aires were disaffected. He set off with ships and a military force, and captured the city. However, the Spanish soon found that the British forces were very weak, rose against them, and expelled them with considerable losses. Popham was reprimanded by court-martial for leaving the Cape unprotected.

On several occasions, large bodies of troops were landed in heavily defended countries. Such attacks included the Egyptian expedition of 1801; Wellington's landings in Portugal in 1808; the attack on Copenhagen in 1807, when the city was forced to surrender by a combination of naval and shore attack; and the Walcheren expedition of 1809. The latter affair involved the landing of 13,000 troops on a Dutch island which controlled the entrance to the Scheldt. The island itself was not heavily defended, and the landings were effected without any great difficulty.

Other operations could be carried out directly with the support of an army, especially when it moved parallel to a coastline. This happened at the very beginning of the Peninsular War, and Wellington later wrote, 'I determined to march towards Lisbon by that route which passes nearest to the sea coast, in order that I might communicate with Captain Bligh of the *Alfred*, who attended the movements of the army with a fleet of victuallers and store ships.'[4] At the end of the same war, the army advanced into France, supported by the navy at the siege of San Sebastian, and by forcing the entry to the River Gironde.

In theory, the capture of a major enemy naval base should have been a great triumph, and a major blow for the enemy; in practice, such operations were never as successful as hoped, and ended in recriminations, and suggestions that opportunities had been missed. The first such case occurred early in the war, when Toulon was taken with the support of French royalists. In fact the operation was a disappointment, and the British force was obliged to retreat after destroying only a small proportion of the French Mediterranean fleet. Another attempt was made at Rochefort in 1808, with the aid of rockets and fireships. The affair ended badly, with Admiral Gambier being accused of timidity in refusing to attack the enemy when he was in confusion.

Shore Bombardment

Ordinary warships could carry out shore bombardment when necessary, but they were not well equipped for it. Large ships had the heaviest guns, but could not come close inshore. 'Their lordships command to observe that although they do not believe that line-of-battle ships could either afford direct assistance by acting against San Sebastian, as they could neither approach the works nor bring their guns to bear on the castle, or that they could occasion any alarm to the enemy for the security of his right or rear.'[5] The guns could not be elevated for long-range fire, the platform was unsteady, and the gun crews were generally untrained in accurate long-distance fire. It was in such circumstances that Sir Howard Douglas decided that the navy had much to learn about accurate gunnery. For sustained shore bombardment, it was far better to use bomb vessels, equipped with mortars, firing shells, and manned by detachments from either the army or the marine artillery. Because of the danger of a premature explosion of the shells, firing was conducted with great care. Most of the shells were kept aboard a tender anchored close to the bomb ketch, and were ferried aboard by a ship's boat. When the shells were aboard the bomb vessel, they were carefully stowed in racks under the mortars, and brought up only when immediately needed. The bomb vessels were operated at anchor, in calm weather, so that they could be aimed accurately.

Landing Techniques

There was no particular doctrine of amphibious warfare, and neither tactical treatises nor manuals on seamanship have much to say about it. Men could be landed by ships' boats, or by specially designed landing craft, wide, flat bottomed, and rowed by seamen. A beach was needed to effect the landing, preferably with little swell — though seamen and soldiers had to land through large breakers on occasion. At Wellington's landing at Mondego Bay in 1808, there were great difficulties.

> A rapid succession of these boats, closely packed with human beings, went tumbling through the surf, discharging on the beach their living cargoes, with little damage beyond a complete drenching. But as the day advanced, the surf increased, and each succeeding boat encountered increasing difficulties in reaching land. At one moment, upwards of twenty boats were struggling with the waves, and an awful anxiety for their fate was experienced... The soldiers, encumbered with their heavy packs, could make but feeble and ineffectual efforts to save themselves.[5]

At least sixty men were lost in this unopposed landing.

It was best to land at dawn, though this often meant that preparations had to begin well in advance. During the Egyptian landings of 1801,

> The boats began to receive the troops at two o'clock in the morning and at three the signal was made for their proceeding to the rendezvous near the *Mondovi*, anchored about a gunshot from the shore where it had been determined they were to be assembled and properly arranged; but such was the extent of the anchorage occupied by so large a fleet, and so great the distance of many of them from any given point, that it was not till nine the signal could be made for the boats to advance towards the shore.[6]

When landing large bodies of troops, it seems to have been normal to form the ships' boats and landing craft in line abreast, with small warships to protect their flanks until the water became too shallow for them. At the landing in Egypt in 1801,

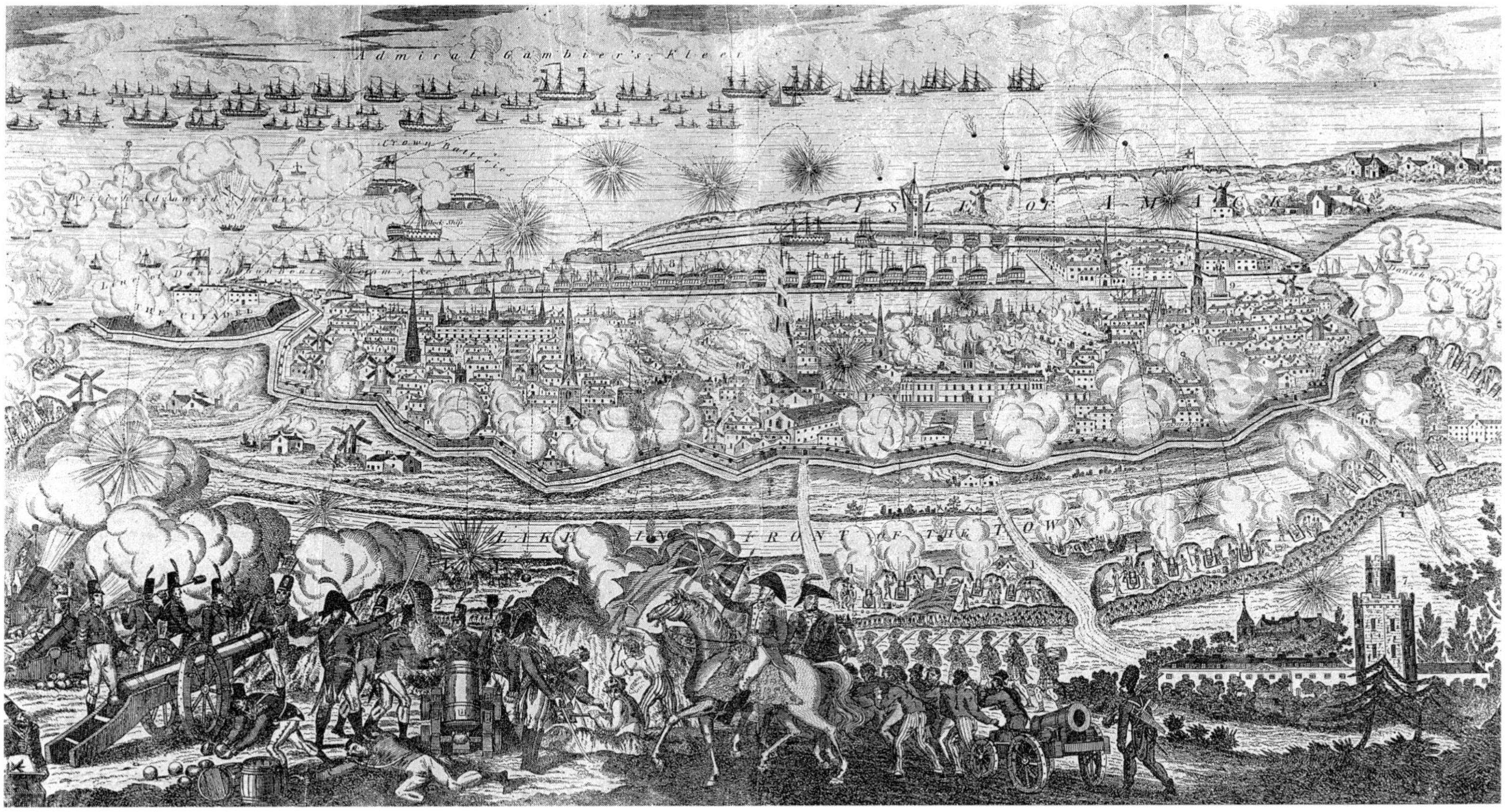

The attack on Copenhagen in 1807. The town is being bombarded mostly from the land, while the ships of the fleet patrol off the coast. National Army Museum

The attack on Egypt in 1801. National Army Museum

Hauling a gun up the side of Diamond Rock. The National Maritime Museum

> The whole line began to move with great celerity towards the beach between the castle of Aboukir and the entrance to the sea . . . the right flank being protected by the *Cruelle* cutter and the *Dangereuse* and *Janissary* gunboats; and the left by the *Entreprenante* cutter, *Malta* schooner and *Negresse* gun vessel, with two launches of the fleet on each wing armed . . . The *Tartarus* and *Fury* were placed in proper situations for throwing shot and shells with advantage; and the *Peterel*, *Cameleon* and *Minorca* were moored as near as possible with their broadsides to the shore.[7]

A code of boat signals had been drawn up for the occasion; for example, number 467 was 'Work as close inshore as possible to cover boats loading or coming off'; number 534 was 'To hoist all boats out'; and number 462 was 'Boats to be provided with lanterns, false fires, rockets, match and co'.[8] The landing was successful, though with heavy casualties.

At Walcheren in 1809, there was a variation in this technique, and it was intended that a line of gunboats should go in ahead of the line of boats.

> Frigates and gunboats being anchored with springs on their cables, to silence the strong batteries of Zoutland and Dykes Hook, with such proportion of rowing gunboats as may be necessary, a line of thirty, and forty, will be formed, and preceding the flat boats with troops, will row directly towards the beach and when within a proper distance for grape shot will open to the right and left for the flat boats to push in and land.[9]

Landing Guns

A favourite technique was to put ships' guns ashore, to bombard enemy positions from a stable base. This was done by Popham on the north coast of Spain in 1812, for example. With considerable skill, a gun was placed on a hill which the enemy regarded as inaccessible to cannon.

> The sea was at this moment breaking with such violence against the rocks at the foot of the hill that it was doubtful if a boat could get near enough to land a gun, but an opportunity offered itself of which Lieutenant

Troops preparing to disembark for the landing at Mauritius. The National Maritime Museum

> Groves availed himself with great activity and got the gun up a short distance by crab, which was so tedious that all the draft bullocks of the army were sent for and 400 men . . . the gun was dragged to the summit of the hill by 36 pair of bullocks, 400 guerrillas and 100 seamen.[10]

An even more notable example was the taking of Diamond Rock, close to Martinique, in 1804. Guns were raised to the summit of the rock to dominate the nearby shipping channel.

> Our enterprising officers and men succeeded in carrying up a line, and, ultimately, a stream cable of the *Centaur*, which was firmly moored by the side of the rock; and with one end of this cable clinched round a projecting rock, and the other on board the ship, a communication was established from one to the other. To the cable a traveller was affixed, similar in principle to that which children put on the string of a kit; to this a 24-pounder was attached, and, by means of tackles, conveyed to the top of the rock, another followed, and at last their carriages, shot, powder, with every article requisite for the support of a commander, two lieutenants and 120 men.[11]

British sailors excelled at such work.

> There is something indescribably animating to the mind of British seamen whenever they are ordered to land with a great gun. The novelty of getting on shore, and the hopes of coming to action, give a degree of buoyancy to their spirits, which carries them to the highest pitch of enthusiasm. A hundred sailors, attached by their canvas belts to a devil-cart, with a long 24-pounder slung to its axle tree, make one of the most amusing and delightful recollections of former days.[12]

Relations with the Army

Relations between admirals and generals depended very much on goodwill on both sides. By the strict letter of the law, there was no provision for putting land forces under the command of a sea officer, or fleets under a general. Disputes between the army and the navy never reached the acrimony that they did in the mid-eighteenth century, when absurd positions often resulted. In many cases, there was quite successful co-operation. On the other hand, there were plenty of cases where divided command created problems. Despite his general approval for the navy's role in the Iberian peninsula, Wellington complained about its level of activity in the latter stages. In 1813, he wrote, 'I complain of an actual want of necessary naval assistance and co-operation with the army, and I believe no man will entertain a doubt who reads the facts stated in my report to the government'.[13] On the naval side, the first lord of the Admiralty wrote, 'Our military officers on the frontiers of Spain do their duty most admirably; but they seem to consider a large ship within a few hundred yards of the shore off San Sebastian as safe a position and as immovable by the winds and waves as one of the Pyrenean mountains'.[11]

At a lower level, even junior officers on troopships could show incredible arrogance to sailors. Aboard the troopship *Duke of York* in 1801, it was logged that 'Col Colvil had openly ordered the sentry at the companion to run his bayonet through the body of the chief mate at any time he'd come that way, or make him go out of his way, though on duty', and 'an officer whose name is Mr Shaugnessy abused the chief mate and knocked him down'.[15]

5 Victory and Defeat

The Habit of Victory

The Royal Navy was consistently successful in battle from 1793 to 1815; 166 British warships were captured or destroyed by enemy action, including five of the line. And 1201 enemy warships were taken or destroyed by the British — 712 French, 172 Dutch, 196 Spanish, 85 Danish, 4 Russian, 15 Turkish, and 17 American. In all, 159 ships-of-the-line, 330 frigates and 50 guns ships, and 712 sloops and smaller vessels were defeated.[1] British victory was not caused by numerical superiority; in general, the combined fleets of Britain's opponents had the numerical advantage, at least until they were defeated in battle. British strategy prevented the various enemy fleets from combining, and this was of great importance; but even so, British commanders were expected to defeat enemy forces much stronger than their own. At Trafalgar the Franco-Spanish force had thirty-three ships to Nelson's twenty-seven, but no-one, least of all the French and Spanish commanders, expected a British defeat. In single-ship actions, it was reckoned that a British ship had a good chance against an enemy of 50 per cent greater gun power and crew.

There were several reasons for these great disparities. The French habit of firing into the rigging accounted for the lesser number of casualties among British crews. The French fleet started off badly in the wars, having been disrupted by the Revolution, and it never fully recovered from this. Though discipline was re-imposed, the ships were held in port by an increasingly tight blockade, and by a high command which preferred not to send them to sea very often. British seamen gained in skill and confidence, while those of France became increasingly demoralised. Some navies, such as the Spanish, suffered from the outdated social infrastructures of their countries. Others, such as the Dutch, were slightly unwilling allies of the French. The American navy suffered from none of these disadvantages, and was therefore able to score dramatic victories. Besides these factors, the Royal Navy had an overwhelming psychological advantage — the 'habit of victory'. Its sailors expected to win. Its commanders adopted daring new tactics, while the enemy timidly formed line to await the onslaught.

Surrender at Camperdown. The National Maritime Museum

The Act of Surrender

Ships were not expected to fight to a finish, and very few were sunk in battle. Once defeat was clearly inevitable, it was permissible for the officers to surrender the ship. If the enemy force was totally overwhelming, and there was no possibility of escape, the resistance might be purely token — firing a broadside and then hauling the flag down. In other cases, a ship was expected to put up a serious fight, and this usually meant that she would have suffered a considerable number of casualties before surrendering.

The actual surrender was done by hauling the ensign down. It was already common to fly two or three ensigns in battle, in case one was shot away. Sometimes, grave mistakes could be made. When the *Chesapeake* surrendered to the *Shannon* after being boarded, a small blue ensign was hauled up over the captured ship. One of the *Shannon's* officers hauled this down to replace it with a larger flag. A gun crew on the *Shannon* saw this, assumed that some Americans were disputing the surrender, and fired into the party.

The next formality was for the captain of the captured ship to surrender his sword to the victorious captain. 'When her captain (a plain-looking sailor man) came on board to deliver up his sword, Sir Richard told him he was a brave fellow for defending his ship so well.'[2] Sometimes the victor would allow the defeated captain to keep his sword. 'On going aboard the *Dessaix*, and presenting my sword to the captain, Christie Palliere, he politely declined taking it, with the complimentary remark that "he would not accept the sword of an officer who had so many hours struggled against impossibility".'[3] The officers might be trusted to this extent, but the crew were not; they were often battened down below decks, with sentries on the hatchways. Some were taken on board the victorious ships; the wounded were treated by the surgeons, sometimes of both sides.

The Penalties of Failure

A British officer whose ship surrendered to the enemy would inevitably face a court-martial, if he survived. Surrender in itself was no crime, if the ship had been properly and gallantly defended, and courts-martial in general were not unfair in assessing this. No captain was penalised for surrender in itself during these years, but any sign of cowardice was severely punished. After Camperdown, Captain John Williams of the *Agincourt* was put to the bottom of the captain's list, and rendered incapable of ever serving at sea again, for 'keeping back and not coming into the fight with the enemy'. Captain Alexander Campbell was also put to the bottom of the list, for not continuing an action with the enemy in 1804, and not exerting enough energy in repairing his ship and getting it back into action. Christopher Laroche was sentenced for not doing his utmost to bring his ship into action with the enemy in 1807, and Captain Claridge of the *Driver* was punished for failing to support the *Horatio* in her action with the French *Junon*.[4] The sentences in all these cases were relatively mild, and did not compare with those of the mid-eighteenth century, when Admiral Byng was shot for the loss of Minorca in 1755, and the senior surviving lieutenant of the *Anglesea* suffered a similar penalty for surrendering his ship in 1745, despite numerous mitigating circumstances. These cases still served as an example to naval officers, and the Articles of War still carried the possibility of death for many offences.

The Rewards of Success

For the crew of a victorious ship, the only material reward was the prize money — though, of course, this was not much for the common seaman, especially from a warship which had resisted strongly. On special occasions, parliament made up for this by voting a cash sum to be distributed in the same way as prize money. After Trafalgar, parliament voted £300,000 for the fleet; with prize money for the four surviving captured ships, each captain got £3362, while a lieutenant got £226, and a seaman £6.10.0.[5] Lieutenants, especially first lieutenants, could expect promotion after a successful action. Captains might be knighted, while a junior admiral could expect a barony or a viscountcy, as Nelson was given after the Nile. A commander-in-chief was entitled to an earldom, as was Jervis after the Battle of St Vincent. Other honours would be showered on victorious officers — freedom of cities, presentation swords, and gold or silver medals. Each would gain a place in history, and all the honour that his profession could confer. Such rewards were highly valued, but commanders were not insulted by being given money in addition; it was quite common for them to be given financial rewards by town councils, chartered companies, and groups of traders.

The Price of Victory

In terms of actual battle casualties, the price of victory in action was relatively low. In at least four single-ship actions — *Crescent* v *Reunion*, *Revolutionaire* v *Unite*, *Indefatigable* v *Virginie* and *Unicorn* v *Tribune*, the French ship was captured without any fatal British casualties at all.[6] In the six major fleet actions, 1483 men were killed, compared with about six times that number of enemy. Trafalgar had the largest 'butcher's bill' of any major action, with 449 killed and 1241 wounded. St Vincent had the smallest — 73 killed and 227 wounded.[7] Death in action was a relatively minor cause of death, a long way behind disease and accident.

Taking a much broader view, the great war with France was expensive in both lives and money. It is estimated that there were 92,386 British naval deaths during those years. Many more men served in the navy against their will, and had their lives affected or even ruined by it. Some, like John Nicol, spent their lives avoiding the press gang, and were ruined economically by this. The taxpayer had to find many millions of pounds, while trade was disrupted and commerce endangered. The wars with France did not disrupt life in the same way as did the twentieth-century wars with Germany, — there was no talk of a 'home front', no rationing, direction of labour or air raids — but there can have been few citizens who were not affected in one way or another.

The Treatment of Prisoners

Most of the officers and men defeated in fleet, squadron or single-ship actions, as well as thousands of merchant seamen, became prisoners of war. Governments had no great wish to keep large numbers of men in idleness at their expense, and in past wars it had been common to exchange prisoners, so that few men spent long periods in captivity; but in the French Revolutionary and Napoleonic Wars, there were several factors which interfered with this practice. In the first place, relations between governments were even worse than in a normal state of warfare. The British government regarded the French revolutionaries with horror, and Napoleon as little better. Communication between them was severely limited. In 1796, a French official wrote, 'The mode in which the present war is carried on, has for a long time prevented the most necessary communication, such as had not ceased to exist between hostile nations at any preceding period. The persons whose lot it has been to suffer most from this interruption, are the prisoners of war on either side.'[8] Secondly, there was a disparity in the numbers involved. Britain had large numbers of naval prisoners from France and her allies; there were far fewer Britons in French prisons, because French naval victories were much rarer. Even when exchanges were arranged, there were discrepancies, as it became difficult to find enough prisoners of suitable rank in the French prisons.

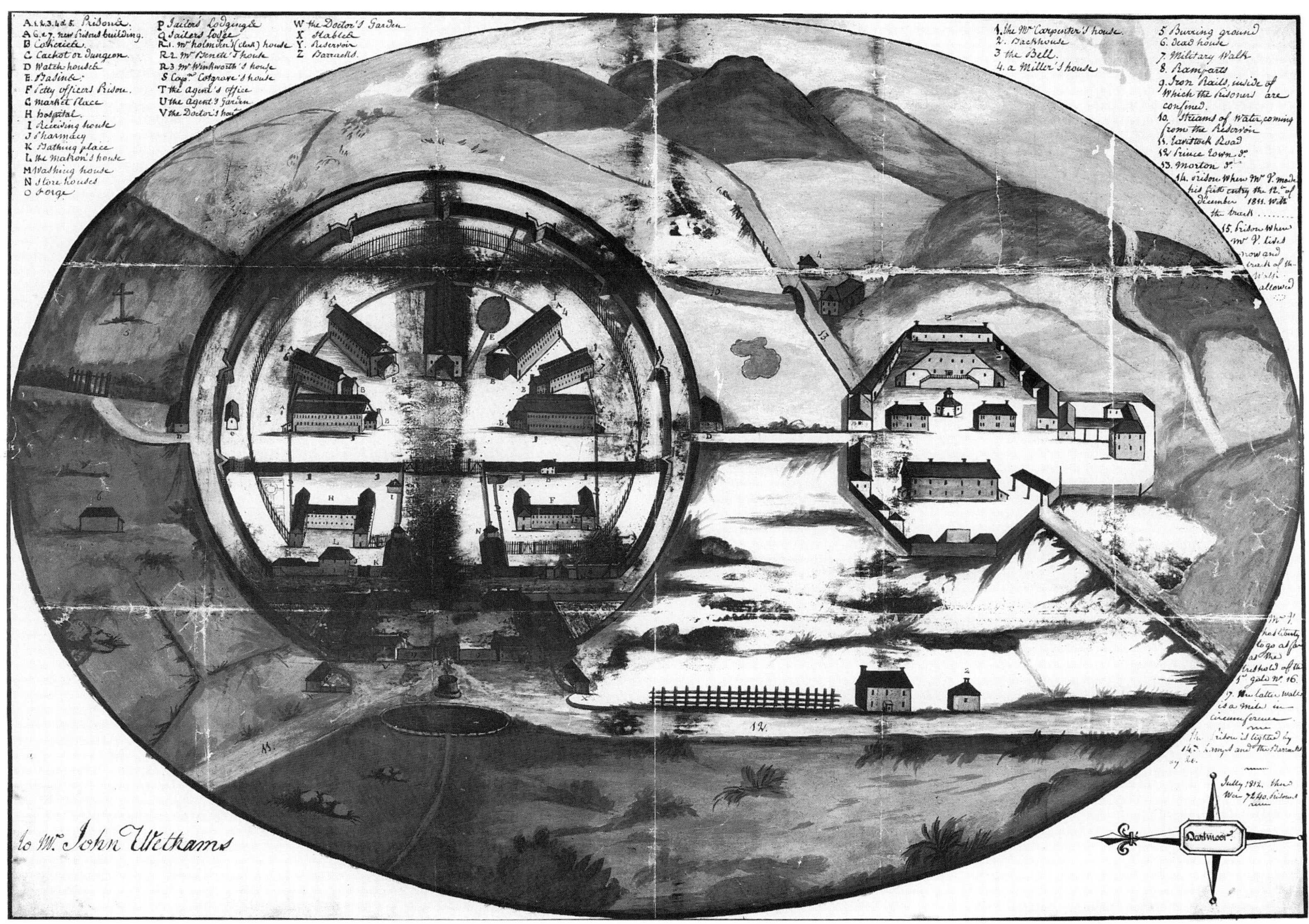

Dartmoor prison, originally built for French prisoners of war in the 1800s. Public Record Office

Prisoners of War in Britain

In Britain, prisoners of war were originally the responsibility of the Sick and Hurt Board, but were transferred to the Transport Board in 1795. Administrators suggested that the latter board was very efficient in its affairs, but this was not always apparent in its dealings with prisoners of war. The British strongly resisted charges that they deliberately mistreated their prisoners of war, and cited evidence that their conduct was no worse than that of the French. 'The charge of cruelty towards French prisoners of war, which has been brought against this country, is utterly void of foundation, and appears to have been fabricated and industriously supported by the enemy for the double purpose of justifying their own ill treatment of British prisoners and of irritating the minds of their countrymen against this nation.'[9]

But prisoners in Britain were certainly subjected to one extra hardship; unlike other countries, the British kept many of their prisoners aboard hulks serving as prison ships in the main naval harbours. According to one French prisoner, 'The difference between the prisons and the hulks is very marked. There is no space for exercise, prisoners are crowded together, no visitors come to see them, and we are forsaken people.'[10] Another witness reports, 'The Medway is covered with men-of-war, dismantled and lying in ordinary. Their fresh and brilliant painting contrasts with the hideous aspect of the old and smoky hulks, which seem the remains of vessels blackened by a recent fire. It is in these floating tombs that are buried alive prisoners of war — Danes, Swedes, Frenchmen, Americans, no matter. They are lodged on the lower deck, on the upper deck, and even on the orlop deck.'[11] A typical prison ship was the *Vryheid*, a Dutch 74 captured at Camperdown. She was moored at Chatham, with a complement of twenty-seven officers and seamen, six boys and forty marines.[12] Another was the *Panther*, an old 60 moored at Plymouth. She had twenty-two in her ship's company, four boys and twenty-six soldiers, later increased to forty soldiers in 1807. The soldiers came from the Royal Veteran Battalion, which had been founded in 1802 from out-pensioners of Chelsea Hospital. The ship's officers included a lieutenant in command, assisted by a master, gunner, boatswain, purser, cook, surgeon, steward, two midshipmen, a master's mate and a clerk.[13]

Other prisoners were housed on shore — often in ancient buildings, such as Portchester Castle, near Portsmouth, and Edinburgh Castle, but also in the newly built prison of Dartmoor. It was customary for 'each prisoner to be furnished with a hammock, a palliasse, a pillow and coverlet'. The hammocks were hung from posts 8ft apart, and in rooms more than 12ft high these could be hung in three tiers.[14] Prisoners employed themselves in craft work, especially making ship

After his surrender, Napoleon is transferred from the Bellerophon *to the* Northumberland, *to be taken to St Helena.* The National Maritime Museum

models from bone and wood. If they were lucky they might be allowed out occasionally to sell them at local markets. Less creative prisoners spent their time gambling. It was said that the French were particularly addicted to this, and that nakedness among them was a result of gambling away their clothes.

As always, officers had much better conditions. Most were allowed to give parole, and therefore to live quietly in towns until exchanged. Commissioned officers were paid at a rate of 1s per day, and other officers at 6d per day in 1796. The definition of an officer was quite wide, and included all ranks down to clerk on a ship of war, officers of merchant ships, and 'passengers of genteel rank'.[15] Notices were posted up in the parole towns to the effect that 'all such prisoners are permitted to walk or ride on the great turnpike road within the distance of one mile from the extreme parts of the town (not beyond the limits of the parish)'. They had to be in their lodgings by 5pm in winter and 8pm in summer.[16]

British Prisoners in France

It is estimated that about 12,000 British prisoners were held in France between 1803 and 1815; a very small proportion of the half million prisoners from all nations who passed through the country during those years. The great majority of British prisoners were naval or merchant seamen.[17] Most were held in northern France, with the fortress at Verdun serving as the main depot. Most officer prisoners were eventually lodged there, including midshipmen, and officers of merchant ships. Other prisoners were taken there to be sorted out and then sent to other prisons in the general area; for example Arras, Valenciennes, Charlemont, Epinal, Metz and Nancy. They were marched in groups escorted by soldiers or gendarmes, and were expected to cover twenty to thirty miles per day. There were other prisoners near the main ports, where new captives were taken in the first instance.

Prisoners were usually kept in old fortresses. They, too, had plenty of stories of ill treatment, and the prisons were certainly not comfortable. The one at Nantes held 400 to 500 men. 'The prison was very much exposed to the inclemency of the weather, their provisions very bad, and insufficient, and particularly the bread bad, and full of sand; and the prisoners were almost in a state of nakedness.' Portanzeau prison near Brest was a quarter of a mile square, with six buildings each 20yds long and 8yds wide, and seven tiers of hammock. It held 1000 men.[18] As in British prisons, there were many deaths from disease.

> Out of our ship's crew we have buried fifty-seven men from 19 March to the last of December 1804, and other ships have suffered in proportion, so that the number of deaths in the prison last year altogether were 813 souls, of the prison putrid fever; this malignant disease was considered to arise from cold, and wet sleeping by night, want and ill usage when all at once arriving at the depot, their daily exercise ceasing . . .[19]

Officers, too, complained of ill treatment. One claimed that 'every man was stripped and plundered of all he had' at Pontibvey prison in Brittany. Futhermore, 'This prison was so small that there was not room for the prisoners to lie down on the floor.' At Quimper prison, a converted convent, 'The allowance was then reduced to three small loaves, weighing about two pounds, *for seven people*, for which they sometimes substituted rice, or horsebeans — the whole of which, however, was barely sufficient to subsist one man.' There were 3678 British prisoners in Quimper, 'besides Dutch, Portuguese and Spaniards, all in a state of starvation and having scarcely any clothes to cover them'.[20]

Victory over France

Napoleon was defeated in 1814, by land campaigns against France. Wellington, victorious in the peninsula, crossed the Pyrenees and defeated the French at Toulouse. To the north, a new coalition had been formed, including Prussia and Austria. Napoleon was defeated at Leipzig in 1813, and had to retreat within the frontiers of France. His enemies followed him, and he was forced to abdicate. Though it was military power which achieved this victory, it was sea power which made it possible. The campaign against Napoleon had gained strength at the extremities of Europe, in Spain, Portugal and Russia. These countries had begun their resistance because of the impositions of the Continental System, and the long blockade had contributed decisively to French defeat.

Napoleon was exiled to Elba, but escaped a year later and resumed his power in France. Press warrants were hastily issued, the fleet began to mobilise, and men taken up by the press gang must have feared another long war like the last one but after a hundred days, Napoleon was defeated at Waterloo, and naval power had little chance to show itself in this campaign. Eventually, he surrendered himself to the Rochefort squadron of the Royal Navy, and had his first close look at his greatest opponent. Aboard the *Bellerophon*, he was shown round the ship, and 'he seemed most struck with the cleanliness and neatness of the men'. He commented, 'What I admire most in your ship, is the extreme silence and orderly conduct of your men.' Of the marines he remarked, 'How much might be done with a hundred thousand such soldiers as these.' But at the same time, he failed to understand the reasons for the French defeat at sea. 'I can see no sufficient reason why your ships should beat the French with so much ease. The finest men-of-war in your service are French; a French ship is heavier in every respect than one of yours, she carries more guns, those guns of a larger calibre, and has a great many more men.'[21] He was taken to Torbay, where the wars with France had begun with the landing of William of Orange in 1688; and then Plymouth Sound, and on to exile on St Helena, where he died in 1821.

The York, *an old 74, serving as a convict ship in 1828. Many of the ships of the great war were reduced to such roles. The ships which had held the French prisoners of war looked rather similar.* From E W Cooke's *Shipping and Craft*

Demobilised sailors, ecstatic at being freed from naval discipline, make their way home by stage-coach. By Cruikshank

Demobilisation

Demobilisation began slowly after the apparent end of the war in 1814, but many ships were kept in commission to deal with the American War, which continued into 1815. By the time that had ended completely, the Hundred Days had begun, and full-scale demobilisation did not begin until the second half of the year. Obviously, it was even further delayed for ships which had to return from overseas stations. On 1 July, there were still 581 ships in commission, and this had been reduced to 368 (of which 198 were at sea) by the beginning of October.[22] In the following years, the navy estimates were reduced: 33,000 men in 1816, and 19,000 in 1817, compared with a wartime peak of 145,000. It was planned to give priority to all seamen who had been in service since 1804 or earlier, though in general men were still paid off ship by ship.[23]

Both in 1801 and 1815, the average seaman was overjoyed at being paid off. John Nicol wrote, 'I was once more my own master and felt so happy. I was like one bewildered. Did those on shore experience only half the sensations of a sailor at perfect liberty, after being seven years on board ship without a will of his own, they would not blame his eccentricities, but wonder he was not more foolish.'[24] But there was a severe recession in postwar Britain, and many went home to unemployment and poverty. Many squandered their back pay within a few days.

> It is truly pitiable and lamentable to see how very few of these honest tars have brought either pay or prize money with them — all is gone — spent, in a few days, what had required months and years to acquire, and now these poor fellows are wandering about London and all the outports, without money and without employment.[25]

Some suggested that it was a mistake to pay off so many men at once.

> I am aware that the Admiralty were anxious to release the seamen after so many years service in the defence of their country, both from a sense of justice to the men and to the country; yet, from the state in which we have seen the poor fellows at every port, so soon after getting their discharge, it is quite obvious that, for their own good, they might have been gradually paid off.[26]

What Remains Today

Of the physical remains of the navy in the Napoleonic Wars, the

Chatham Historic Dockyard. Courtesy of Chatham Historic Dockyard Trust

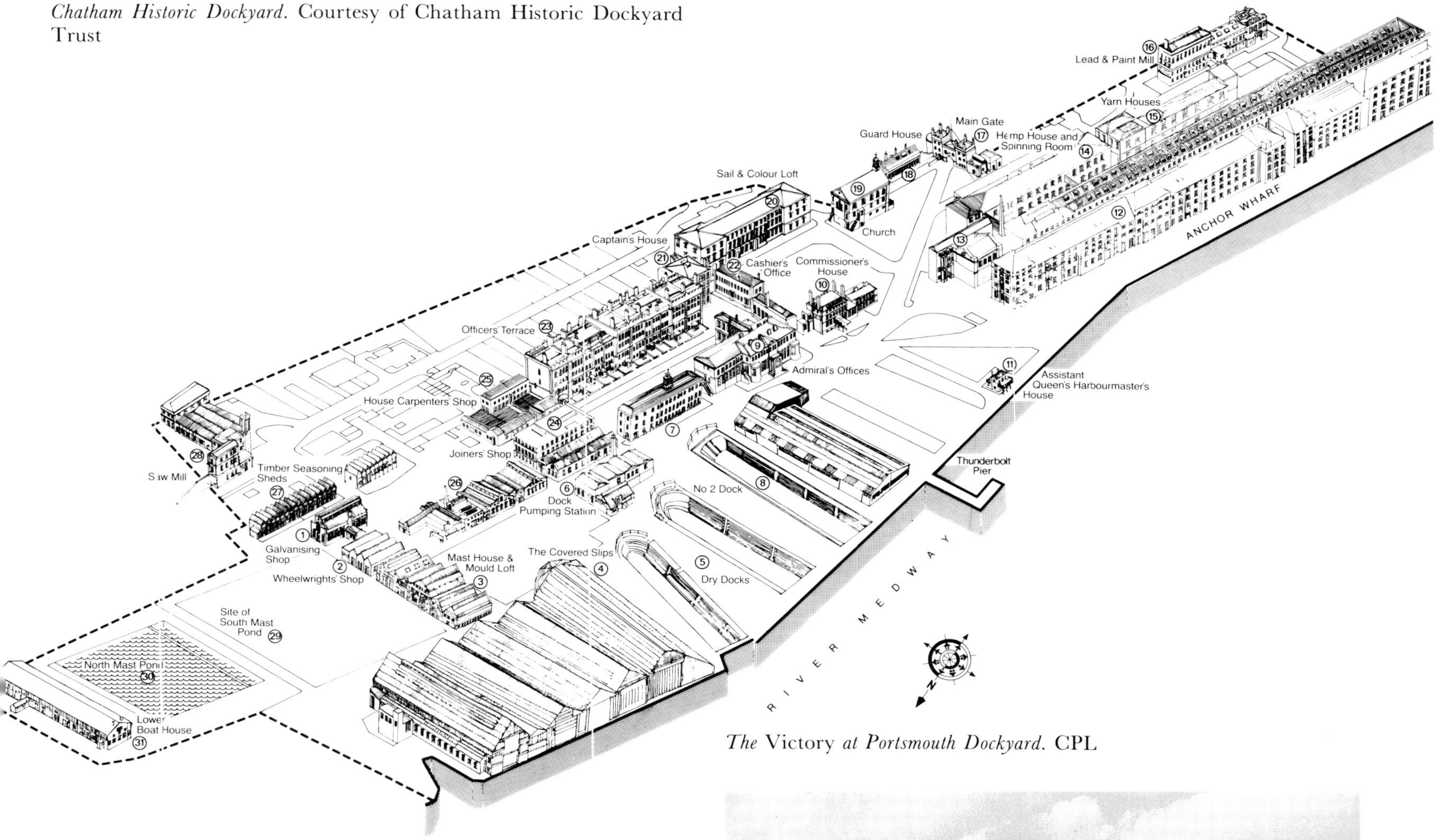

The Victory *at Portsmouth Dockyard.* CPL

most spectacular is, of course, Nelson's flagship the *Victory*. Her historic role was recognised early in the nineteenth century, and she has been deliberately preserved. She is much restored, but there is no doubt about her historical accuracy. She remains in commission as a ship of the Royal Navy, but is open to the public.

Strictly speaking there are no survivors from among the smaller ships of the navy, though two postwar frigates, the *Foudroyant* (ex *Trincomalee*) of 1817, and the *Unicorn* of 1824, are still in existence. Both were built to designs which were in common use before 1815, and give a good idea of the size and layout of such ships. The *Unicorn* is at Dundee, and is open to the public. The *Foudroyant* is currently being restored at Hartlepool. She is very close to a ship of the Napoleonic wars, and unlike the *Unicorn* she does not have the Seppings system of diagonal bracing. Of Britain's opponents' ships, the only real survivor is the USS *Constitution* at Boston; the USS *Constellation* at Baltimore has been heavily restored, and is not really an accurate representation of the ship at any stage in her career.

Apart from whole ships, there are many other ways of finding out about ships of the period. Several wrecks of the time are now being investigated, and eventually they will produce a crop of artefacts which will tell us much about the life of the crew. The golden age of ship models was over by 1793, so contemporary models of warships are quite rare; however, the best of them are to be found in the National Maritime Museum at Greenwich, London. Also housed there are the original plans of most British warships of the period — not just those built in Britain, but also of many captured ships. Some plans show great detail of the structure, fitting and decoration of ships, and are works of art in themselves.

A great deal survives of the buildings used by the navy. The Admiralty building in Whitehall survives, though it is not open to the public. The old Plymouth dockyard was almost entirely destroyed in the Second World War, but much of Portsmouth survived, and can be seen by visitors to the *Victory*. Chatham Dockyard closed in 1984, and is now open to the public. It includes officers' houses, building slips, dry docks, workshops and storehouses. There are demonstrations of rope- and flag-making, and many other exhibitions will be opened over the years. Historic buildings also survive in some of the old overseas yards, at Gibraltar, Malta, Antigua and other places. Greenwich Hospital, now the Royal Naval College, is opposite the National Maritime Museum.

Many artefacts and relics of these years can be seen in the major British museums. The National Maritime Museum has much of interest, including models, manuscripts, artefacts, uniforms, paintings, prints, and draughts. The Royal Naval Museum at Portsmouth has interesting displays on lower-deck life, and is situated opposite the *Victory*. The Royal Marines Museum is also in the Portsmouth area; it is well designed, though perhaps not at its strongest on the period of the Napoleonic Wars. The French navy is represented in the maritime museums in Paris (Musée de la Marine), Rochefort and Brest. The Spanish navy is shown in the museums in Madrid (Museo Naval) and Barcelona.

The written records of Nelson's navy survive in great profusion, in the Public Record Office at Kew and in the National Maritime Museum. There are logs for virtually every day of every ship in commission during these years, recording the many weeks of routine service, as well as the moments of battle. There are thousands of muster books, recording the names and service of almost every man who served. There are letters, reports, medical journals, standing orders, certificates of service, specifications, contracts, and thousands of other items which can give us an intensely detailed picture of life at sea in those years. This book does no more than skim the surface of the subject, and there is a vast amount of material which remains untapped.

Appendices to Parts I, VI, VII, IX and X

Appendix to Part I

Government and Naval Officials, 1793 to 1815

THE KING

George III, reigned 1760–1820
George, Prince of Wales, acted as regent during the illnesses of the king, 1788–9, 1811–20

PRIME MINISTERS

William Pitt the Younger, December 1783 to February 1801
Henry Addington, February 1801 to May 1804
William Pitt the Younger, May 1804 to February 1806
Lord Grenville, February 1806 to March 1807
The Duke of Portland, March 1807 to December 1809
Spencer Perceval, December 1809 to May 1812
Lord Liverpool, June 1812 to 1827

FIRST LORDS OF ADMIRALTY

The Earl of Chatham, July 1788 to December 1794
Earl Spencer, December 1794 to February 1801
The Earl of St Vincent, February 1801 to May 1804
Viscount Melville, May 1804 to May 1805
Lord Barham, May 1805 to February 1806
Charles Grey, February 1806 to September 1806
Thomas Grenville, September 1806 to April 1807
Lord Mulgrave, April 1807 to May 1810
Charles Yorke, May 1810 to March 1812
Viscount Melville, March 1812 to November 1830

CONTROLLERS OF THE NAVY

Henry Martin, March 1790 to September 1794
Sir Andrew Snape Hammond, September 1794 to March 1806
Henry Nicholls, March 1806 to June 1806
Sir Thomas Boulden Thomson, June 1806 to February 1816

SURVEYORS OF THE NAVY

Sir John Henslow and Sir William Rule, February 1793 to June 1806
Sir William Rule and Sir Henry Peake, June 1806 to June 1813
Sir Henry Peake, Joseph Tucker and Sir Robert Seppings, June 1813 to February 1822

Appendix to Part VI

Monthly Pay from 1 January 1807

Rank	*First Rate*		*Second Rate*	*Third Rate*	*Fourth Rate*	*Fifth Rate*	*Sixth Rate and smaller*
	£ s d		*£ s d*	*£ s d*	*£ s d*	*£ s d*	*£ s d*
Captain	32 4 0		26 12 0	23 12 0	18 4 0	15 8 0	16 16 0
Lieutenant	8 8 0	in all rates					
Lieutenant of flagship	9 2 0	in all rates					
Master	12 12 0		11 11 0	10 10 0	9 9 0	8 8 0	7 7 0
Second master	5 5 0		5 5 0	5 5 0	—	—	—
Master of sloop, bomb, brig and cutter	—		—	—	—	—	6 6 0
Master and pilot of gun brig	—		—	—	—	—	5 5 0
Carpenter	5 16 0		5 6 0	4 16 0	3 6 0	3 6 0	3 1 0
Boatswain	4 16 0		4 6 0	3 16 0	3 6 0	3 6 0	3 1 0
Gunner	4 16 0		4 6 0	3 16 0	3 6 0	3 6 0	3 1 0
Purser	4 16 0		4 6 0	3 16 0	3 6 0	3 6 0	3 1 0
Master's mate	3 16 6		3 10 6	3 6 8	2 18 4	2 12 6	2 12 6
Midshipman	2 15 6		2 10 6	2 8 0	2 4 3	2 0 6	2 0 6
Clerk	2 15 6		2 10 6	2 8 0	2 4 3	2 0 6	2 0 6
Schoolmaster	2 15 6		2 10 6	2 8 0	2 4 3	2 0 6	2 0 6
Armourer	2 15 6		2 10 6	2 8 0	2 4 3	2 0 6	2 0 6
Master at arms	2 15 6		2 10 6	2 8 0	2 4 3	2 0 6	2 0 6
Carpenter's mate	2 10 6		2 10 6	2 6 6	2 4 6	2 2 6	2 0 6
Caulker	2 10 6	in all rates					
Ropemaker	2 10 6	in all rates					
Quartermaster	2 5 6		2 5 6	2 2 6	2 0 6	1 18 6	1 18 6
Boatswain's mate	2 5 6		2 5 6	2 2 6	2 0 6	1 18 6	1 18 6
Sailmaker	2 5 6		2 5 6	2 5 6	2 4 6	2 2 6	2 0 6
Gunner's mate	2 5 6		2 5 6	2 2 6	2 0 6	1 18 0	1 16 6
Yeoman of the powder room	2 5 6		2 5 6	2 2 6	2 0 6	1 18 0	1 16 6
Armourer's mate	2 5 6		2 5 6	2 2 6	2 0 6	1 18 0	1 16 6
Corporal	2 5 6		2 2 6	2 0 6	2 0 6	1 18 0	1 16 6
Caulker's mate	2 6 6		2 6 6	2 6 6	2 6 6	—	—
Yeoman of the sheets	2 2 6		2 0 6	1 18 6	1 18 6	1 16 6	1 16 6
Coxswain	2 2 6		2 0 6	1 18 6	1 18 6	1 16 6	1 16 6
Quartermaster's mate	2 0 6		2 0 6	1 18 6	1 18 6	1 16 6	1 15 6
Captain of the forecastle	2 0 6		2 0 6	1 18 6	1 18 6	1 16 6	1 15 6
Captain of the foretop	2 0 6		2 0 6	1 18 6	1 18 6	1 16 6	1 15 6
Captain of the maintop	2 0 6		2 0 6	1 18 6	1 18 6	1 16 6	1 15 6
Captain of the afterguard	2 0 6		2 0 6	1 18 6	1 18 6	1 16 6	1 15 6
Captain of the waist	2 0 6		2 0 6	1 18 6	1 18 6	1 16 6	1 15 6

Rank	*First Rate* £ *s d*		*Second Rate* £ *s d*	*Third Rate* £ *s d*	*Fourth Rate* £ *s d*	*Fifth Rate* £ *s d*	*Sixth Rate and smaller* £ *s d*
Trumpeter	2 0 6		1 18 6	1 15 6	1 15 6	1 15 6	1 14 6
Sailmaker's mate	1 18 6	in all rates					
Quarter gunner	1 16 6		1 16 6	1 15 6	1 15 6	1 15 6	1 15 6
Carpenter's crew	1 16 6		1 16 6	1 15 6	1 15 6	1 15 6	1 15 6
Sailmaker's crew	1 16 6	in all rates					
Gunsmith	1 15 6		1 15 6	1 15 6	—	—	—
Steward	1 15 6		1 15 6	1 15 6	1 13 10	1 10 2	1 9 6
Cook	1 15 6		1 15 6	1 15 6	1 15 6	1 15 6	1 14 6
Steward's mate	1 5 2		1 5 2	1 5 2	1 5 2	—	—
Chaplain	0 19 0	in all rates					

Midshipman ordinary	Swabber	
Volunteer per order	Cooper	
Cook's mate	Able seaman	1 13 6 in all rates
Coxswain's mate	Captain's cook	
Yeoman of the boatswain's store room	Ordinary trumpeter	
Ordinary seaman	Barber	1 5 6 in all rates
Shifter	Gunner's tailor	

Landsman 1 2 6 in all rates
Boy 1st Class £9 0 0 per annum
Boy 2nd Class £8 0 0 per annum
Boy 3rd Class £7 0 0 per annum

Appendix to Part VI

Officers and petty officers of ships, 1807

Rate of ship	*1*	*2*			*3*			*4*			*5*				*6*	
Complement	*837*	*738*	*738*	*719*	*640*	*590*	*491*	*343*	*294*	*284*	*264*	*254*	*215*	*195*	*155*	*135*
No of guns	*100*	*98*	*80L*†	*80*	*74L*†	*74*	*64*	*50*	*44*	*38*	*36*	*32L*†	*32*	*28*	*24*	*20*
Captain	1	1	1	1	1	1	1	1	1	1	1	1	1	1	1	1
Lieutenant	8	8	7	7	6	5	5	4	3	3	3	3	3	2	2	2
Master	1	1	1	1	1	1	1	1	1	1	1	1	1	1	1	1
Second master	1	1	1	1	1	1	1									
Surgeon	1	1	1	1	1	1	1	1	1	1	1	1	1	1	1	1
Carpenter	1	1	1	1	1	1	1	1	1	1	1	1	1	1	1	1
Boatswain	1	1	1	1	1	1	1	1	1	1	1	1	1	1	1	1
Gunner	1	1	1	1	1	1	1	1	1	1	1	1	1	1	1	1
Purser	1	1	1	1	1	1	1	1	1	1	1	1	1	1	1	1
Master's mate	6	4	4	4	3	3	3	2	2	2	2	2	2	2	2	2
Assisant surgeon	3	3	2	2	2	2	2	2	1	1	1	1	1	1	1	1
Midshipman	24	24	24	20	16	16	16	10	8	6	6	6	6	4	4	4
Clerk	1	1	1	1	1	1	1	1	1	1	1	1	1	1	1	1
Schoolmaster	1	1	1	1	1	1	1	1	1	1	1	1	1	1	1	1
Armourer	1	1	1	1	1	1	1	1	1	1	1	1	1	1	1	1
Master at arms	1	1	1	1	1	1	1	1	1	1	1	1	1	1	1	1
Carpenter's mate	2	2	2	1	1	1	1	1	1	1	1	1	1	1	1	1
Caulker	1	1	1	1	1	1	1	1	1	1	1	1	1	1	1	1
Ropemaker	1	1	1	1	1	1	1	1	1	1	1	1	1	1	1	1
Quartermaster	8	8	8	7	6	6	6	4	3	3	3	3	3	2	2	2
Boatswain's mate	4	4	4	3	2	2	2	2	2	1	1	1	1	1	1	1
Sailmaker	1	1	1	1	1	1	1	1	1	1	1	1	1	1	1	1
Gunner's mate	4	4	4	2	2	2	2	1	1	1	1	1	1	1	1	1
Yeoman of the powder room	2	2	2	2	2	2	2	1	1	1	1	1	1	1	1	1
Armourer's mate	2	2	2	2	2	2	2	1	1	1	1	1	1	1	1	1
Corporal	2	2	2	2	2	2	2	2	2	2	2	2	2	1	1	1
Caulker's mate	1	1	1	1	1	1	1	1								
Yeoman of the sheets	4	4	4	4	4	4	4	2	2	2	2	2		1	1	1
Coxswain	1	1	1	1	1	1	1	1	1	1	1	1	1	1	1	1
Quartermaster's mate	6	6	6	5	4	4	4	4	3	3	3	3	3	2	2	2
Captain of forecastle	3	3	3	3	3	3	2	2	2	2	2	2	2	2	2	2
Captain of foretop	3	3	3	3	3	3	2	2	2	2	2	2	2	2	2	2
Captain of maintop	3	3	3	3	3	3	2	2	2	2	2	2	2	2	2	2
Captain of afterguard	3	3	3	3	3	3	2	2	2	2	2	1	1	1	1	1
Captain of waist	3	3	3	3	3	3	2	2	2	2	2	2	2	2	2	2
Trumpeter	1	1	1	1	1	1	1	1	1	1	1	1	1	1	1	1
Sailmaker's mate	1	1	1	1	1	1	1	1	1	1	1	1	1	1	1	1
Quarter gunner	25	23	21	20	20	18	16	13	11	9	8	8	8	7	6	5
Carpenter's crew	12	10	10	8	8	8	8	6	5	5	5	5	5	4	4	4
Sailmaker's crew	2	2	2	2	2	2	2	2	1	1	1	1	1	1	1	1
Gunsmith	1	1	1													
Steward	1	1	1	1	1	1	1	1	1	1	1	1	1	1	1	1
Cook	1	1	1	1	1	1	1	1	1	1	1	1	1	1	1	1
Steward's mate	1	1	1	1	1	1	1	1								
Chaplain	1	1	1	1	1	1	1	1	1	1	1	1	1	1	1	1

Sloops							*Armed sloops*	*Fireships**		*gun vessels*		*Yachts*		*Cutters*		*Bombs*	*Schooners*			*Dispatch cutter*
121	*100*	*95*	*86*	*80*	*70*	*65*	*42*	*56*	*45*	*50*	*45*	*67*	*50*	*60*	*45*	*67*	*60*	*40*	*18*	*17*
1	1	1	1	1	1	1		1	1			1	1			1				
2	2	2	2	1	1	1	1	2	2	1	1	1		1	1	2	1	1	1	1
1	1	1	1	1	1	1		1				1		1		1	1			
							1		1	1	1		1				1			
1	1	1	1	1	1	1		1	1			1	1	1		1	1			
1	1	1	1	1	1	1		1				1	1			1				
1	1	1	1	1	1	1		1				1	1			1				
1	1	1	1	1	1	1		1				1	1			1				
1	1	1	1	1	1	1		1				1				1				
1	1	1	1	1	1	1		1			1	1	1			1			1	1
1	1	1	1	1	1	1	1			1	1				1	1		1		
2	2	2	2	2	2	2	2	2	2	1	1	2	1	2	2	2	2	2	1	1
1	1	1	1	1	1	1	1	1	1	1	1	1	1	1	1	1	1	1		1
1	1	1	1	1	1	1		1	1							1				
1	1	1	1	1	1	1	1	1	1	1	1	1	1	1	1	1	1	1	1	1
1	1	1	1	1	1	1														
2	2	2	2	2	2	2		2	2	1	1	2	1	1	1	2	1		1	
1	1	1	1	1	1	1	1	1	1	1	1	1	1	1	1	1	1	1	1	
1	1	1	1	1	1	1		1	1			1		1		1	1			
1	1	1	1	1	1	1	1	1	1	1	1	1	1	1	1	1	1	1		
1	1	1	1	1	1	1		1	1			1	1			1				
1	1	1	1	1	1	1								1	1					
1	1	1	1	1	1	1		1	1			1				1				
																	1			
1	1	1	1	1	1	1		1	1			1				1				
1	1	1	1	1	1	1		1	1			1	1			1	1			
2	1	1	1	1	1	1	1	1	1	1	1	1	1			1				
2	1	1	1	1	1	1	1	1	1	1	1	1	1			1				
2	1																			
1	1																			
1																				
4	4	4	4	4	3	2								2	2		2	2		
2	2	2	2	2	2	2						1	1		1		1			
1	1	1	1	1	1	1						1	1			1	1			
								1				2		1	1	2	2			
1	1	1	1	1	1	1		1										1		
1	1	1	1	1	1	1		1	1							1				
								1	1					1		1	1			

*Paid as a fifth rate
†Large

Appendix to Part VII

Marine complements

Source: NMM RUSI/36. PRO Adm 2/1190, 2/1199

1795

Rate of Ship	*Captain*	*Subaltern*	*Sergeant*	*Corporal*	*Drummer*	*Private*	*Total*
First	1	2	4	4	2	100	113
Second	1	2	4	4	2	90	103
Third (74)	1	2	2	3	1	70	79
Third (64)	1	1	2	2	1	50	57
Fifth	—	1	1	1	1	30	34
Sixth	—	1	1	1	1	20	24
Sloop of 14 guns	—	1	1	1	—	16	19

1801

Rate of Ship	*Captain*	*Subaltern*	*Sergeant*	*Corporal*	*Drummer*	*Private*	*Total*
First	1	3	4	4	2	131	145
Second, and 80-gun ship	1	3	4	4	2	116	130
Third (74)	1	3	3	3	2	98	110
Third (64)	1	2	2	2	1	72	80
Fourth	—	2	2	2	1	43	50
Fifth (44)	—	2	2	2	1	38	45
Fifth (38, 36)	—	1	1	1	1	36	40
Fifth (32)	—	1	1	1	1	31	35
Sixth	—	1	1	1	1	21	25
Sloop	—	—	1	1	—	13	15

1808

Rate of Ship	*Captain*	*Subaltern*	*Sergeant*	*Corporal*	*Drummer*	*Private*	*Total*
First	1	3	4	4	2	156	170
Second	1	3	3	3	2	138	150
Third (80)	1	2	3	3	2	139	150
Third (74)	1	2	3	2	2	115	125
Third (64)	1	2	2	2	1	82	90
Fourth	—	2	2	2	1	52	59
Fifth (44)	—	2	2	2	1	47	54
Fifth (38, 36)	—	2	2	2	1	41	48
Fifth (32)	—	1	1	1	1	38	42
Sixth (28)	—	1	1	1	1	26	30
Sixth (24)	—	1	1	1	1	26	30
Sloops of 121 men	—	—	1	1	—	18	20
Sloops of the lower class, Gun Brigs of 50 men	—	—	1	1	—	13	15

Appendix to Part IX

Prices of Slop Clothing, 1803

From the purser's account Book of HMS Victory, in the Royal Naval Museum, Portsmouth.

Description	*Cost*
Jackets	7s 2d
Shirts	4s 7d
Shoes	6s
Stockings	2s 3d
Duck trousers	3s
Duck frocks	4s 8d
Woollen trousers	4s
Flannel jackets	3s 2d
Flannel drawers	?
Kersey waistcoats	?
Hats	3s 2d
Blankets	2s 7d
Boys' clothes	
Kersey jackets	4s 6d
Kersey waistcoats	?
Woollen trousers	2s 11d
Stockings	?
Hats	2s 2d
Shoes	3s 5d
Duck trousers	2s 11d
Shirts	3s 3d
Duck frocks	3s 3d
Beds	13s or 16s each

Appendix to Part X

Facilities of the Yards, c1814

	Deptford	*Woolwich*	*Chatham*	*Sheerness*	*Portsmouth*	*Plymouth*	*Total*
Building slips							
First Rates	2	2	3		1	3	11
Third rates	1	1	1		2		5
Frigates	2	1	2	1	1	1	8
Sloop				1	1		2
Total	5	4	6	2	5	4	26
Docks							
Single	1	1	4	2	8	3	19
Double	1	1				1	3
Total no. of docks	2	2	4	2	8	4	22
Total no of ships accommodated	3	3	4	2	8	5	25
Moorings							
Ships-of-the-line			22	11	48	59	140
Frigates	32	14	24	8	31	15	124
Sloops	5	16	5	11	5	5	47
Total	37	30	51	30	84	79	311
Ropeyards	1	1	1		1	1	5
Woodmills					1		1
Metal mills					1		1
Millwright's shop					1		1
No of teams of smiths	17	14	17	6	21	40	115

Dockyard Officers, c1814

Based on tables in Morriss, pp 157–65, 130.

	Deptford	*Woolwich*	*Chatham*	*Sheerness*	*Portsmouth*	*Plymouth*
Commissioner before 1806		*—*		*1*	*1*	*1*
Commissioner after 1806		*1*		*1*	*1*	*—*
Clerks	*2*	*2*	*3*	*3*	*3*	*3*
Master shipwright's department						
Master Shipwright	1	1	1	1	1	1
Clerks	2	3	3	3	3	3
Assistant master shipwrights	2	3	2	1	2	3
Timber master	1	1	1	1	1	1
Clerks	4	5	4	3	7	7
Master boatbuilder	1	1	1	1	1	1
Master mastmaker	1	1	1	1	1	1
Master house carpenter	1	1	1	1	1	1
Master joiner	1	1	1	1	1	1
Master sailmaker	1	1	1	1	1	1
Master smith	1	1	1	1	1	1
Master bricklayer	1	1	1	1	1	1
Master painter	1	1	1		1	1
Master rigger	1	1	1	1	1	1
Master measurer	1	1	1	1	1	1
Clerks	4	5	4	5	10	11
Other principal officers						
Master Attendant	1	1	2	1	3	2
Clerks	1	1	1	2	1	1
Clerks of the cheque	1	1	1	1	1	1
Clerks	6	10	7	8	8	7
Storekeeper	1	1	1	1	1	1
Clerks	7	11	6	7	12	12
Clerk of survey	1	1	1	1	1	1
Clerks	6	9	4	5	8	8
Other officers						
Master ropemaker		1	1		1	1
Clerks		3	1		1	2
Surgeon	1	1	1	1	1	1

Dockyard Workforce c1814

	Deptford	*Woolwich*	*Chatham*	*Sheerness*	*Portsmouth*	*Plymouth*
Boatswain of the yard	1	1	1	1	1	1
Riggers leading man	3	2	4	1	4	6
Riggers	71	55	103	31	176	134
Foreman of shipwrights	3	3	3	2	3	3
Quarterman	35	26	38	14	54	54
Shipwright	513	553	765	249	1374	1257
Boatbuilders' foreman	1	1	1	1	1	1
Mastmakers' foreman	1	1	1	1	1	1
Foreman of caulkers	—	1	—	—	1	1
Quarterman	2	3	5	4	9	5
Caulker	27	39	62	45	119	427
House carpenters' foreman	1	1	1	1	1	1
Leading man	2	4	2	4	1	—
House carpenter	86	16	107	73	243	244
Joiners' foreman	1	1	1	1	1	1
Leading man	2	1	2	2	6	3
Joiner	44	36	73	36	151	104
Bricklayers' foreman	1	1	1	1	1	1
Bricklayer	11	22	37	12	37	56
Labourer	10	20	27	9	42	22
Sailmakers' leading man	3	2	2	1	3	3
Sailmaker	44	27	50	25	74	65
Ropemakers' foreman	—	3	4	—	3	5
Total workers in ropeyard	—	244	398	—	376	379
Smiths' foreman	1	1	1	1	1	2
Fireman	17	14	17	6	21	40
Smith	81	71	102	42	160	192
Scavelmen leading man	2	1	3	1	3	6
Scavelman	38	39	87	39	117	164
Storehouse laborours' leading man	6	4	2	2	3	4
Yard labourers leading man	24	17	7	3	17	20
Yard labourer	610	465	511	148	536	582
Blockmaker	4	3	4	4	7	6
Brazier	1	—	2	—	2	—
Carvers	2	—	1	—	—	—
Cooper	—	1	1	—	1	2
Engine repairer	—	2	—	—	—	—
Founder	—	—	—	—	2	—
Glazier	1	1	1	—	—	—
Hair bed manufacturer	18	10	—	—	—	—
Locksmith	1	2	2	1	2	4
Mason	2	3	5	2	21	29
Messenger	9	10	10	10	16	11
Oakum boys	13	12	21	17	44	45
Oarmaker	1	1	1	1	—	1
Painter	13	15	15	10	47	29
Painters' labourer	—	12	—	5	14	—
Pavier	2	1	—	—	—	—
Pitch heater	1	1	1	1	2	2
Plumber	2	2	4	3	7	5
Sawyer	140	135	167	44	240	208
Teams	19	21	22	9	40	31
Tinman		1			1	1
Treehail mooter		2				
Warder	12	13	20	23	36	26
Waterman	1					
Wheelwright	2	2	2	2	3	3
Employees of:						
Wood mill					94	
Metal mill					66	
Millwright's shop					72	

Sources

NOTE ON SOURCES

Full details of primary and secondary sources are given separately under each chapter where necessary. Otherwise, they are given for the part as a whole. Textual notes are referenced by author and page number, where full details have already been given in the sources. Where a work has not been listed in the primary and secondary sources, full details are given in the textual note. Where such a work is referred to again within the same chapter, it is given as *op cit* and page number.

Abbreviations

Add	Additional Manuscripts in the British Library
Adm	Admiralty papers in the Public Record Office
BL	British Library
NRS	Publications of the Navy Records Society
MM	*Mariner's Mirror*, Quarterly Journal of the Society for Nautical Research
NMM	National Maritime Museum, Greenwich
RUSI	Manuscripts formerly belonging to the Royal United Services Institute, now in the NMM
SNR	Society for Nautical Research.

Part I Background

1 The Wars with France

Secondary Sources

Naval History
Brenton, E P, *The Naval History of Great Britain*, 2 vols 1837
James, W, *The Naval History of Great Britain*, 6 vols 1886
Mahan, A T, *The Influence of Sea Power on the French Revolution and Empire*, 2 vols 1892

General History
Watson, J Steven, *The Reign of George III* 1960.
Kinder H, and Hilgemann, W, *The Penguin Atlas of World History, Vol II: From the French Revolution to the Present* 1978

2 Early naval history

Printed Primary Sources

Various volumes produced by the NRS

Secondary Sources

Baugh, D A, *British Naval Administration in the Age of Walpole*, 1965
Corbett, J, *England in the Seven Years War*, 2 vols, 1907
James, W M, *The British Navy in Adversity*, 1926
Lewis, Michael, *The Navy of Britain*, 1948
Mahan, A T, *The Influence of Sea Power on History*, 1890
Martin, Colin, and Parker, Geoffrey, *The Spanish Armada*, 1988
Oppenheim, M, *The Administration of the Royal Navy, 1509 to 1660*, 1896
Owen, J H, *The War at Sea under Queen Anne*, 1938
Richmond, Rear Admiral Sir H W, *The Navy in the War of 1739 to 48*, 3 vols, 1920
Rodger, N A M, *The Wooden World*, 1986

3 The naval administration

Printed Primary Sources

NRS *Letters of Lord Barham*, vols II and III, 1910
NRS *Letters of Lord St Vincent*, vol II, 1927

Secondary Sources

Collinge, J M, *Navy Board Officials 1660–1832*, 1978
Pool, Bernard, *Navy Board Contracts*, 1966
Rodger, N A M, *The Admiralty*, 1979
Sainty, J C, *Admiralty Officials 1660–1870*, 1975

1 Sainty, pp 102–3
2 Pool, p 114
3 NRS Barham III, p 127

4 Britain and the world

Secondary Sources

Plumb, J H, *England in the Eighteenth Century*, 1963
Watson, J Steven, *The Reign of George III*, 1960
Thompson, E P, *The Making of the English Working Class*, 1963

Kinder H, and Hilgemann, W, *The Penguin Atlas of World History, vol II: From the French Revolution to the Present*, 1978

Part II Ships

Manuscript Sources
Ships' Draughts in the NMM
Progress Books and navy lists, Adm 180 series
Lists of ships and stations, Adm 8 series
RUSI/64, navy list, 1808–16

Printed Primary Sources
Steel, D, Original and Correct List of the Royal Navy, 1793–1815, up to 1814, and official lists thereafter
Derrick, C, *Memoirs of the Royal Navy*, 1806

Secondary Sources
For these chapters, especially II 3 and II 4, I have relied heavily on the ship list prepared by David Lyon of the NMM. I am also grateful for Mr Lyon's comments on the finished chapters.
Charnock, J, *A History of Marine Architecture*, 3 vols, 1800–2
College, J J, *Ships of the Royal Navy, an Historical Index*, vol I, 1969
Fincham, J, *A History of Naval Architecture*, 1852 reprinted 1979
Gardiner, R, 'The First English Frigates' in MM vol LXI, pp 163-72; 'The Frigate Designs of 1755–7' in MM LXIII, pp 51–69. 'Frigate Design in the Eighteenth Century' in *Warship* vol IX, pp 2-12, vol X, pp 80-92 and vol XII, pp 269–277
Lavery, B, *The Ship of the Line*, 2 vols, 1983–4
Lavery, B, *Anatomy of the Ship - Bellona*, 1985
James, W, *Naval History of Great Britain*, 6 vols, 1888
Schomberg, I, *Naval Chronology*, vol IV, 1802
White, D, *Anatomy of the Ship, Diana*, 1987

1 The principles of ship design

1 Lavery, 1983–4 vol I, p 129
2 Ibid
3 Ibid p 132
4 Adm 8/100

2 Ships-of-the-line

1 Derrick, pp 264–5
2 Lavery, 1983–4 vol I, p 140
3 Ibid, p 120
4 Ibid, p 140
5 Ibid, p 121
6 W Falconer, *Marine Dictionary*, 1769, R 1970
7 N Stalkaart, *Naval Architecture*, 1781 pp 135–6
8 Lavery, 1983–4, vol I, p 126

3 Frigates

1 Derrick, pp 264–5
2 James, vol III, table 9
3 Ibid, table 1
4 D Steel, *Naval Chronologist of the Late War*, 1806, p 90
5 Gardiner, MM LXI, pp 163ff

4 Unrated ships and vessels

1 James, vol VI, table 22
2 Ibid
3 Ibid, vol I, p 45
4 Schomberg, vol IV, pp 105–8

Part III Shipbuilding and Fitting

1 Ship construction

Printed Primary Sources
Burney, W, *New Universal Dictionary of the Marine*, 1815, R 1970
Fincham, J, *Introductory Outline of the Practice of Shipbuilding*, 1821
Rees, A, *Naval Architecture*, 1819–20, reprinted 1970
Steel, D, *Elements and Practice of Naval Architecture*, 1805

Secondary Sources
Goodwin, P, *The Construction and Fitting of the Sailing Man-of-War*, 1987
Lavery, B, *Ship of the Line* vol II, 1984
White, D, various articles in *Model Shipwright* on understanding ships draughts and traditional wooden shipbuilding, 1984 to date

1 Lavery, vol I, p 109
2 F Howard, *Sailing Ships of War*, 1979, p 193
3 Quoted in H Baynham, *From the Lower Deck*, 1969, p 45
4 NMM manuscripts COD/21/7

2 Fitting of ships

Secondary Sources
Goodwin, P, *The Construction and Fitting of the Sailing Man-of-War*, 1987
Gardiner, R, 'Fittings for Wooden Warships,' in *Model Shipwright* vols XVII, XIX, XX
Lavery, B, *Arming and Fitting the English Man-of-War*, 1987
May, W E, *The Boats of Men-of-War*, 1974

3 Masts, sails and rigging

Printed Primary Sources
Burney, N, *New Universal Dictionary of the Marine*, 1815, reprinted 1976
Lever, D, *The Young Sea Officer's Sheet Anchor*, 1811, reprinted 1963
Rees, A, *Naval Architecture*, 1819–20, reprinted 1970
Steel, D, *Elements of Mastmaking, Sailmaking and Rigging*, 1974

Secondary Sources
Lees, J, *The Masting and Rigging of English Ships of War 1625–1860*, 1979

1 NMM manuscripts JOD/148
2 Steel, D, *Naval Chronologist of the Late War*, 1806 p 184

4 Armament

Printed Primary Sources
Douglas, H, *Naval Gunnery*, 1820

Secondary Sources
Baker, H A, *The Crisis in Naval Ordnance*, 1983
Blackmore, H L, *The Armouries of the Tower of London, I, Ordnance*, 1976
Gardiner, R, 'Fittings for Wooden Warships, Part 3, Guns' in *Model Shipwright* vol XX, pp 338–53. 'A Note on Naval Guns, 1793 to 1815' in *Model Shipwright* vol XXV, pp 50–1
Lavery, B, *Arming and Fitting the English Man-of-War*, 1987

1 C Derrick *Memoirs of the Royal Navy*, 1806, p 282

Part IV Officers

Manuscript Sources
Adm 6 series, esp, 91–113 – Lieutenants' passing papers

Various ships' draughts in the NMM
Welch and Stalker pattern book in the Victoria and Albert Museum Library, with copy in the NNN RUSI/156

Printed Primary Sources
Admiralty *Regulations and Instructions Relating to His Majesty's Service at Sea* 1806, 1808 editions
Burney, W, *Universal Dictionary of the Marine,* 1815
Gardner J A, (ed. C Lloyd), *Above and Under Hatches,* 1955
Hall, Basil, *Fragments of Voyages and Travels,* 1846
NRS *Captain Boteler's Recollections,* 1942
NRS *Dillon's Narrative,* vol I, 1953, vol II, 1956
NRS *Five Naval Journals, 1787–1817,* ed Thursfield, 1951
Naval Chronicle, 1812, vol XVII, Uniform Regulations in the pp 308–9, and in the *London Gazette,* 1795

Secondary Sources
Lewis, M, *England's Sea Officers,* 1948
Lewis, M, *A Social History of the Navy, 1793–1815,* 1960
Mollo, J, *Uniforms of the Royal Navy During the Napoleonic Wars,* 1965
Fabb, J, and Cassin, J, *Uniforms of Trafalgar,* 1977

1 Officers' entry and training

1 Admiralty, p 140
2 Lewis, pp 97–8
3 NRS *The Keith Papers,* vol III, 1955 p 163
4 Hall, p 6
5 NRS Boteler, p 8
6 Lewis, p 85
7 Burney, p 3
8 Lewis, p 31
9 Gardner, pp 87–9
10 Hall, p 24
11 Quoted in H Baynham, *From the Lower Deck,* 1969 pp 59–60
12 NRS *Five Naval Journals* p 56
13 Hall, p 12
14 NRS *Five Naval Journals* p 250
15 Ibid, p 255
16 NMM PAR/102
17 NRS *Five Naval Journals* p 342
18 Ibid, p 53
19 Hall, p 8
20 NRS Dillon vol I p 66
21 NRS Boteler, p 32
22 Gardner, p 130
23 Gardner, p 111
24 Adm 6/103
25 Hall, p 83
26 NRS Boteler, p 50
27 Gardner, p 131
28 Hall, p 84
29 NRS *The Letters of Lord Barham,* vol III; 1910, pp 389–91
30 NRS Boteler p 49
31 Adm 7/103, 7/108
32 Burney, op cit, p 277
33 NRS *The Keith Papers,* vol II, 1950, p 177

2 Commissioned officers

1 A T Mahan, *The Influence of Sea Power upon History,* 1890, pp 127–8
2 W H Long, *Naval Yarns,* 1899, reprinted 1973, p 117
3 Adm 1/5126
4 Admiralty *Regulations and Instructions,* 1808, p 171
5 J Marshall *Royal Naval Biography* Supplement II, 1828, p 171
6 Quoted in Lewis, *Social History of the Navy,* p 216
7 NRS *The Letters of Lord Barham,* vol III p 284
8 Admiralty *Regulations and Instructions,* 1808, pp 81–2
9 Ibid, p 82
10 Adm 35/1981
11 NRS *The Letters of Lord Barham,* vol III, p 383
12 Adm 8/100
13 Burney, p 5
14 Adm 10/3
15 E P Brenton, *The Life and Correspondence of John, Earl St Vincent,* vol II, pp 399–400

3 Warrant officers

1 Admiralty *Regulations and Instructions,* 1808, p 85
2 W H Long, *Naval Yarns,* 1899, reprinted 1973 p 113
3 Admiralty *Regulations and Instructions,* 1808, p 190
4 Ibid, p 189
5 Ibid, p 87
6 Ibid, p 88
7 C Lloyd and J L S Coulter, *Medicine and the Navy,* vol III, 1961, p 21
8 Burney, p 513
9 Lloyd and Coulter, op cit, p 160
10 Admiralty *Regulations and Instructions,* p 86
11 NRS *The Keith Papers,* vol III, p 317
12 Admiralty *Regulations and Instructions,* p 227
13 Adm 12/24
14 Admiralty *Regulations and Instructions,* p 86
15 W Richardson, *A Mariner of England,* 1908 reprinted 1970, p 121
16 Admiralty *Regulations and Instructions,* p 218
17 Richardson, op cit, p 245
18 Admiralty *Regulations and Instructions,* 1806 p 371
19 NRS *Boteler* p 51

4 Officers' living conditions

1 Fabb and Cassin
2 NRS *Boteler* p 34
3 Ibid, p 43
4 NRS *Five Naval Journals,* p 11
5 NRS *Dillon's Narrative,* p 305
6 NRS *Five Naval Journals,* p 13
7 NRS *Dillon's Narrative,* p 337
8 W Richardson, *A Mariner of England,* 1908, reprinted 1907, p 168
9 NRS *Five Naval Journals,* pp 9–10
10 Ibid, pp 11–12
11 A J Griffiths *Observations on Some Points of Seamanship,* 1828, p 80
12 NRS *Five Naval Journals,* p 25
13 Gardner, p 124
14 Adm 101/120/8
15 NRS *Five Naval Journals,* p 7
16 Richardson, op cit, p 168
17 NRS *Five Naval Journals,* p 10

5 Ship administration

1 Adm 51/1153
2 Admiralty *Regulations and Instructions,* p 112
3 Adm 36/13174
4 R Hay, *Landsman Hay,* 1953, p 49
5 Admiralty *Regulations and Instructions,* p 206
6 Ibid, p 322
7 Ibid, p 323
8 NMM RUSI/36

9 Burney, p 65
10 Lewis, 1960, p 325
11 W Mountaine, *The Seaman's Vade Mecum*, 1756, reprinted 1971, pp 81–2
12 Burney, p 354

Part V Naval Recruitment

Manuscript Sources
Adm 1/579, 580, Reports from Inspectors of Rendezvous
Adm 1, Captain's letters, in the PRO
NMM series ADL/J has various papers on impressment, including press warrants

Printed Primary Sources
Baynham, H, *From the Lower Deck*, 1969
Bechervaise, J, *Thirty-six Years of Seafaring Life*, 1839
Hay, R, *Landsman Hay*, 1953
Leech, S, *A Voice from the Main Deck*, 1843
Nicol, J, *Life and Adventures*, 1922
NRS *Captain Boteler's Recollections*, 1942
NRS *Dillon's Narrative*, vol II, 1956
NRS *Manning Pamphlets 1693-1873*, 1974
Richardson, W, *A Mariner of England*, 1908, reprinted 1970
Robinson, W, or 'Jack Nastyface', *Nautical Economy*, 1836
Spavens, W, *The Narrative of William Spavens*, 1796

Secondary Sources
Hutchinson, J R, *The Press Gang Afloat and Ashore*, 1913
Lloyd, C, *The British Seaman*, 1968
McCord, N, *The Impress Service in North East England During the Napoleonic Wars*, in MM vol LIV, pp 163ff
Brooks, F W, 'Naval Recruiting in Lindsey 1795–7', in *English Historical Review* vol XLIII, pp 231ff

1 The problem of naval recruitment

1 Spavens, p 133
2 A Smith, 1853 *Wealth of Nations*, edited J R McCullough, vol I, p 50
3 Nicol, p 171
4 Bechervaise, p 47
5 Nichol, p 205
6 NRS *Manning Pamphlets*, p 191
7 M Lewis, *Social History of the Navy*, 1960, pp 286, 289
8 NRS *Manning Pamphlets*, pp 347ff
9 BL Harleian Mss, p 163
10 NMM HAR/5
11 Lloyd, pp 155–6
12 J J Sheehan, *History of Kingston-upon-Hull*, 1864, p 148
13 MM vol LIV, p 165
14 NRS *Dillon's Narrative*, vol II, p 11
15 D B S, 'London and the Press Gang' in MM, vol XVI, pp 87–8
16 NRS *Boteler*, p 9

2 The press gang

1 Leech, pp 28–9
2 G V Jackson, *The Perilous Adventures and Vicissitudes of a Naval Officer*, 1927, p 29
3 NRS *Dillon's Narrative*, vol II, p 9
4 Adm 1/579, Admiral's letters, Phillip
5 J J Sheehan, *History of Kingston-upon-Hull*, 1864, p 150
6 Hay, pp 216–17
7 P Bloomfield (ed.), *Kent in the Napoleonic Wars*, 1987, p 119
8 Nicol, p 26
9 W Mark, *At Sea with Nelson*, 1929, p 65
10 J Wetherell, *The Adventures of John Wetherell*, 1954, p 31
11 NRS *The Blockade of Brest 1803–5*, vol I, 1898, p 8
12 Bloomfield, op cit, p 121
13 NRS *Letters of Lord St Vincent*, vol II, 1927, p 23
14 Bechervaise, p 46
15 M A Richardson, *The Local Historian's Table Book*, vol IV, 1844, p 122
16 NRS *Boteler*, p 44
17 Sheehan, op cit, p 150–1
18 Bechervaise, p 45

3 Other methods of recruiting

1 Lloyd, p 93
2 Ibid, p 91
3 Hay, p 34
4 NRS *The Health of Seamen*, 1965, p 265
5 NRS *Manning Phamplets* pp 351–3
6 Adm 12/117
7 Adm 12/147
8 NRS *The Keith Papers*, vol III, p 323
9 Lewis, *Social History of the Navy*, 1960, p 129
10 NRS *The Keith Papers*, vol III, pp 312–3
11 NMM RUSI/249
12 Lewis, op cit, p 200

Part VI Seamen and Landmen

Manuscript Sources
Adm 73 series, esp. 1–36, Greenwich Hospital Admission papers, with summary of each man's career
Courts-martial in PRO Adm 1/5330 to 5450

Printed Primary Sources
Seaman's autobiographies:
Baynham, H, *From the Lower deck*, 1969
Bechervaise, J, *Thirty-six Years of Seafaring Life*, 1839
Hay, R, *Landsman Hay*, 1953
Leech, S, *A Voice from the Main Deck*, 1843
Nicol, J, *Life and Adventures*, 1922
Richardson, W, *A Mariner of England*, 1908, reprinted 1970
Robinson, W, or 'Jack Nastyface', *Nautical Economy*, 1836
Spavens, W, *The Narrative of William Spavens*, 1796
Wetherell, J, *The Adventures of John Wetherell*, 1954
Wilson, R in NRS *Five Naval Journals 1789 to 1817*, 1951, pp 121-276

Other sources:
Admiralty *Regulations and Instructions*, 1806, 1808
NRS *Manning Pamphlets 1693–1873*, 1974

Secondary Sources
Lewis, M, *Social History of the Navy*, 1960
Lloyd, C, *The British Seaman*, 1968
Manwaring, G M and Dobrée, B, *The Floating Republic*, 1935

1 Seaman's conditions of service

1 NRS *The Naval Tracts of Sir William Monson*, vol I, 1902, p 293
2 NRS *Five Naval Journals*, p 243
3 Ibid, p 243–4
4 Burney, *Universal Dictionary of the Marine*, 1815, p 327
5 Ibid
6 NRS *Five Naval Journals*, p 243

7 Adm 73/8
8 Adm 73/27
9 Ibid
10 Ibid
11 Adm 1/99
12 Lewis, pp 47–8
13 Adm 73/27
14 N A M Rodger, *The Wooden World*, 1986, p 125
15 Burney, op cit, pp 336–7
16 Adm 35/99
17 Quoted in Baynham *From the Lower Deck*, p 69
18 Lewis, p 326
19 NRS *The Keith Papers*, vol II, 394
20 Quoted in Baynham, p 136
21 Admiralty Library, Corbett Manuscripts, 121
22 Richardson, p 111
23 NRS *Manning Pamphlets*, p 185
24 Adm 73/8, 27
25 Admiralty *Regulations and Instructions*, 1808, p 120

2 Seamen and petty officers

1 NMM COD/3/10
2 Basil Hall, *Fragments of Voyages and Travels*, vol II 1846, p 67
3 NRS *The Health of Seamen*, 1965, pp 265–6
4 NRS *Five Naval Journals*, p 27
5 J Masefield, *Sea Life in Nelson's time*, first published 1905, 1972 edition, plate 15
6 W H Long, *Naval Yarns*, 1899 reprinted 1973, p 151
7 Adm 73/5
8 Adm 73/8
9 Adm 73/27
10 NRS *Manning Pamphlets*, p 348n
11 NRS *Five Naval Journals*, p 247
12 Ibid
13 NMM WQB/3
14 NRS *Five Naval Journals*, p 10
15 Ibid, p 248
16 Admiralty *Regulations and Instructions*, 1808, p 442
17 W Burney, *Universal Dictionary of the Marine*, 1815, p 376
18 Ibid
19 NRS *Five Naval Journals*, p 246
20 Richardson, p 111
21 Burney, op cit, p 663
22 Ibid, p 92
23 Adm 1/5125
24 Manwaring and Dobrée, pp 262–3

3 Landmen, artificers and servants

1 NMM JOD/11, RUSI/35, NRS *Manning Pamphlets*, pp 352–3
2 NRS *Manning Pamphlets*, pp 350–1
3 Lloyd, p 294
4 NMM COD/3/10
5 Adm 73/27, 13, 8, 5
6 NRS *Manning Pamphlets*, p 191
7 Hay, p 63
8 NRS *Manning Pamphlets*, p 191
9 W Burney, *Universal Dictionary of the Marine*, 1815, p 681
10 Hay, p 33
11 Adm 73/13
12 Adm 73/8
13 Admiralty *Regulations and Instructions*, 1808, pp 121–2
14 Ibid, p 233
15 Adm 73/27
16 Hay, p 138
17 Admiralty *Regulations and Instructions*, 1808, p 232
18 WQB/3
19 Ibid
20 NRS *Five Naval Journals*, p 247
21 Burney, op cit, p 504
22 'Captain in the Royal Navy', *Observations and Instructions for Officers of the Royal Navy*, 1807, p 54
23 Ibid, p 55
24 NRS *Manning Pamphlets*, p 351
25 NRS *Five Naval Journals*, p 246
26 Burney, op cit, p 74
27 Ibid, p 504
28 NRS *Manning Pamphlets*, p 351
29 NRS *Five Naval Journals*, pp 249–50
30 Ibid, pp 11–12
31 Ibid, p 249
32 Ibid, p 247
33 Ibid, p 13
34 Hay, p 63
35 NRS *Five Naval Journals*, p 249
36 NMM RUSI/176
37 W B Rowbotham, 'Soldiers' and Seamen's Wives and Children in HM Ships', in MM, vol XLVII, pp 42–8

4 Mutiny and desertion

1 Adm 12/27F, 12/24
2 Adm 12/24
3 N A M Rodger, *The Wooden World*, 1986, pp 238–9
4 Quoted in Baynham *From the Lower Deck*, 1969, p 23
5 W L Clowes (ed.), *The Royal Navy, a History from Earliest Time to the Present*, vol IV, p 246
6 Adm 12/24
7 C Lloyd and J L S Coulter, *Medicine and the Navy*, vol III, 1961, pp 266–7
8 Quoted in M Lewis, 1960, p 134
9 Quoted in Lloyd, p 192
10 NRS *Five Naval Journals*, p 141

Part VII Marines

Manuscript Sources

NMM OBK/11, Standing Orders for Marines of *Blenheim*, 1796
PRO Adm 96 series, Marine Office Pay Records; Adm 158 series, Description Books; Adm 56 series, Divisional Letter Books, 184 series, Divisional Muster Books.
Royal Marines Museum, Eastney, Portsmouth Letter Book

Printed Primary Sources

Admiralty *Regulations and Instructions Relating to His Majesty's Service at Sea*, 1808
Gillespie, A, *Historical Review of the Royal Marine Corps*, 1803
Donald A J and Ladd, J D, *Royal Marines Records 1793–1836*, 1982
Rees, Thomas, *Journal of Voyages and Travels*, 1822

Secondary Sources

Field, C, *Britain's Sea Soldiers*, 2 vols, 1924
Mollo, J, *Uniforms of the Royal Navy During the Napoleonic Wars*, 1965
Fabb, J, and Cassin, J, *Uniforms of Trafalgar*, 1977

1 Role and organisation

1 A J Marini, 'Parliament and the Marine Regiments 1739', in MM vol LXII, pp 55–65
2 Admiralty *Regulations and Instructions*, 1808, p 422

3 J S Tucker, *Memoirs of the Earl of St Vincent*, 1844, vol I, p 297
4 Ibid, pp 323–4
5 Ibid, vol II, pp 391–2
6 NRS *Manning Pamphlets*, p 387
7 Ibid, p 253
8 NRS *The Spencer Papers*, vol I, 1913, p 200
9 W B Rowbotham, 'Soldiers' and Seamen's Wives and Children in HM Ships' in MM vol XLVII, pp 42–8
10 Adm 157/3
11 Donald and Ladd, p 18
12 Ibid, p 40
13 Royal Marines Museum, Portsmouth Letter Book, 11/10/1803
14 Gillespie, p 2
15 Adm 7/593
16 Rees, p 2
17 *Royal Marines Records*, p 32
18 Adm 7/593
19 W Burney, *Universal Dictionary of the Marine*, 1815 p 339

2 Marines in service

1 W Burney, *Universal Dictionary of the Marine*, 1815 p 339
2 Admiralty *Regulations and Instructions*, 1808, pp 420–1
3 Ibid, p 144
4 NMM OBK/11
5 *Royal Marines Records*, p 13
6 Admiralty *Regulations and Instructions*, 1808, p 419
7 NMM WEL/8
8 Basil Hall, *Fragments of Voyages and Travels*, quoted in Field, vol I, p 288
9 Quoted in Field, p 296–7
10 Brenton, quoted in Field, p 262
11 *Royal Marines Records*, p 22

3 Marine uniform and equipment

1 Adm 49/58
2 NRS *The Letters of Lord St Vincent*, vol II, 1927, p 148n
3 Adm 183/5, 5/6/1802
4 Adm 49/58
5 Royal Marines Museum, Portsmouth Letter Book
6 Mollo, p 42
7 Quoted in Fabb and Cassin, p 35
8 NMM OBK/11

Part VIII Techniques

Printed Primary Sources

Admiralty *Regulations and Instructions Relating to His Majesty's Service at Sea*, 1808
Burney, W, *Universal Dictionary of the Marine*, 1815
Gower, R H, *Treatise on Seamanship*, 1806, 3rd edition 1808
Griffiths, A J, *Observations on Some Points of Seamanship*, 1828
Lever, Darcy, *The Young Sea Officer's Sheet Anchor*, 1808, reprinted 1819, 1963
Purdy, J, *Memoir to Accompany . . . The New Chart of the Atlantic Ocean*, 1821
Steel, D, *The Elements of Mastmaking, Sailmaking and Rigging*, 1974 reprinted 1932

Secondary Sources

Brighton, J G, *Admiral Broke, A Memoir*
Douglas, H, *A Treatise on Naval Gunnery*, 1829
Fullom, S W, *The Life of General Sir Howard Douglas*, 1863
Gilly, W O S, *Narratives of Shipwrecks of the Royal Navy, 1793–1857*, 1864
Harland, J, *Seamanship in the Age of Sail*, 1984
Hewson, J B, *A History of the Practice of Navigation*
Padfield, P, *Guns at Sea*, 1973

1 Basic seamanship

1 Burney, p 103
2 Lever, p 3
3 Burney, p 103
4 Gower, p 131
5 Ibid, p 704
6 Burney, p 333
7 Griffiths, p 158
8 NMM COD/3/10
9 Steel, p 64
10 Ibid, p 68
11 Lever, p 56
12 Burney, p 388
13 Harland, pp 129–30
14 Griffiths, pp 240–1
15 Burney, p 246
16 Gower, p 56
17 Ibid, p 56

2 Ship handling

1 R Sanderson, *Meteorology at Sea*, 1982, p 80
2 NMM CAD/A/6
3 Burney, p 220
4 Ibid, p 160
5 Ibid, p 425
6 Ibid, p 185
7 Ibid, p 194
8 Ibid, p 246
9 Ibid, p 321
10 Ibid, p 556
11 Lever, p 76–7
12 NRS *Logs of the Great Sea Fights*, vol I, 1899, pp 137, 25
13 NMM CAD/A/6

3 Boat and anchor work

1 Griffiths, p 138
2 Burney, p 322
3 B Lavery, *Arming and Fitting*, 1987, p 299
4 Griffiths, p 137

4 Gunnery and fighting

1 Fullom, p 167
2 Burney, p 141
3 NMM JOD/45
4 NMM ADL/G/4
5 Burney, p 142
6 Ibid
7 Douglas, pp 145–6
8 NMM JOD/45
9 NMM JOD/48
10 Ibid
11 Brighton, p 248
12 NMM RUSI/36
13 Adm 1/5129
14 Douglas, p 296
15 Brighton, p 248

16 NMM JOD/48
17 NMM JOD/45
18 Royal Naval Museum, Portsmouth, Ms 981/82
19 NMM JOD/48
20 NMM JOD/45
21 NMM JOD/48
22 NMM JOD/45
23 Ibid
24 Burney, p 46

5 *Navigation*

1 Quoted in A Day, 1967, *The Admiralty Hydrographic Service 1795–1919*, p 334
2 B Lavery, *Arming and Fitting*, p 24
3 Day, op cit, p 334
4 NMM CHA/N/2
5 NMM NVP/7a
6 Burney, p 60
7 A Stevenson, *A Rudimentary Treatise on Lighthouses*, 1850, p 36
8 Ibid, pp 69–70
9 Admiralty *Regulations and Instructions*, 1808, p 200
10 Ibid, p 201
11 NMM Chart no 1165
12 Purdy, p 90
13 Ibid, p 93
14 Ibid, pp 109–10
15 Hewson, p 185
16 Burney, p 118
17 Ibid, p 219
18 Quoted in Purdy, op cit, pp 241–2

6 *Disaster at sea*

1 J Wetherell, *The Adventures of John Wetherell*, 1954, p 8
2 M Lewis, *Social History of the Navy*, 1960, p 442
3 Steel, pp 42–3
4 'Captain in the Royal Navy', *Observations and Instructions for Officers of the Royal Navy*, 1807, p 73
5 NRS *The Journal of Bartholemew James*, 1896, pp 273–4
6 Ibid, pp 288–90
7 Griffiths, pp 174–5
8 *The Trafalgar General Order Book of HMS Mars*, in MM XXII, pp 102–3
9 'Captain in the Royal Navy', op cit, pp 73–4
10 Gilly, pp 4–5
11 Burney, p 226
12 Gower, p 178
13 Gilly, p 88
14 Quoted in Lavery, *Arming and Fitting*, p 68
15 Burney, p 157
16 Griffiths, p 203
17 Burney, p 157
18 D R Hayes, *His Majesty's Late Ship the Invincible*, 1985, p 34
19 *Naval Chronicle*, vol XI, 1804, pp 293–4
20 M Lewis, *Social History of the Navy*, 1860, pp 350–1
21 NRS *The Journal of Bartholemew James*, pp 203–7
22 Lever, p 89
23 Ibid, p 89
24 Lever, p 90
25 R Hay, *Landsman Hay*, 1953, p 186
26 J Wetherall, *The Adventures of John Wetherell*, 1954, p 104

Part IX Shipboard Life

Manuscript Sources

Captain's Orders Books in the NMM:
COD/21/7, *Pegasus*, 1793
HAW/8, *Bellerophon*, 1813–15
JOD/45, Amazon, 1802, kept by J D Skynner
PAR/101, *Prince*, 1800–2
PAR/102, *Amazon*, 1802
ROB/11, sloop *Pylades*, 1813
RUSI/110, *Superb*, 1804
RUSI ER/3/11. *Amazon*, 1799
WQB/3, San Domingo and other ships
WQB/4, *Bacchante*, 1812
WQB/11, *Goliath*
WQB/39. *Indefatigable*, 1812

Other documents in the NMM:
COD/3/8. *Blake's* black list and punishment book
COD/3/10, *Blake's* description book
JOD/148, Diary of Midshipman Pysent, *Gibraltar*, 1809–11
MLN/38/5, crew of the *Caledonia*
RUSI/35 and 36, Journal and Memoranda of Lt Wyke, 1782–99
RUSI/110a, Hammock List for the *Spartiate*, c1805
Documents in the PRO
Adm 1/5125 to 5131, petitions
Adm 1/5330 to 5450, courts-martial

Printed Primary Sources

Seaman's autobiographies:
Baynham, H, *From the Lower Deck*, 1969
Bechervaise, J, *Thirty-six Years of Seafaring Life*, 1839
Hay, R, *Landsman Hay*, 1953
Leech, S, *A Voice from the Main Deck*, 1843
Nicol, J, *Life and Adventures*, 1922
Richardson, W, *A Mariner of England*, 1908 reprinted 1970
Robinson, W, or 'Jack Nastyface', *Nautical Economy*, 1836
Spavens, W, *The Narrative of William Spavens*, 1796
Wetherell, J, *The Adventures of John Wetherell*, 1954
Wilson, R in NRS *Five Naval Journals 1789 to 1817*, 1951, pp 121–276

Other sources:
Admiralty *Regulations and Instructions Relating to His Majesty's Service at Sea*, 1808
'Captain in the Royal Navy', *Observations and Instructions for Officers of the Royal Navy*, 1807 (according to Marshall's *Royal Naval Biography* supplement II, p 48, this was written by John Davie, who was a commander at the time)
McArthur, J, *A Treatise on Naval Courts-Martial*, 1792
NRS *The Health of Seamen*, 1965
NRS *Manning Pamphlets 1693 to 1873*, 1974
'The Trafalgar General Order Book of HMS Mars', in MM XXII, pp 87–104

Secondary Sources

Dickens, G, *The Dress of the British Seaman*, 1957 reprinted 1977
Lewis, M, *A Social History of the Navy 1793–1815*, 1960
Lloyd, C and Coulter, J L S, *Medicine and the Navy*, vol III, 1714 to 1815, 1961

1 *The organisation of the crew*

1 NMM JOD/148
2 NMM WQB/4
3 'Captain in the Royal Navy', p 58

4 W Burney, *Universal Dictionary of the Marine*, 1815, p 619
5 NMM JOD/148
6 Burney, op cit, p 201
7 NRS *Manning Pamphlets*, p 350
8 NMM WQB/3
9 NRS *Five Naval Journals*, p 245
10 Admiralty *Regulations and Instructions*, p 143
11 *Mars* Order Book in MM XXII, p 91
12 NMM WQB/3
13 NMM WQB/4
14 NMM SPB/15
15 NMM WQB/11

2 *The ship's day*

1 NRS *Five Naval Journals*, p 244
2 W Burney, *Universal Dictionary of the Marine*, 1815, p 245
3 NRS *Five Naval Journals*, p 335
4 *Mars* Order Book in MM XXII, p 101
5 NRS *The Keith Papers*, vol II, pp 412–13
6 *Mars* Order Book in MM XXII, p 91
7 Robinson, Quoted in Baynham p 45
8 NRS *Five Naval Journals*, p 244
9 NMM RUSI/110
10 Leech, p 14
11 *Mars* Order Book in MM XXII, p 93
12 NRS *Five Naval Journals*, p 254
13 Quoted in Baynham p 47
14 Ibid
15 NRS *Five Naval Journals*, p 254
16 NMM WQB/40
17 *Mars* Order Book in MM XXII, p 94
18 NRS *Five Naval Journals*, p 336
19 NRS *Health of Seamen*, p 276
20 NMM HAW/8
21 *Mars* Order Book in MM XXII, p 91
22 Ibid, p 88

3 *The necessities of life*

1 NRS *Health of Seamen*, p 270
2 *Mars* Order Book in MM XXII, p 91
3 Quoted in Dickens, p 7
4 NRS *Five Naval Journals*, p 219
5 Ibid, p 364
6 Ibid, p 129
7 NRS *Health of Seamen*, p 266
8 NMM JOD/45
9 Richardson, p 101
10 NRS *Five Naval Journals*, p 178
11 NRS *Health of Seamen*, p 156
12 Adm 1/5125
13 Lloyd and Coulter, p 81
14 Admiralty *Regulations and Instructions*, 1815, p 297
15 W Burney, *Universal Dictionary of the Marine*, 1815, p 40
16 Admiralty *Regulations and Instructions*, p 283
17 Basil Hall, *Fragments of Voyages and Travels*, 1846, p 137
18
19 Hall, op cit
20 Quoted in Baynham, p 271
21 A Griffiths, *Observations on Some Points of Seamanship*, 1828, p 99
22 Quoted in Baynham, p 45
23 Aaron Thomas, *The Newfoundland Journal*, 1968
24 NMM RUSI/110
25 NRS *Five Naval Journals*, p 247
26 Ibid, p 246
27 Quoted in Baynham, p 47
28 G M Manwaring and B Dobrée, *The Floating Republic*, 1935, pp 265–6
29 Lloyd and Coulter, p 325
30 'Captain in the Royal Navy', p 48
31 Burney, op cit, p 184
32 Ibid, p 90
33 NRS *Health of Seamen*, p 157
34 Leech, p 37
35 NMM RUSI ER/3/11
36 Ibid
37 NRS *Five Naval Journals*, p 10
38 Admiralty *Regulations and Instructions*, p 138
39 NMM RUSI/110
40 NMM WQB/40

4 *Rewards and pleasures*

1 G H Manwaring and B Dobrée, *The Floating Republic*, 1935, p 266
2 Adm 1/5126
3 Royal Naval Museum, Portsmouth, Greenhaugh letters
4 Adm 1/5125
5 Adm 1/5127
6 Quoted in Baynham, p 18
7 NRS *Five Naval Journals*, pp 257–8
8 Ibid, p 257
9 NMM JOD/48
10 Quoted in Baynham, p 95
11 Leech, p 26
12 Richardson, pp 105–6
13 W Robinson or 'Jack Nastyface,' *Nautical Economy*, 1836, p 155
14 NMM JOD/11, RUSI/35
15 NRS *Five Naval Journals*, p 8
16 Ibid, p 14
17 Quoted in Baynham, p 94
18 Adm 1/5127
19 Adm 1/5369
20 Admiralty *Regulations and Instructions*, 1747 edition p
21 Admiralty *Regulations and Instructions*, 1808, pp 145–6
22 Lewis, p 281
23 Quoted in Baynham, p 130
24 Ibid, p 68
25 Quoted in C. Lloyd, *the British Seaman*, 1968, p 247
26 Adm 1/5385
27 NMM RUSI/ER/3/11
28 'Captain in the Royal Navy', p 38
29 Adm 1/5125
30 J S Tucker, *Memoirs of the Earl of St Vincent*, 1844, vol I, p 385
31 NRS *Five Naval Journals*, p 70

5 *Medicine and health*

1 Lloyd and Coulter, p 149
2 Lewis, p 420
3 Lloyd and Coulter, p 58
4 NRS *Five Naval Journals*, p 54
5 G M Manwaring and B Dobrée, *The Floating Republic*, 1935, p 65
6 Lloyd and Coulter, p 148
7 Ibid, p 60
8 Adm 101/103/1 and 101/83/3
9 Lloyd and Coulter, p 152
10 Admiralty *Regulations and Instructions*, p 269

11 NRS *Health of Seamen*, p 71
12 *Mars* Order Book in MM XXII, p 97
13 Adm 1/5128
14 Lloyd and Coulter, p 172
15 NMM RUSI/35
16 Lloyd and Coulter, p 61
17 Ibid, pp 58–9
18 Ibid, p 245
19 Lewis, p 248
20 Muster books, Adm 36/13448
21 Adm 1/2920

6 *Discipline*

1 McArthur, pp 27ff
2 McArthur, Article XXXVI
3 NRS *Five Naval Journals*, p 243
4 G M Manwaring and B Dobrée, *The Floating Republic*, 1935, p 247
5 *Mars* Order Book in MM XXII, p 86
6 Adm 1/5367
7 McArthur, pp 54–5
8 Quoted in Baynham, p 63
9 Adm 12/27F
10 Quoted in *The Log Book or Nautical Miscellany*, published by J and W Robins, 1830, p 103
11 J S Tucker, *Memoirs of the Earl of St Vincent*, 1844 vol I, p 309
12 McArthur, p 159
13 Spavens, p 120
14 Quoted in Baynham, p 63
15 Ibid, pp 31–2
16 NRS *Five Naval Journals*, p
17 Ibid, p 66
18 Adm 1/5385
19 Captains' logs, Adm 51/2121
20 NMM COD/3/9
21 McArthur, p 56
22 Adm 1/5125
23 Royal Naval Museum, Portsmouth
24 W Burney, *Universal Dictionary of the Marine*, 1815, p 79
25 C Lloyd, *The British Seaman*, 1968, p 244
26 Quoted in Baynham, p 64
27 NRS *Five Naval Journals*, p 256
28 Quoted in Baynham, p 64
29 NRS *The Keith Papers*, vol III, p 183
30 Quoted in Baynham, p 65
31 Richardson, p 68
32 Adm 1/4366
33 *Mars* Order Book in MM XXII, p
34 Adm 1/5385
35 W Robinson or 'Jack Nastyface', *Nautical Economy*, 1836, p 65
36 Adm 1/5125
37 Ibid
38 A Griffiths, *Observations on Some Points of Seamanship*, 1828, p 107

Part X Dockyards and Bases

Manuscript Sources
Navy Board Papers in Adm 106 series, especially dockyard letters
Dockyard letters and papers in the NMM, CHA and POR series
Admiralty visitations of the dockyards 1801 to 1814, Adm 106/3223 to 3229 and 7/593, 1813–14, with plans
J Rennie's report on proposals for a new dockyard at Northfleet, BL Add 27884
Adm 7/216, victualling instructions, 1806
Adm 112/84 to 159, contracts
Adm 106/3098, regulations for yards, 1806
Adm 180 series, progress books

Printed Primary Sources
W Burney, *Universal Dictionary of the Marine*, 1815, reprinted 1970
NRS *Letters of Lord Barham*, 3 vols, 1906–10
Parliamentary reports, especially:
6th Report of the Commissioners for Naval Enquiry, in House of Commons Reports, Naval, 1803–4, vol III, p 1ff
8th report, in ibid, pp 637ff

Secondary Sources
Beveridge, W, *Prices and Wages in England*, vol I, 1939
Morriss, R, *The Royal Dockyards During the Revolutionary and Napoleonic Wars*, 1983

1 *The work and facilities of the dockyards*

1 R Morriss, pp 108–9
2 D A Baugh, *British Naval Administration in the Age of Walpole*, 1965, p 258
3 Morriss, p 45
4 R J B Knight, 'The Building and Maintenance of the British Fleet During the Anglo French Wars 1688 to 1815', in *Les Marines de Guerre European, XVII-XVIIIe Siecles*, 1985, p 43
5 Morris, p 28
6 NRS *The Barham Papers*, vol III, p 68
7 Morriss, p 24
8 Adm 180/10
9 Ibid
10 Morriss, p 24
11 Adm 180/10
12 Morriss, p 22
13 B Lavery, *Anatomy of the Ship – Bellona*, 1985, pp 11–12
14 Adm 106/3227
15 W Richardson, *A Mariner of England*, 1908, p 306
16 I Schomberg, *Naval Chronology*, vol IV, 1802, p 73
17 Ibid, p 109
18 Ibid, p 62
19 Ibid, p 89
20 Adm 2/114
21 J S Tucker, *Memoirs of the Earl of St Vincent*, 1844, vol I, p 416
22 Morriss, p 44
23 NRS *The Barham Papers*, vol III, p 36
24 Adm 1/882
25 Morriss, p 45
26 8th Parliamentary Report, pp 35–6
27 Burney, p 452
28 8th Parliamentary Report, pp 35–6
29 K V Burns, *Plymouth's Ships of War*, 1972
30 Adm 106/3227
31 8th Parliamentary Report, p 111
32 Ibid, p 219
33 NMM CHA/N/1
34 Adm 106/3098

2 *The dockyard workforce*

1 6th Parliamentary Report, p 5
2 Adm 106/3098
3 Morriss, pp 157–65
4 Burney, p 465
5 Adm 106/3098
6 Ibid

7 Burney, p 505
8 Ibid, p 515
9 6th Parliamentary Report, p 5
10 NRS *Letters of Lord St Vincent*, vol II, 1927, p 181
11 Morriss, p 133
12 Adm 106/3098
13 8th Parliamentary Report, p 295
14 Quoted in Morriss, p 139
15 8th Parliamentary Report, p 121
16 Ibid, p 37
17 8th Parliamentary Report, p 10
18 Adm 106/3098
19 6th Parliamentary Report, p 137
20 8th Parliamentary Report, p 295
21 Adm 106/3227
22 R Morris, 'Labour Relations in the Royal Dockyards 1801–5' in MM vol LXII, p 337
23 B Lavery, *Ship-of-the-Line*, 1984, vol I, pp 123, 130

3 Home anchorages and naval bases

1 BL Add 27884
2 R J B Knight, 'The Building and Maintenance of the British Fleet During the Anglo French Wars 1688 to 1815', in *Les Marines de Guerre European, XVII-XVIIIe Siècles*, 1985, p 35
3 Orkney Record and Antiquarian Society, *Orkney Miscellany* vol IV, p 61
4 J A Gardner, *Above and Under Hatches*, 1955, p 117
5 E P Brenton, *Life and Correspondence of John, Earl St Vincent*, vol II, p 35n
6 NRS *Health of Seamen*, p 237
7 H W Hodges and E A Hughes, *Select Naval Documents*, 1922, pp 212–13
8 *Naval Chronicle* vol XI, 1804, p 12
9 Adm 7/593, p 581
10 NRS *The Blockade of Brest 1803–5*, vol I, 1989, p 228
11 Morriss, p 108
12 Adm 7/593
13 Brenton, op cit, p 180
14 S Bentham, *Statement of Services*, 1813, p 141
15 *Naval Chronicle* vol XXVIII, 1812, p 147
16 Rennie, BL add 27884
17 *Naval Chronicle* vol XI, 1804, p 168
18 NRS *The Letters of Lord St Vincent*, vol II, 1927, p 239

4 Overseas bases

1 Adm 113/125
2 Adm 106/3441
3 Adm 106/3102
4 Morriss, p 224
5 Adm 49/69
6 NRS *The Keith Papers*, vol III, p 216
7 Ibid
8 A V Laferla, *British Malta*, vol I, 1938, p 8
9 Ibid, p 41
10 Ibid, p 7
11 Adm 106/2238, 31/1/1806
12 Morriss, p 4
13 Ibid
14 E P Brenton, *The Naval History of Great Britain*, vol I, 1837, pp 9–10
15 Quoted in G S Graham, *Britain in the Indian Ocean 1810–50*, 1967, pp 24–5
16 Ibid, pp 26–7
17 Ibid, p 32
18 Ibid, p 37
19 Adm 112/13
20 Adm 106/3441
21 Morriss, p 224

5 The victualling organisation

1 NRS *Health of Seamen*, pp 270–1
2 Adm 20/313
3 Burney, p 6
4 Adm 7/216
5 Adm 112/87
6 Adm 112/98
7 Beveridge, p 517
8 Ibid, passim
9 NMM HAL/E3
10 11th Parliamentary Report, 1809, vol VI, p 229
11 Adm 7/593
12 Adm 7/216, p 210
13 Adm 7/593
14 Ibid
15 8th Parliamentary Report, 1803–4, pp 637ff
16 NRS *Health of Seamen*, p 299
17 Adm 7/593
18 13th Parliamentary Report, 1803, vol VI, pp 385ff
19 Adm 7/593
20 Ibid
21 Ibid
22 Adm 112/125
23 Adm 112/13

Part XI Fleets

Manuscript Sources

Fleet lists in Adm 8 series
Signal books in NMM SIG series, especially:
SIG/B/38 and SIG/B/78

Printed Primary Sources

Ship lists
Steel, D, *Original and Correct List of the Royal Navy*, monthly, 1793–1815
The Navy List (the official printed list) begins 1814
Schomberg, I, *Naval Chronology*, vol IV, has many lists for different periods

Other sources
Admiralty *Regulations and Instructions Relating to His Majesty's Service at Sea*, 1808
NRS *The Keith Papers*, vols II and III, 1950–5
NRS *Fighting Instructions 1530 to 1816*, 1905 reprinted 1971
NRS *Letters of Lord Barham*, 3 vols, 1906–10

Secondary Sources

Brenton, E P, *The Naval History of Great Britain*, 2 vols, 1837
Ekins, C, *Naval Battles, 1744–1814*, 1824
James, W, *The Naval History of Great Britain*, 6 vols, 1886
Mahan, A T, *The Influence of Sea Power upon the French Revolution and Empire*, 2 vols, 1892
Perrin, W G, *British Flags*, 1922

1 The distribution of fleets

1 Quoted by A N Ryan, 'The Royal Navy and the Blockade of Brest, 1689–1805, Theory and Practice,' in *Les Marines de Guerre Européenes*, 1985, p 176
2 NRS *The Keith Papers*, vol III, p 228
3 P Bloomfield, *Kent in the Napoleonic Wars*, 1987, pp 103–5
4 Adm 8/71
5 Adm 8/79
6 NRS *The Keith Papers*, vol III, p 3
7 Ibid, p 326
8 Schomberg, pp 637–8
9 NRS *The Barham Papers*, vol III, p 99
10 Adm 8/74
11 NRS *The Keith Papers*, vol III, p 123
12 Ibid, p 113
13 Ibid, p 87
14 Adm 8/95
15 Adm 8/100
16 *Navy List*, 1814
17 Schomberg, pp 725–6
18 Adm 8/71
19 Adm 8/74
20 Adm 8/90
21 Adm 8/100
22 Schomberg, p 457
23 Adm 8/71
24 Adm 8/74
25 Adm 8/90
26 Adm 8/100
27 Schomberg, p 456
28 Ibid, p 100
29 Adm 8/90
30 Adm 8/100
31 Schomberg, pp 444, 445–6
32 Adm 8/100
33 Adm 8/71
34 Admiralty *Regulations and Instructions*, p 69
35 Ibid, p 75

2 Fleet administration

1 Adm 7/212
2 Ibid
3 Admiralty *Regulations and Instructions*, p 381
4 Adm 7/675
5 Ibid
6 Admiralty *Regulations and Instructions*, p 64
7 Ibid, p 63
8 NRS *Letters of Sir T Byam Martin*, vol II, p 57
9 NRS *Letters of Admiral Markham*, 1904, pp 30–1
10 Admiralty *Regulations and Instructions*, p 381
11 NRS *Letters of Sir T Byam Martin*, vol II, p 173
12 *Dictionary of National Biography*, vol XII, p 975
13 W O'Byrne, *A Naval Biographical Dictionary*, 1849, p 869
14 Quoted in *Dictionary of National Biography*, vol XV, p 435
15 Adm 50/49
16 Adm 7/675
17 Ibid
18 Adm 37/1083
19 W Mark, *At Sea with Nelson*, 1929, pp 136–7
20 NRS *Health of Seamen*, p 225
21 Ibid, p 229
22 Admiralty *Regulations and Instructions*, pp 250–1
23 Ibid, supplement
24 J S Tucker, *Memoirs of the Earl of St Vincent*, vol I, 1844, p 241
25 Admiralty *Regulations and Instructions*, p 14
26 Tucker, op cit, p 168
27 Ibid, p 341
28 Ibid, p 423
29 NRS *The Keith Papers*, vol II, pp 412–13
30 G S Parsons, *Nelsonian Reminiscences*, 1843, reprinted 1973, p 41
31 Admiralty *Regulations and Instructions*, p 17

3 Fleet tactics

1 NRS *Fighting Instructions*, p 192
2 Ibid
3 W Burney, *Universal Dictionary of the Marine*, 1815, p 625
4 Ibid, p 236
5 Ekins, eg pp 102–3
6 Ibid, preface
7 NRS *Fighting Instructions*, pp 326–7
8 Ibid, p 215
9 Ibid, p 272
10 Ibid, p 257
11 NRS *Logs of the Great Sea Fights*, vol I, p 12
12 NRS *Fighting Instructions*, pp 290–1
13 Admiralty *Regulations and Instructions*, pp 60–2
14 NMM RUSI/35
15 Admiralty *Regulations and Instructions*, p 13

4 Signals

1 Basil Hall, quoted in Perrin, p 203
2 NMM RUSI/36
3 Adm 7/579
4 NRS *Fighting Instructions*, p 157
5 Perrin, pp 164–5
6 Quoted in ibid, p 180
7 NMM RUSI/36
8 NMM SIG/B/36
9 NMM SIG/B/38
10 NMM WQB/3
11 NMM RUSI/36
12 Adm 7/759
13 Adm 106/3125
14 J A Gardner, *Above and Under Hatches*, 1955, pp 189–90
15 H P Mead, 'The Admiralty Telegraph and Semaphores', in MM vol XXIV. pp 184–203

Part XII The Seaman's World

1 Winds and currents

Printed Primary Sources
Burney, W, *Universal Dictionary of the Marine*, 1815
Hadley, G, 'Concerning the Cause of the General Trade Winds', in *Philosophical Transactions*, vol XXXIV, 1735, pp 58ff
Purdy, J, *Memoir to Accompany the New Chart of the Atlantic Ocean*, 1821
Rennel, J, *Investigation of the Currents of the Atlantic Ocean*, 1832 (written 1820)
Taylor, J, *The Complete Weather Guide*, 1814

Secondary Sources
Admiralty Hydrographic Department, *Ocean Passages for the World*, 1895, 1923, 1973
Maury, F, *Explanations and Directions to Accompany Winds and Charts*, 1853

Sanderson, R, *Meteorology at Sea,* 1982

1 Burney, p 556
2 Purdy, pp 71–2
3 Rennel, pp 152–3
4 Ibid, pp 8–9
5 Purdy, p 59
6 Burney, p 200
7 Taylor, p 46
8 Ibid, p 120
9 Ibid, p 30

2 *The merchant marine*

Manuscript Sources

NMM HNL series, Papers of Michael Henley and Son, shipowners
PRO CUST 17 series, States of Navigation, Commerce and Revenue, 1772 to 1808

Printed Primary Sources

Macpherson, D, *Annals of Commerce,* especially vol IV, 1805
Parliamentary Reports (up to 1800 the references are taken from the Scholarly Resource reprint of the House of Commons Sessional Papers, and the series number is given. After 1800, the volumes in the British Library, Official Publications Room, have been used):
No 4908, 1799, on the Slave Trade
No 4942, 1799, Port of London
No 5036, 1800, on British Herring Fisheries
No 5071, 1800, on the Coal Trade

Secondary Sources

Davis, R, *The Rise of the English Shipping Industry,* 1962 reprinted 1972
Lloyd, C, *The British Seamen,* 1968
Lubbock, B, *The Arctic Whalers,* 1937
MacGregor, D, *Merchant Sailing Ships 1775–1815,* 1983
Parkinson, C N, *Trade in Eastern Seas 1973–1815,* 1937

1 Quoted in Lloyd, *The British Seaman,* p 286
2 PRO BT6/185, Board of Trade miscellaneous papers
3 L A Harper *The English Navigation Laws,* 1939, pp 405–6
4 Macpherson, vol IV, p 336
5 Ibid, p 536
6 Parliamentary Report no 4908, p 135
7 Macpherson, vol IV, p 475
8 Ibid, p 536
9 Parliamentary Report no 5071
10 Macpherson, pp 540–1
11 Parliamentary Report no 5071
12 Parliamentary Report no 5071
13 Ibid, p 139
14 Adm 1/581
15 Parliamentary Report, 5036
16 B Lubbock, p 195
17 PRO CUST 17/18
18 PRO CUST 17/30
19 Parkinson, pp 149 ff
20 Macpherson, p 455
21 Parliamentary Report no 5071
22 R Hay, *Landsman Hay,* 1953, p 194
23 R J B Knight, *Guide to the Manuscripts in the National Maritime Museum,* vol II, 1980, pp 40–2
24 Parliamentary Report no 4942
25 Macpherson, Appendix IV, 'Liverpool'
26 Ibid, 'Hull'
27 Parliamentary Report no 5071
28 P M Kennedy, *The Rise and Fall of British Naval Mastery,* 1976, pp 140–1

3 *Other naval services*

Manuscript Sources

PRO Adm 106/3096, Instructions to Transport Agents, 1803

Printed Primary Sources

NRS *The Keith Papers,* vol III
House of Commons Accounts and Papers, 810, vol XIII, on the Transport Service

Secondary Sources

Chatterton, E K, *Kings Cutters and Smugglers 1700 to 1855,* 1912
Low, C R, *History of the Indian Navy 1613–1863,* 2 vols, 1877
Robinson, H, *Carrying British Mails Overseas,* 1964
Smith, G, *Kings Cutters,* 1983
Woodman, R, *Keepers of the Seas,* 1983

1 House of Commons, Accounts and Papers, 1809, vol IX, p 401
2 M E Condon, 'The Establishment of the Transport Board in 1794', in MM vol LVII, p 180
3 House of Commons Accounts and Estimates, vol XIII, 1810, p 263
4 Adm 106/3096
5 PRO Ministry of Transport papers, MT 223/1
6 House of Commons Accounts and Papers, 1807, vol IV, p 105
7 Adm 106/3096
8 House of Commons, Accounts and Papers, 1810, vol XIII, p 263
9 D Macpherson, *Annals of Commerce,* vol IV, 1805, p 49
10 Chatterton, pp 424–5
11 Ibid, pp 407/8
12 Smith, p 85
13 PRO CUST 20/43
14 Chatterton, p 158
15 Smith, p 112
16 NRS *The Keith Papers,* vol III, p 133
17 MM vol XV, p 420
18 NRS *The Keith Papers,* vol III, pp 146–7
19 Adm 1/581
20 NRS *The Keith Papers,* vol III, p 134
21 Ibid, pp 151–2
22 Woodman, p 184
23 Quoted in ibid, p 24
24 Adm 7/649
25 MM vol LVI, p 213
26 *Court and City Register,* 1807
27 Low, p 539
28 House of Commons, Accounts and Papers, 1807, vol IV, p 105
29 Ibid
30 Robinson, p 313

Part XIII Foreign Navies

1 *The French navy*

Secondary Sources

Crowhurst, P, *The Defence of British Trade 1689–1815,* 1977
Boudriot, J, *The 74-Gun Ship,* translated by D H Roberts, 4 vols, 1986–8
Boudriot, J, numerous articles in *Neptunia* and *Petit Perroquet* since 1968
de La Roncière, C, et al, *Histoire de la Marine,* 1934
Jenkins, E H, *A History of the French Navy,* 1973

Tramond, J, *Manuel d'Histoire Maritime de la France,* 1916

1 J Boudriot, 'L'Artillerie de Mer Francaise, part E, Deux Siècles des Evolutions', in *Neptunia,* 103, pp 33–8
2 V Brun, *Guerres Maritimes de la France,* vol II, 1861, p 644
3 E P Brenton, *The Naval History of Great Britain,* 1837, vol I, p 96
4 J Tramond, p 572
5 P Crowhurst, passim
6 Ibid
7 Ibid, p 21

2 The Spanish navy

Secondary Sources

de Artinaño, G, *La Arquictectura Naval Española,* 1920
Harbron, J D, *Trafalgar and the Spanish Navy,* 1988
Manera Regueyra, E, et al. *El Buque en la Armada Español,* 1981
de Zulueta, J, 'Trafalgar – The Spanish View', in MM vol LXVI, pp 293–318

1 Harbron, p 43
2 de Zulueta, p 295
3 Harbron, p 87
4 de Zulueta, p 297
5 Manera Regueyra, et al, p 259

3 The American navy

Secondary Sources

Chapelle, H I, *The History of the American Sailing Navy,* 1949
Dudley, W S, *The Naval War of 1812, a Documentary History,* vol I, 1985
Maclay, E S, *A History of the United States Navy,* 2 vols, 1894
Roosevelt, T, *The Naval War of 1812,* 1894

1 Roosevelt, p 42
2 Dudley, p 628
3 Roosevelt, p 46
4 Ibid, p 68
5 Dudley, p 504
6 Roosevelt, p 42ff
7 Ibid, p 36
8 Dudley, p 96n
9 Maclay, vol I, p 225

4 Other foreign naval forces

Secondary Sources

Anderson, R C, *Naval Wars in the Baltic,* 1910
Anderson, R C, *Naval Wars in the Levant,* 1952
Berg, H C, and Erichsen, J, *Dankse Orlogskibbe 1690–1860,* 1980
Sokol, A H, *The Imperial and Royal Austro-Hungarian Navy,* 1968
Woodward, D, *Russians at Sea,* 1965

1 W James, *The Naval History of Great Britain,* 1886, vol III, p 42
2 W Burney, *Universal Dictionary of the Marine,* 1815, p 315
3 H Chapman, *Architectura Navalis Mercatoria,* 1968 edition, p 7
4 Anderson, 1910, p 376
5 James, op cit, p 43
6 Burney, op cit, p 315
7 Anderson, 1910, p 276
8 NRS *A Memoir of James Trevenen,* 1959, p 129
9 Anderson, 1952, p 319
10 Ibid
11 Burney, op cit, p 315
12 Sokol, pp 9–10
13 NMM RUSI/176
14 H I Chapelle, *The History of the American Sailing Navy,* 1949, pp 135–6
15 *Naval Chronicle* vol XXXIV, p 327

Part IX Tactics

1 Fighting tactics

Printed Primary Sources

Baynham, H, *From the Lower Deck,* 1969
Burney, W, *Universal Dictionary of the Marine,* 1815 reprinted 1970
Cochrane, T, *Autobiography of a Seaman,* 2 vols, 1860
Richardson, W, *A Mariner of England,* 1908 reprinted 1970

Secondary Sources

Campbell, J, *Lives of the Admirals,* vol VIII, 1815 edition
Padfield, P, *Broke and the Shannon,* 1968
Padfield, P, *Guns at Sea,* 1973

1 Campbell, p 417
2 NMM RUSI/176
3 Quoted in Baynham, p 37
4 Ibid, p 3
5 Burney, p 679
6 Ibid, p 138
7 Cochrane, vol I, p 111
8 C R Low, *Famous Frigate Actions,* 1898, p 103
9 Cambell, p 420
10 Burney, p 348
11 Ibid, p 380
12 F W Maitland, *Surrender of Buonoparte,* 1826, p 96
13 Burney, p 380
14 Richardson, p 216
15 Campbell, p 418
16 Padfield, 1968, p 165
17 Quoted in Baynham, pp 75–6
18 Burney, p 138
19 Cochrane, vol I, p 112
20 Richardson, p 216
21 Quoted in A Friendly, *Beaufort of the Admiralty,* 1977, p 103
22 NRS *The Samaurez Papers,* 1968, p 93

2 Blockade

Printed Primary Sources

Hodges H W, and Hughes, E A, *Select Naval Documents,* 1922
NRS *Letters of Lord Barham,* vol III, 1910
NRS *The Blockade of Brest 1803–5,* 2 vols, 1898–1901
NRS *The Keith Papers,* vols II and III, 1950–5

Secondary Sources

Cooper, G E, 'Methods of Blockade, etc, Employed During the Revolutionary and Napoleonic Wars', in RUSI Journal vol LXI
Ryan A N, 'The Royal Navy and the Blockade of Brest, 1689–1805: Theory and Practice', in *Les Marines de Guerre Européennes,* 1985

1 A T Mahan, *The Influence of Sea Power on the French Revolution and Empire,* vol II, 1892, p 118
2 Ryan, pp 175ff
3 E P Brenton, *The Naval History of Great Britain,* 1837, vol II, pp 61–2
4 NRS *The Letters of Lord Barham,* vol III, p 41
5 NRS *The Keith Papers,* vol III, pp 43–4
6 Ibid, p 195
7 Ibid, p 226

8 NRS *The Blockade of Brest*, vol I, p 344
9 W Robinson, 'Jack Nastyface', *Nautical Economy*, 1836, p 81
10 NMM RUSI/35
11 NRS *The Letters of Lord Barham*, vol III, p 41
12 Ibid, vol II, p 386
13 George Watson, quoted in H Baynham, *From the Lower Deck*, 1969, p 114
14 NRS *The Blockade of Brest*, vol II, p 170
15 Ibid, vol I, p 173
16 Ibid, vol II, p 85
17 J A Gardner, *Above and Under Hatches*, 1955, p 97
18 T Cochrane, *Autobiography of a Seaman*, vol I, 1860, p 77
19 Hodges and Hughes, pp 213–14
20 Padfield, *Broke of the Shannon*, 1968, p 61
21 Quoted in Baynham, op cit, p 48
22 Hodges and Hughes, p 209

3 Convoys and cruisers

Manuscript Sources

Adm 2/1097 to 1114, *Out Letters Relating to Convoys*

Adm 7/64 to 72, Lists of convoys, registers of licences to sail without convoy, etc.

Adm 49/103, *Papers Relating to Signals for Ships Under Convoy, 1805*

NMM RUSI/36, Journals and Memoranda of Lt Wyke, 1782–99

Various convoy signal books in the NMM, esp in the SIG/B series

Secondary Sources

Crowhurst, P, *The Defence of British Trade 1689–1815*, 1977

Mead, H P, 'An Account of the Convoy Drill (Signal) Book', in MM, vol XXXII, pp 42ff

Waters, D W, 'Notes Compiled by Capt R Huddleston, 1912, on Trade Protection, etc, file no 5, *Protection of Trade, 1793–1814*, in NMM WTS/30

1 Adm 8/95
2 NMM WTS/30
3 Adm 49/103
4 NMM WTS/30
5 Ibid
6 C N Parkinson, *Trade in Eastern Seas*, 1937, pp 304–11
7 NMM RUSI/35
8 NMM RUSI/176
9 NMM WTS/30
10 Adm 106/3409, 51/1160
11 W Richardson, *A Mariner of England*, 1908, reprinted 1970, p 137
12 Adm 1/1545
13 NMM RUSI/36, Adm 49/103
14 Adm 49/103
15 Mead, p 47
16 Quoted in NMM WTS/30
17 NMM RUSI/36
18 NMM WTS/30
19 Adm 1/5127
20 Adm 1/5335
21 NMM WTS/30
22 NMM RUSI/35

4 Amphibious operations

Printed Primary Sources

House of Commons, Accounts and Papers, 1810, vol VIII, report on the Walcheren Expedition

NRS *The Keith Papers*, vols II and III, 1950–5

Richardson, W, *A Mariner of England*, 1908 reprinted 1970

Secondary Sources

Brenton, E P, *The Naval History of Great Britain*, 2 vols, 1837

1 Compiled from C G Toogood and T A Brassey, *Index to James, Naval History* 1971
2 NRS *Naval Miscellany* vol IV, 1952, p 367
3 T Cochrane, *Autobiography of a Seaman*, vol I, 1860, pp 321–3
4 House of Commons, Accounts and Papers, 1809, vol XII, p 25
5 NRS *The Keith Papers*, vol III, p 297
6 Ibid, vol II, p 273
7 Ibid, pp 274–5
8 NMM WEL/54
9 House of Commons, Accounts and Papers, 1810, vol VIII, p 332
10 NRS *The Keith Papers*, vol III, p 269
11 Brenton, vol II, p 44
12 Ibid, p 261
13 NRS *The Keith Papers*, vol III, p 298
14 Ibid, p 300
15 Ibid, p 261

5 Victory and defeat

Printed Primary Sources

House of Commons, Accounts and papers, 1798, vol XVIII, Report on the treatment of prisoners of war

Maitland, F L, *The Surrender of Buonoparte*, 1826

Secondary Sources

Abell, F, *Prisoners of War in Britain, 1756–1814*, 1914

Fraser, E, *Napoleon the Gaoler*, 1914

Lewis, M, *Napoleon and his British Captives*, 1962

1 J W Norie, *Naval Gazetteer, Biographer and Chronologist*, 1827, p 534
2 W Richardson, *A Mariner of England*, 1815, p 217
3 T Cochrane, *Autobiography of a Seaman*, vol I, 1860, p 127
4 Adm 12/27c 27d, indices to courts-martial
5 D Howarth, *Trafalgar – The Nelson touch*, 1969, p 243
6 M Lewis, *A Social History of the Navy 1793–1815*, pp 381ff
7 Ibid, p 362
8 House of Commons, Accounts and Papers, p 60
9 Ibid, p 20
10 Quoted in Abell, p 79
11 Dupin, quoted in ibid, p 41
12 Muster book, Adm 36/12681
13 Adm 37/860
14 House of Commons, Accounts and Papers, p 20
15 Ibid, passim
16 Abell, p 287
17 Fraser, p 1
18 House of Commons, Accounts and Papers, pp 57, 60
19 J Wetherell, *The Adventures of John Wetherell*, 1954, pp 138–9
20 W H Long, *Naval Yarns*, 1899, reprinted 1973, pp 176, 178, 182–4
21 Maitland, pp 73, 95, 87, 75
22 D Steel's *Original and Correct List of the Royal Navy, 1793–1815*, list for 1814–15
23 Adm 12/74, 21/3/1815
24 Quoted in H Baynham, *From the Lower Deck*, 1969, p 32
25 *Naval Chronicle* vol XXXIV, p 395
26 Ibid, p 481

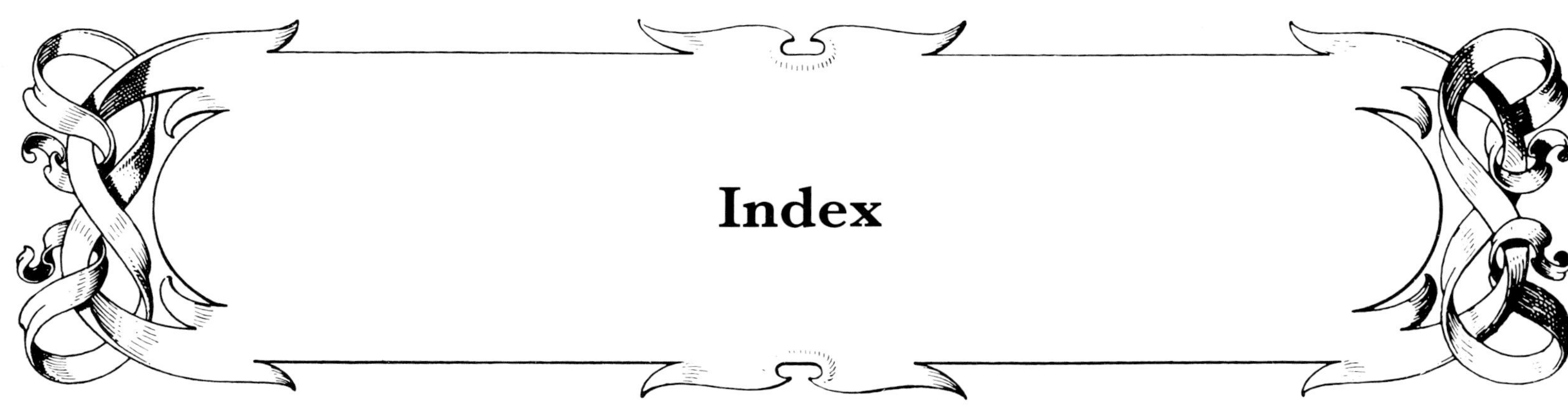

Index

Page numbers in italics indicate illustrations. The original nationality of foreign ships is given in brackets following the name as follows: America - US; Denmark - Den; France - Fr; Netherlands - Neth; Russia - Rus; Spain - Sp; Sweden - Sw. Other ships are British and 'cap' denotes ship captured from the nation indicated.